Conceptualizing the World

Time and the World: Interdisciplinary Studies in Cultural Transformations

Series editor: Helge Jordheim, University of Oslo, Norway

Published in association with the interdisciplinary research program Cultural Transformations in the Age of Globalization (KULTRANS) at the University of Oslo.

Time is moving faster; the world is getting smaller. Behind these popular slogans are actual cultural processes, on global and local scales, that require investigation. *Time and the World* draws on research in a wide range of fields, such as cultural history, anthropology, sociology, literary studies, sociolinguistics, and law, and sets out to discuss different cultures as sites of transformation in a global context. The series offers interdisciplinary analyses of cultural aspects of globalization in various historical and geographical contexts, across time and space.

Editorial board: Andrew Barry, University of Oxford; Richard Baumann, Indiana University; Costas Douzinas, Birkbeck, University of London; Thomas Hylland Eriksen, University of Oslo; Lynn Hunt, University of California Los Angeles; Fazal Rizvi, University of Melbourne; Hartmut Rosa, Jena University; Inger Johanne Sand, University of Oslo; Stefan Willer, Center for Literary and Cultural Research Berlin; Clifford Siskin, New York University

Volume 1
From Antiquities to Heritage: Transformations of Cultural Memory
Anne Eriksen

Volume 2
Writing Democracy: The Norwegian Constitution 1814–2014
Edited by Karen Gammelgaard and Eirik Holmøyvik

Volume 3
Border Aesthetics: Concepts and Intersections
Edited by Johan Schimanski and Stephen F. Wolfe

Volume 4
Conceptualizing the World: An Exploration across Disciplines
Edited by Helge Jordheim and Erling Sandmo

Conceptualizing the World
An Exploration across Disciplines

Edited by
Helge Jordheim and Erling Sandmo

berghahn
NEW YORK · OXFORD
www.berghahnbooks.com

First published in 2019 by
Berghahn Books
www.berghahnbooks.com

© 2019, 2024 Helge Jordheim and Erling Sandmo
First paperback edition published in 2024

All rights reserved. Except for the quotation of short passages for the purposes of criticism and review, no part of this book may be reproduced in any form or by any means, electronic or mechanical, including photocopying, recording, or any information storage and retrieval system now known or to be invented, without written permission of the publisher.

Library of Congress Cataloging-in-Publication Data
Names: Jordheim, Helge, editor. | Sandmo, Erling, editor.
Title: Conceptualizing the world : an exploration across disciplines / Edited by Helge Jordheim and Erling Sandmo.
Description: New York : Berghahn Books, 2019. | Series: Time and the world: interdisciplinary studies in cultural transformations ; volume 4 | Includes bibliographical references and index.
Identifiers: LCCN 2018048856 (print) | LCCN 2018049519 (ebook) | ISBN 9781789200379 (ebook) | ISBN 9781789200362 (hardback)
Subjects: LCSH: History--Philosophy. | Metaphysics.
Classification: LCC D16.8 (ebook) | LCC D16.8 .C66 2019 (print) | DDC 901--dc23
LC record available at https://lccn.loc.gov/2018048856

British Library Cataloguing in Publication Data
A catalogue record for this book is available from the British Library

ISBN 978-1-78920-036-2 hardback
ISBN 978-1-80539-135-7 paperback
ISBN 978-1-80539-407-5 epub
ISBN 978-1-78920-037-9 web pdf

https://doi.org/10.3167/9781789200362

Contents

List of Illustrations   viii

Introduction
        The World as Concept and Object of Knowledge   1
        Helge Jordheim and Erling Sandmo

Part I. Naming the World

Chapter 1.   "World": An Exploration of the Relationship between Conceptual History and Etymology   27
                 Ivo Spira

Chapter 2.   A Multiverse of Knowledge: The Epistemology and Hermeneutics of the *ʿālam* in Medieval Islamic Thought   40
                 Nora S. Eggen

Chapter 3.   Globalization of Human Conscience: A Modern Muslim Case   54
                 Oddbjørn Leirvik

Chapter 4.   Creating World through Concept Learning   66
                 Claudia Lenz

Chapter 5.   Between Metaphor and Geopolitics: The History of the Concept *the Third World*   79
                 Erik Tängerstad

Chapter 6.   On the Dialectics of Ecological World Concepts   94
             Falko Schmieder

Part II. Ordering the World

Chapter 7.   The Emergence of International Law and the Opening of
             World Order: Hugo Grotius Reconsidered   111
             Chenxi Tang

Chapter 8.   "Natural Capital," "Human Capital," "Social Capital": It's
             All Capital Now   123
             Desmond McNeill

Chapter 9.   The Worlds in Human Rights: Images or Mirages?   136
             Malcolm Langford

Chapter 10. Democracy of the "New World": The Great Binding Law
             of Peace and the Political System of the Haudenosaunee
             Confederacy   154
             Lars Kirkhusmo Pharo

Chapter 11. The Immanent World: Responsibility and Spatial
             Justice   168
             Andreas Philippopoulos-Mihalopoulos

Chapter 12. From Critical to Partisan Dictionaries; or, What Is
             Excluded from Today's Flat World Orthodoxies?   182
             Sanja Perovic

Part III. Timing the World

Chapter 13. At Home or Away: On Nostalgia, Exile, and
             Cosmopolitanism   199
             Olivier Remaud

Chapter 14. Extensions of World Heritage: The Globe, the List, and
             the Limes   212
             Stefan Willer

Chapter 15. The End of the World: From the Lisbon Earthquake to
             the Last Days   226
             Kyrre Kverndokk

Chapter 16. Time and Space in World Literature: Ibsen in and out of Sync 240
Tore Rem

Part IV. Mapping the World

Chapter 17. Middle Age of the Globe 255
Alfred Hiatt

Chapter 18. The Champion of the North: World Time in Olaus Magnus's *Carta marina* 274
Erling Sandmo

Chapter 19. The Search for Vínland and Norse Conceptions of the World 286
Karl G. Johansson

Chapter 20. The Cartographic Constitution of Global Politics 299
Jeppe Strandsbjerg

Chapter 21. The Individual and the "Intellectual Globe": Francis Bacon, John Locke, and Vannevar Bush 311
Richard Yeo

Part V. Making the World

Chapter 22. The World as Sphere: Conceptualizing with Sloterdijk 327
Kari van Dijk

Chapter 23. The Fontenellian Moment: Revisiting Seventeenth- and Eighteenth-Century Worlds 339
Helge Jordheim

Chapter 24. Fixating the Poles: Science, Fiction, and Photography at the Ends of the World 356
Siv Frøydis Berg

Chapter 25. The Norwegian Who Became a Globe: Mediation and Temporality in Roald Amundsen's 1911 South Pole Conquest 373
Espen Ytreberg

Index 387

Illustrations

17.1 John of Wallingford, *Globus spericus*. St. Albans, 1258. London, British Library. 256
17.2 Diagrams and world map from Macrobius, *Commentarius in Ciceronis Somnium Scipionis*, thirteenth century. Munich, Bayerische Staatsbibliothek. 259
17.3 World map from Macrobius, *Commentarius in Ciceronis Somnium Scipionis*, tenth century. Vatican City, Biblioteca Apostolica Vaticana. 260
17.4 World map from Macrobius, *Commentarius in Ciceronis Somnium Scipionis*, ca. 1100. London, British Library. 262
17.5 Martin Behaim, *Erdapfel* (1492). Germanisches Nationalmuseum, Nuremburg. 265
17.6 The Psalter map, ca. 1260. London, British Library. 267
18.1 Olaus Magnus, *Carta marina* (1539), detail. Uppsala University Library. 277
19.1 T-O map from Remigius of Auxerre/Isidore of Seville: Commentary on Phocas's *Ars de nomine et verbo*. England, thirteenth century. London, British Library. 287
21.1 Illustration from Francis Bacon's *Sylva sylvarum or a Naturall Historie, in Ten Centuries* ([1627] 1651 edition). Rare Books & Special Collections, University of Sydney Library. 315
21.2 Illustration from Francis Bacon, *Of the Advancement and Proficience of Learning* ([1605] 1640 edition). Rare Books & Special Collections, University of Sydney Library. 315
23.1 Juan Olivar, illustration to the first edition of Fontenelle's *Entretiens*. University of Oslo Library. 342

23.2 Illustration from the Danish 1748 edition of Fontenelle's
     Entretiens. University of Oslo Library. 346
23.3 Illustration from the Danish 1764 edition of Fontenelle's
     Entretiens. University of Oslo Library. 346
23.4 Illustration from the 1780 Berlin edition of Fontenelle's
     Entretiens. National Library of Norway. 347
23.5 Illustration from the 1780 Berlin edition of Fontenelle's
     Entretiens. National Library of Norway. 347
24.1 Frederick W. *Beechey, Winter Harbour*, 1821. National Library
     of Norway. 358
24.2 Unknown photographer/Fridtjof Nansen, Polhavet, 12 July
     1894. National Library of Norway. 364
24.3 Thorvald Nilsen, *Chart over the Immediate Surroundings of the
     South Pole*, 6 February 1912. National Library of Norway. 366
24.4 Lieut. Bowers, *Discovery of Amundsen's tent at the South Pole by
     Captain Scott's party*, 18 January 1912. National Library of
     Norway. 368
25.1 Sverre Halvorsen drawing Roald Amundsen. From the film
     Roald Amundsens sydpolsferd. National Library of Norway. 374
25.2 Roald Amundsen, his crew, and the tent at the approximate
     South Pole on 16 December 1911. Wikimedia Commons. 378

►• Introduction •◄

The World as Concept and Object of Knowledge

Helge Jordheim and Erling Sandmo

At the present moment we are experiencing an extremely prolific and intense discourse on globalization, in terms of processes, movements, and frictions. At the same time, we seem to have only a rather vague idea of the place, or rather the site or the scene, where these processes and movements unfold: *the world*. In contrast to the process of globalization, which seems to be just as open-ended as history itself, the world is limited and absolute. But where are the limits and what do they mean? What can we say about them? The paradoxes brought out by globalization are not, at least not only, products of the digital revolution, not even of modernity, but reveal a whole set of possible emergence histories, genealogies, crisscrossing back in time, often very far back. Nevertheless, the histories of globalization are almost by necessity histories of the present, exposing hidden, older, and often forgotten layers of meaning in the utopian or dystopian discourses on our common global future. How, then, by means of what concepts, representations, tools, technologies, and practices, does the world emerge, or rather is the world brought into being as an object of human experience and activity, and, furthermore, how do these concepts, representations, and so forth deal with the paradoxes and challenges of limited space and unlimited time as well as with the multitude of contrasting genealogies?

One of the briefest, but by no means the worst, definitions of the concept of globalization has been proposed by Manfred Steger: in attempting to "compress" his preliminary results "into a single sentence," he defines globalization as "the expansion and intensification of social relations and consciousness across world-time and world-space."[1] A closer look at the definition, however, shows how it takes a key element for granted. Preoccupied with the processes and relations that unfold within "world time" and "world space," Steger never asks the question that in the end seems to be the most striking one: what is meant by "world-time" or "world-space," or, even more fundamentally, what is meant by "world"?

"Globalization" stems from the verb "to globalize," which seems to presuppose an object, something or someone who globalizes and someone or something that is to be globalized. It is implicitly understood that numerous phenomena are being globalized—such as politics, commerce, and culture, just to mention the major spheres—but globalization is more commonly referred to without any object, as a historical process and movement that consists of everything and everyone. According to Reinhart Koselleck, one of the seminal figures within conceptual history, such as it is practiced today, the phrase has become a *Kollektivsingular*, collective singular,[2] that is, a concept that is only found in the singular form but that nonetheless does not refer to a single, unambiguous subject or object. No matter how much we speak of globalization, it remains unclear who or what is globalizing or being globalized. There are many similar words, such as "progress," "development," and "history," that share the trait of referring to an inexorable and linear development, but whose ultimate end is highly unclear—whether it is lasting peace, freedom and democracy, or catastrophe and ruin.

Should we still wish to inquire into what is being globalized, there is certainly no doubt that language itself has been globalized, and even in a quite literal sense, in that ever more compound words are formed by means of "world" or "global": world citizen, world literature, world heritage, world order, global community, global warming, global health, global justice, and so forth. New such words are constantly being coined, as ever more disciplines, discourses, and epistemological genres seek to explore what is commonly referred to as the "global." Precisely because "globalization" is a collective singular, it can in theory refer to an infinite number of phenomena and objects—that is, the very phenomena and objects that are identified by the new "global" and "world" concepts.

Our discussion so far suggests that we are on the trail of a paradox of sorts. Even as the discussion of globalization becomes ever more widespread in academia, politics, and the newspapers; even as the concept is being expanded to encompass ever new processes, developments, and trends; even as ever new "global" words and concepts are doing the rounds; even as the discourse of globalization is expanding in all these ways, it becomes ever less clear what is the actual site (in both a spatial and a temporal sense) for all these processes and trends, what is the actual scope, the semantic circumference of all these concepts—in short, what "the world" is.[3]

Nevertheless, as this volume is meant to illustrate, "world" is an important concept, maybe even more important now than ever. Using it, we venture to express or understand something about a totality that historically has been crucial in humankind's attempts to see itself from the outside. These attempts—to make ourselves the object of large-scale knowledge and to keep various forms of knowledge together—are becoming increasingly frequent and, indeed, increasingly necessary, as we speak.

This is a book about the world and about its histories of emergence. Paradoxically, it sets out to defend the world, to insist on an importance that may well seem obvious at this point in time, when globalization and discourses on the global seem to be present everywhere. We want to ask where this everywhere *is*, and where it has been, and to point to the necessity of exploring the obvious answer: all over the world. It is such a simple answer, and yet profoundly vague, because it presupposes so many histories and so many different pasts. This haziness is our point of departure. Rather than leaving the world to the present, as this vague and somewhat naïve idea of the sum of all space, we want to study its rich actuality and its potential both for exploration of the past and for understanding the possibilities of the future.

We want to do this in specific ways. There may, as we will suggest in this introduction, be a big history to be told about the emergence, disappearance, and re-emergence of the world, but the world, studied historically, has always been in a state of emergence: the study of its reproductions shows how it has constantly been produced, and the study of the very concept of the world teaches us that it has been and is conceptualized, made conceivable and real, as an object of knowledge. This ongoing process, in different historical manifestations, is our topic, and it is a topic that calls for particular angles and methodologies. We have not wanted to present anthropologies of the world or world views; on the other hand, we do not want to confine us to specific ways of constructing the world, or worlds, or to devote our studies to particular institutions, and our ambition is not to develop systematical analyses of how discourses circulate. In short, the common ground for the studies collected here is not cultural history, history of science, or even history of knowledge, but a broad conceptual history, dealing on the one hand with the history of the concept of the world, and on the other with histories of how the world is conceived as an object of knowledge.

In practice, the distinctions between these historiographical traditions are, of course, difficult to draw. As a whole, though, this book is a work of conceptual history with excursions into a wide range of historical terrains and practices. Its chapters fall into five sections, each revolving around a form of conceptual practice: naming, ordering, timing, mapping, and making. They develop different aspects of the history of concepts and conceptualization. The first deals with the concept of the world in the strong sense, explicitly grounded in conceptual history; the second is concerned with the conceptualization through classifications, systems, and codes; the third and the fourth develop the temporal and spatial dimensions of conceptualization; and the fifth and final section presents studies of conceptualization of the world that are explicit and expressive acts of production.

We begin our introduction with a brief historiographical outline of the concept of the world and with a discussion of "concept" and "metaphor" as analytical, perhaps competing tools. We then move on to an exemplification of the conceptualization of the world as an object of knowledge—in this case in the form of cartography. In the continuation of the maps' character of being a view from both within the world and from nowhere, we move on to a discussion of the idea of the world as an object that can be envisaged and eventually seen from the outside. The two last sections of the introduction suggest a story of the decline and re-emergence of the world as a central, productive concept with a critical potential yet to be fully realized.

The World as Concept—or Metaphor

One of the most sustained attempts to write a history—a social and cultural history, not a purely linguistic or etymological one—about the concept of the "world" was made by the German theologian Hermann Braun in the seventh volume of the lexicon for political language in Germany, *Geschichtliche Grundbegriffe*, in which he contributed a sixty-page entry. Braun opens his history with a few Greek terms, such as *kosmos*, *aion*, and *seculum*, and follows their migrations into Latin, before focusing more intently on the German word *Welt*. However, the writing of conceptual history is something other than conducting etymological studies. Rather than phonetic laws, prefixes, and suffixes, conceptual history pertains to meanings and usage. The precondition for writing the history of "the world" is that we are able to demarcate a field of meaning or area of usage—that is, certain frameworks that help ensure that we are in fact studying the history of the given concept and not merely a disjointed collection of random usages with no inner coherence.

It seems nearly impossible to arrive at a single, unambiguous definition of what we mean by "world." Astronomers will operate with one definition, philosophers another—as will stockbrokers, politicians, athletes, immigrants, and televangelists. Isn't it more or less so that "the world" entirely lacks a conceptual core that can be traced throughout history? In many cases we do not even know whether we are talking about time or space: is the world a globe with a 40,000-kilometer circumference, or is it the number of years, centuries, and millennia that this globe has existed and will continue to exist? "The world" or "the way of the world"? Furthermore, it seems tricky enough to clarify what the concept means today, without inquiring into what it meant two thousand years ago and investigating the conceptual changes it has undergone since.

There is no doubt that "the world" as a concept pushes the methods of conceptual history to the extreme, much as "history," "politics," and "culture" do—only even further, as Braun points out, since "the world" includes and incorporates all of these other concepts. This does not mean that "the world" differs in essence from these other basic concepts. In his introduction to *Geschichtliche Grundbegriffe*, Koselleck points out that what differentiates a concept from a word is precisely that the concept cannot be made unambiguous.[4] Both words and concepts are at the outset ambiguous when we encounter them in current situations or historical sources. However, the words can be made unambiguous by referring to their given context and by clarifying who, what, where, and when; the same cannot be done with concepts. For concepts, in Koselleck's sense of the word, collect, aggregate, and integrate a variety of meanings that often stem from widely differing fields, within widely differing terminologies—it is this very variety of meaning that defines them as concepts. In this sense, "the world" encompasses for instance astrophysical meanings (Earth as a planet in the Milky Way, the third such planet from the Sun, the only one that seems to have signs of intelligent life, and so forth) and political meanings (the world as a system of states that are connected to one another through trade and diplomacy). For a long time "the world" was primarily a religious concept, one that derived its meanings and usages in contrast to "the afterlife," "the kingdom of God," or "heaven." Traces of these meanings remain in the concept of "the worldly," which is also referred to as "the temporal," as a reminder that time itself—transience—was a characteristic of this world.

This brings us to a key element in conceptual history and to a basic premise for this book: concepts are not merely an assembly of contemporary experiences and meanings; past meanings—ones that have become obsolete, been replaced by other concepts, or belong to world views or conceptualizations that we no longer recognize as our own—have also been deposited in concepts and their current usage. Inherent in every concept are several temporal and semantic layers of varying duration.[5] One example would be our current skepticism of notions of "progress" and "development." Many of the results of what we for a long time referred to as "progress," such as industrialization, technological innovation, and the exploitation of natural resources, have turned out to be more a two-edged sword in regard to the climate, the global distribution of wealth, and peaceful coexistence. Without being overly pessimistic, it is possible to assume that historical development is neither linear nor teleological, yet many current concepts of the world base themselves on such a notion of straightforward progress. One example might be "world history." This hardly ever refers to the history of the world per se, but is the history of a shared process that the different parts of the world enter upon at different points in time. As such, it might seem as though the concept of the world is still imbued with a specific philosophy of history, in the guise of meanings and experiences that originated with Christian eschatology as well as with Enlightenment notions of progress[6]—not overtly and explicitly, but as more or less concealed layers of meaning and time that affect our understanding and use of the concept, even though we are not always aware of this. It is a task of conceptual history to uncover such layers of meaning, so that, as Koselleck puts it, "historical clarification" can lead to "political clarity."[7]

However, there is also another way of tackling this problem. It was precisely the chaotic diversity of meanings and usages that led Hans Blumenberg, another German philosopher and historian, to contend that there quite simply is no concept of the world—or, to rephrase his statement, that the world cannot be conceptualized. The concept itself exists, of course, but it is without empirical substance and does not correspond to a specific, human experience. "We have no conception of the totality of being [*Totalität des Seins*]," Blumenberg writes, "but we still use 'the world' as the subject in sentences, just as we do it with 'history.'"[8]

If it is not a concept, then what is "the world"? According to Blumenberg, attempts to describe the world, to describe the very totality of all being, can never result in a concept. Rather, what we end up with will take the shape of a *metaphor*. But this should not be perceived as a negative and unsatisfactory state of affairs; on the contrary, it is metaphors that give structure to the world and open it up for cognition. In his essay on metaphorology (that is, an investigation of metaphors in their historical context and development), Blumenberg discusses two metaphors for the world: *terra incognita* and the incomplete world. When these metaphors appear during the seventeenth century, both are symptomatic of a new and different relationship to the world. Instead of the world being closed, familiar, and complete, the great explorations and the Copernican Revolution made the world open, unfamiliar, and incomplete, something humankind itself can explore and ultimately complete through its combined abilities, curiosity, and scientific and technological innovations.[9]

For Blumenberg, metaphors for the world are what he calls "absolute metaphors," that is, metaphors that cannot be converted to concepts without losing an essential part of their meaning—they are "absolute metaphors for the totality of all being that never is given and that can never be concretized."[10] Blumenberg seems keen on avoiding the very concept of the world—that is, to speak of the world as though it were a concept—even though he himself doubts that this is possible: "Even though I am inclined to believe that we should in the future entirely avoid creating and using statements regarding 'the world,' I doubt whether such an injunction would ever succeed."[11]

In contrast, in this introduction we will argue that rejecting the concept of the world would entail a significant semantic loss—the loss of an opportunity to cast a critical eye on the discourse of globalization. Discussions about globalization further precisely the dream of the incomplete, the as yet undiscovered and unexploited, that was launched with the metaphors *terra incognita* and the incomplete world. The question is whether the semantics continues to be in step with the reality it has been assigned to describe and the intentions it has been assigned to fulfill.

The World as Object of Knowledge

To write the history of the concept of the world, we have to accept that concepts cannot be given a single, unambiguous definition. They are accumulations, aggregates of experiences both past and present, that affect how the concept is used and understood. It is an approach that contains many possibilities, but also certain limitations, at least if we assume that what we are investigating is the world as an object of knowledge—how have people from different eras gone about acquiring knowledge about the world, and to what ends have they used such knowledge? Of course, it is difficult to draw a clear distinction between these two approaches—the world as a concept or a metaphor and the world as an object of knowledge—as they mutually presuppose each other: any knowledge about the world presupposes a concept of the world, and any concept of the world presupposes that the concept refers to something. It is nonetheless possible to say something about the preconditions for representing the world at various points in time, and to show what people have specifically defined as "the world" when this world has been presented to them. An interesting case for discussing the differences and overlaps between conceptualizations and epistemologies are the world maps.[12]

The best preserved of all the world maps prior to the Age of Discovery still hangs where it was created to be hung, in Hereford Cathedral near the English border with Wales.[13] The large, nearly oval map measures 158 x 133 cm and is made of calfskin, probably from a calf that was fattened up with choice fodder for the very purpose of becoming large and developing a particularly soft and exquisite hide. Already from birth this calf was raised to become an image of the world, something it became around the year 1300.

Upon first glance, the map in Hereford Cathedral seems confusing, and the world is hard to recognize for those of us who are accustomed to today's maps and satellite images. The map displays large landmasses centered around an ocean that is replete with islands and images. The ocean reaches its estuary at the bottom of the map, where there is a tiny opening between the landmasses. On either side of this estuary is a narrow, irregular stripe of ocean that encompasses the entire map; this ocean is full of islands, of which the most conspicuous are an archipelago at the bottom left and a circular island at the very top, featuring two miniscule people depicted above a shape that resembles a large, sprawling K. Brief texts and depictions of humans, animals, and buildings have been written and drawn everywhere. Examinations have shown that the map was originally in color and with gilt details, though by now the colors have long since faded; the ocean remains blue, however, and a large, red shape is prominent in the upper right. This is the world, as made clear by the Latin designation for this type of map: *mappa mundi*, a map of the world.

As is frequently the case with ancient maps, we must focus on the Hereford map's center in order to understand what sort of world it represents. The center here is a beautiful, ornate crucifix inside a circle—Jerusalem, the center of Christianity. When we realize this, the geography becomes comprehensible. East is up, west is down: the estuary is the Strait of Gibraltar, the outlet of the Mediterranean Sea. The Nile Delta is recognizable, as are also the British Isles, the archipelago at the bottom left. The large, red shape represents the Red Sea, and we can also make out Scandinavia, decorated with a tiny man on skis, no less.

However, much about the map continues to be alien in another and more profound sense than merely the inexact geography. The circular island at the top is the Garden of Eden, with Adam and Eve. The sprawling K is the common source of the four great rivers of the world: the Phison, the Gehon, the Tigris, and the Euphrates. Eden thereby lies in the very east, where the sun rises. It is also this cardinal point that is closest to the divine, as still testified in modern languages: the Far East is traditionally called—though now with negative connotations—the *Orient*, derived from the Latin word for east, *oriens* (lit. "rising"); turning toward the east, toward the sunrise and the divine, was thus an act of *orientating* oneself. Above Eden and beyond the east on the map we see Christ judging the living and the dead. In the bottom left corner of the edge of the map we see an unusual interpretation of a well-known biblical passage, Luke 2:1 ("And it came to pass in those days, that there went out a decree from Caesar Augustus that all the world should be taxed"), with the distinctive element being that the emperor is depicted as sending forth cartographers. The scene thereby becomes an image of the very knowledge the map presents and of the religious import of this knowledge: it is true, factual knowledge about the world, and the map-making is fundamentally the same as the imperial gathering of knowledge that served as the backdrop for the birth of Christ. The Hereford map provides its viewers a glimpse of the divine.

This makes the map comprehensible as a religious, Christian map of the world, one that displays a world that is defined through its metaphysical coherence. This concept of the world is in other words a concept of order. The map simultaneously reflects another part of this prehistory, namely a concept of something spatial. The Hereford map combines these two aspects of the concept of the world: the Christian world order is allowed to form the space. The parts of the spatial world that are important in the Bible—that is, Israel and the rest of the Middle East from Egypt to Babylon—are according to our more purely geographical objectives greatly blown out of proportion. Their size corresponds to their religious magnitude, thereby also providing ample room for a myriad of miniature scenes from biblical history, such as the Crucifixion, the Tower of Babel, Noah's Ark, and a long, meandering line that represents the Jews' forty-year wander in the desert.

However, the world of the Hereford map is more than that. In addition to the biblical illustrations, there are a host of other miniature images, of mermaids, skiers, rhinoceroses, headless men and cannibals; there is the Labyrinth of Crete and the Pillars of Hercules; there are ships, churches, universities, and mythical rulers. The world is a *heterotopia*, a place where several different times and phenomena from different epistemological systems coexist simultaneously—at least for the viewer.[14] The world is—to use modern, anachronistic concepts—anthropology, history, institutions, and politics, in addition to geography and nature. In other words, orientating oneself in this world also entails orientating oneself among the contrasting concepts of the world, which are all discussed in this book. This world resides not least in the tension between the religious, Christian world and that which merely belongs to the material world, which might even be deceptive and dangerous—the *secular*. The world is the coexistence of transcendent order and temporal multitude, thus mirroring St. Augustine's vision of the eternal City of God immanent in the lives of men.

What the map nevertheless evinces is that the various elements of the world largely have their designated place. Even a heterotopia has its distribution, its system. This system is made apparent not least by the distance from each element to the religion's focal point, Jerusalem. The further away on the map from this focal point, the more prominent is the world's secularity. In this manner the entire world is incorporated in a religious world order that has fixed, everlasting places for all creatures and phenomena. At the same time, it is crucial to understand how the Hereford map contains a myriad of differences, of differing understandings of what "the world" as a concept means, even within a map with a label (*mappa mundi*) that clearly indicates that this is the world. In reality, the various concepts of the world exist not only simultaneously, but also within the same physical representations of the world. Also time is multifaceted, but it can be held together through such a representation, on a map in a cathedral in England.

Most people today would consider geography to be a separate discipline, as an impartial way of representing the world, even though there may still be disagreements concerning how to create the most correct world map. The Hereford map is comprehensible from this "purely" geographical basis, as long as we learn to understand the idea behind these unfamiliar proportions.

One element in particular, however, is conspicuous in its absence from the map: America.

The Europeans discovered America, the "New World," approximately two hundred years after the Hereford map was affixed to the cathedral wall. The discovery resulted of course in an overabundance of new knowledge about the world: about nature, about new dangers and new flora and fauna that could be eaten (or that most certainly should not be eaten), about what could be smoked or drunk, about foreign peoples and possible routes of passage. At the same time, this surfeit of knowledge also led to a crisis of confidence in the idea of the world as a hierarchical order and a religious entity. So much of what had been discovered did *not* have a designated place in the world order, and all this additional knowledge threatened to undermine the entire system, the entire world order.

The world eventually proved fully able to contain all knowledge, and to embrace the spatio-temporal division that followed the European discovery of America—the New World and the Old—but the incorporation, and the subsequent sense of completion of the world as an object of knowledge, was perceived not just as progress. The *Fool's Cap Map* of the world, made around 1590, chillingly reflects the inherent ambivalence of contemporary cartography: the new abundance of geographical knowledge filled the spaces for time and metaphysics. The globe had never been so flat.

This map presents a state-of-the-art world map with a highly detailed American west coast and a vast *terra australis nondum cognita*, "southern land not yet known." Not yet—but soon. The most striking feature of the map, though, is the fact that it is the face of a jester. The world face is framed by the bell-tipped cap of the jester, who also holds a distinctive staff. Above the head, the image is strewn with quotes and sayings on vanity, folly, and madness, under the image's grim heading *Nosce te ipsum*, "Know thyself." All the other sentences state that there is nothing to know, everything is illusion and oblivion. It is still a world, one world, but its melancholic insistence on its own loss of meaning and coherence seems to prefigure a later loss of the sense of the world itself.

The World from Outside

The Age of Discovery vastly expanded the world as an object of knowledge. Even though this expansion could bring with it a certain precariousness of the world, as in the *Fool's Cap Map*, the world remained one and the same. This, however, was about to change. In his *Entretiens sur la pluralité des mondes*, originally published in French in 1686 and immediately translated into both German and English,[15] Bernard de Fontenelle claimed that not one single world existed, but many—indeed, an infinite number of worlds. During a series of conversations, a philosopher and a French noblewoman discuss Copernican cosmology. In place of divine order, harmony, and celestial music, Fontenelle presents a purely mechanical universe on the basis of Cartesian physics. The universe consists of numerous whirlwinds, what Fontenelle terms *tourbillons*; in the center of each one is a star, which planets orbit. But also the planets have their own whirlwinds, something that explains why they in turn have moons orbiting themselves. Already in the title Fontenelle completes his radical conceptual innovation when he refers not to "one world," but to a plurality of worlds. And a world, as quickly becomes evident, is a planet that is populated. It is logically inconceivable, Fontenelle argues, that our planet is the only one that is inhabited. Where other planets exist, there must also be—in line with the tenet of the "infinite plurality of nature," as Fontenelle phrases it[16]—other worlds, other creatures, and other societies. Fontenelle is by no means the first person to propose the idea that there might be life on other planets; on the contrary, this idea has accompanied cosmological speculation ever since the ancient Greeks. However, Fontenelle is the first to achieve such a dissemination throughout the entirety of the European Enlightenment. By means of his work, the world gains an *exterior*, in both an anthropological and a cosmological sense: both our world and its human inhabitants are dislodged from the center of the universe, and characterized by a liminal existence, on the boundary between ourselves and something else. Hence, to be understood it must be seen in its proper context.

One of the earliest and most coherent expositions of this decentralizing movement, both in an epistemological and an anthropological sense, was put forth by the German theologian, philosopher, and author Johann Gottfried Herder, who opened his magnum opus *Ideen zur Philosophie der Geschichte der Menschheit*, 1784-91, with the following statement: "Our philosophy for the history of man, if it is to be worthy of such a name, must start from the heavens." At first glance this idea might seem familiar, but when Herder switches the perspective from the Earth to the heavens, it is not God's omniscience he has in mind. In the opening chapter, which is headed "Our Earth is a star among stars," he declares that "our abode, the Earth, is nothing by virtue of itself, but derives its nature and form, its ability to organize and preserve its creatures, from those powers that extend throughout the entire universe." This means that "we cannot view it by itself in isolation, but only within the choir of worlds of which it is a part."[17]

The idea that an exposition of human history and development cannot begin with humankind and its world but must start off with something that is greater and that encompasses it, something that makes both the Earth and human beings one of several, one of many, is a radical notion even today—or perhaps more correctly, not least today, when new ventures into "deep history" and other large-scale works on global history reinforce the anthropocentrism they set out to criticize. A line may be drawn from Fontenelle's dialogues on the plurality of worlds through Herder's philosophy of history and onward to Alexander von Humboldt, the German explorer, naturalist, and anthropologist, who traveled around Latin America between 1799 and 1804, exploring, surveying, analyzing, describing. His dream was to describe the entire world, a "physical description of the world," as he called it. Toward the end of the 1830s he finally found the time to write such a description. After three decades of traveling and studying geology, botany, physics, chemistry, mineralogy, zoology, astronomy, oceanography, ethnology, and demography, Humboldt certainly did not lack source material; the challenge was rather to create a synthesis, to assemble these diverse pieces in a larger unity, which with some verity might be called the world. Humboldt ultimately opted for a different concept as the title of his work, which was published in five volumes between 1845 and 1862, namely the Greek word *Kosmos*, one of the forerunners of the concept of "the world" and which originally meant "ornament" or "jewelry." But how would Humboldt be able to fashion his chaotic material into a piece of jewelry—what sort of perspective should he assume, what should be his own position? It was impossible to observe the entire world from Berlin—that much was apparent to him. He chose to make the same movement as Fontenelle and Herder before him by using the power of his imagination to, as it were, blast off into the universe:

> We begin in the depths of space, among the most remote nebulae, before gradually descending through the layers of stars that belong to our solar system, to the Earth's sphere, surrounded by air and ocean, its form, temperature, and magnetic tension, and to its abundance of life that unfolds on its surface, stimulated by the light.[18]

Humboldt also explains why he makes this movement of an imaginary descent from the outer confines of the universe and down to Earth. It is thereby no longer "human interests" that forms the basis; on the contrary, the world appears as "part of a whole and is subordinate to this." Only in this manner is it possible to achieve a perspective that is—and here he almost sounds like Nietzsche—"general," "grand and free," and "uninfluenced by motives such as closeness and comfortable sympathy."[19]

In one respect it is a journey into space that Humboldt undertakes, out into the universe and back again—only this journey is neither a physical and technological reality nor a fictional narrative, but a philosophical leap, a movement of the mind, in order to escape both anthropocentrism and terracentrism. A mere hundred or so years later, however, the journey did indeed become technological reality. If we take a century's worth of technological development for granted, there is a more or less straight line from Humboldt to the Apollo 8 spaceflight in 1968, more precisely the moment, broadcast live on television, when the astronauts saw the Earth emerge above the surface of the Moon, as a tiny, blue orb. The view from the Moon toward "the blue planet" was immortalized by astronaut William Anders; the picture he snapped was a global sensation and has subsequently been hailed as one of the most important photographs of all time. It was suddenly possible to gaze upon the world in its entirety—not as something immense and overwhelming, but as a tiny, almost fragile blue orb, one of the Lord's marbles, as it were. Perhaps we might say that the world was thereby subject to a perspective that was precisely typified by "closeness" and "comfortable sympathy," that negates the intellectual distance, the contextualizing gaze, the external perspective that Humboldt wished to achieve. On the other hand, the picture gave rise to a sense of the Earth's vulnerability, which precisely cast doubt on "human interests" as the basis for making the world an object of knowledge.

Today we can repeat this movement—the one that Humboldt enacted through the power of imagination and the written word, and that Apollo 8 carried out with rocket science on a live broadcast—simply by opening Google Earth. Only time will tell in what ways this, too, will change our concepts of the world.

The World that Disappeared

While Fontenelle clearly resonated with the zeitgeist of his era with his dialogues about "the plurality of worlds," Humboldt is already a rare bird, as Braun also notes. The idea that it should be possible to provide a complete "description of the world," which encompasses cosmology, anthropology, and as good as every conceivable natural science, has had to concede defeat to specialization and the partitioning of scientific knowledge into separate disciplines. Already when the final German translation of Fontenelle was published in 1780, the philosophical and literarily speculative dialogues had become a scientific work in a much more modern sense, with extensive, complex footnotes that were atypical for dialogues, containing for example updated measurements of interplanetary distances and planetary rotation periods, calculated by one of Europe's most respected astronomers at the time, Johann Elert Bode from the Royal Academy of Sciences in Berlin. The 1780 German edition was also furnished with new illustrations, with diagrammatic illustrations featuring arrows, numbers, and measurements replacing the original's pictures of amiable marquises strolling among Rococo interiors and almost op art-like representations of a universe full of whirlwinds.[20]

This is of course what is often referred to as scientific progress, but it is precisely this specialization that leads to the disappearance of the world. For

Fontenelle, Herder, and Humboldt, cosmology and anthropology are closely intertwined, to the extent that a statement about the world is also a statement about humankind. It is perhaps only when this close connection between cosmology and anthropology disappears that we realize how important it has been. In this sense, everything that is currently said and written about climate change, emissions, and overconsumption of resources seems to suffer from the lack of a concept of the world that can emphasize and preserve the connection between cosmology (as represented by ecology) and anthropology, or if you will, between the human world and the physical world.

Further developments in the nineteenth and twentieth centuries might perhaps be described as the world disappearing into time, into progress, and—in a certain sense—into history, and thereby to a certain extent becoming removed from the heterogeneous and pluralistic space where Fontenelle allocated it. This conceptual transformation can for instance be illustrated by all the new concepts that emerge—such as "global transportation," "global market," "global audience," "world trade," and "world literature"—that testify to an entirely different world view and to entirely new global conditions than were to be found in the eighteenth and nineteenth centuries. More than anything else, it is striking how much these are *our* concepts, concepts we still use and understand, unlike many of the key concepts from the seventeenth century, such as "world apple" or "world architect." This is in fact one of Koselleck's most important and controversial points: it is precisely during this period between 1750 and 1850, which he refers to as *die Sattelzeit* (roughly "the saddle era"), that our concepts take shape.[21] But the new concepts differentiate themselves from the older ones in that they do not describe more or less static spaces—they are rather concepts of movement, or more precisely concepts of circulation and communication. In that sense they embody the formation of an entirely new semantic framework associated with the concept of the world: the world is no longer something that is more or less given in the form of a religious or cosmologically defined space, but something that is created through human activity: commerce, travel, and other forms of communication and distribution. To all human activity are attached expectations, aspirations, plans, and ambitions, something that in turn infuses concepts with a forward-looking, prognostic, and in some instances almost utopian meaning. What Koselleck calls the "temporalization" of concepts then takes place, something that entails a break with the past and an advance into something new and superior. If we return to the present, it is easy to see the concept of globalization as the latest addition to this series of concepts—a concept of movement and communication, that points toward a future that is utopian for some and dystopian for others.

But when "the world" becomes synonymous with human activity, communication, circulation, and commerce—a goal that humankind is striving to achieve—then a certain set of meanings and epistemological strategies inevitably goes missing, namely everything that pertains to the world as a limited and separate space, that pertains to finitude, scarcity, liminality, and dependence. Or to phrase it another way: the world, such as it took shape for Fontenelle, Herder, and Humboldt, or such as it appeared from the Moon on the picture taken by the Apollo 8 astronaut, disappears as a concept, as a semantic resource we can use to understand ourselves and our own situation. The problems that stem from this semantic loss manifest themselves daily in the media and in political and scientific communication. The evidence suggests that the strongly temporalized, forward-looking concept of globalization, that is, the idea that the world will become one—one market, one state—no longer packs the same punch, or if it does, only in its most dystopian variant, as a catastrophe scenario. It is conceivable that we are in the midst of a new conceptual transformation, not unlike the one that transpired in the Koselleckian *Sattelzeit*. But this time it is temporalization and the belief in progress that are at their journey's end. In order to understand and change our own situation, we need another concept of the world, one that instead of temporal infinity articulates a limited, scarce, and threatened cosmological and anthropological space—a space with an exterior. It is our hope that this book can contribute to the production of new and other concepts.

The Return of the World

In March 1991 US president George H. W. Bush delivered a speech to Congress following the expulsion of Iraqi forces from Kuwait and the end of the Gulf War. In a speech in which the phrase "the world" recurred almost sentence for sentence, Bush declared that the victory of the US-led coalition forces was the beginning of a "new world order." Endorsing Winston Churchill's vision from almost fifty years before, he hailed the defeat of Saddam Hussein as a decisive step in creating a world where the UN's goals could be achieved, a world in which "freedom and respect for human rights find a home among all nations."[22] In the wake of the September 11 attacks a decade later, however, this vision of a new world order appeared to be completely out of touch with reality. Suddenly the world was partitioned in other ways, with new theaters of war and new frontlines, and with a "world order" that none had envisioned only a few years beforehand.

Environmental movements had at this point used the "blue planet" image for decades. In the 1970s and 1980s, the image of the lonely planet adorned the covers of scores, perhaps hundreds, of books on pollution, the threat of nuclear war, and preservation. It signified the planetary dimension of the dangers that loomed large in the future. The conceptualizations of the world that have taken place within the various environmental discourses seem to have become more and more explicit, and the historical awareness of their participants both deeper and more ambivalent. Dipesh Chakrabarty's recent work on historiography and the climate crisis reflects this in an open, almost hesitant manner in its attempts to distinguish and bring together a historical, local guilt, the necessity of a Western *mea culpa* with a responsibility for the future that has to be grounded in a reconceptualization of the world.[23]

As these examples suggest, the world's conceptual "disappearance" has been accompanied by an intense use of that very concept in the political and military discourse, a discourse that has moved as swiftly as the discourse of globalization—and at the same time it is as though the concept of the world has increasingly diminished in substance, even while discussions about the world expand and are transformed ever more swiftly. The question that is thereby raised regards what would be the point, or the potential, in using the concept of "the world" and insisting on this concept having a specific meaning?

One important way to approach this question would be by way of the already discussed notion of exteriority—arguing that the world has an exterior, that our world is merely one of many voices in a choir, only one of many worlds and perhaps even ephemeral. Observing the Earth from outside, Humboldt insists on conceiving of "world" as a totality, with an outside, thus anticipating present debates on climate and environment; on the other hand, Humboldt's important and unsettling notion of solidarity is not limited to our own planet or our own race. The concept of the world can be an opportunity to turn the more recent concept of globalization against itself, to give it an exterior—not least because the concept of the world is so ancient and has so many historical layers of meaning.

If there is a manifest critical potential in the capacity of the concept of "world" to formulate ideas of exteriority, is it then also conceivable that there will be a similar potential in insisting that the world, as a totality, also has an interior? The models are there, in the history we have sketched above, in the world map of the Middle Ages, which so manifestly was based on the idea that the world is created through its essence: the world as a religious order. But could it be an order of a different kind? Who remains on the outside, who is not included, and who is assumed to be strong or weak in contexts where "the world" is conveyed or staged? Are there nonetheless patterns and structures in the use of the concept, even though these are not explicit? A fundamental tenet of Marxism is that capitalism strives toward the global, that the owning class will develop toward becoming a global bourgeoisie. Opposition to capitalism therefore requires a notion of the world as a place of resistance, as a foundation for a different political future. It is striking how the discourse of globalization has focused on domination and ownership as the genuinely global phenomena. A challenge will be to use the concept of the world to articulate ideas about politics and about opposition.

To study how we conceptualize the world, in the past or in the present, can—that is at least the claim of this book—help us express what the world is, as a political, social, and ecological reality in current debates on globalization and a new world order. To articulate and approach the so-called "global challenges," a recent concept coined within the EU and UN systems, including for example poverty, climate change, warfare, and the supply of food and energy, we require a concept of the world that goes beyond the narrowly political, economic, and even anthropological, opening up toward a broader, more comprehensive, and more complex reality—understanding the world from the outside in.

Structure of the Book

One of the basic claims of this book is that the history and the historicity of the world is and has always been a basic element of its conceptualization. The act of "naming" the world is therefore rarely—if ever—a point of pure origin, but an event among many as well as an ongoing process, constantly rekindling earlier conceptualizations. As a methodological approach, this is a basic element of the methodology of conceptual history, as demonstrated by Ivo Spira in the opening chapter of the book's first section, on naming. The other chapters provide specific case studies, each showing how the study of specific historical and social practices of naming can follow different paths. Nora Eggen presents a close reading of how the world is conceptualized in Abū Ḥāmid al-Ghazālī's *Mishkāt al-anwār* (c. 1100) on the basis of earlier Arabic lexicography, zooming in on one specific aspect of one text. In contrast, but in very different ways, Oddbjørn Leirvik and Falko Schmieder explore how concepts of the world are produced and transformed in discourses on conscience and ecology, investigating the world's embeddedness in other histories. Erik Tängerstad's chapter on "the Third World" joins conceptual history with a history of political ideas and shifts the attention toward the strategies of conceptualization, while Claudia Lenz's interest lies in the didactics of conceptualization. Taking Hannah Arendt as her starting point, Lenz studies conceptualization as action with an international teachers' workshop as a case. With her chapter, this book is provided with a guide to a small-scale, ethically grounded practice of the world.

The chapters in the following section, on the ordering of the world, deal with what is already a condition for the practice of "naming," namely that the world has an order, or rather that it can be ordered. The world can be named because there is a something to name, a structured unit, but the questions over the nature, scope, and stability of such orders are dense and complex and invite the open, multidisciplinary reflections demonstrated in the following. Chenxi Tang's chapter highlights the narrative dimension of world order in Hugo Grotius's *De iure belli ad pacis*, a founding text in the history of international law. Grotius argues that the world envisaged by traditional natural law, where humankind shared the resources of nature without any governing authority, was receding as the concepts of property and the state emerged and rose to dominate. This implied a transformation of the *ius gentium* from "law of all peoples" to "law between states," a transformation that in turn heralded a world order in perpetual change and renewal. This instability of the world may seem to be both order and its possible opposite, a flux, a world where the question of order is open and acute. This section's two final chapters, by Andreas Philippopoulos-Mihalopoulos and Sanja Perovic, both use Niklas Luhmann as a starting point for discussions of how notions of a world order rub against the idea of globalization. Philippopoulos-Mihalopoulos does this in a reflection on the concepts of worlding and *Weltgesellschaft* as means to study how a self-observing world system expands and contracts, Perovic in a historical study of the idea of a global convergence of communication. Whereas our present discourse on globalization tends to presume convergence, Pierre Bayle and later Enlightenment thinkers concerned themselves with how the spread of knowledge could spread divergence rather than convergence—an insight that retains its critical-historical potential.

These three chapters frame a trio of case studies. First, Desmond McNeill takes hold of "capital," analyzing how a concept historically deployed to expand economic thinking and to make economic forces more comprehensible has achieved the opposite: the global expansion of an economistic world view and the abstraction of economy. Malcolm Langford examines the intrinsic ideas of the world in human rights, and argues that these rights can be seen as both myth and politics, the two corresponding with pessimistic and optimistic views of the world. Finally, Lars Kirkhusmo Pharo provides a study of the democratic philosophy and political system of the Haudenosaunee Confederacy, universal in its thinking—and established well ahead of corresponding European or colonial democracies.

Just as the ordering of the world seems to be implied in its naming, the next practice, timing, comes across as aspect and expansion of ordering. Any attempt to conceptualize the world as a system of distances, proximities, and communication will also be a reflection on time, which can take almost any number of forms. Progress, backwardness, memory, and longing are but a few of the concepts that have given structure and meaning to the world. In this way, the chapters in this section expand on the preceding discussions of the ordering of the world, the emphasis now to a slightly greater degree on the temporality of space rather than the spatiality of time.

Olivier Remaud's chapter explores one aspect of the relationship between space and time through the study of exile and nostalgia: exile is governed by the feeling of nostalgia, and the exiled individual remains enclosed in his former values and remains at a certain cosmopolitan distance from his present surroundings. A particular, if ephemeral experience of belonging to the world is thus stretched out in time, between the no longer and the not yet. The topic of heritage, and world heritage in particular, could be regarded as the opposite movement, where the past becomes present and the individual, physical place is transformed into what is in principle a global space. Stefan Willer opens—and ends—his chapter with a discussion of the terms "world" and "heritage," highlighting the tensions between the two in the heritage discourse that frames his case study of the "Frontiers of the Roman Empire." In his reading of two Danish-Norwegian texts on the Lisbon earthquake in 1755, Kyrre Kverndokk finds very different conceptualizations of the time of the world. Inspired by Reinhart Koselleck, Kverndokk sees the two texts articulating complementary spaces of experience, horizons of expectation, and modes of explanation—all relating to the interpretation of the earthquake as a world event. Finally, Tore Rem takes issue with the underlying presumptions about the world that can be found in major studies of world literature. Using the early English-language reception of Ibsen as his case, he argues for a more system-like model of the world and for a replacement of a simple center/periphery model with multi-centered perspective. To Rem, this facilitates a more nuanced analysis of the particular historicities and temporality of the various contexts, and he rounds off with a reflection on Ibsen's strategic exile—returning, so to speak, to Remaud's opening motif, now devoid of all nostalgia.

Mapping may seem a very particular kind of practice, compared to the apparently more general "naming," "ordering," and "timing," even when understood as literally as in the chapters in this section. The fact that all its chapters to a large degree focus on premodern European history suggests this even further, but their discussions of what mapping means and entails and of how mapping is an act of conceptualization make them expansions of the preceding topics as much as examples.

Alfred Hiatt examines medieval perceptions of the globe and takes issue with the Heideggerian idea that the ability to see the world from outside is distinctly modern. Taking as a premise that there is no one medieval world view, Hiatt explores how the globe gave a distinct and familiar shape to a range of discussions about the nature of world. The literal study of the medieval globe thus becomes an archway to understanding how the world as a whole—a globe—could be object already to its premodern subjects, its medieval inhabitants. In sharp contrast to Hiatt, Jeppe Strandsbjerg dismisses the idea of a medieval global space, arguing instead that this space needs to be seen as both political and constructed. He then presents a Latour-inspired historical overview of how this "assemblage" of global space is carried out through the treaties of Tordesillas and Saragossa, enabling rather than awaiting European expansion and governance.

Between these two chapters, Erling Sandmo and Karl G. Johansson present mapping as a field of converging knowledges. In Sandmo's chapter the shift from the medieval *mappaemundi* tradition to the Ptolemaic renaissance raises the question of what happens to the temporal aspect of the maps once the projection of "pure" space seems to become the main task of mapping. Using Olaus Magnus's *Carta marina* as his case study, Sandmo discusses how the far North is depicted as a region where different temporalities converge and reveal themselves as world histories. Johansson shares the interest in how the periphery is seen as full of magic and dangers, but his case is older—and concerned with greater distance: the accounts of Vínland in Icelandic sagas. He reads this material in light of existing traditions of knowledge and against what could be understood as both religious and geographical horizons of expectation and shows how discovery was a long-drawn negotiation between old knowledge and new experience.

The last chapter, by Richard Yeo, discusses early modern mappings of the totality of knowledge, conceived by Francis Bacon as "the intellectual globe." As the ideal of universal learning gives way to that of specialist, disciplinary knowledge, knowledge is transformed into a world to be mapped to the benefit of all. Today, we may be losing sight of this world as the single individual is once again alone in the archive.

The final section of the book is about making the world, in the sense of unification, completion, or the opposite movement, dispersion. Kari van Dijk's chapter reflects on the relationship between the almost ahistorical conceptualization of the world as a sphere on the one hand and the historicity of the idea of the world as a whole on the other. Departing from Peter Sloterdijk's work on spheres and globes, van Dijk argues for a concept of the world as a whole never shared by all, despite the fundamental human desire to conceptualize it as a unit.

To Helge Jordheim, the globe takes the apparently immediate form of the *Erdball*, the physical object of the "earth ball." A study of the reception and the translation history of Fontenelle's *Entretiens sur la pluralité des mondes* (Conversations on the plurality of worlds) (1686), this chapter investigates how the plural form decentered the world and stripped it of religious meanings and contexts by making it relative to other planets and their inhabitants. The translations and following revisions of the work sparked a series of debates, political, scientific, and philosophical.

The book ends with two chapters about the poles, conceived as the furthest ends of the world. Siv Berg explores how polar expeditions were prefigured in nineteenth-century fiction—and later staged themselves with appeal to the romantic imagination and to popular mythology. Espen Ytreberg expands the topic of the staging of polar exploration in his study of the mediation of Roald Amundsen's conquest of the South Pole.

Helge Jordheim is Professor of Cultural History in the Department for Culture Studies and Oriental Languages, University of Oslo. He has published widely on eighteenth-century intellectual culture in Europe as well as on the history of concepts and the theory of history. His most recent book is a transnational history of the concepts of civility and civilization, written with an international team of scholars (*Civilizing Emotions*, Oxford University Press, 2015). At present he is writing a book on the cultural history of time in the seventeenth and eighteenth centuries.

Erling Sandmo is Professor of History at the University of Oslo and head of the Norwegian National Library's center for historical cartography. He has published on several aspects of early modern culture, in particular violence, music, and knowledge. His latest books are *Tid for historie: en bok om historiske spørsmål* [Time for History: A Book on Historical Questions] (Universitetsforlaget, 2015) and *Uhyrlig: Sjømonstre i kart og litteratur 1491–1895* [Monstrous: Sea Monsters in Maps and Literature 1491–1895] (The Norwegian National Library, 2017, English and German translations forthcoming).

NOTES

1. Manfred B. Steger, *Globalization: A Very Short Introduction* (Oxford, 2009), 15.
2. Reinhart Koselleck, *Vergangene Zukunft: Zur Semantik historischer Zeiten* (Frankfurt am Main, 1979), 50. Koselleck's most important essays, originally published between 1970 and 2005, have been collected in three volumes: *Vergangene Zukunft: Zur Semantik historischer Zeiten* (Frankfurt am Main, 1979), translated by Keith Tribe as *Futures Past: On the Semantics of Historical Time* (Cambridge, MA, 1985); *Zeitschichten: Studien zur Historik* (Frankfurt am Main, 2000); and *Begriffsgeschichten: Studien zur Semantik und Pragmatik der politischen und sozialen Sprache* (Frankfurt am Main, 2006). Several key essays have been translated by Todd Samuel Presner, Kerstin Behnke, and Jobst Welge as *The Practice of Conceptual History: Timing History, Spacing Concepts* (Stanford, CA, 2002).
3. One of those who have actually discussed this is the sociologist and philosopher Henri Lefebvre, for instance in *The Production of Space*, originally published in French (Paris, 1974) and translated into English (Oxford, 1991), and the essay collection *State, Space, World* (Minneapolis, 2009), which contains translations of several essays from the 1970s and 1980s.

4. Reinhart Koselleck, "Einleitung," in *Geschichtliche Grundbegriffe: Historisches Lexikon zur politisch-sozialen Sprache in Deutschland*, ed. Otto Brunner, Werner Conze, and Reinhart Koselleck (Stuttgart, 1972), xxii.
5. See, for example, Reinhart Koselleck, "Zeitschichten," in Koselleck, *Zeitschichten*, 19–26.
6. This connection between Christian eschatology and modern progressivism is the topic of Karl Löwith's classic *Meaning in History: The Theological Implication of Philosophy of History* (Chicago, [1949] 1957).
7. Koselleck, "Einleitung," xix.
8. Hans Blumenberg, "Beobachtungen an Metaphern," *Archiv für Begriffsgeschichte* 15 (1971): 169.
9. Hans Blumenberg, "Paradigmen zu einer Metaphorologie," *Archiv für Begriffsgeschichte* 6 (1960): 59–68.
10. Ibid., 65.
11. Hans Blumenberg, *Theorie der Unbegrifflichkeit* (Frankfurt am Main, 2007), 38.
12. For an exposition of the history of European maps of the world until the discovery of America, see Evelyn Edson, *The World Map, 1300–1492: The Persistence of Tradition and Transformation* (Baltimore, MD, 2007). For studies of early modern cartography, see for example Jürg Glauser and Christian Kiening, eds, *Text, Bild, Karte: Kartographien der Vormoderne* (Freiburg, 2007); Alfred Hiatt, *Terra Incognita: Mapping the Antipodes before 1600* (London, 2008); and Ute Schneider, *Macht der Karten* (Darmstadt, 2004).
13. The most comprehensive study of the Hereford map is Scott D. Westrem, *The Hereford Map: A Transcription and Translation of the Legends with Commentary* (Turnhout, 2001). See also P. D. A. Harvei, *The Hereford World Map: Medieval World Maps and Their Context* (London, 2006).
14. The classic discussion of the concept "heterotopia" is Michel Foucault's "Different Spaces," originally published in 1967. See Michel Foucault, "Different Spaces," in *Essential Works of Foucault 1954–1984*, vol. 2, *Aesthetics, Method, and Epistemology*, ed. Paul Rabinow (New York, 1998), 175–85.
15. Bernard de Fontenelle, *Entretiens sur la pluralité des mondes* (Paris, 1686). For other editions and translations see the chapter by Jordheim in this volume.
16. Ibid., 62.
17. Johann Gottfried Herder, *Ideen zur Philosophie der Geschichte der Menschheit* (Frankfurt am Main, 1989), 21.
18. Alexander von Humboldt, *Kosmos*, ed. Hanno Beck (Stuttgart, 1978), 48.
19. Ibid., 52.
20. Bernard de Fontenelle, *Dialogen über die Mehrheit der Welten: Mit Anmerkungen und Kupfertafeln von Johann Elert Bode, Astronom der königl. Akademie der Wissenschaften zu Berlin* (Berlin, 1780).
21. Koselleck, "Einleitung," xv.
22. George Bush, *Address before a Joint Session of the Congress on the Cessation of the Persian Gulf Conflict*, 16 March 1991. http://www.presidency.ucsb.edu/ws/?pid=19364, accessed 24 August 2018.

23. See Dipesh Chakrabarty, "The Climate of History: Four Theses," *Critical Inquiry* 35, no. 2 (2009): 197–222.

BIBLIOGRAPHY

Blumenberg, Hans. "Beobachtungen an Metaphern." *Archiv für Begriffsgeschichte* 15 (1971): 161–214.
———. "Paradigmen zu einer Metaphorologie." *Archiv für Begriffsgeschichte* 6 (1960): 59–68.
———. *Theorie der Unbegrifflichkeit*. Frankfurt am Main: Suhrkamp, 2007.
Chakrabarty, Dipesh. "The Climate of History: Four Theses." *Critical Inquiry* 35, no. 2 (2009): 197–222.
Edson, Evelyn. *The World Map, 1300–1492: The Persistence of Tradition and Transformation*. Baltimore, MD: Johns Hopkins University Press, 2007.
Fontenelle, Bernard de. *Entretiens sur la pluralité des mondes*. Paris: C. Blageart, 1686.
Fontenelle, Bernard de. *Dialogen über die Mehrheit der Welten: Mit Anmerkungen und Kupfertafeln von Johann Elert Bode, Astronom der königl. Akademie der Wissenschaften zu Berlin*. Berlin: Christian Friedrich Himburg, 1780.
Foucault, Michel. "Different Spaces." In *Essential Works of Foucault 1954–1984*, vol. 2, *Aesthetics, Method, and Epistemology*, edited by Paul Rabinow, 175–85. New York: New Press, 1998.
Glauser, Jürg, and Christian Kiening, eds. *Text, Bild, Karte: Kartographien der Vormoderne*. Freiburg: Rombach, 2007.
Harvei, P. D. A. *The Hereford World Map: Medieval World Maps and Their Context*. London: British Library, 2006.
Herder, Johann Gottfried. *Ideen zur Philosophie der Geschichte der Menschheit*. Frankfurt am Main: Deutscher Klassiker Verlag, 1989.
Hiatt, Alfred. *Terra Incognita: Mapping the Antipodes before 1600*. London: British Library, 2008.
Humboldt, Alexander von. *Kosmos*. Edited by Hanno Beck. Stuttgart: Brockhaus, 1978.
Koselleck, Reinhart. *Begriffsgeschichten: Studien zur Semantik und Pragmatik der politischen und sozialen Sprache*. Frankfurt am Main: Suhrkamp, 2006.
———. "Einleitung." In *Geschichtliche Grundbegriffe: Historisches Lexikon zur politisch-sozialen Sprache in Deutschland*, edited by Otto Brunner, Werner Conze, and Reinhart Koselleck, xiii–xxvii. Stuttgart: Klett-Cotta, 1972.
———. *The Practice of Conceptual History: Timing History, Spacing Concepts*. Translated by Todd Samuel Presner, Kerstin Behnke, and Jobst Welge. Stanford, CA: Stanford University Press, 2002.
———. *Vergangene Zukunft: Zur Semantik historischer Zeiten*. Frankfurt am Main: Suhrkamp, 1979. Translated by Keith Tribe as *Futures Past: On the Semantics of Historical Time*. Cambridge, MA: MIT Press, 1985.
———. "Zeitschichten." In Reinhart Koselleck, *Zeitschichten: Studien zur Historik*, 19–26. Frankfurt am Main: Suhrkamp, 2000.

———. *Zeitschichten: Studien zur Historik*. Frankfurt am Main: Suhrkamp, 2000.
Lefebvre, Henri. *La production de l'espace*. Paris: Anthropos, 1974. Translated by Donald Nicholson-Smith as *The Production of Space*. Oxford: Blackwell, 1991.
———. *State, Space, World: Selected Essays*. Edited by Neil Brenner and Stuart Elden, translated by Gerald Moore, Neil Brenner, and Stuart Elden. Minneapolis: University of Minnesota Press, 2009.
Löwith, Karl. *Meaning in History: The Theological Implication of Philosophy of History*. Chicago: University of Chicago Press, [1949] 1957.
Schneider, Ute. *Macht der Karten*. Darmstadt: Primus Verlag, 2004.
Steger, Manfred B. *Globalization: A Very Short Introduction*. Oxford: Oxford University Press, 2009.
Westrem, Scott D. *The Hereford Map: A Transcription and Translation of the Legends with Commentary*. Turnhout: Brepols, 2001.

Part I

NAMING THE WORLD

▶• 1 •◀

"World"

An Exploration of the Relationship between Conceptual History and Etymology

Ivo Spira

As a global keyword, *world* has translation equivalents in all major languages.[1] This fact may easily lead one to conclude that there is also a corresponding global concept "world," one that has come to dominate global discourse. It would be hasty, however, to take the translatability of this common English word as conclusive evidence for the hegemony of a universal concept of European origin. Not only do translation equivalents have different ranges of meaning, but they may not even be conceptually identical in the relevant senses. Perhaps this incompatibility can be traced to differing etymologies. After all, the translation "equivalents" have different histories, sometimes radically so, each in its own language. Thus, Greek *kósmos* originally meant "order" (as in "cosmic order") before acquiring the spatial and social sense of "the world (we live in)" in Hellenic Greek, which is very different from the history of English *world*, which originated as a compound of the Germanic bases of *were* ("man," "husband") and *old* ("lifetime," "age").[2] Are these differences in word history, then, evidence for the existence of two entirely different *concepts*, namely "world" and "kósmos"? If so, etymological differences may reflect differences in the way in which different people and cultures understand the world—that is to say, they could be anthropologically significant. And if it turns out that the differences are significant, can the various local or regional concepts still be meaningfully subsumed under a global "world" concept? Even if we postulate this universal concept of "world" (e.g., as the result of the repeated reinforcement of equations like Gk. *kósmos* = Eng. *world*), we are still left wondering whether it is legitimate to make the etymological differences responsible for any tensions we detect in the translation equations. In what follows, I show that while etymology is indeed a subtle and significant factor in the formation of key concepts, it is the historical moments of conceptual definition that determine their meaning and significance.

In this chapter I approach the problem outlined above on two levels. On one level, I look into the etymological origins of words meaning "world" in a number of languages, with the goal of seeing if and how they contribute to the perceived global concept "world." On another level, I offer some reflections on more general questions: (a) How do key concepts arise historically? (b) Does a word's etymology reflect or, alternatively, influence the way in which it conceptualizes something? (c) What is the value of etymological analysis in analyzing a key concept or writing its history? In order to put my brief exploration on a firmer footing, it is necessary to state clearly what I mean by "etymology" and "concept," and, further, how the words to be compared have been selected.

When discussing etymology, it is important to distinguish the actual historical development of a word (*historia ipsa*) from various accounts or interpretations of this development (*historia narrata*). The former is never directly accessible and only approachable by means of the latter. We may further differentiate between scientific and non-scientific etymological interpretations. The former in principle adheres rigorously to historical-critical principles, arriving at a hypothesis of historical development through a systematic consideration of all the evidence in its historical context, relying on all that is known about language change. Of course, that does not in any way guarantee that the resulting interpretations will be historically accurate or even unbiased. They always remain hypotheses embedded in their particular research context. Non-scientific etymological interpretations occur naturally, as they help speakers make sense of the language they speak. Moreover, etymological interpretations of both kinds are useful rhetorically. In practice, the border between scientific and non-scientific etymology is often blurred, since scientific paradigms and available sources change over time, and also since etymological interpretations readily move between the two spheres. Hence it is often a good idea to consider a broad range of possible etymological interpretations, scientific as well as popular, whether the goal is to approach the actual historical development of word forms or simply to investigate the dynamics of form and interpretation.

By "concept" in the narrow sense, I mean a notion that is sufficiently clear to be definable; in an even narrower sense, each concept is determined by its one and only definition, which is the ideal for key concepts in technical texts, for example "voltage." These are usually accessible exclusively through technical terms, and the only valid meaning is licensed by the relevant definitions.[3] Human language, however, is characterized by polysemy, that is to say, words tend to have more than one sense, where senses are semantically and historically interrelated, yet discrete, semantic units (including concepts in the narrow sense).[4] Since speakers habitually make use of the flexibility inherent in linguistic polysemy, one may want to treat a whole cluster of concepts (in the narrow sense) as one overarching super-concept. This happens when speakers exploit the polysemic potential to augment the meaning of a word, so that it can express this super-concept. This turns out to be a very useful way of thinking about social key concepts, because it captures the way in which social keywords actually function—namely as ambiguous symbols, through which the skilled politician may summon multiple definitions and associations according to the context and party utility at any given moment. This is all the more true in a multilingual context, where the concept comes to function as a sort of super-symbol that subsumes (and partly obscures) the differences between the particular concepts that figure in the various translation equations.[5] It is this broader sense of "concept" as super-concept, or super-symbol, that I adopt in this chapter unless otherwise specified. Thus, each concept is treated as potentially multivalent semantically and pragmatically,[6] much in the way Reinhart Koselleck characterizes his *Begriffe*, especially the *Grundbegriffe*, or key concepts.[7]

Turning now to the methodological question of how to identify the words that should be investigated, there are basically two avenues of approach. One approach, which may be called semasiological, is to use the modern super-symbol of the "world" as a starting point and select the translation equivalents that are available for this word in various languages, and then proceed to describe and compare their semantics. The other approach, which may be called onomasiological, is to start with a definition (a concept in the narrow sense), and then find words in different languages that have a sense corresponding to the definition. This procedure is then repeated for each definition that is relevant to an exploration of the super-concept "world." I have resorted to a combination of both approaches in order to get different perspectives.[8]

The modern translation equivalents of English "world" include the following: Standard Chinese *shìjiè* 世界, *tiānxià* 天下, *rénjiān* 人間; Standard Arabic *ʿālam*, *dunyā*; Norwegian Bokmål *verden*; Modern Greek *kósmos*; French *monde*; Russian *mir*, *svet*. This gives us a list of words that are similar enough semantically to function as translation equivalents. In order to investigate their in-language semantics in detail, we would have to go far beyond available dictionaries and look at a broad range of examples in context for each of the words, including, crucially, their occurrence in various kinds of idioms, technical terms, and collocations.[9]

This leads naturally to the other approach, where we can use the set of senses obtained for each of the words in the list to search for, and ask questions about, other words with one or more of those same (or similar) senses. In this way, one will quickly end up investigating whole word fields, so that we might want to consider *universe, cosmos, globe, creation, nature,* and *Earth* in addition to *world*, to take a few examples from English. Investigating the relevant word fields is in any case necessary to get a full picture of a word's place within a language. Eng. *world*, for example, is synonymous with *universe* in the sense of "the whole physical space and everything that is in it," but synonymous with *Earth* in the sense of "the planet Earth, where we live."

We can further enlarge the sample of words to study by applying both of the approaches diachronically. In this way, we will for example find Latin *mundus* by looking at modern English translations of Latin texts from different periods, and Greek *oikoumēnē* and Chinese *tiānxià* 天下 by looking for words with the sense "the known, inhabited world."

After these preliminary remarks, I can now turn to my main topic, which is to investigate the conceptual significance of etymology, or word history, taking English *world* as my point of departure. As a first step, can one identify any patterns in the historical processes of the conceptualization of "world," moving from past to present, from the local to the global? If we find any patterns of conceptualization that are shared between languages, or if we find significant differences, we may venture to suggest that they are anthropologically important, as they reflect similarities and differences in the perception of the world and the construction of the "world" across cultures.

In a survey of words for "world," obtained through the approaches just exemplified, it becomes readily apparent that words or morphemes with the senses "age" (as in Gk. *aiṓn*, Heb. *'ōlam*), "heaven" (Ch. *tiān* in *tiānxià* 天下, lit. "[all] under heaven"), "earth" (Lat. *terra*), "sea" (Ch. *hǎi* in *hǎinèi* 海内, lit. "within the sea"), "create" (Eng. *creation*), or "dwell" (Gk. *oikoumēnē*) recur as constitutive elements across different languages. Combinations also occur, for example Chinese *tiāndì* 天地 (lit. "heaven [and] earth," meaning "universe") and Arabic *al-samāwāt wa-l-'arḍ* ("the heavens and the earth") in the Qur'ān.[10] We can also point to differences in the word histories for words that later become synonyms or translation equivalents. Chinese *tiānxià* 天下 refers to the inhabited world; its denotation thus overlaps with Greek *oikoumēnē* (lit. "the inhabited [earth]"), while the familiar Greek word *kósmos* (lit. "order") only much later became a synonym of *oikoumēnē* via the notion of "cosmic order."

It is tempting to conclude that these elements correspond to cognitive notions that are anthropologically significant in the human conceptualization of the world. Surely the semantic differences and similarities in word structure matter, since it is through these that we name, and hence understand, reality? The imagery and reasoning that underlie the form of words with which we choose to express crucial concepts thus seems to have anthropological relevance. In this light, C. D. Buck's classic *Dictionary of Selected Synonyms in the Principal Indo-European Languages* seems a good starting point for exploring human perception and conceptualization of the world—and, as it happens, "world" is in fact the first synonym group of Buck's dictionary.[11]

There are, however, reasons to be critical of the admissibility of word histories as evidence for "anthropological significance." To begin with, the claim as it stands is too vague. For example, "anthropological significance" could be attached to the way in which the name is derived from words for salient properties of the named entity (salient in the perception of the naming subject, that is); but such significance could equally well be attached to contingent circumstances of the act of naming (the name may have originated as a joke). As long as one is sufficiently clear about what one has in mind, this kind of vagueness probably does not represent a major obstacle.

We may begin by noting that although contingent circumstances certainly play an important role, there is much to be said for the case that speakers *are* constrained by the morphological composition and etymology of the words and phrases they use. Ultimately, this is because the requirement that communication be intelligible and socially acceptable will severely constrain speakers in exercising the power to change their speech at will. This power is in principle arbitrary and unlimited, since you can make up any number of new words or change the meanings you attach to old words whenever you want. But since changing one's language all the time precludes effective communication, speakers in practice reproduce existing norms.[12] There is, in other words, no such thing as an effortless escape from the constraints imposed by the existing senses of linguistic forms. Since this means that the choice between alternative words is constrained by the meaning of their components, we are in principle entitled to derive significance from their morphological and etymological structure. This kind of analysis, however, is valid only as long as we take the historical circumstances of naming into account (a point I will return to below), and only as long as we do not insist on a "scientific," historically accurate etymology as the source of significance, but focus instead on the etymology and structure of words *as understood by the relevant speakers*.

Because of changes in the form of individual words and their frequency of use, specific interpretations of word structure become more opaque to speakers with the passage of time. This naturally also gives rise to alternative interpretations of the same word (reanalysis). The increasing opaqueness of word forms relative to earlier analyses makes it more problematic to derive current conceptual structure from an unearthed (putatively "original") etymological structure the further one gets away from the original naming event.[13]

This means that drawing conclusions about the current meaning of words and concepts from their historically underlying morphological composition is a very risky undertaking, which needs to be conducted with the utmost caution if it is to be attempted at all. The origin of word forms can only provide ancillary evidence for current word meanings or conceptual significance. The etymology of a word tells us *which* resources were marshaled to meet certain expressive needs, without telling us much about *how* or *why*. In particular, formal etymology alone cannot tell us how the different elements were combined in the historical naming event. It may in fact be far from a logical combination of the senses of its components.

Thus, we know that English *world* goes back to Old English *woruld*, which is closely related to Old High German *weralt* and Old Norse *verǫld*. This Germanic word is a compound of the elements found in Old Norse as *verr* ("man," "husband") and *ǫld* ("age," "lifetime"). We can now try to sniff our way back along the trail to Indo-European *$\ast\text{\textit{u̯īros}}$* ("man" < "the strong one") and the root **al-* ("grow; nourish"). We then find other cognates of these roots in other Indo-European languages, such as Latin *vir* ("man") and *alere* ("nourish"). We are now in a position to congratulate ourselves on having convincingly demonstrated the ancient pedigree of the English key concept "world," concluding that it is essentially an ancient Indo-European temporal concept, from which we then attempt to draw wide-ranging anthropological conclusions.

However, it turns out that there is no simple correlation between the keyness of concepts and the history of the word forms that express them. Not only is there no Latin concept **viraltum*, but whereas *vir* did become a key concept in Roman culture, the Germanic cognates of Old Norse *verr* ("man") hardly have any other presence in Germanic languages except English *werewolf*, German *Werwolf*, and similar cognates. Coincidentally, there *is* a relevant Latin key concept, namely *saeculum* ("generation"), but far from being linked to *woruld* by virtue of being a cognate, *saeculum*, augmented by its subsequent biblical sense of "worldly life," licensed the meaning of *woruld* as a key concept. In other words, *saeculum* served as a cultural and linguistic model for *woruld*. Here we see clearly that the *formal* etymological genealogy does not explain the formation of the concept, but that investigating possible models in authoritative texts goes a long way toward a plausible explanation. It is easy to give other examples of the divergence of formal etymological relatedness and conceptual significance. English *Earth* is clearly a prominent cultural keyword, while its cognate Greek *era* is marginal. The culturally central Greek word for "Earth" is *gē* (as in "geography"), of unknown provenance. In Latin we have for example *tellus*, which has the socially and culturally relatively insignificant Old Norse cognate *þilja* ("plank, planking").

Instead of deriving linguistic forms and social institutions from their (reconstructed) Indo-European proto-forms, Émile Benveniste wisely focused on the emergence of the lexical systems of particular languages as correlates of the developments of social and cultural institutions. In his words, "the elements inherited from the common language find themselves incorporated into independent structures which belong to particular languages; hence they [the elements] transform themselves and take on new values among the oppositions which are thus created and which they determine."[14] This means that an etymological analysis, even if it is both scholarly sound and successful in approaching the actual historical development, does not automatically allow us to determine reliably the motivation behind its structure, or what the word meant or how it was actually used. To discover the meaning of a word, we need to consult a corpus of extant texts to see how it was used at a given point in time by certain speakers and, if we are lucky, how it was defined, interpreted, or contested. We are even luckier if we happen to discover pointers to the motivation behind a word's structure in terms of an authentic and relevant account of how it was coined. In the end, it is only in the context of a wider historical and cultural analysis that we stand a chance of finding plausible explanations for the creation or adoption of words to express certain concepts.

In the case of Old Norse *verǫld* (lit. "age of man") and its Germanic cognates, the source of their meaning is basically the Christian concept expressed in Medieval Latin as *saeculum*. But *saeculum* itself was modeled on Greek *aiṓn* ("lifetime," "eternity"), which in turn had been used to translate Hebrew *ʿōlam* ("age," "era").[15] Another word connected with *ʿōlam* is Arabic *ʿālam* ("world"), which may actually be a loanword from Hebrew or Aramaic. It is prominent in the Qur'ān, for example in the divine epithet *rabb al-ʿālamīn* ("Lord of the Worlds"), echoing the Hebrew *ribbon ha-ʿōlamīm*. In Qur'ānic discourse we also find (*al-ḥayāt, al-dār*) *al-dunyā* (lit. "the lower/nearer [life, abode]," that is, "the world of our human, earthly existence"), which contrasts with (*al-dār*) *al-'ākhira* ("the last about," i.e., "the hereafter"), which is temporal in a way reminiscent of Hebrew *ʿōlam*, as in *ha-ʿōlam ha-zeh* ("this age," i.e., "life on earth") and *ha-ʿōlam ha-bā'* ("the world to come").[16] In Modern Arabic, *dunyā* in the sense of "the world we live in" is synonymous with *ʿālam*, albeit with different connotations. But neither of them is necessarily used in a religious sense.

Let us take a different example. In Ancient China, the world where people live was called *tiānxià*, and this was largely taken to be co-extensive with what became the Chinese Empire. The most common modern equivalent in Chinese for English *world* is *shìjiè* 世界 (lit. "generation border"), which has its origin as a translation equivalent for Sanskrit *loka* in the translation of Buddhist texts from the second century CE onward. The modern meanings of the word arose when it was pressed into service as a translation equivalent of English *world*, French *monde*, and German *Welt* in the nineteenth century.

This contrast between a narrow etymology of word forms and a wider investigation of concept formation and conceptual influence within and across languages strongly suggests that the moment in which a word's form and meaning is created, recast, or reproduced—typically by way of an authoritative external model—plays a decisive role in the emergence of keywords. The concept meaning thus ends up by *transcending* the etymology of the concept as a word. We may call this crucial moment of conceptual definition the *formative moment* of the concept within a given language, or perhaps more accurately, within a given speech community.

This, however, requires some qualification. First is the one just mentioned: the continued resonance of earlier senses. To the extent that people are aware of them, these older semantic layers may continue to color their perceptions of the new concept, regardless of whether this was the conceptual innovator's intention or not. Second, the term in question does not become a vehicle for the concept for all speakers at the same time: there is a lag that depends on both social and technological factors.[17] Only if the concept is successfully established will it come to dominate the word (term) that expresses it, and it may eventually trump some or all of its existing senses and etymologies. Third, on the level of scholarship it is important to note that an etymological investigation still has some value, as it shows us which semantic resources were marshaled to form the word(s) that ended up as a vehicle for the new concept. Since the choice of word forms is not arbitrary, etymological and morphological readings that were accessible to relevant speakers at the time of concept formation do have some explanatory potential.

As noted above, it is often the case that the model according to which a concept is formed is external to the language community. An interesting aspect of such impulses from the outside is that the burden of conforming to the existing lexicon, especially the established senses of words, seems to be considerably lessened when a word form is taken from another language (i.e., as a loanword). In one way, this follows naturally from the fact that the loanword is a new element in the recipient language, and as such does not have any interfering, older senses. In another way, the burden is lessened because the community of the source language has its own sources of meaning and authority, for instance in the form of knowledgeable persons, reference works, and sacred texts, which the recipient community can have recourse to. There may also be considerable gains in terms of status if the model language enjoys high prestige. Another reason why it is tempting to take in words from other languages is that one may be highly selective as to which senses are adopted. This is typical in the case of technical terms: the basic sense of *nebula* in Latin is "mist," but in English it is exclusively used in the technical sense of "cloud of gas and dust in outer space," and is not a general synonym of *mist*.

If an existing word is chosen, or a new one constructed from native building blocks, one will have to provide conceptual support in a different way (e.g., through translation, exegesis, or new reference works), and there may moreover be dissonant earlier senses. Older meanings may be activated by a suitable context, that is, a context that selects the older senses. The activation of different senses on different occasions contributes to a kind of semantic osmosis within the word. These older semantic layers may, however, actually be used to good effect in mediating the new (external, foreign) concept, and thus constitute an advantage. One of course also needs to keep in mind that even with an external conceptual or lexical model, the concept may in fact end up being remolded in its replicated form, for example through a redefinition or through other, more subtle forms of appropriation in the new speech community.

So what does the primacy of the formative moment over word history (etymology) mean for the conceptualization of "the world"? It seems plausible that a global concept of "world" in the form of a super-concept does indeed come to dominate the world's languages to the extent that their speech communities orient themselves toward a common global culture. In linguistic terms, this happens when the usage of equivalent terms over time converges on globally dominant discourses. But because of the resonance of older semantic layers and incomplete domination (penetration, coverage), the closest equivalents are likely to remain different in some respects. These differences, however, do not preclude the existence of a global "world" concept—on the contrary, we may think of them as different concepts of "world" that have been integrated into a global symbol as cosmopolitan equivalents, that is, in a symbol that is used to transcend the differences between them, albeit differences that are not quite eliminated. This would then be a sort of global key concept, where key concept is to be understood in the sense of Koselleck's *Grundbegriff*, that is, a global concept that is contested (and hence polyvalent) precisely because it is unavoidable in contemporary public discourse. In other words, this is what a solution to the problem of interlingual etymological dissonance in global concept formation might look like if one chooses to work with Koselleck's conceptual toolbox.

As for the different etymological genealogies of "world" across the globe, the non-arbitrariness of form means that the semantic components "age," "heaven," "earth," "sea," "create," "dwell," "globe," and "man," which recur across languages, may be assumed to reflect either the way in which speakers at some point perceived the world and, additionally, the naming processes themselves.

We may sum up the conclusions of this chapter by turning to the three general questions asked at the beginning of the chapter. Concerning how key concepts arise historically (a), I would suggest that such concepts are formed at crucial moments of concept formation, such as when they appear prominently in a holy text, are taken up by a political movement, or emerge as the cornerstone of a new scientific theory.[18] In many cases the concept is lexicalized in response to some external impulse, such as when a new religion with sacred texts in a foreign language is adopted by speakers of a given language community. This opens up for treating conceptual and lexical developments within a language as firmly rooted in social history, which is to say that it is ultimately impossible to account fully for such developments without considering the cultural and historical context.

As to the relation between conceptualization and etymology (b), a given etymology may clearly *reflect* the conceptual meaning if at least one etymological reading that interprets the concept for speakers is available to speakers at some point in time after the moment of conceptualization. It is then usually not a loanword, unless the source language is well known to the speakers. On the other hand, an etymological reading can also *influence* a conceptualization that occurs at a later stage, either through the resonance of earlier semantic layers, or in the form of an intentional reconceptualization couched in etymological terms. The direction of influence between a given conceptualization and various etymological readings of its term depends on their order in time and the degree to which the term is analyzable for the conceptualizing subject and, of course, whether or not he makes use of the opportunity represented by the reading.

What, finally (c), is the methodological relevance of etymology to conceptual history? Is it of any value in analyzing a concept or writing its history? First, it can be used as evidence for the historical situation at the moment of conceptualization, for example when we identify the model of a loan translation. (Here it is of course essential to look beyond the genealogies of native word forms.) Second, it gives us information about older semantic layers that may resurface either as background resonance, or in the intentional reinterpretations that occur in the contestation of concepts. Third, if the historical circumstances make it plausible, it may constitute evidence of how those who adopted the concept and coined the word perceived that which they chose to lexicalize.

An etymological analysis may thus yield evidence that is useful for conceptual history, but it remains ancillary and can never replace a close reading of relevant primary sources against the background of their historical and cultural context. However, this should not make us blind to the etymological diversity that is evident in the histories of words, even if they end up converging on the same global concept. This is especially true in a multilingual setting, as the abundance of etymological diversity continues to be a resource of potential divergence and reinterpretation.

Ivo Spira is Senior Lecturer in Chinese Studies at Lund University, Sweden. He has been a postdoctoral research fellow and associate professor of Chinese in the Department of Culture Studies and Oriental Languages, University of Oslo. His latest book is *A Conceptual History of Chinese -Isms: The Modernization of Ideological Discourse, 1895–1925* (Brill, 2015), which explores the linguistic and conceptual history of Chinese -isms.

NOTES

1. For further discussions of translation, see in particular the chapter in this volume by Oddbjørn Leirvik.
2. Etymologies are quoted from the following dictionaries, unless otherwise indicated: Germanic languages, *Oxford English Dictionary* online, retrieved 14 February 2014 from http://www.oed.com; Latin, Michiel de Vaan, *Etymological Dictionary of Latin and the Other Italic Languages* (Leiden, 2008); Greek, Robert Beekes, *Etymological Dictionary of Greek* (Leiden, 2010).
3. Technical terms are words or phrases that act as unique, but arbitrary, labels that identify the concepts.
4. The relation between the senses arises through semantic derivation or through association in a given speech situation.
5. This way of looking at translingual key concepts is partly inspired by Lydia Liu's concept of the super-sign, where the meaning of a word is semantically transformed and licensed by a foreign word, usually with the foreign authority behind the transformation being hidden or obscured. Lydia Liu, *The Clash of Empires: The Invention of China in Modern World Making* (Cambridge, MA, 2004), 11–15.
6. Stressing the polysemous nature of words and their consequent multivalence, however, does not in any way exempt one from specifying the polysemous semantic structure by giving a definition for each sense. Similarly, asserting that a given key concept is polysemous does not relieve one of the obligation of specifying its various aspects and uses. In fact, the reverse is true: definitions are necessary in order to make synchronic and diachronic differences explicit.
7. For a brief but very clear exposition of Koselleck's term *Grundbegriff* ("basic concept," i.e., key concept), see Reinhart Koselleck, "Stichwort: Begriffsgeschichte," in *Begriffsgeschichten* (Frankfurt am Main, 2006), 99–105. While the German discipline of *Begriffsgeschichte* has been an important source of inspiration for my work, my remarks here are not exclusively directed at this discipline. My purpose is rather to question the general validity of using word history to draw conclusions about key concepts in society.
8. In line with Reinhart Koselleck, "Begriffsgeschichte und Sozialgeschichte," in *Vergangene Zukunft* (Frankfurt am Main, 1989), 121.
9. Metalinguistic examples (such as comments on usage) are valuable, and one would want to compare these to the explanations in lexicographical works. For modern languages it would also be natural to ask native speakers to explain what the words mean and elicit further examples.
10. For *tiāndì* 天地, see, for example, 惟天地之無窮兮，哀人生之長勤 ("I thought of the limitless vastness of the universe/ I wept for the long affliction of man's life"). 楚辭·5·1/2, quoted in *Thesaurus Linguae Sericae*, ed. Christoph Harbsmeier, text record CC 5.1.0.0.2.0, trans. David Hawkes, retrieved 14 February 2014 from http://tls.uni-hd.de.
11. Carl Darling Buck, *Dictionary of Selected Synonyms in the Principal Indo-European Languages* (Chicago, 1949).

12. Cf. Joseph Vendryes, "Sur l'étymologie croisée," *Bulletin de la Société de Linguistique de Paris* 51 (1955), as quoted in *Etymologie*, ed. Rüdiger Schmitt (Darmstadt, 1977), 171.
13. On the vagaries of word history and also the question of synchronic vs. diachronic interpretation, see Pierre Chantraine, "Étymologie historique et étymologie statique," *Bulletin de la Classe des Lettres et des Sciences Morales et Politiques de l'Académie Royale de Belgique*, 5th ser., 56 (1970): 80–95, reprinted in Schmitt, *Etymologie*, 389–404.
14. Émile Benveniste, *Le vocabulaire des institutions indo-européennes: Sommaires, tableau et index établis par Jean Lallot*, 2 vols (Paris, 1969), 8, my translation.
15. On the history of *Welt, weralt*, and so forth and how the meaning was influenced by Latin models, see J. S. Belkin, "Welt als Raumbegriff im Althochdeutschen und Frühmittelhochdeutschen," *Zeitschrift für Deutsche Sprache* 24, nos. 1–2 (1968): 16–59.
16. *Encyclopaedia of the Qur'ān*, ed. Jane D. McAuliffe (Leiden, 2001–6). s.v. "World."
17. For example, socioeconomic stratification, the density of social networks, and the means of communication.
18. The case is perhaps somewhat different with culturally important concepts that emerge gradually within a speech community over time, as long as they remain uncontested.

BIBLIOGRAPHY

Beekes, Robert. *Etymological Dictionary of Greek*. With the assistance of Lucien van Beek. Leiden: Brill, 2010.

Belkin, Johanna S. "Welt als Raumbegriff im Althochdeutschen und Frühmittelhochdeutschen." *Zeitschrift für Deutsche Sprache* 24, nos. 1–2 (1968): 16–59.

Benveniste, Émile. *Le vocabulaire des institutions indo-européennes: Sommaires, tableau et index établis par Jean Lallot*. 2 vols. Paris: Minuit, 1969.

Buck, Carl Darling. *Dictionary of Selected Synonyms in the Principal Indo-European Languages*. Chicago: University of Chicago Press, 1949.

Chantraine, Pierre. "Étymologie historique et étymologie statique." *Bulletin de la Classe des Lettres et des Sciences Morales et Politiques de l'Académie Royale de Belgique*, 5th ser., 56 (1970): 80–95. Reprinted in *Etymologie*, edited by Rüdiger Schmitt, 389–404. Darmstadt: Wissenschaftliche Buchgesellschaft, 1977.

Encyclopaedia of the Qur'ān. Edited by Jane D. McAuliffe. Leiden: Brill, 2001–6.

Koselleck, Reinhart. *Begriffsgeschichten*. Frankfurt am Main: Suhrkamp, 2006.

———. "Begriffsgeschichte und Sozialgeschichte." In *Vergangene Zukunft*, 107–29. Frankfurt am Main: Suhrkamp, 1989.

Liu, Lydia. *The Clash of Empires: The Invention of China in Modern World Making*. Cambridge, MA: Harvard University Press, 2004.

Oxford English Dictionary online. Retrieved 14 February 2014 from http://www.oed.com.

Schmitt, Rüdiger, ed. *Etymologie*. Darmstadt: Wissenschaftliche Buchgesellschaft, 1977.

Thesaurus Linguae Sericae. Edited by Christoph Harbsmeier. Retrieved 14 February 2014 from http://tls.uni-hd.de.

Vaan, Michiel de. *Etymological Dictionary of Latin and the Other Italic Languages*. Leiden: Brill, 2008.

Vendryes, Joseph. "Sur l'étymologie croisée." *Bulletin de la Société de Linguistique de Paris* 51 (1955): 1–8. Reprinted in *Etymologie*, edited by Rüdiger Schmitt, 168–76. Darmstadt: Wissenschaftliche Buchgesellschaft, 1977.

▶• 2 •◀

A Multiverse of Knowledge

The Epistemology and Hermeneutics of the ʿālam in Medieval Islamic Thought

Nora S. Eggen

Introduction

In medieval Islamic thought, the world was conceptualized as a means of knowledge. Furthermore, existence was perceived as a plurality of worlds, a multiverse. Combining these two ontological ideas, scholars developed theories of differentiated spheres of epistemological and hermeneutical activity. One such scholar in the late eleventh and early twelfth centuries was Abū Ḥāmid al-Ghazālī (d. 1111), a celebrated theologian, jurist, and mystic and a towering figure in subsequent Islamic thought.

How were these ideas of the world constructed? Moreover, how and why did al-Ghazālī formulate a theory of meaning and interpretation using the idea of existence as a multiverse of knowledge with multiple domains? In this chapter I will discuss conceptualizations of the world in medieval Arabic lexicography and examine how these conceptualizations were employed in the thought of al-Ghazālī, with a particular view to his work *Mishkāt al-anwār* and situating the ideas within the larger frame of his work as well as the works of his predecessors.[1]

The World

In medieval Islamic thought the geopolitical world was conceptualized as a collection of "houses" or "abodes" (*diyār*, singular *dār*).[2] According to an early lexicographer, the two most common words for "house," *dār* and *bayt*, differ in that a *dār* is an encircled space protecting the borders from outsiders, while a *bayt* denotes a covered shelter providing protection from natural phenomena such as rain.³ Hence, in its geopolitical use, *dār* referred in classical theories of international relations to a limited geographical entity, a territory with a particular jurisdiction and policy, conventionally labeled by such terms as "abode of Islam" (*dār al-islām*), "abode of war" (*dār al-ḥarb*), "abode of truce" (*dār al-ʿahd*), "abode of security" (*dār al-amān*), and "abode of rebellion" (*dār al-baghy*).⁴ In the medieval cosmology based on the Qurʾān, however, all such geopolitical "abodes" were perceived as temporal and part of the lowest level of existence: earthly life (*al-ḥayāt al-dunyā*, al-Qurʾān 2:86). Its conceptual counterpart was eternal existence, the abode of the afterlife (*al-dār al-ākhira*, al-Qurʾān 6:32).⁵ Earthly, linear time was framed by meta-historical points of reference: the pre-mortal divine covenant accepted by man (al-Qurʾān 7:172; 33:72) and the resurrection day (al-Qurʾān sura 75). The Qurʾānic presentation of the human dwellings in time and space thus has an eschatological focus.⁶

With this cosmological frame and using the Qurʾānic notion *al-ʿālamīn* (1:2 and passim), medieval Islamic scholars formed a perspective on existence that has been understood to suggest a plurality of worlds: existence as a *multi*verse rather than a *uni*verse.

The *ʿālam* in the Qurʾān

In the Qurʾān the word *ʿālam*, often translated as "world,"⁷ occurs exclusively in the sound plural, determinative, grammatically dependent form *ʿālamīn* (genitive case as a *majrūr* or *muḍāf ilayhi*). The word is repeated more than seventy times throughout the text, most commonly in the expression *rabb al-ʿālamīn* ("Lord of the worlds"). The word attracted considerable scholarly attention from the exegetes and lexicographers, who discussed whether the notion refers to a true plurality of realms or species, or whether it is a generic term meaning "all of creation."⁸

Early scholars of the Arabic language considered the existence of homonymous polysemic words to be an intrinsic trait of the language, and in the early exegetical endeavors there was a keen awareness of the polysemic nature of the Qurʾānic language specifically. This polysemy was often referred to as aspects of meaning (*wujūh*), in the sense of co-textually related polysemy (as the terms are distributed throughout the text), as well as in the sense of alternative interpretations of a single passage (levels of meaning). In the books by Muqātil b. Sulaymān al-Balkhī (d. 767) and Abū Hilāl al-ʿAskarī (d. ca. 1010) on such aspects of meaning, we find a wide range of possible references for the word *ʿālamīn*, in its different contexts: jinn and humans, or jinn, humans, and angels (al-Qurʾān 1:2); a particular period (al-Qurʾān 2:122); human beings in the whole human history from Ādam to Judgment Day (al-Qurʾān 21:71);

creation after the time of Nūḥ (al-Qurʾān 37:79); and the people of the Book (al-Qurʾān 3:97).⁹

In the exegesis of the word ʿālamīn in the expression *rabb al-ʿālamīn* (al-Qurʾān 1:2), Simonetta Calderini has identified two main tendencies.¹⁰ In a comprehensive interpretation, the word is considered a plural of a collective, which is already plural in meaning, and the noun thus refers to "all created species," including both animate and inanimate objects. In a selective interpretation, on the other hand, the reference is limited to "created beings endowed with knowledge." This interpretation is based on an alleged etymology of the word (see below), as well as on a morphological argument, as the sound plural form is normally not used for inanimate objects.

Calderini's material is a selection of post-Ghazālian exegesis, but the same tendencies are present in pre-Ghazālian exegesis. Ibn Qutayba (d. 889), an early lexicographer and exegete who wrote on *gharīb al-Qurʾān*, a genre covering both unusual, Arabized, and difficult words and expressions, maintains a selective interpretation and says that the ʿālamūn (nominative case) refers to "categories of spirited beings, and these are humans, jinn and angels. Each category is a world."¹¹ Al-Rāghib al-Iṣfahānī (d. eleventh century), whose work was well known and inspirational to al-Ghazālī, advocates a comprehensive interpretation. In his book on the Qurʾānic vocabulary, he holds that *al-ʿālamīn* includes inanimate objects and states accordingly that there exists the world of the humans, the world of water, and the world of fire.¹²

The Etymology and Semantics of ʿālam

Studies on historical etymology have suggested that the word ʿālam is a loanword. There is little doubt that the root ʿ-l-m is genuinely Arabic, but research literature contests the view that the word ʿālam should derive from this root. Arthur Jeffery has argued that the morphological pattern *fāʿalᵘⁿ* is otherwise not attested as an Arabic morphological pattern, and the fact that the word ʿālam in the Qurʾān occurs solely in the plural may suggest it is a borrowed term. Jefferey admits, however, that there is some uncertainty as to which origin it may have had, noting that in "Hebrew ʿōlam means any duration of time, and in the Rabbinic writings the Aramaic ʿālᵉmā, comes to mean *age* or *world*."¹³ Franz Rosenthal likewise refutes a relation between the root ʿ-l-m and ʿālam,¹⁴ but he does raise the point that "roots common and widely used in Arabic for various facets of mental activity are unusual or, apparently, unknown elsewhere in the close-knit circle of Semitic languages."¹⁵ He suggests that "to know" is a semantic extension peculiar to Arabic of an original, concrete meaning ("way sign") residing in a remote, South Arabian past.

As noted by Walid A. Saleh, etymology may have limited interest for an account of historical semantics.[16] It may, however, serve as an orientation while considering the words in various contexts, and indigenous reflections on provenance throw useful light in our particular case on the meaning historically attributed to the notion of ʿālam. In medieval Arabic lexicography, the word ʿālam was not considered a borrowed term, rather a derivation from the Arabic root ʿ-l-m. In early Arabic lexicography, a semantic relationship between the permutations of a root was suggested. Later on, this idea developed into a full-fledged theory about root meaning that came to be generally accepted, and in one dictionary, the *Muʿjam maqāyīs al-lugha* by Ibn Fāris (d. 1005), root meaning is discussed explicitly.[17] According to this lexicographer, ʿ-l-m is a genuine root with one root meaning: "a characteristic that distinguishes something out from among all other things."[18] From this root derives ʿalāma, which is something that makes something known, a "sign," and ʿalam, a "mark," "flag," or "banner." ʿĀlam is in Ibn Fāris's dictionary another derivation of ʿ-l-m, explained as "every kind among the creatures is an abode or trace (maʿlam) and a sign (ʿalam) in itself." According to Ibn Fāris, it was also said that "al-ʿālam is called such because it encompasses all."[19]

Al-Rāghib al-Iṣfahānī holds that the ʿālam is "that by means of which one knows [something]," thus confirming the view that it originates in ʿ-l-m ("knowledge").[20] He goes on to say that the ʿālam is a noun for the universe with all that it contains of substances and accidents. Its morphological form is likened to other instrumental nouns, as *khātam*, and as such "the ʿālam is an instrument in indication of its Creator."[21] Additionally, al-Rāghib al-Iṣfahānī attests to a tradition traced back to early authorities such as ʿAlī b. Abī Ṭālib (d. 661, fourth caliph and considered the first infallible *imām* in the Shīʿī tradition) and Jaʿfar al-Ṣādiq (d. 702, Ṣūfī authority and considered the sixth infallible *imām* in the Shīʿī tradition), but also with a possible Neoplatonic inspiration, holding existence to be manifested in a macro-cosmos (*al-ʿālam al-kabīr*) and reflected in the micro-cosmos (*al-ʿālam al-ṣaghīr*) of the human being.[22]

Some sources discuss the possibility of two etymologies. ʿĀlam, al-ʿAskarī holds, may be derived from ʿilm ("knowledge") because it refers to beings having knowledge, either creatures with an intellectual faculty (ʿaql), creatures with a soul (*rūḥ*), or, in idiomatic use, people of a particular period (*ahl zaman*). It may, on the other hand, be derived from ʿalāma ("sign"), because it is something that points back to its creator. In this sense, ʿālam would mean the whole of the creation. According to al-ʿAskarī, Arabs sometimes used ʿālam in the sense of "world of the birds," but he did not support this use of the word, holding that ʿālam is an instrumental noun for something out of which one may infer knowledge.[23] In his view, ʿālam is a collective noun that does not have a singular form, as it contains different things.

The Multiverse

The term "multiverse" is coined on the pattern of the term "universe" (from Latin *uni* and *vertere*, "all that which is turning"), and denotes a multiplicity of moving.[24] In recent decades it has been used in philosophy as well as physics, and fiction. In physics it has been used as an analytical concept in a number of theories deriving from the observation that the universe is expanding: as particles move until they are out of reach both empirically and theoretically, they form a number of causally disconnected universes.[25] In fiction some genres accommodate several mental models within the mind of the reader, while others take a multiworld model of reality largely as an ontological given.[26]

The term multiverse is thus not monopolized by any particular discipline or theory. ʿAdī Setia used the term to discuss the question of whether the Qurʾānic term *al-ʿālamīn* refers to multiple worlds within this known universe, or to many other universes or a multiverse beyond.[27] According to Setia, the late twelfth-century philosopher Fakhr al-Dīn al-Rāzī (d. 1209) vehemently supported the idea that there are physical worlds beyond this world, stating that God has infinite power to create thousands of worlds.[28] These ideas had been discussed by philosophers such as Abū Ḥāmid al-Ghazālī a century earlier. He claimed an axiological status to the idea of possible multiple worlds. In response to Ibn Sīnā (Avicenna, d. 1037), who drew on Aristotle's thought that the existence of multiple worlds would be an absurdity, and inspired by the mystic Abū Ṭālib al-Makkī (d. 996), al-Ghazālī formulated a theory of successive possible worlds created in sequence by God from nothing, making up one larger "possible world."[29] Drawing on the historical semantics of the notion *ʿālam* and the idea of a plurality of worlds as an ontological reality, it seems justified to employ the term multiverse generically to refer to a notion of a model of reality corresponding to a mental model.

Abū Ḥāmid al-Ghazālī

A vast research literature investigates different features of the broad-ranging scholarship of Abū Ḥāmid Muḥammad b. Muḥammad al-Ghazālī (d. 1111).[30] His scholarly work comprised authorship of more than seventy works within the diverse fields of philosophy, theology, legal methodology, jurisprudence, ethics, and mystics. It also included teaching activities, most prominently in two periods in the 1090s as the main teacher of the then newly established Niẓāmiyya school in Baghdad, which became, as Omid Safi puts it, both his "greatest podium and his prison."[31] In his time, and beyond, al-Ghazālī was instrumental in consolidating what emerged as a "Sunnī orthodoxy," not least in response to the competing ideas of Muʿtazilī, Shīʿī, and Ismāʿīlī theologies.

Al-Ghazālī wrote the short treatise *Mishkāt al-anwār* (*The Niche of Lights*) toward the end of his life,³² following his refutations of the Avicennian philosophy in *Tahāfut al-falāsifa* (*The Incoherence of the Philosophers*) and his magnum opus *Ihyāʾ ʿulūm al-dīn* (*Revivification of the Religious Sciences*), and followed by his main work on legal methodology *al-Mustaṣfā min ʿilm al-uṣūl* (*The Essentials of Legal Theory*), his autobiographical sketch *al-Munqidh min al-ḍalāl* (*The Deliverer from Error*), and his probably last work, the theological treatise *Iljām al-ʿawāmm ʿan ʿilm al-kalām* (*Preventing the Masses from the Discipline of Theology*).³³ Issues of knowledge and interpretation had been a core concern throughout al-Ghazālī's work, and in *Mishkāt al-anwār* he reiterates and refines his theory of scriptural theological hermeneutics.

A Multiverse Epistemology

Given the idea that the purpose of the world is to be a device for man to know God, the world was in medieval Islamic discourse perceived as a place of moral meaning. A question of concern to al-Ghazālī was how to access this knowledge and moral meaning. He developed a theory of a plurality of worlds, lexicalized with the conceptual pair "the world of sovereignty and witnessing" (*ʿālam al-mulk wal-shahāda*), referring to the phenomenal world available for empirical investigation, and "the world of the unknown and [Divine] sovereignty" (*ʿālam al-ghayb wal-malakūt*), referring to an invisible world. A third category, "the world of almightiness" (*ʿālam al-jabarūt*), is presented in some of al-Ghazālī's other works.³⁴ This last notion is quite elusive. In the *Ihyāʾ*, the world of almightiness is seen as an intermediary realm between the phenomenal and the invisible worlds, likened to "a boat that is moving between the earth and the water."³⁵ However, in his very late, and therefore possibly more conclusive work the *Mishkāt*, neither the epistemology nor the hermeneutics are dependent on this third, intermediate sphere.

The term *ʿālam* is used in a number of other expressions and contexts throughout the work of al-Ghazālī, such as "the world of nature" (*ʿālam al-ṭabīʿa*), pertaining to a particular field of the phenomenal world, or "the world of authority and prophethood" (*ʿālam al-wilāya wal-nubuwwa*) in a discussion on epistemic authority.³⁶ In the *Ihyāʾ*, the sources of sensory impressions are likewise described as "worlds": "The eye trusts the world of colors, the ear the world of sounds, the nose the world of smells, and so forth. The one receiving the information from these worlds and passing them on to the imaginative faculty is like a letter carrier."³⁷

What constitutes a main epistemological and hermeneutical key in the *Mishkāt* is the conceptual pair of the phenomenal and the invisible worlds, with variants of the notions ʿ*ālam al-mulk wal-shahāda* and ʿ*ālam al-ghayb wal-malakūt*. The two notions *mulk* and *malakūt* are, according to the Arabic lexicographers, considered to be derived from the root *m-l-k* denoting strength and soundness.[38] Both terms are Qurʾānic. *Malakūt* appears in the Qurʾān exclusively in connection to the divine and refers to God's dominion over the heavens and the earth (al-Qurʾān 6:75; 7:185; 36:83). The concept of *mulk* refers to sovereignty in a generic way, as in al-Qurʾān 3:26, where the same word is repeated twice, respectively referring to divine and human sovereignty.

Kojiro Nakamura contends that to al-Ghazālī the "worlds of *mulk* and *malakūt* also correspond to this world (*dunyā*) and the afterlife (*ākhira*)."[39] This contention may need a modification. In the *Iḥyāʾ*, al-Ghazālī does not completely identify the two conceptual pairs with each other. They are interconnected in that earthly life belongs to the phenomenal world while the afterlife belongs to the invisible world, in parallel states of being. In terms of human life, however, these are also sequential states of being: "Earthly life is your state before death and the afterlife is your state after death."[40] Thus, al-Ghazālī holds that as situated in earthly life, which belongs to the phenomenal world, the only means human beings have to explain something about the invisible world is by way of similes (*amthāl*).

On this basis I will maintain that al-Ghazālī uses the notion of ʿ*ālam* in various ways pertaining to different categories. On an ontological level, ʿ*ālam* in the *Mishkāt* refers to a "sphere of being" (*kawn*).[41] The two spheres of this earthly life and the afterlife[42] are contrasted to God, who is the only real existence (*al-wāḥid al-ḥaqq*), beyond both. The human spirit may serve as a channel for glimpses of holiness only by "throwing off the two sandals," that is, both this world and the next.[43]

While the phenomenal outward (*ẓāhir*) world is visible to everyone, the invisible, inward (*bāṭin*) world is unattainable for most people, al-Ghazālī holds.[44] Nevertheless, manifestations in the different spheres of knowledge are conceivable by way of different types of light: "the light of seeing" (*nūr al-baṣar*) pertaining to the sensory perception (*ḥiss*) and imaginative faculty (*khayāl*),[45] and "the visionary light" (*nūr al-baṣīra*) pertaining to the intellectual faculty (ʿ*aql*). It is the latter faculty which is the most worthy, al-Ghazālī says, of being designated with this notion of light.[46] The sensory world serves, however, as a ladder to the intellectual world (*al-ʿālam al-ʿaqlī*),[47] which, along with the imaginative faculty, is instrumental in identifying the similes between the phenomenal world and the invisible world, as "there is nothing in this world that is not a parallel (*mithāl*) to something in that world."[48] It should be noted that intellectuality is here not understood as a purely cognitive tool; rather, the intellectual world is identified with the spiritual (*ruḥānī*) world of the invisible.[49]

A Multiverse Hermeneutics

Out of this epistemological scheme of a multiverse grows what may be seen as a hermeneutics of correspondence, and in the *Mishkāt* al-Ghazālī employs this hermeneutical scheme to interpret the "Light verse" (al-Qurʾān 24:35) as well as a prophetic saying. The hermeneutical principle is explained as "a correspondence between the visible world, from which is taken the clay of similes, and the invisible world, from which the spirits of the meanings descend."[50] This theological hermeneutics differs from the formal, legal hermeneutics al-Ghazālī develops in his book *al-Mustaṣfā*, which is geared toward deducing a normative order (*sharīʿa*) from the texts.[51] In the *Mishkāt* the main goal is rather, as David Buchman puts it, to present "the message of attaining nearness to God and its implication in the interpretation of Islam."[52]

According to al-Ghazālī, identifying the similes is possible on different spiritual levels, in the perceptive spirit (*al-rūḥ al-ḥassās*), the imaginative spirit (*al-rūḥ al-khayālī*), the intellectual spirit (*al-rūḥ al-ʿaqlī*), the reflective spirit (*al-rūḥ al-fikrī*), and, ultimately, in the holy prophetic spirit (*al-rūḥ al-qudsī al-nabawī*).[53] Not all of these levels are available to everyone, al-Ghazālī holds, and in his final work, *Iljām al-ʿawāmm ʿan ʿilm al-kalām*, he asserts that most people arrive at their convictions through different methods of demonstration or accepting the arguments of others.[54] Neither does al-Ghazālī claim for himself such a fully equipped interpretational capability. In the interpretation of a certain prophetic saying,[55] he admits to not fully trusting his own ability to understand a reference to the number seventy mentioned. He leaves the ultimate interpretation up to the prophetic ability, although he does seem to prefer a figurative reference, in which the implication is "multitude" rather than the actual number.[56]

Al-Ghazālī advocates here a metaphorical reading, and as Ebrahim Moosa notes, "when pushed he would privilege spirit over body, meaning over utterance."[57] In the *Iḥyāʾ*, however, inward (*bāṭin*), esoteric interpretation reaching too far beyond the outward (*ẓāhir*), linguistic expression is deemed both harmful and forbidden. The result of such esoteric interpretation would be a loss of trust in words, which would render void the benefit even of the words of God and of his prophet, al-Ghazālī holds.[58] Timothy J. Gianotti interprets the concerns of al-Ghazālī within the frames of his "preoccupation with the protection of simple belief."[59] I would suggest a reading focusing on a concern for linguistic stability. Al-Ghazālī admits that linguistic changes inevitably will take place, but warns against allowing linguistic changes to result in recasting the moral order, such as in replacing the praiseworthy with the blameworthy.[60]

To al-Ghazālī, the question of linguistic stability is closely linked to questions of knowledge and of authority, and these statements echo an ideological struggle for epistemic authority. He calls for transparency in the interpretational process, as the esoteric interpretation he disallows is based on absolute epistemic authority, which in al-Ghazālī's scheme is allotted for the prophets only. In this he fiercely opposes the potent contemporary Isma'īlī movement and the Isma'īlī concept of authoritative instruction (ta'līm) on the part of the infallible *imām*.[61] Al-Ghazālī's multiverse of knowledge is conceptualized as a plurality of spheres of epistemological and hermeneutical activity, separate but interlinked and accessible through mental and spiritual endeavor by means of the simile. Through his theory of the multiverse as a model of reality as well as a mental model serving interpretation, al-Ghazālī found a means to accommodate a need for allegorical and pluralistic interpretation while warding off what he deemed harmfully esoteric, and exclusive, interpretation.

Nora S. Eggen is a researcher within Islamic Studies, currently a lecturer at the University of Oslo. Among her latest publications is "Universalized versus Particularized Conceptualizations of Islam in Translations of the Qur'an in Scandinavia," *Journal of Qur'anic Studies* 18, no. 1 (2016) and the edited volume (with Rana Issa) *Philologists in the World: A Festschrift in Honour of Gunvor Mejdell* (Novus forlag, 2017).

NOTES

I would like to thank Stephan Guth for commenting on an earlier draft of this chapter.

1. For further discussions of the dictionary and the encyclopedia, see in particular the chapters by Sanja Perovic and Richard Yeo in this volume.
2. For further discussions of religion, see in particular the chapters by Oddbjørn Leirvik, Chenxi Tang, Kyrre Kverndokk, Alfred Hiatt, Erling Sandmo, and Kari van Dijk in this volume.
3. Abū al-Ḥusayn Aḥmad b. Fāris b. Zakariyā Ibn Fāris, *Mu'jam maqāyīs al-lugha*, ed. 'Abd al-Salām Muḥammad Hārūn ([n.p.], 1979), 2: 310–11.
4. *Al-Mawsū'at al-fiqhiyya* (Kuwait, 1983–2006), 20: 201–20.
5. Binyamin Abrahamov, "World," in *Encyclopedia of the Qur'ān*, ed. Jane Dammen McAuliffe (Leiden, 2006), 5: 552.
6. Angelika Neuwirth, "Cosmology," in *Encyclopedia of the Qur'ān*, ed. Jane Dammen McAuliffe (Leiden, 2001), 1: 449.

7. E. W. Lane, *Arabic-English Lexicon* (Cambridge, 1984), 2: 2141; Abrahamov, "World," 5: 551-52.
8. Abrahamov, "World," 5: 551-52.
9. Muqātil b. Sulaymān al-Balkhī, *Al-Wujūh wal-naẓā'ir fī l-Qur'ān al-karīm*, ed. A. F. al-Mazīrī (Beirut, 2008), 87-88; Abū al-Hilāl al-'Askarī, *Taṣḥīḥ al-wujūh wal-naẓā'ir*, ed. Muḥammad 'Uthmān (Cairo, 2007), 335.
10. Simonetta Calderini, "'Tafsīr' of "ālamīn' in 'rabb al-'ālamīn,' Qurān 1:2," *Bulletin of the School of Oriental and African Studies* 57 (1994): 53-55.
11. Abū Muḥammad 'Abd Allāh b. Muslim Ibn Qutayba, *Tafsīr gharīb al-Qur'ān*, ed. Aḥmad Ṣaqr (Beirut, 1978), 38.
12. Abū al-Qāsim al-Ḥusayn al-Rāghib al-Iṣfahānī, *Al-Mufradāt fī gharīb al-Qur'ān*, ed. Muḥammad Khalīl 'Ītānī (Beirut, 1998), 349.
13. Arthur Jeffery, *The Foreign Vocabulary of the Quran* (Baroda, 1938), 209.
14. Franz Rosenthal, *Knowledge Triumphant: The Concept of Knowledge in Medieval Islam* (Leiden, 1970), 19-20n1.
15. Ibid., 6.
16. Walid A. Saleh, "The Etymological Fallacy and Qur'anic Studies: Muhammad, Paradise, and Late Antiquity," in *The Qur'ān in Context: Historical and Literary Investigations into the Qur'ānic Milieu*, ed. Angelika Neuwirth et al. (Leiden, 2010), 650-98.
17. Rajab 'Abd al-Jawād Ibrāhīm, *Dirāsāt fī al-dalāla wal-mu'jam* (Cairo, 2001), 169, 180.
18. Ibn Fāris, *Mu'jam maqāyīs al-lugha*, 4: 109-10.
19. Ibid., 4: 110.
20. Al-Rāghib al-Iṣfahānī, *Mufradāt*, 349.
21. Ibid., 349.
22. Ibid. See also Yasien Mohamed, "The Classical Islamic Concept of Man as a 'Small World,'" *Afkar* 2 (2001): 87-106.
23. Al-Askarī, *Taṣḥīḥ*, 336-37.
24. Apparently the term "multiverse" was first used to describe the "plasticity and indifference" of visible nature; see William James, "Is Life Worth Living?" *International Journal of Ethics* 6 (1895): 10.
25. Helge Krag, *Higher Speculations: Grand Theories and Failed Revolutions in Physics and Cosmology* (New York, 2011), 258.
26. Karin Kukkonen, "Navigating Infinite Earths: Readers, Mental Models, and the Multiverse of Superhero Comics," *StoryWorlds: A Journal of Narrative Studies* 2 (2010): 40.
27. 'Adī Setia, "Fakhr al-Din al-Rāzī on Physics and the Nature of the Physical World: A Preliminary Survey," *Islam and Science* 2 (2004): 177.
28. Fakhr al-Dīn Muḥammad b. 'Umar al-Rāzī, *Al-Tafsīr al-kabīr aw Mafātiḥ al-ghayb* (Beirut, 2009), 1: 186; cf. Setia, "Fakhr al-Din al-Rāzī," 77.
29. Taneli Kukkonen, "Possible Worlds in the Tahâfut al-Falâsifa: Al-Ghazâlî on Creation and Contingency," *Journal of the History of Philosophy* 38 (2000): 490; Frank Griffel, *Al-Ghazālī's Philosophical Theology* (Oxford, 2009), 225. However, al-Ghazālī draws

on Ibn Sīnā in a number of other ways; see Mesut Okumus, "The Influence of Ibn Sīnā on al-Ghazzālī in Qur'anic Hermeneutics," *Muslim World* 102 (2012): 390–411.
30. For an introduction to the life of al-Ghazālī, see W. Montgomery Watt, *Muslim Intellectual: A Study of al-Ghazali* (Edinburgh, 1963). See also introductory chapters in other works cited in this chapter.
31. Omid Safi, *The Politics of Knowledge in Premodern Islam: Negotiating Ideology and Religious Inquiry* (Chapel Hill, 2006), 107.
32. Abū Ḥāmid Al-Ghazālī, *The Niche of Lights: Mishkāt al-anwār*, ed. Abū al-ʿAlā ʿAfīfī, trans. David Buchman (Provo, 1998). I have in this chapter consulted Buchman's excellent translation, but my translation differs from it on a number of minor points in order to maintain consistency.
33. George F. Hourani, "A Revised Chronology of Ghazālī's Writings," *Journal of the American Oriental Society* 104 (1984): 299–300.
34. A. J. Wensinck, "On the Relation between Ghazālī's Cosmology and His Mysticism," *Mededeelingen des Koninklijke Akademie van Wetenschappen Afdeeling Letterkunde* 75 (1933): 185; Kojiro Nakamura, "Imām Ghazālī's Cosmology Reconsidered with Special Reference to the Concept of 'Jabarūt,'" *Studia Islamica* 80 (1994): 38; Timothy J. Gianotti, *Al-Ghazālī's Unspeakable Doctrine of the Soul: Unveiling the Esoteric Psychology and Eschatology of the Iḥyāʾ* (Leiden, 2001), 151.
35. Abū Ḥāmid al-Ghazālī, *Iḥyāʾ ʿulūm al-dīn* (Beirut, 1993), 5: 124.
36. Abū Ḥāmid al-Ghazālī, *Mīzān al-ʿamal*, ed. Sulaymān Dunyā (Cairo, 1964), 30, 302.
37. Al-Ghazālī, *Iḥyāʾ ʿulūm al-dīn*, 3: 121. Here, as well as in other instances, al-Ghazālī employs the plural *ʿawālim*, not the Qurʾānic plural *ʿālamūn* (nominative case). This does not, however, seem to have a bearing on the theory.
38. Ibn Fāris, *Muʿjam maqāyīs al-lugha*, 5: 351–52. Arthur Jeffery, however, considers *malakūt* to be a loanword from Aramaic; see Jeffery, *The Foreign Vocabulary of the Qurʾan*, 270–71.
39. Nakamura, "Imām Ghazālī's Cosmology Reconsidered," 33.
40. Al-Ghazālī, *Iḥyāʾ ʿulūm al-dīn*, 4: 230, with reference to al-Qurʾān 29:43.
41. Al-Ghazālī, *Mishkāt*, 35.
42. Ibid., 30.
43. Ibid., 26 and 30, with reference to al-Qurʾān 20:12.
44. Ibid., 11.
45. Ibid., 11, 19.
46. Ibid., 19.
47. Ibid., 26.
48. Ibid., 27.
49. Ibid., 25. See more in Gianotti, *Al-Ghazālī's Unspeakable Doctrine*, 120.
50. Al-Ghazālī, *Mishkāt*, 25. See also Martin Whittingham, *Al-Ghazālī and the Qurʾān: One Book, Many Meanings* (London, 2007); Ulrika Mårtensson, "Through the Lens of Modern Hermeneutics: Authorial Intention in al-Ṭabarī's and al-Ghazālī's Interpretations of Q. 24:35," *Journal of Qurʾanic Studies* 11 (2009): 20–48.
51. Whittingham, *Al-Ghazālī and the Qurʾān*, 33.
52. Al-Ghazālī, *Mishkāt*, xxvii.

53. Ibid., 36–37.
54. Abū Ḥāmid al-Ghazālī, *Iljām al-ʿawāmm ʿan ʿilm al-kalām* (Cairo, 1997), 66. For a discussion of al-Ghazālī's division of mankind into different classes, see also Jonathan A. C. Brown, "The Last Days of al-Ghazzālī and the Tripartite Division of the Sufi World: Abū Ḥāmid al-Ghazzālī's Letter to the Seljuq Vizier and Commentary," *Muslim World* 96 (2006): 89–113.
55. The authenticity of this section of the text has been contested; see al-Ghazālī, *Mishkāt*, xxvii.
56. Al-Ghazālī, *Mishkāt*, 44.
57. Ebrahim Moosa, *Ghazālī and the Poetics of Imagination* (Chapel Hill, 2005), 218.
58. Al-Ghazālī, *Iḥyāʾ ʿulūm al-dīn*, 1: 5–6.
59. Gianotti, *Al-Ghazālī's Unspeakable Doctrine*, 62.
60. Al-Ghazālī, *Iḥyāʾ ʿulūm al-dīn*, 1: 45.
61. Farouk Mitha, *Al-Ghazālī and the Ismailis: A Debate on Reason and Authority in Medieval Islam* (London, 2001), 24.

BIBLIOGRAPHY

Abrahamov, Binyamin. "World." In *Encyclopedia of the Qurʾān*, edited by Jane Dammen McAuliffe, 5: 552. Leiden: Brill, 2006.

ʿAskarī, Abū al-Hilāl al-. *Taṣḥīḥ al-wujūh wal-naẓāʾir*. Edited by Muḥammad ʿUthmān. Cairo: Maktaba al-thaqāfa al-dīniyya, 2007.

Balkhī, Muqātil b. Sulaymān al-. *Al-Wujūh wal-naẓāʾir fī l-Qurʾān al-karīm*. Edited by A. F. al-Mazīrī. Beirut: Dār al-kutub al-ʿilmiyya, 2008.

Brown, Jonathan A. C. "The Last Days of al-Ghazzālī and the Tripartite Division of the Sufi World: Abū Ḥāmid al-Ghazzālī's Letter to the Seljuq Vizier and Commentary." *Muslim World* 96 (2006): 89–113.

Calderini, Simonetta. "'Tafsīr' of 'ālamīn' in 'rabb al-ʿālamīn,' Qurān 1:2." *Bulletin of the School of Oriental and African Studies* 57 (1994): 52–58.

Ghazālī, Abū Ḥāmid al-. *Iḥyāʾ ʿulūm al-dīn*. Beirut: Dār al-khayr, 1993.

———. *Iljām al-ʿawāmm ʿan ʿilm al-kalām*. Cairo: Maktabat al-ʿazhariyya lil-turāth, 1997.

———. *Mīzān al-ʿamal*. Edited by Sulaymān Dunyā. Cairo: Dār al-maʿārif, 1964.

———. *The Niche of Lights: Mishkāt al-anwār*. Edited by Abū al-ʿAlāʾ ʿAfīfī, translated by David Buchman. Provo: Brigham Young University Press, 1998.

Gianotti, Timothy J. *Al-Ghazālī's Unspeakable Doctrine of the Soul: Unveiling the Esoteric Psychology and Eschatology of the Iḥyāʾ*. Leiden: Brill, 2001.

Griffel, Frank. *Al-Ghazālī's Philosophical Theology*. Oxford: Oxford University Press, 2009.

Hourani, George F. "A Revised Chronology of Ghazālī's Writings." *Journal of the American Oriental Society* 104 (1984): 289–302.

Ibn Fāris, Abū al-Ḥusayn Aḥmad b. Fāris b. Zakariyā. *Muʿjam maqāyīs al-lugha*. Edited by ʿAbd al-Salām Muḥammad Hārūn. (N.p.): Dār al-fikr lil-ṭibāʿa wal-nashr wal-tawzīʿ, 1979.

Ibn Qutayba, Abū Muḥammad ʿAbd Allāh b. Muslim. *Tafsīr gharīb al-Qurʾān*. Edited by Aḥmad Ṣaqr. Beirut: Dār al-kutub al-ʿilmiyya, 1978.
Ibrāhīm, Rajab ʿAbd al-Jawād. *Dirāsāt fī al-dalāla wal-muʿjam*. Cairo: Dār gharīb, 2001.
Iṣfahānī, Abū al-Qāsim al-Ḥusayn al-Rāghib, al-. *Al-Mufradāt fī gharīb al-Qurʾān*. Edited by Muḥammad Khalīl ʿĪtānī. Beirut: Dār al-maʿrifa, 1998.
James, William. "Is Life Worth Living?" *International Journal of Ethics* 6 (1895): 1–24.
Jeffery, Arthur. *The Foreign Vocabulary of the Quran*. Baroda: Oriental Institute, 1938.
Krag, Helge. *Higher Speculations: Grand Theories and Failed Revolutions in Physics and Cosmology*. New York: Oxford University Press, 2011.
Kukkonen, Karin. "Navigating Infinite Earths: Readers, Mental Models, and the Multiverse of Superhero Comics." *StoryWorlds: A Journal of Narrative Studies* 2 (2010): 39–58.
Kukkonen, Taneli. "Possible Worlds in the Tahâfut al-Falâsifa: Al-Ghazâlî on Creation and Contingency." *Journal of the History of Philosophy* 38 (2000): 479–502.
Lane, E. W. *Arabic–English Lexicon*. Cambridge: Islamic Texts Society, 1984.
Mawsūʿat al-fiqhiyya, al-. Kuwait: Wizārat al-awqāf wal-shuʾūn al-islāmiyya, 1983–2006.
Mårtensson, Ulrika. "Through the Lens of Modern Hermeneutics: Authorial Intention in al-Ṭabarī's and al-Ghazālī's Interpretations of Q. 24:35." *Journal of Qur'anic Studies* 11 (2009): 20–48.
Mitha, Farouk. *Al-Ghazālī and the Ismailis: A Debate on Reason and Authority in Medieval Islam*. London: Tauris, 2001.
Mohamed, Yasien. "The Classical Islamic Concept of Man as a 'Small World.'" *Afkar* 2 (2001): 87–106.
Moosa, Ebrahim. *Ghazālī and the Poetics of Imagination*. Chapel Hill: University of North Carolina Press, 2005.
Nakamura, Kojiro. "Imām Ghazālī's Cosmology Reconsidered with Special Reference to the Concept of 'Jabarūt.'" *Studia Islamica* 80 (1994): 29–46.
Neuwirth, Angelika. "Cosmology." In *Encyclopedia of the Qur'ān*, edited by Jane Dammen McAuliffe, 1: 449. Leiden: Brill, 2001.
Okumus, Mesut. "The Influence of Ibn Sīnā on al-Ghazzālī in Qurʾanic Hermeneutics." *Muslim World* 102 (2012): 390–411.
Rāzī, Fakhr al-Dīn Muḥammad b. ʿUmar al-. *Al-Tafsīr al-kabīr aw Mafātiḥ al-ghayb*. Beirut: Dār al-kutub al-ʿilmiyya, 2009.
Rosenthal, Franz. *Knowledge Triumphant: The Concept of Knowledge in Medieval Islam*. Leiden: Brill, 1970.
Safi, Omid. *The Politics of Knowledge in Premodern Islam: Negotiating Ideology and Religious Inquiry*. Chapel Hill: University of North Carolina Press, 2006.
Saleh, Walid A. "The Etymological Fallacy and Qurʾanic Studies: Muhammad, Paradise, and Late Antiquity." In *The Qurʾān in Context: Historical and Literary Investigations into the Qurʾānic Milieu*, edited by Angelika Neuwirth, Nicolai Sinai, and Michael Marx, 650–98. Leiden: Brill, 2010.
Setia, ʿAdī. "Fakhr al-Din al-Rāzī on Physics and the Nature of the Physical World: A Preliminary Survey." *Islam and Science* 2 (2004): 61–80.
Watt, W. Montgomery. *Muslim Intellectual: A Study of al-Ghazali*. Edinburgh: Edinburgh University Press, 1963.

Wensinck, A. J. "On the Relation between Ghazālī's Cosmology and His Mysticism." *Mededeelingen des Koninklijke Akademie van Wetenschappen Afdeeling Letterkunde* 75 (1933): 183–209.

Whittingham, Martin. *Al-Ghazālī and the Qurʾān: One Book, Many Meanings*. London: Routledge, 2007.

▶• 3 •◀

Globalization of Human Conscience

A Modern Muslim Case

Oddbjørn Leirvik

Most languages, including those that lack a classical parallel to the notion of conscience, have coined words for conscience that have often become an integral part of vernacular usage. Here, as elsewhere, words can also become *concepts*. In the globalization of conscience as a loaded concept, modern ideas about individual integrity and universal community have been influential. The Universal Declaration of Human Rights, which was adopted by the United Nations in 1948, seems both to express a distinctively modern understanding of human conscience and to further inspire conscience-oriented discourses among intellectuals around the globe. In the preamble, the declaration states that "disregard and contempt for human rights have resulted in barbarous acts which have outraged the conscience of mankind."[1] The formulation implies that there are certain violations of human integrity that—right across cultural and religious divides—can be recognized as crimes against humanity. In this way, the preamble implies in fact a "world community" responding in unison to abhorrent acts deemed to be inhuman and to grave violations of rights perceived to be universal.

The implicit reference of the preamble is of course the world wars of the twentieth century. Whereas the preamble depicts the dark background of a renewed discourse on conscience, the declaration itself refers to conscience in positive terms, as in Article 1: "All human beings are born free and equal in dignity and rights. They are endowed with reason and conscience and should act towards one another in a spirit of brotherhood." Both in the preamble and in Article 1, conscience is referred to as the seat of a shared, universal knowledge—of good and evil, of right and wrong. The focus is upon morally binding knowledge with the other, as expressed by the connection that is made in Article 1 between the voice of conscience and the spirit of brotherhood. But the Universal Declaration also reflects the idea of the free individual, as expressed in Article 18. Here, conscience is referred to as the inviolable property of the individual. Correspondingly, freedom of conscience is seen as a right that every individual holds: "Everyone has the right to freedom of thought, conscience and religion." Both dimensions of the notion of conscience—integrity of the self and morally binding knowledge with the other—are thus solidly present in the Universal Declaration of Human Rights.

Against the possible suspicion that conscience is only a Western concept, it is interesting to note that the reference to conscience was in fact proposed by a Chinese member of the drafting committee. In his eyes, the Christian or Western notion of conscience paralleled the Confucian concept of *jen*, expressed by a word that is composed of the signs for "human being" and "two"—meaning something like "two-man-mindedness" or "consciousness of one's fellow men."[2]

Further developments of the notion of conscience from the mid twentieth century could in fact be read as a process of accelerating globalization, in which "conscience" denotes a universal bond capable of shaping and consolidating a world community.

Another milestone in the mid twentieth century's globalization of conscience is Mahatma Gandhi's active use of the concept in his moral, religious, and political philosophy. Against divisive notions of religious belonging, Gandhi saw belief in God as something deeply personal that—by virtue of being anchored in every individual—transcended the confines of religious communities: "God is conscience."[3] Correspondingly, he confessed his inspiration from the teachings of several religions: Hinduism, Buddhism, Zoroastrianism, Islam, and Christianity.[4] For Gandhi, the voice of conscience was also intimately linked with the virtue of non-violent, passive resistance.[5] Gandhi's distinctive contribution to the globalization of conscience as a loaded notion was thus, first, to emphasize conscience's faith-transcending nature, and second, to link conscience with the virtue of non-violence, as reflected in the notion of "conscientious objection." In both respects, he seems to have been a major source of inspiration for Muslim intellectuals in Egypt, writing in the 1950s and with a similar focus on a faith-transcending, non-violent notion of conscience.

Some Notes on Conscience's Conceptual History

Before turning to the modern Muslim case indicated above, some reflections on conscience's history of ideas in Christian ethics and European philosophy are in order.[6] The ancient roots of the concept are found with the classical Greek philosophers and in the New Testament, more specifically in the Pauline epistles. In both Greek and Latin, conscience means "knowing with," as reflected by the constructs *syn-eídēsis* and *con-scientia*. In medieval times, and in conjunction with Paul's remarks in his Epistle to the Romans, conscience was often associated with the notion of a divinely imbued natural law, as in Romans 2:14–15:

> When Gentiles who have not the [Jewish] law do by nature what the law requires, they are a law to themselves, even though they do not have the law. They show that what the law requires is written on their hearts, while their conscience also bears witness and their conflicting thoughts accuse or perhaps excuse them.

In modernity, the notion of conscience has acquired some distinctively new aspects. On the one hand, it has been coupled with strong notions of individuality such as moral autonomy (as in Kant's identification of conscience with the inner judge) or personal authenticity (as in Rousseau, who saw conscience as the divine voice within). On the other hand, conscience has also been associated with modern notions of sociality, as with Hegel and Feuerbach. According to Feuerbach, conscience is also stripped of its divine reference, signifying simply the internalized bond between I and You:

> Conscience is "knowing with." To such a degree is the imprint of the Other woven into my self-consciousness, my self-image, that even the expression of what is more than anything else my own, my innermost, the conscience, becomes an expression of socialism, communality.[7]

As can be seen from the above quote, Feuerbach notes that etymologically, conscience means "knowing with." In the European history of ideas, the notion of conscience has revealed what might seem to be an inherent *tension* between conscience's two aspects of "knowing by oneself" and "knowing with the other." Conscience refers not only to something known intimately by oneself, but also to relationships with distinctive others and to something that can be known together with them. Conceptually, it could actually be argued that the notion of conscience intimately *joins* the ambition of being true to oneself with the recognition of a moral bond with others (what Feuerbach terms "communality").

From a history of ideas perspective, the concept of conscience thus joins a concern for individual freedom with the idea of a universal moral community (*allgemeine Kirche*, as Kant had it) that transcends communal bonds of a more parochial kind. It should be noted, however, that the sense of community implied in conscience as knowing with others is not necessarily of a universal nature. In many discourses, conscience is felt to be a *communitarian* bond, informed by specific confessional insights. In modernity, however, conscience seems to have become a key notion for expressing a type of moral community that is perceived as *universal*, as expressed by the notion of a "global ethic."[8] In this sense, modern references to human conscience often articulate one's belonging to "the world" (emblematically expressed in the Universal Declaration of Human Rights) rather than to a confined community, whether religious or otherwise.

Conscience in Arabic

During the nineteenth century, and more or less contemporary with Feuerbach's divestment of conscience's divine clothing, the notion of conscience was also included in ethical discourses outside the orbit of Western Christianity. It is in the mid nineteenth century that modern Arabic coins a distinct word for conscience, preferably by use of the word *damīr*, which in classical Arabic refers to innermost knowledge. Although many of the ideas associated with the European notion of conscience can be found in Islamic ethics, classical Islam lacks a comparable concept that joins individuality and sociality. But with modernity comes also the coining of a particular Arabic word for conscience. Dictionaries as well as other literary evidence indicate that the word *damīr* gradually acquires this meaning from the first half of the nineteenth century onward, competing to some extent with the word *wijdān*, which more strongly connotes emotional knowledge.[9]

Given its classical reference to innermost knowledge, the coining of *damīr* as conscience in modern Arabic indicates a strong inward orientation, toward a moral voice within. However, when a word becomes a concept, there is more at play than mere etymology. As Koselleck has taught us, "a word becomes a concept when the plenitude of a sociopolitical context of meaning and experience in and for which a word is used can be condensed into one word."[10] In a contextual view, the coining of *damīr* as conscience coincides more or less with translations of European philosophy into Arabic, and—notably—with new developments in biblical Arabic.[11] It seems in fact that Arabic translations of the Bible in the nineteenth century have been instrumental in imbuing *damīr* with ideas associated with the concept of conscience. With the exception of Hispano-Arabic Bibles, Arabic Bible translations in the premodern period preferred other words than *damīr*, such as *niyya* ("intention") or *basīra* ("insight"), when translating *syneídēsis*. The decisive change in biblical Arabic came with the Protestant, so-called Bustani–van Dyck Bible translation, which was published in Beirut from 1860 onward. In all relevant verses this new translation rendered *syneídēsis* with *damīr*. In the wake of the Bustani–van Dyck Bible, other Bible translations (for instance the Jesuit Bible from 1878) made the same decision.[12]

Supported by contemporary lexicographical evidence, it is quite probable that developments in biblical Arabic were one of the main factors in the linguistic process toward a general use of *damīr* for moral consciousness or conscience in Modern Standard Arabic, as well as in colloquial Egyptian Arabic. In this perspective, it could in fact be argued that the coining of *damīr* as conscience reflects Christian–Muslim interaction in the modern context, in the context of modern nationalist projects that downplayed religious difference to the benefit of national belonging.

In Egypt, biblical Arabic contributed toward a semantic and conceptual development that was taken a step further when reform-minded Arab intellectuals of the early twentieth century (Muslims as well as Christians) employed either *damīr* or *wijdān* when rendering conscience in their reception of European philosophy and in their elaborations on Christian or Islamic ethics.[13]

Faith-Transcending Conscience: Modern Egyptian Examples

In previous research I have examined how the notion of conscience (*damīr*) was used by three Muslim intellectuals writing in the 1950s and 1960s. This was an era marked not only by nationalist trends in politics but equally by internationalism (as in Egypt's involvement in the Non-Aligned Movement) and faith-transcending orientations in ethics in tune with President Nasser's secular orientation. Whereas more recent developments from the 1970s onward have tended to segregate Muslims and Christians in their mutual concentration on Islamic or Coptic authenticity, respectively, the 1950s and 1960s were marked by a much more open exchange of intellectual ideas between adherents of the two religions, reflecting Egyptian nationalism at its Nasserite height, internationalism, and a universalistic orientation in ethics that seems also to have been much inspired by human rights discourses.

The authors I have been researching are ʿAbbas Mahmud al-ʿAqqad (1889–1964), Khalid Muhammad Khalid (1920–96), and Kamil Husayn (1901–77), all of them prominent Muslim intellectuals. In their writings on religion, philosophy, and ethics, the notion of conscience (*damīr*) is strikingly central.

Muhammad and Christ, Together on the Road

A recurrent motif in al-ʿAqqad's writings, inspired by Thomas Carlyle's modern classic *On Heroes and Hero-Worship* from 1841, is the role of the genius in transforming society from stagnation to modern dynamism. In his book *ʿAbqariyyat Muhammad* ("The Genius of Muhammad"), which was published in 1942, the notion of conscience already plays a central role.

Indicative of his universalism, al-'Aqqad claims that Muhammad, when properly understood, has a natural (and faith-transcending) appeal to the human conscience. On a distinctively modernist note, he adds that those who deny Muhammad's inner qualities and outward achievements reject not only the greatness of Muhammad but the progress of humankind toward a perfect balance of inner and outward qualities as well.

In 1953, al-'Aqqad published a similar book, *'Abqariyyat al-Masīh* ("The Genius of Christ"), which was republished as *Hayāt al-Masīh* ("The Life of Christ") in 1957.[14] Al-'Aqqad's biography of Christ has been widely acclaimed as a groundbreaking Muslim approach to the life of Christ, not least because of its reliance on the New Testament gospels. In this book, 'al-Aqqad praises Christ for preaching "the law of love and conscience" (*sharī'at al-hubb wa-l-damīr*). In al-'Aqqad's view, Christ's law of love and conscience was advanced as a religious and ethical alternative to "the law of outward forms and appearances" that prevailed in his time.[15] By these expressions, al-'Aqqad twists (and expands) the very notion of Sharia in a faith-transcending direction. A typical modern reformer, he mobilizes both Christ and Muhammad in what he calls a *jihād* of conscience against petrified religion and authoritarian forms of moral authority.

Apparently, al-'Aqqad's interest in Christ was not restricted to a historical presentation of Christ as a law reformer in Judaism. There are many indications that his book about Christ should also be read as a critique of rigorous attitudes and superficial literalism among traditionalist Muslim scholars (*'ulamā'*). This shines through in his employment of terms referring to traditional Islamic offices such as *fuqahā'* (jurists), *'ulama'* (learned scholars), and *huffāz* (those who know the Qur'an by heart).[16] His discourse of conscience is thus rallied in a larger project of modernized ethics that may be characterized as an "inward turn forward."

In tune with Hans Küng's later notion of "a global ethic,"[17] mid-nineteenth-century discourses about conscience among Muslim intellectuals in Egypt thus implied openness toward learning from other religious traditions. This is even more conspicuous with Khalid Muhammad Khalid, whose general orientation was not toward human geniuses but rather, in tune with Nasser's socialism, toward "the common people." In 1958, he published a book replete with references to human conscience, with the telling title *Ma'an 'alā al-tarīq: Muhammad wa-l-Masīh* ("Muhammad and Christ: Together on the Road").[18] Here, he speaks of the integrity of human conscience as the uniting bond between the two prophets and their adherents:

> That is exactly what I want to say to those who believe in Christ and those who believe in Muhammad: If you are sincere, the proof of your faith is that today, one and all of you embark upon the task of protecting the human being ... protecting life![19]

In this book, both Muhammad and Christ are praised for their uprightness and honesty of conscience. Indicative of his universalistic concern, Khalid also credits Christ for having liberated human conscience from its imprisonment by racial and nationalist prejudice. His brothers are those who know the will of the Lord, regardless of their nationality and origin: "In brief, this is the position of Christ regarding human conscience."[20] Reflecting the globalization of a conscience-based discourse in the wake of the Universal Declaration of Human Rights, Khalid depicts both Christ and Muhammad as vigorously defending human rights—the right of subsistence as well as the right of conscience.[21]

In Khalid's presentation, the virtues of the two prophets seem almost to be complementary. Whereas Christ, as in al-'Aqqad, is portrayed as a liberator of individual consciences, Muhammad is praised for his combination of personal integrity and political engagement. For all Khalid's admiration of Christ and his conscience-based, entirely non-violent ethics, it is obvious that the well-balanced perfection of the divine message is left to Muhammad. In this respect, the modern notion of human progress clearly works in favor of Muhammad, who in this sense took the message of Christ a step forward.

In 1963, five years after his book on Muhammad and Christ, Khalid rallied the entire history of religion and philosophy to join, as his new book proclaimed, "Human Conscience on Its Journey Toward Its Destiny" (*Ma'a al-damīr al-insānī fī-masīrihi wa-masīrihi*).[22] In his previous book, Khalid had already invoked a wide array of spiritual authorities in his call for human authenticity, freedom of conscience, and progress. In his grand narrative of human progress from 1963, he adds a number of new actors ranging from the ancient Egyptians to Gandhi. Together with prophets and philosophers, they are portrayed as joining hands in a great chain of champions in the progressive rule of human conscience. In this narrative, the conscientious discourses of the prophets are carried forward and further developed by modern philosophers—and Gandhi.

Muhammad and Christ, United in Gandhi?

In Khalid's books, the influence from human rights language is obvious. With a view to global impulses, it is also interesting to note his references to Gandhi's non-violent activism as a perfect synthesis of the person- and society-related messages of Christ and Muhammad respectively.

The example of Gandhi also received much attention from al-'Aqqad. In 1948, he wrote an entire book about Gandhi, in which the notion of '*insāniyya*, "humanity," is strikingly central.[23] In his book from 1942 about the genius of Muhammad, al-'Aqqad had already noted that "in our time" there is much talk about Gandhi and his non-violent, passive resistance, which is said to originate either from Tolstoy or from Hindu and Buddhist ethics. Al-'Aqqad notes that many have suggested that non-violence is quite different from what Islam teaches. According to al-'Aqqad, however, that is not the case: the practice of Muhammad was in fact a model of diplomacy and of friendly contracts and truces.[24]

In Khalid's grand narrative of conscience from 1963, the final chapter is left to Gandhi. Khalid emphasizes that with Gandhi non-violence was not merely preached as an ideal but practiced as an efficient method of political change. Khalid seems in fact to regard the intentionalism of Christ and the more political orientation of Muhammad as being merged in the conscience-based practice of Gandhi, a practice that shook the world and had tangible political consequences: "Human conscience now reached the peak of its integrity, and it moved across the stage of the major events of our age, materializing in the person of its devoted son Mahatma Gandhi."[25]

A More Pessimistic Outlook

In the books of the third author in my modern Egyptian case, Kamil Husayn, conscience is also referred to as a uniting bond across religious divides. With al-'Aqqad and Khalid, conscience is seen almost as a modernizing motor, on the road toward a brighter future for humanity. With Husayn, there is a much darker undertone than in his colleagues' more optimistic elaborations on conscience. In his book *City of Wrong: A Friday in Jerusalem* (published in Arabic as *Qarya zālima* in 1954), Husayn meditates on the drama of Good Friday, a controversial theme between Muslims and Christians since Muslims generally believe that Christ was not actually crucified. Husayn's way around this interreligious conundrum is to write about the *intention* to crucify, which the Qur'an also asserts. Husayn's take on this drama is to depict Good Friday as the day when human conscience was crucified:

> When they resolved to crucify him, it was a decision to crucify the human conscience and extinguish its light. They considered that reason and religion alike laid upon them obligations that transcended the dictates of conscience.[26]

In a more positive mode, Husayn sees it as the essential task of conscience to keep reason within its moral boundaries, and to resist religiously motivated violence. His main interest, however, is to warn against the dire consequences of silencing conscience: "There is no evil afflicting humanity which does not derive from this besetting desire to ignore the dictates of conscience."[27] In the novel, Husayn dramatizes the inner conflicts of the Jewish leaders and the representatives of Roman authority. Because of political rationality or religious (communal) allegiance, they all denied their inner voice when resolving to have Christ crucified. Throughout the novel, Husayn insists that conscience in the proper sense only exists in the individual, and he is adamant that religion may only affect society in a positive way by nurturing virtuous individuals who are loyal to the guiding and curbing voice of their conscience.[28]

What could have been the impetus behind Husayn's decision to make crucifixion of conscience such a crucial theme in *City of Wrong*? According to his biographer Harold Vogelaar, the book should first of all be read in the light of the shattering experience of World War II, as "an emotional, literary reaction to that catastrophic event," movingly depicting "the utter failure of traditional religion to prevent it."[29] His translator Kenneth Cragg, on the other hand, sees in Husayn's novel an implicit Muslim self-criticism in which the rule of conscience is critically related to controversial issues in contemporary Islam such as religious authority, community consensus, and violent punishments.[30] In any case, the perspective is universalistic, in a warning mode reminiscent of the preamble of the Universal Declaration of Human Rights.

Visions of World Community versus Confrontational Identity Politics

The works of al-'Aqqad, Khalid, and Husayn were produced in the heyday of Egyptian nationalism and in the reconstructive spirit of the postwar world community, that is, in a cultural climate conducive to visions of Muslims and Christians focusing on shared humanity and cooperating for the common good. Fifty years later, dialogical and cooperative visions are heavily challenged by confrontational identity politics, making it much less likely today to see books with such titles as *Muhammad and Christ: Together on the Road*. In Egypt, the focus has long shifted from shared human or Egyptian values to (from the 1970s onward) an overriding concern for Coptic or Muslim authenticity, as reflected in expressions such as "Christian conscience" and "Muslim conscience."[31]

In a climate more oriented toward knowing by oneself as separate, religious communities (in Egypt and elsewhere), the inclusive discourses of al-'Aqqad, Khalid, and Husayn deserve to be remembered. Their contribution to the globalizing of human conscience had its shortcomings, however. For instance, it was more a literary effort on the part of Muslim intellectuals than a real dialogical process between Muslim, Christian, and secular-minded citizens. Their innovative writings seem also to have remained a rather elitist discourse, in contrast to the wide-ranging effects of Muslim and Christian revivals and the strong communitarian tendencies in the general populace from the 1970s onward.

Whether or not the Arab Spring has revived human conscience across religious divides remains to be seen. The globalization of human conscience in the mid nineteenth century may nonetheless serve as inspiration for renewed discourses of global ethics, against contrary tendencies both in Egypt and on the global scene.

Oddbjørn Leirvik is Professor of Interreligious Studies, Faculty of Theology, University of Oslo. His books include *Human Conscience and Muslim-Christian Relations: Modern Egyptian Thinkers on al-damīr* (Routledge, 2006), *Images of Jesus Christ in Islam* (Continuum, 2010), and *Interreligious Studies: A Relational Approach to Religious Activism and the Study of Religion* (Bloomsbury, 2014).

NOTES

1. For The Universal Declaration of Human Rights, see http://www.un.org/en/uni versal-declaration-human-rights/. For further discussions of human rights, see in particular the chapter by Malcolm Langford in this volume.
2. Tore Lindholm, "Article 1: A New Beginning," in *The Universal Declaration of Human Rights: A Commentary*, ed. Asbjørn Eide et al. (Oslo, 1992), 33.
3. Mahatma Gandhi, *The Mind of Mahatma Gandhi*, ed. R. K. Prabhu and U. R. Rao (Madras, 1946), 27, 39. For further discussions of religion, see in particular the chapters by Nora Eggen, Chenxi Tang, Kyrre Kverndokk, Alfred Hiatt, Erling Sandmo, and Kari van Dijk in this volume.
4. Gandhi, *Mind of Mahatma Gandhi*, 90.
5. Ibid., 78.
6. Lars Bo Bojesen and Jan Lindhardt, *Samvittigheden* (Copenhagen, 1979); cf. Oddbjørn Leirvik, *Human Conscience and Muslim-Christian Relations: Modern Egyptian Thinkers on al-damīr* (London, 2006), 25–38.
7. Ludwig Feuerbach, "Zur Ethik: Der Eudämonismus," in *Sämtliche Werke*, vol. 10, *Schriften zur Ethik und nachgelassene Aphorismen* (Stuttgart, 1960), 282, my translation.
8. Hans Küng, ed., *Yes to a Global Ethic* (London, 1996).
9. Oddbjørn Leirvik, "Conscience in Arabic and the Semantic History of *damīr*," *Journal of Arabic and Islamic Studies* 9, no. 2 (2009): 18–36.
10. Reinhart Koselleck, *Futures Past: On the Semantics of Historical Time* (Cambridge, MA, 1985), 84.
11. For further discussions of translation, see in particular the chapter by Ivo Spira in this volume.
12. Leirvik, "Conscience in Arabic."
13. Leirvik, *Human Conscience and Muslim-Christian Relations*, 83–89.

14. F. Peter Ford Jr., *'Abbas Mahmud al-'Aqqad: The Genius of Christ*, ed. and trans. F. Peter Ford Jr. (Binghamton, NY, 2001).
15. 'Abbas Mahmud al-'Aqqad, *Hayāt al-Masīh* (Cairo, [1957] 1996), 105.
16. Ibid., 108, 115.
17. Küng, *Yes to a Global Ethic*.
18. Khalid Muhammad Khalid, *Ma'an 'alā al-tarīq: Muhammad wa-l-Masīh* (Cairo, [1958] 1986).
19. Ibid., 7, my translation.
20. Ibid., 114.
21. Ibid., 78, 91.
22. Khalid Muhammad Khalid, *Ma'a al-damīr al-'insānī fī masīrihi wa-masīrihi* (Cairo, 1963).
23. 'Abbas Mahmud al-'Aqqad, "Rūh 'azīm al-Mahatmā Ghāndī," in *Les oeuvres complètes de A. M. al-Akkad*, vol. 20, *Al-majmū'a al-kāmila li-l-mu'allafāt al-'ustādh 'Abbās Mahmūd al-'Aqqād* (Beirut, [1948] 1981), 275, 333.
24. 'Abbas Mahmud al-'Aqqad, *'Abqariyyat Muhammad*, in *'Islāmiyyāt* (Cairo, [1942] 1985), 54–58.
25. Khalid, *Ma'a al-damīr*, 222.
26. M. Kamel Hussein, *City of Wrong: A Friday in Jerusalem*, trans. Kenneth Cragg (Oxford, 1994), 29.
27. Ibid., 30.
28. Ibid., 212.
29. Harold Vogelaar, "Religious Pluralism in the Thought of Muhammad Kāmil Hussein," in *Christian–Muslim Encounters*, ed. Yvonne Y. Haddad and Wadi Z. Haddad (Gainesville, 1995), 414.
30. Cragg, in Hussein, *City of Wrong*, 17–18.
31. Leirvik, *Human Conscience and Muslim-Christian Relations*, 192–209.

BIBLIOGRAPHY

'Aqqad, 'Abbas Mahmud al-. *'Abqariyyat al-Masīh*. Cairo: Dār nahdat Misr, [1953] n.d.
―――. *'Abqariyyat Muhammad*. In *'Islāmiyyāt*. Cairo: Dār al-ma'ārif, [1942] 1985.
―――. *Hayāt al-Masīh*. Cairo: Dār nahdat Misr, [1957] 1996.
―――. "Rūh 'azīm al-Mahatmā Ghāndī." In *Les oeuvres complètes de A. M. al-Akkad*, vol. 20, *Al-majmū'a al-kāmila li-l-mu'allafāt al-'ustādh 'Abbās Mahmūd al-'Aqqād*. Beirut: Dār al-kitāb al-lubnānī, [1948] 1981.
Bojesen, Lars Bo, and Jan Lindhardt. *Samvittigheden*. Copenhagen: Berlingske forlag, 1979.
Carlyle, Thomas. *On Heroes and Hero-Worship*, 1911 [1841]. London, Melbourne and Toronto: Wardlock & Co.
Feuerbach, Ludwig. "Zur Ethik: Der Eudämonismus." In *Sämtliche Werke*, vol. 10, *Schriften zur Ethik und nachgelassene Aphorismen*, 1960 [1911-1913], edited by W. Bolin und F. Jodl. Stuttgart: Frommann Verlag Günther Holzboog, 1969.

Ford, F. Peter, Jr. *'Abbas Mahmud al-'Aqqad: The Genius of Christ*. Studies in Contemporary Philosophical Theology 1, edited and translated by F. Peter Ford Jr. Binghamton, NY: Global Publications, 2001.

Gandhi, Mahatma. *The Mind of Mahatma Gandhi*. Edited by R. K. Prabhu and U. R. Rao. Madras: Oxford University Press, 1946.

Hussein, M. Kamel. *City of Wrong: A Friday in Jerusalem*. Translated by Kenneth Cragg, from *Qarya zālima*. Oxford: Oneworld, 1994.

Khalid, Khalid Muhammad. *Ma'a al-damīr al-'insānī fī masīrihi wa-masīrihi*. Cairo: Maktabat al-'angilū al-misriyya, 1963.

———. *Ma'an 'alā al-tarīq: Muhammad wa-l-Masīh*. Cairo: Dār thābit, [1958] 1986.

Koselleck, Reinhart. *Futures Past: On the Semantics of Historical Time*. Cambridge, MA: MIT Press, 1985.

Küng, Hans, ed. *Yes to a Global Ethic*. London: SCM Press, 1996.

Leirvik, Oddbjørn. "Conscience in Arabic and the Semantic History of *damīr*." *Journal of Arabic and Islamic Studies* 9, no. 2 (2009): 18–36.

———. *Human Conscience and Muslim-Christian Relations: Modern Egyptian Thinkers on al-damīr*. London: Routledge, 2006.

———. "Muhammad, Christ and Modern Consciences." *Studies in Interreligious Dialogue* 18, no. 2 (2008): 129–52.

Lindholm, Tore. "Article 1: A New Beginning." In *The Universal Declaration of Human Rights: A Commentary*, edited by Asbjørn Eide et al., 31–54. Oslo: Scandinavian University Press, 1992.

Vogelaar, Harold. "Religious Pluralism in the Thought of Muhammad Kāmil Hussein." In *Christian–Muslim Encounters*, edited by Yvonne Y. Haddad and Wadi Z. Haddad, 411–24. Gainesville: University Press of Florida, 1995.

⊱ 4 ⊰

Creating World through Concept Learning

Claudia Lenz

Introduction

How does world or *worldliness* emerge when teachers and teacher trainers with different national, religious, and institutional backgrounds exchange their views on key concepts of multiculturalism and, subsequently, investigate their varying meanings in contemporary and historical contexts?

This chapter takes its starting point in a phenomenological notion of *world* as it is introduced in the political thinking of Hannah Arendt. Here, *world* is related to the fact of human plurality and constituted through action. This qualifies language as the necessary medium for action to evolve, through which (inter)action is mediated and can be expressed. In the thinking of Arendt, language is an essential precondition for worldliness, since it is the medium through which the different perspectives that go along with human plurality are shared and exchanged. The individual human being gains a sense of reality and has the chance to experience this reality as meaningful as (and only if) it takes part in the intersubjective process of making sense of this reality. Language is the living matrix that transfers the traces of previous action to future generations. It is this transmission of experience through language that can be taken into consideration by new generations when they create their own action and their unique worldliness.

Further, the chapter sets out to transfer these qualities of worldliness to the field of education, or more precisely to concept learning.[1] How can the exploration of concepts become a source of *worldliness* and contribute to the learner's capacity to take part in and build the realm of common affairs? I will introduce an approach to concept learning inspired by two different fields: on the one hand the theoretical and methodological fundaments of intercultural education, on the other conceptual history. The systematic exploration of the different meanings that concepts have in differing contexts and how these meanings have emerged and changed over time, I will argue, can become a source of critical thinking, mutual understanding, and political agency.

The last part of the chapter links these theoretical reflections to a case study. In a workshop for teachers and teacher trainers from various European countries, participants explored key concepts related to intercultural education. The methodology of the workshop was based on the principles of participation, reflection, and dialogue. The analysis of the empirical data collected during the workshop suggests, first, that the collaborative concept exploration resulted in an experience of "world" emerging among people with extremely diverse backgrounds, and second, that the diversity was a necessary condition of this worldliness.

Hannah Arendt's Phenomenological Notion of "World"

In *The Human Condition* (1958), Hannah Arendt unfolds her understanding of the specific qualities of human existence as being marked by the ideas of *natality* and *plurality* and realized through *action*.[2]

Arendt's thinking was strongly informed by Martin Heidegger and the philosophy of existence. Regarding the specific, yet limited freedom that stems from being a part of nature and bound to it without being completely determined by it, Arendt considered death not as the ultimate signifier framing human existence (*Sein zum Tode*) but the opposite. The doubleness of the fact that we are born—the *biological* act of "coming to the world" corresponds with a *symbolical*, social birth that needs to be realized through participation in "worldly affairs"—is expressed in the concept of *natality*. As humans we bring new, unprecedented actions to the already existing realm of human affairs. This capacity to not only continue and repeat what has always been there, but to make a difference and to *be* different from everyone who has inhabited the world before us leads to the other signifier of human existence—plurality:

> Action would be an unnecessary luxury, a capricious interference with general laws of behavior, if men were endlessly reproducible repetitions of the same model, whose nature or essence was the same for all and as predictable as the nature or essence of any other thing. Plurality is the condition of human action because we are all the same, that is, human, in such a way that nobody is ever the same as anyone else who ever lived, lives, or will live.[3]

Through her or his actions, each human being becomes a unique representative of mankind. Only through action (which means acting *together* with other irreducible unique humans) can the full potential to be human be realized. Even the realm for action is constituted *through* action—this is world in its immaterial sense, to be distinguished from world as constituted by material objects. In contrast to a positivistic notion of reality, there is no pre-existing reality or world with fixed, objective meanings for Arendt. Continuous interactions and negotiations of how the world should be and how its material and immaterial substance should be created form the crucial condition for the realization of both human existence and worldliness. Another element in Arendt's theory of worldliness is interesting in the context of this chapter: the notion of plurality is closely related to the notion of *in-between*. As the communicative, social experience of being different from each other constitutes us as human beings, we create a common realm of objects that are shared and keep us at a distance at the same time:

> To live together in the world means essentially that a world of things is between those who have it in common, as a table is located between those who sit around it; the world, like every in-between, relates and separates men at the same time.[4]

The building blocks of worldliness are not only and not even in the first place physical objects. Since it is constituted and maintained through interaction, world needs language as the medium of human expression and self-realization, that is, the stories that are told as a result of human action and the meanings that are attributed to this action by people and negotiated and contested. So, it is language that bears and reflects plurality, it constitutes the in-between—or its collapse:

> Men in the plural, that is, men in so far as they live and move and act in this world, can experience meaningfulness only because they can talk with and make sense to each other and to themselves.[5]

Summing up, the emergence of world in the sense of Hannah Arendt requires *shared spaces* of human experience and articulation, which means spaces in which human plurality and *difference(s)* can be expressed, experienced, and acknowledged. These spaces need to be created and constantly maintained by the kind of interaction that is not dominated by instrumentality but provides the possibility to create new and unprecedented ways of "making sense" of and creating reality.

Under these conditions, a common and at the same time dynamic (since constantly negotiated) framework of meaning emerges, which is not a product of theoretical sophistication but rooted in the common experience of (inter)action. World in this sense is fragile, and in contrast to the world of material objects it disappears if it is not constantly re-established through "action" and articulated by a shared language that still reflects human plurality. For Arendt, history has shown that worldliness can collapse under the condition of totalitarian rule, when ideology and terror suppress and eliminate plurality and establish *same-ness*: the total hegemony of *one* truth and the total power of *one* rule.

Intercultural Education: The Space "between" as the Realm of Encounter and Self-Reflection

How is world in Arendt's sense created in our times, with growing international and global interdependencies, informed by new, mediatized forms of communication and interaction?

Following Arendt, this new, globalized situation has the potential to create new ways of interconnectedness and worldliness, creating a common human realm for negotiation and decision making. However, the new, globalized reality is accompanied by threats against this kind of cosmopolitan vision. On the one hand, globalized capitalism means also homogenizing commodity culture. Consumerist homogenization seems to find its denial by the xenophobic insistence on the radically or culturally different "Other." On the other hand, the embracement of diversity and "hybridity" of cultural identities resulting from global migration are counteracted by the reinvention of rigid and excluding group identities. Neoliberal, globalized realities are accompanied by anxieties. In this situation, education can play a crucial role in preparing young generations to use the opportunities and realize the potentials of pluralist and diverse societies. The aim of intercultural education is to support learners in developing an "increased awareness of subjective cultural context (world view), including one's own, and developing greater ability to interact sensitively and competently across cultural contexts."[6]

Intercultural education is informed by a dynamic understanding of culture (and of identities being formed within *and* between cultures). If cultures and identities are not static but emerging and changing through continuous human interaction, being able to handle the contents and concepts that inform notions of identity, belonging, and difference becomes a crucial precondition for social and political participation. The role of education is to equip learners with the necessary capacities, understanding, and skills and also motivate them to take part in this ongoing process.

The field of intercultural education is constituted by a broad range of academic, formal, and non-formal educational approaches and institutional networks, and it is informed by policies at national and international levels.[7] Still, some common principles can be identified:

- *Mutual respect* and *multi-perspectivity*. Being able to consider phenomena from different points of view and being willing to understand the contexts

in which different systems of meaning and cultural expression emerge is a necessary precondition for respectful dialogue and interaction in diverse societies.
- *Self-reflexivity* and *critical thinking*. Intercultural understanding is often associated with being aware of the specificities and "peculiarities" of other cultures (the "Other"). Beyond that, intercultural education also challenges the learner's own assumptions and prejudices about the other, and focuses on the processes and modes of *constructing* the understandings, imaginaries, and identifications related to "the self" and "the other" and to "one's own" and "other" cultures.

It is evident that these principles correlate with the preconditions of *worldliness* in Hannah Arendt's sense—the critical work of "taking a distance" from the notions of sameness and the opening of the realm *in between* in which plurality of cultural and political expressions can unfold and interact.

But how should this kind of self-reflexive endeavor be possible without investigating the ways in which the realities of selfness and otherness are not only constructed and maintained but also transformed by and through language? Some specific competences related to the understanding of concepts, namely the capacity to reflect and negotiate their multilayered meanings, are part and parcel of what could be called "intercultural competence." Without being able to handle the complexity and dynamics of concepts and their crucial function in social and political processes, people will not be able to take an active part in the societies in which they live. In order to be an agent and co-creator of a shared world, the individual needs to be able to take part in the construction of a shared realm of meaning and action.

Concept Learning Becomes Reflexive

Different assumptions regarding the meanings of the concepts that organize our social, cultural, and political life may have profound implications for human interaction.[8] Being aware of the differences in the meanings ascribed to such concepts, as well as of the contexts in which these different meanings emerge and the consequences they have, means thus to be able to understand different ways of *conceptualizing the world*, and, on these grounds, to take part in it. What, then, should concept learning look like in order to prepare the ground for critical thinking, political experience, and action?

First of all, *misunderstandings* should not merely be considered as obstacles that need to be surmounted. The variety of ways of "making sense" of terms and concepts is an important resource for learning processes. An educational approach leaning toward the principles of critical thinking, (self-)reflection, and multi-perspectivity, as introduced above, will not seek to give the "final answers" to questions of definition. Instead, it should provide instruments that enable learners to investigate the possible meanings of concepts, reflect on the conditions that inform their own and others' ways of understanding, and negotiate "reasonable" and "adequate" definitions (which, by nature, have to be working definitions, dynamic and bound to contexts) with others.

A learning methodology, which operationalizes these principles, should make use of what has been described in the "transmission of experiences of human action from the past" in and through concepts. This idea, taken from Hannah Arendt's political theory, corresponds with the thinking of Reinhart Koselleck around conceptual history. Koselleck contends that concepts are containers of historical experience and that this experience, which condensates in language, can be unpacked and studied in systematic ways.[9] As suggested in the introduction to the present volume:

> concepts are not merely an assembly of contemporary experiences and meanings; past meanings ... have also been deposited in concepts and their current usage. Inherent in every concept are several temporal and semantic layers of varying duration.

Transferred to the field of concept learning, the contours of a very effective methodology become visible, including the following aspects.

Reflecting Individual Pre-assumptions

The first step is taking stock of the individual learners' own understanding and interpretation of the concept. What has influenced this understanding? Has it changed over time, related to biographical experiences and/or circumstances?

This stage of the learning process is of great importance because it places the learner at the center of his/her own learning process and at the same time creates an awareness regarding the dynamic ways of understanding and interpreting concepts in different/changing contexts.

Synchronic Analysis

The next step is the exploration of understandings and definitions of concepts in different contexts. What are the contexts in which concepts are interpreted and used differently (e.g., national/linguistic contexts but also religion, politics, literature, and science)? Which circumstances influence their meaning, and in which ways are they contested?

This element of the methodology is crucial for the ability to take different perspectives and acknowledge how the meanings of concepts are informed by contexts. It is also a precondition for critical reflection about the validity and legitimacy of different understandings/definitions.

Diachronic Analysis

In a last step, different meanings and uses over time will be explored. When does the concept occur, and in which ways is its emergence linked to historical developments and events? Is there a continuous development, or can ruptures and contradictory developments be described?

This dimension of the methodology is indispensable for the reflection of the interdependence of language/meaning and social reality—and, related to this, the possibility of radical historical change through human action.

In the following, the application of these methodological principles in educational practice will be demonstrated. It will be highlighted how this way of concept learning allows learners to reflect and interact in ways that result in *worldliness* in the sense of Hannah Arendt.

The Case Study

Concept learning was a core element of the "From Division to Diversity" workshop held in Falstad, Norway, in September 2011.[10] Nineteen participants (teachers and teacher trainers) from sixteen European countries took part in this one-week training course. The theme of the training was intercultural education, related to historical and contemporary ways of dealing with diversity. The topic of the workshop was addressed through the *content* of different sessions (e.g., national minorities in Norway and religious diversity, and a visit to the deaf museum in Trondheim) but also through a workshop on methodology. Participatory and collaborative learning methods were applied in order to create positive experiences related to interactions in diverse contexts and to raise awareness regarding the creative and intellectual potential emerging from diversity within a learning group. In this context, concept learning—organized according to the principles introduced above—seemed to be a suitable element of the workshop.

The development of a dynamic "workshop glossary," dealing with some key concepts in the context of the training, was included as a cross-cutting element in the workshop program. At several stages of the training, participants worked individually or in groups in order to "unpack" the diachronic and synchronic layers of meanings related to one of the concepts of *normality*, *minority*, or *multiculturality*. These three concepts seemed to be feasible in order to create an awareness regarding the immense impact of certain key concepts on systems of belonging and exclusion. At the same time, these concepts are linked to political agency and the mobilization of political action. We will come back to this point.

In a first step of the concept work, the participants were invited to write down their individual notions of one concept they had chosen. This is a very important element of the methodology, and a crucial one in the light of the generation of "worldliness." By encouraging the participants to take their own assumptions regarding the concepts seriously (and relating the later stages of the work back to this first step), the relevance of the participants' individuality and the authority of their (pre-)knowledge was stressed. Traditional education often focuses on replacing the learner's "incomplete" or even "wrong" assumptions with "complete" or "correct" knowledge. In that perspective, the notion of plurality of possible interpretations and the chance to explore the origins and consequences of these differences further gets lost. Here, exactly this exploration was intended.

This exercise was followed by group work in which the individual assumptions were shared and the participants were tasked with trying to generate a common working definition of their concept on the basis of these aspects. All three groups had clearly identified the normative and descriptive dimensions related to the concept of normality, minority, or multiculturality, respectively, as well as the consequences of different ways of defining the terms for power relations and "social engineering." The group working on multiculturality, however, strived to separate their concept from other concepts such as diversity, multiculturalism, and interculturalism. A productive discussion followed, focusing on the extent to which the fuzziness of the concept and its openness toward neighboring concepts is a part of its politicization—making it even more crucial to investigate "who" is using this concept, how, and in which contexts. Moreover, it became clear that especially the component "culture" in multiculturality needs further exploration in order to determine the identity strategies and politics related to its uses. In this situation, Koselleck's idea "to alienate the concepts through past experiences" in order to "sharpen consciousness of the present; such historical clarification may lead to a more enlightened political discourse" was well received by the participants.[11]

In the following sections, some aspects of the working process will be highlighted that show in which ways *worldliness* emerged among the participants. We will concentrate on the concept of minority since the two groups working with the concept came to very different ways of historicization—based on their different composition—which opened up interesting perspectives on the contradictory potential to politicize and mobilize the concept in contemporary contexts.

Exploring the Concept of Minority

Two groups of five participants each worked on the concept of minority. During the first session, it became evident that the presence of two Muslim participants (both of whom were educated theologians) in the first group created a different focus in that group than in the other group. In particular, the experience of a Bosnian teacher trainer, who had experienced the war in the Balkans in the 1990s, shed a particular light on what it means to be a religious minority and how the war and the following foundation of separate nation-states dramatically changed the majority-minority relations and the notions of the concept of minority in that region.

In the second group, differing personal experiences of politicization and political engagement informed the discussion. People had been engaged in different types of anti-racist or experimental artist work in the past. The notion of "black is beautiful" related to the civil rights movement in the United States was an important reference point regarding the possibility that a minority position can be related to pride and the struggle for rights rather than to inferiority. In the light of the notion of worldliness discussed above, this group work fulfilled two of its elementary conditions: the participants gathered as different but equal individuals in order to generate a common, deeper understanding through particular and partly incongruent experiences related to the concept of minority.

The different compositions of the groups became especially interesting in the second step of the group work, when the participants were asked to systematize the different understandings/definitions of their concept along contemporary contexts (synchronic) and historical developments (diachronic). The groups created a table, the so-called speaker position chart, indicating which contexts at which times had influenced the understanding/interpretation of "minority." This realm of worldliness—which so far was composed of the collected "realm of experiences" of the participants—was extended in the next step, when broader contemporary and historical contexts that inform the meanings of the concept of minority were explored.

The first group focused on the different notions of minority and majority, resulting from a religious framework in the Ottoman Empire or in the framework of the nation-state predominant from the nineteenth century. These different frameworks, and hence their different insights, generated different mechanisms or systems of belonging and exclusion. Moreover, the changing significance of ethnicity as marker of majority-minority status was discussed by that group. This seemed especially interesting with regard to contemporary racist discourses in Europe, in which religion seems to become more relevant than ethnicity as a signifier of minority status.

The discussion of the second group moved, as one might expect after the more personal exchange in the first step, in another direction. In their historical exploration, the group did not go as far back in time as the first one—in fact, they only looked back as far as the 1940s. Within this relatively short period, major events and developments influencing the understandings of the concept of minority were identified. Cultural and social events as well as scientific and political developments that have contributed to the acknowledgment of minority rights were identified (such as "black is beautiful" in the United States, research on injustice against the Sami people in Norway, and rising awareness regarding sexual minority rights). The group also noted the importance of transnational political processes and major legal documents recognizing minority rights (the United Nations, the Council of Europe, and the European Union). In summary, the ways in which the concept of minority was mobilized and politicized in order to empower marginalized groups was at the center of the group's interest.

For both groups, a point made previously became evident: through sharing individual understandings and experiences, the participants became aware of not only the variety of meanings with which the concept of minority can be associated, but also its impact on discourses of belonging and systems exclusion as well as the mobilization of political agency and the establishment of fundamental rights.

In regard to the concept of worldliness, the group came to insights that are in line with Hannah Arendt's thinking, which identifies worldliness as one of the preconditions of political action: the acknowledgment of plurality and the communicative establishment of "world" is the basis for solidarity and "acting in concert."

Conclusion: Worldliness and the Realm of Plural Meanings

As the discussion of the workshop results has shown, the systematic investigation of key concepts can open a broad variety of concrete insights into the layers of meaning embedded in these concepts. But more relevant than the concrete knowledge about relevant historical contexts contributing to a change of meanings is the process of meta-cognition: the insight into the dynamic and contested character of concepts, the notions of identity and power related to it, and hence the potential to support the learner's agency through concept learning.

Worldliness I

As indicated earlier, worldliness in Hannah Arendt's sense depends on the experience and acknowledgment of plurality. In order to realize the potential of human agency, there needs to be a realm where unique subjects (inter) act as equals. Arendt would call such a sphere of encounters a "pre-political" sphere, since it is the condition *sine qua non* for political action even if it does not show all the qualities of political action.

In the setting of the teacher training introduced above, these qualities were fully realized. Since the learning process was not at any point organized as a competition (for the "right" solution or "smarter" answer), it was centered on the authority and validity of individual experiences and interpretations. Even if the final aim of the process was to go beyond these pre-understandings and reflect them within a variety of contexts and in the light of historical developments, they were indispensable in order to generate common insights and reflections. At the end of the process, it was up to each individual participant to reflect and make up her or his mind regarding the degree to which the encounter with the plurality of meanings would change personal orientations.

Worldliness II

Just as the focus on the personal opened up for the pre-political dimensions of worldliness, the focus on the contemporary contexts and historical developments touched upon the full political sense of worldliness. As the example of reflections on the concept of minority has shown, worldliness has been not only a signifier of inferiority and submission but also a symbol of a struggle for pride and collective rights. This awareness of the contestedness of a concept, in accordance with Arendt's ideas, is an awareness of the potential and power of human action. The emergence of worldliness in this sense means to empower learners, since it enables them to read/understand and *use* concepts as elements of political struggle. Of course, this notion of worldliness was limited because of the context. During a training course lasting only one week, the participants did not start or even plan joint political action. But in times of European and global professional and political interaction and organization, it should not be underestimated that these teachers and teacher trainers in some way or another compose and become part of "networks" and "communities" that share values, reflections, and know-how related to the implementation of educational practice that aims to prepare learners to become inhabitants of the world for which they take responsibility since they are aware that it is up to them to create it.

I will give the last word to a Bosnian participant, who describes her experience as such:

> I value the fact that I started questioning the concepts I use every day. It was empowering to realize how concepts are used to mobilize people, even in education. On the other hand, the use of the concepts makes us, in a way, a part of ever changing society as well, empowering us to influence it.[12]

Claudia Lenz works as a professor at the Norwegian School of Theology, where she teaches social science in the teacher education program. She is also affiliated to the Centre for Studies of Holocaust and Religious Minorities in Oslo as a Research Professor. Her main fields of research are historical consciousness, memory culture, and history didactics, as well as prejudice and processes of constructing the Other. Recent publications include "Human Rights Education and History Education: A Congeniality of Souls?" in *Crossing Borders: Combining Human Rights Education and History Education*, ed. Claudia Lenz, Sanna Brattland, and Lise Kvande (Lit Publishers, 2016).

NOTES

1. For further discussions of education and didactics, see in particular the chapter by Alfred Hiatt in this volume.
2. Hannah Arendt, *The Human Condition* (Chicago, 1958).
3. Ibid., 8.
4. Ibid., 7.
5. Ibid., 4.
6. Milton J. Bennett, "Defining, Measuring, and Facilitating Intercultural Learning: A Conceptual Introduction to the *Intercultural Education* Double Supplement," *Intercultural Education* 20, no. 4 (2009): 3; see also *T-Kit 4: Intercultural Learning* (Strasbourg, 2002), 34.
7. E.g., Ireland: "National Council for Curriculum and Assessment," retrieved 23 August 2018 from https://www.ncca.ie/en; Council of Europe, "Intercultural Education in the New European Context, Declaration Standing Conference of European Ministers of Education 2003," retrieved 20 March 2013 from http://storicamente.org/sites/defau lt/images/figures/2009/ora_di_religione/ora_di_religione_2009_02.pdf; UNESCO, "UNESCO Guidelines on Intercultural Education," retrieved 23 August 2018 from http://unesdoc.unesco.org/images/0014/001478/147878e.pdf.
8. The following sections describe the educational approach of the project Concept Learning for Empowerment through Analysis and Reflection (CLEAR, formerly the Intercultural Glossary Project, IGP). However, since CLEAR is not the object of the case study on which this chapter focuses, and has only informed the approach applied in the case study, it will not be further discussed here. Information about the CLEAR project is available at www.clear-project.net.
9. See for instance Reinhart Koselleck, "'Space of Experience' and 'Horizon of Expectation': Two Historical Categories," in *Futures Past: On the Semantics of Historical Time*, trans. Keith Tribe (New York: Columbia University Press, 1983), 256.
10. Helge Jordheim, "Historicizing Concepts, Reflecting Identities: The Potential of Conceptual History for Intercultural Education," lecture held at the Pestalozzi workshop, "From Division to Diversity: Educational Challenges Related to Past and Present," Falstad, Norway, 19 September 2011. The workshop was part of the activities of the Pestalozzi Programme, which is the Council of Europe's training

and capacity-building program for education professionals; for more information, see "Pestalozzi Programme," retrieved 8 February 2018 from https://www.coe.int/en/web/pestalozzi.
11. Reinhart Koselleck, "Introduction and Prefaces to the Geschichtliche Grundbegriffe," trans. Michaela Richter, in *Contribution to the History of Concepts* 1, no. 6 (2011): 16.
12. Quote from the report sent by the participant to the Pestalozzi Programme after the workshop.

BIBLIOGRAPHY

Arendt, Hannah. *The Human Condition*. Chicago: University of Chicago Press, 1958.

Bennett, Milton J. "Defining, Measuring, and Facilitating Intercultural Learning: A Conceptual Introduction to the *Intercultural Education* Double Supplement." *Intercultural Education* 20, no. 4 (2009): 1–13.

Jordheim, Helge. "Historicizing Concepts, Reflecting Identities: The Potential of Conceptual History for Intercultural Education." Lecture held at the Pestalozzi workshop "From Division to Diversity: Educational Challenges Related to Past and Present," Falstad, Norway, 19 September 2011.

Koselleck, Reinhart. "Introduction and Prefaces to the Geschichtliche Grundbegriffe." Translated by Michaela Richter, in *Contribution to the History of Concepts* 1, no. 6 (2011): 1–37.

———. "'Space of Experience' and 'Horizon of Expectation': Two Historical Categories," in *Futures Past: On the Semantics of Historical Time*. Translated by Keith Tribe. New York: Columbia University Press, 1983.

T-Kit 4: Intercultural Learning. Strasbourg: Council of Europe Publishing, 2nd ed. 2018. Retrieved 23 August 2018 from https://pjp-eu.coe.int/documents/1017981/10762748/PREMS+042218+T-kit4+WEB.pdf/37396481-d543-88c6-dccc-d81719537b32.

▶• 5 •◀

Between Metaphor and Geopolitics

The History of the Concept *the Third World*

Erik Tängerstad

The Third World is a commonly used reference when discussing political and socioeconomic aspects of the contemporary world order. Although it is not used as frequently as it was during the latter half of the Cold War era, it remains a well-known demarcation within contemporary discourses. The aim of this chapter is to present the conceptual history of the term *the Third World*.

Tiers Monde and Third World

The French term *le Tiers Monde* was coined in 1952 in an attempt to challenge and change the then prevailing Cold War discourse. The difference between the French words *tiers* ("a third of the whole") and *troisième* ("third") should be noticed. The concept alluded to the Tiers État (the Third Estate) before the French Revolution, not to a series of one, two, three, and so forth.

It was the French intellectual and demographer Alfred Sauvy who coined the term *Tiers Monde*. He wanted to present a new political option for France beyond the prevailing Cold War discourse, and to point out that the vast majority of the world's population lived outside and beyond the competing spheres led by the United States and the Soviet Union. Sauvy also thought that France, as a colonial empire, could side neither with the United States nor with the Soviet Union. Indeed, in France of the early 1950s one could find a widespread urge to find a third stance beyond what was perceived as the basically Manichean Cold War discourse. Sauvy responded by using a metaphor:

> One could console oneself, if one wanted, with the gaudy proof of an advance bigger than that of capitalism, but not so foolishly made. And perhaps, it could be that the First World [*premier monde*], at its fervent pace, all human

solidarity besides, cannot remain insensitive to the slow and irresistible, humble and ferocious, pressure toward life. Because in the end, this Third World [tiers monde], ignored, exploited, and despised, like the Third Estate [tiers état], wants to become something too.[1]

The way in which Sauvy let his concept *Tiers Monde* allude to the Third Estate is explicit. At the time, most francophones would have identified the reference to Emmanuel-Joseph Sieyès's (a.k.a. the Abbé Sieyès) renowned 1789 pamphlet *What Is the Third Estate?* (*Qu'est-ce que le Tiers état?*) and its famous conclusion:

1 What is the Third Estate? Everything.
2 What is it in the present political order? Nothing.
3 What does it want? To become something.

Sauvy later confirmed that his formulation, "the Third World ... wants to become something too," referred to Sieyès's pamphlet.[2] One reason for him to choose the *Tiers Monde* metaphor was precisely that in France of the 1950s it was easily recognized as an allusion to the Tiers État. Since it functioned as an advertisement, the metaphor helped promote his political ideas.

Within France's distressed situation during the 1950s—in the midst of multiple crises—and because of Sauvy's status as a famous researcher and debater, the term *Tiers Monde* spread rapidly among center-left French intellectuals. These primarily Paris-based intellectuals expected nothing less than seeing the supposedly emerging *Tiers Monde* taking shape as a politically active global force that could overthrow the then present world order. *Tiers Monde* tended to become a signifier for *the others—those whom we are not*. It was not seen as an inimical other, however, but instead as an ally in the struggle against the Cold War conflict between the United States and the Soviet Union.

On the whole, these French academics and intellectuals were not against the colonial system as such. Instead, they wanted to see colonialism remaining the cornerstone in an upcoming global welfare system based on the rule of law. The issue was to find a solution with which to improve the colonial system, not to abolish it. In 1953, for example, Sauvy wrote:

> Colonialism gets bad press, because of its past, but also, all too often, because of its present. The formula, however, is one of great efficiency. It is a sort of patronage, a collaboration that is asymmetrical, without doubt, but also reciprocal. From the viewpoint of efficiency, then, it would be necessary to wish for the establishment of such relations, if they did not already exist. But they can only be justified on the expressed condition of accelerating development, of giving protected populations superior conditions to those of independent populations. Otherwise, it is difficult to see what kind of justification could be given before the near unanimous court of world opinion.[3]

The Bandung Conference

In April 1955, President Sukarno of Indonesia summoned Asian and African (but not Latin American) leaders to a conference to be held in Bandung. Contrary to a commonly held supposition, the terms *Third World* and *Tiers Monde* were not used at the conference. The often-heard claim that the Bandung Conference should have been the birthplace of the *Tiers Monde*—the moment when the Third World came into existence as a unified political force—does not hold sway. In 1955–56, instead, the group of researchers and intellectuals around Sauvy in Paris took the Bandung Conference to be the expected event at which their awaited *Tiers Monde* started to emerge. It was in Paris, not in Bandung, that Sauvy's term *Tiers Monde* was projected onto the conference, thereby laying the foundation for the still purported idea that the conference was the birthplace of the organized Third World. In 1956, social anthropologist Georges Balandier manifested this projection when editing an anthology titled *Le "tiers monde."* The volume attempted to analyze the world in the wake of the Bandung Conference and included a contribution by Sauvy, who in this case nevertheless refrained from using the term *Tiers Monde*.[4]

During the latter half of the 1950s, parallel with the escalating war in Algeria and the continuing destabilization of France, the usage of the term *Tiers Monde* increased. At the time, the concept came to signify the upcoming Non-Aligned Movement, including countries such as Yugoslavia. Users of the term were opening up for a position that could counteract the discourse of the Cold War, a position to be known as the Non-Aligned Movement. Already in the early 1960s, however, discourses changed in unforeseen ways. In 1963 Sauvy wrote:

> When the expression *le Tiers Monde* was first used in 1952 it applied more clearly than today to a certain part of the globe; its political definition and its economic-demographic definition since then have been separated.
> On the political level, the *Tiers Monde* is to be understood as relatively developed countries outside of the two blocs [of the Cold War], such as Yugoslavia; on the economic-demographic level, it contains countries such as China and Albania, as well as Guinea and perhaps even Cuba. Principally, it is this [latter] aspect of the expression that interests us here.[5]

By differentiating between Yugoslavia and Albania, Sauvy signaled the break-up of a supposed political and socioeconomic unity that he had believed in during the 1950s, but that he could no longer substantiate in the early 1960s. To Sauvy, the term *Tiers Monde/Third World* was not a geographical marker, since Yugoslavia and Albania were neighboring countries. And since both Yugoslavia and Albania were placed in Europe, Sauvy's notion of the

Tiers Monde/Third World did not mark out any European/non-European delimitation.

Frantz Fanon and the Concept of the *Tiers Monde*

Because of the politically malfunctioning Fourth Republic, the downfall of the French economy, and the disastrous and violent dissolution of the French colonial empire, France in the late 1950s was exhausted. In particular, the wars in Indochina and Algeria became a source of civil unrest in (mainland European) France. A question that proved particularly contentious was whether Algeria was a French colony or an African part of mainland France. Taken together, the various crises threatened to collapse France into an outright civil war. At that time Frantz Fanon took up and transformed the concept *le Tiers Monde*. The translation of his book *Les damnés de la terre* (1961) as *The Wretched of the Earth* in 1963 was pivotal to the transformation of the French *Tiers Monde* into the English *Third World*, and into equivalent concepts in other languages.

Frantz Fanon (1925–61) was from Martinique in the French West Indies.[6] During World War II, he, as the patriotic Frenchman he thought himself to be, volunteered and fought under General de Gaulle. He took part in the D-Day invasion and was later decorated for bravery in combat. After the war he remained in France to study medicine. He became frustrated, however, when noticing that because of his skin color others in France did not regard him to be their French compatriot. Instead, he was looked upon as a foreigner and a Negro. Fanon nevertheless managed to be recognized as a contemporary intellectual, not least because of his 1952 book *Peau noire, masques blancs* (*Black Skin, White Masks*).[7] In late 1953 he was appointed director of the psychiatric hospital in Blida, outside of Algiers in Algeria, just before the outbreak of the Algerian War. Fanon found himself in the delicate position of having to treat both torturer and tortured. In 1957 he broke with the French Republic, with which he had hitherto identified. He and his wife and son fled to Tunis in Tunisia, where he started working for the Algerian Front for National Liberation (FLN). However, because he basically remained a French intellectual (he sometimes called himself European) who was neither Arab nor Muslim, and because he did not speak Arabic, let alone English, he remained at the organization's fringe.

In 1959 Fanon published a compilation of his articles entitled *L'an V de la révolution algérienne*, which was reprinted in 1966 as *Sociologie d'une révolution (l'an V de la révolution algérienne)*.[8] It was translated into English and published under slightly different titles: *Studies in a Dying Colonialism* and *A Dying Colonialism*.[9] These titles miss the book's central point of reference.

As indicated by the French title, more faithfully translated as "Year V of the Algerian Revolution," Fanon referred to the revolutionary calendar of the French Revolution, according to which the year 1792—the founding of the republic—was set as Year Zero of the new world order. Subsequently 1793 became Year I, 1794 became Year II, and so forth. The Algerian revolt started in 1954. When referring to 1959 as Year V of the Algerian Revolution, Fanon was thus explicitly alluding to the French Revolution. Indeed, the basic theme of this book is that the colonialist French Republic had effectively forfeited its revolutionary heritage. Fanon made the point that the true heir of the French Revolution was the struggling Algerian nation, not the present French Republic.

Les damnés de la terre

Fanon's last book, *Les damnés de la terre*, took the same stance as *L'an V de la révolution algérienne*. But instead of claiming that it was the Algerian nation that now was the true heir and successor of the French Revolution, he based his argument on the *Tiers Monde*. He thereby managed to use Sauvy's term contrary to Sauvy's intention, yet at the same time remaining true to the metaphor of *Tiers Monde* being the global Tiers État of the twentieth century. While Sauvy looked upon the *Tiers Monde* as an ally in the struggle to mend and resurrect French colonialism, Fanon used it as a counter-concept when overthrowing the system of colonialism at large.

At the age of thirty-five, Fanon was diagnosed with malignant leukemia. Instead of undertaking the prescribed cure, he, assisted by his wife Josie Fanon, wrote his most famous book, *Les damnés de la terre*. The book was published in Paris in early December 1961, only days before Fanon's death. After a week it was banned in France.

In 1960, Jean-Paul Sartre had published *Critique de la raison dialectique* (*Critique of Dialectical Reason*).[10] Sartre argued that the colonial system was violent to its core, and that there could be no colonial system free of violence and oppression. He claimed that when a violent revolt or protest occurred within the colonial system, it was wrong to see it as acts of random violence. Any protest, instead, should be regarded as an expression that mirrored the latent and oppressive violence used when installing and maintaining the colonial system. The only way to dismantle the colonial system and free man from its violent oppression was through the use of counter-violence. In this book Sartre never applied the term *Tiers Monde*.

Fanon read Sartre's book and accepted the presented conclusion. The first and the longest chapter in *Les damnés de la terre* discussed methods to fight violent oppression by using counter-violent methods. Fanon in 1961, unlike

Sartre in 1960, made active use of the term *Tiers Monde*, although he did not define the term. Instead, he embedded it in his text. In the book's first chapter, "De la violence," it is suddenly stated—here in the English translation from 1963—that "each *jaquerie*, each act of sedition in the Third World [*tiers monde*] makes up part of the picture framed by the Cold War."[11] Fanon indicated that the *Tiers Monde* was the vanguard of the ongoing world revolution of modernization—a revolution that had started with the French Revolution. He hinted that people arguing like Sauvy were mistaken, since the solution to the problems created by the colonial system could never be found in attempts to come to a compromise with that system. He thereby used the term *Tiers Monde* as a counter-concept with which he could challenge Sauvy's concept *Tiers Monde*—which itself had originated as a counter-concept challenging the Cold War discourse.

Knowing full well that the concept *Tiers Monde* was made up by socio-liberal intellectuals around Sauvy, Fanon turned the entire notion on its head when writing that "Europe is literally the creation of the Third World."[12] He thereby managed to be true to the metaphor of the *Tiers Monde/Third World* being the Tiers État of the twentieth century, as well as turning Sauvy's stance on its head. According to Fanon, people like Sauvy were not defending the ideals of the French Revolution, since colonialism, in any form, ran counter to the ideals of universal liberty, equality, and fraternity. The only way to free oneself from colonial violence was by fighting colonialism with counter-violence. In this book, Fanon also became the first to indicate the stance *we of the Tiers Monde/Third World*:

> So we see that the young nations of the Third World are wrong in trying to make up to the capitalist countries. We are strong in our own right, and in the justice of our point of view.[13]

Fanon's use of the pronoun "we" should be noticed here. Sometimes, as in the first sentence quoted above, "we" refers to the detached readers of his book. At other times, as in the second sentence, it refers to the group of people he was writing about. Constantly mixing the positions of *we—the detached reader* and *we who present ourselves through the text's narrative*, Fanon managed to integrate his readers into his text. He thereby invoked his readers in the statement he was making, turning them into *we of the Tiers Monde/Third World*. It should be noted that the book was written in French and published in Paris by a left-leaning publishing house, Maspero. Fanon probably expected his readers to be French or francophone intellectuals, whom he could influence by provoking self-criticism. He was not especially trying to reach non-Europeans, and he certainly did not exclude French intellectuals.[14]

In *Les damnés de la terre*, Fanon turned "Tiers Monde" into a concept that would mark out a new phase in the continuing globalization of modernity, which had started with the French Revolution. The book's title alluded to the revolutionary battle song "The Internationale," which in its French original begins "Debut, les damnés de la terre." The song was written and first sung during the Paris Commune of 1871.[15] Even if the reference was clear to most francophone intellectuals of the 1960s, it became obscured when translated into other languages.

Sartre's Preface

Fanon had been inspired by Sartre's *Critique de la raison dialectique*. During his stay in France in the early 1950s, Fanon had met Sartre in person a few times, and he contributed to Sartre's journal *Les Temps Modernes*. In 1961, Fanon asked Sartre to write a preface to *Les damnés de la terre*, and Sartre accepted. In addition, the first chapter, "De la violence," was published in the May 1961 issue of *Les Temps Modernes*.[16] In the preface, apparently for the first time, Sartre used the term *Tiers Monde*, which he enclosed in quotation marks.[17] In most translations of the book, these quotation marks have been removed so that Sartre's usage of the term appears more similar to Fanon's than it originally was. It should be noted that while Fanon used *Tiers Monde* as a concept with which he could involve the readers of the text, Sartre nevertheless managed to remain detached. He wrote about the tone of Fanon's book: "The tone is new. Who dares to speak thus? It is an African, a man from the 'Third World,' an ex-'native.'"[18]

Sartre—despite knowing that the book's author was a French intellectual from Martinique—turned Fanon into one of *the Others*, not one of *us*: Sartre saw Fanon as a black man, not as a Frenchman. Although writing in the same volume, Sartre in his preface used the term differently than Fanon did. According to Fanon, the *Tiers Monde* was the force that would overcome present colonialist Europe and pave the way not only for a post-colonialist Europe, but also for an entirely "New Man" beyond racism and any notion of "human races." Fanon's *Tiers Monde* was an inclusive concept: everyone, regardless of "race," could take part in the process of pursuing the ongoing globalization of modernity. Sartre's conceptualization of the *Tiers Monde* was different. He made a stark distinction between *us* and *them*, that is, between the white, colonizing Europeans and the non-white, colonized peoples of the so-called *Tiers Monde*. He even stated that the conflict between *us* and *them* was, and had to be, a violent one, in which *they* were to kill *us*.[19]

Sartre thus turned Fanon into a *non-white, non-European ex-native* who was teaching his fellow *non-white, non-European ex-natives* how to become an integrated *Tiers Monde* that could crush and kill *us* white (first and foremost French) Europeans. According to Sartre, Fanon was a prophet and a forerunner for an emerging *Tiers Monde*. But Fanon—dying of leukemia—distanced himself from that role.[20]

Even though both Fanon and Sartre were using Sauvy's term *Tiers Monde* in the same book, they turned it into two different counter-concepts that both opposed Sauvy's original concept. The distinctions between different usages of the term *Tiers Monde* may be tacit, but it proves important with regards to how the term was to be received, especially in translations.

Fanon and Worsley

In 1960, Peter Worsley had been traveling through Africa. In Accra, the capital of newly independent Ghana, he attended sessions held by the All-African People's Congress and overheard a speech by Fanon, who spoke in French. Afterward Worsley approached Fanon, with whom he became friends.[21]

Worsley wrote for the journal *New Left Review*. Heavily influenced by Sartre's *Les Temps Modernes*, it had been founded earlier the same year, in 1960. By that time, Sartre's journal had published articles containing the expression *Tiers Monde*. In early 1961, as mentioned, the first chapter of the still unpublished *Les damnés de la terre*—the one in which Fanon introduces his notion of the *Tiers Monde*—had appeared in *Les Temps Modernes*. In late 1961, *New Left Review* published an article covering the emerging Non-Aligned Movement and its recent Belgrade Summit, followed by a related article written by Worsley. Under the headline "Revolution of the Third World," Worsley aimed at placing the Belgrade Summit in historical context, although he did not use the term "Third World" when doing so.[22] He described the Belgrade Summit as a successor to the 1955 Bandung Conference, using terms such as "the non-aligned Powers," "the neutral, ex-colonial Powers," and "the New Powers." He thereby included Yugoslavia in the group of countries he was talking about. Since the article's headline was "Revolution of the Third World," a reader would be prone to integrate Yugoslavia into the concept "Third World." Since the article stood in the context of the 1961 Belgrade Summit, a reader would also be likely to understand the term as synonymous with the Non-Aligned Movement.[23]

This understanding was to be changed in two years' time. In 1963 the concept sparked a debate in the *New Left Review*. Geographer Keith Buchanan contributed an article titled "The Third World: Its Emergence and Contours," writing that the "most striking political development of the last two decades has been the emergence of what French geographers and social scientists term the Tiers Monde—the Third World." He called it "a great bloc of countries" existing outside of Europe and North America: "All are poor, most are backward, all are either crippled by lack of development or deformed by exploitative development. They contain an aggregate population of almost two thousand million people—two-thirds of the world total." After quoting a passage from Sartre's preface, Buchanan stated that his main source was Fanon's *Les damnés de la terre*.[24]

Under the headline "Third World or Third Force?" Michael Barratt Brown criticized Buchanan. He wrote that the term "Third World" threatened to divide the world proletariat. He meant that there existed no substantial evidence that the European proletariat was actively exploiting the peoples of the supposed Third World. He made an explicit qualification at this point, however: he might have missed out substantial information, since he had not read Fanon's *Les damnés de la terre*.[25]

Buchanan answered that the Western working class was uninterested in the wellbeing of non-Western working classes, and that the European proletariat was only interested in its own welfare while not caring for conditions in the Third World. He explicitly raised the claim that it was high time to break up the obsolete idea of a single world proletariat. He sided with what he called the *Third World* against what he perceived to be a decadent European proletariat.[26]

Worsley's *The Third World*

In the early 1960s Peter Worsley not only contributed to the *New Left Review*, he also re-contemplated his academic career. As a trained social anthropologist, he saw that there were increasing options for sociologists. Deciding to take the leap from social anthropology to sociology, Worsley wrote a book titled *The Third World*. He aimed at presenting the social structures leading from a colonial to a post-colonial world order, focusing his study on the term "Third World," though he never formally defined the term. Worsley made it clear that the term was a translation of the French *Tiers Monde*, and he especially referred to Fanon's usage of the concept. To Worsley, the Third World was a loose compilation of colonialized and post-colonialized parts of the world.[27]

Unlike most readers of *Les damnés de la terre*, Worsley chose to stick to Fanon's text, leaving Sartre's preface aside. Although he came to the conclusion that the conflict between what he called "Euro-America" and the "Third World" was profound and characterized by mutual distrust, he did not reach the Sartrean conclusion that the conflict could only be overcome through bloodstained world revolution in which *they* were to kill *us*. However, Worsley let his notion of the Third World be cemented in a distinction between *us and them*, between *us in Euro-America and the others in the Third World*.

The term "Third World" entered the social sciences around the mid 1960s. In 1966, for example, Oxford University Press published at least two academic titles containing the term. J. D. B. Miller, an Australian professor of International Relations, published *The Politics of the Third World*, recognizing the French origin of the term:

> "The Third World" ... [is] derived from the French *tiers monde* and used to describe those countries which are plainly neither Communist nor Western. Some countries clearly belong to it and others, just as clearly, do not: India and Indonesia are undoubtedly in, Norway and Australia undoubtedly out. Problems of definition arise, however, not with these obvious cases, but with the marginal ones, of which we may choose Israel and Japan.[28]

Irving Louis Horowitz, an American professor of sociology, did not acknowledge the term's French origin. In his book *Three Worlds of Development*, Horowitz introduced a novelty, namely the notions of the *First World* and the *Second World*:

> The First World of the United States and its Western Allies, the Second World of the Soviet Union and its Eastern Bloc Allies, and the Third World of the non-aligned, but variously committed nations of Latin America, Asia, and Africa.[29]

Semantic Logic and World-Naming

Some five years after *Third World* had been introduced as a concept in the English language, *First World* and *Second World* were added to make a complete set. In most language discourses, a *third* calls out for a *first* and a *second*, hence the notion of a *Third World* seemed to presuppose the existence of a *First World* and a *Second World*. For as long as the etymological connection between the *Tiers Monde* and the Tiers État was recognized, there was no need for such additional notions. The need for such worlds appeared only when the connection between the concept *Third World* and its French origin *Tiers Monde* was lost; it was only then that a logical urge for a *first* and a *second* manifested itself. And these *lost worlds* were immediately found and identified within the Cold War discourse.

The very term that in the French discourse of the early 1950s had emerged as a metaphor when trying to break up the Manichean logic of the Cold War had in the Anglo-American academic discourse of the mid 1960s become a geopolitical marker within the logic of the Cold War discourse. It was a marker that not only functioned when corroborating that discourse, but was also used when affirming the positivist notion of a transcendence between human knowledge and external reality: the Third World became conceived as an objectively existing part of the world out there in the physical geography, beyond languages and discourses. The concept came to verify a distinction between *us* and *them*. The poor and underdeveloped people of the world lived in the *Third World*, which was located *far away from us* in Western Europe and North America. The concept was thus used when creating what was seen as an objective distinction between *us here in the developed world* and *the others over there in the underdeveloped, yet developing Third World*.

Erik Tängerstad is a teacher, historian, and author. He is affiliated with the Department of History at Lund University, Sweden, and currently teaches history, politics, philosophy, and the Swedish language at Birkagårdens folkhögskola in Stockholm, Sweden. His fields of research span popular culture and film history, as well as the political history of the twentieth century, and he has published, among other things, on the Swedish Vietnam movement in the 1960s, the use of popular film in the German political context in the 1920s, and the concepts of *bildning* (Swedish) and *Bildung* (German). His latest book is an essay in Swedish on the contemporary refugee situation, titled *På Flykt – en essä om politiskt sönderfall* (Korpen, 2016).

NOTES

1. Alfred Sauvy, "Trois mondes, une planète," *L'Observateur*, 14 August 1952, 14. To illustrate the Manichean division of the world along East-West demarcations, Sauvy took the divided Germany as a point of reference. He claimed that not only the Germans but also humanity at large was paying a high price in the then ongoing Cold War, my translation.
2. In an interview, Sauvy explained: "In 1951, I had, in a Brazilian review, come across the mentioning of three worlds; however, it did not employ the expression *Third World* [*Tiers Monde*]. That expression I coined and used for the first time when writing in the French weekly journal *L'Observateur*. … I transposed in this way Sieyès's famous phrase about the Third Estate during the French Revolution." Seloua Luste Boulbina, "Les états postcoloniaux et l'indépendance des sujets," *Revue québécoise de droit international* (November 2012): 35n4. The full remark, in French, has been cited on various websites, for example Alfred Sauvy, "Note sur l'origine de l'expression 'Tiers Monde,'" retrieved 11 March 2014 from http://www.jaibhim.hu/trois-mondes-une-planete/, my translation.
3. Alfred Sauvy, *L'Europe et sa population* (Paris, 1953), 206, my translation.
4. Georges Balandier, ed., *Le "tiers monde": Sous-développement et développement* (Paris, 1956). The quotation marks in the book title around *"tiers monde"* should be noted. In a 2003 interview, Balandier commented on the term *tiers monde*: "This expression

has had a global success. It has however generally been misunderstood. To us, it never qualified a third group of nations, besides the two blocs (the capitalist and the soviet), during the Cold War. No, instead it was a reference to the third estate during *l'Ancien Régime*, that part of society that refused to remain 'nothing', according to the pamphlet of the Abbé Sieyès. The term was designed for the nations that claimed to become inscribed in history." Quoted after Boulbina, "Les états postcoloniaux," 36, my translation.

5. Alfred Sauvy, *Théorie générale de la population*, vol. 1 (Paris, 1963), 270. The quotation is taken from the book's English-language summary.
6. On Fanon's biography, see David Macey, *Frantz Fanon: A Life* (New York, 2000), and Alice Cherki, *Frantz Fanon: Portrait* (Paris, 2000), translated by Nadia Benabid as *Frantz Fanon: A Portrait* (Ithaca, NY, 2006).
7. Frantz Fanon, *Peau noire masques blancs: Préface (1952) et postface (1965) de Francis Jeanson* (Paris, 1965). The book was translated by Charles Lam Markmann as Frantz Fanon, *Black Skin, White Masks* (New York, 1967).
8. Frantz Fanon, *L'an V de la révolution algérienne* (Paris, 1959); Frantz Fanon, *Sociologie d'une révolution (l'an V de la révolution algérienne)*, 4th ed. (Paris, 1966). The publisher of the first edition, François Maspero, started his publishing business in 1959 by publishing works on the then ongoing conflict in Algeria.
9. Frantz Fanon, *Studies in a Dying Colonialism*, trans. Haakon Chevalier (New York, 1965), later retitled *A Dying Colonialism* (New York, 1967).
10. Jean-Paul Sartre, *Critique de la raison dialectique: Précédé de questions de méthode* (Paris, 1960).
11. Frantz Fanon, *The Wretched of the Earth*, trans. Constance Farrington (New York, 1963), 75.
12. Ibid., 102.
13. Ibid., 105.
14. Peter Worsley made this point in 1972. About Fanon's choice of language and publisher, he wrote: "Far from duplicating his message on cheap paper, writing it in Arabic, Swahili, Hindi or Malay, and distributing it to the peasants and sub-proletarians of the Third World, he wrote it in French and published it in Paris so that it could be read by Western intellectuals. His influence on the Third World has therefore been quite small. It has been in the heartlands of developed capitalism that he has been influential: in the revival of direct action in Paris and Berlin, but above all in the Black ghettos of the United States where his books have sold in the thousands." Peter Worsley, "Fanon and the 'Lumpenprolitariat,'" *Socialist Register* 9 (1972): 219.
15. Among other things, the revolutionaries of the Paris Commune returned to the use of the revolutionary calendar, that is, the same calendar that Fanon had alluded to in the title of his book *L'an V de la révolution algérienne*.
16. Frantz Fanon, "De la violence," *Les Temps Modernes* 181 (1961): 1453–93.
17. Jean-Paul Sartre, preface to Frantz Fanon, *The Wretched of the Earth*, trans. Constance Farrington (New York, 1963), 7–26.
18. Ibid., 9.

19. Ibid., 10–18. This is not to say that Sartre was a racist, but rather that he was writing within a racist discourse that he did not fully recognize or reflect in the same manner that Fanon did.
20. When the second French edition of *Les damnés de la terre* was to be launched in 1967, Josie Fanon, Frantz Fanon's widow and co-writer, refused to have Sartre's preface included. Indeed, the 1967 French edition of the book is the only one without Sartre's preface.
21. Worsley, "Fanon," 193.
22. Peter Worsley, "Revolution of the Third World," *New Left Review* I/12 (November–December 1961): 18–25. It should be noted that the term *the Third World* only appeared in the headline. It was probably one of the editors who wrote that headline. This was the last issue of *New Left Review* edited by Stuart Hall before Perry Anderson took over as editor.
23. In this issue of *New Left Review*, the article previous to Worsley's was titled "The Belgrade Conference." In that article, David Ross lamented that so many neutral and non-aligned countries did not attend the summit: "It is a pity that other countries could not have been brought into the group, which is already disparate. For instance Austria, Switzerland and Laos are all neutrals by statute; others absent included Sweden, Finland, the Irish Republic, Sierra Leone, Nigeria, Israel, Jordan, many ex-French colonies, Liberia (in fact, nearly all the Monrovia group)." David Ross, "The Belgrade Conference," *New Left Review* I/12 (November–December 1961): 12–17. It should here be noted that the common denominator for Ross was that the countries in question were formally neutral in the Cold War, not that they were ex-colonies. His notion was immediately, although only implicitly, challenged by Worsley, who tried to make the character of being an ex-colony the common denominator. The status of Yugoslavia was the test case: was Yugoslavia in 1960–61 considered to be a Third World country or not? The way that question was answered defined the term *the Third World*.
24. Keith Buchanan, "The Third World: Its Emergence and Contours," *New Left Review* I/18 (January–February 1963): 5.
25. Michael Barratt Brown, "Third World or Third Force?" *New Left Review* I/20 (Summer 1963): 32–36. It should be noted that he constantly wrote "Third World" within quotation marks, which Buchanan did not do.
26. Keith Buchanan, "Bingo or UNO? Further Comments on the Affluent and Proletarian Nations," *New Left Review* I/21 (September–October 1963): 29.
27. Peter Worsley, *The Third World*, 2nd ed. (Chicago, 1967), ix–x, 242, 260ff. This preface is dated "29 September, 1963," that is, parallel in time with the aforementioned *New Left Review* debate between Buchanan and Barratt Brown. In his preface, Worsley thanked a number of people, among them Barratt Brown, but not Buchanan.
28. John Donald Bruce Miller, *The Politics of the Third World* (Oxford, 1966), x.
29. Irving Louis Horowitz, *Three Worlds of Development: The Theory and Practice of International Stratification* (New York, 1966), 1.

BIBLIOGRAPHY

Balandier, Georges, ed. *Le "tiers monde": Sous-développement et développement*. Paris: Presses Universitaires de France, 1956.

Barratt Brown, Michael. "Third World or Third Force?" *New Left Review* I/20 (Summer 1963): 32–36.

Boulbina, Seloua Luste. "Les états postcoloniaux et l'indépendance des sujets." *Revue québécoise de droit international* (November 2012): 33–42.

Buchanan, Keith. "Bingo or UNO? Further Comments on the Affluent and Proletarian Nations." *New Left Review* I/21 (September–October 1963): 21–29.

———. "The Third World: Its Emergence and Contours." *New Left Review* I/18 (January–February 1963): 5–23.

Cherki, Alice. *Frantz Fanon: Portrait*. Paris: Seuil, 2000. Translated by Nadia Benabid as *Frantz Fanon: A Portrait*. Ithaca, NY: Cornell University Press, 2006.

Fanon, Frantz. *L'an V de la révolution algérienne*. Paris: François Maspero, 1959.

———. *Black Skin, White Masks*. Translated by Charles Lam Markmann. New York: Grove Press, 1967.

———. *Les damnés de la terre: Préface de Jean-Paul Sartre*. Paris: François Maspero, 1961.

———. "De la violence." *Les Temps Modernes* 181 (1961): 1453–93.

———. *Peau noire masques blancs: Préface (1952) et postface (1965) de Francis Jeanson*. Paris: Seuil, 1965.

———. *Sociologie d'une révolution (l'An V de la révolution algérienne)*. 4th ed. Paris: François Maspero, 1966.

———. *Studies in a Dying Colonialism*. Translated by Haakon Chevalier. New York: Grove Press, 1965. Later retitled *A Dying Colonialism*. New York: Grove Press, 1967.

———. *The Wretched of the Earth*. Translated by Constance Farrington. New York: Grove Press, 1963.

Horowitz, Irving Louis. *Three Worlds of Development: The Theory and Practice of International Stratification*. New York: Oxford University Press, 1966.

Macey, David. *Frantz Fanon: A Life*. New York: Picador, 2000.

Miller, John Donald Bruce. *The Politics of the Third World*. Oxford: Oxford University Press, 1966.

Ross, David. "The Belgrade Conference." *New Left Review* I/12 (November–December 1961): 12–17.

Sartre, Jean-Paul. *Critique de la raison dialectique: Précédé de questions de méthode*. Paris: Gallimard, 1960.

———. Preface to *The Wretched of the Earth*, by Frantz Fanon, 7–26. Translated by Constance Farrington. New York: Grove Press, 1963.

Sauvy, Alfred. *L'Europe et sa population*. Paris: Les Éditions Internationales, 1953.

———. "Note sur l'origine de l'expression 'Tiers Monde.'" Retrieved 11 March 2014 from http://www.jaibhim.hu/trois-mondes-une-planete/.

———. *Théorie générale de la population*. Vol. 1. Paris: Presses Universitaires de France, 1963.

———. "Trois mondes, une planète." *L'Observateur*, 14 August 1952, 14.

Worsley, Peter. "Fanon and the 'Lumpenprolitariat.'" *Socialist Register* 9 (1972): 193–230.
———. "Revolution of the Third World." *New Left Review* I/12 (November–December 1961): 18–25.
———. *The Third World*. 2nd ed. Chicago: University of Chicago Press, 1967.

▸• 6 •◂

On the Dialectics of Ecological World Concepts

Falko Schmieder

In their introduction to this volume, the editors invite the contributors to illuminate the paradox of how the complex, heterogeneous, and infinite dynamics of globalization gives rise to the idea and reality of a limited, finite—and thus vulnerable—world. One context in which this problem of the development of a counter-concept to globalization plays a major role is the more recent discourse on ecology.[1] Today, whenever we think about the relationship between globalization as a primarily economically driven process and as a world consciousness that is informed by the limitedness and vulnerability of the world, we do so under the conditions of a fundamental crisis of the societal relationship to nature. A political expression of this crisis can be found in the demand to establish a sustainable society, which implies that the current evolution of society cannot be maintained; in other words, our society as it exists and develops today is not future-compliant. And yet, although this insight has existed for decades, we seem no closer to curbing those trends. On the contrary, it seems that under the conditions of the perpetual economic crisis, alternative developmental possibilities are lost from sight again, and political interest focuses instead on strengthening and extending those very structures that, from an ecological point of view, must be seen as highly problematic.[2]

Being aware of the pertinence of this problem, I wish to focus my attention on the formation of the modern ecology movement, since this movement was the first to both politicize and discuss the contradiction between economic expansion and limited planetary resources. In so doing, it established a multitude of new world concepts and global metaphors that remain relevant to today's discourses. First, I would like to highlight an epistemic disruption, the "Copernican turn" of the ecological consciousness, as it were. The second step will then be to trace the attempts of ecological thinking to redress the allegedly problematic relationship of expansive globalization and integrative world consciousness by analyzing the basic metaphors and theoretical models implemented.

From its very inception, the modern capitalist economic system was accompanied by complaints about its wasteful and exploitative relationship with nature. The concept of sustainability itself provides an early example of such a critique; sustainability was coined in 1713 by the mining engineer and forest scientist Hans Carl von Carlowitz.[3] The coinage of the term occurred in connection with his experience of the overuse of forests, which made it clear that wood supplies would eventually be exhausted if traditional practices were maintained. In addition to resource crises, the pollution of rivers and air through the use of coal was a permanent source of concern. Despite the persistent reflections on the over-exploitation of nature (and their apparent similarities to current discourse), it is important to remember that the difficulties in relation to nature were discussed in very different forms throughout the development of capitalism.[4] The most dramatic break was the emergence of modern ecology in the 1960s, which differs fundamentally from the preceding paradigm of conservationism.[5]

The first central epistemic difference between modern ecology and conservationism is that people are no longer seen in opposition to nature, be it as nature's lawyer, doctor, or helper, but are instead themselves conceived as a vulnerable and endangered part of nature, or, alternatively, as a microcosm. As Rachel Carson states in her classic book *Silent Spring*, published in 1962, "There is also an ecology of the world within our bodies."[6] The background for this transformation of the (collective) consciousness concerning man's place in nature was the release of radioactive materials during nuclear weapon tests, which, through the food chain, also penetrated the human body. Shortly thereafter, other substances, whose origins were civilian rather than military, such as heavy metal and pesticides, were detected in the human body too. This transformed the effects of nature upon humankind from the indirect (i.e., scarcity resulting from overconsumption of resources) as it was understood within the paradigm of conservationism, into a direct physical effect on humankind within the frame of modern ecology.

The second epistemic difference contained within the shift from conservationism to modern ecology is the globalization of the problem. While the traditional conservationism was engaged with local problems, modern ecology engages with the whole world understood as a single endangered unit. The history of the concept "ecology" demonstrates this tendency toward universalization. Not even a century after Ernst Haeckel introduced the concept of ecology in his manifesto *The History of Creation* in order to define a specific branch of biology,[7] ecology already functioned as an enormously politicized scientific and, at the same time, popular umbrella term referring to the global ecosystem.

The situating of humankind within nature, when combined with the globality of the problem, finally results in a third difference from conservationism: the eminently political character of the ecological movement. Based on the local restriction of the problems and the fixation on phenomena of external nature ("out there"), traditional conservationism had strong aesthetic components and was essentially static and conserving in character, for it focused on protecting, preserving, and nursing nature; nature was to be protected over and against man's interference. For the modern ecological discussion, these differences no longer exist—the distinction between mankind and nature has been destroyed and with it the possibility of constructing an antagonistic binary. Because human existence is, at the same time, a cause *for* nature's disturbed metabolism and also affected *by* this same disturbance, man's ideal relationship with nature can no longer be a matter of simply preserving nature, but instead must involve the practical change of dominant societal relationships with nature. The connection between anti-nuclear or peace movements on the one hand, and environmental movements on the other, demonstrates this tendency within modern ecology toward politicization. After the first deployment of nuclear bombs, the problem arose that from that day forward, it was necessary to take into account capacities of destructiveness that were, potentially, of infinite size and, as a result, related to the whole globe. The shock caused by the technical possibility of the globe's destruction is at the heart of the 1950s nuclear debate.[8] For the first time in world history, humanity as a whole appeared to be at risk. Faced with the possibility of humanity's own extinction, it is no coincidence that under these circumstances the unity of humanity has often been expressed in the biological category "species." According to Arthur Koestler, "Our time is unique. Before the thermonuclear bomb, man lived with the idea of his death as an individual; from now on, humanity lives with the idea of its death as a species."[9] This inevitably changed the definition of war. The still very young category "World War" received a new meaning; a World War III waged with nuclear and hydrogen bombs, it was speculated, could leave no survivors. This concern for the world as a whole, a characteristic feature of the discourse on nuclear weapons, was also a central theme of the early ecology movement, which in part developed out of the anti-nuclear movement. As it became clearer that the threat of radioactive fallout was part of a much more comprehensive problem, perception patterns and concepts of the anti-nuclear discourse were transferred into the environmental discourse. The example that perhaps best demonstrates this transfer is the concept of the "population bomb."[10] The seemingly exponential growth of the population in the "underdeveloped countries" was thus portrayed as a threat as devastating as the explosion of an atomic bomb. Viewed more generally, this heritage mainly finds expression in the often-recognized apocalyptic tone of the early ecology movement, a tone clearly perceptible within the writings of Barry Commoner, one of the pioneers of the ecology movement. In his 1963 book, *Science and Survival*, he writes: "I believe that world-wide radio-active contamination, epidemics, ecological disasters, and possibly climatic changes would so gravely affect the stability of the biosphere as to threaten human survival everywhere on the earth."[11] Institutionally, this transition can also be seen in the transformation of the St. Louis Committee for Nuclear Info, which in the 1960s exchanged the term "Nuclear" for "Environmental."[12]

On the other hand, the connection of the anti-nuclear movement and ecology discourse should not be overstated; the shock-like experience of the early ecological movement is the result of the historically unprecedented paradox that the general endangering of life conditions is no longer exclusively connected to war, a political state of emergency, or large-scale technological accidents. Instead of the result of an "exceptional" state, threats to human survival can now be conceived as undesirable "side effects" of the regular economic reproduction of society. The productive force is discovered to be simultaneously a destructive force, and the suspicion grows that the negative effects of economy begin to outweigh the positive effects. From the perspective of conceptual history, it is illuminating that the concept of progress, one of the leading terms of the nineteenth century, is now notably used almost exclusively in quotation marks, meaning that it is systematically called into question.[13] The shocking experience, that the destructive effects are side effects of economic production, condenses in the now-tired formula of standing at a turning point in history.[14] The most fundamental message of the ecological consciousness is "that infinite expansion is impossible on a finite planet."[15] More specifically, the central contradiction is seen in the fact that the activities within the context of a globalized capitalist economy, which relies on infinite growth, must get caught in a fundamental, necessarily escalating contradiction with the naturally limited resources of the earth, so that "sooner or later," the survival conditions of humankind are in danger. In Commoner, it reads: "We have come to a turning point in the human habitation of the earth. For the first time in history, the future of the human race is now in serious question."[16] The secretary-general of the United Nations, Sithu U Thant, used almost the same words.[17] The late but rapid spread of this perception has two primary sources. On the one hand, it is the result of the neglect of nature within economic theory and a fundamental belief in progress, which assumed nature as an almost inexhaustible and infinitely available substratum. On the other hand, it is, most practically, due to the enormously expanded range of technological progress, which new weapon systems show perhaps most clearly, but can also be witnessed in the development of a postwar consumption culture, which introduced both new consumption patterns, and with them previously unknown side effects, forms of damage, and follow-up problems. While the history of economic theory since Adam Smith was concerned with the formation and increasing compression of a world market, ecological thinking reformulates this process of globalization as a process of increasing destruction, which, spatially and temporally, becomes increasingly unlimited;[18] radioactive clouds are carried away from their origin and cause damage even in distant regions, with effects that extend far into the future. Such problems push ecology toward a global perspective that emphasizes the interdependency of all natural processes. The holism of ecology is in part expressed in the concept of a "total environment," and therefore is necessarily entailed in the discourse of the effects of nature on mankind. The formula is: "Every part depends on another one; all are related to the movement of the whole." In parallel, the enormously increased effects and influence of man, who now is understood as a "geological factor,"[19] reinforces the perspective of the finiteness of the resources and the vulnerability of the whole of nature. One of the most central concepts to the holism of ecology is the concept of a global ecosystem, a concept that combines the experiences of interdependency and the effect of the whole on the individual and appears as a polemical counter-concept to the expansionism of globalization. A typical feature of early discourse on ecology was the mutual exclusivity of the expansionary logic of economics and the cyclical rhythms of nature. This contradiction was condensed in a variety of new public images and metaphors that are still present in today's discourses: the medical analogy that compares economic expansion with a blindly spreading cancer,[20] highlighting the life and will that globalization seems to have independent of mankind; an economic analogy that refers to a growing indebtedness to nature and future generations;[21] a social-psychologizing analogy that compares globalization with a suicidal course;[22] a biological analogy in which it is a parasitism,[23] and so on. In all cases, economic development that is addicted to permanent growth increasingly affects its own natural preconditions. The family resemblance of these images lies in the fact that they not only name the contradiction between the economic and ecological logics, but they call for immediate action to eliminate this contradiction.

In the history of ideas, the onset of the so-called age of ecology[24] meant moving into a historical phase where humankind knows that its previous course is not future-compliant and comes with catastrophic consequences. Against this backdrop, the ecological discourse is confronted mainly with three tasks: first, the scientific analysis of the global ecosystems, that is, the global interdependencies and limits of nature; second, the politicization of public awareness with the aim of a change of consciousness and values; and third, the practical implementation of the ecological findings on behalf of the elimination or, at least, amelioration of the contradiction of globalization and ecological requirements. In this chapter, I can only briefly outline each of these problems, with the focus on the contradiction between the expansive globalization and a finiteness-referring world consciousness serving as a guide.

The conviction of the early ecology movement in the finiteness of the earth was, at the time, hardly based on empirical experiences in an ecological sense. Rather, it was a theoretical generalization of local experiences or the anticipation of universal crises, resulting from the projection of existing trends. It was uncontroversial that the exponential logic of growth "sooner or later" would come up against natural limits and could not be continued forever. The recording of ecological impact factors and the development of models that allow the discovery of the limits of the carrying capacity of the earth was seen as a priority task in the scientization of ecology. These efforts resulted in, among other things, the concept of the "ecological footprint," which can be applied to individuals as well as states or the global community as a whole.[25] The definition of this concept once again expresses the contradiction between economic and ecological logic very distinctly; graphical depictions showed how many earths would be needed to supply the resources humankind requires, while more recent studies have concluded that human resource consumption exceeds the ecological capacity of the earth by about 20 percent.[26]

The new concept of world balance proved to be productive in another way, as it led to a dense web of worldwide connected survey stations. The collection and analysis of information on temperature, carbon dioxide, oxygen, and other factors made possible the discovery of so-called "tipping points" in earth history; beyond that, it enabled a modeling of the historical development of the global climate, which in turn permits the prediction of future trends. The 2°C maximum increase in average global temperature declared by today's politics would be unthinkable without these conceptual preconditions, which were stimulated by the concept of global natural balance.

As I have pointed out, in modern ecology the cognition of the global nature of the problem coincides with the cognition of the effects on humankind itself. But this insight is at first only based on the logical theorem of the impossibility of a permanent expansive growth; an ecological parallel to the world economy crisis was not in sight. The gulf between the logical theorem of the impossibility of limitless growth and the empirical experience of a growing wealth was compensated for with a universalizing rhetoric that contemporary commentators mocked as an evangelical "One big union."[27] Nearly every book on the early ecological debate contains the argument that society's development produces problems that "increasingly concern mankind as a whole," and respectively "increasingly affect common interests." In connection with this constitution of a universal subject affected by ecological change, the ecology movement has produced a wide range of new world concepts or, if it referred to already existing ones, loaded them with new meanings. One can find concepts like "family of mankind," "world community," or "world society."[28] With these ecological umbrella terms, which constitute homogeneous collective subjects, correspond concepts that aim at new political forms of organization meant to face the depicted new challenges. In this context, concepts like "world government," "Environment Security Council," or "world domestic politics" can be found. Complementary to new political forms of organization, new political agendas, referring to the whole of the globe, were suggested, among them the so-called Earth Charter,[29] the development of "world or earth ethics,"[30] or the demand for the formation of an "earth company."[31]

The strong normative charge of these concepts is the result of the ecology movement's conception of a historically unprecedented problem combined with a historically unprecedented transformation of society's interaction with nature. Previous political revolutions all operated within the paradigm of progress or growth; the ecological turn forced a rejection of precisely this paradigm. Insofar as the individual, with its structure of needs, is a part of this growth economy, this implies the need for self-discipline and self-transformation. The great variety of emotionally powerful images created by the ecology movement can be seen in this context as an attempt to force individuals to distance themselves from a self-centered mindset and to generate a greater sense of collective responsibility and solidarity.

One of the best-known images is "Spaceship Earth,"[32] a complement of the "blue planet" picture taken by American astronauts during the Apollo 8 space mission, the image that enabled humankind to see their home planet from the outside for the first time. While the image of the blue planet represents the uniqueness and vulnerability of the earth, creating a uniform object against the darkness of outer space, "Spaceship Earth" more specifically aims at the mutual dependency of the crew members on one another as well as in relation to their unusual habitat. If the flight is to be continued without complications, the image insinuates, the interactions of the crew must be exactly adjusted to the requirements of this highly complex, artificial habitat.

A second popular image also rests on new technological circumstances, namely the image of the "global village,"[33] which is connected to hopes of equal access and distribution and aims at a transparent economy no longer independent on individuals, but rather serving their needs. However, the metaphor of the global village becomes increasingly less applicable as the processes of globalization reinforce the tendency toward urbanization, sharpening the contrast between metropolis and countryside. The implications of the new globalized media systems for the formation of a new world consciousness or a new world citizen consciousness also work on another level, in that the new media make otherwise unknown and silent suffering as well as disastrous living conditions in distant parts of the world visible. Underneath the claim of universal participation, this level emphasizes the possibility of an identification with the victims of the acceleration of globalization, which could be a step toward the formation of a new collective identity.[34]

The popular slogan "Think globally, act locally"[35] holds a similar mediating position; in a general way, it demands concrete actions be carried out with awareness of their potentially worldwide consequences, as discovered by ecology. More specifically, it could also be understood as a new categorical imperative: act only in such a way that the consequences of your actions do not exceed the ecological capacity of the earth, and that your actions can provide the standard for a universal economy.

Finally, the politicization of public awareness also finds its expression in numerous forms of the institutionalization of ecology. The interest in the formation of a new world consciousness is often already expressed in the labels and titles of these institutions; examples include the magazine *Panscope* or the society Friends of the Earth, which was founded in 1969 and whose members were among the organizers of the so-called Earth Day, a kind of World Environment Day, which took place for the first time in 1970 under the motto "reclaiming the planet."[36]

Earth Overshoot Day represents a similar form of critical remembrance, aimed at the contradiction between economic and ecological categories and based on the concept of the ecological footprint: it marks the day each year when the ecological capacity of the earth allegedly is being exceeded. For example, in 2012 this ecological capacity was surpassed on 23 August.

Despite the pathos surrounding the universalizing aspects of ecology, it is undeniable that there is no uniform political subject that could achieve the desired reform agenda of ecology, or that in empirical experience no homogeneous, shared influence of the environment on the individual can be observed. Moreover, the processes of globalization have led to marked differences in both the causes and the effects of the ecological problems within the so-called world community. Globalization thus is not only recognized as an expansive process but also as one that permanently produces and reproduces social tension. While pop star Sting blessed his audience with the verse "One world is enough for us all," a report by the Brundtland Commission titled *Our Common Future*, which implemented the obligation to sustainability as a political aim, begins with a sentence that more reflects the real conditions of globalization: "The Earth is one but the world is not."[37] The empirical data speaks for itself: a small part of the world population claims a large part of the resources, and while one part is concerned about the future availability of resources, the other part even today lives below or near the level of subsistence. Not by chance, other concepts, paralleling the invention of "one big union" concepts, have emerged, emphasizing just these differences. Among these, the construct of the "Third World," which in its 1952 original context appeared in Alfred Sauvy's phrase "Three worlds, one planet,"[38] became particularly influential. Another important opposition was the distinction between industrial and developing countries, respectively between developed and underdeveloped countries. The basic phrase of the ecology movement, that the present development is not sustainable, that is, not future-compliant, was transformed by political lobbyists of the industrial countries into the realization that the development of the underdeveloped countries could not be carried out according to the model of the industrialized countries. This results in a glaring contradiction between the proclaimed universalism of Western values and the claimed impossibility of the generalization of Western lifestyles. In political practice, this corresponds with the particularism of the leading industrial countries, which, through institutions like the World Bank or the International Monetary Fund, dictate the terms of trade of the world market. Answering the question of whether India, after independence, aimed for the same living standard as Great Britain, Mahatma Gandhi replied: "It took Britain half the resources of this planet to achieve its prosperity. How many planets will a country like India require?"[39] What Gandhi did not anticipate was the internal momentum of globalization, which today offers India the perspective to become a "global player" like its neighbor China.

This leads us to questions and interesting oppositions that, until today, characterize the relation between industrial and threshold countries and block an effective implementation of economic knowledge. Today, just as was the case in the 1970s, it still seems that for many representatives of the developed countries, the ecology discourse is a means of dictating the development of the underdeveloped countries in accordance with the interests of the leading industrial countries. American economic historian Robert Heilbroner, in reference to the fact that the main causes of the global food crisis were not physical limits to production but social conditions of distribution, expressed a fundamental critique of the pathos of universality:

> When men can generally acquiesce in, even relish, the destruction of their living contemporaries, when they can regard with indifference or irritation the fate of those who live in slums, rot in prison, or starve in lands that have meaning only insofar as they are vacation resorts, why should they be expected to take the painful actions needed to prevent the destruction of future generations, whose faces they will never live to see?[40]

The contradictions cited by Heilbroner have elsewhere been identified through the deconstruction of the images of a unified world community. In regards to the image of "Spaceship Earth," it has been noted that space travel is the most advanced product of that very same technical subjection of nature that is confronted with its insufficient sustainability by the ecology discourse. The rocket, with its vertical take-off and initially linear trajectory, also symbolizes the process of the decoupling of globalization from its material preconditions. A permanent reference point of the critics concerns the contradiction between the enormous costs of the space programs and the small sums that are being spent to aid development or for ecological concerns. Another potential critique reminds us of the image's origin as a by-product of the bitter interstellar arms race through the expansion of the so-called Cold War into space. The Cold War as necessary prerequisite for the ecological icon of the blue planet is hardly a suitable representation for the unity of humankind, characterized as it is by mutual threat and bloc confrontation. A final objection refers to the strict hierarchy observed on board actual spaceships, which contradicts the claimed or intended equality of the earth's inhabitants. These objections led to the development of the lifeboat as a more realistic counter-model, one that embraces an agonistic logic of struggle and thus reflects the real balance of power and the economic conflicts of interests.[41]

It is not necessary to mention that comparable points of criticism can be made against the other world concepts and global metaphors. But to finish, let me briefly call to mind some conceptual interventions that point to an unsettled critical heritage of the ecology discourse. One of these elements is the construct of the "over-developed nations," which appears as an alternative to the normative opposite pair "developed vs. underdeveloped" and sets both of them into a new relation, for now the developed country no longer appears as the standard but as the main problem for further development. This new concept, inspired by the concept of the "affluent society" introduced by Kenneth Galbraith in 1958,[42] implies that the main responsibility for ecological change lies with the industrial nations. A second intervention is the demand for alternative concepts to the gross national product (GNP), which is accused of serving as a fetishized scale for societal wealth in the context of globalization. While the GNP is based on a purely quantitative concept of growth, indices have been suggested that are instead orientated toward qualitative factors such as literacy rates, health condition, or the life satisfaction of a particular populace.

Falko Schmieder is a researcher on the project "Theory and Concept of an Interdisciplinary Conceptual History" at the Zentrum für Literatur- und Kulturforschung Berlin. His publications include *Überleben: Historische und aktuelle Konstellationen* (ed., Fink, 2011); *In Gegenwart des Fetischs: Dingkonjunktur und Fetischbegriff in der Diskussion* (ed. with Christine Blaettler, Turia+Kant, 2014); *Freud und Adorno: Zur Urgeschichte der Moderne* (ed. with Christine Kirchhoff, Kadmos, 2015); and *Begriffsgeschichte und historische Semantik: Ein kritisches Kompendium* (with Ernst Müller, Suhrkamp, 2016).

NOTES

1. For further discussions of ecology, see in particular the chapter by Desmond McNeill in this volume.
2. See Frederick Buell, *From Apocalypse to Way of Life: Environmental Crisis in the American Century* (New York, 2004).
3. See Ulrich Grober, *Die Entdeckung der Nachhaltigkeit: Kulturgeschichte eines Begriffs* (Munich, 2010), 111–21.
4. For further discussions of capitalism, see in particular the chapter by Desmond McNeill in this volume.
5. See Björn-Ola Linnér, *The Return of Malthus: Environmentalism and Post-War Population-Resource Crisis* (Isle of Harris, 2003), xii.
6. Rachel Carson, *Silent Spring* (Boston, MA, 1962), 170.
7. Ernst Haeckel, *Natürliche Schöpfungsgeschichte* (Berlin, 1879).
8. See Herman Kahn, *On Thermonuclear War* (Princeton, NJ, 1960); Bertrand Russell, *Common Sense and Nuclear Warfare* (London, 1959); Bertrand Russell, *Has Man a Future?* (London, 1961).
9. Arthur Koestler, *The Ghost in the Machine* (London, 1967), 322.
10. For some aspects of the history of the concept, see Pierre Desrochers and Christine Hoffbauer, "The Post War Intellectual Roots of the Population Bomb: Fairfield Osborn's 'Our Plundered Planet' and William Vogt, 'Road to Survival' in Retrospect", *Electronic Journal of Sustainable Development* 1, no. 3 (2009): 37–61.
11. Barry Commoner, *Science and Survival* (New York, [1963] 1966), 146.
12. See Barry Commoner, *The Closing Circle: Nature, Man, and Technology* (New York, 1980), 200.
13. See for instance Kenneth W. Mann, *Deadline for Survival: A Survey of Moral Issues in Science and Medicine* (New York, 1970), viii.
14. Mihajlo Mesarovic and Eduard Pestel, *Mankind at the Turning Point* (New York, 1974).
15. Warren A. Johnson and John Hardesty, *Economic Growth vs. the Environment* (Belmont, CA, 1971), 200.
16. Commoner, *Science and Survival*, 146.
17. See U Thant, quoted in Richard Jolly et al., eds., *UN Contributions to Development Thinking and Practice* (Bloomington, 2004), 125.
18. See Ulrich Beck, *Risk Society: Towards a New Modernity* (London, 1992).
19. See Fairfield Osborn, *Our Plundered Planet* (Boston, MA, 1948), 32.
20. See Robert L. Heilbroner, "Growth and Survival," *Foreign Affairs: An American Quarterly Review* 51, nos. 1–4 (October 1972–July 1973): 141.
21. See Erik Paredis et al., *The Concept of Ecological Debt: Its Meaning and Applicability in International Policy* (Ghent, 2008).
22. See Leslie Roos, ed., *The Politics of Ecosuicide* (New York, 1971).
23. See William Vogt, *Road to Survival* (London, 1949), 44, 59.
24. Donald Worster, *Nature's Economy: The Roots of Ecology* (San Francisco, 1979), 339.

25. Mathis Wackernagel et al., "Tracking the Ecological Overshoot of the Human Economy," *Proceedings of the Academy of Science* 99, no. 14 (2002): 9266–71.
26. See Donella Meadows, Jørgen Randers, and Dennis Meadows, *Limits to Growth: The 30-Year Update* (White River Junction, VT, 2004), xiv.
27. See Gladwin Hill, "A Not So Silent Spring," in *The Crisis of Survival*, ed. the Editors of *The Progressive* (Madison, WI, 1970), 221.
28. On this concept, see Gerhard Hirschfeld, *The People: Growth and Survival* (Chicago, 1973).
29. Peter Blaze Corcoran and A. James Wohlpart, eds, *A Voice for Earth: American Writers Respond to the Earth Charter* (Athens, 2008).
30. Robert F. Harrington, *To Heal the Earth: The Case for an Earth Ethic* (Surrey, BC, 1990).
31. Jack Randall, *The Shepherds of Earth* (Baltimore, MD, 2006), 33.
32. See Kenneth Boulding, "The Economics of the Coming Spaceship Earth," in *Environmental Quality in a Growing Economy*, ed. Henry Jarrett (Baltimore, MD, 1966), 3–14; R. Buckminster Fuller, *Operating Manual for Spaceship Earth* (Carbondale, 1969).
33. Marshall McLuhan, *The Gutenberg Galaxy: The Making of Typographic Man* (Toronto, 1962).
34. Jeremy Rifkin's thesis of a worldwide culture of empathy continues this expectation in the present but also shows the limits of this attempt; see Jeremy Rifkin, *The Empathic Civilization: The Race to Global Consciousness in a World in Crisis* (New York, 2009).
35. See Ernst Schumacher, *Small Is Beautiful: A Study of Economics As If People Mattered* (London, 1993).
36. See National Staff of the Environmental Action, ed., *Earth Day—The Beginning: A Guide for Survival* (New York, 1970).
37. The report can be found online at http://www.un-documents.net/our-common-future.pdf (accessed 18 February 2018).
38. Alfred Sauvy, "Trois mondes, une planète," *L'Observateur*, no. 118 (14 August 1952), 14.
39. Mahatma Gandhi, quoted in Shridath Ramphal, *Our Country, the Planet: Forging a Partnership for Survival* (Washington, DC, 1992), 195.
40. Robert L. Heilbroner, *An Inquiry into the Human Prospect* (New York, 1974), 143.
41. See Garrett Hardin, "Living on a Lifeboat," *BioScience* 24, no. 10 (October 1974): 561–68.
42. John Kenneth Galbraith, *The Affluent Society* (Boston, MA, 1958).

BIBLIOGRAPHY

Beck, Ulrich. *Risk Society: Towards a New Modernity*. London: Sage, 1992.
Boulding, Kenneth. "The Economics of the Coming Spaceship Earth." In *Environmental Quality in a Growing Economy*, edited by Henry Jarrett, 3–14. Baltimore, MD: Johns Hopkins University Press, 1966.

Brecht, Bertolt. "Radiotheorie." In *Schriften zur Literatur und Kunst*, vol. 1, edited by Werner Hecht, 127–147. Berlin: Aufbau-Verlag, 1966.
Buell, Frederick. *From Apocalypse to Way of Life: Environmental Crisis in the American Century*. New York: Routledge, 2004.
Carson, Rachel. *Silent Spring*. Boston, MA: Houghton Mifflin, 1962.
Commoner, Barry. *The Closing Circle: Nature, Man, and Technology*. New York: Bantam, 1980.
———. *Science and Survival*. New York: Viking, [1963] 1966.
Corcoran, Peter Blaze, and A. James Wohlpart, eds. *A Voice for Earth: American Writers Respond to the Earth Charter*. Athens: University of Georgia Press, 2008.
Desrochers, Pierre, and Christine Hoffbauer. "The Post War Intellectual Roots of the Population Bomb: Fairfield Osborn's 'Our Plundered Planet.'" *Electronic Journal of Sustainable Development* 1, no. 3 (2009): 37-61.
Fuller, R. Buckminster. *Operating Manual for Spaceship Earth*. Carbondale: Southern Illinois University Press, 1969.
Galbraith, John Kenneth. *The Affluent Society*. Boston, MA: Houghton Mifflin, 1958.
Grober, Ulrich. *Die Entdeckung der Nachhaltigkeit: Kulturgeschichte eines Begriffs*. Munich: Antje Kunstmann, 2010.
Haeckel, Ernst. *Natürliche Schöpfungsgeschichte*. Berlin: Georg Reimer, 1879.
Hardin, Garrett. "Living on a Lifeboat." *BioScience* 24, no. 10 (October 1974): 561–68.
Harrington, Robert F. *To Heal the Earth: The Case for an Earth Ethic*. Surrey, BC: Hancock House, 1990.
Heilbroner, Robert L. "Growth and Survival." *Foreign Affairs: An American Quarterly Review* 51, nos. 1–4 (October 1972–July 1973): 139-153
———. *An Inquiry into the Human Prospect*. New York: W. W. Norton, 1974.
Hill, Gladwin. "A Not So Silent Spring." In *The Crisis of Survival*, edited by the Editors of *The Progressive*, 9–11. Madison, WI: Scott, Foresman, 1970.
Hirschfeld, Gerhard. *The People: Growth and Survival*. Chicago: Aldine, 1973.
Johnson, Warren A., and John Hardesty. *Economic Growth vs. the Environment*. Belmont, CA: Wadsworth, 1971.
Jolly, Richard, Louis Emmerij, Dharam Ghai, and Frédéric Lapeyre, eds. *UN Contributions to Development Thinking and Practice*. Bloomington: Indiana University Press, 2004.
Kahn, Herman. *On Thermonuclear War*. Princeton, NJ: Princeton University Press, 1960.
Koestler, Arthur. *The Ghost in the Machine*. London: Hutchinson, 1967.
Linnér, Björn-Ola. *The Return of Malthus: Environmentalism and Post-War Population-Resource Crisis*. Isle of Harris: White Horse Press, 2003.
Mann, Kenneth W. *Deadline for Survival: A Survey of Moral Issues in Science and Medicine*. New York: Seabury, 1970.
McLuhan, Marshall. *The Gutenberg Galaxy: The Making of Typographic Man*. Toronto: University of Toronto Press, 1962.
Meadows, Donella, Jørgen Randers, and Dennis Meadows. *Limits to Growth: The 30-Year Update*. White River Junction, VT: Chelsea Green, 2004.
Mesarovic, Mihajlo, and Eduard Pestel. *Mankind at the Turning Point*. New York: E. P. Dutton, 1974.

National Staff of the Environmental Action, ed. *Earth Day—The Beginning: A Guide for Survival*. New York: Bantam, 1970.
Osborn, Fairfield. *Our Plundered Planet*. Boston, MA: Little, Brown, 1948.
Paredis, Erik, Gert Goeminne, Wouter Vanhove, Frank Maes, and Jesse Lambrecht. *The Concept of Ecological Debt: Its Meaning and Applicability in International Policy*. Ghent: Academia, 2008.
Ramphal, Shridath. *Our Country, the Planet: Forging a Partnership for Survival*. Washington, DC: Island, 1992.
Randall, Jack. *The Shepherds of Earth*. Baltimore, MD: Publish America, 2006.
Rifkin, Jeremy. *The Empathic Civilization: The Race to Global Consciousness in a World in Crisis*. New York: J. P. Tarcher, 2009.
Roos, Leslie, ed. *The Politics of Ecosuicide*. New York: Holt, Rinehart, and Winston, 1971.
Russell, Bertrand. *Common Sense and Nuclear Warfare*. London: Allen & Unwin, 1959.
———. *Has Man a Future?* London: Penguin, 1961.
Sauvy, Alfred. "Trois mondes, une planète," *L'Observateur*, no. 118 (14 August 1952): 14.
Schumacher, Ernst. *Small Is Beautiful: A Study of Economics As If People Mattered*. London: Blond&Briggs, 1993.
Vogt, William. *Road to Survival*. London: Victor Gollancz, 1949.
———. "'Road to Survival' in Retrospect." *Electronic Journal of Sustainable Development* 1, no. 3 (2009): 37–61.
Wackernagel, Mathis, Niels B. Schulz, Diana Deumling, et al. "Tracking the Ecological Overshoot of the Human Economy." *Proceedings of the Academy of Science* 99, no. 14 (2002): 9266–71.
Ward, Barbara, and René Dubos. *Only One Earth: The Care and Maintenance of a Small Planet*. London: André Deutsch, 1972.
Worster, Donald. *Nature's Economy: The Roots of Ecology*. San Francisco, CA: Sierra Club, 1977.

Part II

ORDERING THE WORLD

▸• 7 •◂

The Emergence of International Law and the Opening of World Order

Hugo Grotius Reconsidered

Chenxi Tang

The rise of the sovereign state in early modern Europe, together with the discovery of the New World and the division of the Western Church, shattered the traditional cosmos and the medieval *respublica christiana*, making it necessary to reconceive world order. In the decades around 1600, jurists trained in various traditions—humanistic, scholastic, or otherwise—tried to come up with a legal code for the world of sovereign states. The result of their endeavors was the founding of international law, which on the conceptual level took the form of a redefinition of *ius gentium*, replacing its traditional meaning of "law of all peoples" in Roman jurisprudence with a new meaning of "law between states."[1] A key figure in the founding of international law was Hugo Grotius. In *De iure belli ac pacis* (1625), Grotius states that "by mutual consent it has become possible that certain laws should originate as between all states, or a great many states; and it is apparent that the laws thus originating had in view the advantage, not of particular states, but of the great society of states. And this is what is called the law of nations [i.e., international law], whenever we distinguish that term from the law of nature."[2] International law, particularly in its Grotian formulation, makes it possible to conceive of world order as international legal order. This chapter examines this new conception of world order, focusing on a hitherto rarely studied dimension of it: narration. There are two narratives underlying Grotius's international law: a narrative of the emergence of property from common ownership, and a narrative of the emergence of the state through the collective agreement of individuals. According to these narratives, the world has departed from its primeval condition, in which humankind, without civil authority, shared the bounty of nature in common. It has been moving toward a condition shaped by property rights and the state without, however, ever being able to reach an end. The world is caught in an endless transition. The new world order as conceived by Grotius is new not only in the sense that it is different from previous conceptions of order, but above all in the sense that it is an order that ceaselessly renews itself. There may be no better term with which to describe the picture he paints of the world than the worn-out "modern condition."

The Rise of International Law

Up to the turn of the sixteenth century, world order had been guaranteed by the universal, immutable laws of nature. It had been a matter of natural order. Inspired by Stoic ideas, Cicero understood the world as a *civitas communis deorum atque hominum*, that is, a well-ordered community abiding by unchanging laws that issue from the divine yet are recognized by humans, because humans are endowed with the divine faculty of reason.[3] These laws animating the world as a whole are the laws of nature: according to Cicero, "law in the proper sense is right reason in harmony with nature. It is spread through the whole human community, unchanging and eternal, calling people to their duty by its commands and deterring them from wrong-doing by its prohibitions."[4] In the meantime, the Roman jurist Ulpian spoke of *ius naturale* as "that which nature has taught to all animals."[5] The Latin Middle Ages amalgamated the Christian divine law with the natural law as conceived by Roman philosophers and jurists.[6] Thomas Aquinas consummated the ancient tradition of natural law, not only by weaving together a whole from the various strands of this tradition—pagan and Christian, philosophical, theological, and juridical—but also by setting off, in his orderly, scholastic manner, natural law against other kinds of law. In *Summa Theologica*, he defines law as the rational ordering of things. The rational pattern of all the things in the universe, laid down by God, is the eternal law. Because the rational creature is part of the order of the universe, there must be a portion of the eternal law that governs its conduct and determines its end. The participation of the rational creature in the eternal law is called natural law, establishing the rational order of earthly life. It comes in a variety of commands and prohibitions, which are supposed to be in force in all human societies regardless of faith (because it is not the divine law) and despite local particularities (because it is not human law), which cannot be changed and are ingrained in the hearts of men. The order ordained by the law of nature thus conceived epitomizes the idea of *ordo* at the heart of medieval thought. Thomas spoke of a twofold order: "the one, whereby a created thing is directed to another, as the parts to the whole, accident to substance, and all things whatsoever to their end; the other, whereby all created things are ordered to God."[7] As well as designating the ordered relation of creatures with one another, the natural law instantiates the ordered relation to God, for it is grounded in the eternal law. The order of the human world is predicated upon divine order.

In the sixteenth century, the ancient tradition of natural law began to decline, as attested to by the reinvigorated Thomist movement—the so-called later scholasticism. Confronted with the juridical issues raised by the conquest of the New World, Spanish theologians Francisco de Vitoria and Domingo de Soto shifted the attention of the discourse of natural law from objective order to the subject, thereby reconceiving world order as constituted by the negotiation of subjective claims. In the context of the Counter-Reformation, Jesuit thinkers such as Luis de Molina and Francisco Suárez advocated the primacy of free will, going a step further in thinking of world order, both theologically and juridically, in subjective and voluntarist terms. The notion of the objective order of nature gave way to a notion of man-made and hence volatile world order. The transformation of natural law reached a turning point in Grotius, as he combined the emphasis of later scholastic jurisprudence on subjective natural rights with tenets of reason of state. The discourse of reason of state, which took shape in the sixteenth century, unmoored the state from all ethical or religious norms and regarded expediency and the maximization of interest as the overarching principles of the state. Grotius was a vociferous proponent of reason of state.[8] Unlike other thinkers of reason of state, however, he sought to bring reason of state to bear on natural law. In the first step, he applied the tenets of reason of state to the individual and thus identified self-preservation and self-interest as the driving forces of human actions. He then defined, in the jurisprudential language of subjective rights, the preservation of life and property as the basic rights given to each human being by nature. In the third step, he translated right into law, turning self-preservation and self-interest—"the first principle of the whole natural order"—into the "fundamental law" of nature, the foundation of "justice and equity."[9] Once the fundamental law of nature is established, Grotius argued, all the laws of nature can be deduced by reason without recourse to transcendent divine agencies. This natural law theory broke with the ancient tradition and so was destined to acquire the epithet "modern" in later times.[10]

Grotius's new conception of natural law includes a theory of the state, which in turn enables the rise of international law. Although an individual has by nature certain rights and must observe the laws of nature, he cannot prevent others from infringing on his rights and violating the general laws of nature. As a consequence, individuals institute, by a collective agreement, an authority for the purpose of enforcing their natural rights. This authority is the state. Once instituted, states relate to each other in the same way as individuals do in the natural order, so that they need to abide by the laws of nature as well. Apart from whatever voluntary agreements states might enter with one another, the law governing the relationship between states is no different from natural law. Grotius calls this law between states *ius gentium*, but it is clear that he completely restructures the typology of laws laid down by Roman jurisprudence. *Ius gentium* is no longer a branch of law next to natural law, but coincides by and large with natural law, even though it might contain additional voluntary elements. At the same time, with states as its subjects, *ius gentium* is no longer private law, but becomes public law. Its grounding in natural law lends it universal validity, so that the international legal order that it aims to establish stands now for world order.

Narratives of Property

Grotius's new model of world order as international legal order is developed not merely by reinventing natural law, but also by means of narration. Two narratives are crucial to it: that of the emergence of property from common ownership, and that of the emergence of the state through the collective agreement of individuals.

Property is the crux of Grotius's natural and international law, for he deems the right to acquire, retain, and defend property to be a fundamental principle of the natural order, applicable to individuals and states alike. This conception of property is grounded in a narrative. At the beginning of the world, human beings shared everything in common: "soon after the creation of the world, and a second time after the Flood, God conferred upon the human race a general right over things of a lower nature.... In consequence, each man could at once take whatever he wished for his own needs, and could consume whatever was capable of being consumed." The enjoyment of this universal right was constrained only by one condition: "whatever each had thus taken for his own needs another could not take from him except by an unjust act." Such a primitive state of common ownership was characterized by the "great simplicity" of life and the "mutual affection" among men. It could still be seen, according to Grotius, in people living in "extreme simplicity," as in "certain tribes in America," and in communities based on affection as exemplified by "a goodly number who live an ascetic life."[11] In the course of time, however, people became less and less satisfied with the simple and innocent life, Grotius argues, as they gained more knowledge and pursued various kinds of arts. The primitive common ownership seemed less and less feasible, because men "were not content to feed on the spontaneous products of the earth, to dwell in caves, to have the body either naked or clothed with the bark of trees or skins of wild animals, but chose a refined mode of life; this gave rise to industry, which some applied to one thing, others to another." Meanwhile, mutual affection gave way to rivalry and ambition. The increasing "lack of justice and kindness" militated against common ownership as well. As a result of these developments, things became subject to private ownership. This happened by means of "a kind of agreement, either expressed, as by division, or implied, as by occupation."[12]

Grotius's narrative of the emergence of property rights from common ownership draws on a key doctrine of the ancient tradition of natural law—the doctrine that at the beginning of the world all things belonged to men in common. In *De officiis* (44 BC), Cicero postulates that reason and speech unite all men into a natural community. In the fellowship of the whole human race,

> the common ownership of all things which nature has brought forth for men's joint use must be preserved, in the sense that private possessions as designated by statutes and by civil law are to be retained as the laws themselves have ordained, while the rest is to be regarded, in the words of the Greek proverb, as "all things shared by friends." ... Arising out of this are the general maxims "Do not prevent access to running water," "Let all who want it take the fire from your fire," "Give honest advice to one in doubt."[13]

This doctrine persisted throughout the ancient tradition of natural law, as *Decretum Gratiani* and Thomas Aquinas's *Summa Theologica* attest to.[14]

Grotius returns to the traditional natural-law doctrine of common ownership, but only in order to draw an opposite conclusion. Whereas the ancient tradition deems common ownership to lie in the nature of things and private property to be imposed by positive laws, Grotius attempts to prove that private property is a matter of natural law as well. In chapter 12 of *De Indis* (1604), later published separately as the controversial *Mare Liberum* (1609), Grotius first concurs with the ancients that in distant days all things were at the disposal of mankind at large, and then continues: "it is evident, however, that the present-day concept of distinctions in ownership was the result, not of any sudden transition, but of a gradual process whose initial steps were taken under the guidance of nature herself." Many things, he points out, are consumed by use, either in the sense that they admit of no further use after being consumed by one person or in the sense that they are less fit for additional service. Such consumption represents the first step toward private ownership. Later this basic concept is extended "by a logical process" to other movable as well as immovable things, either because the use of such things is indirectly bound up with consumption, or because these things are not sufficient for indiscriminate use by all.[15] The taking possession of ownerless things or things common to all is called occupation in Roman law. In *De iure belli ac pacis*, Grotius describes the process by which things become subject to private ownership as a voluntary act of agreement, which can take the form of either division or occupation. Grotius stresses that this process, rooted as it is in a physical act of attachment, is a natural one. The forces that propel it—the human desire to lead "a more refined mode of life" as well as the ensuing erosion of "justice and kindness"—arise from the course of nature. Consequently, the law established on this matter "was patterned after nature's plan" as well.[16] It is a dictate of the law of nature that everyone should be allowed to acquire and retain property, and that no one may seize possession of that which has already been taken into the possession of another. Whoever takes away another person's property must return it or face punishment. The natural order is a lawful order of property relations.

At first glance, Grotius's narrative of the transition from common ownership to private property looks like the narratives of world ages that had existed since the very beginning of European literature. In *Works and Days* (eighth century BC), the Greek poet Hesiod tells of the first race of men in the Golden Age, when there was no toil, no misery, no old age, and no property. But this idyllic state declined, going through the Silver and Bronze Ages until it reaches the Iron Age in the present. Amid the general toil and misery, the present Iron Age needs to "hearken to Right" above anything else.[17] The right of property thus comes into being. Ovid's retelling of the Hesiodic narrative in *Metamorphoses* (8 AD) makes this explicit. Whereas in the Golden Age men shared the bounty of nature in common, the Iron Age witnessed the birth of property: "And on the ground, common till then and free / As air and sunlight, far across the fields / By careful survey boundaries were marked."[18]

Without making metaphoric use of the hierarchy of metals, Grotius seems to tell the same story. However, the Grotian narrative relates the beginning of time to the present time in such a way as to create a temporal structure entirely different from that of the Hesiodic and Ovidian narratives. The transition from the Golden Age to the Iron Age is a steady decline, with the Silver and Bronze Ages being traversed in between. The Grotian narrative gets rid of all the intermediate stages of time, so that only the beginning and the present remain. With only two points left on its trajectory, time loses its direction. Grotius makes no attempt to envision any third point—such as a possible future condition—from which to determine the direction of time. In his narrative, time seems instead to circle fitfully back and forth between a putative beginning and the present.

According to the Grotian narrative, common ownership at the beginning of time continues into the present in vestigial forms. First, certain things in the world cannot become subject to private ownership. The prime example of this is the ocean, which resists occupation and possession, for it is so inexhaustible as to suffice for any possible use by all peoples for drawing water, fishing, and sailing; it also resists division, as no boundaries can be drawn on it. This view, formulated initially in *De Indis* to justify the Dutch forays into Asia and to combat the Portuguese monopoly of the Asian trade, developed later into the famous "free sea" doctrine. Second, certain things that are capable of being occupied or in fact have been occupied nonetheless suffice for general use by other persons without detriment to the owner. This fact gives rise to the right of innocent use, for example the use of running water and passage over land and river. Grotius extrapolates therefore the right of free travel and migration, including the right of refugees to reside permanently in another country.[19] As vestigial forms of the common, things not capable of being owned, as well as things capable of being owned but susceptible to innocent use, perform an important function for private ownership. They figure as the medium through which men can access the still unoccupied things—the so-called *res nullius*—in remote areas, occupying them, dividing them, and turning them into private property, and through which man can go to other men, trading their property with one another. Colonial settlers and traders from Europe need the free sea to sail to other corners of the world, and they need to claim the right of free travel in doing so. Without such a medium, men would be tethered to their necessarily limited possessions, leaving a great share of the vast store of nature forever unoccupied, forgoing the enjoyment of novel properties, thereby mired in a perpetual stasis. For this reason, the said vestigial forms of the common actually represent the enabling conditions for private property.

There is yet another vestigial form of the common, which has a quite different, indeed an opposite effect on private property according to Grotius. It is the reversion to common ownership under extraordinary circumstances: "in direst need the primitive right of user revives, as if community of ownership had remained, since in respect to all human laws—the law of ownership included—supreme necessity seems to have been excepted."[20] Necessity suspends the right of property and resuscitates common ownership. The concept of necessity is an integral part of the discourse of reason of state. Reason of state is wont to ride roughshod over law and morality in the name of necessity. By invoking necessity, then, Grotius leaves the right of property in the international arena at the mercy of reason of state. Common ownership at the beginning of time seems to be lodged at the heart of private property, threatening to upend it in case of urgent need.

Taken together, the vestigial forms of the common indicate that the beginning of time is by no means irretrievably lost but persists in the present, either enabling private property or suspending it. Conversely, the present time existed already in an embryonic form in the beginning. Grotius agrees with Hesiod, Ovid, as well as ancient natural law theorists that the bounty of nature was originally given to men in common, but he contends that men could not enjoy all that nature has to offer unless they trade readily available products: "owing to the fact that the distances separating different regions prevented men from using many of the goods desirable for human life ... passage to and fro was found to be a necessity."[21] Geographical proximity to things created a primordial form of property. One man gave products in his own region to another man in the expectation that the other would give him products from his own region. Exchange, then, was the precondition for common ownership. By the same token, commerce in the age of private property enables men to enjoy a share in many, if not all, things, so that "one person's lack might be remedied by means of another person's surplus."[22] For this reason, Grotius passionately defends free trade as a practice in conformity with and indeed dictated by nature. Through free trade, private ownership paradoxically carries out the plan of nature to give all things to all men, always approximating, if never entirely restoring, the common.

The common continues to be in force in the present time of private property, while private property strives, by means of free trade, toward the common at the beginning of time. In Grotius's narrative, the transition from common to private ownership has not yet been, and can never be, completed. As far as men's relationship to things is concerned, the world is still and will always be in transition, beginning anew all the time. To be sure, private ownership has emerged. But it is haunted by the specter of common ownership that either serves as the enabling condition for acquiring new properties or suspends property rights in case of necessity, so that it can be said to be still in the making. At the same time, it pursues no end beyond itself, which would complete its making. By insisting on the capacity of commerce for making all things accessible to all people, Grotius seems to hold up the common as the end of private ownership, but the restoration of a golden age or abolition of private property in the future is certainly out of the question. The unfinished quality of private ownership means that property rights is not a matter settled once and for all, but one constantly subject to challenge and contestation. It is therefore no accident that Grotius's discussion of property rights is bound up with his discussion of the right to war. War is a means of defending, among other things, one's right to property in case it is challenged and contested. Settlement brought about by peace is always a temporary condition followed by new conflicts and hence new wars.

As a fundamental principle of the natural order, property rights apply to both the individual and the state. If the subject of rights is the state, the natural order takes the form of international order. In his discussions of natural law, Grotius postulates a primeval condition in which individuals have to defend their natural rights to life, limb, and property on their own. With a view to "self-protection through mutual aid" and to "equal acquisition of the necessities of life," they established the civil state "by a general agreement."[23] Such an account of the institution of the state is at once a contractualist theory and a narrative. As a narrative, it places the establishment of the state in time. At the beginning of the world, "God, who created all things in the image of His own perfection, created not a state but two human beings."[24] In the course of time, the number of mankind increased, so that the natural power was vested in the heads of households. Later on, individuals brought the state into being through a collective agreement in order to protect their rights and secure justice. Grotius's narrative of the emergence of the state turns out to have the same temporal structure as his narrative of the emergence of property.

First of all, just as certain things are left in common ownership after the establishment of private property, natural rights of the individual, including the right to execute his own natural rights, may continue to be in force after the establishment of the state. In *De Indis*, Grotius argues that "whatever there was of law at the world's beginning, prior to the establishment of states, must necessarily have continued to exist afterward among those human beings who did not set up courts for themselves, and for whom … 'might is the measure of right.'"[25] He proceeds to suggest that this is still the case among some peoples of the present day. In *De iure belli ac pacis*, he concedes that "the license which was prevalent before the establishment of courts has been greatly restricted," but he does so in order to highlight the fact that "there are circumstances under which such license even now holds good, that is, undoubtedly, where judicial procedure ceases to be available."[26] Grotius names two possibilities: the temporary suspension and the continuous unavailability of judicial procedure. Judicial procedure is suspended temporarily "when one cannot wait to refer a matter to a judge without certain danger or loss." This is the case of emergency, similar to the revival of common ownership in direst need. Judicial procedure can be continuously unavailable either in law or in fact: "in law, if one finds himself in places without inhabitants, as on the sea, in a wilderness, or on vacant islands, or in any other places where there is no state; in fact, if those who are subject to jurisdiction do not heed the judge, or if the judge has openly refused to take cognizance."[27] There are places outside of any jurisdiction just as there are things not subject to any private ownership. Freedom from jurisdiction is similar, though not identical, to freedom from private ownership. The sea is free in both senses. The de facto dissolution of existing jurisdiction happens in times of civil unrest, rebellion, or simply general chaos.

If natural rights of the individual persist in vestigial forms after the establishment of the civil state, the superior authority of the state may, conversely, be resisted and even actively combated by its subjects in certain circumstances. "As a general rule," Grotius stresses, "rebellion is not permitted."[28] This rule, however, tacitly leaves open the possibility of resistance in cases where the state authority fails to perform its agreed-upon function of maintaining public tranquility. Indeed, Grotius lists a wide range of circumstances in which the right of resistance may be conceded. Apart from extreme necessity, they involve mostly violation of the collective agreement underlying the state. One may resist a king who alienates the kingdom or otherwise turns against the whole people. One may also resist a king who transgresses the conditions of his exercise of power in some way, for instance if he violates a clause inserted in the grant of power, or if he seeks to arrogate a part of sovereign power that does not belong to him. Above all, one may resist a usurper of sovereign power. In all these cases, active resistance returns the state to the moment of its founding.

In Grotius's narrative, mankind has departed from its primeval natural condition and established the civil state without being able to leave behind entirely the natural condition, while the civil state already established runs the risk of dissolving through the active resistance of its subjects. Just like the transition from common ownership to private property, the transition from the natural condition to the civil state has not yet been completed, and can never be so. Both the narrative of the emergence of property and that of the emergence of the civil state portray the human world as caught up in an eternal in-between condition without offering any prospect of an end. The Grotian narratives spell the end of the end. The world depicted by them is devoid of any transcendent purpose. Yet it is relentlessly dynamic in its radical immanence, as neither private property nor the state is a stable condition, but are constantly in the making, constantly emerging.

The emergence of international law as the law between states around 1600 led to a new conception of world order as international order, replacing the traditional conception of world order as articulated by the ancient natural law theory. The very notion of order had changed. Whereas order was considered immutable and eternal in the traditional conception, the new model saw order as fundamentally open. The state as the subject of international order is no fixed entity, but something unfinished and still emerging, and the right to property—the crux of the relation between states no less than that between individuals—is likewise unfinished and still emerging. International order is thus doubly volatile, with the instability of the state and the uncertainty of property rights magnifying and aggravating each other. In fact, one cannot help wondering whether it is possible at all to speak of order without postulating an end. Thomas Aquinas, as mentioned above, speaks of a twofold order: the order of creatures in relation to one another, and the order of creatures toward God. It is only through their ordered relation to a divine end that creatures can have an ordered relation to one another. Without an end, the relations of things or those of persons to one another could never stabilize into an order. There would be at most an endless process of ordering. Any equilibrium—or peace—is doomed to be temporary, to be succeeded by new strife. One can only hope that at least strife follows certain rules. Grotius's *De iure belli ac pacis* culminates in formulating these rules—the law of war or *ius in bello*. But what authority could enforce these rules at all? This question, unanswerable within the theoretical framework designed by Grotius, or for that matter by any other jurist of the time, points to the intrinsic paradox of international law, which was not resolved until the establishment of international institutions in the twentieth century.

Chenxi Tang is Professor of German at University of California at Berkeley. His recent research includes a two-volume project on international law and literature. The first volume, *Imagining World Order: International Law and Literature in Early Modern Europe, 1500-1800*, is scheduled to appear with Cornell University Press in fall 2018. *Imagining World Order II: International Law and Literature, 1789-1918* will follow soon.

NOTES

1. For further discussions of law, see in particular the chapters by Malcolm Langford and Lars Kirkhusmo Pharo in this volume.
2. Hugo Grotius, *De iure belli ac pacis*, trans. Francis Kelsey (Oxford, 1925), Prolegomena 17.
3. Cicero, *De legibus*, 1.23.
4. Cicero, *De re publica*, 3.33. Cf. *The Republic and The Laws*, trans. Niall Rudd (Oxford, 1998), 68.
5. *Digesta*, 1.1.1.3. Cf. Theodor Mommsen and Paul Krueger (eds.), *The Digest of Justinian*, trans. Alan Watson (Philadelphia, 1985), I.1.1.3, 4.
6. For further discussions of religion, see in particular the chapters by Nora Eggen, Oddbjørn Leirvik, Kyrre Kverndokk, Alfred Hiatt, Erling Sandmo, and Kari van Dijk in this volume.
7. Thomas Aquinas, *Summa Theologica*, trans. the Fathers of the English Dominican Province (Notre Dame, IN, 1981), Ia, q.21, a.1.
8. See Richard Tuck, *Philosophy and Government, 1572-1651* (Cambridge, 1993), 154-201.
9. Hugo Grotius, *Commentary on the Law of Prize and Booty*, ed. Marine Julia van Ittersum, trans. Gwladys Williams (Indianapolis, 2006), 21.
10. For a comparison between the ancient and the modern tradition of natural law, see Merio Scattola, "Models in History of Natural Law," *Ius Commune* 28 (2001): 91-159.
11. Grotius, *De iure belli ac pacis*, 2.2.2.1.
12. Ibid., 2.2.2.4-5.
13. Cicero, *De officiis*, 51-52. Cf. Cicero. *On Obligations*, trans. P. G. Walsh (Oxford, 2001), 19
14. *Decretum Gratiani*, D. 8, pars. 1; Aquinas, *Summa Theologica*, IIaIIae 66, a. 2.
15. Grotius, *Commentary*, 317.
16. Ibid., 318.
17. Hesiod, *Theogony and Works and Days*, trans. M. L. West (Oxford, 1988), 40-43.
18. Ovid, *Metamorphoses*, trans. A. D. Melville (Oxford, 1987), 1.137-39.

19. Grotius, *De iure belli ac pacis*, 2.2.12–17.
20. Ibid., 2.2.6.
21. Grotius, *Commentary*, 354.
22. Ibid.
23. Ibid., 36.
24. Ibid., 137.
25. Ibid., 138.
26. Grotius, *De iure belli ac pacis*, 1.3.2.1.
27. Ibid.
28. Ibid., 1.4.2.

BIBLIOGRAPHY

Aquinas, Thomas. *Summa Theologica*. Translated by the Fathers of the English Dominican Province. Notre Dame, IN: Christian Classics, 1981.

Cicero. *On Obligations*. Translated by P. G. Walsh. Oxford: Oxford University Press, 2001.

———. *The Republic and The Laws*. Translated by Niall Rudd. Oxford: Oxford University Press, 1998.

Grotius, Hugo. *Commentary on the Law of Prize and Booty*. Edited by Marine Julia van Ittersum, translated by Gwladys Williams. Indianapolis: Liberty Fund, 2006.

———. *De iure belli ac pacis*. Translated by Francis Kelsey. Oxford: Oxford University Press, 1925.

Hesiod. *Theogony and Works and Days*. Translated by M. L. West. Oxford: Oxford University Press, 1988.

Mommsen, Theodor, and Paul Krueger (eds.), *The Digest of Justinian*. Translated by Alan Watson. Philadelphia: University of Pennsylvania Press, 1985.

Ovid. *Metamorphoses*. Translated by A. D. Melville. Oxford: Oxford University Press, 1987.

Scattola, Merio. "Models in History of Natural Law." *Ius Commune* 28 (2001): 91–159.

Tuck, Richard. *Philosophy and Government, 1572–1651*. Cambridge: Cambridge University Press, 1993.

▶• 8 •◀

"Natural Capital," "Human Capital," "Social Capital"

It's All Capital Now

Desmond McNeill

Introduction

We are well accustomed to recognizing the power of capitalism in shaping the world in material terms.[1] Equally powerful is the concept of capital itself in shaping our relationship to the world. Capital—in its various manifestations—seems to encompass almost every aspect of our lives: our relation to nature, to each other, and even to ourselves. Today, we talk not only of "natural capital" but also "human capital" and "social capital"—and indeed other capitals. Such terminology encourages an economistic, technocratic, and market-oriented worldview, which is powerfully dehumanizing.

The concept of natural capital frames our thinking about the environment—as a resource to be exploited. The concept of human capital encourages us to think of improvements in health and education not so much as beneficial for human wellbeing but as productive investments. And the concept of social capital treats social relations as something measurable, which can be empirically shown to contribute to economic growth. In each case, the concept encourages a dehumanized, alienated perspective on the world, such that nature, we ourselves, and our relations with others are seen in instrumental terms—as means to an economic, materialist end.

This situation is ironic for two reasons. First, in each case the original intention in introducing the term was to widen the scope of economic thinking, but instead these phenomena have simply been incorporated into the arena of economics and the market. Second, the aim was to make these phenomena more visible, more "real," by calling them capital, but the current financial crisis has highlighted how "unreal" capital is—increasingly far removed from the material. Today's economic system has largely become disengaged from nature and from humanity, yielding huge profits to a very small group while failing to enhance the wellbeing of a large proportion of the population.

The first half of this chapter briefly examines what is meant by natural, human, and social capital as well as the implications of using these terms. The second half explores more critically what is involved in the phenomenon of naming, drawing on Marx's analysis in *Capital*. For Marx—in the first chapter of volume I of *Capital*—capital is the ultimate fetish, the final outcome of a "logico-historical" process that begins with the fetishism of the commodity. The lasting significance of Marx's work, I suggest, is his sophisticated critical analysis of capitalism, seen as a comprehensive system of shared beliefs, a mystifying worldview that serves the interests of capitalists and can best be understood by analogy with religion. The subtitle of *Capital, A Critique of Political Economy*, could equally well have been *A Critique of Economic Categories*, the title of a work by his collaborator Engels, for one of Marx's most profound insights was the power that these categories exert. Although he rejected the excesses of Hegelian idealism, Marx recognized that concepts can nevertheless have real power, just as the fetish of West Africa has real power over those who believe in it.

We may, I suggest, gain valuable insights into the situation we encounter today from Marx's critical analysis of capitalism and of the mystification, exploitation, and alienation that the system carries with it. I begin by examining the three types of capital of my title.

Natural Capital

"Natural capital" refers to the stock of natural ecosystems. It is *nature*—but seen through an economic lens.[2] The concept of natural capital was first used by E. F. Schumacher in his famous 1973 book *Small Is Beautiful: A Study of Economics As If People Mattered*. This is ironic, because he was trying to counter the dominance of an economistic, market-oriented approach; what in fact happened is that the concept was taken up by mainstream economists in the late 1980s and built into their econometric models. Today it is widely used by researchers, non-governmental organizations, national and regional governments, and international agencies, linked to the concept of environmental accounting and, more recently, payment for environmental services. Even a critic of mainstream economics, the ecological economist Robert Costanza, seems to adopt the term, despite noting its inherent weakness. He writes:

> The economies of the earth would grind to a halt without the services of ecological life support systems, so in one sense their total value to the economy is infinite. However, it is instructive to estimate the "incremental" or

"marginal" value of ecosystem services—the estimated rate of change of value with changes in ecosystem services from their current levels.[3]

The term "natural capital" is a good example of how a word can frame thought, and hence also action—a phenomenon that has been studied in terms of neo-Gramscian theory.[4] Our perception of nature is surely changed if we call it "capital." We come to regard it as an economic resource on which an economic value can be placed, and indeed *is* placed, when public decisions—regarding, say, building a road through a national park—are based on the estimated economic value of the "nature" that is lost.

Human Capital

The term "human capital" is of slightly older vintage and refers to the resources embodied in people—not so much their brute force, but their skills, education, and physical health. The term is economistic, portraying human beings as inputs into the production process. The value of a person is thus perceived in instrumental terms, related to a productive purpose.

At least since the time of Adam Smith, economists have recognized that acquired abilities and improved health affect productivity, but it was in the early 1960s that the theory of human capital became formalized, in the work of economists Jacob Mincer, Theodore Schultz, and the Nobel laureate Gary Becker.[5] Becker developed a theoretical model for deciding whether to invest in, for example, a college education. In the model, the direct costs (tuition, books, etc.) and indirect costs (forgone income while at college) are measured against the benefits (measured as the additional earnings resulting from a college education). If the benefits exceed the costs, the investment should occur. The benefits of education are here seen purely in terms of increased earnings.

The concept of human capital has been warmly embraced by national and international bureaucracies. One example is the Organisation for Economic Cooperation and Development (OECD), as described by the United Nations Educational, Scientific and Cultural Organization (UNESCO) in their background report to the World Education Forum 2000:

> Interest in the human capital theories dating from the work of Schulz, Becker and others in the sixties has been renewed: work began in the second half of the decade on human capital indicators in response to the 1996 OECD Ministerial Council request. For the purpose of this activity, human capital was defined as "The knowledge, skills, competence and other attributes embodied in individuals that are relevant to economic activities." ... Major international studies were carried out during much of the nineties [in which] the core theme might be summarised as a growing need for a workforce

> displaying highly intelligent, flexible, knowledge-based production and information processing capability, together with resourcefulness, initiative and skill in group problem solving. (UNESCO 2000).[6]

The term received an added boost thanks to work by economists on growth theory, and more specifically on so-called endogenous growth models. According to an authoritative source,

> the newer classical growth models incorporated formally Schultz's insight, and related work on accounting for growth by Hollis Chenery and colleagues at the World Bank pointed to the contribution of more skilled workers with more human capital to increased productivity and growth. The more recent endogenous growth models are even more emphatic.[7]

In the field of health, also, the concept of human capital has become very influential. It has led, *inter alia*, to the establishment of the Health as Human Capital Foundation, whose mission is "to promote the Health as Human Capital paradigm, bring market solutions to healthcare, and support organizations in aligning incentives, information, and choice." This approach, they write,

> relies heavily on economic principles that explain how and why people make choices regarding health and work .... Our goal is to produce evidence and insights that lead to market solutions that apply to both the healthcare cost and quality problems in the US, and to employers' needs to efficiently recruit and retain valued employees.[8]

In the language of human capital, education and health are thus seen not as valuable in themselves, but as instrumentally serving the overarching objective of increased economic performance—at both the national and individual levels. What is lost here is humanity, as well as the idea that education and good health may be valuable in themselves.

Social Capital

The third concept that I shall briefly discuss is social capital. While human capital refers to individual persons, social capital refers to connections between individuals—social networks and the norms of reciprocity and trustworthiness that arise from them. In that sense, social capital is closely related to what some have called "civic virtue."

Although the term had been used earlier (in a rather different sense) by the sociologist Pierre Bourdieu, this concept really "took off" in the late 1990s after it was used by the political scientist Robert Putnam in *Making Democracy Work: Civic Traditions in Modern Italy*, his 1993 comparative study of the economic fortunes of northern and southern Italy. The concept, as presented by Putnam, became swiftly and astonishingly popular among academics and the wider reading public. It was also warmly embraced by economists, with active support from the World Bank. It has in recent years been applied in a number of different fields, including the study of management. According to Portes, describing the development of the term, "the journey was fast, explaining major social outcomes by relabeling them with a novel term, and then employing the same term to formulate sweeping policy prescriptions."[9]

Elsewhere I have presented the results of a bibliometric analysis of the use of "social capital" in six different realms: academic journals, doctoral theses, non-academic journals, newspapers, World Bank publications, and UN publications.[10] From this analysis, two important points of relevance to this chapter emerge. First, the term became extremely significant when it was taken up by economists in the World Bank. Second, the concept has been largely ignored, or even resisted, by anthropologists—though this has made little difference to its appeal to policy-makers since economists are far more influential. For economists, the introduction of social capital is a broadening of the agenda, incorporating into earlier theoretical models an enhanced understanding of institutions in the wider sense. By contrast, anthropologists tend to see this rather as squeezing a phenomenon that has been much studied and is well understood into the narrow confines of an inappropriate discipline.[11]

As with the concepts of natural and human capital, however, we may ask: why do they become dominant? And how does this affect both our worldview and that of policy-makers? These terms become dominant largely because of the appeal they have to bureaucrats, locked in a world of measurement and management. To quote the World Bank:

> The Social Capital Initiative aims to contribute to both the conceptual understanding of social capital and its measurement. … The lack of conceptual clarity stands in the way of the measurement of social capital, and the variety of existing definitions makes it inherently difficult to propose a list of indicators. Instead, indicators will have to evolve as the conceptual and, *more important*, the operational definition of social capital are developed.[12]

Thus, the appeal of a concept such as social capital is that it can be "operationalized," usually implying quantification; indicators are developed for measuring "social capital" in order not only to test the relationship between this and economic performance, but also to assess the success of a program of "building" social capital.

In each of these three cases—natural capital, human capital, and social capital—the term was taken up enthusiastically by economists and bureaucrats, without effective protest from social scientists or anyone else. The potential dangers—of commodification and dehumanization—were rarely recognized.

Analysis

How is it that such categories, and more generally such a way of thinking, have become so dominant? In seeking to answer this question I draw inspiration from Marx and his analysis of commodities and the economic concepts of profit, rent, and interest. I believe that Marx's ideas are still capable of shedding light on how power is exercised—not "hard" power, directly and explicitly applied, but "soft" power, exercised in ways of which we are unaware: both those who gain and those who lose in the unequal global market economy.

The most basic category, for Marx, was the commodity itself, which is why the first chapter of *Capital* deals with what many regard as the rather obscure concept of commodity fetishism. The commodity is a strange hybrid, a material thing set in a system of social relations. It has value—not inherently, but because people believe it has value. In order to understand and communicate this point, Marx used the analogy with religion, for the power of the belief system that creates and maintains the fetish of the commodity is similar to the power of religion. As Marx puts it in the first chapter of *Capital*, volume I,

> There (with commodities) it is a definite social relation between men, that assumes, in their eyes, the fantastic form of a relation between things. In order, therefore, to find an analogy, we must have recourse to the mist-enveloped regions of the religious world. In that world the productions of the human brain appear as independent beings endowed with life, and entering into relation both with one another and the human race. So it is in the world of commodities with the products of men's hands. This I call the Fetishism which attaches itself to the products of labour, so soon as they are produced as commodities, and which is therefore inseparable from the production of commodities.[13]

Rather more accessible than his analysis of the commodity is Marx's critique of other economic concepts such as profit, rent, and interest. Marx's thesis was not simply that the profit of the capitalist is exploitative, through the extraction of surplus value, but that this exploitation is concealed by the way in which the phenomenon is portrayed. Profit seen as a return on capital does not appear to be exploitative, nor rent as the return to land. But Marx challenges such terms—as meaningless as "a yellow logarithm," as he puts it in *Theories of Surplus Value*.[14] Yet this is how profit is commonly portrayed and understood. And because such terms as rent and profit are used and unquestioned, the social relations that they reflect are concealed. Marx argued that these social relations are exploitative; this is his central criticism of capitalism.

But he also argued that capitalism leads to alienation, and it is this that I wish to emphasize in this chapter, as I shall explain.

It was in recognizing the importance of the social aspect of labor that Marx most effectively distinguished his theory of value from that of Ricardo. In his own works, he emphasized not simply the quantitative but also what he called the qualitative aspect of value. He does not, of course, ignore the material— quite the reverse. But he was keenly aware that economics is concerned with things and people set in a social context. This "social context" may be seen as a system of relations within which material things are located, and from which they cannot be torn with (conceptual) impunity. Indeed, this is an enlightening way of analyzing social phenomena generally, and commodity fetishism more specifically.

Marx's understanding of value as inherently social contrasts with that of later economists. Walras is one of the most famous of those who, at the beginning of the twentieth century, transformed political economy into neoclassical economics. Walras writes as follows:

> Thus any value in exchange, once established, partakes of the character of a natural phenomenon, natural in its origins, natural in its manifestation and natural in essence. If wheat and silver have any value at all, it is because they are scarce, that is, useful and limited in quantity—both of these conditions being natural.[15]

What is going on here may be described in very broad terms as "depoliticization." For it is not merely the social relations that are concealed, but more specifically relations of power: political relations. These are, according to Marx, exploitative social relations, based on unequal access to power, that appear to be natural—and hence go unchallenged.

Marx might thus be seen as promoting what could be called "a conspiracy theory of concept formation," arguing that this fetishism is a deliberate and self-serving mystification, which capitalists engage in, served by their tame economists—or "hired prize-fighters," as Marx described them.[16] In places, it seems that Marx is tempted by this view. For example, he quotes with approval the analogy that Luther draws with the monster Cacus in his discussion of usury: "An excellent picture, it fits the capitalist in general, who pretends that what he has taken from others and brought into his den, emanates from him, and by causing it to go backwards he gives it the semblance of having come from his den."[17] And: "To the vulgar economist who desires to represent capital as an independent source of value ... this form [i.e., interest] is of course a godsend."[18]

But in *Capital*, Marx's views about the role of the capitalist and the economist are ambivalent. He is clear that the capitalist benefits from this mystification, but he seems to suggest that the capitalist is as unaware as anyone else of the "reality" that Marx reveals with his analysis. And he does not explicitly claim that the "bourgeois economist" is aware of the situation either.

Nor am I suggesting that the mainstream economist of today is aware of the significance of so widely applying the term "capital," of the implications of extending the realm of economics and the market into every aspect of human life. But I do claim that these categories are of enormous significance: they "frame" the way that we see the world, and hence also our actions.

In his attack on Proudhon's *Philosophy of Poverty*, Marx criticizes Proudhon on the grounds that he "has not grasped that, in accordance with their productive forces, these men also produce the social relations amid which they manufacture cloth and linen. Still less has he understood that men ... also produce ideas, categories, that is to say the abstract ideal expression of these same social relations."[19] I fully agree. But Marx also criticizes Proudhon for erroneously believing that "one must change the categories and the consequences will be a change in the existing society."[20] Here I beg to differ. I believe that to change our categories does indeed change our perceptions, and hence changes existing society. Indeed, I am suggesting that Marx's own writings can be used to justify my claim.

Economists today play a powerful role in establishing the dominant categories that I describe in this chapter: of natural, human, and social capital. I am not claiming that economists are aware of the role that they play, or that there is a total lack of critical voices even within "mainstream economics." But the majority contribute to the process of depoliticization by maintaining the myth that economics is a "positive science." And the work of economists appeals to bureaucrats and politicians, because it appears to provide a rigorous, quantitative, neutral basis on which to take controversial decisions.

Does this matter? I suggest that it does, because being subject to this economistic worldview comes at a cost—to our humanity. In Marx's time, and still today in many parts of the world, the categories of rent, profit, and interest conceal exploitation. But in the rich North, I suggest, the danger of the economistic worldview is rather different: that it leads to alienation. My criticism of the terms natural capital, human capital, and social capital is not that they conceal exploitative relations, but that intrinsic values are replaced by instrumental values—with the overriding imperative being increased economic growth measured in aggregate money terms. My claim is that these categories conceal the humanity, and the sociality, of human beings.[21]

In the first of the 1844 manuscripts, *Wages of Labor*, Marx describes the various forms of alienation that result from capitalism: alienation from his product, from his productive activity, from his species-being, and from other men. Labor is clearly seen as the key to man's species-being: "It is just in his work upon the objective world, therefore, that man really proves himself to be a *species-being*."[22] Today, at least for those in the rich part of the world, production through labor—man's "work upon the objective world"—is not so crucial; consumption is perhaps equally important for modern man's species-being.[23] However, thanks to the power of an economistic worldview, also in this "world of consumption," we are alienated—from nature, from ourselves, and from others.

While some, such as Althusser, suggest that alienation is a concept of the young Marx that plays no part in his mature works, my own view is quite the opposite: the concept of alienated labor is of great importance in *Capital*.[24] It may perhaps be used in his earlier works only as a sociological concept, but in *Capital* it is integrated with the economic in the concept of the value-form. There are indeed some clear parallels between fetishism and alienation, with each starting out as rather loose terms, but, in the course of Marx's writings, becoming both more rigorously defined and more allied with the central economic argument in Marx's *Capital*.

What is driving this process of alienation? The answer, I suggest, is the god of economic growth. The unquestioned purpose of life, it seems, is increased consumption. For people living on one or two dollars a day, we have no reason to challenge this imperative. But one may have cause to wonder when the same imperative drives the rich and prosperous, and not only because of the ultimate material incompatibility between economic growth and the environment. The concern I express in this chapter is the process of dehumanization that accompanies this focus on growth, encouraged by the economistic terminology of natural, human, and social capital.

As I have briefly demonstrated, concepts such as these powerfully influence how we think. But are we not free to use other terms, to perceive our world in other than economic, instrumental terms? It seems to be no easy matter. Two recent examples are relevant. In order to justify why human rights merit our concern, the World Bank finds it necessary to argue in instrumental terms, presenting evidence of how promoting human rights contributes to economic growth. And Jeffrey Sachs's 2001 report for the World Health Organization, *Macroeconomics and Health: Investing in Health for Economic Development*, manifests the same tendency.[25]

Our modern world is increasingly "framed" by concepts such as those described here: the dehumanizing categories of the economist and the bureaucrat. They "comprehend" the world in a certain way and seek to change it in a certain way, with the purpose of achieving enhanced efficiency and competitiveness in the market. This is not, I suggest, the result of the malign or self-interested actions of a powerful and privileged group. But the forces seem to be hard to resist, and the outcome is a continuing process of dehumanization. It seems that we have little choice but to play the game and use the concepts; little chance to change the rules of engagement.

Marx claimed that mystical terms, such as "profit" presented as "return on capital," serve the interests of those in power (the capitalists), and that economists play the role of their "hired prize-fighters." What is concealed by these terms, and more broadly by the belief system that supports capitalism, is, for Marx, exploitation: the extraction of surplus value. My argument in this chapter is that in the modern age of capitalism we encounter a similar mystification—in other economic categories that shape the way we see the world and hence how we act in it. I have exemplified this by reference to the three capitals and argued that the effect is dehumanizing; that by our tacit acceptance of these categories we commit ourselves to the worldview that goes with such a terminology; and that we alienate ourselves from nature, from ourselves, and from the rest of humanity. "What's in a name?" one may ask. In this case, I suggest, a great deal.

Desmond McNeill is Research Director at the Centre for Development and the Environment (SUM), University of Oslo, Norway. He has published extensively on global governance and the power of economics. His books include: *Global Institutions and Development: Framing the World?* (ed. with M. Bøås, Routledge, 2007); *Development Issues in Global Governance: Market Multilateralism and Public-Private Partnerships* (with B. Bull, Routledge, 2009); and *Global Poverty, Ethics and Human Rights: The Role of Multilateral Organisations* (with A. St. Clair, Routledge, 2012).

NOTES

1. For further discussions of capitalism, see in particular the chapter by Falko Schmieder in this volume.
2. For further discussions of ecology, see in particular the chapter by Falko Schmieder in this volume.
3. Robert Costanza, Ralph d'Arge, Rudolf de Groot, et al., "The Value of the World's Ecosystem Services and Natural Capital," *Nature* 387 (1987): 253.
4. Morten Bøås and Desmond McNeill, eds, *Global Institutions and Development: Framing the World?* (New York, 2004), 1.
5. Jacob Mincer, "Investment in Human Capital and Personal Income Distribution," *Journal of Political Economy* 66 (1958): 281–302; Theodore Schulz, "Investment in Human Capital," *American Economic Review* 5 (1961): 1–17; Gary Becker, *Human Capital: A Theoretical and Empirical Analysis, with Special Reference to Education* (Chicago, 1964).
6. UNESCO. "Trends and Issues from an OECD Perspective: Western Europe and North America." http://www.unesco.org/education/wef/en_leadup/rmeet_europ_ass_we na.shtm, 2000, accessed 1 January 2008, defunct per August 2018.

7. Nancy Birdsall, "Human Capital and the Quality of Growth," *Development Outreach* 3, no. 1 (2000): 14.
8. Wendy D. Lynch and Harold H. Gardner, *Aligning Incentives, Information, and Choice: How to Optimize Health and Human Capital Performance* (Cheyenne, WY, 2008), 233.
9. Alejandro Portes, "Social Capital: Its Origins and Applications in Modern Sociology," *Annual Review of Sociology* 24 (1998): 21.
10. Desmond McNeill, "Social Capital and the World Bank," in Bøås and McNeill, *Global Institutions and Development*, 108–23.
11. For a powerful critique of social capital, see Ben Fine, *Social Capital versus Social Theory: Political Economy and Social Science at the Turn of the Millennium* (New York, 2001).
12. World Bank, *The Initiative on Defining, Monitoring and Measuring Social Capital*, Social Capital Initiative Working Paper 2 (Washington, DC, 1998), 11, emphasis added, retrieved 3 February 2018 from http://documents.worldbank.org/curated/en/111741468767413539/text/292800PAPER0In1defining010sci0no-02.txt.
13. Karl Marx, *Capital: A Critique of Political Economy*, vol. 1 (Moscow, 1954), 77.
14. Karl Marx, *Theories of Surplus Value, Part III* (Moscow, 1971), 798.
15. Léon Walras, *Elements of Pure Economics* (London, 1954), 69.
16. Marx, *Capital*, 25.
17. Marx, *Theories of Surplus Value*, 536.
18. Ibid., 462.
19. Karl Marx, *The Poverty of Philosophy* (Moscow, 1975), 174.
20. Ibid., 176.
21. Desmond McNeill, "Social Capital or Sociality? Methodological Contrasts between Economics and Other Social Sciences," in *Economics and Social Sciences: Complements, Competitors, Accomplices?* ed. Stavros Ioannides and Klaus Nielsen (Cheltenham, 2007), 163–84.
22. Karl Marx, *Economic and Philosophic Manuscripts of 1844* (Moscow, 1977), 74.
23. Desmond McNeill, *Fetishism and the Value-Form: Towards a General Theory of Value* (Oslo, 2011).
24. Louis Althusser, *For Marx* (London, 1977).
25. World Health Organization, *Macroeconomics and Health: Investing in Health for Economic Development: Report of the Commission on Macroeconomics and Health* (Geneva, 2001).

BIBLIOGRAPHY

Althusser, Louis. *For Marx*. London: New Left Books, 1977.

Becker, Gary. *Human Capital: A Theoretical and Empirical Analysis, with Special Reference to Education*. Chicago: University of Chicago Press, 1964.

Birdsall, Nancy. "Human Capital and the Quality of Growth." *Development Outreach* 3, no. 1 (2000): 4–17.

Bøås, Morten, and Desmond McNeill, eds. *Global Institutions and Development: Framing the World?* New York: Taylor & Francis, 2004.
Costanza, Robert, Ralph d'Arge, Rudolf de Groot, et al. "The Value of the World's Ecosystem Services and Natural Capital." *Nature* 387 (1987): 253–60.
Fine, Ben. *Social Capital versus Social Theory: Political Economy and Social Science at the Turn of the Millennium.* New York: Routledge, 2001.
Lynch, Wendy D., and Harold H. Gardner. *Aligning Incentives, Information, and Choice: How to Optimize Health and Human Capital Performance.* Cheyenne, WY: Health as Human Capital, 2008.
Marx, Karl. *Capital: A Critique of Political Economy.* Vol. 1. Moscow: Progress Publishers, 1954.
———. *Economic and Philosophic Manuscripts of 1844.* Moscow: Progress Publishers, 1977.
———. *The Poverty of Philosophy.* Moscow: Progress Publishers, 1975.
———. *Theories of Surplus Value, Part III.* Moscow: Progress Publishers, 1971.
McNeill, Desmond. *Fetishism and the Value-Form: Towards a General Theory of Value.* Oslo: Published by the author, 2011.
———. "Social Capital or Sociality? Methodological Contrasts between Economics and Other Social Sciences." In *Economics and Social Sciences: Complements, Competitors, Accomplices?* edited by Stavros Ioannides and Klaus Nielsen, 163–84. Cheltenham: Edward Elgar, 2007.
———. "Social Capital and the World Bank." In *Global Institutions and Development: Framing the World?* edited by Morten Bøås and Desmond McNeill, 108–23. New York: Taylor & Francis, 2004.
Mincer, Jacob. "Investment in Human Capital and Personal Income Distribution." *Journal of Political Economy* 66 (1958): 281–302.
Portes, Alejandro. "Social Capital: Its Origins and Applications in Modern Sociology." *Annual Review of Sociology* 24 (1998): 1–24.
Putnam, Robert. *Making Democracy Work: Civic Traditions in Modern Italy.* Princeton, NJ: Princeton University Press, 1993.
Schulz, Theodore. "Investment in Human Capital." *American Economic Review* 5 (1961): 1–17.
Schumacher, E. F. *Small Is Beautiful: A Study of Economics As If People Mattered.* New York: Harper, 1973.
UNESCO. "Trends and Issues from an OECD Perspective: Western Europe and North America." http://www.unesco.org/education/wef/en-leadup/rmeet_europ_ass_wena.shtm, 2000, assessed 1 January 2008, defunct per August 2018
Walras, Léon. *Elements of Pure Economics.* London: Allen & Unwin, 1954.
World Bank. *The Initiative on Defining, Monitoring and Measuring Social Capital.* Social Capital Initiative Working Paper 2. Washington, DC: World Bank, 1998. Retrieved 3 February 2018 from http://documents.worldbank.org/curated/en/111741468767413539/text/292800PAPER0In1defining010sci0no-02.txt.

World Health Organization. *Macroeconomics and Health: Investing in Health for Economic Development: Report of the Commission on Macroeconomics and Health.* Geneva: WHO, 2001.

▶• 9 •◀

The Worlds in Human Rights

Images or Mirages?

Malcolm Langford

The "world" is nowhere and everywhere in human rights. On one hand, the phrase conjures up images, stories, memories of particular places, people, and claims—of political prisoners, persecuted minorities, invidious discrimination, brutal displacement, angry property owners or neglect of the most vulnerable. Whether the place of struggle, contestation, or victory is close or distant in time and space, the phrase commonly invokes a concrete-enough representation.

Such particularity is essential to the teleological animus of human rights: to force the public, the powerful, to lower their gaze from the general, the aggregate, the statistical, the synthesis, the other, so that they can see the individual. As Dworkin puts it: "Individual rights are political trumps held by the individuals. Individuals have rights when, for some reason, a collective goal is not a sufficient justification for denying them what they wish, as individuals, to have or to do, or not a sufficient justification for imposing some loss or injury upon them."[1]

On the other hand, human rights are all about the world.[2] They invoke, represent, and radiate an entire moral and political universe. They carry an *image* of the world with *all humans* on some equal plane (a physical world), with the message that these rights are *beneficial* for all (a moral world), constitute a means of seeing, imagining, or imposing a new world *order* (a political world), and are proclaimed or invoked on the grounds that the authority or speaker can *represent* the preferences of the world (an epistemic world).

In her historical articulation of the logic of human rights, Hunt captures in a classical manner these first two world-like concepts:

> Human rights requires three interlocking qualities: rights must be *natural* (inherent in human beings); equal (the same for everyone); and universal

(applicable everywhere). For rights to be human rights, all humans everywhere in the world must possess them equally and only because of their status of human beings.[3]

More constructivist and legal perspectives of human rights also give prominence to the third. According to Beitz, human rights are "requirements whose object is to protect urgent individual interests against certain predictable dangers" under "typical circumstances of life in a *modern world order* composed of states" to which "political institutions" must respond.[4]

Human rights have achieved a resoundingly deeper worldwide acceptance in the last few decades. They have emerged as a dominant international discourse, a global *lingua franca*, or even a "worldwide secular religion."[5] Simmons argues that we find today "an increasingly dense set of international rules, institutions and expectations regarding the protection of individual rights" that is more significant "than at any point in human history."[6]

This exponential rise of "human rights" in late modernity has spurred a surfeit of disciplinary research, including in history. The most common approach in history is to sketch a *longue durée*: human rights are a contingent but connected outcome of struggles and intellectual thought that stretch back at least a few centuries to the Enlightenment and possibly earlier to early Christendom or the Greek stoics.[7] These stories have their dissenters. In Moyn's revisionist account, for instance, human rights are a wholly recent phenomenon, an idea that broke through substantively and strategically in the 1970s due to the dissolution of utopian alternatives.[8]

It is not the intention of this brief chapter to engage with the contested conceptual and empirical histories of human rights.[9] However, the emerging histories of human rights provide a useful departure point in asking what the role of the world is in understanding and explaining the rise of human rights. Does the embedment of an idea of the world in the concept explain both its popularity and contingency? More particularly, might it help explain what many of these causal theories struggle with: how to explain the (more significant) expansion of human rights discourse and institutionalism since the end of the 1980s? These questions are taken up in the first part of the chapter.

At the same time, human rights constitute a paradigm under constant critique. Skepticism is often expressed in philosophical or empirical tones but is often rooted in or framed by an understanding of the moment and circumstances of the historical emergence of human rights. An interesting way of perceiving some skeptical perspectives is to see them as a challenge to the ontological and normative conceptions of world embedded in the concept. Do human rights represent or constitute a world of autonomous and disembodied individuals; or a world made in the image of the West formed by global hegemonies?[10] Looked at this way, we might ask, does the geographic imaginary of human rights, with its ambition of representing the world, ultimately constitute the Achilles heel of the concept? Does the attempt to stretch a moral and political map so far render the image prone to caricature and irrelevance? Or does it represent the only map available in a world that no longer seamlessly fits into any other cartographic boundary or scale? This is addressed in the second half of the chapter.

The World as a Stage

In the most familiar narrative of human rights, the concept is mobilized to set moral limits or declare basic moral aspirations for all. This move is appealing since invocation of the concept makes a particular claim resistant to the mores of context and power, whether cultural, political, or economic. The French king, the English colonialist, the transatlantic slave trader, the Latin American autocrat, or the Soviet communist was forced to contend with not only a "view from elsewhere,"[11] in Adam Smith's moral theory, but a "view from everywhere."

In this register, human rights might provide a means to reset the boundaries of the world in two ways: moral and physical. It responds possibly to what Jordheim and Sandmo call in the introduction the "disappearance of the world" in modernity. But it is not only the "physical world" of the environment that can be quickly submerged by "scientific progress," as they focus on. It is also the physical world of living breathing *homo sapiens* and their moral world of the permissible and desirable. In that sense, it is not surprising that human rights and environment share much in common: human rights were partly built on the idea of "the natural" (a successor to the idea of natural rights)[12] and in the last few decades both have birthed international movements and a core of global, albeit fragile, values.

This twining of moral and physical conceptions of the world can be seen in human rights' etymological history. When the phrase entered the lexicon in English it was often used as an expression of outrage toward acts against individuals who are not citizens or men but those who share, with the outraged, only their mere humanity,[13] humanity as an ontological category distinct from the divine and the animal. Thus, US President Thomas Jefferson in 1806 used this particular expression of rights, rather than, say, the rights of man, in referring to the practice of enslavement:

> I congratulate you, fellow citizens, on the approach of the period at which you may interpose your authority constitutionally, to withdraw the citizens of the United States from all further participation in those violations of human rights which have been so long continued on the unoffending inhabitants

of Africa, and which the morality, reputation, and the best interests of our country, have long been eager to proscribe.[14]

But these human rights were limited—slaves were not to be accorded further rights in the American polity.

In French, there was greater potency for the phrase or a set of phrases to convey greater agency on all humans and thus a thicker moral conception of the world. The "rights of humanity" in French, which was used more broadly in the eighteenth century, mirrored to a certain extent Jefferson's thin conception, but not always. More particularly, *droit de l'homme* (the rights of man), which found a place in the 1789 French Declaration, held greater potency. The use of "man" rather than "humanity" hinted at a narrower application but it was clearly less passive, signaling a thicker and less biological view of humanity and its just moral demands.[15]

In her reading, Hunt captures this use of the thicker meaning in the appeal by a Protestant pastor to the French king in 1787, who uses all variations of the term in arguing that a proposed law concerning religious freedom was not robust enough:

> We know today what natural rights are, and they certainly give to men much more than this edict accords to Protestants ... The time has come when it is no longer acceptable for a law to overtly overrule the rights of humanity that are very well known all over the world.[16]

However, this more substantive view of rights succumbed to the liberal nationalism of the nineteenth century. It was the rights of citizens, and men as gendered beings, that were prominent and the site of most political and rights-based struggles.

Only in the Universal Declaration of Human Rights of 1948 (UDHR) did the different streams of burgeoning rights begin to coalesce under the more universalistic "human rights." The justification was based on a sense of moral outrage, an articulation of what all humans in the world could accept, a boundary of permissibility, as well as a thicker understanding with rights as basic moral and political objectives.[17] In the opening preambular paragraphs, it states (with emphasis added):

> Whereas disregard and contempt for human rights have resulted in barbarous acts which have outraged the conscience of mankind, and the *advent of a world* in which human beings shall enjoy freedom of speech and belief and freedom from fear and want has been proclaimed as the highest aspiration of the common people...

This account of the rise of human rights is, in essence, too functionalist for Moyn.[18] Until recently,[19] he argued that the state has been the pre-eminent space in which rights found their expression, meaning, and institutionalization, whether it be the national liberalism of the nineteenth century or the democratic liberalism (and national communism) of the twentieth century. Moreover, the centrality of the state limited their international and global expansion. Indeed, Moyn sees the UDHR as the premier illustration of the almost non-existent emergence of human rights. The 1945 UN Charter institutionalized a system of realist statist power politics, most notably in the form of the vetoes and limited membership of the Security Council. Human rights were demoted to a few perfunctory references followed by the non-binding UDHR. While a number of key treaties were then drafted and approved by 1965 and 1966, this opening for human rights was brief. By 1949, Cold War pragmatism, resurgent national sovereignty, and economic development soon emerged as prevailing international discourses.

In the 1970s, human rights re-emerged in global discourse, and established itself more deeply as a global practice.[20] In the midst of global economic uncertainty and weakened superpowers, the championing of human rights by non-governmental organizations (NGOs) suddenly gained unprecedented attention. It was aided by the Helsinki conference, in which communist countries officially condoned civil and political rights, and the USA under President Carter, which ushered human rights, including economic and social rights, into its foreign policy. Moyn argues that what was critical in this period is that other grand international utopias dissolved, as political activists in the West and East settled on a more limited but seemingly achievable and important agenda:

> There is no way to reckon with the recent emergence and contemporary power of human rights, without focusing on their utopian dimension: the image of another, better world of dignity and respect that underlies their appeal, even when human rights seem to be about slow and piecemeal reform. But far from being the sole idealism that has inspired faith and activism in the course of the human events, human rights emerged historically as the last utopia—one that became powerful and prominent because other visions imploded.[21]

One way of understanding Moyn's account is that he sees the idea of the political world in human rights as constitutive, not additive. If human rights are not politicized, institutionalized, or legalized in an internationalist manner, then they offer no more than noise or mere rhetoric in everyday politics. His conception of human rights requires the third world "world order," that Beitz speaks of in his definition of human rights. The key variable for Moyn is the state. In the fields of politics and international relations, the empirical conception of the world has been overwhelmingly statist: it, along with the empire, has been the central unit. Even in China, where the idea of the world was traditionally expansive—"infinite in space and time with the Chinese emperor's palace at the center"—a "society of states had long been a concept in the Chinese mind."[22]

In its normative posture, international relations does open up for new pictures, new visions of the world. When it moves beyond mere problem-solving into a more critical modus, such normativity "contains an element of utopianism in the sense that it can represent a coherent picture of an alternative order," although it is limited to "feasible transformations of the existing world."[23] Thus, the "intersubjective" empiricized understandings of the world give way to "collective images of social order," which differ as to both the "nature and legitimacy of prevailing power relations, the meanings of justice and public good, and so forth."[24]

The idea of an alternative political world order based on human rights is comparatively new. Few of the early movements and struggles were transnational and the leading cosmopolitan of the time, Immanuel Kant, possessed a rather restricted view of a world community. The ideologies of capitalism and communism were much more clear-sighted in their institutional and political vision of world order. However, in the twentieth century this dimension soon became more apparent, initially with the fragile League of Nations and its Permanent Court of International Justice adjudicating minority rights disputes, and found clear if vague expression in the UDHR. The draft title of the declaration was consciously switched from "International" to "Universal" and Article 29 made the audacious claim that "Everyone is entitled to a social and international order in which the rights and freedoms set forth in this Declaration can be fully realized."[25]

The political world of human rights, in which political authority to define and enforce them was not axiomatically linked with the state (as, for example, the ideas of civil rights, citizenship rights, minority rights, and self-determination rights more clearly are), was thus increasingly the subject of imagination and proclamation. Human rights fitted well with Cox's idea of a "feasible transformation of the existing world,"[26] which is what made them attractive, to activists and experts in the 1930s and 1940s and to publics and politicians from the 1970s.[27] The idea that the political space for contesting and realizing human rights claims was not confined to the state but encompassed the world (both international and transnational) lay the groundwork for human rights to be deployed by activists and states alike, and from the 1980s an array of international and regional courts and bodies and a cascading series of detailed standards and treaties deepening and broadening the UDHR.

Of course, this new political world of human rights is as thin as the early imaginings of the physical and moral worlds of human rights. The international order lacks courts with enforcement powers, armies and police, tax collectors, and a phalanx of journalists. It is a multilevel world order where states still possesses considerable power.

However, what both of these historical accounts lack is an explanation of the rise and rise of human rights from the 1980s. Indeed, even if one is sympathetic to Moyn's account of the surge of human rights in the 1970s, it is clearly empirically overstated. In his epilogue, Moyn tries to account for the "global human rights revolution" from the 1980s through a kind of path dependency, a historical institutionalism or auto-cataclysm. Human rights emerged as the only legitimate ideology on the global scene in the 1970s and it is natural that they are then forced to take on new challenges:

> The very neutrality that allowed for human rights to survive in the 1970s, and prosper as other utopias died, also left them with a heavy burden later. ... Partisans of the human rights idea were forced to confront the need for political agenda and programmatic vision. ... Human rights were forced to move not simply from morality to politics, but also from charisma to bureaucracy.[28]

This expansion was aided in Moyn's view by a diverse group of actors—from international and local activists to European federalists, international lawyers, as well as anti-communist Western politicians—that brought human rights "to new geographic areas around the globe."[29]

However, Moyn's account of the present era of human rights seems too limited. It is not just that the world is a mere stage in which human rights can and must find expression—international and transnational spaces of discourse, action, law, and institutionalization.[30] Increasingly, the world is the only relevant political unit and, equally, the political world is pluralistic rather than multilevel (i.e., state-international). What occurs in the 1980s is the rise of the world as a political, economic, and cultural unit. The processes of globalization were underway. What is interesting is that human rights, at least as understood by Moyn, appear to have gained most *resonance* in those spaces in which the state has withered. The most active human rights court in the world lies in Europe, which has integrated enormously in the last three decades through the European Union. At the other end of the scale are the least integrated regions (the Middle East and Asia), at least politically, which have very underdeveloped international spaces for human rights. Along the scale, one finds the same pattern: weak integration and human rights systems in Africa, stronger integration and courts in West Africa (facilitated by the Economic Community of West African States, ECOWAS), and finally Latin America with its inter-American system of human rights that most approximates Europe.[31] This might not be an empirical surprise but it is notable that human rights thicken in more integrated international spaces—the idea of the world in human rights seems to make it a closer fit.

But it is more than the integration of states. The political world is more pluralistic. It is a world of non-state actors—both peripheral and global. Broader social forces, in the shape of intergovernmental organizations, individuals, transnational corporations, non-governmental organizations, indigenous peoples, and militias, have not only become subjects of international law but have exhibited clearly the ability to affect and contest power relations, making them competitors to the state as political units. However, what all these entities lack is the power of legitimate and independent law-making. Intergovernmental institutions come the closest, with state-based participation directly or through governance control, but these intergovernmental organizations increasingly act independently and must make choices on values, standards, and law. It is the age of neo-medievalism, a phenomenon where "overlapping and concurrence of multiple legitimate authorities take place inside the same decision-making framework"[32] that is "held together by a duality of competing universalistic claims," particularly those of the nation-state system and the transnational market economy.[33] It is in these spaces that human rights often emerges as the only or dominant discourse (with widely varying degrees of social and institutional integration) that seeks to reflect ideas of justice or a principled response to utilitarian logic. The World Bank or a Malian militia can dismiss the laws of a particular state as peripheral or parochial, but they can do this less with human rights that carry a global imprimatur.

And it may go beyond actual political spaces to imagined, felt, or weakly legalized ones. One of the intriguing aspects of international and comparative law in the last decade is the transfusion of international norms among the judiciary, including on human rights. The growing "harmonization" of interpretation suggests that judges and lawyers view themselves and the cases before them as part of a present, even if hazy, worldwide legal community or complex.[34]

This picture paints, however, a rather one-way relationship: the universalism inherent in human rights (as global norms with global backing) provides them with opening and leverage in new global spaces. But the relationship may be recursive: human rights are constitutive of new orders—they only gain legitimacy, instrumentality, and coherence through human rights. One illustration of this is Thornhill's sociological constitutionalism. He argues that the constitutional formula of rights + constituent power, representing "a set of institutions able to act in abstracted autonomy," first facilitated the statist modern political system as it "separated itself from the external/personalistic pre-state political apparatus of feudalism, and it became able, as a state, to form a distinct political domain, in which power was autonomously transmitted in a generalizable manner across temporally and geographically extensive societies."[35] Thornhill takes this a step further when he argues that rights, particularly judicial constitutionalism, have been equally constitutive of the new global order: it "makes available a structure for the circulation of power which enables power to be applied in reasonable consistency across multi-centric geographical territories."[36]

The World as a Stooge

The above account is mostly sympathetic to the idea or role of human rights as representing or constituting the 'world'. But they are no stranger to critique. What is interesting for the present purposes is that much skepticism resides, in essence, in the embedded conceptions of the world. In his *Visions of World Community*, Bartelson concedes, for instance, that "every effort to impose a given set of values on the existing plurality of communities in the name of a common humanity is likely to be met with resistance on the grounds of its very own particularity. From this point of view, a real and genuine world community is a dream incapable of realization."[37]

A classical objection to human rights is cultural relativism. Human rights may present a distorted picture of the world by elevating autonomous individuals to the center stage of social existence. For instance, Mutua states:

> The human rights corpus views the individual as the center of the moral universe, and therefore denigrates communities, collectives, and group rights. ... This is a particularly serious problem in areas of the world where group and community rights are deeply embedded both in the cultures of the peoples, and exacerbated by the multinational nature of the post-colonial state. ... This runaway notion of individualism, which is a central tenet to liberalism, has retarded the capacity of human rights thinkers to moderate selfishness with community interests.[38]

Mutua lacerates the legitimacy of the normative vision of the UDHR, arguing that "non-Western views were largely unrepresented" and that "it was presumptuous and shamelessly ethnocentric for the UDHR to refer to itself as the 'common standard of achievement for all peoples and all nations.'"[39]

This cultural relativity critique has had some purchase in international debates over Asian values and African values. At the local or communal level, it may also represent a significant obstacle to limiting the spread of at least explicit human rights approaches.[40] But the critique is somewhat over-caricatured since group rights have been a prominent part of the human rights story: some of today's most prominent movements are the indigenous rights movement and peasant rights movements, while equality and social rights norms have ensured that a range of collective demands are also recognized.[41] It is also important to query whether states who raise these critiques always possess the democratic legitimacy in making them. Moreover, the non-Western contribution to the UDHR should not be overlooked. A worldwide study preceded the drafting and World War II affected Asia and other parts of the world and produced intellectuals and diplomats who were equally enamored of the concept.[42] Inclusion of human rights in the UN Charter was strongly demanded by small states, which were wary of the enhanced powers of the five large powers under the UN Charter. Glendon notes that "the Great Powers were not going to take the initiative in making human rights a centerpiece of their postwar arrangements" as it was "not in their interest to do so."[43] However, a disparate coalition of "smaller" states—from Brazil to Lebanon, Australia, and the Philippines—and more than forty NGOs lobbied the San Francisco Conference for a more emphatic recognition of human rights within this international sphere.[44]

But perhaps more important is the misunderstanding of the self in human rights. Mutua equates autonomy with selfishness as if human rights were a concept encased by neoclassical economics. Hunt acknowledges that a shift in the idea of self was a condition precedent for human rights but argues that it was the rise of the autonomous *and* empathetic self in the mid eighteenth century that was crucial. This was generated not only by accounts of atrocity (and arguably economic and demographic changes) but also by the breakthrough of the modern novel in the mid eighteenth century. The growing middle class and elites could feel for and identify with very differently situated individuals:

> The magical spell cast by the novel thus turned out to be far reaching in its effects …. Readers learned to appreciate the emotional intensity of the ordinary and the capacity of people like themselves to create on their own a moral world. Human rights grew out of the seedbed sowed by these feelings…. [People] learned this equality, at least in part, by experiencing identification with ordinary characters who seemed dramatically present and familiar, even if ultimately fictional.[45]

The way out of the conundrum may be to avoid a single lens in viewing individual autonomy. Human rights may be aspirational but they are not (and arguably should not be) a thick projection of the ideal community or good life. They are as much (if not primarily) a critical (and affective) norm by which to evaluate and/or resist unjust arrangements, relationships, and institutions. This perspective is boldly captured by Douzinas. In his cosmopolitan and *liberational* account, his axiom of cosmopolitan justice is respect for the "singularity of the other" and an individual's "bare sovereignty." His cosmopolitanism to come "extends beyond nations and states" and human rights are summoned to "attack the omnipotence of the sovereign, humanitarianism, the brutality and excess of its unlimited power."[46] While he protests against thick community, he is committed to relation rather than bare autonomy: one exists through relating to the "existence of others, to other existences, and to the otherness of existence." This form of encounter is thoroughly within the present and includes the task of resistance: "What binds me to an Iraqi or a Palestinian is not membership of humanity, citizenship of the world or of a community but a protest against citizenship, against nationality and thick community.... What binds my world to that of others is our absolute singularity and total responsibility beyond citizen and human, beyond national and international."[47]

The second critique is more challenging. Human rights present nothing of a "world made new," to take the phrase of one of the founding drafters of the Universal Declaration of Human Rights, Eleanor Roosevelt, but rather constitute a vision of the "world in our image," a projection of Western, liberal or neoliberal ideas. Human rights are the unwitting handmaiden for the project of globalization, strengthening and legitimating it. This critique brings into sharp relief the fourth and rather different idea of the world connected with human rights posited at the beginning of this chapter: the epistemic world. Every claim to represent the existence, meaning, or application of a human right is based on epistemic assumptions that one can "know," "project," or "design" this world: its physicality, its morality, its political order. The abstractness and part normativity of human rights appears to leave enormous openings for considerable epistemic flexibility. It provides a resource to those who are empowered to fill it with content.

However, this causal understanding equally presents a challenge for claims of Western bias. As we shall see, in short and long waves of time, human rights are punctuated by cycles of *contestation*, *consensus*, and *appropriation*. There is often deep disagreement over the relevance, selection, or strength of human rights that is resolved by some sort of agreement, which then opens the way for selected and appropriated use in politics, bureaucracy, and law, and thus new contestation. How these cycles play out and in what direction is largely an empirical question—the different ideational resources contained within human rights have led in different directions with different intensities.

In the drafting of the UN Charter and UDHR, there was an immense struggle by the great powers to not only minimize references to human rights but to favor particular types of rights. However, this was overcome by small states, NGOs, and influential individuals.[48] The UDHR may reveal some Western bias but it was certainly far from what Western countries demanded, particularly the many economic and social rights.

However, human rights were quickly appropriated for more clearly ideological or nationalist purposes in the Cold War period, with the West invoking international civil and political rights and the East economic and social rights. While many in the Soviet bloc had abstained during the voting on the UDHR, the UN human rights chief commented that if "one were to judge by their frequent references to it" in international politics, an "uninitiated person might well think the Soviets had voted for the Declaration."[49] The appropriation was also not confined to states; it occurred from below as well. Projects like the European Convention on Human Rights were clearly an attempt to represent the world as conceived by Western Europeans, but these countries suddenly found their own citizens equally eager to use the Convention against them by using the Strasbourg court or in claims for political and legal reforms. However, recent archival research shows how select Southern states were essential in promoting the first wave of human rights conventions.[50]

In the second period, from the 1970s, this pattern of appropriation was partly altered and produced less contestation. For example, a slew of new international human rights-oriented instruments emerged on humanitarian obligations, women's rights, prohibitions on torture, and children's rights in which the East and West often battled to promote their particular vision of human rights within a document, as opposed to working to slow down the progress of legal development. This was possibly strengthened after the fall of the Berlin Wall as numerous constitutions of the South and East recognized all international human rights in a relatively balanced fashion.

However, it is also possible to see the more appropriating and neoliberal hand of human rights in the last two decades. The third wave of democracy from the 1980s could be characterized as a "Janus faced transition that embraced political democratization and economic liberalization."[51] The rise of globalization led to the promotion of investor and trade rights in international law, increasingly recognized and promoted as human rights.[52] But again, the last two decades have been characterized by a thickening of a range of other human rights in different societies and in international affairs. For instance, attempts by the Bush administration to weaken some rights (e.g., protections against torture) and strengthen others (e.g., foreign investor rights) met with such resistance that the United States was forced to recalibrate its stance within the substantive and procedural limits of the UN system.[53]

Thus, the answer to the politicization of rights may be a politics of rights—affirming some interpretations and uses, attacking others. As Douzinas argues:

> What must be attacked is the theological mask of sovereignty, represented today by the hegemonic power rather than its pale homonymic imitations ... we must be aware that we cannot fight sovereignty and the nation-state in general without risking giving up the principles of equality and self-determination to the emerging super-sovereign. These principles were inaugurated by, with and against national sovereignty. They are today an indispensable barrier against ideological, religious, ethnic or capitalist hegemonies which masquerading as universalism or cosmopolitanism, claim the dignity of the cosmos that is nothing more than a marketplace or the moral rationalisation of particular interests. When a hegemon attacks the weakened sovereigns around the world, resistance may demand supporting the local against the global.[54]

Conclusion

Ideas of the world are intrinsic and embedded in human rights. They have served as a recursive stage: human rights not only demarcate new physical, moral, and political worlds but our imagination or acknowledgment of these worlds limits the space in which human rights has traction. At the same time, the idea of the world in human rights may be but a stooge, neither emancipatory or universal but rather a vehicle for a more particularist and weaker vision of the world: individualist, liberalist, or formalist.

In this sense, the world may be a deceptive mirage or empowering image, an appropriation or a resource—a dualism that mirrors Scheingold's "myths" and "politics" of rights. In his view, rights were both a myth, that promised liberation while being anchored to conservative and entrapping political discourse, bureaucracy, and legal modalities,[55] and a form of politics, being "political resources of unknown value in the hands of those who want to alter the course of public policy."[56] Human rights may be a "world in our image," darker and manipulative, or a "world made new," optimistic and political.

Which visions of the world have and will triumph may be an open question. But at the very least, the cosmopolitan idea of rights highlights the present dystopic world and promises a modestly better one. A dissonance of visions that are not too far apart. Promoting human rights is thus a fine art. Imagining a world that is new enough to inspire action but realistic enough to instill commitment; detailed enough that it guides action and avoids perverse appropriations but vague enough that it permits particularity and vernacularity.

The challenge is to have a good map. Not the limited cartographic or political map of the West's Columbus who ended up colliding with the rest of the world; and not the detailed map of Suarez's imaginary empire where the "College of Cartographers evolved a Map of Empire that was of the same scale as the Empire and coincided with it point for point" so that it was soon judged "cumbersome" and was gradually "abandoned to the Rigours of sun and Rain."[57] If human rights are to play a role, it is to provide a vision of the world that is critical and anti-dystopic (rather than necessarily utopian)—a non-exclusive map that highlights the dangerous rocks and reefs rather than the sunny and gentle climes.

Malcolm Langford is Professor of Public Law at the University of Oslo and Co-Director of the Centre on Law and Social Transformation at the University of Bergen and Chr. Michelsen Institute. He has published widely in law, economics, and political science. His publications include *Social Rights Jurisprudence* (Cambridge University Press, 2008), *Socio-Economic Rights* *in South Africa: Symbols or Substance?* (with B. Cousins, J. Dugard, and T. Madlingozi, Cambridge University Press, 2014), "Rights, Development and Critical Modernity," *Development and Change* 46, no. 4 (2015), and *Research Methods in Constitutional Law: A Handbook* (with David Law, Edward Elgar, 2019).

NOTES

1. Ronald Dworkin, *Taking Rights Seriously* (Cambridge, MA, 1977), xi.
2. For further discussions of human rights, see in particular the chapter by Oddbjørn Leirvik in this volume.
3. Lynn Hunt, *Inventing Human Rights* (New York, 2007), 21.
4. Charles R. Beitz, *The Idea of Human Rights* (Oxford, 2009), 109, emphasis added.
5. Elie Wiesel, "A Tribute to Human Rights," in *The Universal Declaration of Human Rights: Fifty Years and Beyond*, ed. Yael Danieli et al. (Amityville, NY, 1999), 3–4.
6. Beth A. Simmons, *Mobilizing for Human Rights: International Law in Domestic Politics* (New York, 2009), 3.
7. Micheline Ishay, *The History of Human Rights: From Ancient Times to the Globalization Era* (Berkeley, 2008).
8. Samuel Moyn, *The Last Utopia: Human Rights in History* (Cambridge, MA, 2010).
9. Indeed, the debate is partly sideshow on account of the different definitions of human rights employed by the protagonists: see for instance G. Bass, "The New Old Thing," *New Republic*, 20 October 2010; Samuel Moyn, "On the Genealogy of Morals," *The Nation*, 17 April 2007. As pointed out in the next section, this split is partly hinged on the different conceptions of the world in human rights.
10. Another world-centered critique is omitted for reasons of space. Human rights might represent a decoupled world of formalism and symbolism, rhetorical adornments and ineffective institutions. Does it therefore really correspond to the deep moral aspirations of, say, the Universal Declaration or it is rather a stale, de-peopled formal world of rules, procedures, distant institutions, legal elites? They are particularly irrelevant to the needs of the poorest and excluded: Joshua Castellino, *Social Inclusion & Human Rights: Implications for 2030 and Beyond. Background Paper for the High-Level Panel of Eminent Persons on the Post-2015 Development Agenda*, UN Sustainable Development Solutions Network, 15 January 2013, http://unsdsn.org/wp-content/uploads/2014/02/130114-Social-Exclusion-and-Human-Rights-Paper-for-HLP.pdf. There is no doubt that human rights face particular problems of enforcement and some institutions are skewed toward the rights of the more powerful, but research has also found significant impacts from the existence and use of human rights and associated mechanisms: e.g., Simmons, *Mobilizing for Human Rights*; Varun Gauri and Daniel M. Brinks, *Courting Social Justice: Judicial Enforcement of Social and Economic Rights in the Developing World* (New York, 2008).
11. For a resurrection of Smith's notion of the "view from elsewhere" in political theory, see Amartya Sen, *The Idea of Justice* (Cambridge, MA, 2009).

12. However, human rights have also become deeply enmeshed with modernity such that they are today better understood as containing naturalist and modernist elements. See Beitz at n. 4.I
13. Hunt, *Inventing Human Rights*, 22.
14. Quoted in Hunt, *Inventing Human Rights*, 21.
15. Ibid., 22–26.
16. Quoted in Hunt, *Inventing Human Rights*, 26.
17. It should be noted that like many defenses of human rights it was also twinned with an instrumental claim. The preceding paragraph states: "recognition of the inherent dignity and of the equal and inalienable rights of all members of the human family is the foundation of freedom, justice and peace *in the world*." Retrieved 28 August 2018 from http://www.un.org/en/universal-declaration-human-rights/; emphasis added.
18. Moyn, *The Last Utopia*.
19. In his latest book, Moyn appears to partially retreat from this position. He acknowledges the transnational and partly global character of human rights before the 1970s. See Samuel Moyn, *Not Enough: Human Rights in an Unequal World* (Cambridge, MA, 2018).
20. Beitz, *The Idea of Human Rights*.
21. Moyn, *The Last Utopia*, 4.
22. Yaqing Qin, "Why Is There No Chinese International Relations Theory?" *International Relations of the Asia-Pacific* 7, no. 3 (2007): 313–40.
23. Robert W. Cox, "Social Forces, States and World Orders: Beyond International Relations Theory," *Millennium: Journal of International Studies* 10, no. 2 (1981): 126–55, at 130.
24. Ibid., 136.
25. Mary Ann Glendon, *A World Made New: Eleanor Roosevelt and the Universal Declaration of Human Rights* (New York, 2001).
26. Robert W. Cox, "Social Forces, States and World Orders: Beyond International Relations Theory," 130.
27. Moyn privileges exclusively the latter in the *The Last Utopia* but acknowledges the former in *Not Enough*.
28. Moyn, *The Last Utopia*, 213, 219.
29. Ibid., 221.
30. For further discussions of law, see in particular the chapters by Chenxi Tang and Lars Kirkhusmo Pharo in this volume.
31. There are of course exceptions, such as North America with NAFTA (North American Free Trade Agreement), or SADC (the Southern African Development Community), which created and then abolished its court after the first decision against Zimbabwe.
32. Hedley Bull, *The Anarchical Society* (New York, 2002), 254–55, quoted in Cecilia M. Bailliet, "What Is to Become of Human Rights Rule-Based International Order within an Age of Neo-Medievalism?" in *Non-State Actors, Soft Law and Protective Regimes: From the Margins*, ed. Cecilia M. Bailliet (Cambridge, 2012), 95–124.
33. Jörg Friedrichs, "The Meaning of New Medievalism," *European Journal of International Relations* 7, no. 4 (2001): 475.

34. Anne-Marie Slaughter, "A Typology of Transjudicial Communication," *University of Richmond Law Review* 29, no. 1 (1994–95): 99–137.
35. Christopher Thornhill, "Contemporary Constitutionalism and the Dialectic of Constituent Power," *Global Constitutionalism* 1, no. 3 (2012): 369–404, 397.
36. Ibid., 396.
37. Jens Bartelson, *Visions of World Community* (Cambridge, 2009), 2.
38. Makau W. Mutua, "Human Rights and Powerlessness: Pathologies of Choice and Substance," *Buffalo Law Review* 56 (2008): 1029.
39. Makau W. Mutua, "The Ideology of Human Rights," *Virginia Journal of International Law* 36 (1996): 589.
40. On the challenges of speaking of rights in community-based training programs on AIDS in South Africa, see Peris Jones, *AIDS Treatment and Human Rights in Context* (London, 2009).
41. See, e.g., Daniel P. L. Chong, *Freedom from Poverty: NGOs and Human Rights Praxis* (Philadelphia, 2010).
42. Glendon, *A World Made New*.
43. Ibid., 10.
44. For an extended summary of the literature on this point, see Malcolm Langford, "Critiques of Human Rights", *Annual Review of Law and Social Science* 14 (2018), available at https://www.annualreviews.org/toc/lawsocsci/14/1.
45. Hunt, *Inventing Human Rights*, 58.
46. Costas Douzinas, *Human Rights and Empire: The Political Philosophy of Cosmopolitanism* (London, 2007), 245.
47. Ibid., 295.
48. Glendon, *A World Made New*.
49. Ibid.
50. Steven Jensen, *The Making of International Human Rights: The 1960s, Decolonization, and the Reconstruction of Global Values.* (Cambridge, 2016).
51. Adam Habib, "Political Power: Social Pacting, Human Rights and the Development Agenda," in *Symbols or Substance? The Role and Impact of Socio-Economic Rights Strategies in South Africa*, ed. Malcolm Langford et al. (Cambridge, 2013), 137.
52. Malcolm Langford, "Cosmopolitan Competition: The Case of International Investment," in *Cosmopolitan Justice and Its Discontents*, ed. Cecilia M. Bailliet and Katja Franko Aas (London, 2011), 178–204; Ernst-Ulrich Petersmann, "Introduction and Summary," in *Human Rights in International Investment Law and Arbitration*, ed. Pierre-Marie Dupuy et al. (Oxford, 2009), 3–42.
53. José E. Alvarez, "Contemporary International Law: An 'Empire of Law' or the 'Law of Empire,'" *American University International Law Review* 24, no. 5 (2009): 811–42.
54. Douzinas, *Human Rights and Empire*, 295.
55. Stuart A. Scheingold, *The Politics of Rights: Lawyers, Public Policy and Social Change* (Ann Arbor, 1974).
56. Ibid., 7.
57. Jens Bartelson, *Visions of World Community* (Cambridge, 2009), vi.

BIBLIOGRAPHY

Alvarez, José E. "Contemporary International Law: An 'Empire of Law' or the 'Law of Empire.'" *American University International Law Review* 24, no. 5 (2009): 811–42.

Bailliet, Cecilia M. "What Is to Become of Human Rights Rule-Based International Order within an Age of Neo-Medievalism?" In *Non-State Actors, Soft Law and Protective Regimes: From the Margins*, edited by Cecilia M. Bailliet, 95–124. Cambridge: Cambridge University, 2012.

Bartelson, J. *Visions of World Community*. Cambridge: Cambridge University Press, 2009.

Bass, G. "The New Old Thing." *New Republic*, 20 October 2010.

Beitz, Charles R. *The Idea of Human Rights*. Oxford: Oxford University Press, 2009.

Bull, Hedley. *The Anarchical Society*. New York: Columbia University Press, 2002.

Castellino, Joshua. *Social Inclusion & Human Rights: Implications for 2030 and Beyond. Background Paper for the High-Level Panel of Eminent Persons on the Post-2015 Development Agenda*. UN Sustainable Development Solutions Network, 15 January 2013. http://unsdsn.org/wp-content/uploads/2014/02/130114-Social-Exclusion-and-Human-Rights-Paper-for-HLP.pdf.

Chong, Daniel P. L. *Freedom from Poverty: NGOs and Human Rights Praxis*. Philadelphia: University of Pennsylvania Press, 2010.

Cox, Robert W. "Social Forces, States and World Orders: Beyond International Relations Theory." *Millennium: Journal of International Studies* 10, no. 2 (1981): 126–55.

Douzinas, Costas. *Human Rights and Empire: The Political Philosophy of Cosmopolitanism*. London: Routledge-Cavendish, 2007.

Dworkin, Ronald. *Taking Rights Seriously*. Cambridge, MA: Harvard University Press, 1977.

Friedrichs, Jörg. "The Meaning of New Medievalism." *European Journal of International Relations* 7, no. 4 (2001): 475–501.

Gauri, Varun, and Daniel M. Brinks. *Courting Social Justice: Judicial Enforcement of Social and Economic Rights in the Developing World*. New York: Cambridge University Press, 2008.

Glendon, Mary Ann. *A World Made New: Eleanor Roosevelt and the Universal Declaration of Human Rights*. New York: Random House, 2001.

Habib, Adam. "Political Power: Social Pacting, Human Rights and the Development Agenda." In *Symbols or Substance? The Role and Impact of Socio-Economic Rights Strategies in South Africa*, edited by Malcolm Langford, Ben Cousins, Jackie Dugard, and Tshepo Madlingozi, 131–155. Cambridge: Cambridge University Press, 2014.

Hunt, Lynn. *Inventing Human Rights*. New York: W. W. Norton, 2007.

Ishay, Micheline. *The History of Human Rights: From Ancient Times to the Globalization Era*. Berkeley: University of California, 2008.

Jones, Peris. *AIDS Treatment and Human Rights in Context*. London: Palgrave Macmillan, 2009.

Langford, Malcolm. "Critiques of Human Rights", *Annual Review of Law and Social Science*, 14 (2018), available at: https://www.annualreviews.org/toc/lawsocsci/14/1

———. "Cosmopolitan Competition: The Case of International Investment." In *Cosmopolitan Justice and Its Discontents*, edited by Cecilia M. Bailliet and Katja Franko Aas, 178-204. London: Routledge, 2011.
Moyn, Samuel. *Not Enough: Human Rights in an Unequal World*. Cambridge, MA: Harvard University Press.
———. *The Last Utopia: Human Rights in History*. Cambridge, MA: Harvard University Press, 2010.
———. "On the Genealogy of Morals." *The Nation*, 17 April 2007.
Mutua, Makau W. "Human Rights and Powerlessness: Pathologies of Choice and Substance." *Buffalo Law Review* 56 (2008): 1027-1034.
———. "The Ideology of Human Rights." *Virginia Journal of International Law* 36 (1996): 589-657.
Petersmann, Ernst-Ulrich. "Introduction and Summary." In *Human Rights in International Investment Law and Arbitration*, edited by Pierre-Marie Dupuy, Francesco Francioni, and Ernst-Ulrich Petersmann, 3-42. Oxford: Oxford University Press, 2009.
Qin, Yaqing. "Why Is There No Chinese International Relations Theory?" *International Relations of the Asia-Pacific* 7, no. 3 (2007): 313-40.
Scheingold, Stuart A. *The Politics of Rights: Lawyers, Public Policy and Social Change*. Ann Arbor: University of Michigan Press, 1974.
Sen, Amartya. *The Idea of Justice*. Cambridge, MA: Harvard University Press, 2009.
Simmons, Beth A. *Mobilizing for Human Rights: International Law in Domestic Politics*. New York: Cambridge University Press, 2009.
Slaughter, Anne-Marie. "A Typology of Transjudicial Communication." *University of Richmond Law Review* 29, no. 1 (1994-95): 99-137.
Thornhill, Christopher. "Contemporary Constitutionalism and the Dialectic of Constituent Power." *Global Constitutionalism* 1, no. 3 (2012): 369-404.
Wiesel, Elie. "A Tribute to Human Rights." In *The Universal Declaration of Human Rights: Fifty Years and Beyond*, edited by Yael Danieli, Elsa Stamatopoulou, and Clarence J. Dias, 3-4. Amityville, NY: Baywood, 1999.

10

Democracy of the "New World"

The Great Binding Law of Peace and the Political System of the Haudenosaunee Confederacy

Lars Kirkhusmo Pharo

Indigenous American Knowledge Systems and the "World"

It is generally acknowledged that foods, animals, plants, agricultural techniques, and medicines from "America" or the so-called New World greatly benefitted the hypothetical Old World. Indigenous American knowledge systems, science, and philosophies are, however, not equally recognized. For example, whereas the concept and positional value of zero came to Europe first in the twelfth century through the Hindu-Arabic numeral and positional system, a mathematical and numerological system consisting of the concept of zero was independently invented in Mesoamerica. The Mesoamerican mathematical and philosophical concept of zero is recorded in the classic Maya (c. 200–c. 900) inscriptions as *mih*, signifying "nothing," though the symbol for the digit zero as placeholder in a place-value system was possibly conceived by the much earlier Olmec civilization.[1]

Another example of an independent innovation in America is a sophisticated system of accounting and recordkeeping employing the method of checks and balances founded upon a decimal place system of numeration in the Andes of South America. This system is recorded on *khipus* (i.e., dyed knotted strings for communication) of the Inka Empire (1438–1535). The principles of debit and credit, forming the double-entry system of accounting, constitute the two fundamental aspects of financial transactions in the bookkeeping system invented in Italy in the formative period of European capitalism.[2]

Democratic political systems with universal moral values existed in precolonial America and do not exclusively adhere to the European political heritage later disseminated to the world. This political idea and institution has accordingly an Indigenous American origin. In this chapter, I give a brief example of the political philosophy and system of democracy of an Indigenous American intellectual tradition, later conferred to colonizing descendants from Europe who constructed the political constitution of the United States of America at the end of the eighteenth century.

Democracy *avant la lettre* in America

From the beginning of the sixteenth century, various nations from Europe—with the English, Spanish, French, Russian, Dutch, and Portuguese as the foremost representatives—invaded and later conquered the vast continent to be known as "America." There is a Eurocentric mythology of American ("New World") historiography, that *history* begins after the arrival of Christopher Columbus in 1492:[3]

> A great myth that has been used to justify and to sustain the seizure of North and South America from native peoples is that what was "discovered" on this continent by Europeans was a wilderness, a "new world." The New World: fresh, virginal, unaltered by human hands. And in consequence of believing in the unspoiled nature of the land found here, all culture on this continent was considered then, and is considered now by many, to have been transplanted from the "advanced" civilization of Europe, the "Old World."[4]

Despite the destructive impact of colonial European and the later post-colonial nation-states of the Americas, there are extant numerous and different types of religious, philosophical, linguistic, and cultural systems of the many (c. 42 million) Indigenous peoples of the American continent. The Oglala Lakota professor Vine Deloria Jr. reminds us that the European designation "America" is not self-evident or undisputed: "When asked by an anthropologist what the Indians called America before the white man came, an Indian said simply, 'Ours.'"[5] Moreover, among quite a few Indigenous peoples, North America is called "Turtle Island."

There is a widespread assumption that Indigenous political systems represented so-called timocracies (from Gr. *timē*, "honor, worth, value," and *kratia*, "power, rule by") or societies where ideas about the "naturalness" and "correctness" of inequality and hierarchy are legitimized.[6] A concept of democracy does, however, exist *avant la lettre* in the political philosophies, systems, and practices of Indigenous peoples of America before the European arrival.

The Great Binding Law of Peace (GBLP) or *Kayáneñhsä'kóna* (Onondaga) constitution and the democratic political system of the Haudenosaunee (a.k.a. Iroquois) Confederacy of North America came into being many centuries before the European invasion.[7] European travelers and Jesuit missions provide the earliest written accounts about the Confederacy, which substantiate that it was created before the European invasion of the seventeenth century.[8] But according to Haudenosaunee tradition it was formed far earlier.[9]

The GBLP outlines principles of a democratic consensus system.[10] Furthermore, it proclaims equality among human beings and between genders, as well as peace with foreign nations—values of universal, inalienable human rights and inherent human dignity later expressed in the United Nations Declaration of Human Rights of 1948.[11] The Haudenosaunee ("People of the Long House") Confederacy is perhaps the oldest functioning democracy in the world. As the one of few independent reservations in North America, the Onondaga—just south of the city of Syracuse, New York—remains the democratic meeting place for the Grand Council of Chiefs, the traditional religious-political ruling body for the Haudenosaunee.

The Longhouse serves as the seat of government of the Grand Council of Chiefs, selected in accordance with the time-honored democratic system. Laws or ideas that come before the council are presented in the Indigenous language.[12] It is therefore notable that there were no democratic institutions but (absolute) monarchies and republican oligarchies in Europe when the Europeans colonized America. Moreover, the political models of Ancient Greece and Rome had imperfect democracies, since not only the majority of men but also women were excluded. Direct democracy in the Greek *polis* was restricted to participant, eligible citizens, whereas the Roman Republic was oligarchic (patrician/plebeian).

Democratic Principles of the Political Philosophy and System of the Haudenosaunee Confederacy

To conceptualize the category of democracy and its constitutional and institutional structures is complicated. There is no consensus on how to define democracy and democratic institutions although various conceptions and models have been established.[13] Democracy (from Gr. *demos*, "people," and *kratos*, "power") can be defined as a system of government where the people, free and with equal rights, participate in making decisions. In the following I will concisely outline democratic principles that exist in the political philosophy and polyarchic government of the Haudenosaunee.[14]

As a constitution, the GBLP formulates a political vision, defining the institutions and fundamental morals for the Confederacy. But it is also a supra-national legal constitution. The constitution of the GBLP expresses unity in diversity, where every nation's tradition and identity are secured. It is both a political and religious democratic system with ritual-religious institutions. Each nation and representative chiefs enjoy equal authority in the Confederacy, which shall stay together as a family in the Longhouse.[15]

The democratic principles of the Haudenosaunee Confederacy signify an egalitarian civil society, a society for the public good of every individual. There are equal rights for people without regard to culture, religion, language, ethnicity, or gender. The Haudenosaunee Confederacy can be categorized as a consensus and pluralist representative democracy, with civil (individual) liberty, freedom of speech, freedom from political persecution by government, and the rule of law including accountability (effective checks on rulers) and minority rights.[16] Metaphors of "single mind" and "single person" in Haudenosaunee languages refer to the consensus system. When a decision by the council has been passed, it comes with the backing of all chiefs in agreement and is said to be "of one mind."[17]

The original five nations of the Haudenosaunee established a democratic system of government led by the Grand Council of Chiefs consisting of fifty *hoyane* ("good minds," also known as "sachems") from each nation as representative chiefs to the council.[18] "Condolence" is a foundational ritual process of the Longhouse. It is also the way new chiefs, *hoyane*, are installed in their offices. They are approved after being questioned about qualifications.[19]

Haudenosaunee women have continuously lived with great status and authority in a matrilineal society.[20] The clan mothers are fundamental in the political system. They appoint male delegates or deputies (*hoyane*) to represent the clan at tribal meetings and at the council. The men of the clan later give their approval of the appointment. The fifty chiefs, who have an equal say, collaborate with clan mothers and the clans to ensure the preservation and wellbeing of the Haudenosaunee. In council they are the voice of the people.[21] Once a man is selected to be a *hoyane*, he holds that position for life, but he can be removed from office if he does not fulfill his responsibilities to the nation and the clan. Women (i.e., clan mothers) control the laws that constrain the conduct of the chiefs. They have the obligation to depose a chief if he breaks the rules.[22]

There are strict rules of conduct for the representative chiefs.[23] Democratic procedures are established in council after due protocol.[24] Consultations within the clan are later debated at the Grand Council.[25] Matters are discussed between the different nations and clans before the *hoyane* unanimously agree on the decision. This political process of public debate and consensus embodies a judicial-political checks-and-balances system, with a possible veto, between the nations. Unity is secured at every level of the parliamentary procedure. As the Firekeepers, the Onondaga nation give the subject for discussion to the other nations, where it is discussed according to a complicated procedure before the opinion is announced by the *Tadodaho*,[26] according to the consensus principle of the council.[27]

The GBLP states that the chiefs must put forward particularly important matters to the people for decision. The people can instigate impeachment, charges of treason, forward opinions and laws to the council, and remove *hoyane* from the League's council:

> Whenever a specially important matter or a great emergency is presented before the Confederate Council and the nature of the matter affects the entire body of the Five Nations, threatening their utter ruin, then the Lords of the Confederacy must submit the matter to the decision of their people and the decision of the people shall affect the decision of the Confederate Council. This decision shall be a confirmation of the voice of the people.[28]

The council depends therefore upon the will of the people.[29] The duties of the appointed chiefs secure the welfare of women and men of the Confederacy. The chiefs guarantee, moreover, the political rights of all people.[30] Every member of society, without regard to sociopolitical status or class, enjoys a protection of the rights of individual beings, including freedom from fear and want and freedom of speech and religion.[31] Furthermore, there is an ideal of communal property rights and sharing of resources. Everyone is related: men, women, young people, and children.[32]

Let me summarize the above-mentioned fundamental democratic principles of the Haudenosaunee Confederacy. There is an ideal of human social and political relations based on consensus and communication, where every human being enjoys equal rights.[33] Furthermore, there is participation and inclusiveness, with formally guaranteed political and civil rights and liberties. These are vital for ensuring the citizens' ability to control political processes through a judicial checks-and-balances system, which signifies a separation of powers.[34] The governmental system has institutions with political accountability ensuring that elected officials follow the interests of constituents, rather than personal interests.[35] There is also accountability that secures direct interaction between politicians and citizens concerning legislation and implementation.[36]

The Haudenosaunee political system can be classified as not only a representative and pluralist but also a deliberative democracy with the aforementioned fundamental consensus principle, where public reasoning focused on the common good motivates political decisions among informed and competent participants who are open to persuasion.[37] It can also be categorized as an egalitarian democracy with civil liberties and rights, which is a key feature for political empowerment as well as political and social equality.[38] There is a principle of communal property rights, religious freedom, and gender and ethnic equality. It signifies a system of inclusive citizenship where citizens and permanent residents enjoy the protections of the law.[39]

Conflict studies of democracy and interstate conflict hypothesize that there is an obvious relationship between democracy and peace.[40] Equality, rules for making decisions, and laws for peaceful relations between nations are stated in the judicial-political doctrine of the GBLP.[41] It announces the "Good Message," the "Power," and the "Peace" to separate nations and people with no regard to culture, ethnicity, religion, or language. Every nation shall be one under the Great Law. Peace will unite all people but with equal authority between nations.[42] Peace is the foundation of the government and a vigorous lifestyle based on living in harmony with the (natural) world. The GBLP provides a model of freedom for all on the basis of a balance of responsibilities in an egalitarian system. Peace is recognized as being built upon law and justice. Righteousness practiced between people and nations, where the symbol of peace is metaphorically conceived as a tree with roots to the four cardinal directions of the world, represents an extension of its message to the people of the world.[43] A much later, related, and essential reference document to the GBLP, outlining equivalent universal moral principles, is the Universal Declaration of Human Rights of 1948, later followed and complemented in 2007 by the United Nations Declaration on the Rights of Indigenous Peoples.[44]

Epistemology of Political Philosophies and Practices of the World

In America it is to a certain extent only Europeans and their descendent colonizers that have enjoyed the symbolic prestige of having complex political traditions and systems. As noted, it is common in political science to claim that the idea of democracy was exclusively constructed in Ancient Greece and later developed by European philosophy and national governments from the late eighteenth century. In line with this lack of knowledge, non-Anglo-American political democratic institutions have been largely ignored in the scholarly literature. This is demonstrated in the conceptualizing of the idea of democracy in America from Alexis de Tocqueville's *De la démocratie en Amérique* (1835–40) to Samuel Huntington's *Who Are We? The Challenges to America's National Identity* (2004).

Even though the French nobleman Tocqueville observed with admiration the egalitarian tradition and practices among Native Americans, in *De la démocratie en Amérique* he claims that Indigenous peoples were all equal and free but as opposed to Anglo-Americans they did not possess a democratic government. Tocqueville maintains that Indigenous peoples are Americans but not democratic ("Ils sont américains sans être démocratiques") and are therefore not relevant to his analysis of democracy in the United States.[45] Tocqueville displays a lack of knowledge and intellectual curiosity—similar to later political scientists, sociologists, anthropologists, and historians—not only about the confederacy system of the Haudenosaunee but also of political institutions of other Indigenous nations of North and South America.

In his book *Who Are We? The Challenges to America's National Identity* (2004), the professor of political science Samuel P. Huntington emphasizes that the United States was founded by English settlers from the beginning of the seventeenth century. They created a distinctive culture and language (i.e., American English). The "American Creed," as expressed by Thomas Jefferson, is the result of the settler culture of the Anglo-Protestants who established American society in the seventeenth and eighteenth centuries, featuring English concepts of rule of law and the limits of government power, representative government, private property, work ethic, a legacy of European art, literature, philosophy, music, and Protestant moral values of individualism, liberty, and equality.[46] In particular, Protestantism, with its many denominations, constitutes the heart of American culture and the American Creed, whose "Protestant origins make America unique among nations."[47] The American Creed as the "core component of American identity" constitutes a liberal democratic principle. The creedal component, writes Huntington, represents "American exceptionalism" according to various observers from America and Europe. Now this exceptionalism has become "universalism" as democracy has become globally accepted as the rule of government.[48] Huntington argues that the political and religious (Protestant) idea of democracy, if not exclusively an "Old World" notion, is the product of the creation of a unique constitution and unprecedented political system by Anglo colonizers originating from the "Old World" but created in the colonial and post-colonial "New World."

Interestingly, Karl Marx and Friedrich Engels differed in this respect from traditional European and Anglo-American political historiography. On the basis of the American anthropologist Lewis Henry Morgan's study *Ancient Society: Researches in the Lines of Human Progress from Savagery through Barbarism to Civilization* (1877), Marx wrote the commentary *Die ethnologischen Exzerpthefte* (The Ethnological Notebooks) between 1880 and 1882.[49] In *Der Ursprung der Familie, des Privateigenthums und des Staats* (The Origin of the Family, Private Property and the State) from 1884, Engels used the notes from Marx's manuscript and outlined the "democratic assembly" with equal votes for men and women in the Iroquois (Haudenosaunee) council. Furthermore, Engels claims that their GBLP was a "public constitution."[50] It is indeed remarkable that neither Marx nor Engels conducted field research in America but were still able to distinguish aspects of the Haudenosaunee democratic constitution and political practices. But their observations have mainly gone unnoticed by scholars.

Frances Jennings maintains the significant Indigenous impact on American colonial and post-colonial political history, while Jack Weatherford argues that democracy in the United States is influenced by Native American political traditions and values.[51] According to certain scholars, the democratic principles of the GBLP influenced the United States constitution of 1787 and the constitutional democracy of the United States.[52] In 1988, the US Senate and House of Representatives passed Concurrent Resolution 331 acknowledging the Haudenosaunee Confederacy's influence upon the Founding Fathers and the contribution of its democratic principles in making the US constitution.[53] In his speech during the 2013 White House Tribal Nations Conference, President Barack Obama stated, "I think we could learn from the Iroquois Confederacy, just as our Founding Fathers did when they laid the groundwork for our democracy."[54]

Surprisingly, and most unfortunately, this important political contribution to world history is largely unknown within academia and among the general public. A "globalized world" requires at least elementary knowledge and recognition of the (moral) philosophical and political traditions and influence of the American Indigenous peoples. In this regard, the education systems of national governments have a fundamental responsibility, which they have to this date failed to fulfill.

Lars Kirkhusmo Pharo is Professor of Religions and Ethics at Nord University. His recent publications include *The Ritual Practice of Time: Philosophy and Sociopolitics of Mesoamerican Religious Calendars* (Brill, 2013), Moral Knowledge in Early Colonial Latin America. 53-94. Helge Wendt (ed.) (MPIWG). *The Globalization of Knowledge in the Iberian Colonial World* (Max-Planck-Institut für Wissenschaftsgeschichte, 2016), *Concepts of Conversion: The Politics of Missionary Scriptural Translations* (Walter De Gruyter, 2017), and "Multilingualism and Lingua Francae of Indigenous Civilizations of America" 467-519. *Studies in Multilingualism, Lingua Franca, and Lingua Sacra*, ed. Markham J. Geller and Jens Braarvig (Max-Planck-Institut für Wissenschaftsgeschichte, 2018).

NOTES

1. Nikolai Grube and Werner Nahm, *A Sign for the Syllable* mi (Washington, DC, 1990); John S. Justeson, "Numerical Cognition and the Development of 'Zero' in Mesoamerica," in *The Archaeology of Measurement: Comprehending Heaven, Earth and Time in Ancient Societies*, ed. Colin Renfrew and Iain Morley (Cambridge, 2010), 49-50.
2. Gary Urton, "Sin, Confession, and the Arts of Book and Cord-Keeping: An Intercontinental and Transcultural Exploration of Accounting and Governmentality," *Comparative Studies in Society and History* 51, no. 4 (2009): 801-31.

3. Oren R. Lyons and John C. Mohawk, eds., *Exiled in the Land of the Free: Democracy, Indian Nations, and the US Constitution* (Santa Fe, NM, 1992).
4. Peter Matthiessen, "Foreword," in Lyons and Mohawk, *Exiled in the Land of the Free*, xi.
5. Vine Deloria Jr., *Custer Died for Your Sins: An Indian Manifesto* (Norman, 1988), 166.
6. Roy A. Rappaport, *Ritual and Religion in the Making of Humanity* (Cambridge, 1999), 426–27; Stephen D. Houston and Takeshi Inomata, *The Classic Maya* (Cambridge, 2009), 43.
7. The five original nations of the Haudenosaunee were the Mohawks, Oneidas, Onondagas, Cayugas, and Senecas (the Tuscaroras joined the Confederacy in 1722/23). The Haudenosaunee became the greatest indigenous power in colonial America, with a homeland that spanned northern New York between the Hudson and Niagara Rivers and an influence that extended from the Ottawa River to the Chesapeake Bay and from New England to Illinois. The GBLP came into being long before the English Bill of Rights (1689), the American Declaration of Independence (1776), and the French Declaration of the Rights of Man (1798).
8. Bruce G. Trigger, "Early Iroquoian Contacts with Europeans," in *Northeast*, ed. Bruce G. Trigger (Washington, DC, 1978), 344–56; Hanni Woodbury, "Introduction," in *Concerning the League: The Iroquois League Tradition as Dictated in Onondaga by John Arthur Gibson*, by John Arthur Gibson, ed. and trans. Hanni Woodbury, with Reg. Henry and Harry Webster (Winnipeg, 1992), xi. Cf. William M. Beauchamp, ed., *Moravian Journals Relating to Central New York 1745–1766* (Syracuse, NY, 1916); Frances Jennings, ed., *The History and Culture of Iroquois Diplomacy: An Interdisciplinary Guide to the Treaties of the Six Nations and Their League* (Syracuse, NY, 1985); Reuben G. Thwaites, ed., *The Jesuit Relations and Allied Documents: Travel and Explorations of the Jesuit Missionaries in New France, 1610–1791*, 73 vols. (Cleveland, OH, 1896–1901).
9. "Timeline," Onondaga Nation website, retrieved 2 February 2018 from http://www.onondaganation.org/history/timeline/.
10. Woodbury, "Introduction," xi, xxvi; Gibson, *Concerning the League*, 251–63.
11. Lars Kirkhusmo Pharo, "The Concepts of Human Dignity in the Moral Philosophies of Indigenous Peoples of the Americas," in *Cambridge Handbook of Human Dignity: Historical Traditions, Philosophical Interpretations, Legal Implementation and Contemporary Challenges*, ed. Marcus Düwell et al. (Cambridge, 2014), 147–155; Lars Kirkhusmo Pharo, "The Council of Valladolid (1550–1551): A European Disputation about the Human Dignity of Indigenous Peoples of the Americas," in Düwell et al., *Cambridge Handbook of Human Dignity*, 95–101.
12. Cf. Woodbury, "Introduction."
13. See Ian Shapiro, *The State of Democratic Theory* (Princeton, NJ, 2003); David Held, *Models of Democracy* (Cambridge, 2006); Michael Coppedge and John Gerring, with David Altman et al., "Conceptualizing and Measuring Democracy: A New Approach," *Perspectives on Politics* 9, no. 2 (2011): 247–67.
14. Robert A. Dahl, *A Preface to Democratic Theory* (Chicago, 1956).
15. Woodbury, "Introduction," xxvii; Gibson, *Concerning the League*, 304–11.

16. Dahl, *A Preface to Democratic Theory*; Held, *Models of Democracy*; Coppedge et al., "Conceptualizing and Measuring Democracy." For further discussions of law, see in particular the chapters by Chenxi Tang and Malcolm Langford in this volume.
17. Woodbury, "Introduction," xxv n50; Gibson, *Concerning the League*, 39–40, 221.
18. Woodbury, "Introduction," xxviii; Gibson, *Concerning the League*, 325–26, 334–45.
19. Woodbury, "Introduction," xxviii, xlix–l; Gibson, *Concerning the League*, 348–418, 697–701.
20. Sally Roesch Wagner has examined how the Haudenosaunee influenced the nineteenth-century women's rights movement in the United States. Sally Roesch Wagner, *Sisters in Spirit: Haudenosaunee (Iroquois) Influences on Early American Feminists* (Summertown, TN, 2001).
21. Woodbury, "Introduction," xxviii–xxxi; Gibson, *Concerning the League*, 418–22, 460–64, 497–502.
22. Woodbury, "Introduction," xxix; Gibson, *Concerning the League*, 450–57.
23. Woodbury, "Introduction," xxvi; Gibson, *Concerning the League*, 450–57.
24. Woodbury, "Introduction," xxvi; Gibson, *Concerning the League*, 252–63.
25. Donald A. Grinde, "Iroquois Political Theory and the Roots of American Democracy," in Lyons and Mohawk, *Exiled in the Land of the Free*, 235–36.
26. The *Tadodaho* is the religious leader, principal Onondaga chief, and the Firekeeper of the Confederacy.Woodbury, *Onondaga-English/English-Onondaga Dictionary*, 811.
27. Elisabeth Tooker, "The League of the Iroquois: Its History, Politics and Ritual," in Trigger, *Northeast*, 429.
28. Arthur C. Parker, *The Constitution of the Five Nations or The Iroquois Book of the Great Law* (Ohsweken, ON, [1916] 2006), 55.
29. Grinde, "Iroquois Political Theory," 236.
30. Parker, *Constitution of the Five Nations*, 34–40.
31. P. A. W. Wallace, *The White Roots of Peace* (Ohsweken, ON, [1946] 1998), 57–58.
32. Woodbury, "Introduction," xxix; Gibson, *Concerning the League*, 38–39, 457–60.
33. Gibson, *Concerning the League*, 210.
34. E.g., Larry Diamond and Leonardo Morlino, *Assessing the Quality of Democracy* (Baltimore, MD, 2005); Ronald Inglehart and Christian Welzel, *Modernization, Cultural Change and Democracy: The Human Development Sequence* (Cambridge, 2006).
35. Simeon Djanknov et al., "Courts," *Quarterly Journal of Economics* 118, no. 2 (2003): 453–517.
36. Inglehart and Welzel, *Modernization, Cultural Change and Democracy*.
37. Held, *Models of Democracy*; Coppedge et al., "Conceptualizing and Measuring Democracy."
38. Robert A. Dahl, *Democracy and Its Critics* (New Haven, CT, 1986); Robert A. Dahl, *Dilemmas of Pluralist Democracy* (New Haven, CT, 1982); Coppedge et al., "Conceptualizing and Measuring Democracy."
39. Coppedge et al., "Conceptualizing and Measuring Democracy," 253–57.
40. Bruce Russet and John Oneal, *Triangulating Peace: Democracy, Interdependence and International Organizations* (New York, 2001).

41. Woodbury, "Introduction," xxix–xxx; Gibson, *Concerning the League*, 440–46, 458–60.
42. Woodbury, "Introduction," xx, xxvii; Gibson, *Concerning the League*, 14–15, 27–33, 37–41, 304.
43. Wallace, *White Roots of Peace*, 32, 34–35, 66.
44. Pharo, "Concepts of Human Dignity"; Pharo, "Council of Valladolid."
45. Alexis de Tocqueville, *De la démocratie en Amérique* (Paris, [1835–40] 1986), 1: 65, 95, 467.
46. Samuel P. Huntington, *Who Are We? The Challenges to America's National Identity* (New York, 2004), xv–xvi, 40–41, 59–80.
47. Ibid., 63; 62–69.
48. Ibid., 257.
49. Karl Marx, *The Ethnological Notebooks of Karl Marx (Studies of Morgan, Phear, Maine, Lubbock)*, ed. Lawrence Krader (Assen, 1972). Cf. Carol L. Bagley and Jo Ann Ruckman, "Iroquois Contributions to Modern Democracy and Communism," *American Indian Culture and Research Journal* 7, no. 2 (1983): 53–72
50. Friedrich Engels, *The Origin of the Family, Private Property and the State* (London, [1884] 2010), 120, 124–30, 158–59; Marx, *Ethnological Notebooks*, 145–46, 162–73.
51. Frances Jennings, *The Ambiguous Iroquois Empire: The Covenant Chain Confederation of Indian Tribes with English Colonies* (New York, 1990); Frances Jennings, *The Invasion of America: Indians, Colonialism, and the Cant of Conquest* (Chapel Hill, 2010); Jack Weatherford, *Indian Givers: How Native Americans Transformed the World* (New York, 2010).
52. Carol L. Bagley and Jo Ann Ruckman, "Iroquois Contributions to Modern Democracy and Communism," *American Indian Culture and Research Journal* 7, no. 2 (1983): 53–72; Gregory Schaaf, *The US Constitution and the Great Law of Peace: A Comparison of Two Founding Documents* (Santa Fe, NM, 2004).
53. It was written into the Congressional Record. John C. Mohawk and Oren R. Lyons, "Introduction," in Lyons and Mohawk, *Exiled in the Land of the Free*, 1–12.
54. "Remarks by the President at Tribal Nations Conference," Archived Obama White House Website, 13 November 2013, retrieved 6 August 2018 from https://obamawhitehouse.archives.gov/realitycheck/the-press-office/2013/11/13/remarks-president-tribal-nations-conference.

BIBLIOGRAPHY

Bagley, Carol L., and Jo Ann Ruckman. "Iroquois Contributions to Modern Democracy and Communism." *American Indian Culture and Research Journal* 7, no. 2 (1983): 53–72.

Beauchamp, William M., ed. *Moravian Journals Relating to Central New York 1745–1766*. Syracuse, NY: Dehler Press, 1916. Reprinted in 1976 by AMS Press.

Coppedge, Michael, and John Gerring, with David Altman et al. "Conceptualizing and Measuring Democracy: A New Approach." *Perspectives on Politics* 9, no. 2 (2011): 247–67.

Dahl, Robert A. *Democracy and Its Critics.* New Haven, CT: Yale University Press, 1986.
———. *Dilemmas of Pluralist Democracy.* New Haven, CT: Yale University Press, 1982.
———. *A Preface to Democratic Theory.* Chicago: University of Chicago Press, 1956.
Deloria, Vine, Jr. *Custer Died for Your Sins: An Indian Manifesto.* Norman: University of Oklahoma Press, 1988.
Diamond, Larry, and Leonardo Morlino. *Assessing the Quality of Democracy.* Baltimore, MD: Johns Hopkins University Press, 2005.
Djanknov, Simeon, Rafael La Porta, Florencio Lopez-de Silanes, and Andrei Shleifer. "Courts." *Quarterly Journal of Economics* 118, no. 2 (2003): 453–517.
Düwell, Marcus, Jens Braarvig, Roger Brownsword, and Dietmar Mieth, eds. *Cambridge Handbook of Human Dignity: Historical Traditions, Philosophical Interpretations, Legal Implementation and Contemporary Challenges.* Cambridge: Cambridge University Press, 2014.
Engels, Friedrich *The Origin of the Family, Private Property and the State.* London: Penguin Classics, [1884] 2010.
Gibson, John Arthur. *Concerning the League: The Iroquois League Tradition as Dictated in Onondaga by John Arthur Gibson.* Edited and translated by Hanni Woodbury, with Reg. Henry and Harry Webster. Winnipeg: Algonquian and Iroquoian Linguistics, 1992.
Grinde, Donald A. "Iroquois Political Theory and the Roots of American Democracy." In *Exiled in the Land of the Free: Democracy, Indian Nations, and the US Constitution*, edited by Oren R. Lyons and John C. Mohawk, 227–80. Santa Fe, NM: Clear Light Publishers, 1992.
Grube, Nikolai, and Werner Nahm. *A Sign for the Syllable* mi. Research Reports on Ancient Maya Writing 33. Washington, DC: Center for Maya Research, 1990.
Held, David. *Models of Democracy.* Cambridge: Polity Press, 2006.
Houston, Stephen D., and Takeshi Inomata. *The Classic Maya.* Cambridge World Archaeology. Cambridge: Cambridge University Press, 2009.
Huntington, Samuel P. *Who Are We? The Challenges to America's National Identity.* New York: Simon & Schuster, 2004.
Inglehart, Ronald, and Christian Welzel. *Modernization, Cultural Change and Democracy: The Human Development Sequence.* Cambridge: Cambridge University Press, 2006.
Jennings, Frances. *The Ambiguous Iroquois Empire: The Covenant Chain Confederation of Indian Tribes with English Colonies.* New York: W. W. Norton, 1990.
———. *The Invasion of America: Indians, Colonialism, and the Cant of Conquest.* Institute of Early American History & Culture. Chapel Hill: University of North Carolina Press, 2010.
———, ed. *The History and Culture of Iroquois Diplomacy: An Interdisciplinary Guide to the Treaties of the Six Nations and Their League.* Syracuse, NY: Syracuse University Press, 1985.
Justeson, John S. "Numerical Cognition and the Development of 'Zero' in Mesoamerica." In *The Archaeology of Measurement: Comprehending Heaven, Earth and Time in Ancient Societies*, edited by Colin Renfrew and Iain Morley, 43–53. Cambridge: Cambridge University Press, 2010.

Lyons, Oren R., and John C. Mohawk, eds. *Exiled in the Land of the Free: Democracy, Indian Nations, and the US Constitution*. Santa Fe, NM: Clear Light Publishers, 1992.

Marx, Karl. *The Ethnological Notebooks of Karl Marx (Studies of Morgan, Phear, Maine, Lubbock)*. Edited by Lawrence Krader. Assen: Van Gorcum, 1972.

Matthiessen, Peter. "Foreword". In *Exiled in the Land of the Free: Democracy, Indian Nations, and the US Constitution*, edited by Oren R. Lyons and John C. Mohawk. Santa Fe, NM: Clear Light Publishers, 1992.

Mohawk, John C., and Oren R. Lyons. "Introduction." In *Exiled in the Land of the Free: Democracy, Indian Nations, and the US Constitution*, edited by Oren R. Lyons and John C. Mohawk, 1–12. Santa Fe, NM: Clear Light Publishers, 1992.

Morgan, Lewis Henry. *Ancient Society: Researches in the Lines of Human Progress from Savagery through Barbarism to Civilization*. New Brunswick, NJ: Transaction, [1877] 2000.

Parker, Arthur C. *The Constitution of the Five Nations or The Iroquois Book of the Great Law*. Iroquois Reprints. Ohsweken, ON: Iroqrafts, [1916] 2006.

Pharo, Lars Kirkhusmo. "The Concepts of Human Dignity in the Moral Philosophies of Indigenous Peoples of the Americas." In *Cambridge Handbook of Human Dignity: Historical Traditions, Philosophical Interpretations, Legal Implementation and Contemporary Challenges*, ed. Marcus Düwell et al., 147–155. Cambridge: Cambridge University Press, 2014.

———. "The Council of Valladolid (1550–1551): A European Disputation about the Human Dignity of Indigenous Peoples of the Americas." In *Cambridge Handbook of Human Dignity: Historical Traditions, Philosophical Interpretations, Legal Implementation and Contemporary Challenges*, ed. Marcus Düwell et al., 95–101. Cambridge: Cambridge University Press, 2014.

Rappaport, Roy A. *Ritual and Religion in the Making of Humanity*. Cambridge: Cambridge University Press, 1999.

Roesch Wagner, Sally. *Sisters in Spirit: Haudenosaunee (Iroquois) Influences on Early American Feminists*. Summertown, TN: Book Publishing Company, 2001.

Russet, Bruce, and John Oneal. *Triangulating Peace: Democracy, Interdependence and International Organizations*. New York: W. W. Norton, 2001.

Schaaf, Gregory. *The US Constitution and the Great Law of Peace: A Comparison of Two Founding Documents*. Santa Fe, NM: Center for Indigenous Arts and Cultures, 2004.

Shapiro, Ian. *The State of Democratic Theory*. Princeton, NJ: Princeton University Press, 2003.

Thwaites, Reuben G., ed. *The Jesuit Relations and Allied Documents: Travel and Explorations of the Jesuit Missionaries in New France, 1610–1791*. 73 vols. Cleveland, OH: Burrows Brothers, 1896–1901. Reprinted in 1959 by Pageant.

Tocqueville, Alexis de. *De la démocratie en Amérique*. Paris: Gallimard, [1835–40] 1986.

Tooker, Elisabeth. "The League of the Iroquois: Its History, Politics and Ritual." In *Northeast*, edited by Bruce G. Trigger, 418–41. Washington, DC: Smithsonian Institution, 1978.

Trigger, Bruce G. "Early Iroquoian Contacts with Europeans." In *Northeast*, edited by Bruce G. Trigger. Washington, DC: Smithsonian Institution, 1978, 344–356.

———, ed. *Northeast*. Handbook of North American Indians 15. Washington, DC: Smithsonian Institution, 1978.

Urton, Gary. "Sin, Confession, and the Arts of Book and Cord-Keeping: An Intercontinental and Transcultural Exploration of Accounting and Governmentality." *Comparative Studies in Society and History* 51, no. 4 (2009): 801–31.

Wallace, P. A. W. *The White Roots of Peace*. Iroquois Reprints. Ohsweken, ON: Iroqrafts, [1946] 1998.

Weatherford, Jack. *Indian Givers: How Native Americans Transformed the World*. New York: Broadway, 2010.

Woodbury, Hanni. "Introduction." In *Concerning the League: The Iroquois League Tradition as Dictated in Onondaga by John Arthur Gibson*, by John Arthur Gibson, edited and translated by Hanni Woodbury, with Reg. Henry and Harry Webster, xi–lxi. Winnipeg: Algonquian and Iroquoian Linguistics, 1992.

Woodbury, Hanni. *Onondaga-English/English-Onondaga Dictionary*. Toronto. University of Toronto Press. 2003.

▶• 11 •◀

The Immanent World

Responsibility and Spatial Justice

Andreas Philippopoulos-Mihalopoulos

What World before Globalization?

Niklas Luhmann famously came up with a concept of globalization that preceded the term. *Weltgesellschaft* ("world society") is a non-totalizing, non-unifying understanding of the world as a continuous process of folding and unfolding.[1] The concept hardly constitutes a leap from Luhmann's narrower understanding of society (rather than *world* society) as a world without outside, namely a continuous inside that expands or contracts and that in so doing extends its topology.[2] Luhmann's world is one of communications between systems rather than one of material extensions, but materiality is an inherent feature of the theory's expected development, as I have argued elsewhere, in the sense that the seeds for a material autopoiesis are already included in the original theory both of biological autopoiesis and Luhmann's sociological version.[3] What is of interest here is that Luhmann's society is never seen in its ontological status but only and always as an epistemological construction. The theory of autopoiesis, namely *self-creation*, that Luhmann employed from biology reserves a pivotal role for the observer ("anything said is said by an observer," in Maturana and Varela's words), and Luhmann has continued on this level of observation of reality, albeit by positing a system as an observer.[4] Although the observation point is not a privileged one, it still assumes that a certain distance is posited between the observer and the world. For this reason, an observer can never apprehend the whole world because she would necessarily have to include herself in the observation. But her own body, the materiality of her own systemic presence, remains a blind spot, the necessary blind spot of any observation that enables observation and disables totality.

Observation, however, can be seen as the ethical responsibility of each system of which society consists. Law, politics, religion, science, media, and so on observe the world and how parts of the world observe each other. I choose to call this a responsibility because this is the only way in which systems can carry on with their autopoiesis, that is, their continuous generation of themselves. A system has the *responsibility* to carry on operating, to maintain its topology of *here*. Simply put, autopoiesis is survival, and each system has only one objective (and one responsibility): to survive, namely autopoietically to reproduce itself and its elements. Observation is the only way in which a system can carry on its autopoiesis without risking falling into solipsism. Observation opens up the possibility of change and development, since it is the basic tool of cognitive openness of the system. The latter is always found in a simultaneous co-dependency with normative closure, which means that the system can only understand what is already part of its operations and never anything that lies outside, at least not until "translated" into its own systemic language. This, counterintuitively, makes observation only and always self-observation, since the system manages to observe what it manages to observe and nothing more. What a system does not manage to observe remains the *environment* for the system, that is, an unknown and inaccessible quantity to the system. Nevertheless, at any point the system can extend its topology by (self-)observing, thus incorporating parts of its environment within the system.

The systemic incorporation of chunks of its environment within its boundaries is the system's *worlding*. A world unto itself, the system's worlding never ceases. While carefully eavesdropping on its own entrails, the system expands and contracts materially and cognitively. Every systemic foray into the environment is an exercise in worlding, and in that sense also othering: the system always becomes other than itself, moving away from its previous boundaries and into a new state of systemic topology. Any prediction of how society develops can only be based on the careful observation of the shifting boundaries of each system. For this is all that systems do: observe. And this is why they cannot directly affect each other, regulate their impact on each other, or indeed control each other. Observation is always self-observation, an openness trapped in closure, a necessary illusion of transcendence amidst blocks of immanence. But how can closures come together and reproduce immanence? How can all these hermits produce a world? This is the reason for which Luhmann's society is nothing more than a happenstance, an improbability that happened to happen and continues to happen for as long as it manages to. Society is an aggregation of its systems and receives its limits from the boundaries of its systems. Little more than an absence of environment, a hole in the environmental chaos of miscommunication, a nebulous formation that sustains itself as a bunch of communications huddled together. This is what society is, namely "a system totally and exclusively determined by itself."⁵ In a beautiful fragment of dialogue between Jean-François Lyotard and Luhmann, the immanence of the world was shared. Lyotard recounts: "It was possible for us to form a small common front against the waves of ecologist eloquence. A two-sided front. There is no Nature, no *Umwelt*, external to the system, he explained."⁶

Luhmann molds his theory into a vessel that accommodates both self-limitations and the altogether surprising apparition of otherness within, in the double form of worlding and othering. For as soon as worlding appears as solipsistic closure, othering dilutes it. This dilution, paradoxically, does not come through openness but through a deepening of closure and the fumbling for openness within: an oxygen shaft that connects the darkness of the blind system to worlding. The world becomes other by bringing everything within the world. But is this not a completed, achieved all-inclusiveness? Is this not finally a synthesis, society as maximum, world as totality? Almost, bar one little point: the point from which the *impossibility* to observe the totality becomes observable. An ontological epistemologist, if the pun is forgiven, is one that leaves oneself outside the world. The result is double: on the one hand, since this is the only way of observing the world, one severs the world and constructs the illusion of outside. Here is the world; there I am, looking at the world. All the observers become autopoietic Little Princes that land on earth while still retaining the observational distance afforded to them by their own planet somewhere up there (where? one does not know—this will remain a blind spot). On the other hand, in leaving oneself out, one risks losing the necessary illusion of all-inclusiveness. One necessity versus another, Antoine de Saint-Exupéry versus Niklas Luhmann. Both grand but necessary illusions, incubated in carton boxes in which sheep bleat and the world is bleeding.

The collapse of the illusion is perhaps a risk worth taking, although not before the future bleeding of the world is firmly included in the system. Luhmann has already engulfed both the spatial and temporal horizon of society within society by qualifying the latter as the *Weltgesellschaft*, or "world society."⁷ *Weltgesellschaft* is a horizontal plane of flows of closure and whirls of self-observation that slowly but fairly steadily moves toward its future production of autopoiesis. The concept of a horizontal world as the orientation of society means that no system, whether national or regional, orients itself on a merely local basis. This is not a refusal to acknowledge local differences. On the contrary, such differences are contained in their fragmented potentiality as part of a functionally differentiated horizon that expands or contracts depending on its empty content. Indeed, the world is the horizon of any self-observation. Since, however, self-observation is internal, so is the world. Each system is a world unto itself. Each systemic boundary is an event of internalization of *Weltgesellschaft*, constituting at the same time the only locus in which *Weltgesellschaft* can present itself ontologically. This is the grand paradox of autopoiesis as ontologizing epistemology: each system is a soliloquizing epistemological observer that ontologizes its observations as the only thing that exists, or as Luhmann puts it, "systems operate under the illusion of contact with the environment—at least while they observe that they observe and not how they observe."[8] Accordingly, the world is posited ontologically in each system, and operates as a spatial and temporal systemic horizon. In parallel to this, Luhmann posits another level of observation, that of second order, which affords the necessary distance to look at *Weltgesellschaft* as a whole, with its various systems observing each other. This is the observation of *how* (in Luhmann's quote above) others observe, rather than *what* they observe, and only impressionistically a more privileged point of view. In fact, no observation can include the locus from which observation takes place. Whether first or second order, observation generates multiple blind spots, all of which guarantee the non-synthetic nature of society.

Weltgesellschaft appears to be the equivalent of a systemic fate, as inaccessible as it is inevitable. Its contribution to contemporary sociology can be found especially in its dialogue with globalization: as a predating concept (since, rather famously, Luhmann's shot at globalization discourse through the concept of *Weltgesellschaft* took place earlier than the discourse itself), *Weltgesellschaft* describes the totality while destabilizing its totalization.[9] To put it more concretely, the characterization of the world from one systemic point of view (the economic) as it often happens in globalization is a totalizing totality. On the other hand, *Weltgesellschaft* is the impossibility of replacing the multiplicity with a simplifying unity. For this reason, I suggest that *Weltgesellschaft* remains an untranslatable concept, as opposed to the readily "meaningful" *globalization*. The German concept *Weltgesellschaft* remains untranslatable into English because no translation can offer the unity of difference between the epistemological whispering of *Weltgesellschaft* and the ontological booming of "globalization."

Weltgesellschaft is not unlike Jean-Luc Nancy's dialogue between *mondialisation* (another untranslatable concept) and globalization.[10] This can be schematically put as, on the one hand, *mondialisation* as world-forming (or "the creation" of the world, as Nancy puts it, which is deprived of "any form of production in the sense of a fabrication that supposes a given, a project, and a producer," and which properly speaking "only depends on itself, while this 'self' is given from nowhere but from itself") and, on the other, globalization as suppression of this world-forming and the "enclosure in the undifferentiated space of a unitotality."[11] *Weltgesellschaft* is a description of something that produces itself without cause, direction, or any possibility of external "vision." I have dealt with the concept of world society and its ramifications for knowledge elsewhere.[12] Here, I would simply like to quote at length one of the most powerful descriptions of the concept, interestingly not by Luhmann but by Jean Clam:

> The topology of world society is the topology of paradoxical surfaces, of surfaces which re-enter themselves and make it impossible to distinguish the inside from the outside, the engulfing from the engulfed, the penetrating from the penetrated. This topology is the re-entry of the world into itself: the world as an extensive, sequential space for a non-entangling deployment of self and other re-enters itself as an all-present, non-sequential, paradoxical space of a constantly accomplished entanglement of a self and other.[13]

This "non-sequential, paradoxical" all-inclusiveness is worlding at work. While the world is worlding, alterity is constantly called forth from the folds of the present, creating one immanent yet infinite surface on which the self is no different from the other. This surface topology of the world is produced through the mechanism of *re-entry*, namely the reappearance, within the system, of the difference between system and environment.[14] Through these continuous interruptions, totality is destabilized, while its epistemology fragments into observational shards and its ontology folds and unfolds across the surface of immanence.

Where in the World to Begin?

Whatever the choice of beginning, it will seem unfair. Why privilege this space over that as a space of beginning, soon to be seen as origin? Why privilege this particular direction emanating from the point of beginning, soon to be seen as center? A solution might be to avoid beginning altogether (à la Deleuzian stuttering) or to accept the arbitrariness of beginning as Luhmann does. *Weltgesellschaft* has no fixed beginning and consequently no origin, center, or direction. It is a multiplication of systemic ontologies from which different autopoietic responsibilities emerge. In ethical terms, this means that responsibility is to be located in the process of multiplication. As I have mentioned, there is a fractal responsibility of observing, namely carrying on one's autopoiesis through othering, which is nothing else than pushing one's cognitive boundaries always further. But in a second-order observation, namely the how rather than the what, the responsibility becomes an autopoietic continuation of the process. Responsibility is the proliferation of systemic ontologies. Seen on the wider material surface, responsibility becomes an issue of justice. As Jean-Luc Nancy writes:

> How to do justice, not only to the whole of existence, but to all existences, taken together but distinctly and in a discontinuous way, not as the totality of their differences, and differends—precisely not that—but as these differences

together in a multiple way, if one can put it this way, or as a multiple together, if we can state it even less adequately ... —and held by a *co-* that is not a principle.[15]

The question of justice emerges from responsibility and precisely the kind of responsibility that does not emanate from one center, one pivot, or one unity of totalizing synthesis, but from within the crisscrossing corridors of observational flows that, however, have nowhere to go but to turn inside, to their infinite immanence of worlding. However, since all worlding is at the same time othering, the responsibility of being in the world is the autopoietic continuum of positing alterity in its ultimate presence as part of the world, yet otherworldly. The proliferation of *just heres* spreads across the surface of the world and emits its own need for just emplacement, corresponding to the obligations of other *heres* not only not to impede but indeed to guarantee their just emplacement. I have written on the spatiality of justice elsewhere, and among the various dimensions of the concept I would like to emphasize here the diffused responsibility of differentiated emplacement, that is, to put it in autopoietic terms, that only one system can occupy the exact topology of its worlding at any point in time.[16] This is not merely functional differentiation in the traditional Weberian/Luhmannian sense, namely the arbitrarily attributed point of differentiation among the various societal systems, such as law, politics, religion, economy, and so on, as well as the consequent disappearance of any vantage point from which one ideologically imposing description of society could emerge.[17] On the contrary, it goes directly to the material heart of the world. Justice is a question of material, spatial, and temporal emplacement and as such can only take place when its place is guaranteed by a reciprocal enforcement of rights of emplacement. This is a spatial justice that does not accept that state law or globalized constitutional forces can do a better job than the archipelagos of *heres* among them, in their reciprocal force of emplacement.

Spatial justice, therefore, emerges in the space of responsibility par excellence, namely not the center, the periphery, the boundary, or the beyond, but the space of the middle. The middle cannot be seen as a synthetic space between system and environment, nor indeed as an innocuous dialectical compromise in view of the impossibility of synthesis. The middle is a force against the material harking for origin, centrality, and boundaries. In French *milieu*, the middle is both environmental and interstitial—and this is how Deleuze and Guattari employ the concept.[18] They use the example of grass in order to describe it. Just as grass has no one root, central part, or limits to its expansion, in the same way to begin in the middle is to find oneself folded between the multiplicity of the world without a discernible origin, a specific center, and determined territorial limits.[19] The world is all there is and can be, itself an infinite plane of folds that unfold while othering, creating perspectives, systems, and bodies in a flurry of virtual generation. To be thrown into this orgasmic multiplicity is to be an ant ambling in the grass: one loses one's origin, one's preconceived ideas of location and destination, one's belief in the importance of the center. One is lost in a horizontal plane of movement, indeed what Deleuze and Guattari have called *plane of immanence*. On the plane, everything works as grass, as opposed to a tree with its defined root, trunk, and volume. As Deleuze and Guattari write, "arborescent systems are hierarchical systems with centers of significance and subjectification."[20] For this reason, they urge us to "make rhizomes, not roots, never plant! Don't sow, grow offshoots!"[21]

Offshoots and rhizomes are characteristics of the plane of immanence that, for Deleuze and Guattari, constitutes the world. Rhizomes specifically embody the posthuman understanding of humanity as a horizontal, trans-species, heterogeneous growth in a constant process of worlding. Worlding is not a linear, vertical construction, but a movement on a surface where any modulation is absorbed, closed in, and eventually spread. At the same time, although to position oneself in the space of the middle is a solid ethico-political responsibility that denies the primacy of hierarchies, the space in the middle itself is not a moral position. Neither necessarily "good" nor "bad," neither positive nor problematic, the space in the middle is a space of struggle—in this case, against origins, boundaries, centers. It is indeed the space of spatial justice, the terrain on which different claims for just emplacement are rehearsed and run in conflict or in parallel with each other, constituting assemblages with the materiality of their own bodies as well as that of the actual spaces in which they take place. This happens because the space in the middle is a space of encounters with other bodies, a space in which one's body affects and is affected by other bodies, and within this movement of affect, the body is deemed "good" or "bad." It is significantly not a space of *judgment*, of secure values, of fixed constructions. Rather, the space in the middle is precisely *in the middle*, neither this nor that side: judgment takes sides, institutes boundaries, emanates from a specific originary authority, and constructs centralities of power concentration. The middle is the space of justice, namely the space *between* the bodies and *of* the bodies, which determine the negotiation through their own positioning. As Deleuze writes, "there exists a justice that is opposed to all judgment, according to which bodies are marked by each other, and the debt is inscribed directly on the body following the finite blocks that circulate in a territory."[22] This might sound brutal, and it is indeed inspired by Antonin Artaud's theatre of cruelty. It is, however, much less cruel than the machines of judgment that fix bodies in inescapable arborescent hierarchies that reproduce the oppression of a better place outside, an escape route that is meant to pacify the horrors of the present.

The space in the middle, therefore, is full immanence, full materiality, and full immersion. It is not a boundary and therefore is not flanked by sides. It simply is, a fold amidst folding. Likewise, it offers no direction: just as the leaves of grass move with the wind, the space in the middle consists of the *encounter* between the grass and the wind. An encounter for Deleuze pushes the encountered parties out of their comfort zone of categories and identities, and throws them in a "mad becoming."[23] The grass becomes wind and moves along the wind's breath, the wind becomes grass and spreads itself on the ground: becoming itself is pushed deeper in the middle, as it were. Finally, the space in the middle offers no chronology and no external causality: all is interfolded in simultaneity and immanence. The wind becomes the grass, the grass becomes tomorrow's grass, its beginning is in the middle, in the space of here, manically flapping around its movement. Deleuze and Guattari use the example of the wasp and the orchid: "The orchid deterritorializes by forming an image, a tracing of a wasp; but the wasp reterritorializes on that image. The wasp is nevertheless deterritorialized, becoming a piece in the orchid's reproductive apparatus. But it reterritorializes the orchid by transporting its pollen. Wasp and orchid, as heterogeneous elements, form a rhizome."[24]

How does othering occur on the plane of immanence? Let me change register briefly.[25] In his book on Leibniz, *The Fold*, Deleuze folds his thought into Leibniz's fragments and gives us the *fold* itself, a concept that unfolds through Deleuze's work determining the relation between inside and outside, and with it subjectivity, materiality, and the world at large. The Leibnizian figure of the monad with its formula "no windows" is the site of the fold: a monad is "an inside without outside," but the outside is folded within.[26] The monad is filled with the folds of the outside, "but it includes them in its closure and all its actions are internal."[27] This internal doubling

> is not a doubling of the One, but a redoubling of the Other. It is not a reproduction of the Same, but a repetition of the Different. It is not an emanation of an "I," but something that places in immanence an always other or a Non-self. It is never the other who is a double in the doubling process, it is a self that lives me as the double of the other. I do not encounter myself on the outside, I find the other in me.[28]

This is Deleuze's way of moving away from the obvious dialectic potential of the inside/outside: immanence, doubling of difference, lack of synthesis, lack of historical move toward the bridging of the inside and the outside. On the contrary, inside and outside are contiguous, interfolding, echoing with the difference of difference but never to be told apart. From the inside (but is there anywhere else?), the space of the monad is a closed system that ingests its environment and converts it into its own materiality. The othering of the monad is by definition included in the monad, repeated internally as difference within.

The monad is unmirrored, its windows are blocked and the world is silent. It is "a unity that envelops a multiplicity," as Deleuze writes.[29]

Fold autopoiesis into the Deleuzian fold. A folding autopoiesis is an autopoiesis of difference and environmental proliferation, where enclosure means openness, immanence means flight, and where system and environment are the repetition of difference without reaching identity yet without being ontologically different from each other.[30] The outside is neither inferior to the inside nor dialectically opposite to it ("an opposition is no longer in question").[31] Just as the two are not arranged in hierarchy, in the same way the two can never be directly conciliated or neatly fused. Just like the Luhmannian *Weltgesellschaft*, the Leibnizian/Deleuzian baroque lacks synthesis. Polyphony shutters chambers and facades, making the house one with the wind, a veil that reveals while billowing. Levels, floors, folds in folds enveloping and developing anti-dialectically, with one task only: "how to continue the fold, to have it go through the ceiling, how to bring it to infinity."[32] This is the autopoietic task par excellence, a task that supersedes duty or mission and folds in the movement of the systemic innards. How to carry on, to continue making (*poein* = "to make, to create") oneself, to take the poetics of oneself through the ceiling and to the horizon, to open oneself to the vastness of the present? The autopoietic monad is not *in* the world but *for* the world: "closure is the condition of being for the world," guaranteeing the world's infinity through the monad's own finitude.[33] The inside folds the outside into its closure, and in doing so it guarantees the infinite potential of worlding and othering: it guarantees the world by excluding the world or rather by hyper-including it, by squeezing the world into a room. A counterintuitive teleology no doubt, but for this reason also routinely chopped up and brought to systemic measure. Autopoiesis embodies—*is* the body of—an "internal destiny" that makes the system "move from fold to fold, or what makes machines from machines all the way to infinity."[34] Autopoiesis is the continuous inclusion of the outside as a guarantee for the outside to carry on. To take an example, politics exist so that society can carry on. Yet, as far as the political system is concerned, autopoiesis exhausts itself in the topology of the system, like lapping waves at a lake's edge. Autopoiesis is the world, and there is nothing outside this. The causality of this responsibility to carry on remains incomplete, an atrophied limb turning back in, a blind teleology. As the space of absolute immanence, the monad contains the world.

The End Is Nowhere

All responsibility is one of emplacement. Being *for* the world is the ultimate emplacement of the struggle for spatial justice. This is a justice of space that extends in the world and its othering. Worlding generates other worlds as part of this world, and in so doing generates also a proliferation of directions, addresses, and velocities of responsibility. In a world without outside, the main ethical responsibility is that of positioning oneself in a way that would allow worlding and othering to carry on. This entails both claiming one's position in a pivotal vector of responsibility allocation, and withdrawing from potentially problematic ethical assemblages. It entails never abandoning the space in the middle, yet equally never succumbing to the space in-between, that fetishized third space that, in its attempt to avoid dialectics, manages to reinforce it. It entails never dwelling on origin and destination, yet entertaining the necessary illusions of attributions, in full awareness of both the necessary and the illusionary nature of such attributions.

Where does this responsibility end? The answer is *nowhere*. The challenge of the fold is to carry on folding and unfolding, worlding and othering. The challenge of this world is to carry on othering while retaining strong positions of responsibility in the strife for spatial justice. All lines lead further inside. Deleuze and Guattari have called them *lines of flight*, creative unfoldings that push the limits of the world further out but from the inside.[35] A line of flight is the mapping of the necessity of the illusion. As Peter Hallward writes on Deleuze's line of flight, "it must lead out of the world. Does this mean a return to transcendence, a leap into an otherworldly beyond? Not at all: 'out' doesn't mean 'beyond.' Extra-worldly doesn't mean other-worldly. To move virtually out—to *out*—involves neither actual externality nor a transcendent ideal; the outing is a line of flight."[36] Lines of flight circulate between the other worlds within the world, linking virtualities, originary and futuristic, and generating a net of responsibility that enables emplaced movement. One is creative within this world, pushing the limits of the world always further, finding escape routes that remain loyal to the plane of immanence on which they circulate while generating other worlds and thus extending the world. But these are not oppositional directions, nor are they part of a grander synthetic schema. Remember, there is nowhere to stand and stare outside this. The total is incomplete. Nor can the total have any space for negativity. The negative is not the precondition for the world. A monad is pulsating with fullness: *this* is the precondition for the world, the irrepressible monadic fullness. According to Hallward, quoting from Deleuze,

> only affirmation can create new values, and in the end "affirmation takes the place of all negations"—but affirmation can only replace negation if there is nothing left of negation. Negation must first negate itself. Negation must exhaust itself and vanish, leaving not so much as its empty place. Negation must leave nothing of its place other than the possibility of a wholly different place: the place itself must change, until "there is no longer any place for another world."[37]

Perhaps this is the main reason for which the world must be conceptualized without an outside. Whether properly outside, as Heidegger's Nothing that determines Being, or ingested inside, as an internalized environment, the outside remains a determining negativity. Negativity brings the need to cross over, a transcendence of sorts that is always privileged over the *here* of the material world. What is invariably left behind is the praxis of justice, a justice relegated in the future (a justice to come) or a mere contingency (justice may or may not arrive). In a world without outside, however—that is, a world that is worlding and othering in the blind autopoietic teleology of carrying on—justice is both infinite (a strife) and *just here*, always present on the vectors of responsibility that trammel the various worlds, carved and impressed on the bodies that inhabit the world and through which, in its turn, responsibility animates the world. This is the only body we have, this is the only world we have. But as Spinoza says, "no one knows what a body can do."[38] We begin in the space of the middle, the pulsating space of responsibility toward the process of carrying on, and we carry on to the infinity of space within this world. As Hallward writes, "only the creature can overcome its own creatural limitations. This overcoming will involve experimentation and invention, the configuration of new actualities or bodies and new assemblings of bodies."[39] The autopoietic body, just as the autopoietic world, is a matter of creation without a creator. The process of carrying on and overcoming one's seeming limitations is experimental and essentially creative. But it can only begin *here* and end nowhere. To paraphrase Spinoza, no one knows what the world can do.

Andreas Philippopoulos-Mihalopoulos, LLB, LLM, PhD, is Professor of Law and Theory at the University of Westminster, and Director of the Westminster Law and Theory Lab. He is the author of *Absent Environments* (Routledge, 2007), *Niklas Luhmann: Law, Justice, Society* (Routledge, 2010), and *Spatial Justice: Body, Lawscape, Atmosphere* (Routledge, 2014), as well as editor of several books.

NOTES

This chapter is a version of the larger article "The World without Outside," *Angelaki: Journal of the Theoretical Humanities* 18, no. 4 (2014): 165–77, and is published here with thanks.

1. Niklas Luhmann, "World Society as a Social System," in *Dependence and Equality: A Systems Approach to the Problems of Mexico and Other Developing Countries*, ed. R. Felix Geyer and Johannes van der Zouwen (Oxford, 1982), 131–138.

2. For my treatment of this and Luhmann in general, see Andreas Philippopoulos-Mihalopoulos, *Niklas Luhmann: Law, Justice, Society* (London, 2010).
3. Andreas Philippopoulos-Mihalopoulos, "Critical Autopoiesis: The Environment of the Law," in *Law's Environment: Critical Legal Perspectives*, ed. Ubaldus de Vries and Lyana Francot, (The Hague, 2011), 45–62.
4. Humberto Maturana and Francisco Varela, *Autopoiesis and Cognition: The Realization of the Living* (Dordrecht, 1972), 9.
5. Niklas Luhmann, *Die Gesellschaft der Gesellschaft* (Frankfurt am Main, 1997), 95.
6. Jean-François Lyotard, *Political Writings*, trans. Bill Readings and Kevin Paul Geiman (Minneapolis, 1993), 81.
7. Luhmann, "World Society." For a more "synthetic" understanding in terms of the world, see, e.g., Hans-Georg Moeller, *Luhmann Explained: From Souls to Systems* (Chicago, 2006), 52ff.; Geyer and van der Zouwen, *Dependence and Equality*; David Roberts, "Paradox Preserved: From Ontology to Autology. Reflections on Niklas Luhmann's *The Art of Society*," *Thesis Eleven* 51, no. 1 (1997): 53–74.
8. Luhmann, *Die Gesellschaft*, 93.
9. For the distinction, see Moeller, *Luhmann Explained*.
10. Jean-Luc Nancy, *The Creation of the World or Globalization*, trans. François Raffoul and David Pettigrew (Albany, 2007).
11. Ibid., 51, 28.
12. Andreas Philippopoulos-Mihalopoulos, "The Successful Failing of Legal Theory," in *Decolonisation of Legal Knowledge*, ed. Amita Dhanda and Archana Parashar (London, 2009), 44–63.
13. Jean Clam, "What is Modern Power?" in *Luhmann on Politics and Law: Critical Appraisals and Applications*, ed. Michael King and Chris Thornhill (Oxford, 2006), 160.
14. Luhmann, *Die Gesellschaft*.
15. Nancy, *Creation of the World*, 61.
16. Andreas Philippopoulos-Mihalopoulos, "Spatial Justice: Law and the Geography of Withdrawal," *International Journal of Law in Context* 6, no. 3 (2010): 1–16.
17. Niklas Luhmann, *Social Systems*, trans. John Bednarz Jr. (Stanford, CA, 1995).
18. Gilles Deleuze and Félix Guattari, *A Thousand Plateaus: Capitalism and Schizophrenia*, trans. Brian Massumi (London, 1988).
19. For further discussions of territory, see in particular the chapters by Stefan Willer and Jeppe Strandsbjerg in this volume.
20. Deleuze and Guattari, *A Thousand Plateaus*, 16.
21. Ibid., 24.
22. Gilles Deleuze, *Essays Critical and Clinical*, trans. Daniel W. Smith and Michael A. Greco (London, 1997), 127–28.
23. Gilles Deleuze, *Difference and Repetition*, trans. Paul Patton (London, 2004), 141.
24. Deleuze and Guattari, *A Thousand Plateaus*, 10.
25. Gilles Deleuze, *The Fold: Leibniz and the Baroque*, trans. Tom Conley (London, 2006).
26. Ibid., 31.
27. Ibid., 34.

28. Gilles Deleuze, *Foucault*, trans. Sean Hand (Minneapolis, 1988), 98.
29. Deleuze, *The Fold*, 25.
30. Deleuze, *Difference and Repetition*.
31. Deleuze, *The Fold*, 35.
32. Ibid., 39.
33. Ibid., 28.
34. Ibid., 8.
35. Deleuze and Guattari, *A Thousand Plateaus*.
36. Peter Hallward, *Out of This World: Deleuze and the Philosophy of Creation* (London, 2006), 57.
37. Ibid., 57, quoting from Deleuze, *The Fold*, 65.
38. Baruch Spinoza, *Ethics*, trans. G. H. R. Parkinson (Oxford, 2000), 3, P2 Sch.
39. Hallward, *Out of This World*, 90.

BIBLIOGRAPHY

Clam, Jean. "What Is Modern Power?" In *Luhmann on Politics and Law: Critical Appraisals and Applications*, edited by Michael King and Chris Thornhill, 145–62. Oxford: Hart, 2006.

Deleuze, Gilles. *Difference and Repetition*. Translated by Paul Patton. London: Continuum, 2004.

———. *Essays Critical and Clinical*. Translated by Daniel W. Smith and Michael A. Greco. London: Verso, 1997.

———. *The Fold: Leibniz and the Baroque*. Translated by Tom Conley. London: Continuum, 2006.

———. *Foucault*. Translated by Sean Hand. Minneapolis: University of Minnesota Press, 1988.

Deleuze, Gilles, and Félix Guattari. *A Thousand Plateaus: Capitalism and Schizophrenia*. Translated by Brian Massumi. London: Continuum, 1988.

Geyer, R. Felix, and Johannes van der Zouwen, eds. *Dependence and Equality: A Systems Approach to the Problems of Mexico and Other Developing Countries*. Oxford: Oxford University Press, 1982.

Hallward, Peter. *Out of This World: Deleuze and the Philosophy of Creation*. London: Verso, 2006.

Luhmann, Niklas. *Die Gesellschaft der Gesellschaft*. Frankfurt am Main: Suhrkamp, 1997.

———. *Social Systems*. Translated by John Bednarz Jr. Stanford, CA: Stanford University Press, 1995.

———. "World Society as a Social System." In *Dependence and Equality: A Systems Approach to the Problems of Mexico and Other Developing Countries*, edited by R. Felix Geyer and Johannes van der Zouwe, 131–138. Oxford: Oxford University Press, 1982:

Lyotard, Jean-François. *Political Writings*. Translated by Bill Readings and Kevin Paul Geiman. Minneapolis: University of Minnesota Press, 1993.

Maturana, Humberto, and Francisco Varela. *Autopoiesis and Cognition: The Realization of the Living*. Dordrecht: Reidel, 1972.
Moeller, Hans-Georg. *Luhmann Explained: From Souls to Systems*. Chicago: Open Court, 2006.
Morin, Edgar. "From the Concept of System to the Paradigm of Complexity." *Journal of Social and Evolutionary Systems* 15, no. 4 (1992): 371–85.
———. *La méthode: La nature de la nature*. Paris: Seuil, 1977.
Nancy, Jean-Luc. *The Creation of the World or Globalization*. Translated by François Raffoul and David Pettigrew. Albany: State University of New York Press, 2007.
Philippopoulos-Mihalopoulos, Andreas. "Critical Autopoiesis: The Environment of the Law." In *Law's Environment: Critical Legal Perspectives*, edited by Ubaldus de Vries and Lyana Francot, 45–62. The Hague: Eleven International, 2011.
———. *Niklas Luhmann: Law, Justice, Society*. London: Routledge, 2010.
———. "Spatial Justice: Law and the Geography of Withdrawal." *International Journal of Law in Context* 6, no. 3 (2010): 1–16.
———. "The Successful Failing of Legal Theory." In *Decolonisation of Legal Knowledge*, edited by Amita Dhanda and Archana Parashar, 44–63. London: Routledge, 2009.
Rilke, Rainer Maria. *Ahead of All Parting: Collected Poetry and Prose*. Edited and translated by Stephen Mitchell. New York: Modern Library, 1995.
Roberts, David. "Paradox Preserved: From Ontology to Autology. Reflections on Niklas Luhmann's *The Art of Society*." *Thesis Eleven* 51, no. 1 (1997): 53–74.
Spinoza, Baruch. *Ethics*. Translated by G. H. R. Parkinson. Oxford: Oxford University Press, 2000.

▶• 12 •◀

From Critical to Partisan Dictionaries; or, What Is Excluded from Today's Flat World Orthodoxies?

Sanja Perovic

A common supposition of globalization discourses is the idea of a shared process of world history. Thus, Friedman describes globalization as the outcome of a "triple convergence" in which the world is increasingly organized according to one standard, united by new communication systems such as the World Wide Web and enabled by ever greater participation of the world's population in "horizontal collaboration."[1] Such optimistic accounts of a "flat," "homogeneous," "horizontal" world, however, overlook the key characteristic of any world, namely that it functions as a unity of meaning only if it remains a closed system.[2] To have a world, one must take into account the existence of a horizon, a boundary demarcating the limits and exclusions that are the condition for identifying a common stock of knowledge. Whereas globalization pundits typically equate the planetary globe with one world and "one global future,"[3] their critics insist that the term "world" can only be used in the plural. In order to counter the "finality" and "teleology" of globalization discourses, the terms "world" and "worlding" have been coined to reflect the insight that action and interaction require choice and a reduction of theoretical possibilities, and this is only possible if social worlds are differentiated from one another.[4]

At first glance, it appears easy to deconstruct the optimism of globalization cheerleaders. There is no "global standpoint" that can be identified with a given subject, nor is there a "global culture." Conflicts continue to persist, and there appears to be little consensus, much less convergence, over their meaning and outcome. Moreover, by insisting so loudly on the powers of convergence, globalization pundits fail to acknowledge a key aspect of our contemporary relation to knowledge. This is the realization that, ever since the nineteenth century, the cost of advancement in any given field of knowledge has been a loss of vision of the whole. As Luhmann reminds us, each discipline has constructed its own reality in an autonomous manner, and each remains coherent only to the extent that it remains blind to other, competing descriptions. Thus, biologists, physicists, and neuroscientists each construct their version of "nature" according to their own descriptions, just as law, economics, and anthropology each define "society" in their own way. But if critics of globalization are right to insist that there is no global standpoint from which to view the world as a whole, they, in turn, fail to sufficiently acknowledge its corollary: that whatever coherent vision remains is not derived from expert culture but from mass media, which mediates much of what counts as "world knowledge" today.[5] Moreover, in the absence of any one, authoritative system of knowledge, the convergence of common opinion is often the only evidence we have that our knowledge of the world matches reality. This raises two related questions. First, from what subject position do we assess and critique a reality that increasingly takes on the form of a global, interconnected world? Second, given near universal communicability, can we distinguish a critical reflection on the world from the reproduction of common opinion, and if so, how?

To address these questions, I propose to go back to the early modern period when the discovery of the world as something to be mapped and explored in its entirety (as a globe) was also accompanied by an intense awareness of the limits of human knowledge. For alongside this newfound ability to imagine the world as one globe, there also emerged a radical skepticism about the ability of any one description of the world to sustain itself on its own terms. This is especially evident in the critical dictionary, one of the first genres in which a "global" but also "critical" relation to knowledge emerged. The late seventeenth and eighteenth centuries have been dubbed the "great age of the dictionaries"[6] because the genre of the dictionary or the encyclopedia (the two terms remained largely undifferentiated) captured so precisely a historical moment in which a belief in the powers of reason to map all knowledge of the world coincided with the impossibility of maintaining any such unity in the face of the increasing growth and differentiation of world descriptions.[7] On the one hand, a dictionary or encyclopedia represents a closed world in which each entry is defined by relation to another in a string of potentially endless loops (indeed, the word "encyclopedia" etymologically refers to a "chain" or "circle" of all learning, or *padeia*, in the world). By aiming to collect and link the sum total of all learning, a dictionary or encyclopedia presupposes that knowledge exists as a whole, even if only ideally. On the other hand, the proliferation of dictionaries during this period reflects the increasing realization that no one person or group could conceptualize such a total understanding. In order to compensate, therefore, for this lost vision of a whole, a new kind of "critical" dictionary emerged. This is one that used the arbitrary order of the alphabetical index to encourage the reader to construct his or her own path through the text, thereby making and remaking their own system of world knowledge according to their own perspective.

In what follows, I trace the reception of the critical dictionary from Pierre Bayle's *Dictionnaire historique et critique* (1697) to the partisan dictionaries of late eighteenth and early nineteenth century France in order to consider how critical thinking—and awareness of self-reference more generally—became the goal of any attempt to define a system of world knowledge. In so doing, I aim to show how the critical dictionary evolved from a representation of world knowledge to offering competing descriptions of what Luhmann has called "world society."[8] I conclude by suggesting that this notion of a critical (heterodox) relation to world knowledge offers a useful corrective to our current overreliance on categories of convergence as a way of understanding the worlding of the globe.

From Pierre Bayle to the *Encyclopédie*

It is arguably Pierre Bayle who first identified the fundamental problem of all convergence theories, namely that universal communicability is evidence neither of reason nor of convergence because reason is capable of producing incompatible theories about the world. Bayle lived at a time when the conflict between different religious sects, each with their own claims to truth, made consensus impossible. But as Kojève notes, what distinguished Bayle from his contemporaries was his articulation of a new problem, namely that reason itself, and not just false belief, produced incoherence because it could express incompatible theories about the world.[9] If reason at best produces many meaningful worlds and never one truth, this raises doubts about whether human reason is ever capable of adjudicating between competing truth claims.

In stark contrast to our present-day globalization pundits, for whom universal communicability (typically attributed to such technology as the internet) is unproblematically taken as evidence of convergence, Bayle identified communication as part of the problem. Not only did the numerous journals and gazettes (the new media of his day) distort events of the recent past, making it impossible to distinguish truth from rumor, error, or outright fiction, they also exacerbated the problem of groupthink, "our irresistible tendency toward agreement."[10] Moreover, because this communicability functions as its own form of authority, it gives rise to what Elisabeth Labrousse has called the "fatal paradox of education," namely that we are quick to judge when it comes to justifying our own prejudices and slow to go against what we have been taught.[11]

The problem of the relation between reason and the world is thus twofold. It concerns the all-too-easy communicability of pseudo-reason on the one hand and the contradictory claims made by rational discourse on the other. Bayle's response was to construct what he called a "dictionary of errors." By identifying errors in existing dictionaries, most notably Louis Moreri's *Grand dictionnaire historique* (1674), Bayle attempted to distill whatever glimmers of truth remained behind. This is because the likelihood of convergence was highest in the corroboration of adversaries rather than the consensus of people who thought alike.[12] Whereas naïve assumptions of convergence tend to replicate commonplace beliefs, "every philosophical dispute supposes that the contesting parties agree on certain definitions."[13] Moreover, in identifying dissent as the locus of any potential agreement, Bayle also revealed the failure of reason to rationally illuminate a world. For, as Bayle explained, it is much easier to use reason to destroy a belief that one denies than to establish what one affirms.[14]

The outcome was a wholly new kind of dictionary, what Richard H. Popkin has called a *Summa Sceptica* of contemporary thought, in which theological doubts were placed alongside biographical information, obscene anecdotes, and moral philosophy.[15] Significantly, Bayle was careful to distinguish a dictionary, which he defined as an arbitrary collection of exempla, from any concept of a system. The arbitrary order of the alphabet ensured that the author never posed as a spiritual guide, for without "following any system, any method, any order," the maker of dictionaries "acts as if he were tossing off his views like a pin in a field [and] makes it well enough known that he does not care to have any followers at all."[16] The dictionary was such a felicitous genre because it combined the encyclopedic criterion of completeness with the awareness that there is no third-person perspective from which to synthesize and validate the representation of knowledge as a whole. In other words, the critical dictionary contains many worlds but no globe because there is no "objective," "planetary" perspective from which the whole can be unified.

In his own *Dictionnaire philosophique* (1764), Voltaire praised Bayle for being a *bon juge* and for valorizing the role of the critic as a *juge, estimateur*, and *arbitre*.[17] The use of the term *arbitre* is revealing. As the etymology of the French term suggests, *arbitre* refers both to a referee, someone who adjudicates between competing terms, and to someone who is free to exercise their *libre arbitre* ("free will"). Thanks to the dictionary's arbitrary order of classification, the reader is called upon to freely judge, that is, to exercise her *libre arbitre*. At the same time, this arbitrary order does not mean the complete absence of all method. In other words, even if Bayle insisted that his biographical dictionary was without a properly defined method or system, it nonetheless presupposed a mapping of knowledge. More than a mere collection of exempla, it presupposed a procedure (Bayle used the judicial metaphors of prosecution and defense), a series of steps to be taken in order for any "world" to be revealed.

This conception of world knowledge as world-making differs from our contemporary globalization discourse in two key respects. It assumes that the increased communicability of knowledge produces the potential for divergence rather than convergence of opinion, and furthermore that there is no global subject position, no Hegelian "I that is We" from whose perspective these conflicting worldviews might be unified. Both aspects appear in Diderot and d'Alembert's famous *Encyclopédie* (1751–72). With over 70,000 articles and 250 collaborators, the *Encyclopédie* was the first text to acknowledge the importance of large-scale knowledge and the need to keep together increasingly specialized fields in a period of unprecedented growth. The sheer number of collaborators alone reflected a new understanding of world knowledge as something co-constructed. If there was an eighteenth-century example of a "horizontal, flat world," then this was it. It was also arguably the first text to engage the reader in the co-construction of knowledge by insisting that each reader trace his or her own path through the encyclopedia. To encourage the reader's autonomy, Diderot and d'Alembert organized the encyclopedia alphabetically and proposed that every article be cross-referenced as thickly as possible with a potentially unlimited number of other articles. The encyclopedia thus became a text "written" by the reader, who selected which path to take in the absence of a third-person, global perspective of the encyclopedia as a whole. D'Alembert's famous image for this system of cross-references was the *mappemonde*: there will be as many itineraries through the *Encyclopédie*'s articles as projections of the world map. In an equally famous image, he contrasted this image of the encyclopedia as a world map with the real time of critical thinking, which is more like a labyrinth through which we grope blindly: "The general system of the art and sciences is like a type of labyrinth, a twisting path that the mind embarks upon without knowing too well which route to take."[18]

Strictly speaking, neither the map nor the labyrinth was a new image for an encyclopedia. Ephraim Chambers, from whom Diderot and d'Alembert borrowed both the idea of an alphabetical index and the system of cross-references, had already used the image of the map.[19] Rather, what is innovative is the use of the world map not just to represent large-scale knowledge but also as a method for critical thinking more generally. This is captured in d'Alembert's dual reference to two ultimately incompatible images of the map. The first evokes the rational hope for a universal order; the second recalls the older medieval image of the labyrinth with its connotations of irregularity, blindness, and even despair. This suggests that world knowledge and individual knowledge can never be fully synchronized, because each presupposes a different frame of reference. The world map represents the total field of possible knowledge available at any given time, while knowledge itself is actualized from the perspective of the individual reader, who follows one path through the labyrinth while remaining blind to other possible paths. The intelligible world is always smaller than the actual world because it requires closure and awareness of one's position as a partial observer.

Diderot's own description of the *Encyclopédie* used the revealing geographical analogy of the Old and New Worlds to describe the creation of a *mundus intelligibilis*. "The cross-references," Diderot states, "will serve as itineraries in these two worlds, in which the visible can be considered like the Old World and the Intelligible like the New."[20] This assertion can be understood in two ways. First, that the intelligible world reveals what the Old World cannot—that there are as many different ways of classifying and understanding objects as there are ways of observing the world. Second, that knowledge must take into account not just multiple perspectives on *one world*, but also the coexistence of multiple worlds and ways of linking past and future (old world and new worlds).

At the same time, Diderot acknowledged the limits of such ambitions. Every act of reason requires us to redraw the connection between old and new worlds. Yet the danger of all dictionaries is that they fix what, from the perspective of the future, might appear not as a "truth" but merely the expression of a *sensus communis*: "we realize at every moment that those expressions we understand the least are the ones we use the most. ... All we ever do is repeat what we have heard our entire life."[21] This brings us back again to the old definition of the encyclopedic dictionary as a book of commonplaces, that is to say, a collection that is not just arbitrary but also unthinking. In this sense every dictionary, in order to remain critical, must combat its own ambition to offer a total representation of world knowledge by acknowledging its partial construction.

Combat des Dictionnaires: From Impartiality to the Partisan Perspective

Bayle's critical dictionary and the *Encyclopédie* both embraced limitation as essential for the production of meaning in a world of increasingly large-scale knowledge. This in turn produced a new model of critical thinking that privileged the autonomy of reason and the individual reader over that of consensus and shared opinion. In contrast to today's globalization discourses—which presuppose an increasingly expanding "global contemporary," a sort of endless present in which there is no future except for ever tighter networks of the same—both these early modern critical dictionaries emphasized plural futures, thereby keeping the future itself open as a speculative horizon.[22] By the mid eighteenth century, the plurality of such world descriptions resulted in the proliferation of all kinds of dictionaries, including dictionaries of heresies, hermeticism, and even love.[23] This raises the question: how did the dictionary, an englobing genre if there ever was one, come to express opposition to establishment values?

To answer this question, we must take into account not just the influence of Bayle's critical dictionary but also the wider move against Classical theories of language that had taken place by the late seventeenth and early eighteenth centuries. When Furetière initiated his move against the dictionary project of the French Academy, he rejected the Classical assumption that there existed a natural language corresponding to a "world community" of (Christian) mankind. The French Academy had compiled its dictionary partly to "cleanse language of the obscenities contracted either through popular usage or the throngs of the *Palais*."[24] Furetière, in contrast, rejected this normative assumption that a proper language reflected the manners of a good society, as did Bayle, who wrote the anonymous preface to Furetière's *Dictionnaire universel* after his death. Instead, both writers aimed to be "global rather than selective,"[25] uncoupling language from its exemplary function of representing the society of *les grands* (in French tellingly designated by the term *le monde*). In other words, by upscaling or expanding the parameters of world knowledge, these dictionaries also downscaled the norms associated with the small world of the select few. They thereby came to express what Luhmann calls "world society," that is to say, a society in which normative self-description is no longer possible.[26]

Whereas for Furetière and Bayle, the "englobing" perspective continued to be associated with impartiality, by the mid eighteenth century the dictionary became increasingly associated with a heterodox standpoint, especially in France. The following three examples demonstrate how the englobing function of the critical dictionary came to be associated with a partisan position. The first is Le Roux's *Dictionnaire comique, satyrique, critique, burlesque, libre et proverbial* (1718–86), published three times over the century and censored each time. Dedicated to the everyday language of the city of Paris, this lexicographical dictionary used the burlesque to align itself with all the "dissidents du bon usage."[27] It aimed not to correct language but to compile the multiple and contradictory meanings of common expressions, expanding the parameters of speech and the communities associated with it. Its heterodox tendency is evident in such entries as *glose* and *gloser*. Instead of referring to the original meaning of "gloss" as a commentary on scripture, Le Roux defines it as "an unclear explanation that muddles the text instead of shedding light on it"; "to gloss" is to "critique, mock, satirize, find fault with, monitor, examine, and correct."[28] The rejection of normative self-description is also found in such terms as *citoyen* ("citizen"), which is defined first as a *bourgeois* exercising "bourgeois rights" and secondarily as a term designating the children of a household, or "the little citizens we believe to have fathered."[29] Similarly, humanity is defined with the popular expression *reposer son humanité*, referring to the act of making oneself comfortable, and having commodities with which to do so at one's disposal.[30]

If Le Roux used the "englobing" perspective to capture the plurality of idioms, Voltaire's *Dictionnaire philosophique* (1764) was famously reductive. With just 118 entries, Voltaire's dictionary is too short to function either as a dictionary of words or an encyclopedia of concepts. Instead it englobes in a different way: by demonstrating the declarative function of all dictionaries, which is to establish a worldview. Voltaire uses the dictionary genre first and foremost as an argument rather than as source material, asking his readers to map new relations between concepts that are effectively generalized into a new vision of reality. The same terms and "often the same references"[31] are repeated in different articles and in so doing function very much as "catchwords" (the English term that came to denote political slogans around 1794, according to the Oxford English Dictionary). It is significant that before the term "catchword" came to reflect a partisan standpoint, it referred to a lexicographical tool used in eighteenth-century dictionaries and reference books. A term is "caught up and repeated" when the first word of the following page is also inserted on the preceding page, much like Voltaire catches up and repeats the same terms in different articles, in this case the new catchwords of Enlightenment *philosophie*. Here too the global planetary perspective is invoked not to articulate an ultimate point of convergence, but to emphasize a dissenting stance that requires the ability to see one's world from the outside. Voltaire thus begins the article on *catéchisme chinois* by describing the earth's globe as "infinitely smaller than a grain of sand in comparison with the millions of billions of universes,"[32] before proceeding to use the geographically distant worlds of China, Japan, and India as a foil to critique the Judeo-Christian West.

Of course, such an "impartial" stance was itself partial, a point well understood by Voltaire's detractors. As Nonnotte's *Dictionnaire philosophique de la religion* (1772) makes clear, every inclusion also functioned as its own kind of exclusion. Even the innocuous term "tolerance" was nothing but a "specious veil" under which to hide "invectives, complaints, and rants against Christians."[33] Rebutting each of Voltaire's catchwords, Nonnotte accused Voltaire of spreading a new kind of dogma on three counts. First, Voltaire allegedly did so by turning all truth claims into linguistic propositions and thereby collapsing the crucial distinction between "evidence" and "interpretation," inherited from the scriptural tradition. As a result, terms are defined by other terms in a self-referential and ultimately vicious circle.[34] Second, whereas in the scriptural tradition the evidence was weighed up against the credibility of witnesses (something still evident in Bayle), here all claims to reason are "attested by unknown strangers, vagabonds, impassioned, self-interested, or suspect people."[35] In other words, to possess truth one cannot be a vagabond, with no fixed address, because without a proprietary relation to speech all claims risk being unsubstantiated opinions or, worse, the ideological effect of interested parties seeking to substitute appearance for reality. Finally, without a belief in authority and the credibility of witnesses, there is no way to escape the realm of opinion. We return once more to the problem of communicability: how do we ensure that our reason reflects more than just common opinion in the absence of any authoritative structure?

Conclusion: Global vs. Counter-Histories

This chapter began by suggesting that the critical dictionary offers a useful corrective to the current faith in the powers of convergence. Whereas convergence theories presuppose a global world that is (at least implicitly) coextensive with a uniform public sphere and a homogeneous linear time of a single "world history," the critical dictionary demonstrates how it is primarily through the acknowledgment of competing publics that the commonplaces of "public opinion" can be challenged. Whereas globalization advocates often assume that synchronization alone—more and more people participating in a single global present—is sufficient evidence of the totality and unity of a single, shared world, the early modern *combat des dictionnaires* was characterized by the proliferation of multiple, contemporaneous, unsynchronized worlds existing side by side, at times to their mutual exclusion. In this sense, the critical dictionary functioned as a type of counter-history, defined by Amos Funkenstein as the "systematic exploitation of the adversary's most trusted sources against their grain" with the aim of distorting "the adversary's self-image, his identity through the deconstruction of his memory."[36] Such counter-history was possible so long as the critical dictionary, while postulating to collect the sum total of world knowledge on any given field, never attempted to be geographically coextensive with the planetary globe. There always remained the potential to adopt another position, either by forging new links within an existing dictionary or by constructing another world description.

Of course, by the time of the French Revolution, this link between a global account of "world knowledge" and (multiple) selective descriptions of a "world society" became uncoupled. This is evident in such late eighteenth-century publications as Sylvain Maréchal's *Dictionnaire des athées anciens et modernes* (1798), a biographical dictionary that listed all the partisans of atheism throughout history, self-declared or not. Maréchal's delineation of an alternate world society of atheists was intended as an oppositional concept, the demarcation of an "us" that takes a stand against dominant reality (here the return of Catholicism as a de facto state religion). In a similar vein, if from an opposing political standpoint, the reactionary *Dictionnaire laconique, véridique et impartial, ou Étrennes aux démagogues sur la Révolution française* (1791) attacked the "catchwords" of revolutionary rhetoric, by redefining *patrie* and *patriotisme* as slogans "empty of meaning" and cross-referencing *liberté* and *constitution* with *licence* and *anarchie*.[37] Several decades later, one finds a rejoinder in the *Petit dictionnaire Ultra* (1823), which for its part challenged the definition of *patriotisme* by stating that "it is by mistake that this word has been included in the dictionary of the *ultra*, as there is no such expression in their language."[38]

"Englobing" without being "global," all three post-revolutionary dictionaries attempted to rewrite history according to their own criteria and self-understanding in a radically unreproducible manner. In this sense they differed from the scientific dictionaries and encyclopedias that became the mainstay of a nineteenth-century disciplinary division of knowledge in which each field maintained its commitment to a "neutral," "objective" account of knowledge on condition that it remain blind to other competing descriptions. Whereas scientific dictionaries mask the performative function of claims to account for "world knowledge," the critical dictionary, with its projections of alternate, and competing, world societies, maintains a heterodox relation to the established order, thereby revealing objectivity and neutrality to function as a silent orthodoxy. Indeed, the tradition of the critical dictionary continues in France, stretching from Flaubert's posthumously published *Dictionnaire des idées reçues* (1913), exploring the dead-ends of commonplace thought and political language, to Bataille's "Dictionnaire critique" (first appearing in his 1929 art review *Documents*), consisting entirely of personal terms (*abattoir, black birds, oeil*), to more recent publications such as *Chirac de A à Z: Dictionnaire critique et impertinent* (1995) or *Le Pen de A à Z* (1995).

By emphasizing the importance of self-reference, these critical dictionaries expose, if only *a contrario*, the fictive character of the current discourse about globalization. Of course, there is no denying the empirical reality of increasingly dense networks of global exchange. However, globalization remains fictive so long as it assumes the planetary perspective of a world without borders. In other words, it remains fictive insofar as it functions as a totality without unity, that is to say, an ideology rather than a meaningful "world." In the end, there is no easy way to distinguish between opinion and reason in an increasingly mediatized and globalized consumer society. However, what this brief reconsideration of the "age of the dictionaries" makes clear is how communicability maintains an authoritative hold on thought by conflating the distance between world and globe. At the very least, this should remind us of the importance of keeping apart these two concepts: that of a global (planetary) perspective that can be used to see (human, cultural) worlds from the outside but from which there is no place to locate a particular perspective, and that of the world, which is always limited, partial, and in the last instance, personal.

Sanja Perovic is Reader in the Department of French at King's College London. She is the author of *The Calendar in Revolutionary France: Perceptions of Time in Literature, Culture, and Politics* (Cambridge University Press, 2012) and has published widely on the aesthetics and politics of time, from the early modern period to the present.

NOTES

1. Thomas Friedman, *The World Is Flat: The Globalized World in the Twenty-First Century* (London, 2006), 204–33.
2. See Niklas Luhmann, *Social Systems*, trans. John Bednarz Jr. with Dirk Baecker (Stanford, CA, 1995), 69–70.
3. Amartya Sen, quoted by Friedman, *The World Is Flat*, 54.
4. Rob Wilson and Christopher Leigh Connery, eds, *The Worlding Project: Doing Cultural Studies in the Era of Globalization* (Santa Cruz, CA, 2007), 7, 97, 212.
5. Niklas Luhmann, "Deconstruction as Second-Order Observing," in *Theories of Distinction: Redescribing the Description of Modernity*, ed. William Rasch (Stanford, CA, 2002), 107.
6. Pierre Rétat, "L'âge des dictionnaires," in *Histoire de l'édition française*, ed. Roger Chartier and Henri-Jean Martin (Paris, 1984), 186.
7. For further discussions of the dictionary and the encyclopedia, see in particular the chapters by Nora Eggen and Richard Yeo in this volume.
8. Luhmann, *Social Systems*, 432.
9. Alexandre Kojève, *Identité et réalité dans le Dictionnaire de Pierre Bayle*, ed. Marco Filoni (Paris, 2010), 193.
10. Elisabeth Labrousse, *Pierre Bayle: Hétérodoxie et rigorisme*, 2nd ed. (Paris, 1996), 71. My translation.
11. Ibid., 76.
12. Ibid., 18–20.
13. Pierre Bayle, *Historical and Critical Dictionary: Selections*, trans. Richard H. Popkin (Indianapolis, 1991), 411.
14. Pierre Bayle, "Arriaga," in *Historical and Critical Dictionary*, 26.
15. Richard H. Popkin, "Introduction," in Bayle, *Historical and Critical Dictionary*, ix.
16. Bayle, *Historical and Critical Dictionary*, 397.
17. Voltaire, "Dictionnaire philosophique et critique," in *Oeuvres complètes de Voltaire* (Paris, 1860), 13: 50.
18. "Discours préliminaire," in Denis Diderot and Jean le Rond d'Alembert, eds, *Encyclopédie, ou dictionnaire raisonné des sciences, des arts et des métiers, etc.* (Paris,

1751–72), available at the University of Chicago, ARTFL Encyclopédie Project (Spring 2013 Edition), ed. Robert Morrissey, http://encyclopedie.uchicago.edu/. Henceforth *Encyclopédie*.

19. See Richard Yeo, "A Solution to the Multitude of Books: Ephraim Chamber's *Cyclopaedia* (1728) as 'the Best Book in the Universe,'" *Journal of the History of Ideas* 64, no. 1 (2003): 61–72.
20. Entry "Encyclopédie," in *Encyclopédie*. Online, retrieved 23 August 2018 from https://artflsrv03.uchicago.edu/philologic4/encyclopedie1117/navigate/5/2355/.
21. Ibid.
22. For this definition of the global contemporary, see Peter Osborne, "Global Modernity and the Contemporary," in *Breaking Up Time: Negotiating the Borders between Present, Past and Future*, ed. Chris Lorenz and Berber Bevernage (Göttingen, 2013), 82.
23. See Giorgio Tonelli, *A Short-Title List of Subject Dictionaries of the Sixteenth, Seventeenth and Eighteenth Centuries*, ed. Eugenio Canone and Margherita Palumbo (Florence, 2006).
24. Quoted by Paul Pellison-Fontanier, *Histoire de l'Académie française* (Paris, 1700), 26: "Nettoyer la langue des ordures qu'elle a contractées ou dans la bouche du peuple ou dans la foule du Palais."
25. Rétat, "L'âge des dictionnaires," 190.
26. Luhmann, *Social Systems*, 432.
27. Monica Barsi, "Introduction," in Philibert Joseph Le Roux, *Dictionnaire comique, satyrique, critique, burlesque, libre et proverbial (1718–1786)*, ed. Monica Barsi (Paris, 2003), xii.
28. Le Roux, *Dictionnaire comique*, 350: "une explication qui n'est pas fort clair, qui embrouille le texte au lieu de l'éclairer … pour critiquer, railler, satyriser, trouver à rédire, à contrôler, examiner et corriger."
29. Ibid., 158: "de petits citoyens dont on croît être père."
30. Ibid., 385.
31. On these references, see Christiane Mervaud, *Le dictionnaire philosophique de Voltaire* (Oxford, 1994), 73–76.
32. Voltaire, *Oeuvres complètes*, 12: 494: "infiniment moins qu'un grain de sable en comparaison de ces millions de milliasses d'univers."
33. Claude-Adrien Nonnotte, *Dictionnaire philosophique de la religion, où l'on établit tous les points de la Religion, attaqués par les Incrédules, & où l'on répond à toutes les objections par l'auteur des erreurs de Voltaire* (Liège, 1772), 657.
34. See Mervaud, *Dictionnaire philosophique*, 98.
35. Nonnote, *Dictionnaire philosophique*, 524: "attesté par des inconnus, des vagabonds, des hommes passionnés, intéressés ou suspects."
36. Amos Funkenstein, "History, Counterhistory and Narrative," in *Probing the Limits of Representation: Nazism and the "Final Solution"*, ed. Saul Friedländer (Cambridge, MA, 1992), 69.
37. *Dictionnaire laconique, véridique et impartial, ou Étrennes aux démagogues sur la Révolution française* (Paris, 1791), 27–28, 13.

38. Charles-R.-E. de Saint-Maurice Mongie, *Petit dictionnaire Ultra: précédé d'un Essai sur l'origine, la langue et les oeuvres des Ultra* (Paris, 1823), 69: "C'est par erreur que ce mot a été compris dans le dictionnaire des ultra; il n'est point d'usage dans leur langue."

BIBLIOGRAPHY

Bataille, Georges, "Dictionnaire critique", in *Documents: Doctrine, archéologie, beaux-arts, ethnographie* 1929–30. Available as *Dictionnaire critique*. Paris: Éditions Prairial, 2016.

Bayle, Pierre. *Historical and Critical Dictionary: Selections*. Translated by Richard H. Popkin. Indianapolis: Hackett, 1991.

Dictionnaire laconique, véridique et impartial, ou Étrennes aux démagogues sur la Révolution française. Paris, 1791.

Diderot, Denis, and Jean le Rond d'Alembert, eds. *Encyclopédie, ou dictionnaire raisonné des sciences, des arts et des métiers, etc.* Paris, 1751–52. Available at the University of Chicago, ARTFL Encyclopédie Project (Spring 2013 Edition), edited by Robert Morrissey. Retrieved 28 August 2018 from http://encyclopedie.uchicago.edu/.

Flaubert, Gustave, *Dictionnaire des idées reçues*. Paris: Ligaran, 2015 [1913].

Friedman, Thomas. *The World Is Flat: The Globalized World in the Twenty-First Century*. London: Farrar, Straus, and Giroux, 2006.

Funkenstein, Amos. "History, Counterhistory and Narrative." In *Probing the Limits of Representation: Nazism and the "Final Solution"*, edited by Saul Friedländer, 66–81. Cambridge, MA: Harvard University Press, 1992.

Hecht, Emmanuel, and François Vey, *Chirac de A à Z: Dictionnaire critique et impertinent*. Paris: Albin Michel, 1995

Kojève, Alexandre. *Identité et réalité dans le Dictionnaire de Pierre Bayle*. Edited by Marco Filoni. Paris: Gallimard, 2010.

Labrousse, Elisabeth. *Pierre Bayle: Hétérodoxie et rigorisme*. 2nd ed. Paris: Albin Michel, 1996.

Le Roux, Philibert Joseph. *Dictionnaire comique, satyrique, critique, burlesque, libre et proverbial (1718–1786)*. Edited by Monica Barsi. Paris: Champion, 2003.

Luhmann, Niklas. "Deconstruction as Second-Order Observing." In *Theories of Distinction: Redescribing the Description of Modernity*, edited by William Rasch, 94–112. Stanford, CA: Stanford University Press, 2002.

———. *Social Systems*. Translated by John Bednarz Jr. with Dirk Baecker. Stanford, CA: Stanford University Press, 1995.

Maréchal, Sylvain. *Dictionnaire des athées anciens et modernes*. Paris, 1798.

Mervaud, Christiane. *Le dictionnaire philosophique de Voltaire*. Oxford: Voltaire Foundation, 1994.

Mongie, Charles-R.-E. de Saint-Maurice. *Petit dictionnaire Ultra: précédé d'un Essai sur l'origine, la langue et les oeuvres des Ultra*. Paris, 1823.

Nonnotte, Claude-Adrien. *Dictionnaire philosophique de la religion, où l'on établit tous les points de la Religion, attaqués par les Incrédules, & où l'on répond à toutes les objections par l'auteur des erreurs de Voltaire.* Liège, 1772.

Osborne, Peter. "Global Modernity and the Contemporary." In *Breaking Up Time: Negotiating the Borders between Present, Past and Future*, edited by Chris Lorenz and Berber, Bevernage, 69-84. Göttingen: Vandenhoeck & Ruprecht, 2013.

Pellison-Fontanier, Paul. *Histoire de l'Académie française*. Paris, 1700.

Rétat, Pierre. "L'âge des dictionnaires." In *Histoire de l'édition française*, edited by Roger Chartier and Henri-Jean Martin, 232–245. Paris: Promodis, 1984.

Tonelli, Giorgio. *A Short-Title List of Subject Dictionaries of the Sixteenth, Seventeenth and Eighteenth Centuries.* Edited by Eugenio Canone and Margherita Palumbo. Florence: Olschki, 2006.

Voltaire. *Oeuvres complètes de Voltaire.* Paris: Hachette, 1860.

Warin, Olivier, *Le Pen de A à Z.* Paris: Albin Michel, 1995

Wilson, Rob, and Christopher Leigh Connery, eds. *The Worlding Project: Doing Cultural Studies in the Era of Globalization.* Santa Cruz, CA: New Pacific Press, 2007.

Yeo, Richard. "A Solution to the Multitude of Books: Ephraim Chamber's *Cyclopaedia* (1728) as 'the Best Book in the Universe.'" *Journal of the History of Ideas* 64, no. 1 (2003): 61–72.

Part III

TIMING THE WORLD

▶• 13 •◀

At Home or Away

On Nostalgia, Exile, and Cosmopolitanism

Olivier Remaud

The Latin word for "elsewhere" is *alibi*. An alibi is used to establish innocence. By using an alibi, a person provides proof that he or she was not at the scene of a crime as it was being committed. Living in exile can often mean experiencing the presumption of guilt. This feeling does not only come from others; it is also anchored in our inner selves as an echo of general suspicions. These doubts multiply at all levels of being, to the point that the concerned individual ends up partaking in the same questioning put to him by others: what were my motives for leaving the country? What events inspired me to flee the land of my birth? Was I right not to stay? Bertolt Brecht spoke out against this diffuse sense of suspicion, criticizing the exile's feeling that he must constantly justify his presence.[1]

Exile is rarely voluntary. However, there are many people who interpret it as such. The exile is forced to provide alibis in order to clear his name of an alleged fault, distance himself from a supposed responsibility, and at times dispel the suspicion that he is complicit with the unspeakable authorities of the enemy. The exile is immediately thrown into a masquerade. At times, these masks are imposed on him when someone or other improperly interprets his reasons for arriving in the place of exile; at other times the exile uses these masks to cover himself in order to fight the lies that defame him. The worst of these disguises are surely those that the exile himself creates in order to respond to his astonishment at the ambivalence he feels toward his own loyalties. In fact, no newly arrived foreigner can immediately adopt what Alfred Schütz calls the "thinking as usual" of the group that receives him. This becomes even more improbable if he is kept in the limbo of suspicion. And it is precisely this suspicion that gives rise to resentment. If exile sometimes causes people to take a different and more tolerant view of those around them, it is also the moment when these legends are born, when narratives are invented to allow the exile to confront the real world and its prejudices.

Edward Said refuted the humanist account of exile for at least two reasons. On the one hand, by making the exiled figure a hero, the literature of exile does not consider the real-life attitudes that reflect the character of an era. And yet the general appearance of the present is marked by mass displacements. How can we provide a positive interpretation for all these forced migrations? Personal experiences must be distinguished from literary experiences. We should acknowledge these differences in several ways. The exile of a renowned author is not the same as that of an undocumented refugee from the countryside. Furthermore, exile plays a critical role in the making of nationalism. Most nationalisms arise "from a condition of estrangement,"[2] from the solitude imposed by exile. Many overcome this solitude only by falling into the trap of discourses of national pride. Adhering to an ideology is a way for the exile to reconstitute his broken life, to get back a shred of his future, and to recreate a universe of values. According to Said, "much of the exile's life is taken up with compensating for disorienting loss by creating a new world to rule."[3] Although the exile is a foreigner himself, the fact of his exile reinforces his sense of the group or even hostility toward other foreigners. It thus occurs that exiles themselves become the reason for other cases of exile.

The analysis of mechanisms of "long distance nationalism," to use Benedict Anderson's phrase, from the point of view of the dehumanizing link between exile and what Said calls "defensive nationalism," depends on a complex alchemy of filiations.[4] Yet one does not always look to create compensatory ideologies. Before paving the way for such ideologies, nostalgia provides a strange occasion to remark on the uselessness of the social contract.

Generally speaking, the loss of civic obligations linked to the land of origin weakens the import of initial loyalties. In exile, loyalties appear more "volatile" than ever, as Judith Shklar points out. The feeling of betrayal toward the motherland only serves to reinforce this volatile character. Once obligations disappear, can one continue to love the country that has denounced the terms of the civic contract? What does it mean to no longer feel loyalty toward one's nation? Shklar notes that opting for a *tabula rasa* is an illusion, as the ghosts of nostalgia always accompany exiles:

> The German Jews ... could retain no conceivable obligation to Germany even after the destruction of the Nazi state, and only a handful returned. They also had no grounds for loyalty, since their erstwhile fellow citizens had abandoned them with such alacrity. One can look at their condition in Lockean terms. Both contracts had been broken, the first between members of society as well as the second between citizens and the state. They were betrayed at both levels, excluded from civil no less than from political society. Personal ties of fidelity remained occasionally and so did nostalgia. "How

shall I sing the Lord's song in a strange land?" sang an exile in the saddest of Old Testament Psalms. And for many of them that is what exile came down to.[5]

To use the terminology of John Locke, we must make clear that the destruction of the civic contract abolishes two concurrent social dynamics. On the one hand, there is no longer mutual consent between the members of a given society. And yet it is impossible to collectively imagine, in the absence of mutual consent, a passage from the state of nature to civil society. On the other hand, contrary to what Locke advocated, there is no longer any reason to prefer the rule of the majority to the absolute authority of a governing body. Nevertheless, only the figure of the majority of the social body can represent legitimacy and ensure that civil society is no worse than the state of nature. The contract between citizens and the state therefore rests partially on an act of faith in plurality. This remains conditional. It is lost as soon as the majority considers that the government no longer fulfills its duties, the same presupposition that underscores the doctrine of the separation of powers. Consequently, the revocation of the contract of association as much as that of the contract of conditional submission—to which Shklar alludes—in effect sends the exile into a new kind of state of nature. Since the obligations that are derived from the two contracts disappear, the exile has the feeling when he arrives in another society that he has to restart *ex nihilo* the cycle of civility. In the aforementioned case of totalitarian Germany, this task seems all the more incongruous as the principle of the division of powers was abandoned to the benefit of a single body and as the exile received no heritage from the rogue government.

The power of nostalgia finds its principal source of nourishment in the annulment of the political cycle by totalitarian regimes. It feeds on the destruction of the equilibrium between obligations and loyalties. It also incites people to search through the archives of their original culture to find elements of a potential heritage. It is enough that the feeling of political nullity is reinforced and affects the heart of personal memories to make loyalties even more "volatile." It is then that the "intermittences of the heart" evoked by Marcel Proust surge forth. In the face of the slowness of social approbation, which he nonetheless wishes to obtain, the exile tends to withdraw into the intimacy of his memories and explore their furthest recesses. Forced to leave the public domain that he previously frequented, he finds himself confronted by the numerous secrets of his person.

In exile, the rapidity acquired from custom suddenly finds itself broken. However, customs are no less enduring; they simply transform themselves. Custom becomes a system of recurring images. Removed from its original framework, it becomes unrealized and finds a new base in the submersed area of sensorial memory. The more the sensations that accompany the act of remembering accumulate and are made precise, the more the effort of willpower slackens. From this point on, willpower gives way to the plentiful flow of images. Without looking to recall the aroma of a flower that one once smelled on the wayside of a forest path, willpower surges forth with surprising precision, at times uncanny in its seizure of consciousness. Images such as these are the traces of a past world. When they return, they are not subject to any periodicity. They know no predetermined cycle. They do not follow any rhythm—if by this we mean a precisely regular cadence—and are consequently unpredictable. But they always invite the exile to cherish the effort of remembering, which gives off so much emotional warmth. It is as though the exile substituted one act of faith for that other act of faith, evoked by Locke, which acts as the cement of civil society. The exile begins to attribute particular virtue to the state of passivity, as he waits for the reminiscence that links him to the world of the past. He does not turn to the past; it is rather the past that constantly turns to him and that aims to overtake him. Strictly speaking, this is the ghostly force of memory. Haunted by ghosts from his past existence, the exile imbues the past with a reality that it never possessed, with a particular weightiness. The weight of memories proves to be as substantial as the past injustice It is this passage of time that imposes itself on his willpower in a chaotic and insistent manner. It is this force that renders the exile incapable of enjoying the present. Compared to what came before, the presence has no substance.

Giacomo Leopardi already emphasized, in his own way, the "volatility" of the relationship that many travelers have with the present:

> As humankind is in the habit of upbraiding present things, and praising those which are past, so most travelers, while they are travelling, love their native place and somewhat angrily prefer it to wherever they find themselves. Having returned to their native place, with the same anger they value it less than all the other places where they have been.[6]

The exile whose life is governed by nostalgia is not a traveler whose movements are subject to dissatisfaction. In both cases, the past overcomes the present, but for the traveler the past is lighter than it is for the exile. While the former plays with the affective registers of time and space, to the extent that he values only what he can enjoy indirectly, the latter is tied to one past and to one place in particular. If Leopardi's traveler frees himself with ease from the hold of his native land, the exile is hard pressed to act in the same way. Nostalgia is not only a matter of temporality, it is also a matter of place. The sentiments of the exile are more firmly anchored than those of the simple traveler.

For the exile, nostalgia represents the trump card of his emotional geography. It singles out memories by reinforcing contrasts and creating relief.

In nostalgia, no two memories are alike—even if a familial air unites them all. Previously unnoticed details, which revive a dream lived long ago and which have nothing in common with any other detail, spring up in memory. The exile sees everything in nothing (while Leopardi's traveler sees nothing in everything). Nostalgia takes great care to distinguish memories from one another. It sharpens insight into the differentiated treasures of memory. Exile thus incites every exile to become the Christopher Columbus of his own sea of hidden memories. But nostalgia also divides the world into a lived world and a remembered world. It mounts ghosts on every street corner and reveals the spectral nature of a vicariously seen reality. The exile really lives nowhere because he is always everywhere at once, leading a second life daily obsessed with internal voices of the past. The isolated exile feels connected to an "atmospheric Elsewhere," to a vaporous image of his distant homeland that makes his presence in the world an absent one. Thus, as Vladimir Jankélévitch notes, the nostalgic man, "troubled by the gentleness of his soul's vagueness, captivated by the alibis of the past, is a kind of sleepwalker among us."[7] The paradox of the "multipresence" described by Jankélévitch points to the impossibility of omnipresence. Forced to live in one place, even though he would still like to live in another, the exile charges his imagination with the task of allowing him to overcome this impossibility. Recurring images and interior voices provide the individual with a sense of victory over passing time. But this is ephemeral, because the exile quickly understands that nostalgia is in fact its own cause and that he has no power as long as he remains in its grip. Jankélévitch also observes that it is not necessary to previously have been happy to become nostalgic; it is sufficient to have been there and to associate that place with the experience of estrangement. The simple fact of estrangement makes a thing inaccessible. In becoming inaccessible, the thing acquires an aura of ideality. Without putting thought into it, the exile forms an excessive attachment. Thus, "closed nostalgia," which signifies the singular desire to return to one's country, finds its complement in an "open nostalgia," which responds to the inevitable disappointment of return with an indeterminate need for new movement.[8] As for me, I associate the dialectic of closed and open with the unbearable weight of nostalgia that makes the exile dependent upon his universe of images.

No return can truly make up for a departure. Certain departures even proscribe recovering from the pain of exile. We cannot go back in time. We cannot restore the old order of things. This is why nostalgia is the mother of all memories of exile. In order to compensate, she re-enchants the domain of memory. But the price of this re-enchantment is high. On the one hand, the exile isolates himself in his memories of his culture of origin. On the other hand, he can come to believe that it is always preferable to flee since he will never again know his motherland. The pinnacle of nostalgia is thus eternal wandering. Often, exile designates neither the loss of the motherland nor the disappearance of the love that one harbors for it, but rather the fact that "loss is inherent in the very existence of both."[9] The sense of a consubstantial loss of life reinforces the solipsistic tendency of the exiled mind. This results in fragmented identities and catastrophes of history that have produced a pileup of memories in such a way that the present and the past become incommensurable. Thus, the exile is still not Leopardi's traveler. If one can acquire knowledge of the past through displacement, the other discovers that his knowledge of memory comes from the past itself and that the boundaries between the living and the dead are permeable. The imaginary world of the exile is made of simulacra, flashbacks, and connections between events.

Seen thus, nostalgia presents a double risk. On the one hand, the exile often feels disgusted with himself when he sees himself as too passive. On the other hand, he is still unable to rid himself of his passivity, so dear to him are his memories. Nostalgia encloses the individual in the complicated folds of his past intimacy. It does not allow him to evolve his identity in the future. It happens then that he considers a potentially nominalist relationship with the world around him. In exile, knowledge of the world is refracted through the prism of a particular place, of a singular history. One might object that this is the distinctive character of the global human condition.[10] But the situation of exile prompts other questions: are the memories that nostalgia rouses transmissible? Is the exile, gripped by nostalgia, capable of recognizing memories other than his own?

Exile destroys the social significance of individual biographies. In his displacement, the exile is stripped bare. Forbidden to practice his trade elsewhere, he loses his professional status. Exile dissociates the individual from his past training, from experience he has acquired, and from his potentially accumulated wisdom. It brings him back to the atmosphere at the beginning of his career, making him hesitate before the path he will choose, like an adolescent who does not know what conduct to adopt in the adult world. Exile depreciates and humiliates the individual. It makes him fall from the rank that he has worked toward all his life. Thus, the exile appears to those in the society that receives him as an individual devoid of a past:

> Only the ways in which his fathers and grandfathers lived become for everyone elements of his own way of life. Graves and reminiscences can neither be transferred nor conquered. The stranger, therefore, approaches the other group as a newcomer in the true meaning of the term. At best he may be willing and able to share the present and the future with the approached group in vivid and immediate experience; under all circumstances, however, he remains excluded from such experiences of its past. Seen from the point of view of the approached group, he is a man without a history.[11]

Nostalgia aims to compensate for this denial of history—at least for the concerned individual. By the force of memories, it creates the fictional impression of reordering. Each person thus recalls the time when he enjoyed a status. Retrospectively, nostalgia reorders and returns a minimum of dignity. It matters little that one recognizes it as artificial. In the condition of exile, nostalgia is the archetypal feeling of useful fictions.

In the order of social relationships, the double means that the previous status is not considered and that it is only the object of private memories, inciting the exile to act as a "social pariah," to use Hannah Arendt's term. And yet the social pariah is obsessed with trying to change his identity. Most German émigrés did not wish to be categorized as "refugees." They much preferred the terms "newcomers" or "immigrants."[12] The reason is simple: the word "refugee" is enough to evoke a past that the social pariah forces himself to silence.

The exile described by Arendt in her 1943 article "We Refugees" fights against what I have called the unbearable weight of nostalgia. It is this nostalgia that effectively inspires him on the contrary to forget his past: to eschew German in favor of English, to not mention concentration camps at the risk of sounding like a pessimist incapable of finding his place in an American society bound by optimism. But what is silenced by day reappears by night, haunts the mind, feeds nightmares, and ultimately pushes toward suicide. The equation between silence and suffering and the eloquence of his denial push the exile to leave the world. He can silence what pains him and display the conduct of a person who never had to suffer. When he has lost all familiarity with daily life, in which the former profession for which he was respected becomes pointless, when his adopted language is insufficient to meet the spontaneous demands of his mind, and when a large part of his family has disappeared in death camps or ghettos, the forced optimism of what Arendt viewed as assimilationists has much in common with a magic recipe whose ingredients are poisonous. Arendt observes that no justification appears in the suicide letters left behind. Here, she sees proof of the harshness of opinions in society, the sign of the reign of masks that imply superficial behavior meant to hide an original sin. Arendt's exiles are the Jews for German Nazis; *boches* ("krauts") for the French allied with Vichy, who imprison them on this account; and suspicious individuals for the many Americans who do not bestow their confidence on those who try too hard to obtain it. The result is a generalized state of confusion in which the catalyzing power of nostalgia, which stimulates the capacity to react and weakens the aptitude to do so, is implicitly proven. From this point on, nothing prohibits these "first *prisonniers volontaires*" of history from instituting themselves as their own demiurges. But no one imagines how absurd it is to want to recreate a world inside a world that rejects all new departures:

> Man is a social animal and life is not easy for him when social ties are cut off. Moral standards are much easier kept in the texture of a society. Very few individuals have the strength to conserve their own integrity if their social, political and legal status is completely confused. Lacking the courage to fight for a change of our social and legal status, we have decided instead, so many of us, to try a change of identity. And this curious behavior makes matters much worse. The confusion in which we live is partly our own work. ... A man who wants to lose his self discovers, indeed, the possibilities of human existence, which are infinite, as infinite as is creation. But the recovering of a new personality is as difficult—and as hopeless—as a new creation of the world.[13]

This passage announces themes that will be reprised in Arendt's trilogy on totalitarianism. Social pariahs effectively know this "loneliness" to the point that they want to abandon their identities. They live this uprooting that robs the individual of his place in the world, conceals him from the gaze of others, and finally renders him useless, superfluous, outside the world, deprived not only of his social status but also his human existence. They confirm the thesis according to which "loneliness," unlike solitude, is never more apparent than when they are in the company of others. Significantly, most of them also see a horizon of social and intellectual redemption for the exile. Even when Edward Said maintains that the sadness implied by exile is insurmountable, that the chagrin caused by distance is too hard to bear, and that real exile comes from an irreversible loss, he suggests that

> seeing "the entire world as a foreign land" makes possible originality of vision. Most people are principally aware of one culture, one setting, one home; exiles are aware of at least two, and this plurality of vision gives rise to an awareness of simultaneous dimensions, an awareness that—to borrow a phrase from music—is *contrapuntal*. ... Thus both the new and the old environments are vivid, actual, occurring together contrapuntally. There is a unique pleasure in this sort of apprehension, especially if the exile is conscious of other contrapuntal juxtapositions that diminish orthodox judgments and elevate appreciative sympathy. There is also a particular sense of achievement in acting as if one were at home wherever one happens to be.[14]

Ernst Bloch, on the other hand, identifies two types of exiles that both seem unpleasant to him: in one case, those who take to hating Germany and the German language by opting for accelerated Americanization; and in the other, those who still believe in a better Germany that does not resemble its current disfigured form, and who create an isolate of German culture in the heart of America. These two types represent two forms of "false radicalism" that contradict the plural identity of the United States. The most appropriate attitude is thus the one that maintains "double loyalties" (and not "divided loyalties") by the combined exercise of memory and confidence in the future. Significantly, Bloch concludes his lecture with the figure of Abraham Lincoln and human rights. Even though in the original German version of his speech he proves to be critical of prevailing capitalism to the point of imagining the possibility of a return to Germany, thus affirming his essential fidelity to his European heritage, he acknowledges his debt to American society. Between forced mimicry and the refusal of assimilation, the proper moral attitude is

> as far from insipid intrusion as it is from introverted foreignness. The German refugee writer brings his roots with him: a mature language, an old culture. He brings these values to America. And he remains faithful to them not by making museum-pieces out of them, but by testing and quickening his powers of expression on the new stuff of life.[15]

The promotion of this double affiliation counteracts the deleterious effects of nostalgia. "Contrapuntal" consciousness is not the ghostly consciousness described by Jankélévitch. Rather, it provides the exile with a sense of self-confidence that authorizes him to penetrate the maze of daily life, where contingency reigns, where no social status is assured, where what seems normal is not guaranteed to last, and where what should be accepted immediately—a protective cultural model—always poses a problem. Freed from the unbearable weight of nostalgia, the individual becomes capable of finding his way in the labyrinth of a new world. Orientation in the labyrinth is a sign of a cosmopolitan identity in progress.[16]

Arendt's and Said's attention to the theme of recreating a world serves to underscore the need, felt by all exiles, to substitute a universe of meaning for the former real world, which has since become intangible. And yet their analyses differ. Said interprets such a need at times as the origin of what Eric Hobsbawm and Terence Ranger call an "invented tradition," and at other times in terms of writing that provides a sense of refuge.[17] As for Arendt, she insists on the ability to start over and the absolute necessity of conserving one's identity. Faced with the difficulty of remaining oneself in exile, she adds that refugees "driven from country to country represent the vanguard of their peoples—*if they keep their identity*" (my italics).[18] The exclusion of Jews from legal society in the nineteenth century did not prevent certain figures from assuming the role of "conscious pariahs." Arendt cites Heinrich Heine, Rahel Varnhagen, Bernard Lazare, and Franz Kafka. The vigilance of these representatives of Jewish tradition should have even served as a lesson to the whole of Europe as it headed toward chaos. It is they who constitute the first avant-garde.

In defending the virtues of self-equality, Arendt indirectly rejoins one of the moral presuppositions that affirm the ancient Cynics' reflections on exile. According to Diogenes of Sinope, the exile must equally remain faithful to himself. There are at least two reasons for this. On the one hand, exile is only rarely the fruit of dishonesty for respectable people. Thus, shame should not affect the exiled or banished person but rather those who were the cause of his eviction. On the other hand, the country that betrayed its own citizens no longer signifies any greatness. There is no reason to remain unduly attached to it. Constant and detached, the exile is a citizen of the world. For Epictetus, he is even an envoy from the gods, an explorer, or even an observer who—following the example of Diogenes when he was sent to Philip II after the Battle of Chaeronea—returns to his fellow countrymen in order to show them their faults and help correct them (*Discourses*, 3.22.23–25). As a citizen of the world and a messenger of humanity, the exile also distinguishes himself by his outspokenness, which allows him to occupy a position in the interstices of politics, where his courage for truth is distinguished from routine behavior. This is certainly an avant-garde attitude.

If nostalgia is the feeling that governs the condition of exile, it consequently tends to stall the individual in the closed universe of his former values. Since the new society often considers these same values useless, nostalgia prevents the exile from reducing the "fundamental discrepancies" that emerge from the confrontation between cultural models. It does not help him introduce himself into the milieu whose codes and conducts he does not master. Its gravity constantly draws him in. It weighs him down and prevents him from "jumping from the stalls to the stage" in order to pass from the status of a "former onlooker" to a "member of the cast," to use Alfred Schütz's expressions. Nonetheless, Schütz contends, it is only in this way that a newly arrived individual "enters as a partner into social relations with his co-actors, and participates henceforth in the action in progress."[19] For the exile, as for all strangers, there is no other way to (again) become cosmopolitan. It is necessary to be a member of the cast and unburden oneself in order to make a decisive step out of the zone of nostalgia and become involved in the theater of public action. Then nostalgia can be recuperated by being considered in a self-reflexive light, which means a capacity to achieve distance from one's homeland in a particular manner.

Olivier Remaud is a Research Professor at the School for Advanced Studies in Social Sciences (Ecole des Hautes Etudes en Sciences Sociales) in Paris. His recent publications include *Solitude volontaire* (Albin Michel, 2017); *Un monde étrange* (PUF, 2015); and the co-edited *Faire des sciences sociales* (EHESS Press, 2012, 3 vols) and *War and Peace* (Duncker & Humblot, 2010), with Soraya Nour.

NOTES

1. See for instance Bertolt Brecht, *Bertolt Brecht: Poems 1913–1956*, ed. Ralph Manheim and John Willett (London, 1987), 301.
2. Edward Said, "Reflections on Exile," in *Reflections on Exile and Other Essays* (London, 2001), 173–86, 176.
3. Ibid., 181.
4. Cf. Benedict Anderson, "Exodus," *Critical Inquiry* 20, no. 2 (1994), 326.
5. Judith N. Shklar, "Obligation, Loyalty, Exile," *Political Theory* 21, no. 2 (1993): 193.
6. Giacomo Leopardi, *Thoughts*, in *Thoughts; and The Broom*, trans. John G. Nichols (London, 2002), 25.
7. Vladimir Jankélévitch, *L'irréversible et la nostalgie* (Paris, 1983), 346–47, my translation.
8. Ibid., 349–52 and 360–67.
9. Said, "Reflections on Exile," 185.
10. See Roland Robertson, *Globalization: Social Theory and Social Culture* (London, 1992).
11. Alfred Schütz, "The Stranger: An Essay in Social Psychology," *American Journal of Sociology* 49, no. 6 (1944): 502.
12. Hannah Arendt, "We Refugees," in *Altogether Elsewhere: Writers on Exile*, ed. Marc Robinson (Boston, MA, 1994), 110. On this point, Seyla Benhabib has some useful terminological reminders: "One becomes a *refugee* if one is persecuted, expelled or driven away from one's homeland; one becomes a *minority* if the political majority in the polity declares that certain groups do not belong to the supposedly 'homogeneous' people; one is a *stateless person* if the state whose protection one has hitherto enjoyed withdraws such protection, as well as nullifying the papers it has granted; one is a *displaced person* if having been once considered a refugee, a minority, or a stateless person, one cannot find another polity to recognize one as its member, and remains in a state of limbo, caught between territories, none of which desire one to be its resident." See Seyla Benhabib, *The Rights of Others: Aliens, Residents, and Citizens* (Cambridge, 2004), 54. Original emphasis.
13. Arendt, "We Refugees," 116–17. For a general commentary on this text, see Wolfgang Heuer, "Europe and Its Refugees: Arendt on the Politicization of Minorities," *Social Research* 74, no. 4 (2007): 1159–72.
14. Said, "Reflections on Exile," 186. For Said, the "scrupulous subjectivity" of contrapuntal conscience is an alternative to "mass society." It is embodied in the act of writing, which then becomes the unique refuge possible in a world where everything is proven to be provisional (for the exile) and prefabricated (for society). It is accompanied by a moral worthy of Marcus Aurelius (185–86): "Regard experiences as if they were about to disappear. What is it that anchors them in reality? What would you save of them? What would you give up? Only someone who has achieved independence and detachment, someone whose homeland is 'sweet' but whose circumstances make it impossible to recapture that sweetness, can answer those questions. (Such a person would also find it impossible to derive satisfaction from substitutes furnished by

illusion or dogma.)" Said here comments on Hugo of St. Victor's remarks. Erich Auerbach previously analyzed them in his essay "Philologie der Weltliteratur," and Said emphasized the extent to which Auerbach's drafting of *Mimesis* while in exile in Istanbul demonstrates "the executive value of exile, which Auerbach was able to turn into effective use" (Edward Said, "Secular Criticism," in *The World, the Text, and the Critic* [Cambridge, MA, 1983], 8). By affirming that he would not have been able to write this book at home among all of his books, Auerbach (according to Said) confirms that exile produces a creative distance in regard to the native culture. In this sense, the exile is less a product of his time than the most vivid actor of his own culture. Moreover, such is the meaning of "criticism."

15. Ernst Bloch, "Disrupted Language—Disrupted Culture," *Direction* 2, no. 6 (1939): 18. The sense of "double loyalties" is also used by Tzvetan Todorov: "Exile is fruitful if one belongs to both cultures at once, without identifying itself with either" (*The Conquest of America: The Question of the Other* [New York, 1985], 250).
16. Schütz, "The Stranger," 506: "The cultural pattern of the approached group is to the stranger not a shelter but a field of adventure, not a matter of course but a questionable topic of investigation, not an instrument for disentangling problematic situations but a problematic situation itself and one hard to master."
17. Cf. Eric Hobsbawm and Terence Ranger, eds, *The Invention of Tradition* (Cambridge, 1983).
18. Arendt, "We Refugees," 119.
19. Schütz, "The Stranger," 503.

BIBLIOGRAPHY

Anderson, Benedict, "Exodus," *Critical Inquiry* 20, no. 2 (1994): 326.
Arendt, Hannah. "We Refugees." In *Altogether Elsewhere: Writers on Exile*, edited by Marc Robinson, 110–119. Boston, MA: Faber and Faber, 1994.
Auerbach, Erich, "Philologie der Weltliteratur," in *Weltliteratur: Festgabe für Fritz Strich zum 70. Geburtstag*, ed. Walter Muschg and E. Staiger (Bern: Francke, 1952), 39-50.
Benhabib, Seyla. *The Rights of Others: Aliens, Residents, and Citizens*. Cambridge: Cambridge University Press, 2004.
Bloch, Ernst. "Disrupted Language—Disrupted Culture." *Direction* 2, no. 6 (1939): 16–19.
Brecht, Bertolt, *Poems 1913–1956*, edited by Ralph Manheim and John Willett, translated by Edith Anderson, Lee Baxendall, Eva Bornemann et al.,. London: Meuthen, 1987.
Heuer, Wolfgang. "Europe and Its Refugees: Arendt on the Politicization of Minorities." *Social Research* 74, no. 4 (2007): 1159–72.
Hobsbawm, Eric, and Terence Ranger, eds. *The Invention of Tradition*. Cambridge: Cambridge University Press, 1983.
Jankélévitch, Vladimir. *L'irréversible et la nostalgie*. Paris: Champs-Flammarion, 1983.
Leopardi, Giacomo. *Thoughts*. In *Thoughts; and, The Broom*, translated by John G. Nichols, XVIII – 93. London: Hesperus, 2002.
Robertson, Roland. *Globalization: Social Theory and Social Culture*. London: Sage, 1992.

Said, Edward. "Reflections on Exile." In *Reflections on Exile and Other Essays*, 173–86. London: Granta Books, 2001.

———. "Secular Criticism." In *The World, the Text, and the Critic*, 1–30. Cambridge, MA: Harvard University Press, 1983.

Schütz, Alfred. "The Stranger: An Essay in Social Psychology." *American Journal of Sociology* 49, no. 6 (1944): 499–507.

Shklar, Judith N. "Obligation, Loyalty, Exile." *Political Theory* 21, no. 2 (1993): 181–97.

Todorov, Tzvetan. *The Conquest of America: The Question of the Other*. New York: Harper Row, 1985.

▶• 14 •◀

Extensions of World Heritage

The Globe, the List, and the Limes

Stefan Willer

Today the concept of "the world" is extremely effective in cultural policy, especially in the World Heritage program, promoted by the United Nations Educational, Scientific and Cultural Organization (UNESCO) and executed by all kinds of national and regional authorities and institutions. In this chapter I argue that the effectiveness of this powerful "world" concept needs to be analyzed and problematized. In a first step I will examine the semantic and functional scope of both relevant terms, "world" and "heritage," focusing on the tension between the extensional project of incorporating cultural traditions on a global level, and the intensional, content-based idea of heritable universal cultural values. Second, I will sketch a case study regarding a specific site on the World Heritage List, namely the "Frontiers of the Roman Empire." This transnational site, which comprises Hadrian's and Antonine Walls in England and Scotland, and the so-called Limes frontier in south-west Germany, serves as an example for the practices of limitation that are operative in defining the actual extensions of World Heritage. To conclude, I will raise some questions regarding the globality and/or universality of cultural heritage today.

Inheriting World Culture

When defining a term such as "world," we can distinguish an intensional and an extensional meaning. The intension is the content of a term, more specifically its necessary qualities and characteristics; the extension is the range and scope of a term, regarding the sum total of everything the term covers. As for "world," its intensional qualities traditionally have to do with the classical eighteenth-century ideas of universality and cosmopolitanism, where worldliness is some kind of task that has to be pursued in a potentially infinite progress.¹ Of course, we might also think of all kinds of restricted and exclusive uses in which what is called "world" actually only refers to a very small part of it—*le monde* of the French *ancien régime* for instance, which designated the "fashionable society," the "beautiful people."²

By contrast, the extension of the world seemingly can be described without drawing on any philosophical or sociological concepts, since it is determined geographically, or astronomically. This extensional world—as far as terrestrial matters are concerned—is quite simply the planet Earth, our globe.³ But of course this determination and delimitation is conceptual, philosophical, and political as well. Thus, the extension (extensiveness) of the world as globe has to do with the reality of a limited, finite, and vulnerable world, and with the idea of One World, which is and has to be enough for all of us—hence the increasing importance of *sustainability* as a main political and cultural concern (to which I will return).

As to World Heritage, "world" obviously indicates the global extension of the current heritage policy, which is supposed to be valid and prestigious *worldwide*. What is registered on the famous UNESCO World Heritage List is a certain number of particular domains. Most of them are attributed to distinct nations, and many of them are in public ownership. All of them are said to belong, as the preamble of the 1972 UNESCO Convention Concerning the Protection of the World Cultural and Natural Heritage has it, to "all the peoples of the world," adding up to "the world heritage of mankind as a whole."⁴ This ideal or idealistic kind of ownership makes quite evident that the concept of World Heritage cannot be told apart from the intensional, content-based concepts of "world" mentioned before—which especially regards the basic idea of *inherited* cultural values that are to be passed on to following generations. For this is what the signatory states committed themselves to in 1972: "the identification, protection, conservation, presentation and transmission to future generations of the cultural and natural heritage."⁵

Linking heritage to the concept of generations obviously means using both a legitimizing and a naturalizing argument. He or she who is declared heir is adjudged a legitimate place in a line of succession, whereas others are delegitimized. This holds true not only for individuals, but also for groups, societies, and whole cultures. To better understand why the discourse about World Heritage has become so prominent in global cultural policy, it is helpful to go further into the problem of transgenerational inheritance, which is at the core of the heritage discourse. The intrinsically linked concepts of inheritance and of generations—especially "future" generations—have many aspects and prerequisites that do not easily fit with globality or the discourse on globalization.

Generation is a key concept to describe modern relations of time, society, and individuality.⁶ One of the most important features of its use is the designation of history and society as something natural. Speaking in terms of "generation," contingent and variable processes of social change can be narrated as if they were self-evident and self-reproductive, for the pattern of subsequent generations can be regarded as the epitome of natural reproduction. Nonetheless, intergenerational relationships can also be conceived of as the paradigmatic confrontation between obsolete and innovative political orders. Especially in the French and American Revolutions, the "new" and "forthcoming" generations were invoked against any logic of the *ancien régime*. Obviously, generations can be regarded as exemplary social agents in both continuity and conflict. When in the decades around 1800 the concept of generation started its political career, it was seen as the motor of innovation, and of the path to an emphatically open future—which should be kept in mind for the "future generations" of World Heritage.

The concept of *inheritance*, again, integrates cultural, social, and scientific aspects.[7] All economic, material inheritance is something cultural; on the other hand, discourses and practices of cultural inheritance are loaded with economic problems and interests. Also when biological *heredity* is concerned, the strict boundary between a "natural" and a "cultural" perspective can hardly be maintained. Knowledge about biological heredity itself has its cultural history, and it surely has its cultural effects (one of which is that biodiversity has become an issue of cultural heritage). Even when we stick to cultural *heritage* in the narrower sense, we cannot ignore the natural, or naturalizing, aspects. The whole idea of designating cultural traditions a matter of inheritance in the first place, that is, of a transfer that is guaranteed by the shift from generation to generation, is another instance of historical change understood as something natural. This might be the reason why today's discourse about cultural heritage is so widely accepted and why the idea of cultural values being passed on to following generations, who will then become the cultural heirs, seems so plausible and so pertinent. This is all the more true since the heritage discourse can easily be translated into the current conception of intergenerational relationships in terms of *sustainability*.

Sustainability surely is one of the most topical political tasks with regard not only to cultural heritage, but also to economies, social systems, and the environment on a global scale.[8] What is at stake here is a certain relationship between space and time, which are brought together in a very special and unique way, mixing political arguments and particular interests with an almost metaphysical rhetoric. According to the political claim of sustainability, the state of the globe—signifying a maximum of space—shall be saved and secured for future generations—signifying a maximum of time. Conservation, being the main concern of the protagonists of World Heritage, is obviously connected to this kind of maximum spatio-temporality. In a 2003 article, Francesco Bandarín, the then director of the UNESCO World Heritage Centre in Paris, linked sustainability and conservation to the idea of survival.

"Sustainability," Bandarín stated, "remains the key to both the survival of World Heritage and its credibility." He then continued: "Conservation is by definition long term—not for a year or two, but for ever."[9] In this perspective, survival means no less than eternal life; and sustainability means keeping something up *forever*.

UNESCO thus argues for a general application of its cultural concept of sustainability, understood as the epitome of futurity. "World" in World Heritage addresses the problem of the reach and the validity of the cultural heritage policy, for this policy is supposed to operate and to be accepted worldwide. Now a series of questions emerges: how can globality be reconciled with other territorial entities operative in cultural heritage discourses and practices, such as the state, the country, or the site?[10] What is a "heritage site" in the first place, and where does it end? How can such a site actually be delimited, that is, told apart from its surroundings that are not part of World Heritage? What is the connection between this territorial delimitation of every single site and the numeric limitation of sites on the famous World Heritage List? And—given the listing of more and more sites, and the propagation of more and more additional heritage programs—is there really a limit to the extensions of World Heritage?

Incidentally, in the UNESCO vocabulary the term "site" is used alternately not only with "place," but also with "property."[11] This word, "property," again conveys the basic concept of culture as a valuable and transmissible heritage. The fact that "property," "place," and "site" are interchangeable indicates that, in World Heritage, cultural economy and questions of space and topography are closely connected. In the administration of this topographical economy, UNESCO, being not actually a global, but rather an *international* organization, relies on *nations* as entities that can be clearly told apart from each other, and which the UNESCO terminology refers to as "states parties." Thus, the proclamation of World Heritage produces an international rivalry of cultural excellence. "The list" being the canonical form of presentation makes perfectly clear that World Heritage is actually not an open and inclusive concept, but is explicitly based on closure and limitation. With this, we touch the controversial status of cultural heritage—quite different from the harmonized idea of an integral cultural treasure from the past belonging to "mankind as a whole." Instead, a constant evaluation and valorization process is going on in order to find out what is part of that treasure, in other words what is on the World Heritage List, and what is not.

To defend this kind of decision, the UNESCO conventions and publications make frequent use of concepts of representation and exemplarity. This concerns above all the ten selection criteria for the denomination of a heritage site, according to which "sites must be of outstanding universal value." Hence it is imperative that they "represent a masterpiece of human creative genius," or "bear a unique or at least exceptional testimony to a cultural tradition," or "be an outstanding example of a type of building, architectural or technological ensemble or landscape which illustrates (a) significant stage(s) in human history," or "contain superlative natural phenomena or areas of exceptional natural beauty and aesthetic importance," or "be outstanding examples representing significant on-going ecological and biological processes."[12]

It is remarkable that the 1972 convention text here simply interchanges "exceptional," "outstanding," and "exemplary" ("example") without making any effort to differentiate these notions—which is just another instance for the finding that the logic of exemplarity and the logic of exception have very much in common.[13] In this vein, the very characterization of "standing out" is not only a matter of quality, but also of territoriality and delimitation, for it has to be substantiated in every single case how that which "stands out" can be marked off from its immediate surroundings. Thus, the place is being distinguished from the regular affairs, from the normal economies and life circumstances; it is becoming exemplary in the Latin meaning of the word: *ex-imere*, "to take out." This is why the following example is of special interest: "Frontiers of the Roman Empire" is a case in which a limitation itself has become a site.

Safeguarding Imperial Frontiers

The World Heritage site "Frontiers of the Roman Empire" consists of three vast borderline formations: the more than 100-km-long Hadrian's Wall in northern England, the 60-km-long Antonine Wall in Scotland, and the Limes whose relics have been found within a range of five hundred kilometers in south-west Germany between the Rhine and the Danube. While the British sites are unquestionably monuments—although partly in ruins—the Limes has become mostly invisible over the course of the centuries. But it is precisely the invisibility that makes it an exemplary site, significantly different from usual monuments like churches or historical city centers. Thus, the acceptance of the Limes epitomizes the idea of turning frontiers into a site—which, again, can be interpreted as a symbolic limiting value of world cultural policy, following the Latin words *limes* and *limen*, which not only mean "borderline" or "threshold," but also the "limiting value" in its mathematical sense.

The history of this World Heritage site started with the acceptance of Hadrian's Wall onto the List in 1987. From the 1990s, meetings were held by preservationists from other countries on whose territories Roman remains had been excavated. In 2003 these preservationists founded the so-called Bratislava Group, which aimed at establishing the "Frontiers" as a transnational site. The Group recommended gradually comprising into this site all of the fortifications found in Europe, North Africa, and Asia Minor, indicating the maximum circumference of the Roman Empire in the second century AD (between Emperors Trajan and Septimius Severus). What should be identified, protected, and conserved was not only each single site but also the multilocality of these sites and, along with it, the historical idea of the Roman Empire as both a universal and a global empire of its time. Quite sagaciously, the Roman self-conception as "imperium sine fine,"[14] as "endless" in time and space (eternal and infinite), should be presented precisely by emphasizing the *ends* of the empire: its territorial limits, indicating at the same time the temporal limitation of this as of all other empires.

The years following the foundation of the Bratislava Group saw two nominations: the Limes was proposed in 2004/2005, the Antonine Wall in 2007/2008. After being evaluated by the International Council on Monuments and Sites (ICOMOS), UNESCO's most important certification organization regarding cultural monuments, both applications were approved. The Limes was put on the List by the World Heritage Committee in 2005, the Antonine Wall in 2008. In its 2005 recommendation, ICOMOS explicitly advocated further nominations, "initially in Europe, but in due course perhaps also in Africa and Asia."[15] Obviously the peripheral positioning of a "transboundary" site occupying the very space of the antique fortifications was acknowledged as an idea with future potential, creating an ongoing exception from the basic rule of World Heritage sites belonging to separate "states parties."

The transboundary site can be understood to somehow revive the idea of the Roman Empire, which, in its very quality of empire, exceeds (and historically precedes) the narrow boundaries of nation-states. Moreover, the creation of a transboundary site means integrating different historical traditions in the interpretation of the Roman remains.[16] These have not always been seen as part of the Roman heritage: Hadrian's Wall, for instance, was formerly understood as a stronghold of the British against the Scots. From this reception-historical view, concepts of World Heritage date back to very different ways of making sense of leftovers from the past, comprising practices that were not at all about safeguarding, but about very concrete, material forms of appropriation. Hadrian's Wall was being used as a stone quarry for several centuries (which is why Roman stones have often been found in churches and cloisters); the Limes became practically forgotten while it vanished into the soil, which is why it was often used as building ground, even (and above all) in the 1950s and 1960s.

Since the early modern period, however, the Roman remains were not only exploited but also thoroughly researched. The Limes was successively examined in its historical course, first by individual scholars, later by learned societies (*Altertumsvereine*), and finally by the German Reichs-Limeskommission founded by historian Theodor Mommsen in 1892. Ever since, historical studies about the limits of the Roman Empire must also be seen as specific appropriations of the past. This is evident for the historicist approaches of the late nineteenth century when the Limes became a political issue after the formation of the German empire after 1871—hence the decision of Emperor Wilhelm II to have the Saalburg fort reconstructed in 1897. By contrast, more recent and differentiated research about "frontier history" dismissed the idea of a strict and fortified borderline and embraced the concept of the frontier as "contact zone" between Romans and other populations.[17]

Current efforts at safeguarding are obviously less constructivist than former historical appropriations, which is mainly due to a preservationist shift of paradigm around 1900 when art historians claimed that there should be conservation instead of restoration or reconstruction.[18] In the twentieth century, "historical restorations" like the Saalburg fort became more frequently condemned by the experts. Ever since, what has to be preserved is not a reconstructed original state but rather the status quo—that is, the state in which a site is, in the very moment when it is declared a monument, including as much as possible from the complete diachronic development of this site. The relevant "Venice Charter" ("International Charter for the Conservation and Restoration of Monuments and Sites," 1965, a direct forerunner of the 1972 UNESCO World Heritage convention) says that "the valid contribution of all periods to the building of a monument must be respected, since unity of style is not the aim of a restoration."[19] Another article of that same charter states that the process of restoration "must stop at the point where conjecture begins."[20]

This standard leads to interesting consequences in the case of the Limes. According to historical and archaeological authenticity, one would award the Heritage status only to the former Limes line in its present state of a mostly invisible ground monument, given the Venice Charter slogan that "Ruins have to be maintained."[21] Any embellishment or restoration would have to be considered false, including the historicizations from the late nineteenth century. But these restorations are in fact an integral part of the World Heritage site, even though, according to today's state of the art, they are historical mistakes. Moreover, it is precisely for this reason that they can be historicized and included into Heritage, as ICOMOS stated in the evaluation:

> ICOMOS considers that the Roman remains need to be differentiated from reconstructions. Whereas reconstructions carried out in the nineteenth century can be said to now have a certain historical interest, it does not consider that reconstructions carried out since the inception of the Venice Charter can be considered authentic or of sufficient value as to be included in the nomination.[22]

Since today's "historical interest" certainly includes the nineteenth century, past changes of the antique site can be included into this very site. At the same time, ICOMOS sets a clear historical boundary beyond which the "heritability" of reconstructions definitely ends. This boundary is—quite remarkably—"the inception of the Venice Charter," that is, the codification of today's preservationist regime. Everything restored or reconstructed after this time must be regarded inauthentic and valueless, according to the ICOMOS formulation. This kind of distinction is characteristic of UNESCO and its appointed organizations. They concede the validity of reconstructions only up to a certain point, drawing a line that is at the same time temporal and spatial: "Those parts of the Limes that have been reconstructed since 1965, together with development over and above Roman remains, should be excluded from the nomination and treated as a buffer zone."[23]

This logic of inclusion and exclusion implies a strict definition of where the Limes territory begins and where it ends, which would require the exact measurement of each sector of meadow or forest identifiable as Limes. Even if this is archaeologically impossible, on a conceptual level it leads to the factual restoration of the Limes as the strict borderline it probably never was. The more interesting concept of the "contact zone," instead, can be recognized only in the "buffer zone" excluded from the actual site. And even this buffer zone ends where future changes should be put into practice: "Any further reconstructions ... could risk putting the site under threat."[24] Threat and danger are the emphatically negative concepts the Heritage program uses to designate its other. On the World Heritage website, every entry to the List bears a "Reporting Trend" (formerly called "Threat Intensity Coefficient"), based on "the frequency at which the World Heritage Committee has deliberated over this property."[25] If the resulting threat reaches a certain degree, the relative monuments appear on the sub-list of "World Heritage in Danger,"[26] which is the last resort before completely excluding a site from the List.

One should keep in mind that this strict way of preventing danger refers back to the historical situation in which UNESCO was founded. After World War II, the destruction not only of monuments but of cultural values on a much broader scale was a plain reality. It was this extreme caesura that created the desire to safeguard cultural tradition from further threats—hence the institutional success and productivity of UNESCO and its many programs. But it must also be stated that the original motive of protection has turned into a broad range of administrative and bureaucratic mechanisms that have to be executed by the "states parties" and the actors on the heritage sites. Often this seems to create a rivalry in prevention, since the national and local institutions hurry on ahead to prevent any admonitions or restrictions from the World Heritage Committee. The understanding of heritage as "sustainable conservation for future generations," as quoted above, finally tends to become a threat itself, endangering a more flexible concept of transgenerational inheritance, in which bequest and appropriation have to be dialectically negotiated.

Revisiting Cosmopolitanism

The Limes case demonstrates how a given territory, when declared a Heritage Site, is somehow isolated from the rest of the world, from the normal topography, in order to gain a special status. Obviously, there is a tight connection between the numeric limitation of the sites on the Heritage List and the territorial delimitation of every single site. In general, the necessity of delimitation is in a certain contrast with the aspiration of the World Heritage program to consider cultures *globally*, that is, to incorporate, if possible, all of the traditions and regions worldwide. This is precisely where the two different concepts of "world" again intertwine: intensional and extensional, universality and globality. For the presumed *universality* of the idea of World Heritage is supposed to lead to a *global* normal distribution of cultural values—whereas it is taken for granted that globality, that is, a designation of extensiveness, really matches universality, a designation of content. The "world" of World Heritage, in this sense, is the globe on which the heritage sites must be situated in an equitable way, until the distribution of sites in, say, East Africa has reached the density of South-West Europe (France and Italy being the top nations as far as the number of sites on the List is concerned). Of course, one could not reach this density by applying the criteria that were up to date in the 1970s when the classical monuments such as cathedrals and castles were listed—hence the ongoing redefinition of what is "outstanding," and the propagation of additional heritage programs, such as Documentary Heritage (since 1992), Underwater Cultural Heritage (since 2001), and Intangible Heritage (since 2003).

All of these programs—especially the latter—are supposed to be less Eurocentric and to allow for a more global distribution of properties. Still they are universal and unifying in the formulation of their criteria of relevance. At which point it is important to notice that universality is not such an innocent concept. The universal—as the intensional concept of what "the world" is or should be—can be translated as transnational or "transboundary," but for most of the time it has been put into practice by single nations. Thus, it has often led to practices of cultural appropriation that proceeded in an expansive and aggressive way, touching other nations' properties and the boundaries of their territories. This concept of national universalism (or of universalist nationalism) originated in the French Revolution, when the first genuinely modern attempts to create a national cultural heritage, a *patrimoine culturel*, proceeded in legitimized practices of disappropriation.[27]

This not only concerned the formerly privileged classes in France itself, but also the territories gained in the post-revolutionary and Napoleonic wars. The Louvre was intended to be a national museum and at the same time a universal cultural site that was to be filled with art objects from European and non-European countries.[28] Following this example, museums all over Europe in the nineteenth century were conceived of as places in which world culture was to be collected. These collections followed unifying, universal cultural pretensions such as public education and intercultural comparison—but still, the very act of collecting meant taking something away from where it had been situated before, to remove it from a specific place of the world (a site on which it had been "site-specific") to another place where it became an object in a series of other objects, from other places. Conversely, in today's postcolonial condition, we are witnessing an ongoing and, as it may seem, infinite discussion about looted art and restitutions, concerning almost all of Europe's and North America's museums. Most of the relevant cases concern the *belonging* of cultural property, the ways in which artifacts can be attributed to a certain place, on the one hand, and to a certain people, or groups of people, on the other. At the core of these controversies, again, lies a complex and problematic relationship between time and space: if something was once taken away from a territory now belonging to a certain state that did not exist back then, does this generate a title of property for this actual state?

This matter has been discussed as a challenge to globalization in the 2006 book *Cosmopolitanism* by Princeton philosopher Kwame Anthony Appiah. With this programmatic heading, Appiah develops what could be called an ethics of globalization. Speaking of culture, heritage, and property, Appiah not only states that for ancient artifacts and archeological findings the actual proprietors are hard to determine, since there is—as he says—"no continuity of title" from whichever antiquity to our present.[29] He also calls into question the legalistic connection between culture, value, and ownership as such. In his view, an object's cultural value can never be fully captured by its value as private or public property. Linking *culture* to *belonging* at all might always already lead us in the wrong direction. In this context, Appiah makes an interesting and innovative statement about restitution. From the "cosmopolitan" perspective, restitution does not mean sending every object home, but seriously starting to circulate world culture worldwide: "It is a fine gesture to return things to the descendants of their makers, … but it certainly isn't a duty. You might also show your respect for the culture it came from by holding on to it because you value it yourself."[30] Only this kind of valuation and respect should be experienced by as many people as possible.

If we take Appiah's stance—which has been harshly criticized[31]—as an up-to-date cosmopolitan attitude, then cultural globalization would mean something different from what UNESCO is promoting. The World Heritage business is about singling out and safeguarding as many particular and "outstanding" cultural artifacts and expressions as possible. Thus, they have to remain in their particularity in order to justify, retrospectively, why they have been picked out in the first place. Understanding globalization as cosmopolitanism, on the other hand, would mean opening up local cultures to global change instead of presupposing that they have to be authentic or identical. This would require a less conservative, perhaps also less sustainable approach—an approach, however, that would be more pragmatic and more open to future changes in the idea of what "heritage" and "world" actually mean. The "world" of World Heritage, in this sense, would not only be the globe on which the heritage sites must be situated in an equitable way, but also the space and time in which the cultural goods are being negotiated. This could be a possible way to reconcile intensional and extensional definitions of "the world," without simply harmonizing them. At the least, it would mean taking the UNESCO convention's claim seriously, that the objects, the monuments, artifacts, and "intangible" practices on the various Heritage lists really belong "to all the peoples of the world."

Stefan Willer is Professor at the Institute of Cultural History and Theory at the Humboldt-Universität and co-director of the Center for Literary and Cultural Research in Berlin. Among his book publications are *Prophetie und Prognostik* (co-edited with Daniel Weidner, Fink, 2013), *Erbfälle: Theorie und Praxis kultureller Übertragung in der Moderne* (Fink, 2014) and *Futurologien: Ordnungen des Zukunfswissens* (co-edited with Benjamin Bühler, Fink, 2016).

NOTES

1. See Louis-Charles Fougeret de Monbron, *Le cosmopolite ou Le citoyen du monde* (Bordeaux, [1750] 1970).
2. See Michel Figeac, *L'automne des gentilshommes: Noblesse d'Aquitaine, noblesse française au Siècle des Lumières* (Paris, 2002).
3. For further discussions of the globe, see in particular the chapters by Alfred Hiatt, Jeppe Strandsbjerg, Kari van Dijk, Helge Jordheim, Siv Frøydis Berg, and Espen Ytreberg in this volume.
4. Convention Concerning the Protection of the World Cultural and Natural Heritage, UNESCO, retrieved 3 August 2018 from whc.unesco.org/archive/convention-en.pdf, "Preamble."
5. Ibid.
6. Ohad Parnes, Ulrike Vedder, and Stefan Willer, *Das Konzept der Generation: Eine Wissenschafts- und Kulturgeschichte* (Frankfurt am Main, 2008).

7. See Stefan Willer, Sigrid Weigel, and Bernhard Jussen, eds, *Erbe: Übertragungskonzepte zwischen Natur und Kultur* (Berlin, 2013); Stefan Willer, *Erbfälle: Theorie und Praxis kultureller Übertragung in der Moderne* (Munich, 2014).
8. See Klaus Mathis, ed., *Efficiency, Sustainability, and Justice to Future Generations* (Dordrecht, 2011).
9. Francesco Bandarin, "Protecting Heritage," *Our Planet* 14, no. 2 (2003): 12.
10. For further discussions of territory, see in particular the chapters by Andreas Philippopoulos-Mihalopoulos and Jeppe Strandsbjerg in this volume.
11. For further discussions of property, see in particular the chapter by Chenxi Tang in this volume.
12. "The Criteria for Selection," UNESCO, retrieved 3 August 2018 from http://whc.unesco.org/en/criteria/.
13. See Jean-Claude Milner, "L'exemple et la fiction," in *Transparence et opacité: Littérature et sciences cognitives*, ed. Tibor Papp and Pierre Pica (Paris, 1988), 173–81; Giorgio Agamben, *Homo Sacer: Sovereign Power and Bare Life*, trans. Daniel Heller-Roazen (Stanford, CA, 1998).
14. Virgil, *Aeneid*, 1.279.
15. "Frontiers of the Roman Empire," UNESCO, retrieved 3 August 2018 from http://whc.unesco.org/archive/advisory_body_evaluation/430ter.pdf, 167.
16. Cf. Tilmann Bechert, "Limes, Hadrianswall," in *Der Neue Pauly: Enzyklopädie der Antike: Rezeptions- und Wissenschaftsgeschichte* 15.1, ed. Manfred Landfester (Stuttgart, 2001), cols. 149–56; Egon Schallmayer and Wolfgang Schmidt, "Limes, Limesforschung," in Landfester, *Der Neue Pauly* 15.1, cols. 156–70.
17. Cf. already Theodor Mommsen's conceptual differentiations ("Der Begriff des Limes" [1894], in *Historische Schriften*, vol. 2 [Berlin, 1908], 456–64), then Owen D. Lattimore's distinction of "frontier of inclusion" vs "frontier of exclusion (*Studies in Frontier History: Collected Papers 1928–1958* [Paris, 1962]) and Benjamin Isaac's dismissal of the idea that *limes* had ever designated a defended border (*The Limits of Empire: The Roman Army in the East* [Oxford, 1990]). See also Gerhard Waldherr's notion of "contact zone" (*Der Limes: Kontaktzone zwischen den Kulturen* [Stuttgart, 2009]).
18. See Georg Dehio and Alois Riegl, *Konservieren, nicht restaurieren: Streitschriften zur Denkmalpflege um 1900* (Braunschweig, 1988).
19. "The Venice Charter," ICOMOS, retrieved 3 August 2018 from https://www.icomos.org/charters/venice_e.pdf, art. 11.
20. Ibid., art. 9.
21. Ibid., art. 15.
22. "Frontiers of the Roman Empire," UNESCO, retrieved 3 August 2018 from http://whc.unesco.org/archive/advisory_body_evaluation/430ter.pdf, 167.
23. Ibid.
24. Ibid.
25. "Frontiers of the Roman Empire," UNESCO, retrieved 3 August 2018 from http://whc.unesco.org/en/list/430/indicators/.
26. "List of World Heritage in Danger," UNESCO, retrieved 3 August 2018 from http://whc.unesco.org/en/danger/.

27. See Bénédicte Savoy, *Patrimoine annexé: Les biens culturels saisis par la France en Allemagne autour de 1800* (Paris, 2003).
28. See Ulrike Vedder, "Museum/Ausstellung," in *Ästhetische Grundbegriffe: Historisches Wörterbuch*, vol. 7, ed. Karlheinz Barck et al. (Stuttgart, 2005), 161–65.
29. Kwame Anthony Appiah, *Cosmopolitanism: Ethics in a World of Strangers* (New York, 2006), 122.
30. Ibid., 131.
31. Cf. "Cosmopolitan Theft," *Greekworks* (blog), 6 May 2006, retrieved 3 August 2018 from http://www.greekworks.com/content/index.php/weblog/extended/cosompolitan_theft/.

BIBLIOGRAPHY

Agamben, Giorgio. *Homo Sacer: Sovereign Power and Bare Life*. Translated by Daniel Heller-Roazen. Stanford, CA: Stanford University Press, 1998.

Appiah, Kwame Anthony. *Cosmopolitanism: Ethics in a World of Strangers*. New York: W. W. Norton, 2006.

Bandarin, Francesco. "Protecting Heritage." *Our Planet* 14, no. 2 (2003): 11–12.

Bechert, Tilmann. "Limes, Hadrianswall." In *Der Neue Pauly: Enzyklopädie der Antike: Rezeptions- und Wissenschaftsgeschichte* 15.1, edited by Manfred Landfester, cols. 149–56. Stuttgart: Metzler, 2001.

Dehio, Georg, and Alois Riegl. *Konservieren, nicht restaurieren: Streitschriften zur Denkmalpflege um 1900*. Braunschweig: Vieweg, 1988.

Figeac, Michel. *L'automne des gentilshommes: Noblesse d'Aquitaine, noblesse française au Siècle des Lumières*. Paris: Champion, 2002.

Fougeret de Monbron, Louis-Charles. *Le cosmopolite ou Le citoyen du monde*. Bordeaux: Ducros, [1750] 1970.

Isaac, Benjamin. *The Limits of Empire: The Roman Army in the East*. Oxford: Clarendon Press, 1990.

Lattimore, Owen D. *Studies in Frontier History: Collected Papers 1928–1958*. Paris: Mouton, 1962.

Mathis, Klaus, ed. *Efficiency, Sustainability, and Justice to Future Generations*. Dordrecht: Springer, 2011.

Milner, Jean-Claude. "L'exemple et la fiction." In *Transparence et opacité: Littérature et sciences cognitives*, edited by Tibor Papp and Pierre Pica, 173–81. Paris: Cerf, 1988.

Mommsen, Theodor. "Der Begriff des Limes" (1894). In *Historische Schriften*, vol. 2, 456–64. Berlin: Weidmann, 1908.

Parnes, Ohad, Ulrike Vedder, and Stefan Willer. *Das Konzept der Generation: Eine Wissenschafts- und Kulturgeschichte*. Frankfurt am Main: Suhrkamp, 2008.

Savoy, Bénédicte. *Patrimoine annexé: Les biens culturels saisis par la France en Allemagne autour de 1800*. Paris: Maison des Sciences de l'Homme, 2003.

Schallmayer, Egon, and Wolfgang Schmidt. "Limes, Limesforschung." In *Der Neue Pauly: Enzyklopädie der Antike: Rezeptions- und Wissenschaftsgeschichte* 15.1, edited by Manfred Landfester, cols. 156–70. Stuttgart: Metzler, 2001.

Vedder, Ulrike. "Museum/Ausstellung." In *Ästhetische Grundbegriffe: Historisches Wörterbuch*, vol. 7, edited by Karlheinz Barck et al., 148–90. Stuttgart: Metzler, 2005.

Waldherr, Gerhard. *Der Limes: Kontaktzone zwischen den Kulturen*. Stuttgart: Reclam, 2009.

Willer, Stefan. *Erbfälle: Theorie und Praxis kultureller Übertragung in der Moderne*. Munich: Fink, 2014.

Willer, Stefan, Sigrid Weigel, and Bernhard Jussen, eds. *Erbe: Übertragungskonzepte zwischen Natur und Kultur*. Berlin: Suhrkamp, 2013.

▶• 15 •◀

The End of the World

From the Lisbon Earthquake to the Last Days

Kyrre Kverndokk

The earthquake that struck Lisbon on 1 November 1755 was probably the first globally mass-mediated disaster in history. From Lisbon the news spread around Europe and eventually to the various European colonies. The news reached Paris on 22 November, London and Amsterdam on 26 November, and on 8 December accounts of the devastation in Lisbon reached Copenhagen.[1] The accounts were shocking. The disaster was seemingly meaningless and put the religious and moral order of the world on trial.[2] Clergymen, scientists, and philosophers all over Europe strived to make some sense out of the senseless and to re-establish some sort of cosmological order.[3] Numerous pamphlets, poems, sermons, and philosophical inquiries discussed the moral and religious order of the world. In these attempts, notions of the world as such were articulated. These texts expressed certain understandings of how the world was interconnected in temporal, spatial, and cosmological senses.

This chapter will examine two such texts written far away from Lisbon, namely in Copenhagen: a poem by the theologian Christian Henrik Biering and a geological analysis by the theologian and scientist Erik Pontoppidan. These two texts have not been selected because they were considered to be of particular importance in their time or because of their historical importance, but rather because they manifest quite different ways of reasoning about the cause of the disaster. Written within radically different genres, they represent two well-established traditions of interpretation in early modern Europe. Produced far away from the disaster area, these texts have to claim some sort of general implications of the earthquake in order to make the disaster relevant for the Dano-Norwegian reader. By focusing upon the relationship between contemporary incidents and the future—the end of the world, to be precise—they articulate notions both of the world as an enclosed whole and of universal time. This chapter will discuss what kind of conceptualizations of the globe are articulated in these two texts, with a special emphasis on the texts' temporal dimensions.

The analysis draws on Koselleck's concepts for discussing the changing notion of temporality in so-called *Neuzeit*. Koselleck claims that the difference between experiences and expectations has increasingly expanded in modern history. The fundamentally new experiences and discoveries of the Renaissance triggered this process, but even though shocking events like the Reformation, the Copernican Revolution, and the discovery of the New World produced a consciousness of a difference between past experiences and coming expectations, the process first truly accelerated in the eighteenth century. Koselleck argues that the future and the past were interconnected as long as the Christian eschatology defined an absolute limit for the horizon of expectations.[4] The world was regarded as fundamentally immutable, and the timescale of the world was regarded as fixated within the framework of God's plan. Hence, it was possible to productively use the experiences of the past as an analytical tool to understand the present as well as the future. However, this changed radically when it became possible to imagine a new horizon of expectations, without a fixed end. When an open future replaced the eschatology, the *horizon of expectations* was separated from the *space of experiences* as an autonomous temporal category. In this chapter, however, I do not discuss an open future; instead, I will use Koselleck's temporal categories *horizon of expectations* and *space of experiences* to examine temporal notions *within* the framework of the eschatology.

The Earthquake as a Divine Sign

The author Christian Henrik Biering (1729–1804) is long since forgotten. In the mid 1750s he was a recently graduated theologian and tried to succeed as an author. His literary debut was the 158-stanza poem *Poetic Thoughts on the Destruction of Lisbon by the Inaudible Earthquake on All Saints' Day 1755*.[5] The reception of the poem was mixed: one reviewer was quite positive,[6] while another was almost sarcastic in his critique.[7] However, it is not the literary quality that makes the poem interesting, but rather its insistence on interpreting the earthquake as a divine sign.

The poem was written within the early modern genre of accident and disaster poetry, a genre that assumed a direct, causal connection between the victims' sinful actions and righteous, divine punishment.[8] Such poems worked as pedagogical reminders of the crucial importance of piety. In his attempt to explain how the Lisbon earthquake works as such a reminder, Biering describes in detail the sin that triggered the wrath of God. Biering uses the time of the disaster, All Saints' Day, to establish a scene of sins. He portrays an imagined saints' procession through the streets of Lisbon in rather censorious terms:

> Look, All Saints' Day, when what is unholy,
> When pictures and bones are displayed, cultivated, honored
> When one, as runaway cattle, the everlasting invokes,
> When often bones of thieves are declared saintly.
>
> When the all-knowing GOD, the great creator
> Must see his honor so shamefully defiled ...[9]

Biering obviously despises such papist practices. He claims that this kind of idolatry was just like the Israelites' dance around the Golden Calf. Hence, by referring to Exodus 32:1–14 he characterizes the religious practice of Lisbon not merely as papist but also as pagan—this was what provoked the wrath of God.

Biering's use of biblical analogies is based on an early modern typological thinking.[10] This kind of reasoning assumed that contemporary events had their prefigurations in scripture. Biblical narratives represented universal truths and worked productively as analytic tools to understand contemporary events. Hence, the present was not considered to be essentially different from the past, but was all incorporated in God's plan. The typological interpretive practice was epistemologically grounded on exemplarity. Examples were useful communicative vehicles because they connected a concrete case with an abstract maxim.[11] In early modern Europe, examples such as biblical narratives were not merely rhetorical tools, but worked as moral points of orientation in life. New example narratives could also be produced, for instance by authorizing an interpretation of an incident with references to biblical prefigurations. When Biering compared the saints' procession in Lisbon to the Israelites' dance around the Golden Calf, it was not just a rhetorical analogy, but also a method for understanding the character of the sins of Lisbon and for emphasizing the exemplarity of the earthquake.

Biering presents the earthquake as an edifying narrative about idolatry, sin, and divine punishment. But for this narrative to work as a general example, it has to be placed into a larger pattern. After establishing the devastation of Lisbon as an example, he systematically widens the disaster scene and the scene of sins. He asks rhetorically if Lisbon is to be blamed alone, and answers no: the earthquake has been experienced all over Portugal and Spain, and there have also been quakes in France, Italy, and even in Great Britain. Hence, all of Europe has to bear the guilt. He asks again whether Europe is to bear this guilt alone, and the answer is again no: there have been accounts of earthquakes from Africa as well as America. According to Biering, there have not yet been any accounts of earthquakes from Asia, but such accounts are likely to appear, fitting the worldwide pattern of divine punishments he is drawing.

Every continent—the entire world—was hit by earthquakes, or as he puts it: "Oh! Look, now the entire Earth's globe is trembling."[12] The earthquake is a divine sign that concerns everyone.

Then follow four stanzas in which Biering explicates how the earthquake must be interpreted as a divine sign, as "a picture of the Lord's judgment," that is, as a prediction of Judgment Day:

> If no sign is given now, no sign shall ever come:
> Now the wind terrible, now the sea and waves roiling,
> Now is heard battle and war in all the fields of the world,
> Now fright, anxiety, and fear follow all feet and hearts.
>
> Now the Earth's globe is trembling, even bursting in two,
> Yes! Look, now signs are seen in the clear realm of the sun,
> Now fire rages and in wrath asks: What now?
> Should we not ask what this might mean?
>
> There is no doubt, thus God's words spake:
> Wake ye up, ye complacent peoples of Earth!
> Wake up from your complacency, you smug Earth!
> To the East, West, yea even South and North!
>
> Oh! Wake you up, oh! Consider!
> You who are now seeing the last age of the world;
> See here a picture of the Lord's judgment,
> See the terror when Earth and heaven are falling.[13]

The art of reading omens is ancient, both as an intellectual and a vernacular practice. This kind of interpretive practice was especially theorized and widely performed in intellectual circles in the sixteenth and seventeenth centuries. In the semiotic worldview of the Renaissance, nature was considered a divine text, God's book of nature. It was assumed to be possible to read God's plan directly out of nature, and natural phenomena were interpreted as divine signs in light of the Bible.[14] Hence, dramatic and peculiar phenomena in nature could be interpreted as omens predicting a forthcoming major disaster, most often Judgment Day. Omen interpretations, structured as narratives and framed as examples, were modeled after eschatological verses of the Bible. When interpreted as eschatological signs, seemingly meaningless phenomena were transformed into significant signs. Even though the intellectual practice of reading omens was not as prevalent in the mid eighteenth century as in the preceding centuries, the Lisbon earthquake was still widely examined as a divine sign predicting the end of the world.

The ominous character of the earthquake is authorized by a web of intertextual references in both the stanzas and in a number of footnotes. First of all, Biering points out how the earthquakes in Lisbon and elsewhere have to be interpreted in light of eschatological verses of the Bible. The question "Should we not ask what this might mean?" is answered in a footnote with references to both Matthew 24:3 and Luke 21:25. The two lines "Yes! Look, now signs are seen in the clear realm of the sun" and "now the sea and waves roiling" are also paraphrases of the same verse from the Gospel of Luke. In this way, he underlines the similarity between the eschatological prefiguration and the divine sign.

The interpretation of a natural phenomenon as an omen was not only authorized by references to scripture. Another way to authorize the certainty of the omen was to place it in a larger pattern of divine signs. This is exactly what Biering does, when in the footnotes to these four stanzas he lists a number of rare incidents that had occurred recently in addition to the earthquake: major floods in France, Italy, and Spain; five moons in the sky over Poland; rain as red as blood in Locarno, Switzerland; and a ball of fire, with a twenty-fathom-long tail, streaking across the sky over Växjö, Sweden.[15] All these occurrences were commonly acknowledged as divine signs, and all of them were prefigured in the Bible. It is fascinating how Biering so intensely sticks to a rather old-fashioned semantic interpretative practice in his attempt to understand the earthquake. In anticipating criticism, however, he finds it crucial to remark: "But I would not like to be considered a person who makes any falling star into a supernatural sign."[16] Biering was a man of the Enlightenment, but he was still convinced that all these rare incidents could only be explained as a pattern of eschatological signs.

The poem interconnects the world as a spatial and temporal whole through the Lisbon earthquake. By first systematically placing the earthquake into a global pattern of earthquakes, and second placing these earthquakes into a web of divine signs in nature, the Lisbon earthquake is given universal significance. Hence, the Lisbon earthquake works as a keyhole for gazing into God's plan and what time will bring. One implication of his reading is that just like the divine punishment struck Lisbon, the Lord's final judgment will eventually also strike Denmark. The last few stanzas are formulated as a prayer addressed to the Lord himself, asking for strength in faith and piety in anticipation of the Last Days, and more importantly for the Lord to spare the kingdom of Denmark-Norway and its sovereign from harsh punishment and severe suffering. Thus, the focus is no longer global but local, as the earthquake is transformed into a Dano-Norwegian concern.

The temporality of the poem is strictly defined within the framework of God's plan. The semiotic reading of the earthquake demonstrates how the past, the present, and the future until the end of the world are understood as concurrent categories. Strictly speaking, it is not the future that Biering is looking into, but Providence. However, what goes beyond the Last Judgment is a radically different story. In general, expectations beyond this point were directed to the hereafter. Hence, such expectations could not be based on previous experiences, since they were not part of this world.[17] The poem does not articulate any such expectations and does not mention the hereafter.

The Geological Pathway to the Last Days

The theologian Erik Pontoppidan (1698–1764) is often referred to as the chief ideologist of state pietism under the regime of Christian VI (1730–46). However, later in life he also worked extensively as a scientist. He was a member of the Academy of Sciences and Letters in Copenhagen and from 1755 was the pro-chancellor of the University of Copenhagen.[18] His book about the Lisbon earthquake—titled *Preliminary Meditations Concerning the Natural Cause of the Many and Great Earthquakes, Plus the Extraordinary Weather Phenomena That Lately Have Taken Place Both in and outside Europe*—is one of his least-known scientific works.[19]

Pontoppidan's approach to the earthquake is radically different from Biering's. The book is occupied with the so-called mechanical principles behind the earthquake. Pontoppidan claims that soon after 1 November 1755, and long before the accounts of the earthquake reached Copenhagen, he had predicted the occurrence of a tremendous earthquake somewhere in the world. This prediction was, he claims, strictly based on scientific knowledge, and the book was an attempt to explain how such a prediction was possible.[20] He draws a clear distinction between scientific predictions and religious divinations as ways to seek insight into Providence. Biering's poem was published a few months before Pontoppidan finished his book, and even though Pontoppidan does not explicitly refer to Biering's poem, he most certainly knew it. He explicitly criticizes those who interpret the earthquake as a divine sign, and he criticizes the assumptions of a direct moral causality between a sinful Lisbon and God's punishment. However, he does not exclude a religious superstructure.

Along with scientists like Carl Linnaeus, Pontoppidan advocated the physico-theology of the mid eighteenth century.[21] His scientific project was to write updated scientific knowledge into a theological framework.[22] Almost parallel to the book on the Lisbon earthquake, he wrote *Treatise on the Novelty of the World*,[23] in which he discusses the age of the world. In the early eighteenth century there were only two possible opinions about the age of the world: biblical time and classical notions of eternity.[24] Biblical chronology, however, was soon to be expanded by leading scientists like Buffon, and it would eventually collapse under severe scientific pressure. However, the classical notion of eternity was still the main counter-position to the biblical timescale when Pontoppidan wrote his *Treatise*. His objective was to convince the reader that the biblical time span was the only possibility and that the world had to be six thousand years old. This was done by emphasizing the transmutations and developments of the natural world.[25] I regard Pontoppidan's *Treatise on the Novelty of the World* and his book on the Lisbon earthquake to be parts of the same physico-theological project. While the *Treatise* is mostly occupied with the age and historical development of the Earth, the latter book is concerned with the future development until the Last Days.

In Pontoppidan's book on the Lisbon earthquake, the theological arguments are put aside until the last few pages. The main concern is the geological constitution of the globe. He operated within so-called Earth theory, a scientific tradition that attempted to explain the creation, development, and also often the end of the world.[26] Pontoppidan was well oriented in the European scientific debates and newly developed Earth theories.[27] His influences included the seventeenth-century scientist Athanasius Kircher's work *Mundus subterraneus* (1664–65), for the most part read through the Danish topographer Lucas Debes' presentation of his theories in *Description of the Faroe Islands*.[28] Furthermore, the contemporary Norwegian scientist Jens Christian Spidberg had developed a well-founded theory about the geological causes of the Lisbon earthquake.[29] Pontoppidan was in correspondence with him and based his thesis quite directly on Spidberg's work.

There had been an ongoing geological debate in the late seventeenth century and throughout the eighteenth century between the *neptunists*, who considered water to be the primary force in the creation and development of the Earth, and the *vulcanists*, who considered fire to be the driving force. According to Rhoda Rappaport, however, it is a simplification to draw a sharp line between these positions: most of the eighteenth-century scientists acknowledged the importance of both elements, and the disagreement mainly concerned whether the center of the globe contained an enormous water basin or a central fire.[30] Pontoppidan, however, maneuvered around this discussion. Rather than discuss the center of the globe, he was interested in the mid layers between the center and the surface. Along with Spidberg, Debes, and Kircher, he claims that the mid layers of the globe consist of a complex of subterranean cellars and vaults filled with combustible materials. These cellars and vaults, he writes, could be as large as the largest city and were assumed to be interconnected by an enormous system of ducts. According to Pontoppidan, continuous fires ran through these cellars, vaults, and ducts, and constantly moved from one vault to another. For Pontoppidan, the final cause of earthquakes is divine, but he locates the natural cause in this subterranean system. He claims that if combustible material in one vault burned out, the entire construction was weakened and the ceiling of the vault would simply collapse. Such major subterranean collapses cause earthquakes, he claims, and could even cause the Earth's crust to burst. According to his theory, this was exactly what must have happened somewhere in the ocean outside of Lisbon.

Pontoppidan emphasizes that Madeira was reported to have disappeared into the ocean, and although he immediately remarks that this had turned out to be merely a rumor, it is almost as if he wished it were true, as it would have fit his argument very well. However, he adds, some smaller Spanish islands had in fact disappeared into the ocean.[31]

Accounts of the Earth's crust bursting were widespread across Europe after the Lisbon earthquake. On 16 January 1756, for instance, the only Danish newspaper at the time reported that both the Azores and Madeira had disappeared.[32] This was most certainly Pontoppidan's source, but of equal importance to such accounts were the biblical descriptions of similar incidents. Both the book of Numbers 16:30–32 and Psalms 106:17 describe how the earth opens and men and buildings vanish into the abyss.[33] Though Pontoppidan does not explicitly refer to such biblical examples, frame the Lisbon earthquake as a divine example, or examine nature as God's book of nature, it is possible to get a glimpse of an underlying typological way of thinking in his emphasis on the collapse of the Earth's crust.

Pontoppidan's implicit references to the Bible are part of what he calls the a priori reasons for his Earth theory. However, most of his book rather presents what he calls the a posteriori proofs of the same theory.[34] He identifies a long range of natural phenomena as such proofs. While Biering is occupied with reading natural phenomena as communicative signs,[35] Pontoppidan is occupied with understanding the natural causes, or what Aristotle termed efficient causes, behind the same kind of phenomena. Pontoppidan, like Biering, uses the term "sign" to some extent, but the term refers exclusively to indexical signs, indicating a causal connection between the sign and its natural causes. Hence, the term "sign" seems to work synonymously with his use of the term "proof."

One kind of proof was flood wave accounts. Observations of such waves had been reported from several places along the European coastlines, and even from some Norwegian lakes. Pontoppidan was convinced that these waves were caused by the Lisbon earthquake. He assumed that the Earth's underground was perforated not only with cellars, vaults, and ducts filled with combustible material, but also with a similar system of ducts containing water. This was assumed to be a complex, worldwide system interconnecting all lakes and oceans around the globe. He argued that when the Earth's crust had cracked somewhere outside of Lisbon, large amounts of water were led through these ducts and pumped with great force into oceans and lakes, causing flood waves. It was the accounts of these flood waves, combined with his scientific knowledge about the worldwide complex of subterranean water connections, that had initially led Pontoppidan to assume that a major collapse in the Earth's crust had occurred somewhere in the world.[36]

Just like Biering, Pontoppidan bases his argument on a number of earthquake accounts from around the world. He especially emphasizes an earthquake in Iceland in September 1755 and an earthquake in the Moroccan city of Fez on 1 November that same year. He regards these earthquakes to be caused by a chain reaction in the underground fires, explaining that the fires had moved from the ground underneath Iceland to the ground underneath Morocco. He calculates the distance between Iceland and Fez to be 900 to 1,000 Danish miles.[37] Hence, the distance between these two earthquakes documents the scale and range of the subterranean complex of cellars, vaults, and ducts. Moreover, he enumerates other rare incidents that had occurred recently, such as "hurricanes, sulfur vapor, glowing signs in the air, rumbling sounds, and alarms underground."[38] While Biering carries out a semiotic reading of such incidents, Pontoppidan is concerned with their geological causes. Like Biering, Pontoppidan also refers to the reddish rain in Switzerland, but while Biering is interested in its symbolism, reading it as a sign, Pontoppidan focuses on the red substance, which he explains as sulfuric rain or ashes.[39] He considers it to be waste material from the subterranean fires, and uses it as proof of how volcanoes work as chimneys for these fires. He claims that the fire activity had recently intensified, especially underneath Europe. Therefore, he argues, the number of volcanoes in Europe will eventually increase.

The leading Earth theorists in the seventeenth century had argued that the topography of the Earth had been shaped as a consequence of major catastrophes, especially the Deluge.[40] During the eighteenth century, however, processes of gradual transformation were introduced as explanatory factors in the science of geology.[41] Pontoppidan was a process-oriented Earth theorist and claimed that the geology of the Earth had changed continually from the Earth's creation to the present. This argument was influenced by the works of the contemporary geologist Anton Lazzaro Moro.[42] Moro emphasized the importance of the volcanoes for the geological development of the Earth, and hence also emphasized how the globe was in constant flux.[43] Leaning on Moro's ideas, Pontoppidan even argued that the geological processes were speeding up. The increased activity in the underground fires would cause more frequent subterranean collapses in times to come. The fire would eat its way through the Earth's crust and would eventually cause the final conflagration. In the late seventeenth and early eighteenth centuries, the idea of the final conflagration was widely recognized among influential Earth theorists such as Thomas Burnet and William Whiston, Isaac Newton's successor at the University of Cambridge. The idea of the conflagration was generally based on the eschatological descriptions in the Second Epistle of Peter 3:6–7. However, Pontoppidan consciously refrains from modeling his explanations of the conflagration on biblical descriptions.[44] He does not present it as a miracle, but as a mechanical process, although he still considered the conflagration to be under divine control. Hence, geological time and God's plan are two sides of the same coin in his understanding of the final conflagration.

To Pontoppidan, the Lisbon earthquake was not merely a local concern and not merely an earthly concern. His scientific approach is one reason he rejects the sinfulness of Lisbon as an explanation for the earthquake. Another reason was most likely theological, founded on the Lutheran doctrine of the original sin. He did not, however, reject sin as the final divine cause. One of his physico-theological objectives was to counter the worldview of Spinozists and atheists by drawing on scientific arguments.[45] At the end of the book, he explicitly attacks what he terms "the mockingbirds of religion" that were thriving as never before.[46] In this way, he claims that the earth's geology evolves in line with religious and moral decay, thereby relating geological time to historical time. The argument is universally formulated and is not related to any particular catastrophe or any particular kingdom or city. The underground fires will eventually lead to the end in an irreversible and global process.

In Pontoppidan's cosmology, the final conflagration certainly meant the end of this world. It did not imply the end as such, however, and he argues elsewhere that the conflagration would mean a transformation of the Earth into a millennial kingdom.[47] In line with Biering, Pontoppidan also recommends piety and prayer as a means of preparing for the Last Days and for what follows after.

The Future: The Time Prior to Judgment Day

Both Biering and Pontoppidan emphasize the universal character of the Lisbon earthquake as a disastrous incident pointing toward the end of the world. However, their way of reasoning about the earthquake operates on two different cosmological levels: Biering is concerned with the divine, final cause of the earthquake, while Pontoppidan discusses the efficient or natural causes. Biering reads the earthquake symbolically, while Pontoppidan is concerned with the physical processes behind it.

These rather dissimilar ways of reasoning about the relation between the earthquake and the Last Days draw on different temporal understandings. In Biering's case, the course of events in Lisbon works as a narrative and argumentative focal point. His reading of divine signs is based on an assumption of the world as fixed and predefined in God's plan. Hence, the biblical past can be productively used to understand the present, and likewise, present events can foretell the upcoming, final disaster; it is not the future he is gazing into, but Providence.

Pontoppidan, on the other hand, is barely interested in the devastation of Lisbon as such. The earthquake is to him a crucial temporal event in the history of the Earth, pointing toward future geological changes that will lead to the end of the world. Unlike Biering, it is not Providence he is gazing into, but rather the earthly future. Arguing that the geological changes of the world are accelerating, Pontoppidan expects the earthly future to be different from the present; hence, the historical-geological mutability of the world makes it impossible to base expectations for the future on experiences of the past. In his thinking, the past and the future are no longer of the same kind. It is possible to get a glimpse of a qualitatively new temporal consciousness in his approach to the future. Pontoppidan represented a new kind of geology that focused on how the Earth continually transforms—a kind of geology that would soon exceed the limits of the biblical time span. For Pontoppidan, however, the earthly changes were still occurring within a fixed biblical timeframe: the Earth was six thousand years old, and he presumed that it was not going to be much older.

Kyrre Kverndokk is Professor of Cultural Studies in the Department of Archaeology, History, Cultural Studies and Religion at the University of Bergen, Norway. He has published on the cultural history of natural disasters, Holocaust memory, and the history of folklore studies. He is currently working on a project on notions of temporality in climate change discourses.

NOTES

1. T. D. Kendrick, *The Lisbon Earthquake* (Philadelphia, 1956), 213–14; Theo D'Haen, "On How Not to Be Lisbon If You Want to Be Modern: Dutch Reactions to the Lisbon Earthquake," *European Review* 14, no. 3 (2006): 351–58; *Kiøbenhavnske Danske Post-Tidender* [newspaper], 8 December 1755, 1.
2. For further discussions of religion, see in particular the chapters by Nora Eggen, Oddbjørn Leirvik, Chenxi Tang, Alfred Hiatt, Erling Sandmo, and Kari van Dijk in this volume.
3. Gunnar Broberg, *Tsunamin i Lissabon: Jordbävningen den 1 november 1755, i epicentrum och i svensk periferi* (Stockholm, 2005), 36.
4. Reinhart Koselleck, *Futures Past: On the Semantics of Historical Time* (Cambridge, MA, 1985), 276–77.
5. Christian Henrik Biering, *Christian Henric Bierings poetiske Tanker over Lissabons Ødeleggelse ved det uhørlige Jordskiælv paa Alle Helgens Dag 1755* (Copenhagen, 1756).
6. *Kiøbenhavnske nye Tidender om lærde og curieuse Sager* [journal], 8 April 1756, 117–18.
7. *Efterretninger om nye Bøger og lærde Sager i Danmark og Norge* [journal], March 1756, 115–17.

8. Jørgen Sejersted, "Ulykkesdiktning på 1600-tallet: Noen norske eksempler fra 1627 til 1702," in *Overdådighet og død i barokken*, ed. Hall Bjørnstad and Mette Nygård (Oslo, 2002), 115.
9. Biering, *Poetiske Tanker*, 11. Translated by John C. Anthony.
10. Northrop Frye, *The Great Code: The Bible and Literature* (New York, 1982).
11. John Lyons, *Exemplum: The Rhetoric of Example in Early Modern France and Italy* (Princeton, NJ, 1989), 5; Anne Eriksen, Ellen Krefting, and Anne Birgitte Rønning, eds, *Eksempelets makt: Kjønn, representasjon og autoritet fra antikken til i dag* (Oslo, 2013), 9.
12. Biering, *Poetiske Tanker*, 52.
13. Ibid., 53.
14. Nils Gilje and Tarald Rasmussen, *Norsk idéhistorie*, vol. 2, *Tankeliv i den lutherske stat* (Oslo, 2002), 203-33.
15. Biering, *Poetiske Tanker*, 53.
16. Ibid., 53.
17. Compare Koselleck, *Futures Past*, 277.
18. Brita Brenna, "Negotiating the History of the World," in *Negotiating Pasts in the Nordic Countries: Interdisciplinary Studies in History and Memory*, ed. Anne Eriksen and Jon Vidar Sigurdsson (Lund, 2009), 125-29.
19. Erik Pontoppidan, *Uforgribelige Betænkninger over den naturlige Aarsag til de mange og store Jord-Skiælv, samt det usædvanlige Veirlig, som nu paa nogen Tid er fornummet, baade i og uden for Europa* (Copenhagen, 1756).
20. Ibid., 5-6.
21. Tore Frängsmyr, *Geologi och skapelsetro: Föreställningar om jordens historia från Hiärne till Bergman* (Stockholm, 1969), 220.
22. Brenna, "Negotiating the History of the World," 132-35.
23. Erik Pontoppidan, *Afhandling om Verdens Nyehed eller Naturlig og Historisk Beviis paa at Verden ikke er af Evighed, men maa, For nogle tusende Aar siden, have taget sin Begyndelse, Tienlig til Bestyrkelse for de Christnes Troe om den Bibelske Histories Sandhed* (Copenhagen, 1757).
24. Rhoda Rappaport, *When Geologists Were Historians, 1650-1750* (Ithaca, NY, 1997), 190.
25. Brenna, "Negotiating the History of the World," 132-35.
26. Ibid., 135; Norman Cohn, *Noah's Flood: The Genesis Story in Western Thought* (New Haven, CT, 1999).
27. Brenna, "Negotiating the History of the World," 136.
28. Lucas Jacobsøn Debes, *Faeroae et Faeroa reserata: Det er Færøernis oc Færøeske Indbyggeris Beskrifvelse, udi hvilken føris til Liuset adskillige Naturens Hemeligheder oc nogle Antiqviteter, som her til Dags udi Mørcket hafver været indelugte, oc nu her opladis, alle curieuse til velbehagelighed* (Copenhagen, 1673).
29. Jens Christian Spidberg, "Historisk og physisk Relation om det mærkværdige Jordskielv i Norge, Lisabon og andre Stæder den 1 Novembr. 1755," *Det københavnske Selskabs Skrifter*, no. 7 (1758): 101-12.
30. Rhoda Rappaport, "The Earth Sciences," in *The Cambridge History of Science*, vol. 4, *Eighteenth-Century Science*, ed. Roy Porter (Cambridge, 2002), 427.

31. Pontoppidan, *Uforgribelige Betænkninger*, 8–9.
32. *Kiøbenhavnske Danske Post-Tidender* [newspaper], 16 January 1756, 2.
33. Matthias Georgi, "The Lisbon Earthquake and Scientific Knowledge in the British Public Sphere," in *The Lisbon Earthquake of 1755: Representations and Reactions*, ed. Theodore E. D. Braun and John B. Radner (Oxford, 2005), 86.
34. Pontoppidan, *Uforgribelige Betænkninger*, 51.
35. Søren Kjørup has suggested the term "communicative sign" as a generic term for what Pierce terms icons and symbols. Søren Kjørup, *Semiotik* (Fredriksberg, 2002).
36. Pontoppidan, *Uforgribelige Betænkninger*, 6.
37. Ibid., 9–10, 20. A Danish mile was 7,532.48 meters long.
38. Ibid., 11.
39. Ibid., 27.
40. Cohn, *Noah's Flood*.
41. Anne Eriksen, *Topografenes verden: Fornminner og fortidsforståelse* (Oslo, 2007), 51.
42. Pontoppidan, *Afhandling om Verdens Nyehed*, 71.
43. Rappaport, *When Geologists Were Historians*, 223.
44. Gina Dahl, "Bibelsk tid: Pontoppidans jordhistorie," *Bjørgvin, Kyrkjehistorisk årbok*, no. 1 (2004): 79.
45. Brenna, "Negotiating the History of the World," 134.
46. Pontoppidan, *Uforgribelige Betænkninger*, 91.
47. Brenna, "Negotiating the History of the World," 138; Pontoppidan, *Afhandling om Verdens Nyehed*, 175; *Kiøbenhavnske nye Tidender om lærde og curieuse Sager* [newspaper], 4 November 1756, 357.

BIBLIOGRAPHY

Biering, Christian Henrik. *Christian Henric Bierings poetiske Tanker over Lissabons Ødeleggelse ved det uhørlige Jordskiælv paa Alle Helgens Dag 1755.* Copenhagen, 1756.

Brenna, Brita. "Negotiating the History of the World." In *Negotiating Pasts in the Nordic Countries: Interdisciplinary Studies in History and Memory*, edited by Anne Eriksen and Jon Vidar Sigurdsson, 121–49. Lund: Nordic Academic Press, 2009.

Broberg, Gunnar. *Tsunamin i Lissabon: Jordbävningen den 1 november 1755, i epicentrum och i svensk periferi.* Stockholm: Atlantis, 2005.

Cohn, Norman. *Noah's Flood: The Genesis Story in Western Thought.* New Haven, CT: Yale University Press, 1999.

Dahl, Gina. "Bibelsk tid: Pontoppidans jordhistorie." *Bjørgvin, Kyrkjehistorisk årbok*, no. 1 (2004): 67–83.

Debes, Lucas Jacobsøn. *Faeroae et Faeroa reserata: Det er Færøernis oc Færøeske Indbyggeris Beskrifvelse, udi hvilken føris til Liuset adskillige Naturens Hemeligheder oc nogle Antiqviteter, som her til Dags udi Mørcket hafver været indelugte, oc nu her opladis, alle curieuse til velbehagelighed.* Copenhagen, 1673.

D'Haen, Theo. "On How Not to Be Lisbon If You Want to Be Modern: Dutch Reactions to the Lisbon Earthquake." *European Review* 14, no. 3 (2006): 351–58.

Efterretninger om nye Bøger og lærde Sager i Danmark og Norge (Journal, Copenhagen 1756–57).

Eriksen, Anne. *Topografenes verden: Fornminner og fortidsforståelse.* Oslo: Pax, 2007.

Eriksen, Anne, Ellen Krefting, and Anne Birgitte Rønning, eds. *Eksempelets makt: Kjønn, representasjon og autoritet fra antikken til i dag.* Oslo: Scandinavian Academic Press, 2013.

Frängsmyr, Tore. *Geologi och skapelsetro: Föreställningar om jordens historia från Hiärne till Bergman.* Stockholm: Almquist & Wiksell, 1969.

Frye, Northrop. *The Great Code: The Bible and Literature.* New York: Harcourt Brace Jovanovich, 1982.

Georgi, Matthias. "The Lisbon Earthquake and Scientific Knowledge in the British Public Sphere." In *The Lisbon Earthquake of 1755: Representations and Reactions*, edited by Theodore E. D. Braun and John B. Radner, 81–96. Oxford: Voltaire Foundation, 2005.

Gilje, Nils, and Tarald Rasmussen. *Norsk idéhistorie.* Vol. 2, *Tankeliv i den lutherske stat.* Oslo: Aschehoug, 2002.

Kendrick, T. D. *The Lisbon Earthquake.* Philadelphia: J. B. Lippincott, 1956.

Kiøbenhavnske nye Tidender om lærde og curieuse Sager (Journal, Copenhagen 1749–66).

Kjørup, Søren. *Semiotik.* Fredriksberg: Roskilde Universitetsforlag, 2002.

Koselleck, Reinhart. *Futures Past: On the Semantics of Historical Time.* Cambridge, MA: MIT Press, 1985.

Lyons, John. *Exemplum: The Rhetoric of Example in Early Modern France and Italy.* Princeton, NJ: Princeton University Press, 1989.

Pontoppidan, Erik. *Afhandling om Verdens Nyehed eller Naturlig og Historisk Beviis paa at Verden ikke er af Evighed, men maa, For nogle tusende Aar siden, have taget sin Begyndelse, Tienlig til Bestyrkelse for de Christnes Troe om den Bibelske Histories Sandhed.* Copenhagen, 1757.

———. *Uforgribelige Betænkninger over den naturlige Aarsag til de mange og store Jord-Skiælv, samt det usædvanlige Veirlig, som nu paa nogen Tid er fornummet, baade i og uden for Europa.* Copenhagen, 1756.

Rappaport, Rhoda. "The Earth Sciences." In *The Cambridge History of Science*, vol. 4, *Eighteenth-Century Science*, edited by Roy Porter, 417–35. Cambridge: Cambridge University Press, 2002.

———. *When Geologists Were Historians, 1650–1750.* Ithaca, NY: Cornell University Press, 1997.

Sejersted, Jørgen. "Ulykkesdiktning på 1600-tallet: Noen norske eksempler fra 1627 til 1702." In *Overdådighet og død i barokken*, edited by Hall Bjørnstad and Mette Nygård, 111–34. Oslo: Emilia, 2002.

Spidberg, Jens Christian. "Historisk og physisk Relation om det mærkværdige Jordskielv i Norge, Lisabon og andre Stæder den 1 Novembr. 1755." *Det københavnske Selskabs Skrifter*, no. 7 (1758): 101–12.

▶• 16 •◀

Time and Space in World Literature

Ibsen in and out of Sync

Tore Rem

There will always be a variety of asymmetries and reciprocities involved in a particular text's accommodation into world literature, with the asymmetries no doubt being more salient when the movement is from periphery to center. While certain centers can be extremely powerful in terms of consecration, the concept of a "Greenwich Mean Time" of literature, as introduced by Pascale Casanova in her influential study *The World Republic of Letters* (1999), is nevertheless a problematic one at best.[1] The introduction of the notion of a standard or absolute temporality, one inhabited by the norm and the power to consecrate, may hide as much as it discloses. In creating only one, consecrating Greenwich meridian of literature, Casanova hides the similar work done in other centers, that is, other than Paris. Moreover, such a concept cements the binary of center and periphery, thus indirectly always placing the periphery as secondary or subsidiary. The work of the periphery stands in danger of being deleted, and that in spite of protestations to the contrary.

Center-periphery relations are primarily temporal relations, and with ideas of such relations come ideas about the center being ahead of the periphery, about the periphery lagging behind and striving to catch up. The importance of particular centers clearly also depends on the peripheries in question, and the relative importance both of centers and peripheries is subject to historical change. In a significant contribution to the field of world literature, Mads Rosendahl Thomsen has, for example, argued that Scandinavian literature becomes a sub-center of world literature in the period 1880–1900.[2] But it is nevertheless, even here, worth asking: from what perspective? Sub-centers reverse, for the time being, the dominant temporal dimension, and thus clearly make periodization difficult and complex. It is true that Ibsen's *A Doll's House* (1879), Strindberg's *The Red Room* (1879), and Jacobsen's *Niels Lyhne* (1880) first appeared at the beginning of this period, but at this stage they were primarily works of Scandinavian literature, and not yet of "world literature."[3] Such decentering, then, valuable and necessary as it is, introduces complex temporalities that transcend the dichotomy of discontinuity/continuity. Franco Moretti has persuasively argued that new literary forms, or at least novelistic forms, most often come into being in the center, and that they are then adapted to and by the peripheries.[4] But how can we understand the center, and its responses, when this innovation happens in the periphery, as it does in Henrik Ibsen's case? The case of Ibsen, I would argue, may help us rethink, and perhaps reconceptualize, center-periphery relations within a world literary system.

My aim in questioning Casanova's account is, then, not to debunk Paris's relative importance as a literary center, but to replace one centrist perspective with a multi-centered perspective, one informed by the perspective of the periphery. It is important that we remind ourselves of such particularities and distinctions; if not, we easily end up ignoring the specificity and variability of the world (or worlds) to which world literature belongs. It is, furthermore, worth "provincializing" the centers of literary consecration, to give a nod to Dipesh Chakrabarty (while acknowledging that the world of this chapter to a large extent means late nineteenth-century Europe), whether they be Paris, London, or Berlin. In that way it may to a greater extent be possible to acknowledge the intricate circuits of world literature, the crucial contributions to literary innovation from the peripheries, as well as the problems inherent in a number of inherited narratives.

In reflecting on some of the challenges involved in thinking about how literary novelty enters the center from the periphery, as well as on the notions of "world" that inevitably are involved in the creation of world literature, I would like to focus on Ibsen's early English-language reception. More particularly, this chapter will examine the work of the man credited with having been Ibsen's first mediator in and into English, Edmund Gosse. In spite of the Norwegian playwright's somewhat earlier reception in Germany, English was to become the main vehicle for Ibsen's way into the world, and, because of its later status as the world's first truly global language, English would become crucial for his continued place in the circuits of world literature and drama. Gosse has perhaps received more than his fair share of honor in later accounts of this process, but my aim here is to examine his concepts of Ibsen, literature, and the world somewhat more closely. Contrary to standard narratives of Ibsen's way into world literature—generally told with the slight triumphalism of retrospective, canonical certainty and often from the perspective of a particular center—I hope to show that both the "world" and the "Ibsen" at stake in the playwright's early English-language reception may have differed from those of later versions. By so doing, I would urge us to pay attention to the historical particularity of both texts and concepts, that is, if we want to do justice to the complex mechanisms of world literature, and not least to those pertaining to the often fraught relationships between centers and peripheries.

The first substantial article on Henrik Ibsen in the English language, "Ibsen, the Norwegian Satirist," was a strong attempt at placing the Norwegian writer at the center of European, if not world, culture. In 1873, the young English critic Edmund Gosse, having worked his way through *Love's Comedy*, *Brand*, and *Peer Gynt*, sought to communicate Ibsen's achievements to the readers of the *Fortnightly Review*. "There is now living at Dresden a middle-aged Norwegian gentleman," began Gosse, effectively communicating the foreign writer's cosmopolitanism, as well as his acceptability to English standards.[5] "Where shall we look for a young great poet among continental nations?" he continued, and listed a few candidates, none of whom were deemed qualified as "world-poets." The answer lay, no doubt surprisingly to nearly every British reader, to the north: "It is my firm belief that in the Norwegian, Henrik Ibsen, the representative of a land unknown in the literary annals of Europe, such a poet is found."[6]

How are we to understand such a claim about Ibsen, made in Britain already in 1873, only a year after his name had first appeared in English? Literary historians have tended to see Gosse as prophetic, a pioneer who immediately recognized Ibsen's greatness and his status as world literature. Such an understanding establishes a teleology, from this early English discoverer of Ibsen to the playwright who, two decades later, achieves broad international recognition and is gradually taken up into world literature. Such a perspective is not merely anachronistic, however; it ignores the different temporalities involved in the canonization of world literature, the asymmetries between center and periphery, as well as the composite meanings of the concept itself.[7] The history of international reception and canonization in world literature is, as Rosendahl Thomsen reminds us, "marked by considerable discontinuities."[8]

Speaking to Johann Peter Eckermann in January 1827, Goethe had famously expressed a strong interest in foreign literature, based on his belief that "poetry is the universal possession of mankind," and, with a claim for a particular futurity, that "the epoch of world literature is at hand."[9] With the publication of Eckermann's *Gespräche mit Goethe in den letzten Jahre seines Leben* in 1835, the term *Weltliteratur* began to be more widely circulated, very soon also in Britain. In fact, the first recorded use of this concept in English comes, not too surprisingly, from the German-oriented Thomas Carlyle. Already in 1831, in the *Edinburgh Review*, Carlyle registered his hope, put in the form of a question, that, "Instead of isolated, mutually repulsive National Literatures, a World Literature may one day be looked for?"[10] But Goethe's concept of *Weltliteratur* did at the very least contain two related if different meanings: one of the idealist kind (referring to "a perceived transformation of cultural space," it insisted on something that was, while stressing the fact that it was still primarily to come),[11] and one related to a more materialist understanding, that is, of a new network of international intellectual exchange, of texts "actively present within a literary system beyond that of its original culture," to quote David Damrosch.[12]

Gosse's claim in "Ibsen, the Norwegian Satirist," I would argue, could at this point in time only be made from the center (or *a* center). It was, furthermore, related to romantic notions of Norway that the impact of a later Ibsen would do much to modify. Gosse referred to a land with "a healthy population, unexhausted and unrestrained," suggesting that this was the future: "here, if anywhere, human nature may hope to find a just development."[13] Gosse seems not, at this stage, to be the least troubled by any thought that Ibsen's obscure, northerly origins might be irreconcilable with his Europeanness, or even with a status as world-poet. Such doubts would, however, be at the forefront of Ibsen's later European receptions.

Whose and which "world" is this world of the world-poet? It is one obviously related to the idealist meaning of Goethe's concept of *Weltliteratur*. Ibsen has at this point, in 1873, hardly been translated outside of Scandinavia. His "world-poetry" may at best be understood as being part of an ideal "international conversation" among great writers,[14] and has nothing or little to do with actual reception; alternatively, or as well, it is a poetry of great potentiality, of the future. In a poem addressed to Ibsen, and written in the same year, Gosse noted: "Your verses lie like gems that hide / In coffers sealed from English eyes."[15] There is, then, as of yet an occult quality to Ibsen, not in terms of his status as national literature, where he can be clearly seen and his greatness recognized, but as world literature. In this case, I would suggest, we ought also to ask "which Ibsen?" What is the relationship between Gosse's Ibsen of 1873 and the Ibsen who in the 1890s was hailed as one of Europe's three greatest living writers, with Zola and Tolstoy? More generally—and this is a question that lies outside the scope of the present chapter, but that is central to my interest in a peripheral and multi-centered perspective on world literature—how was it possible for a "representative of a land unknown in the literary annals of Europe," to quote Gosse, to achieve this literary status in such a relatively short time?

Gosse's "centrist" perspective of course comes across as benign and cosmopolitan, even as it inevitably assumes a power to define both the universal and the literary, whereas many later perspectives from the center would, in acting from similar premises, be severely hostile, attempting to exclude Ibsen from the same categories.

Noting that Gosse's Ibsen, the Ibsen of *Love's Comedy*, *Brand*, and *Peer Gynt*, was a different Ibsen than "Ibsen, the Father of Modern Drama" does not of course mean that later narratives have distinguished between the two. One reference work, David Pickering's *Dictionary of the Theatre* (1988), will have to suffice as an example of how later accounts have tended to conflate Ibsen at home with Ibsen abroad, albeit in a number of significantly different ways. Under the heading "Henrik Ibsen," *Dictionary of the Theatre* claims that "*Brand* and *Peer Gynt* soon became internationally recognized for their technical mastery, psychological insight, and bleakness of vision."[16] Quite apart from the fact that it is highly questionable whether *Peer Gynt* (1867) is characterized by "bleakness," the chronology here is completely wrong. While there were a few early translations of *Brand* and *Peer Gynt*, these works did not receive "international" acclaim until after Ibsen's breakthrough with the social problem plays in the late 1880s and early 1890s. While *Brand* and *Peer Gynt* certainly established the playwright's reputation at home, in terms of world literature they—*Peer Gynt* in particular—were a secondary phenomenon, with canonization following only after Ibsen had been recognized as the inventor of the modern prose play. The perspective of this *Dictionary of the Theatre*, based as it clearly is on secondary sources, is thus benevolently retrospective and its effect stabilizing, approaching as it does Ibsen as a writer safely settled at the center of the canon. But this inevitably leads to an elimination of the historical differences between periphery and center, quite apart from an unreflective acceptance of a certain version of the "author function."

While Gosse had simply asserted Ibsen's status as world-poet in 1873, the matter was undecided for much longer and still open to debate in his British reception two decades later. Typically, and in representative fashion, the critic of *The Academy*, Sir Frederick Wedmore, identified the problem: "If Ibsen were an Englishman, I should say that he was provincial, I should say that he was suburban."[17] Many critics, such as William St. Leger, tried to degrade Ibsen by referring to his nationality, wondering how "the maunderings of nookshotten Norwegians" with their "provincial improprieties" could ever be a "revelation" to cosmopolitan Englishmen.[18] Ibsen was irrelevant, and in some accounts his works did not even count as literature. Wedmore's two accusations, of provincialism and suburbanity, are found again and again in the conservative criticism of Ibsen around this time; indeed, many of Ibsen's British champions had to admit that there was something to this line of attack, feeling the need to respond to it. Ibsen's peripheral and provincial status, in short, became a key problem in this British reception, as it did in a number of European countries. Seen as a conspicuously provincial writer, it was the often difficult negotiation between Ibsen's perceived particularity (his Norwegianness) and his appeal (or what was considered his universality) that came to dominate his first receptions in Britain, Germany, and France.

A new dynamic was introduced when new Ibsen plays were beginning to be published in synchronization in a number of European countries in the 1890s.

Even if the battles over a more ideal notion of his status as world literature—akin to Gosse's claim from the early 1870s, although applied to a quite different form of literature, a different Ibsen—would rage for a little while longer, the very distribution of Ibsen plays, in book form and as performance, was making him into world literature in the other, more material sense. Almost upon publication, each new Ibsen play began to circulate beyond its original national context, and not just in one or two foreign cultures. *Hedda Gabler* (1890) was the first play to be published nigh simultaneously in Copenhagen, Berlin, Paris, and London, with this fact being advertised in the first editions. Perhaps these are, indeed, the first "world events," or at least Europe-wide events, of world literature.

Pascale Casanova presents Ibsen as an exemplary writer, a cultural outsider received into the center (i.e., Paris), and thus consecrated. But while it is possible to make claims about one center's relative importance in relation to other centers, this account, I would argue, "protests too much." It invests too much, in Ibsen's case, in bringing out one particular center's perspective, in spite of Casanova's awareness of what she calls "the ethnocentric blindness of these centers."[19] Casanova shows little awareness of the importance of Ibsen's Scandinavian consecration, of his preference for Italy and Germany as places of exile, of Germany's mediating role, or of the central significance of London and English literature in the ultimate process of canonization and world distribution.

In making her claims, Casanova typically finds quotations that seem to support her case, as when she refers to Ibsen's impatience about being received in the French capital, calling Paris, in a *Le Figaro* interview of 1893, "the real heart of the world."[20] But such flattery was conventional for Ibsen, and Casanova's aim—that of portraying Paris as the main source of literary autonomy—means that she is blind to the perspectives of other centers, as well as Ibsen's own periphery, his Norwegian contexts of origin. Ibsen, it should be noted, expressed very similar views about other centers in letters to his English and German mediators. In 1872, he told Gosse that "being introduced into the English world of reading is for me the main thing"; it was one of his "dearest literary dreams."[21] When he wrote to his German translator Julie Ruhkopf four years later, he claimed that "but my greatest interest is after all to have my books distributed in Germany."[22] Ibsen at one point called Paris an almost unthinkable dream, referring to the "so inaccessible Paris," but this last observation runs counter to the claim, incidentally made from the center, that Paris was, and was considered, the most receptive of capitals.[23] The most solid account of the reception of Scandinavian literature in Paris during these decades, Stellan Ahlström's *Strindbergs erövring av Paris* (Strindberg's Conquest of Paris), paints quite a different picture, one of strong resistance and much hostility.²⁴ At certain points Ibsen, furthermore, expressed a clear disinterest in or skepticism about Paris, such as when he questioned the writer John Paulsen as to why he was staying for so long in the French capital—why not choose Germany instead?²⁵ In 1888, a Norwegian man of the theater, Johan Irgens Hansen, suggested that it was the Germans who would effect Ibsen's academic canonization, as they had done with Shakespeare. The Germans were the most universal of nations from this Scandinavian perspective, and had a special mission as "the interpreter of our common European culture."²⁶ It is hard from this to see how Paris would represent Greenwich Mean Time in Ibsen's case, and that even in hindsight, and even when ignoring the author's own perspective. Considering the relative status of Ibsen within various world canons, it is clear that he enjoys a higher status in the English-language world canon, and in the German, than he does in the French, and there are, furthermore, few signs of him having traveled from French into English or German.

In short, the making of Ibsen as world literature includes many elements that do not adhere to Casanova's spatial model, or that remain unaccounted for. In a number of ways, the making of Ibsen as world literature was more complex. First, Casanova does not pay sufficient attention to the dynamics of the Scandinavian book and theater market, that is, the internal sources of autonomy that were accessible to Ibsen from the time of *Brand*. From a relatively early stage, Ibsen was able to stop writing for newspapers and to devote himself entirely to his plays, normally publishing these at two-year intervals. In the 1890s, when he was established as one of Europe's greatest living writers, most of his income still came from Scandinavia. Second, Ibsen's exile, a biographical fact that in most influential accounts has been the subject of overdetermined readings, took place in Italy and Germany, not in France. He seems almost deliberately to have avoided Paris, in contrast to Scandinavian colleagues such as August Strindberg, Bjørnstjerne Bjørnson, and Jonas Lie. Third, it was Germany that was the first country or language culture outside of Scandinavia to receive Ibsen. And fourth, London and the English language became of central importance to Ibsen's larger international breakthrough and to his canonization, world distribution, and later status as world literature. Allowing for his usual habit of keeping his mediators happy, Ibsen seems to have seen the importance of the latter already in 1891, when he thanked William Archer for what he had done for his literature in "all of the great British territory—and through this also much wider than that."²⁷

When a "peripheral" author gains recognition as world literature, the periphery's own work, and investment in the authorship, is typically rendered invisible. It is clear that the stress on the asymmetry between Ibsen and his native land, and more generally Scandinavia, has been exaggerated. On the contrary, it could be argued that Ibsen acquired a considerable degree of autonomy in the Danish-Norwegian book market, and this also seems to have been his own perspective. Already in 1870, Ibsen thanked his Danish publisher Frederik V. Hegel for what he had done for him in Denmark, noting the impact this had had on his reception in Norway. Such "secure ground" was necessary, he noted, particularly for an author such as himself who would always have to "risk much."[28] It was this connection to a Danish publisher that made it possible for him "to live without worry" for his "calling," as he formulated it to another correspondent a year later.[29]

After his strong involvement in the earliest, and rather ineffectual, phase of Ibsen's reception in Britain, Edmund Gosse left off writing about the Norwegian playwright in 1879, and picked up again only ten years later, when others had helped Ibsen toward his first real British breakthrough. In hindsight this may look like a strategic mistake. Gosse did not write about *A Doll's House, Ghosts, An Enemy of the People, The Wild Duck,* or *Rosmersholm* when these first appeared between 1879 and 1886. But this Ibsen was not, I hope to have made clear, Gosse's Ibsen, not his "world-poet," and Gosse had been unprepared for Ibsen's developments, already resisting the writer's turn to prose in *Emperor and Galilean*. Even if Gosse in the 1890s adjusted his earlier views somewhat, he could still not help missing the "lovely creations" of Ibsen's youth.[30] He had initially held Ibsen up as a healthy alternative to a decadent center, while the same center would now, for a while, label Ibsen precisely as decadent and degenerate, in short, as modern.

Gosse's last extended consideration of Ibsen came in *Ibsen*, a short monograph published in 1907. Here he reminded his readers that he had been the first to write about the Norwegian playwright in English, albeit choosing not to revisit his more particular arguments about the "world-poet."[31] In a fairly reserved portrayal, Gosse stressed that Ibsen primarily belonged to Norway and that he was best understood at home, but he now also observed that it was the playwright's "determination to use prose" that had aided him "vastly in his dissemination" and had created his appeal "to the whole world." From one perspective, the "world-poet" of 1873 had been, as it were, "unworlded" in the very process of being "worlded." It was not Gosse's Ibsen but a later Ibsen, one whom Gosse had initially resisted, who had by this time started circulating as world literature, beginning to lead what David Damrosch calls "an *effective* life" as world literature.[32]

"World literature will always be a world literature as seen from a particular place," Rosendahl Thomsen notes, and this place, we might add, inevitably also involves a time.[33] In studying the movements of world literature, and the canonization of works of world literature, it is necessary to pay attention to the particular logics and histories of different national fields. Two examples of the displacements and discontinuities of the world literary system must suffice here. The first relates to the order in which Ibsen's plays were introduced.

While his status in the Danish-Norwegian field had already been secured through earlier works like *The Pretenders*, *Brand*, and *Peer Gynt*, in Britain his breakthrough came with the publication of later plays such as *A Doll's House* and *Ghosts*. How did that shape the different perceptions of the writer in these two fields, both then and later? There is also the matter of generational differences internal to each field in question. While Knut Hamsun in 1891 attacked Ibsen for writing an old-fashioned and psychologically one-dimensional literature that a new generation had to break with and overcome, a much younger James Joyce ten years later held Ibsen up as an ally of the young and as a great model. Such highly dissimilar attitudes can hardly be explained by way of a change in Ibsen's texts in the intervening years; they must be related to the differences and temporal displacements between the Scandinavian and the British literary fields. Ibsen's position at home led to Hamsun's counter-position at the same time as the playwright's work was being appropriated by the avant-garde in France and Britain.

The rhetoric of center and periphery organized the international appropriations of Ibsen in his own time, and it has continued to organize our understandings of him and of his career. It is worth maintaining an emphasis on the realities of center-periphery asymmetries, including the power inequality involved in all such relations, a world literary system that is, in Moretti's terms (drawing on Immanuel Wallerstein's world systems theory), "profoundly unequal."[34] Our inherited models have also clearly created blind spots. One of these relates to the aforementioned focus on exile. As Narve Fulsås has pointed out, in choosing his places of exile Ibsen did not seek European modernity; on the contrary, he ended up in Counter-Reformation Europe, far away from intellectual and economic centers of modernity, like Paris and London.[35] There is, furthermore, little evidence of Ibsen involving himself in his new local environments, with Munich as a partial exception. Exile seems for him primarily to have been a matter of achieving a degree of social distance from the small-town conditions at home, while nevertheless writing for home, in other words for the European periphery.[36] Ibsen would stress the wider view, the fresher air, and at one point noted that staying abroad also meant the possibility of "a greater clarity through comparison."[37] When Casanova "centers" the world republic of letters in Ibsen's case, she relies heavily on the importance of French literary life as a model of autonomy, but it seems more sensible in Ibsen's case to discuss the *relative* position of Paris, and to examine the different functions performed by the different centers in which he was received and appropriated. In Ibsen's case, the power of defining the universal, or at the very least the literary, seems to have belonged as much, if not more, to Berlin and London, and even to Copenhagen, as it did to Paris.

Tore Rem is Professor of English Literature in the Department of Literature, Area Studies and European Languages at the University of Oslo. He has published extensively on British and Scandinavian nineteenth- and twentieth-century literature. His most recent books include *Hva skal vi med humaniora?* [Why the Humanities?] (with Helge Jordheim et al., Fritt Ord, 2014); *Knut Hamsun: Reisen til Hitler* [Knut Hamsun: The Journey to Hitler] (Cappelen Damm, 2014); and, with Narve Fulsås, *Ibsen, Scandinavia and the Making of a World Drama* (Cambridge University Press, 2018).

NOTES

I would like to extend my thanks to Helge Jordheim and Narve Fulsås for their perceptive comments on this chapter.

1. See Pascale Casanova, *The World Republic of Letters*, trans. M. B. DeBevoise (Cambridge, MA, 2004), 87.
2. Mads Rosendahl Thomsen, *Mapping World Literature* (London, 2008).
3. See Narve Fulsås, "Ibsen, Europa og det moderne gjennombrotet i nordisk litteratur," *Historiska och litteraturhistoriska studier* 86 (2011): 35–60.
4. Franco Moretti, "Conjectures on World Literature," *New Left Review* 1 (2001): 54–68.
5. Edmund Gosse, "Ibsen, the Norwegian Satirist," *Fortnightly Review* 19 (1 January 1873): 74.
6. Ibid., 88.
7. Mads Rosendahl Thomsen writes of "the temporal differentiations in the idea of world literature"; see *Mapping World Literature*, 3.
8. Ibid., 2.
9. Quoted in David Damrosch, *What Is World Literature?* (Princeton, NJ, 2003), 1.
10. Quoted under "world literature" in *Oxford English Dictionary*, retrieved on 8 August 2018 from http://www.oed.com/view/Entry/230262?redirectedFrom=world+literature#eid13857022.
11. See Stefan Hoesel-Uhlig, "Changing Fields: The Directions of Goethe's *Weltliteratur*," in *Debating World Literature*, ed. Christopher Prendergast (London, 2004), 33.
12. See John Pizer, *The Idea of World Literature* (Baton Rouge, 2006), 11; Damrosch, *What Is World Literature?* 4.
13. Gosse, "Ibsen, the Norwegian Satirist," 75.
14. Fritz Stich, "Goethe and World Literature," quoted in Christopher Prendergast, "The World Republic of Letters," in Prendergast, *Debating World Literature*, 2.
15. Edmund Gosse, "To Henrik Ibsen in Dresden," in *On Viol and Flute* (London, 1873), 142.
16. David Pickering, *Dictionary of the Theatre* (London, 1988), 250.
17. Frederick Wedmore, "Ibsen in London," *The Academy* 35 (15 June 1889): 419–20.
18. William St. Leger, "Dialogue" [with Justin Huntly McCarthy], *Black & White* 1 (21 March 1891): 222.

19. Casanova, *World Republic*, 23.
20. Ibid., 162.
21. Henrik Ibsen to Edmund Gosse, 2 April 1872, in Henrik Ibsen, *Henrik Ibsens skrifter: Brev*, ed. Narve Fulsås, retrieved from http://ibsen.uio.no/brev.xhtml on 8 August 2018. All translations from the letters are mine.
22. Henrik Ibsen to Julie Ruhkopf, 17 March 1876, in Ibsen, *Brev*.
23. Henrik Ibsen to Moritz Prozor, 25 October 1889, in Ibsen, *Brev*.
24. Stellan Ahlström, *Strindbergs erövring av Paris: Strindberg och Frankrike 1884–1895* (Uppsala, 1956).
25. Henrik Ibsen to John Paulsen, 20 September 1879, in Ibsen, *Brev*.
26. "Den europeiske Fælleskulturs Fortolker"; Johan Irgens Hansen, quoted in Fulsås, "Ibsen," 56.
27. Henrik Ibsen to William Archer, 29 April 1891, in Ibsen, *Brev*.
28. Henrik Ibsen to Frederik V. Hegel, 2 July 1870, in Ibsen, *Brev*.
29. Henrik Ibsen to Carl Christian Hall, 27 February 1871, in Ibsen, *Brev*.
30. See Ronald Gray, *Ibsen: A Dissenting View* (Cambridge, 1977), 202.
31. Edmund Gosse, *Ibsen* (London, 1907), 265.
32. Damrosch, *What Is World Literature?* 4; emphasis in the original.
33. Rosendahl Thomsen, *Mapping World Literature*, 1.
34. Moretti, "Conjectures on World Literature," 54.
35. Fulsås, "Ibsen."
36. Henrik Ibsen to Bjørnstjerne Bjørnson, 28 December 1868, in Ibsen, *Brev*. Ibsen here advised Bjørnson to travel, "Baade fordi Afstanden giver større Synsvidde og fordi man selv paa samme Tid er Godtfolk ude af Syne" ("Both because the distance affords a broader vista and because one is simultaneously out of sight of the bourgeoisie").
37. Henrik Ibsen to Kristian Elster, 25 March 1880, in Ibsen, *Brev*.

BIBLIOGRAPHY

Ahlström, Stellan. *Strindbergs erövring av Paris: Strindberg och Frankrike 1884–1895*. Uppsala: Almqvist & Wiksell, 1956.
Casanova, Pascale. *The World Republic of Letters* [1999]. Translated by M. B. DeBevoise. Cambridge, MA: Harvard University Press, 2004.
Damrosch, David. *What Is World Literature?* Princeton, NJ: Princeton University Press, 2003.
Eckermann, Johann Peter. *Gespräche mit Goethe in den letzten Jahre seines Leben* [1835], edited by Christoph Michel et co. Frankfurt am Main: Deutscher Klassiker Verlag, 1999, vol. 12.
Fulsås, Narve. "Ibsen, Europa og det moderne gjennombrotet i nordisk litteratur." *Historiska och litteraturhistoriska studier* 86 (2011): 35–60.
Gosse, Edmund. *Ibsen*. London: Hodder and Stoughton, 1907.
———. "Ibsen, the Norwegian Satirist." *Fortnightly Review* 19 (1 January 1873): 74–88.

———. "To Henrik Ibsen in Dresden." In *On Viol and Flute*, 142. London: Henry S. King, 1873.

Gray, Ronald. *Ibsen: A Dissenting View*. Cambridge: Cambridge University Press, 1977.

Hoesel-Uhlig, Stefan. "Changing Fields: The Directions of Goethe's *Weltliteratur*." In *Debating World Literature*, edited by Christopher Prendergast, 26–53. London: Verso, 2004.

Ibsen, Henrik. *Henrik Ibsens skrifter: Brev*. Edited by Narve Fulsås. Retrieved 8 August 2018 from http://ibsen.uio.no/brev.xhtml.

Moretti, Franco. "Conjectures on World Literature." *New Left Review* 1 (2001): 54–68.

Oxford English Dictionary, http://www.oed.com.

Pickering, David. *Dictionary of the Theatre*. London: Sphere Books, 1988.

Pizer, John. *The Idea of World Literature*. Baton Rouge: Louisiana State University Press, 2006.

Prendergast, Christopher. "The World Republic of Letters." In *Debating World Literature*, edited by Christopher Prendergast, 1–25. London: Verso, 2004.

Rosendahl Thomsen, Mads. *Mapping World Literature*. London: Continuum, 2008.

St. Leger, William. "Dialogue" [with Justin Huntly McCarthy]. *Black & White* 1 (21 March 1891): 222.

Wedmore, Frederick. "Ibsen in London." *The Academy* 35 (15 June 1889): 419–20.

Part IV

MAPPING THE WORLD

⊢• 17 •⊣

Middle Age of the Globe

Alfred Hiatt

Around 1258 a monk drew an image of the world. The monk, John of Wallingford, was a member of the Benedictine monastery of St. Albans, a few miles north of London, an institution renowned for its historiographical, literary, and scientific achievements. His image—contained in a miscellaneous manuscript that includes excerpts from various chronicles, calendrical material, and a well-known map of England by John's contemporary at St. Albans, Matthew Paris—consists of two halves (Figure 17.1). On the left, occupying most of the Northern Hemisphere, is the known world. It is divided into eight climatic zones: the seven known to classical antiquity, commencing at the equator with the "region of the Indians" (*clima Indorum*), then the regions of the Ethiopians or Moors, Egyptians, Jerusalemites (whose city is central), Greeks, Romans, and Franks, before, in a modernizing touch, adding an eighth *clima*, that of England, Ireland, and "northern parts."

On the right, beneath the equator, are two statements of theory. One informs the reader that a sea at the equator divides the world in two, and constitutes "a third part of the whole earth, which is a spherical globe" (*est tercia pars tocius terre que est globus spericus*). At the center of the world, the statement continues, there is an inferno or abyss, the source of all waters "that surround the globe of the earth like white around the yoke in an egg" (*que sunt circa globum terre sicut albumen circa uitellum in ouo*). And then, in a kind of non-sequitur, the inscription concludes that "when we have day they have night. When we have winter, they have summer" (*Quando nos habemus diem illi noctem. Quando nos hiemem illi estatem*). This final remark is explained somewhat by the second inscription, which alludes to the notion that the equatorial region was one of intense heat: "It is not known if this middle part, which is beyond the torrid part, is inhabited, for no-one ever crossed from that part to us, nor from us to them" (*Hec media pars que est ultra torridam si*

256 • Alfred Hiatt

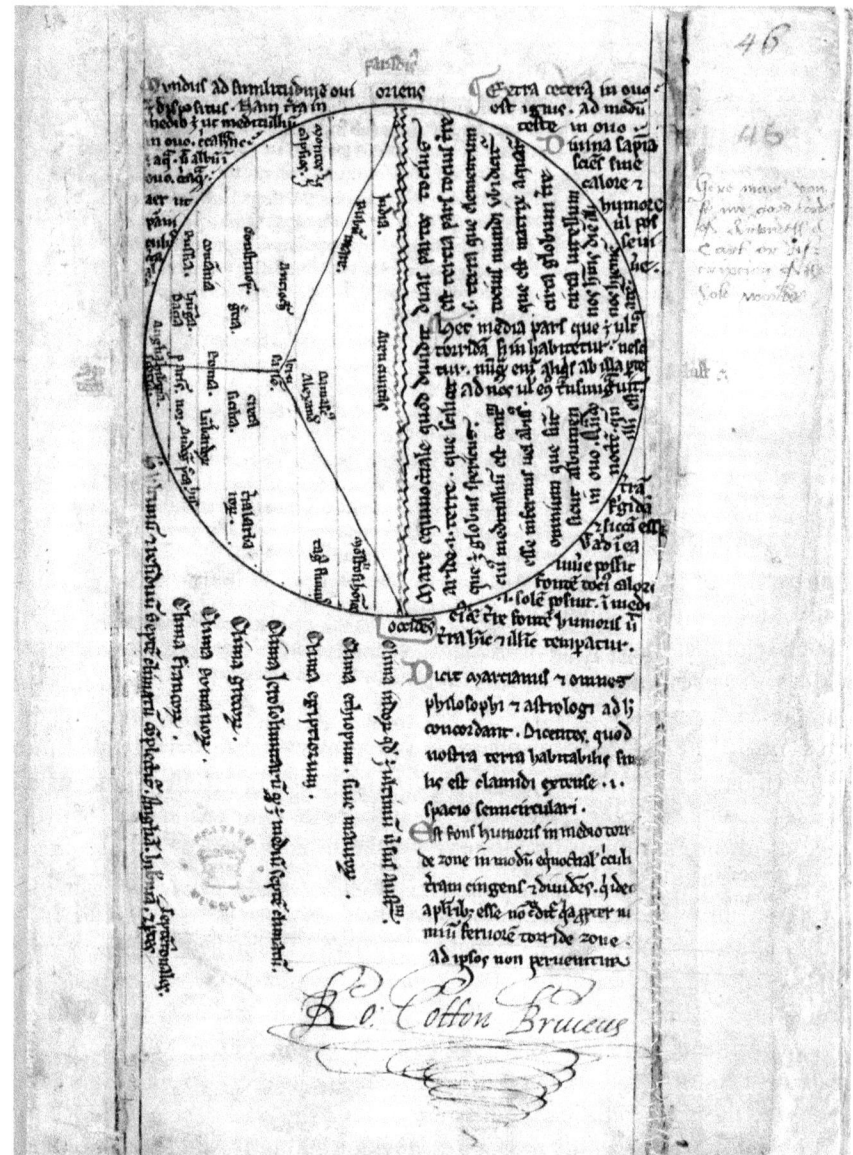

Figure 17.1. John of Wallingford, *Globus spericus*. St. Albans, 1258. London, British Library, Cotton MS Julius D.VII, f. 46r. © The British Library, published with permission.

in habitetur nescitur. Numquam enim aliquis ab illa parte ad nos uel econtra transmigrauit).[1]

Some of the concerns and ideas about the world held by a learned person around the middle of the thirteenth century emerge from John's image. There are fundamental questions about the relationship between the known world and parts beyond and about the balance between earth and water, and there is a particular interest in people who, it is imagined, may live on the other side of the earth. Undeniably, John of Wallingford conceived of the world as a sphere, a *globus spericus*. He sought to represent that globe as an image, both in writing and in visual form, in order to explain the theories and debate that animated a great deal of thirteenth-century argument about the nature of things, and that would go on to preoccupy natural scientists in the fourteenth and fifteenth centuries.

In the context of a reconsideration of the meaning of the global, this medieval representation of the *globus spericus* raises two necessary questions.[2] First, in what ways has the idea of a spherical earth functioned *historically* as a means for thinking about, and representing, unknown peoples, places, and lands? And second, what model of change might we posit for thinking about the many different manifestations of the image of the globe? If we do not adopt a banal explanation of inexorable progress from ignorance to knowledge, how do we, for example, explain the emergence of something called "the globe," and its attendant concepts of "the global," globalization, and so forth? In this chapter I approach these questions through a consideration of two manifestations of "premodern" global thinking. I consider, first, the significance of the antipodes for medieval European conceptions of the earth; and second, the terrestrial globe as a pedagogical tool and material object in the Middle Ages.[3] These topics, I suggest, not only contradict ill-informed assumptions about medieval spatial thought and representation; more fundamentally, they demand a more nuanced understanding of the representation of the world as a pluralistic practice that evades schematic periodization.

Feet

The very term "antipodes" carries the idea of an opposing foot. Although this word could, during the Middle Ages, be understood to refer to a monstrous person with a foot reversed (that is, facing back to front, as it is in Isidore of Seville's *Etymologiae*), it was more normally understood as referring to conjectured people on the other side of the earth who, in St. Augustine of Hippo's dismissive words, supposedly "make their footsteps against our feet" (*aduersa pedibus nostris calcare uestigia*).[4] But what precisely was meant by "the other side of the earth"? According to certain divisions of the earth in classical antiquity, the world could be divided into four quadrants, only one of which consisted of the known world. Strictly speaking, then, the "antipodes" referred to the portion of the earth diametrically opposite Europe, Africa, and Asia.[5] In the course of the transmission of the idea, however, the term antipodes began to be applied to the other two unknown segments: the quadrant beyond the equator, due south of the known world, and the underside of the Northern Hemisphere, sometimes thought of as the "western antipodes."[6] The notion of the anti-podes, opposed feet, ultimately won out in popular and scientific terminology over its classical and medieval rivals—such as *antoikoi* ("opposite the ecumene") and *antikthones* ("opposite earthers"). "Antipodes" of course carried particular implications that these rivals did not. To whom did those opposed feet belong? Humans? Animals? Monstrous races? Were they cast in the image of Europeans, their customs and beliefs aligned, or in some way inverted?

Early Christian authors articulated two principal concerns about the other side of the earth.[7] One was based on a literal understanding of "antipodes": the rhetorician and Christian apologist Lactantius asked in the fourth century whether "there was anyone so foolish as to believe that there are men whose feet are above their heads?" (*aut est quisquam tam ineptus qui credat esse homines quorum uestigia sint superiora quam capita*).[8] The more influential view, expressed by Augustine, found the notion of the antipodes not literally but theologically impossible. Augustine reasoned that, since the size of the ocean made it impossible for people in the known world to travel to the other side of the earth, the word of God could not have been transmitted to antipodeans. Scripture asserted that all humanity was descended from Adam, and that the apostles had spread Christianity to the ends of the earth;[9] both of these assertions were difficult to reconcile with the notion of inhabited land at the antipodes.

But the antipodal feet—the conjectured sign of corresponding others—never went away. One reason for this persistence was the profound attempt made by scholars over several centuries to preserve and understand the image of the world transmitted by classical scientific and literary works. Of particular importance in this regard was Cicero's "Dream of Scipio" (*Somnium Scipionis*), the text with which the Roman statesman and rhetorician concluded his work *De re publica* in the first century BC. The "Dream," or the "Somnium," which contains a description of the world including those parts beyond Roman power, received a substantial commentary around AD 430 from the Roman philosopher Macrobius, who used diagrams to explain the concepts that underlay Cicero's description. These included a representation of the position of the earth within the cosmos, at the center of seven planetary circles; the division of the earth into zones (Figure 17.2); and a map, designed to show the sources of the Mediterranean, the Red Sea, and the Indian and Caspian Seas, the shape of the known world, and its relationship to the unknown space of the Southern Hemisphere.[10] Naturally, the image changed as it was copied.[11] Typically, though, Macrobius's map shows a schematic division of the earth into five zones: cold (*frigida*) and uninhabitable zones

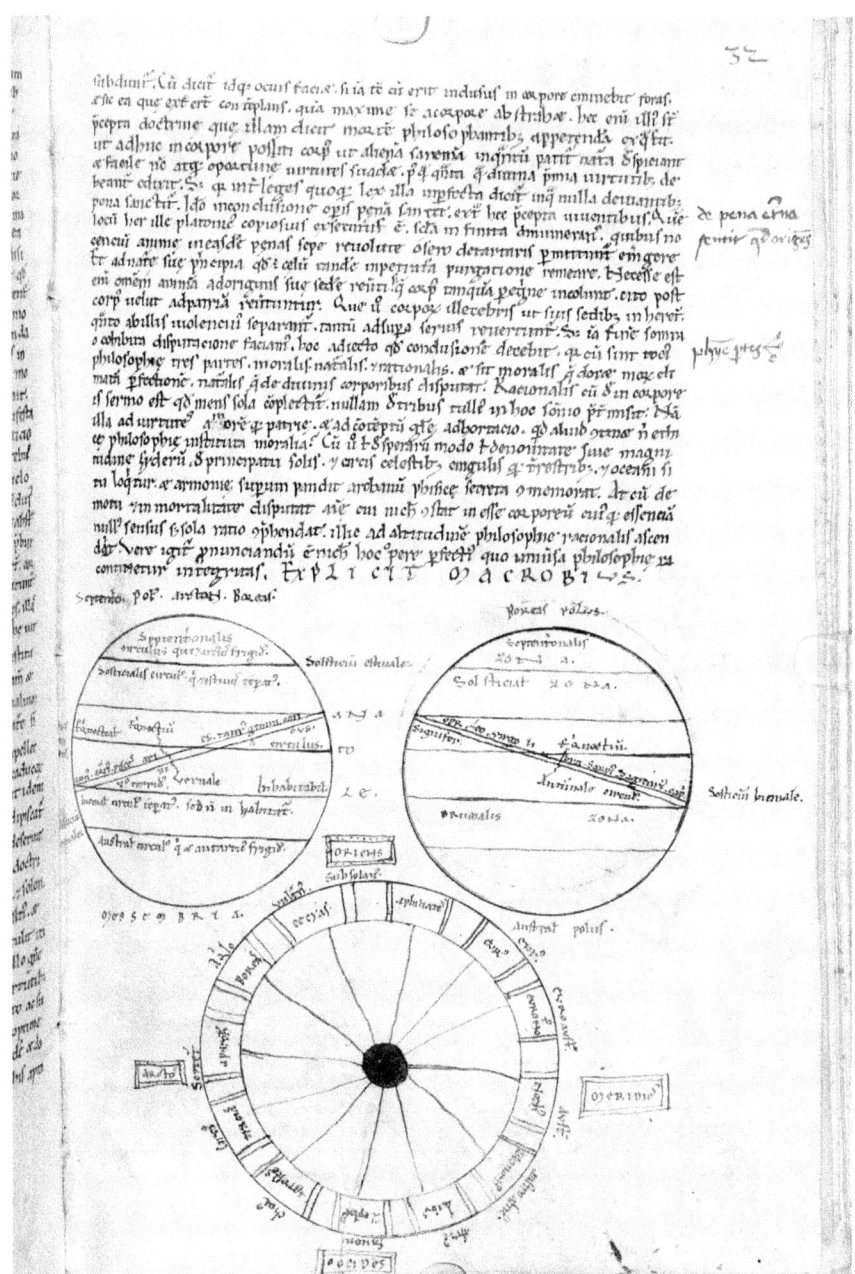

Figure 17.2. Macrobius, *Commentarius in Ciceronis Somnium Scipionis*. Collection of diagrams including *globus terre* and zonal diagrams, and a world map, copied at Tegernsee, thirteenth century. Munich, Bayerische Staatsbibliothek Clm 18208, f. 32r, published with permission.

at the far north and south; a hot (*torrida*) or "burnt up" (*perusta*) zone in the center, containing an equatorial ocean; and two temperate zones, one in the north and one in the south (Figure 17.3). This map forms an integral part of a large number of extant manuscripts of Macrobius's *Commentarius*; at a rough estimate, there are around 150 copies of the image dating from the tenth to the fifteenth centuries. It therefore must be regarded as one of the most widespread and—within learned circles—familiar medieval images of the world. It represents a received tradition, certainly, but one that could be juxtaposed

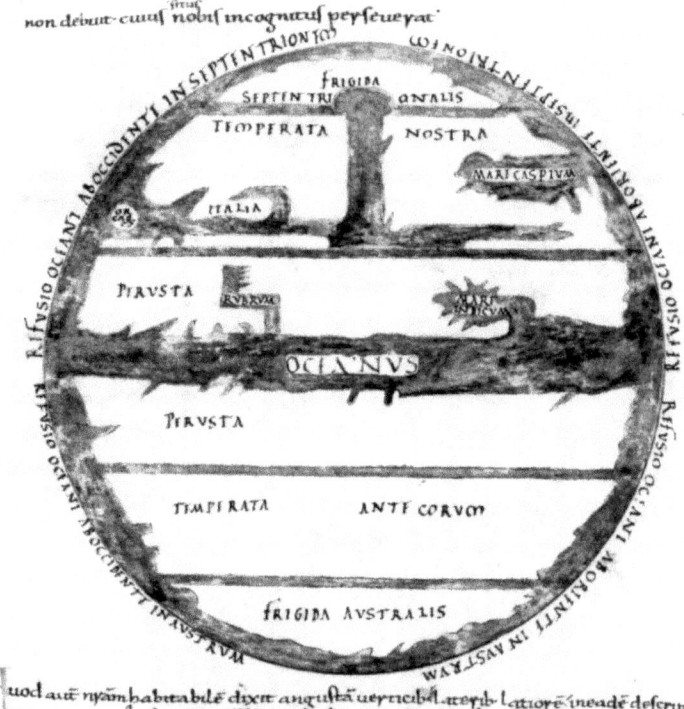

Figure 17.3. Macrobius, *Commentarius in Ciceronis Somnium Scipionis*. World map, tenth century, copied at the abbey of Saint Nazarius of Lorsch. Vatican City, Biblioteca Apostolica Vaticana, MS Palat. lat. 1341, f. 86v, published with permission.

provocatively against other received traditions, such as Augustine's denial of antipodal inhabitation. Above all, the map of Macrobius witnesses ongoing attempts to explain and represent the world in its entirety. This is a world that cannot be traversed, because of the extent of ocean and the extremes of heat and cold at its center and poles, but it is one that can be comprehended by means of the image.

Earth and Water

A central purpose of the map of Macrobius was to show how different parts of the world were conjoined through the operation of natural forces. A standard feature of the map is the presence of inscriptions around the image, indicating the flows (*refusiones*) of water from the equatorial ocean, continually burnt up by the sun's heat, and continually replenishing, to the North and South Poles. The image, in other words, is designed to show a global system of oceanic tides. On a limited number of copies of the map, the theory is expressed in the form of a longer text that appears within the equatorial ocean (Figure 17.4): "[This is] the equinoctial ocean, which flows in equal measure through the lower and upper parts of this [central] zone making the entire world into four islands, inaccessible to each other."[12] This depiction of water flows suggests another mode of global thinking, one not primarily concerned with human habitation, but rather with oceanic currents. To get some sense of the vitality of this way of conceiving the world during the height of popularity of Macrobius's *Commentarius* in the twelfth and thirteenth centuries, it is helpful to turn to the work of the philosopher William of Conches.

William of Conches was the product of the study of natural philosophy that flourished in the schools of the early twelfth century. The methods of that study included careful commentary on non-Christian texts: William's works include glosses on Plato's *Timaeus* and Macrobius's *Commentarius*, as well as Boethius's *De consolatione philosophiae*. In his *Philosophia* (ca. 1125–30), and its later redaction the *Dragmaticon philosophiae* (1144–49), William adapted Macrobius's distillation of Neoplatonic cosmology to provide an impressively supple discussion of the relationship between "our habitable" part of the world and peoples in other places. His discussion of the world is necessarily schematic, but at the same time keen to avoid rigidities; in this section of the *Philosophia* and later *Dragmaticon*, William thinks unambiguously in global terms. Water, he explains, moves across the equator and around the world. So too, as a consequence, do winds: Boreas, the north wind, arises from the clash of waters at the pole, and while it starts cold in the north, it has become hot by the time it passes through the torrid zone and reaches the Southern Hemisphere; the opposite process occurs for Auster,

Figure 17.4. Macrobius, *Commentarius in Ciceronis Somnium Scipionis*. World map, ca. 1100. London, British Library, Egerton MS 2976, f. 62v, published with permission.

the south wind.[13] Experience is different in different parts of the world. It is the condition of sphericity that while some have day, others have night; that certain stars are visible to one people, but not to another; and that while one set of peoples endures winter, another basks in summer.[14] The theory William discusses was not new, but it is one he needed to position in relation to his own time. The *Dragmaticon* is presented in the form of a dialogue between a *dux* (duke), an intellectually curious secular ruler, and his teacher, the *philosophus*. The former at times presents religious objections, at times acts as a disgruntled reader of classical literature, and occasionally voices some of the wilder theories of natural philosophy. At one point he requests that the philosopher prove that the earth is round; at another that it does not move.[15] Evidently, in the context of dialogue between pupil and master, the sphere is a concept that can be represented, shown in diagrammatic form, and subjected to various thought experiments. What would happen if a hole were drilled through the earth's surface from one end to the other, asks the duke, and a stone dropped into that hole? (The stone would descend to the middle of the earth and reside there, replies the philosopher.[16]) The *globus spericus* in this energetic theorization becomes an object of study. Graspable and external to the enquiring philosopher, its workings are open to question, debate, and inspection.

In the thirteenth and fourteenth centuries, new theories about the relationship between land and water were disseminated widely within scholarly circles. Under the influence of Aristotle's works of natural history, particularly his *De caelo*, the proposition arose that the extent of land on the earth might be restricted to the known world. According to the Aristotelian theory of elements, since earth was heavier than water, it followed that the sea should cover the land.[17] How to explain the presence of any exposed land was therefore a serious problem for scholastic natural science in the later Middle Ages, and a staple of debate at the University of Paris and other *studia*. Were there two separate centers of gravity for the earth and for water, allowing a small portion of earth to protrude? Did water exist in the inner parts of the earth (*in visceribus terrae*), mixing with air through evaporation, with the result that the size of the earth exceeded the volume of water?[18] These topics continued to possess an intimate connection with the question of habitation, since on their answer depended the fate of the antipodes. Was there, in the end, any land to inhabit (land, that is, uncovered by water) in the regions of the world beyond Europe, Asia, and Africa?[19]

Such questions were, at one level, wholly abstract. At another, though, they were related to practical questions of travel, and even political expansion. In the thirteenth century both Albertus Magnus and Roger Bacon urged the possibility of exploration beyond the equator.[20] Their certainty that such exploration was possible arose directly from a second key contribution of Aristotelian science, as mediated through Arabic texts: the dismantling of the notion of an impassable torrid zone at the equator. The revised theory, as conveyed by Avicenna, among others, held that equatorial regions were the most temperate on earth.[21] Rather than zonal division, an alternative mode of cartographic depiction showed the known world divided into *climata*, beginning with the equator, at the center of which could be found the hypothetical city of Arīn (the *Aren ciuitas* on John of Wallingford's map).

Rigid models of scientific progress, in which one theory categorically replaces another, seem particularly unhelpful in assessing these understandings of the world. A more accurate account of intellectual history would allow for the coexistence of contradictory theories and images of the world, not necessarily in states of mutual antagonism. Thus, the theory of zonal division with its equatorial torrid zone persisted into the sixteenth century, while at the same time the division of *climata* from the equator through the Northern

Hemisphere, with neither torrid nor frigid zones, gained currency in learned circles. Nor were such revisions of the image of the world restricted to a scholarly elite. Fantasies of circumnavigation arose, long before the achievement of such feats was possible. In the 1240s the popular cosmographical treatise *L'image du monde* by Gossouin of Metz included a description of two men who start at the same point on the globe, walk in opposite directions "as a fly would walk around a round apple" (*comme une mouche iroit entour une pomme reonde*), and meet on the opposite side of the earth.[22] A similar scenario in Nicolas Oresme's fourteenth-century scientific textbook, *Le livre du ciel et du monde*, where the walker begins and ends in Rouen, was the source for the account in John Mandeville's *Livre des merveilles du monde* of a young man who sets off for India and eventually reaches an island where his own language is spoken.[23]

As the preceding discussion should indicate, there was not a single medieval "view of the world." Old authorities remained potent, but the old authorities actually provided multiple points of view with regard to the relationship between known and unknown parts of the world, and between land and sea. Within the field of natural science, the globe was subject to debate and imagination. Possessed of an intellectual function, it could be traversed in the mind, even if—as it had been for Cicero's Scipio—it remained a symbol of the restraint, rather than the full expression, of political ambition.

Ages of the Globe

The earliest surviving terrestrial globe is the so-called *Erdapfel* (lit. "earth apple"), completed by the Nuremburg cosmographer Martin Behaim in 1492 (Figure 17.5). It is a spectacular specimen, colorful, filled with pictorial representations of peoples, ships, and marine life, and with a vast amount of text.[24] Its propitious date gives Behaim's globe a curiously ambivalent status. An embodiment of the plenitude of geographical knowledge available in Europe by the end of the fifteenth century, it is at the same time an image of the world about to be radically revised by the discovery of the Americas. The survival of this artifact, while of great significance for a proper understanding of spatial representation at the end of the fifteenth century, has had the less happy consequence of obscuring a longer history of the representation of the world on globes.[25] There is evidence to suggest that Behaim's *Erdapfel* stands not at the beginning but rather in the midst of a tradition of crafting terrestrial globes. Prior to the fifteenth century, references to such objects are rare and tantalizing, but they nevertheless allow a glimpse of an often unremarked aspect of medieval cosmography, one of some importance for an appreciation of the history of global thinking.

Figure 17.5. Martin Behaim, *Erdapfel* (1492). Germanisches Nationalmuseum, Nuremburg, published with permission.

In an early eleventh-century German commentary on Boethius's *De consolatione philosophiae* produced in the monastery of St. Gall, one of the monks, Notker (ca. 950–1022), devoted a lengthy note to the size and inhabitation of the earth. He explained the division of the earth into zones, their correspondence to the zones of the celestial spheres, and the extent of the known world as far as the northernmost island of Thule. These aspects of the earth's shape could be understood, Notker went on, by looking at the globe (*spera*) that was recently made at St. Gall under Abbot Purchart, a statement that helps to date the globe to Purchart's abbacy from 1001 to 1022.[26] When placed so that the North Pole was viewed from above, the six zodiacal signs of the north became visible, but the six of the south were hidden. Notker also commented that from the globe the positions of all peoples could be observed, making it possible to understand Boethius's reference to the known part of the world as a "fourth portion" of the earth.[27] This *spera* has in the past been understood to have been a celestial globe (that is, a globe of the heavens), an identification supported by Notker's description of the position of the signs of the zodiac. On the other hand, the reference to the position of peoples suggests a terrestrial globe. Moreover, the passage of Boethius's *De consolatione* on which Notker was commenting describes the limited extent of the known world, a topic more likely to call for a globe showing the earth rather than the skies.[28] The question cannot, perhaps, be resolved conclusively, but Notker's reference to the globe in terms of zodiacal signs and population certainly suggests the possibility of complementary relationships between terrestrial and celestial globes,[29] the latter of which are known to have existed since at least the tenth century. It also provides an insight into how a globe could be handled by the intellectually curious, or by a teacher (Notker himself was a *magister*) instructing his students within the monastery.

A little over a century later, an important early translator of Arabic scientific texts into Latin, Hermann of Carinthia, devoted an extensive passage in his treatise *De essentiis* to describing a series of calculations of the earth's surface that could—in his opinion—only usefully be conducted by using a globe (*globulus spericus*). Hermann instructs his readers to construct such a globe since his argument cannot be shown on a plane surface (*in plano*). It is not known whether Hermann or his readers actually did make a globe, but the passage at least affirms the currency of the concept. The primary purpose of the globe in this instance was not to show places or peoples, or even the coastal outline of the known world. Instead, it facilitated measurement, and the calculation of the portion of the globe occupied by the known parts of the world: Europe, Asia, and Africa.[30]

The contexts in which these two references to globes occur are telling. The artifacts are invoked for educational purposes, perhaps to function alongside celestial globes. To that pedagogical tradition of making and discussing globes should be added the widespread medieval iconography in which a sphere, marked with the three parts of the world, was shown in the hands of a secular ruler. This deployment of the world image to indicate temporal power was the secular counterpart of representations in which Christ was shown embracing, encompassing, or holding a world image, as a sign of salvation (Figure 17.6).[31]

Middle Age of the Globe • 267

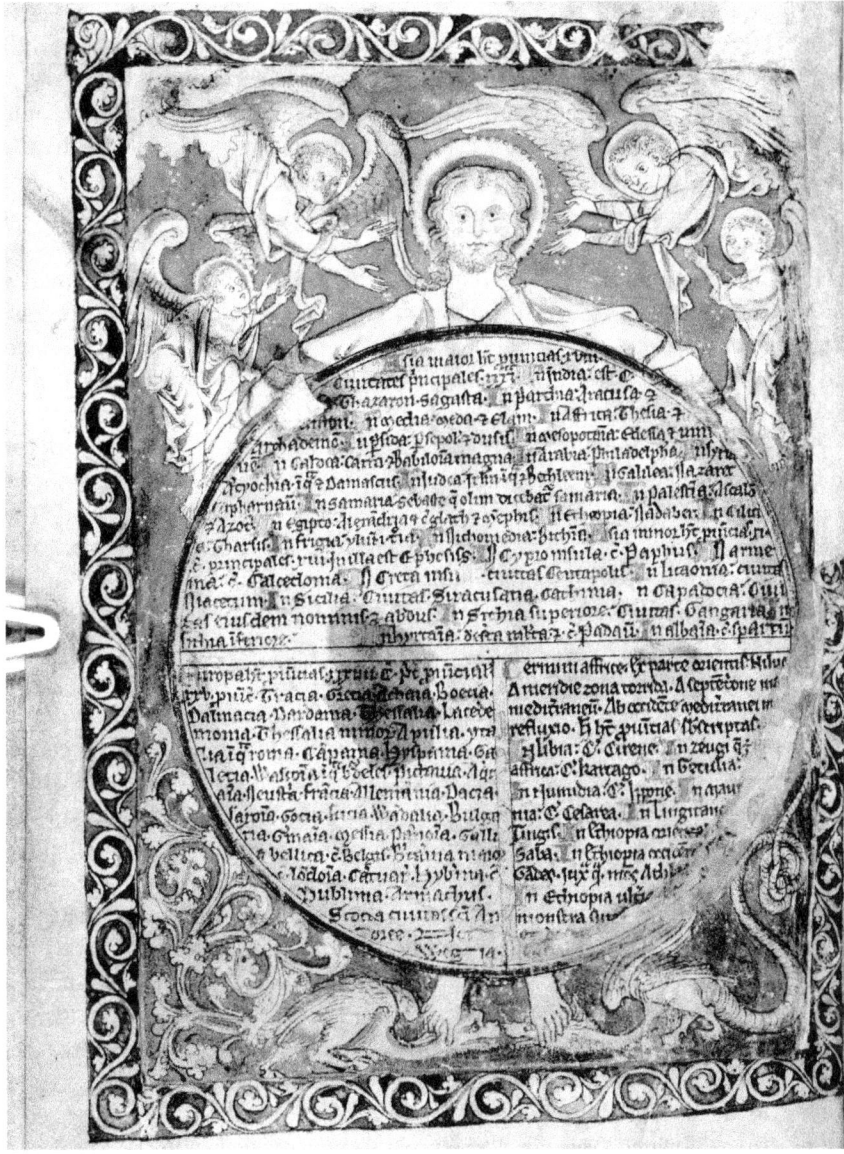

Figure 17.6. The Psalter map, ca. 1260. London, British Library, Additional MS 28681, f. 9v, published with permission.

Within these pedagogical and ideological functions, a fine balance might be perceived between self-knowledge and self-aggrandizement; between the globe as sign of possession, and as sign of absence, in the form of the portions of the world unknown to European power.

This question of the unknown, and the expansion of the known, was critical to the development of the globe as a material object in the fifteenth century. Several factors, including the rediscovery of classical texts and the effects of travel and exploration, worked to extend the known world some considerable distance beyond the limits traditionally ascribed to it. In the east, sources such as Marco Polo and the Venetian traveler Niccolò de' Conti provided a much fuller picture of the world, including details of Southeast Asia beneath the equator.[32] Portuguese exploration of the west coast of Africa and particularly of the Atlantic during the fifteenth century similarly expanded the world image to the south and west, while in the north, cartographers were able to supply details of Scandinavia and Russia unknown to their classical sources. These sources now included Claudius Ptolemy's second-century AD *Geographia*, which was translated from Greek to Latin in the first decade of the fifteenth century, contributing both the framework for a mathematically-based cartography, and—of more immediate interest for its humanist readers—a particularly valuable source of ancient toponyms.[33] The known world, in other words, was starting to expand beyond classical and medieval frames of representation, and one response to this revised image of the world may have been the development of globes. There is convincing, if indirect evidence for at least two terrestrial globes from the first half of the fifteenth century, neither of which has survived. The earliest of these globes was made by the French doctor and instrument maker Jean Fusoris, to accompany a treatise on the sphere he wrote in 1432. In this treatise, Fusoris refers to a *boule ronde*, which he states he has made himself and which he invokes to explain certain principles regarding the size and shape of the earth.[34] Just a few years later, between 1440 and 1444, another terrestrial globe was constructed for Philip the Good, duke of Burgundy, and it was apparently still in the duke's possession at his death in 1467.[35] Yet another plausible reference to terrestrial globes appears in a south German manuscript of the mid fifteenth century, like the preceding two instances intimately connected with the reception of Ptolemy's *Geographia*.[36] These records suggest that while terrestrial globes might be crafted in order to accompany a scientific treatise, increasingly in the fifteenth century they were commissioned to function as prized artifacts owned by a powerful patron, such as a duke, a king, or even a pope. The renowned German cartographer Nicolaus Germanus is known to have made a pair of globes, one terrestrial and one celestial, for the Vatican in 1477.

There was, in short, nothing new about the idea of the globe in 1492. As a symbol of power, of disdain for power, of divine wisdom, and as a material object, it was part of a system of understanding the world. It was a symbol and a system always subject to debate, and here it seems important to note the often unremarked significance of intellectual interests and controversies in changing perceptions of the globe. From these debates about the relationship between land, water, and wind and about the human habitation of the earth, navigators, politicians, artists, and writers of fiction took their cue. It may also be the case, however, that in the fifteenth century we witness an important spark in which interest in the globe, which can be traced from classical antiquity through the Middle Ages and into modernity, took a new turn, in which the *globus spericus* began to move from the university hall or monk's notebook into the chambers of powerful men, and from there, eventually, into ordinary homes as a point of reference at once graspable, comprehensible, and familiar.

The preceding discussion might strike a reader as a doggedly literalist approach to the question of how the world was conceptualized in the European Middle Ages. Preoccupied with maps and globes, I have allowed little or no space for non-material understandings of the physical world. Nor—it might be added—have I even begun to consider the existence of religious conceptions of the world that necessarily interact with, but always aim to transcend, mundane space. "The founding event of the modern age is the conquest of the world as picture," asserted Heidegger, and as he made clear, he was not thinking of a picture of the world but "the world comprehended as picture" (*nicht ein Bild von der Welt, sondern die Welt als Bild begriffen*).[37] To insist that there were pictures of the world in the Middle Ages is therefore to miss his point (after all, he said nothing about maps), and perhaps to miss the points of many others who have posited similarly decisive breaks between modernity (*Neuzeit*) and previous ages.[38] It is the *Welt/Lebensanschauung* that is in question, and that for Heidegger marked an unbridgeable separation between the new time and the old. And yet literalism may not be quite the inappropriate response it first seems. From where, after all, do these pictures of the world emerge, if not from a capacity to comprehend the world as picture? Did the medieval European who imagined himself standing foot to foot with a hypothetical antipodean not view the picture at once from outside and from within? Is it so "impossible" that he conceived the world as an object and himself (and the antipodean) as subject, in the manner apparently only realized in modernity?[39] These questions are not intended to deny change, or to doubt its profundity, but to propose a narrative without bombast (and without the vestiges of a fatalistic Romanticism), in which the possession of terms such as "subject," "world picture," "new," or "global" does not reside exclusively in a particular age. A multiplicity of images emerges from an examination of the representation of the world in the Middle Ages; numerous ways of defining the space of the world, open to interpretation and adaptation. In comparison, it is certain modern conceptions of the globe, and the global, that begin to look fixed, static, and homogenizing.

Alfred Hiatt is a reader in Medieval English Literature at Queen Mary, University of London. He is the author of *The Making of Medieval Forgeries: False Documents in Fifteenth-Century England* (British Library, 2004) and *Terra Incognita: Mapping the Antipodes before 1600* (British Library, 2008). He has longstanding interests in spatial representation, the medieval reception of classical texts, and early humanism; he is currently editing a multi-authored volume on *Cartography between Europe and the Islamic World 1100–1500*.

NOTES

1. All translations are my own, unless otherwise stated.
2. For further discussions of the globe, see in particular the chapters by Stefan Willer, Jeppe Strandsbjerg, Kari van Dijk, Helge Jordheim, Siv Frøydis Berg, and Espen Ytreberg in this volume.
3. For further discussions of education and didactics, see in particular the chapter by Claudia Lenz in this volume.
4. Isidore of Seville, *Etymologiarum sive originum libri XX*, ed. W. M. Lindsay (Oxford, 1911), 11.3.24–25; Augustine, *De civitate dei*, ed. B. Dombart and A. Kalb, 2 vols (Turnhout, 1955), 16.9.
5. Geminus, *Introduction aux phénomènes*, ed. Germaine Aujac (Paris, 1975), 16.1; Cleomedes, *Caelestia (ΜΕΤΕΩΡΑ)*, ed. Robert Todd (Leipzig, 1990), 1.1.215–28.
6. Peter Martyr, *Selections from Peter Martyr*, ed. and trans. Geoffrey Eatough (Turnhout, 1998), 498.
7. For further discussions of religion, see in particular the chapters by Nora Eggen, Oddbjørn Leirvik, Chenxi Tang, Kyrre Kverndokk, Erling Sandmo, and Kari van Dijk in this volume.
8. Lactantius, *Divinae Institutiones*, 3.23, in *Opera omnia*, ed. Samuel Brandt and Georg Laubmann (Vienna, 1890).
9. Augustine, *De civitate dei*, 16.9.
10. Macrobius, *Commentarii in Somnium Scipionis*, ed. James A. Willis (Leipzig, 1963), book 2.
11. Alfred Hiatt, "The Map of Macrobius before 1100," *Imago Mundi* 59 (2007): 149–76.
12. British Library, MS Egerton 2976, f. 62v: *Occeanus equinoctialis qui se per inferiores et superiores partes huius zone equaliter diffundit faciens iiii insulas ex toto orbe terrarum inaccessibiles sibi*.
13. William of Conches, *Philosophia*, ed. and trans. Gregor Maurach (Pretoria, 1980), 3.10–11; William of Conches, *Dragmaticon philosophiae*, ed. Italo Ronca (Turnhout, 1997), 5.9.
14. William of Conches, *Philosophia*, 4.2–3; *Dragmaticon*, 6.3–5.
15. William of Conches, *Dragmaticon*, 6.2.2, 2.6.7.
16. Ibid., 2.6.10.
17. Aristotle, *De caelo (On the Heavens)*, trans. W. K. C. Guthrie (London, 1939), 2.4 [287a–b].

18. John Buridan, *Expositio et quaestiones in Aristotelis De caelo*, ed. Benoît Patar (Louvain, 1996), 410–17; Albert of Saxony, *Quaestiones in Aristotelis De caelo*, ed. Benoît Patar (Louvain, 2008), 437–47.
19. Buridan, *Expositio et quaestiones*, 414; Albert of Saxony, *Quaestiones*, 445.
20. Albertus Magnus, *Opera omnia*, vol. 2, *De natura loci*, ed. Paul Hossfield (Aschendorf, 1980), 1.7; Roger Bacon, *The "Opus maius" of Roger Bacon*, ed. John Henry Bridges (Oxford, 1897), 1.301–5.
21. Avicenna, *A Treatise on The Canon of Medicine of Avicenna Incorporating a Translation of the First Book*, trans. O. Cameron Gruner (London, 1930), 61.
22. Gossouin of Metz, *L'image du monde de Maitre Gossouin*, ed. Oliver H. Prior (Lausanne, 1913), 93.
23. Nicolas Oresme, *Le livre du ciel et du monde*, ed. Albert D. Menut and Alexander J. Denomy, trans. Albert D. Menut (Madison, 1968), 576–77; John Mandeville, *Mandeville's Travels: Texts and Translations*, ed. Malcolm Letts (London, 1953), 2.333.
24. E. G. Ravenstein, *Martin Behaim: His Life and His Globe* (London, 1908).
25. Patrick Gautier Dalché, "Avant Behaim: Les globes terrestres au XVe siècle," *Médiévales* 58 (2010): 43–61.
26. Notker the German, *Boethius: De consolatione philosophiae*, ed. Petrus W. Tax (Tübingen, 1986–2009), 1.97.
27. Ibid.
28. Ibid., 2.7 (*prosa*).
29. Christine Hehle, *Boethius in St. Gallen: Die Bearbeitung der "Consolatio philosophiae" durch Notker Teutonicus zwischen Tradition und Innovation* (Tübingen, 2002); *au contraire* Gautier Dalché, "Avant Behaim," 47–48.
30. Hermann of Carinthia, *De essentiis*, ed. and trans. Charles Burnett (Leiden, 1982), 216–17.
31. Danielle Lecoq, "Image du pouvoir: Globe céleste ou globe terrestre de l'Antiquité au Moyen Âge," in *Le globe et son image*, ed. Catherine Hofmann et al. (Paris, 1995), 7–29.
32. Angelo Cattaneo, *Fra Mauro's Mappa Mundi and Fifteenth-Century Venice* (Turnhout, 2011), 188–225.
33. Patrick Gautier Dalché, *La géographie de Ptolémée en Occident (IVe–XVIe siècle)* (Turnhout, 2009).
34. Patrick Gautier Dalché, "Jean Fusoris et la géographie: Un astronome, auteur d'un globe terrestre, à la découverte de Ptolémée," in *Humanisme et culture géographique à l'époque du concile de Constance: Autour de Guillaume Fillastre*, ed. Didier Marcotte (Turnhout, 2002), 161–75.
35. Jacques Paviot, "La mappemonde attribuée à Jan van Eyck par Fàcio: Une pièce à retirer du catalogue de son œuvre," *Revue des Archéologues et Historiens d'art de Louvain* 24 (1991): 57–62.
36. Gautier Dalché, "Avant Behaim," 52–53.
37. Martin Heidegger, "Die Zeit des Weltbildes," in *Gesamtausgabe*, vol. 5, *Holzwege*, ed. Friedrich-Wilhelm von Herrmann (Frankfurt am Main, 1977), 94, 89.

38. Paul Zumthor, *La mesure du monde: Représentation de l'espace au Moyen Âge* (Paris, 1993), 51.
39. Heidegger, "Die Zeit des Weltbildes," 89–90.

BIBLIOGRAPHY

Albert of Saxony. *Quaestiones in Aristotelis De caelo*. Edited by Benoît Patar. Louvain: Peeters, 2008.
Albertus Magnus. *Opera omnia*. Vol. 2, *De natura loci*. Edited by Paul Hossfield. Aschendorf: Monasterii Westfalorum, 1980.
Aristotle. *De caelo (On the Heavens)*. Translated by W. K. C. Guthrie. London: Heinemann, 1939.
Augustine. *De civitate dei*. Edited by B. Dombart and A. Kalb. 2 vols. Corpus Christianorum, Series Latina 47-48. Turnhout: Brepols, 1955.
Avicenna. *A Treatise on The Canon of Medicine of Avicenna Incorporating a Translation of the First Book*. Translated by O. Cameron Gruner. London: Luzac, 1930.
Bacon, Roger. *The "Opus maius" of Roger Bacon*. Edited by John Henry Bridges. 2 vols. Oxford: Clarendon Press, 1897.
Buridan, John. *Expositio et quaestiones in Aristotelis De caelo*. Edited by Benoît Patar. Louvain: Peeters, 1996.
Cattaneo, Angelo. *Fra Mauro's Mappa Mundi and Fifteenth-Century Venice*. Turnhout: Brepols, 2011.
Cicero. *De re publica*. Edited by K. Ziegler. Leipzig: Teubner, 1964.
Cleomedes. *Caelestia (ΜΕΤΕΩΡΑ)*. Edited by Robert Todd. Leipzig: Teubner, 1990.
Gautier Dalché, Patrick. "Avant Behaim: Les globes terrestres au XVe siècle." *Médiévales* 58 (2010): 43–61.
_____. *La géographie de Ptolémée en Occident (IVe–XVIe siècle)*. Turnhout: Brepols, 2009.
_____. "Jean Fusoris et la géographie: Un astronome, auteur d'un globe terrestre, à la découverte de Ptolémée." In *Humanisme et culture géographique à l'époque du concile de Constance: Autour de Guillaume Fillastre*, edited by Didier Marcotte, 161–75. Turnhout: Brepols, 2002.
Geminus. *Introduction aux phénomènes*. Edited by Germaine Aujac. Paris: Les Belles Lettres, 1975.
Gossouin of Metz. *L'image du monde de Maitre Gossouin*. Edited by Oliver H. Prior. Lausanne: Librairie Payot, 1913.
Hehle, Christine. *Boethius in St. Gallen: Die Bearbeitung der "Consolatio philosophiae" durch Notker Teutonicus zwischen Tradition und Innovation*. Tübingen: Max Niemeyer Verlag, 2002.
Heidegger, Martin. "The Age of the World Picture." In *The Question Concerning Technology and Other Essays*, translated by William Lovitt, 115–54. New York: Garland, 1977.
_____. "Die Zeit des Weltbildes." In *Gesamtausgabe*, vol. 5, *Holzwege*, edited by Friedrich-Wilhelm von Herrmann, 75–113. Frankfurt am Main: Vittorio Klostermann, 1977.

Hermann of Carinthia. *De essentiis*. Edited and translated by Charles Burnett. Leiden: Brill, 1982.
Hiatt, Alfred. "The Map of Macrobius before 1100." *Imago Mundi* 59 (2007): 149–76.
Isidore of Seville. *Etymologiarum sive originum libri XX*. Edited by W. M. Lindsay. 2 vols. Oxford: Clarendon Press, 1911.
Lactantius. *Opera omnia*. Edited by Samuel Brandt and Georg Laubmann. 2 vols. Vienna: Bibliopola Academiae Litterarum Caesareae Vindobonensis, 1890.
Lecoq, Danielle. "Image du pouvoir: Globe céleste ou globe terrestre de l'Antiquité au Moyen Âge." In *Le globe et son image*, edited by Catherine Hofmann, Danielle Lecoq, Ève Netchine, and Monique Pelletier, 7–29. Paris: Bibliothèque nationale de France, 1995.
Macrobius. *Commentarii in Somnium Scipionis*. Edited by James A. Willis. Leipzig: Teubner, 1963.
Mandeville, John. *Mandeville's Travels: Texts and Translations*. Edited by Malcolm Letts. 2 vols. London: Hakluyt Society, 1953.
Notker the German. *Boethius: De consolatione philosophiae*. Edited by Petrus W. Tax. 3 vols. Tübingen: Max Niemeyer Verlag, 1986–2009.
Oresme, Nicolas. *Le livre du ciel et du monde*. Edited by Albert D. Menut and Alexander J. Denomy, translated by Albert D. Menut. Madison: University of Wisconsin Press, 1968.
Paviot, Jacques. "La mappemonde attribuée à Jan van Eyck par Fàcio: Une pièce à retirer du catalogue de son œuvre." *Revue des Archéologues et Historiens d'art de Louvain* 24 (1991): 57–62.
Peter Martyr. *Selections from Peter Martyr*. Repertorium Columbianum 5, edited and translated by Geoffrey Eatough. Turnhout: Brepols, 1998.
Ravenstein, E. G. *Martin Behaim: His Life and His Globe*. London: Philip, 1908.
William of Conches. *Dragmaticon philosophiae*. Edited by Italo Ronca. Turnhout: Brepols, 1997.
———. *Philosophia*. Edited and translated by Gregor Maurach. Pretoria: University of South Africa, 1980.
Zumthor, Paul. *La mesure du monde: Représentation de l'espace au Moyen Âge*. Paris: Seuil, 1993.

▶• 18 •◀

The Champion of the North

World Time in Olaus Magnus's *Carta marina*

Erling Sandmo

The world maps left to us from medieval Western Europe, the *mappaemundi*, are strangers to our time. It is their conception of time that gives them their strangeness. They are not projections of geographical space in our sense, but images of a world where space and time converge. The most famous example is the Hereford *mappa mundi* from Hereford, England, made around 1300 and still located in the cathedral there. These singular, mounted maps contain themselves. This simple fact opens the historical difference between medieval and present cartography. Portability is a defining trait of the modern map; it is made for movement. The Hereford map is made for contemplation, for immersion in a world where time and space are one.

The unity of space and time is most conspicuous in the case of the Holy Land, which—to us—is wildly out of proportion in the Hereford *mappa mundi*, taking up 30–40 percent of the surface of the depicted globe. It has been claimed that the space allotted to the world of the Bible was determined by the number of images and texts that fill it, but the idea that its proportions are adjusted in order to accommodate history seems to miss the basic point: the extension of the Holy Land is temporal as much as "purely" spatial.[1]

The other elements of the Hereford *mappa mundi* are ordered according to their distance from Jerusalem. The map is encyclopedic: the entire space of the world is filled with visual and textual information on natural history, mythology, anthropology, and current issues, from the terror of the Mongols to the splendor of the university in Paris. It is also a depiction of the physical world with mountains, rivers, islands, and oceans—although it is first and foremost a map of the terrestrial world surrounding the Mediterranean.

The proportions of the Hereford *mappa mundi* are relative to its spiritual and historical center, Jerusalem. A century later, European cartography was transformed by the reinvention of the Greek geographer Ptolemy and his work on the projection of the globe. This new cartography was based on the principle that the world could be represented in purely spatial terms. Space and time became distinct dimensions of the world, with geography and history destined to become the respective ways of studying and ordering them. Time was banished from the map. Where did it go?

Olaus Magnus and the Displacement of Time

This chapter is a case study in the cartographic representation of time after the Ptolemaic turn. My case is the extant works of the Swedish bishop and humanist Olaus Magnus (1490–1557). The first was the *Carta marina*, a map of present-day Scandinavia and the North Sea region published in Venice in 1539. The map includes a short text in Latin that was expanded in an explanatory booklet, the *Opera breve*, published both in German and Italian.[2] Olaus's ultimate work was the *Historia de gentibus septentrionalibus*, "History of the Northern Peoples," published in Rome in 1555 and illustrated partly with coarse reproductions of the images from the map.[3]

The detailed and exact map was a major event in the history of the cartography of Northwestern Europe. Still, Olaus kept the encyclopedic aspirations of the *mappaemundi* alive. The *Carta marina*, like the Hereford map, presents a wealth of information on natural history, daily life, political conflicts, history, and, above all, religion. The map had a message, and the message was vehemently anti-Lutheran.[4]

Olaus was a priest who made his career under the new Swedish king, Gustav Vasa. Gustav had led a rebellion against Christian II, king of Denmark-Norway and Sweden, in the wake of the so-called Stockholm Bloodbath, Christian's massacre of his opponents among the Swedish elite. The rebellion led to the fall of Christian and to the dissolution of the Nordic union. Gustav proved to be an able king, but his relationship with the church was uneasy. The archbishop, Gustav Trolle, was widely seen as Christian's co-conspirator and responsible for the massacre.

In 1523, Olaus traveled to Rome to lobby for the appointment of his brother Johannes as a new archbishop. The mission was a spectacular failure. First, the pope, Clement VII, was not willing to dismiss Gustav Trolle, and second, it became clear that the new Swedish regime was going Lutheran.

Olaus never returned to Sweden. His brother joined him in Danzig (Gdansk), where they lived for almost ten years under the protection of the city council during a period of intense and violent conflict between Lutherans and Catholics.[5] From there, the brothers traveled to Italy, where Johannes was eventually appointed nominal archbishop of Sweden. After his death, Olaus took over the title and became the last Swedish Catholic archbishop for almost four hundred years. In 1554 he also published Johannes's *Gothorum Sveonumque historia*, a history of the Swedish Goths.

This is the immediate religio-political context of the *Carta marina*. The map displays Scandinavia as a battlefield in the war between the true church (i.e., the Roman Catholic Church) and emerging Lutheranism—at a time when it was still feasible that these states could be saved. All the states are supplied with stylized portraits of their kings, each equipped with a suitable verse from the Bible. The faithful are praised while the others are chastised, warned, or encouraged. This network of kings, then, may be said to constitute not only the imbedded politics of the map, but a temporal dimension. It is a level of biblical allegory, where the politics of contemporary Northern Europe is seen as a reflection of the landscape of the Bible, that which had been the very surface of the medieval *mappaemundi*.

This temporal and religious landscape emerges on the *Carta marina* in different ways and places. The most striking example is the North Sea. The ocean was a new space in Ptolemaic cartography, present by a necessity that had not been there for the makers of the *mappaemundi*. Water was empty, eventless, void—and a space for new kinds of signification. Olaus's North Sea is populated by spectacular monsters gathered from classical natural history, local knowledge, and religious propaganda, juxtaposing different embodied temporalities.[6] The juxtaposition transformed the North Sea into a condensed world, a space where monsters signifying Roman antiquity surfaced between creatures from medieval travel accounts, contemporary religious propaganda, and local wildlife. The map would also align the North Sea region with the Americas, the newly discovered world that was constantly being mapped and remapped for a wide European audience. Olaus was picturing the North as a part of the world in an age of discovery, but he was also inscribing the world in the North. This was achieved not least by juxtaposing different times in the same space.

The *Carta marina* was an attempt to establish the Northern countries and the North Sea as an object of knowledge by means of analogy. The analogy between the North and the New World lies in the abundance of strange natural phenomena, the images of savages and heathens, and the common appeal to wonder. The presence of scenes and creatures known from classical natural history ties the North Sea to the Mediterranean and to the classical heritage that was so fundamental to Renaissance culture.

Embodying Time: Starkater and the Lion

The sea may be the most obvious place to look for Olaus Magnus's world time, but I will spend the remainder of this chapter on time ashore, in the far North,

Figure 18.1. "Starkater, Swedish champion." Detail from Olaus Magnus's *Carta marina* (1539). Courtesy of Uppsala University Library. http://art.alvin-portal.org/alvin/view.jsf?file=6964.

in the land of the heathen Lapps or Sami. At the very top of the *Carta marina*, we see a large, bearded man carrying two stone tablets. He is obviously Moses, bringing God's Law to the people. However, he is not Moses, or not quite. He is *Starcaterus pugil Sueticus*, "Starkater, Swedish champion." The legend adds only that he was "once famous in all Europe."[7] The Italian *Opera breve* notes that he carries two tablets inscribed with Gothic letters, and the German version specifies that they were "inscribed with Gothic letters many centuries ago, to commemorate that many bellicose and valiant men had lived in his country."[8]

Olaus's acquisition of Starkater as a Swedish hero was a bold move. The mythical Starkater is one of the most spectacular figures of the *Gesta Danorum* (*The History of the Danes*) written by Saxo Grammaticus early in the thirteenth century. He is there a Danish Hercules rather than a Danish Moses, an invincible warrior, blessed with a poetic gift and magical invincibility, cursed with an uncontrollable fury and the inability to be a member of human society.[9] Olaus was obviously taken with Saxo's story but did not feel the obligation to respect Starkater's historical nationality. He simply transferred Starkater to Sweden and gave him a major part in his own account of the history of his own people.[10] The *Historia*, however, does not see Starkater in the religious light that radiates from the map.

There are no Israelites on Olaus's map. Starkater, carrying both the law and a huge sword, is moving toward the Sami, who are performing two different heathen rituals: a wedding ceremony and the worship of a red flag or a banner—the equivalent of the golden calf. Olaus describes both rituals in the later *History*.

At least three levels of time merge in the far North: the biblical time of the Old Testament, embodied by Moses; the time of ancient Nordic history, embodied by Starkater; and, finally, the more or less present time of the heathen Sami as discovered by the Christian Swedes. The confrontation between Starkater and the Sami is clearly religious, with Starkater carrying the representation of true faith, the law. However, this law is very different from the one Moses originally brought down from Mount Sinai. The runic inscription simply identifies Starkater himself: *Starcaterus pugil Sueticus*. His name is the law, the divine message to the Sami—who, being about to receive it, show themselves to be the Israelites in the desert, a chosen people who have been led astray but who will, eventually, return to their path.

The Israelites of the Old Testament were able to continue because God's commandments were their guiding light and the sign of their common calling and identity. Starkater's name would give the Sami a common past and a common future. The Sami need to recognize that they were destined to be part of Swedish history, to join in the cause embodied by its champion: to restore the true church.

Starkater does not walk alone. At his feet stands a snarling animal with one clawed front paw raised. The Latin legend tells us nothing about what kind of beast we are dealing with, but the German *Opera breve* adds that "under derysen ist gezaigt ain thier hayst grymklau genant ist in seyner griefs als ain uuolff und ist stets zorni," that is, it is an animal called *grymklau*—"grim claw"—which is the size of a wolf and always angry. The Italian version, too, identifies this as a *Grun Klo*, but compares it to a bear or a lion, not to a wolf. Olaus makes no mention at all of the animal in the *Historia*, but it re-emerges in the first volume of Conrad Gesner's *Historia animalium* (1551), where the image is obviously derived from the *Carta marina* and the text from the *Opera breve*.[11] Gesner classifies the animal as a *lupus scythicus*, a Scythian wolf; the German translation (1563) retains the name *grimmklauw*. In any case, the animal does not seem to have been conceived by Olaus as a *grymklau* or indeed named by him at all, but added to the *Opera breve* by his unfortunately unknown agents.[12] This fact makes it tempting to ask if Olaus was not imagining and imaging something well beyond the natural history embodied in the *grymklau*. The animal certainly looks more like a lion than anything else, and my proposition would be that this is the Lion of the North, prophesied by Jeremiah:

> Set up the standard toward Zion: retire, stay not: for I will bring evil from the north, and a great destruction. The lion is to come up from his thicket, and the destroyer of the Gentiles is on his way; he is gone forth from his place to make thy land desolate; and thy cities shall be laid waste, without an inhabitant. (Jer. 4:6–7)

Olaus maps a literal interpretation of Jeremiah, placing the lion as far north as possible, very close to the magnetic North Pole. It is not just the Lion of the North, it is the emblem of the symbolic, religious North. The lion was to be used, famously, by King Gustavus Adolphus as a symbol of Swedish power during the Thirty Years War a century later, but its function on the *Carta marina* is different: it is a symbol not of the Swedes, but of the global significance of the space they inhabit. Together with the Moses/Starkater figure, the lion serves to represent the far North as a space where the eternal history of the Bible is present, where the forces of good and evil face each other.

The lion can also be seen as a specific emblem of the end of time. That is of course the immediate, biblical reference, but Olaus would also have been concerned with the idea and fear that the collapse of the universal church would bring about the end of the world—hence the vision of the great destroyer.[13] It is a vision that becomes the *pièce de resistance* of the map as an attempt to lay out the North as a significant, signifying space, a region where historical and religious signs emerge and can be mapped. In that sense, it may be said to take over the function of the Holy Land in the *mappaemundi*.

The Separation of Times and Spaces

However, the epistemology of the map had changed. The medieval *mappaemundi* are juxtapositions of different times. Paradoxically, the fact that these times have spatial form separates them completely from each other. The only connection between the Mongols roasting an enemy in Scythia and the Israelites' crooked path through the desert is that they can both be found on the same map. Their spatial separation shows that they have no common history. They do not inhabit the same time. This kind of spatio-temporal separation was dissolved as an effect of the Ptolemaic revolution, as geography and history became complementary dimensions of human knowledge. This paved the way for the "pure" geography of later cartography, but it was also an important precondition for later historicist thought and the idea that the past is not only fundamentally different from the present, but irretrievably gone.

In the works of Olaus Magnus, both the *Carta marina* and the *Historia*, the two ways of thinking about time and space intersect. The scene with Starkater, the lion, and the Sami provides a particularly dense example of the intersection. On the one hand, the figures from the Old Testament tell the spectator that the far North was a particular kind of terrain, unlike the landscapes of present-day animals, hunters, kings, and volcanoes. Moses did not belong in Copenhagen, Oslo, or Stockholm. Being Moses, he belonged to a particular, separate, desolate space. On the other hand, the map is a system of historical continuities. It shows Moses interacting with the Sami population, even commanding them to return to the history of the Swedes. These Sami are not confined to the space of Moses/Starkater and the lion. The map shows them warring, skiing, hunting, traveling in sleighs, and even riding reindeer, all over the Ostrobothnian region. This freedom to move in space mirrors their temporal freedom, their continued presence in history.

This historicity is developed in the *Historia* in books 3, "On the Superstitious Worship of Demons by the People of the North," and 4, "On the Wars and Customs of the Pagan Dwellers in the Wild and their Neighbors." Here, too, the peoples of the northernmost lands are lit from two different angles. First, Olaus attempts to understand their customs and characters by way of classical analogy; second, he embeds them in his story of the Christianization of Northern Europe and argues that contemporary paganism can be seen as remains of the ancient Norse religion.[14] This story is wonderfully complex and ambiguous. Olaus moves unpredictably between retelling pagan legends twice removed, as reports of stories told and believed by others, and telling of magic that had been very real indeed.

> How proficient some women among the people of the North once were in magical skills I shall show by means of a few instances. … When King Hading was at dinner, [a woman], carrying stalks of hemlock, was observed to raise her head from the ground near to a brazier and, extending the lap of her garment, to ask in what part of the world such fresh plants had grown in winter-time. As the king desired to know, she wrapped him in her mantle and vanished away with him under the earth. When she had shown him the wonders of the lower regions, she at last restored him to the upper world.[15]

There was, in other words, a grand history in which the Sami had a place, quite independent of whether or not they themselves were aware of it or willing to accept it, but Starkater came to them to draw them into the history of the Catholic Church. At the same time, Olaus in his *Historia* insists that the story of the far North was not just one of Christianization and its obstacles; it was also a story about the gradual weakening of pagan magic, as signaled above by the almost wishful "once," a distance that emerges in several of the accounts of Northern sorcery: "Finland, the northernmost land, together with Lappland, was once during pagan times as learned in witchcraft as if it had had Zoroaster the Persian instructor in this damnable science."[16]

Olaus's historical tapestry brings together the great story of universal Christendom, a regional history of the progress of Christianization, a history of the decline of magic, and a meditation on how the great Swedish past has become invisible to its own people. They go about their daily lives without realizing that the ground beneath their feet is a land of wonders, heroes, and eternal struggles. All this merges in the far North, as Starkater, the Lion of the North, and the pagans face each other. Starkater is the magnificent embodiment of all these dimensions. The rituals of the Sami threaten to unleash the lion and thus the destruction of the entire world—the map is a warning of impending doom.

It is on this scale that we must read Olaus Magnus's works, not least the map, which depicts and localizes the dangers that are facing mankind. The richness of the map and the *Historia* serves to convince his audience of the splendor and consequent importance of the Northern countries—that is, of Sweden—but the deepest drama, the ultimate signified of all these signs, can be seen only on the map: the end of time.

The Geography of Vision

The *Carta marina* is a visionary map, a revelation of the ultimate implication of the Lutheran takeover of the Nordic countries. The region becomes the focal point of universal history. In geographical terms, it may not be more—or less—than an impressively exact representation of a certain, limited space; in temporal terms, it is a map on a larger scale, a map of the battlefield where the future of the world was being decided.

Could the world be saved from the lion and from the destruction of all things? Olaus's identification of the Lion of the North with the North as such implies that the great threat had to be fought on its own home ground, and stopped—in the North. Curiously, but logically, the task then is the Christianization of the Sami, a process that is one with their re-entry into Swedish history. At this point in the *Historia*, Olaus himself steps forward:

> We must constantly pray that, since the harvest is plenteous, [God] will deign to send out capable and effectual labourers at the right season. If I too seemed needed, I should never refuse to undertake such sacred labour, in case God in his majesty should vouchsafe to put it into the heart of the king of Sweden to allow me, whose most burning desire it is, to perform so excellent a work; since I assumed the title of archbishop to those parts eleven years ago, I have unceasingly desired it, for the honour of God on high and the everlasting safety of all those who dwell there. Nor could I doubt that with His help I should increase the number of this kingdom's subjects in places which I have seen in the past to be highly suitable, so that areas where no one now lives I should within ten years turn into a fit and ample habitation for many thousands of people.[17]

The Lutherans blame the Catholics for the persistence of paganism, says Olaus, but this is a "false and sacrilegious" accusation. Catholicism is the true faith and its followers remain loyal, provoking the hatred and envy of the "infamous Lutherans."[18] In other words, in the absence of Moses—that is, the Catholic Church—those who needed its leadership have strayed from the path. The Lutherans stand between the people and their spiritual leader, the Catholic archbishop—namely Olaus Magnus himself, and his brother Johannes before him. Both wanted to return to Sweden, both wrote major histories, both were exiles, so to speak, on Mount Sinai. Starkater's stone tablets are the perfect image of the dual message of history and religion: he is not only his own historical self and the biblical Moses, but also the Magnus brothers, with the aging but still living Olaus begging to be allowed to return and lead his people to the Promised Land.

The religious and historical imagery of the *Carta marina* simultaneously becomes cosmological and personal. The figure of Starkater carries the entire span: he is both past and future, estranged historian and mankind's potential savior. This interpretation finds support in the map, but it may not have been the only interpretation even to Olaus's contemporaries—such as the translators of the *Opera breve*, who insisted on seeing the creature as a *grymklau*, an animal without any obvious religious significance. This view seems to have become the norm, more or less explicitly, since the image from the map is reproduced as a "Scythian wolf" in later works such as Gesner's *Historia animalium* (1551) and Edward Topsell's *The History of Four-Footed Beasts and Serpents* (1658).

Still, the centuries pass without the Scythian wolf looking like anything other than a lion. And there can be no doubt that the wolves that are indisputably there on the *Carta marina* are of a very different species. The map, quite simply, gives no evidence for the claim that it is a wolf. As we have seen, Olaus does not mention the beast at all, neither in the *Opera breve* nor in the *Historia*. One of the chapters on Starkater is illustrated with a reproduction of the image of the champion and the beast, but the text is silent.

The Silence of the Maps

One of the most intriguing dimensions of Olaus's work is the relationship between the map and the texts. But the relationship is difficult to grasp, since the map is practically silent and challenges us to interpret its images on our own. The connections between the *Carta marina* and the *Historia* are obvious—they deal with the same region, and the book is illustrated throughout with images from the map. However, the map's explicit religious polemic and the Devil have left the *Historia*, and this is telling, in light of the sixteen years that passed between 1539 and 1555. In the course of that period, with Olaus himself in the midst of events, the religious division of Europe went from strong possibility to undisputable fact. The Northern countries were among the first Lutheran states. This explains why the underlying religious epistemology of the map was toned down and phased out, paving the way for a more classically oriented history and natural history. The original message no longer held power or realism.

The silence of the map makes it a necessary but uncertain exercise to wonder what the drawings meant and to trace the gaps between text and image. The danger, of course, is the natural inclination to reach for commonsensical interpretations—the way I do here, when insisting that the animal is a lion because it looks like one. But what is left for us, except comparison and silences? The animal not only looks like a lion; it does not look remotely like any other animals on the map or in the book—and there is no mention of it in the texts that can be identified clearly as Olaus's works. It shares this silence with the tablets that turn Starkater into Moses, with his proximity to the heathens, with Olaus's biblical messages to the kings, in short, with almost every element that can be said to embody different temporalities. This movement away from the heterochronia seems to begin at the moment of the publication of the *Carta marina*. The two versions of the *Opera breve* both seem to play down this complexity of time, erasing the multilayered strangeness of its conception of the world as both spatial and temporal.

The *Carta marina* grapples with time on several levels, within the strict spatial framework of Ptolemaic geography. This chapter has studied a few elements of the map's depiction of the far North, where several layers of temporality overlap: classical mythology, biblical and Norse history, the history of the Sami, and contemporary Sweden. These overlaps converge in the figure of Starkater, who also embodies Olaus Magnus's desire to synchronize the temporalities and bring the Sami into the common history of a nation that in turns needs to return to its true faith. The lion, as I interpret it, is the embodiment of the end of time, an heir to the images of the Last Judgment that surrounded the old *mappaemundi*. This presence of temporality transforms the *Carta marina* from a map of a small region to a map of the world, with its imagery of local and universal time. This world was still a spatio-temporal continuum, but time was fading fast.

Erling Sandmo is Professor of History at the University of Oslo and head of the Norwegian National Library's centre for historical cartography. He has published on several aspects of early modern culture, in particular violence, music, and knowledge. His latest books are *Tid for historie: en bok om historiske spørsmål* [Time for History: A Book on Historical Questions] (Universitetsforlaget, 2015) and *Uhyrlig: Sjømonstre i kart og litteratur 1491–1895* [Monstrous: Sea Monsters in Maps and Literature 1491–1895] (The Norwegian National Library, 2017, German ed., *Ungeheuerlich*, 2018).

NOTES

1. Cf. Naomi Klein, *Maps of Medieval Thought: The Hereford Paradigm* (Woodbridge, 2001).
2. The German version is titled *Ain kurze Auslegung und Verklerung der neuuen Mappen von den alten Gœttenreich und andern Nordlenden sampt mit den uunderlichen dingen in land und uasser darinnen begriffen biss her also klerlich nieintuuelt geschriben* (A brief exposition and explanation of the new map of the old Gothic kingdom and other Northern countries along with the wonderful things on land and in water as known at present, clearly described for the first time) with no date, publisher, or place given; the Italian bears the nearly identical title *Opera breve, laqvale demonstra, e dechiara, ouero da il modo facile de intendere la charta, ouer del le terre frigidissime di Settentrione: oltra il mare Germanico, doue si contengono le cose mirabili*, also with no date, publisher, or place given. Both versions are included in Herman Richter, *Olaus Magnus Carta Marina 1539*, Lychnos-bibliotek 11.2 (Lund, 1967). Quotes are from the original text with my own translations. The original translators are unknown.
3. The two surviving copies are kept at the State Library in Munich and the University Library in Uppsala. Both are available as online, high-resolution scans: http://daten.digitale-sammlungen.de/~db/bsb00002967/images/ and http://art.alvin-portal.org/alvin/view.jsf?file=6964. References to Olaus Magnus's *Historia* are to books and chapters, hereafter by numbers only. English quotations are from the Hakluyt Society edition (Olaus Magnus, *Historia de gentibus septentrionalibus*, ed. P. G. Foote [London, 1996–98]); Latin original quotations are from the first edition.
4. For further discussions of religion, see in particular the chapters by Nora Eggen, Oddbjørn Leirvik, Chenxi Tang, Kyrre Kverndokk, Alfred Hiatt, and Kari van Dijk in this volume.
5. See Kurt Johannesson, *The Renaissance of the Goths in Sixteenth-Century Sweden: Johannes and Olaus Magnus as Politicians and Historians* (Berkeley, 1982), 28.
6. For further discussions of monsters and monstrosity, see in particular the chapters by Karl G. Johansson and Siv Frøydis Berg in this volume.
7. "Si dipinge Starchatero gigante suetico gia nominatissimo in tutta la Europa fra doe colone descritte con Gothice littere." Olaus Magnus, *Carta marina*.
8. "Hie ist ainer uon den alten risen Starcaterus gena(n)t hat zuay staine tafeln zu ainer gedechtnus das in den landen seindt uil streitperlicher menner geuesen un(n) man-hait mit gettischen buchstaben beschribe(n) uor uil hundert iaren an gezaigt." *Ain kurze Auslegung*, letters D.C.
9. Olaus, too, draws the parallel, and calls Starkater "a second Hercules" (*Historia*, 5.4).
10. Starkater is the subject of six chapters, 3–9, of Olaus's *Historia*.
11. P. 156b. Cf. Sachiko Kusukawa, "The Sources of Gessner's Pictures for the *Historia animalium*," *Annals of Science* 67, no. 3 (2010): 308.
12. A possible explanation for the German addition is that it links the image of the beast to classical literature. In *The Histories* (4.105), Herodotus writes about a particular Scythian tribe, the Neuri, where "once a year every one ... becomes a wolf for a few days and changes back again to his former shape." The addition thus provides the map

with yet another of many examples of how creatures and natural phenomena from the classical literature re-emerge both on the *Carta marina* and in the *Historia*.
13. Cf. Reinhart Koselleck, "Modernity and the Planes of Historicity," in *Futures Past: On the Semantics of Historical Time* (New York, 2004), 9–25.
14. This theory remained important and is basic to Johannes Schefferus's influential study of the Sami or Lapps, *Lapponia* (Frankfurt am Main, 1673).
15. Olaus Magnus, *Historia*, 3.15: "Artem magicam apud Septentrionales populos quanturn calluerint olim mulieres aliquot, paucis exemplis ostendetur. ... Hadingo Rege cœnante, alia eiusdem artis fœmina cicutarum gerula, propter foculum humo caput extulisse conspecta, porrectoque finu percontari visa, qua mundi parte tam recentia gramina brumali tempore fuissent exorta: cujus cognoscendi cupidum Regem proprio obvolutum amiculo, refuga secum sub reiras adduxit: ostensisque infernalium regionum monstris: tandem mundo restituit."
16. Ibid., 3.16: "Hoc præmisso, quod hæc extremi Aquilonis regio Finlandia, ac Lapponia, ita erat docta maleficiis olim in paganismo, ac si Zoroastren Persam in hac damnata disciplina præceptorem habuisset."
17. Ibid., 4.19: "Interea tamen & assidue petendum erit, ut cum messis multa sit, idoneos & efficaces operarios emittere dignetur in tempore opportuno. Et si ego viderer necessarius, nunquam recusarem tam pium subire laborem, ubi divinæ maiestati in cor Regis Svetiæ immittere dignaretur, ut sineret me iuxta ardentissimum desiderium meum adimplere tam optimum opus, quenadmodum annis XI suscepto Archiepiscopali titulo illarum regionum incessanter cupieram, pro honore excelsi Dei, & omnium incolarum perpetua securitate. Nec dubitarem eius auxilio ita augere regnicolas in locis olim per me visis aptissimis, ut ubi nemo iam habitat, intra decennium habitationem capacem, & idoneam redderem, pro pluribus hominum millibus commodissime habitaturis."
18. Ibid., 4.20.

BIBLIOGRAPHY

Johannesson, Kurt. *The Renaissance of the Goths in Sixteenth-Century Sweden: Johannes and Olaus Magnus as Politicians and Historians*. Berkeley: University of California Press, 1982.
Klein, Naomi. *Maps of Medieval Thought: The Hereford Paradigm*. Woodbridge: Boydell Press, 2001.
Koselleck, Reinhart. "Modernity and the Planes of Historicity." In *Futures Past: On the Semantics of Historical Time*: 9–25. New York: Columbia University Press, 2004.
Kusukawa, Sachiko. "The Sources of Gessner's Pictures for the *Historia animalium*." *Annals of Science* 67, no. 3 (2010): 303–28.
Olaus Magnus. *Historia de gentibus septentrionalibus*. Edited by P. G. Foote. London: Hakluyt Society, 1996–98.
Richter, Herman. *Olaus Magnus Carta Marina 1539*. Lychnos-bibliotek 11.2. Lund: Almqvist & Wiksell, 1967.
Schefferus, Johannes. *Lapponia*. Frankfurt am Main: Christian Wolff, 1673.

⊱• 19 •⊰

The Search for Vínland and Norse Conceptions of the World

Karl G. Johansson

In the late tenth century a new land was found in the west of Greenland by Norse sailors. The land they found was soon abandoned, perhaps due to conflicts with the people they encountered. Their experiences seem, however, to have been remembered in oral tradition and were subsequently forged into written narratives. The written sources of the Norse travels in the northern parts of the Atlantic Ocean from the thirteenth and fourteenth centuries provide good examples of how information that does not conform to current views must be treated in one of two ways: it is either assimilated and explained within the current world view or it initiates changes in this view.

Conceptions of the world and speculations of the unknown are universal. In every culture there is an interplay between what is known, and therefore forms the current world view, and new information that will either be assimilated or cause changes in the existing world view.[1] The two so-called Vínland sagas, *Grœnlendinga saga* and *Eiríks saga rauða*, both primarily assimilate the new information to the contemporary world view by using models found in Continental tradition, at the same time as they add traditional knowledge of the lands in the west.

It is today difficult to distinguish Norse tradition from Continental influences in the extant works. They are obviously part of the same tradition of geographical description. But if the two narratives are compared to earlier narratives of mythical lands and the periphery of the known world, some new light could perhaps be shed on the ways in which they present Norse awareness of real lands within the European horizon of knowledge. In the following, two main strategies of assimilation will be pointed out: first, the promise of Paradise and green pastures; second, the periphery as a place of danger, magic, and unknown creatures. Both these strategies, I argue, are similar to what we see in other contemporary geographical descriptions; the periphery has to be conquered by the Christian Church, and Paradise is to be found at the outermost part of the world, out of reach for human beings in this life.

When the Icelandic chieftain and author Snorri Sturluson in the prologue to his major chronicle about the Norwegian kings, *Heimskringla* (lit. "the earth's round"), describes the world as he perceives it, his description could very well have been based on a so-called T-O map (see Figure 19.1). Snorri, born around 1179 and writing in the 1220s, shows a clear awareness of current speculations about the world. The prologue describes the known world:

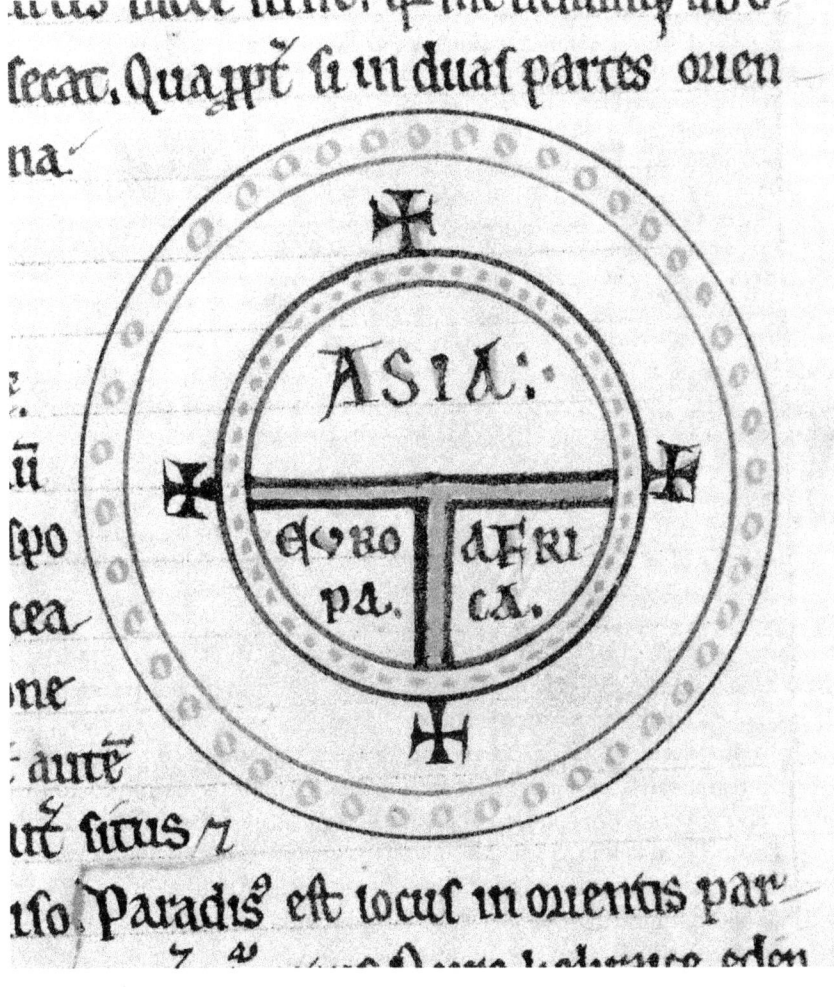

Figure 19.1. T-O map from Remigius of Auxerre/Isidore of Seville: Commentary on Phocas's *Ars de nomine et verbo*. England, third quarter of the thirteenth century. Courtesy of British Library (BL Royal 12 F IV f. 135v). http://www.bl.uk/catalogues/illuminatedmanuscripts/ILLUMIN.ASP?Size=mid&IllID=43047.

> The earth's round, on which mankind lives, is much indented. Great seas cut into the land from the ocean. We know that a sea goes from the Norva Sound [the Strait of Gibraltar] all the way to Jórsalaland ["Jerusalem Land," Palestine]. From this sea a long arm extends to the northeast which is called the Black Sea. It separates the three parts of the world. The part to the eastward is called Asia; but that which lies to the west of it is called by some Europe, by others Eneá. North of the Black Sea lies Svíthjóth the Great or the Cold. Some men consider Svíthjóth the Great not less in size than Serkland the Great ["Saracen Land," North Africa], and some think it is equal in size to Bláland ["Blackman's Land," Africa]. The northern part of Svíthjóth is uncultivated on account of frost and cold, just as the southern part of Bláland is a desert because of the heat of the sun. In Svíthjóth there are many large provinces. There are also many tribes and many tongues. There are giants and dwarfs; there are black men and many kinds of strange tribes. Also there are animals and dragons of marvellous size. Out of the north, from the mountains which are beyond all inhabited districts, a river runs through Svíthjóth whose correct name is Tanais [the Don]. In olden times it was called Tana Fork or Vana Fork. Its mouth is in the Black Sea. The land around the Vana Fork was then called Vana Home or the Home of the Vanir. The river divides the three continents. East of it is Asia, west of it Europe.[2]

The medieval world view that was common to Snorri Sturluson and his contemporaries in Iceland and the general European tradition can be exemplified by a description found in chapter 14 of Isidore of Seville's *Etymologiae*, entitled *De terra et partibus* ("The Earth and Its Parts"):

> The *Orbis* ["circuit," i.e., the world] gets its name from the roundness of a circle, since it is like a wheel ... Because of this, the Ocean flowing around it is contained in a circular limit, and it is divided in three parts, one part being called Asia, the second Europe, and the third Africa.[3]

It is not too farfetched, I would contend, to suggest that Snorri Sturluson knew a text quite similar to this one when he formed his prologue to *Heimskringla*, or at least was well acquainted with its world view. He describes the land surrounded by the ocean and divided into three continents with the Mediterranean and Black Seas forming a center. This view of the known world would persist throughout the Middle Ages, until it was finally challenged both by new knowledge about Asia and Africa and by the European discovery of a new continent on the other side of the Atlantic Ocean. Snorri and his contemporaries were well acquainted with European learning and speculation. The Icelandic elite, no less than that of other peripheral parts of Europe, had constant contacts with centers of learning. It is in this period that we find the narratives of Vínland, a land west of Greenland. Knowledge of continuous lands along the Atlantic shore was most likely available not only in Iceland but throughout Scandinavia from the time when Norse people settled in Greenland and briefly also in L'Anse aux Meadows in Newfoundland. This knowledge was subsequently confronted with mythical narratives of lands in the west and soon assimilated into this genre. In this assimilation process it was necessary to adjust the indigenous information so that it did not contradict the world view represented by Snorri's account, that is, the contemporary world view of the Christian Church.

Greenland in itself was probably difficult enough to explain within the tripartite world. All earlier accounts of this island describe it as part of the Eurasian landmass, connected to another more or less mythical periphery, Bjarmaland ("Land of the Bjarmar"). This understanding of Greenland would persist also in post-Columbian times, as exemplified by the map of the northern Atlantic shoreline produced by the Icelander Sigurður Stefánsson in the late sixteenth century. Here not only Greenland but also the subsequent lands of Helluland ("Stone-slab Land"), Markland ("Forest Land"), and Skrælingaland ("Land of the Skrælings") are connected to other European peripheries, Riseland ("Land of the Giants"), Jotunheimar ("Land of the Jotuns [i.e., Giants]"), and the already mentioned Bjarmaland, before we reach Promontorium Vinlandiæ.

The two main Old Norse narratives of the new lands in the west, *Grœnlendinga saga* and *Eiríks saga rauða*, are today dated to the first half of the thirteenth century by most scholars. There have, however, been suggestions both for a later date for one or both of the sagas, as well as for later additions and changes due to the continuous revisions of texts typical of manuscript culture. The *Grœnlendinga saga* is today only extant as a part of the large kings' saga compilation found in Flateyjarbók (GKS 1005 fol), a manuscript dated to 1387–95, while *Eiríks saga rauða* is preserved in Hauksbók (AM 544 4to) from the first decade of the fourteenth century and the manuscript AM 557 4to from around 1420–50.[4] The geographical descriptions found in the two sagas, therefore, cannot with certainty be used for establishing the world view of thirteenth-century Icelanders. Here I choose to accept the thirteenth-century dating with some caution.

There is a longstanding debate about whether the name *Vínland* means "Land of Vines," as suggested by the two medieval narratives, or "Land of Meadows." Today most scholars seem to agree that the explanation of the name found in the sagas should be accepted, and there still seems to be a consensus that there has actually existed a land known to the Norse in the first decades of the eleventh century as Vínland.[5] I will not discuss this further in this context. Here I rather suggest that the name should be understood as part of the mythical narrative of lands in the periphery, dangerous or paradisical, the land where grapes grow and fields are ripe.[6]

There are other early sources testifying to the knowledge of Vínland but they are generally rather sparse in their descriptions. In the Icelandic

Íslendingabók, dated to 1122–33, we find the first Icelandic mention of Vínland and its inhabitants:

> There they found human buildings both in the eastern and western parts of the land and broken boats made from hides and stone tools. From this it could be seen that the kind of people who lived in Vínland and were called Skrælings by the Greenlanders had been there.[7]

The author, Ari Þorgilsson, seems, however, to have known the work of the German cleric Adam of Bremen who wrote half a century earlier about a land in the west called Vínland, even if Adam's focus is a bit different:

> He also spoke of yet another island that had been discovered by many people in this ocean. It is called Vinland, because wild vines grow there and produce an excellent wine. There is also corn for bread in abundance there without the need to sow, a fact that I have not learned from false rumors but from the trustworthy knowledge of the Danes.[8]

It is obvious that there are problems related to determining in which direction a tradition, oral or written, has moved. It seems most plausible, however, to suggest that the idea of a land in the west with wild grapes and fantastic beings has been influenced by biblical traditions, and that Adam of Bremen may very well be one of the sources for the forming of the mythical narratives of Vínland, and perhaps also of the name itself. This would indicate that the short passage above, based on European myths of paradisical islands in the west, has been part of the incitement to create stories of wine and wheat in the Norse thirteenth century, stories that have been combined with the narratives of Skrælings as these are mentioned by Ari. Ari seems, judging from his above description, to be the one with more direct information of Inuit people (the matrix for all "Skrælings").

The two sagas relating the discovery of Vínland by Leifr Eiríksson both present the main traits of the story of exploration, but with different perspectives and bias. In *Eiríks saga rauða* the land is described as Paradise, that is, the saga adapts the first of the two strategies suggested above, here in the Hauksbók version:

> Once he had made ready, Leifr set sail. After being tossed about at sea for a long time he chanced upon land where he had not expected any to be found. Fields of self-sown wheat and vines were growing there; also, there were trees known as maple, and they took specimens of all of them. Some trees were so large that they were used in building houses.[9]

In this saga there is no mention of the reason for the name *Vínland*; the land is described as rich in valuable resources, and the description of vines and self-sown wheat indicates its paradisical status. It is only later in the narrative, when Leifr has told about the new lands after his return to Greenland, that the name appears:

> In Brattahlíð there was much talk about going out to find Vínland the Good, and it was said that there must be good opportunities to be found. And as a result Karlsefni and Snorri prepared their ship in order to sail for the land in the spring.[10]

Eiríks saga rauða also mentions another land further to the west named Hvítramannaland, or the Great Ireland:

> They [i.e., two Skræling children abducted by the Norse] spoke of another land, across from their own. There people dressed in white clothing, shouted loudly and bore poles and waved banners. This people assumed to be Hvítramannaland ["the Land of the White Men"] or Great Ireland.[11]

Here there are clear references to other European traditions, such as the tales of Brendan, that mention paradisical islands in the ocean, at the same time as there are geographical notions reminiscent of what is found in other geographical descriptions from the same period. Hvítramannaland is mentioned in various contexts in the Norse material, and it seems to be understood as Christian and a place in close proximity to Paradise; the men in white clothing waving banners would remind us of a Christian procession.[12]

In *Grœnlendinga saga* the discovery of the new lands is described in a quite different way. This saga introduces Bjarni Herjólfsson as the first sailor to find new lands, although without going ashore. Bjarni is on his way to Greenland to visit his father when he drifts off course in a fog, and when the fog rises he and his crew spot land they have never heard of. On Bjarni's order they do not go ashore, but sail past three lands before they finally reach Greenland. It is only later that Leifr Eiríksson decides to sail in the other direction along the coastline that Bjarni has discovered. The saga relates the sailing in three stages. First, they reach the land spotted last by Bjarni:

> They sailed up to the shore and cast anchor, put out a boat and rowed ashore. There they found no grass, but large glaciers covered the highlands and the land was like a single flat slab of rock from the glaciers to the sea. This land seemed to them of little use. Leifr then spoke: "As far as this land is concerned it can't be said of us as of Bjarni, that we did not set foot on shore. I am now going to name this land and call it Helluland ["Stone-slab Land"]."[13]

The description of the land is matter of fact and seems to provide a reasonably true image of what we could expect travelers in these parts to have encountered. We could most likely consider this description, therefore, to be based on local knowledge of the northern parts. The second land is presented as more prosperous:

> This land was flat and forested, sloping gently seaward, and they came across many beaches of white sand. Leifr then spoke: "This land shall be named for what it has to offer and called Markland ["Forest Land"]."[14]

But still the description is rather rational and matter of fact. Markland was most likely an area known for its resources more or less throughout the Middle Ages. This land of forests was important as a place to gather timber and other natural riches.

When Leifr and his crew reach the third land, the naming does not take place in the same way and according to the same principles. In this land they spend some time and discover the wild grapes and good pastures. One day a German slave called Tyrkir disappears, and when they finally find him he is in good spirits. The saga relates how Tyrkir has found trees with grapes that are highly appreciated by Leifr; they start collecting both vines and grapes to take with them. It is only when they are ready to set sail and return to Greenland, however, that Leifr provides a name for the land:

> When spring came they made the ship ready and set sail. Leifr named the land for its natural features and called it Vínland.[15]

In a recent article, Judith Jesch has argued well for the narrative in *Grænlendinga saga* being a more genuine description of the sailing routes along the North Atlantic coastline. Jesch argues that the description of the various lands is based on real knowledge of sailing and navigation.[16] This argumentation I find convincing, with only one exception, and this concerns Vínland. In the case of Helluland and Markland, the names indicate features that can be seen when approaching the land from the sea. This would be valuable for the sailor looking for points of direction along the coast. Jesch argues that the name Iceland could be explained in concordance with this principle, as the first thing seafarers see when arriving from Norway is the ice on Vatnajökull. Greenland poses a problem here, as it seems to have done already for the saga writers; the above-mentioned *Íslendingabók* recounts how Eiríkr rauði named it Greenland to make it more inviting for settlers.[17] Jesch suggests that the name *Vínland* should be explained in a similar way and seems to accept it as an original name.[18] She appears to be in some doubt on this point, however, and states:

> The name *Vínland*, however, begins to take us out of the realm of exploration and into the realm of imagination. Even Adam of Bremen knew about it; indeed he provides the earliest evidence for the name, less than a century after it was bestowed.[19]

My suggestion here is that *Vínland* is a later invention, perhaps even bestowed by Adam himself, and that the name originally was part of the mythology, and not, as Jesch suggests, part of mythologizing the geographical knowledge.[20] My suggestion is supported by the descriptions of the periphery found in Adam's work. When he reaches the outermost lands in his account of the world, Adam relates European tradition rather than actual knowledge with descriptions of rare creatures and strange and dangerous people:

> There you can find Amazons, and cynocephali, and Cyclops, who have one eye in front, as well as those that Solinus calls himantopods who run on one leg, and those who enjoy eating human flesh.[21]

This could be directly compared to the descriptions of the uniped in *Eiríks saga rauða* as well as to the accounts of Skrælings, the native people.[22] The uniped appears in a short sequence where it kills Þorvaldr, one of the sons of Eiríkr rauði, with an arrow. The description is short but the saga writer is in no doubt about the assailant's identity:

> One morning Karlsefni and his men caught sight of a spot in a clearing that shimmered toward them, and they called out to it. It moved, and it turned out to be a uniped.[23]

The Skrælings are generally described as human beings. In their actions, however, they are typical of the people on the margins of the world found in many medieval sources. They are savage in their ways and depicted as ugly, with dark skin and black hair. In both sagas the natives use magic, which is always a trait found among peoples in the periphery (and found also in Greenland among the pagan Norse), and in their encounters the Norse experience a number of supernatural events. One example is when Guðríðr in *Grœnlendinga saga* meets a woman who speaks Norse and appears and disappears without any plausible explanation:

> A shadow fell across the doorway, and a woman in a black tunic entered. She was rather short with a shawl and red-brown hair, and she was pale and had large eyes so that no-one has ever seen bigger eyes in a human head. The woman went to where Guðríðr was seated and said: "What's your name?" "My name is Guðríðr. And what's your name?" [Guðríðr asked]. "My name is Guðríðr," the woman answered. ... Then Guðríðr heard a great blast, and the woman was gone.[24]

Carolyne Larrington has suggested that this is a way for the saga author or the tradition he renders to present the indigenous people as linguistically challenged.[25] I would suggest that the supernatural event in this case rather points in the direction of Guðríðr's future as a Christian forerunner, when she returns to Iceland from a pilgrimage and becomes the rather anachronistic first nun in Iceland, more than a century before the first female convent was established in 1185.[26] My contention is therefore that Guðríðr has a vision of a holy woman. The woman is dressed in a way that could remind us of the dress of a nun and she has large eyes like the ones found in icons. In 1295 a new convent was founded at Reynistaðir where Guðríðr is said to have spent her last days as a nun; the vision therefore could be seen not only as a personal one, but it also in a sense legitimizes the Christian house on the site. Shortly after this event the Norse colonizers, on Karlsefni's suggestion, leave Vínland and return to Greenland.

If the two sagas I have discussed so far seem to primarily use European narratives of more or less paradisical lands that lie west of the known world, they also open the possibility of a more geographical explanation, still in close connection to general medieval strategies of describing the peripheral parts of the known world. Both sagas do contain geographical information, but none of them explicitly tries to place the new lands in the tripartite world. Rather, they seem to indicate that both Greenland and the three new lands—Helluland, Markland, and Vínland—form a single large landmass and that Greenland is connected in the east to Bjarmaland, the fantastic land in outermost Europe where many of the *fornaldarsögur* (legendary sagas) are staged. Already the earliest descriptions of the North Atlantic geography, however, refer to Africa as being placed in the continuation from Greenland. The description in *Historia Norwegie*, a work from the late twelfth century, is interesting in this context.

> This country [i.e., Greenland], discovered, settled and confirmed in the Catholic faith by Icelanders, marks the western boundary of Europe, and almost touches the islands off Africa, where the Ocean tides surge in.[27]

It is significant that *Historia Norwegie* mentions *insulas Africanas* ("African islands"), which echoes Adam of Bremen's description of Vínland as an island. This understanding of the new land as forming a part of the known world in the east seems to be carried further in the fourteenth century, and now the outermost periphery of the new land is placed firmly in Africa. In a description of the known world found in the manuscript AM 194 8vo from the fourth quarter of the fourteenth century, the land is speculatively connected to Africa:

> [From] Bjarmaland there is a wide wilderness in the north until Greenland appears. South of Greenland is Helluland, then Markland. From there it is not far to Vínland the Good, which by some is said to be a part of Africa; and if this is right, then the ocean falls in between Vínland and Markland.[28]

Helluland and Markland are connected to Europe while Vínland is at the peak of Africa. This could indicate that Markland was still a land known by seafarers from Iceland and Greenland, while Vínland is on the other side of the *úthaf* ("outer sea"), and at this time a mythical land, far removed from the known world. It would take another hundred years until the new continent was accepted and the old European world view was finally outdated.

Karl G. Johansson is Professor of Old Norse Philology at the University of Oslo, Norway. He has published widely on various topics of Scandinavian philology, concerning both eastern and western Scandinavia. Johansson has been involved in a number of large projects: the so-called Vadstena projects (2003–2006) concerning the Birgittine monastery in Vadstena, Sweden; a project on translated and indigenous romantic literature in Norway and Iceland from the thirteenth to the fifteenth century (2007–2010); and most recently (2013–2017) a project studying the translation and use of Bible texts in the Scandinavian Middle Ages.

NOTES

1. For studies of the cartographic and geographic discussions of the Middle Ages, see, e.g., Alfred Hiatt, *Terra Incognita: Mapping the Antipodes before 1600* (Chicago, 2008); Evelyn Edson, *The World Map, 1300–1492: The Persistence of Tradition and Transformation* (Baltimore, MD, 2007).
2. Lee M. Hollander, trans., *Heimskringla: History of the Kings of Norway by Snorri Sturluson* (Austin, 1964), 6; *ÍF 26 = Snorri Sturluson: Heimskringla 1*, Íslenzk fornrit 26, ed. Bjarni Aðalbjarnarson (Reykjavík, 1941), 9–10: *Kringla Heimsins, sú er mannfólkit byggvir, er mjǫk vágskórin. Ganga hǫf stór ór útsjánum inn í jǫrðina. Er þat kunnigt, at haf gengr frá Nǫrvasundum ok allt út til Jórsalalands. Af hafinu gengr langr hafsbotn til landnorðrs, er heitir Svartahaf. Sá skilr heimsþriðjungana. Heitir fyrir austan Ásíá, en fyrir vestan kalla sumir Európá, en sumir Eneá. En norðan at Svartahafi gengr Svíþjóð in mikla eða in kalda. Svíþjóð ina miklu kalla sumir menn eigi minni en Serkland it mikla, sumir jafna henni við Bláland it mikla. Inn nørðri hlutr Svíþjóðar liggr óbyggðr af frosti ok kulða, svá sem inn syðri hlutr Blálands er auðr af sólarbruna. Í Svíþjóð eru stórheruð mǫrg. Þar eru ok margs konar þjóðir ok margar tungur. Þar eru risar, ok þar eru dvergar, þar eru blámenn, ok þar eru margs konar undirligar þjóðir. Þar eru ok dýr ok drekar furðuliga stórir. Ór norðri frá fjǫllum þeim, er fyrir útan eru byggð alla, fellr á um Svíþjóð, sú er at réttu heitir Tanais. Hon var forðum kǫlluð Tanakvísl eða Vanakvísl. Hon kømr til sjávar inn í Svartahaf. Í Vanakvíslum var þá kallat Vanaland eða Vanaheimr. Sú á skilr heimsþriðjungana. Heitir fyrir austan Ásíá, en fyrir vestan Európá.*
3. Isidore of Seville, *Etymologiarum sive originum libri XX*, ed. W. M. Lindsay (Oxford, 1911), 14.2: *Orbis a rotunditate circuli dictus, quia sicut rota est. … Undique enim Oceanus circumfluens eius in circulo ambit fines. Divisus est autem trifarie: e quibus una pars Asia, altera Europa, tertia Africa nuncupatur.*
4. For recent discussions about the dating, see Andrew Wawn and Þórunn Sigurðardóttir, eds, *Approaches to Vínland: A Conference on the Written and Archaeological Sources*

for the Norse Settlements in the North-Atlantic Region and Exploration of America (Reykjavík, 2001).
5. For a recent survey, see Alan Crozier, "The *Vinland Hypothesis: A Reply to the Historians," *Gardar: Årsbok för Samfundet Sverige-Island i Lund-Malmö* 29 (1999): 37-66; cf. Carolyne Larrington, "'Undruðusk þá, sem fyrir var': Wonder, Vínland and Mediaeval Travel Narratives," *Mediaeval Scandinavia* 14 (2004): 91-114.
6. For a general study of medieval conceptions of Paradise on Earth, see Alessandro Scafi, *Mapping Paradise: A History of Heaven on Earth* (Chicago, 2006).
7. ÍF 1 = *Íslendingabók: Landnámabók*, Íslenzk fornrit 1, ed. Jakob Benediktsson (Reykjavík, 1968), 13-14: *Þeir fundu þar manna vistir bæði austr ok vestr á landi ok keiplabrot ok steinsmíði þat es af því má skilja, at þar hafði þess konar þjóð farit, es Vínland hefir byggt ok Grænlendingar kalla Skrælinga.*
8. Adam of Bremen, *Hamburgische Kirchengeschichte/Gesta Hamburgensis Ecclesiae Pontificum*, ed. Bernhard Schmeidler, 3rd ed. (Hannover, 1917), 275: *Preterea unam adhuc insulam recitavit a multis in eo repertam oceano, quae dicitur Winland, eo quod ibi vites sponte nascantur, vinum optimum ferentes. Nam et fruges ibi non seminatas habundare non fabulosa opinione, sed certa comperimus relatione Danorum.*
9. ÍF 4 = *Eyrbyggja saga; Brands þáttr ǫrva; Eiríks saga rauða; Grænlendinga saga; Grænlendinga þáttr*, Íslenzk fornrit 4, ed. Einar Ól. Sveinsson and Matthías Þórðarson (Reykjavík, 1935), 211: *Lætr Leifr í haf ok er lengi úti ok hitti á lǫnd þau, er hann vissi áðr enga ván til. Váru þar hveitiakrar sjálfsánir ok vínviðr vaxinn. Þar váru þau tré, er mǫsurr heita, ok hǫfðu þeir af þessu ǫllu nǫkkur merki, sum tré svá mikil, at í hús váru lǫgð.*
10. Ibid., 221: *Í Brattahlíð hófusk miklar umræður, at menn skyldi leita Vínlands ins góða, ok var sagt, at þangat myndi vera at vitja góðra landkosta; ok þar kom, at Karlsefni ok Snorri bjuggu skip sitt at leita landsins um várit.*
11. Ibid., 234: *Þeir sǫgðu þar liggja land ǫðrum megin, gagnvart sínu landi, er þeir menn byggðu, er váru í hvítum klæðum ok báru stangir fyrir sér, ok váru festar við flíkr ok œpðu hátt, ok ætla menn, at þat hafi verit Hvítramannaland eða Írland it mikla.*
12. For a discussion of these references, see, e.g., Björn Þorsteinsson, "Some Observations on the Discoveries of the Norsemen," *Saga-Book* 16 (1962-65): 187. For the most recent treatments, see Larrington, "Wonder, Vínland and Mediaeval Travel Narratives," and Else Mundal, "Hvítramannaland and Other Fictional Islands in the Sea," in *Isolated Islands in Medieval Nature, Culture and Mind*, ed. Torstein Jørgensen and Gerhard Jaritz (Budapest, 2011), 81-87.
13. ÍF 4, 249: *Þar sigla þeir at landi ok kǫstuðu akkerum ok skutu báti ok fóru á land ok sá þar eigi gras. Jǫklar miklir váru allt it efra, en sem ein hella væri allt til jǫklanna frá sjónum, ok sýndisk þeim þat land vera gœðalaust. Þá mælti Leifr: "Eigi er oss nú þat orðit um þetta land sem Bjarna, at vér hafim eigi komit á landit. Nú mun ek gefa nafn landinu ok kalla Helluland."*
14. Ibid., 250: *Þat land var slétt ok skógi vaxit, ok sandar hvítir víða, þar sem þeir fóru, ok ósæbratt. Þá mælti Leifr: "Af kostum skal þessu landi nafn gefa ok kalla Markland."*
15. Ibid., 253: *Ok er várar, þá bjuggusk þeir ok sigldu burt, ok gaf Leifr nafn landinu eptir landkostum ok kallaði Vínland.*

16. Judith Jesch, "Naming and Narratives: Exploration and Imagination in the Norse Voyages Westward," in *The World of Travellers: Exploration and Imagination*, ed. Kees Dekker et al. (Leuven, 2009), 61–79.
17. *ÍF 1*, 13.
18. Jesch, "Naming and Narratives," 66.
19. Ibid., 71.
20. Ibid., 72.
21. Adam of Bremen, *Gesta Hamburgensis Ecclesiae Pontificum*, 257: *Ibi sunt Amazones, ibi Cynocephali, ibi Ciclopes, qui unum in fronte habent oculum; ibi sunt hii, quos Solinus dicit Ymantopodes, uno pede salientes, et illi, qui humanis carnibus delectantur pro cibo.*
22. For further discussions of monsters and monstrosity, see in particular the chapters by Erling Sandmo and Siv Frøydis Berg in this volume.
23. *ÍF 4*, 232: *Þat var einn morgin, er þeir Karlsefni sá fyrir ofan rjóðrit flekk nǫkkurn, sem glitraði við þeim, ok œpðu þeir á þat. Þat hrœrðisk, ok var þat einfœtingr.*
24. *ÍF 4*, 262: *þá bar skugga í dyrin, ok gekk þar inn kona í svǫrtum námkyrtli, heldr lág, ok hafði dregil um hǫfuð ok ljósjǫrp á hár, fǫlleit ok mjǫk eygð, svá at eigi hafði jafnmikil augu sét í einum mannshausi. Hon gekk þar at, er Guðríðr sat, ok mælti: "Hvat heitir þú?" segir hon. "Ek heiti Guðríðr; eða hvert er þitt heiti?" "Ek heiti Guðríðr," segir hon. ... þá heyrði Guðríðr brest mikinn, ok var þá konan horfin.*
25. Carolyne Larrington, "Wonder, Vínland and Mediaeval Travel Narratives," 106.
26. *ÍF 4*, 269.
27. *Historia Norwegie*, ed. Inger Ekrem and Lars Boje Mortensen, trans. Peter Fisher (Copenhagen, 2003), 54: *Qua patria* [Greenland] *a Telensibus reperta et inhabitata ac fide catholica roborata terminus est ad occasum Europæ, fere contingens Africanas insulas, ubi inundant oceani refluenta.*
28. Ólafur Halldórsson, ed., *Grænland í miðaldaritum* (Reykjavík, 1978), 79–80: *[Af] Bjarmalandi ganga lönd óbyggð of norðurætt, unz við tekur Grænland. Suður frá Grænlandi er Helluland, þá er Markland; þá er eigi langt til Vínlands hins góða, er sumir menn ætla að gangi af Afríka, og ef svo er, þá er úthaf innfallanda á milli Vínlands og Marklands.*

BIBLIOGRAPHY

Adam of Bremen. *Hamburgische Kirchengeschichte/Gesta Hamburgensis Ecclesiae Pontificum*. Edited by Bernhard Schmeidler. 3rd ed. Hannover: Hahnsche, 1917.

Björn Þorsteinsson. "Some Observations on the Discoveries of the Norsemen." *Saga-Book* 16 (1962–65): 173–91.

Crozier, Alan. "The *Vínland* Hypothesis: A Reply to the Historians." *Gardar: Årsbok för Samfundet Sverige-Island i Lund-Malmö* 29 (1999): 37–66.

Edson, Evelyn. *The World Map, 1300–1492: The Persistence of Tradition and Transformation*. Baltimore, MD: Johns Hopkins University Press, 2007.

Hiatt, Alfred. *Terra Incognita: Mapping the Antipodes before 1600*. Chicago: University of Chicago Press, 2008.//
Historia Norwegie. Edited by Inger Ekrem and Lars Boje Mortensen. Translated by Peter Fisher. Copenhagen: Museum Tusculanum Press, 2003.//
Hollander, Lee M., trans. *Heimskringla: History of the Kings of Norway by Snorri Sturluson*. Austin: University of Texas Press, 1964.//
ÍF 1 = Ari Þorgilsson: *Íslendingabók: Landnámabók*. Íslenzk fornrit 1, edited by Jakob Benediktsson. Reykjavík: Hið íslenzka fornritafélag, 1968.//
ÍF 4 = *Eyrbyggja saga; Brands þáttr ǫrva; Eiríks saga rauða; Grœnlendinga saga; Grœnlendinga þáttr*. Íslenzk fornrit 4, edited by Einar Ól. Sveinsson and Matthías Þórðarson. Reykjavík: Hið íslenzka fornritafélag, 1935.//
ÍF 26 = *Snorri Sturluson: Heimskringla 1*. Íslenzk fornrit 26, edited by Bjarni Aðalbjarnarson. Reykjavík: Hið íslenzka fornritafélag, 1941.//
Isidore of Seville. *Etymologiarum sive originum libri XX*. Edited by W. M. Lindsay. 2 vols. Oxford: Oxford University Press, 1911.//
Jesch, Judith. "Naming and Narratives: Exploration and Imagination in the Norse Voyages Westward." In *The World of Travellers: Exploration and Imagination*, edited by Kees Dekker, Karin Olsen, and Tette Hofstra, 61–79. Leuven: Peeters, 2009.//
Larrington, Carolyne. "'Undruðusk þá, sem fyrir var': Wonder, Vínland and Mediaeval Travel Narratives." *Mediaeval Scandinavia* 14 (2004): 91–114.//
Mundal, Else. "Hvítramannaland and Other Fictional Islands in the Sea." In *Isolated Islands in Medieval Nature, Culture and Mind*, edited by Torstein Jørgensen and Gerhard Jaritz, 81–87. Budapest: Central European University Press, 2011.//
Ólafur Halldórsson, ed. *Grænland í miðaldaritum*. Reykjavík: Sögufélag, 1978.//
Scafi, Alessandro. *Mapping Paradise: A History of Heaven on Earth*. Chicago: University of Chicago Press, 2006.//
Wawn, Andrew, and Þórunn Sigurðardóttir, eds. *Approaches to Vínland: A Conference on the Written and Archaeological Sources for the Norse Settlements in the North-Atlantic Region and Exploration of America*. Reykjavík: Sigurðar Nordal Institute, 2001.

20

The Cartographic Constitution of Global Politics

Jeppe Strandsbjerg

Introduction: The Cartographic Assemblage of Global Space

There was no global space prior to it being assembled through cartographic means from the fifteenth to the seventeenth centuries. By this, I mean that the notion of the globe had little impact on the political organization of space. When the globe first came to play a role, it emerged as an abstract—conceptualized but yet largely unknown—spatial referent.[1] That the globe was merely an abstract figure that would come to guide spatial thinking and politics in the proceeding centuries underlines a curious trend within social science, namely that it is taken as given that the globe is a natural space of humankind, whereas specific political spaces such as territory are considered historically contingent particularities.[2] The claim put forward in this chapter is that far from being a natural space that brings unity to humankind, global space is as political and constructed as any other social space.

While the concept of the globe is, of course, a precondition for global politics, the conceptualization in itself was of little use for navigating and capturing the globe as a stage for European ambitions. We often downplay the significance of the lengthy, arduous work of making the globe cartographically present at the European courts. When political practice expanded to a global scale, it required that global space was made practically known; otherwise it would not be possible to act on it. Following the Treaty of Tordesillas in 1494, both the Spanish and the Portuguese courts strived to develop techniques of global mapping. The treaty codified an intellectual and practical move that rendered the globe political and at times a universal, or singular, world stage for their competition.[3] In response, both Iberian courts launched large institutional cartographic projects to establish a new global reality of space that would allow long-distance exploitation and governance. These processes demonstrate how the globe was surveyed, recorded, and calculated—that is, mapped—in order to become a familiar space that allowed global politics to develop. And this, I argue, should be understood as a cartographic assemblage of a global space where "empirical observations" were gradually fitted into an epistemic framework based on an abstract vision of the globe.

Rather than thinking of the globe as a natural space, we can talk about a spatial reality being realized historically through cartographic assemblages. The concept of space embraces a notion of positioning, that is, both a relationship to others and a relationship between people and their material environment. As such, space signifies a social relation to the environment that has to be mediated through social practice, including technology. The point is that if space is a social relation, then a notion of social totality (in the shape of the globe) cannot rest on a notion of natural spatial unity as an ontological fact. Instead, the globe as a single stage for human interaction had to be constructed.

In making this argument, I draw on historical and geographical accounts such as Denis Cosgrove's *Apollo's Eye* (2003) and Jerry Brotton's *Trading Territories* (1997), and interpret these within a Latourian understanding of the relationship between space and cartography.[4] This implies that in order for a phenomenon (e.g., space) to be real, it has to be fabricated as an autonomous thing. In that process, space becomes a knowable phenomenon that appears differentiated from other things. Historically, cartography played a key role in the process that rendered space autonomous. Cartography embodies a set of practices that mediates between our material environment, technological oeuvre, and conceptualizations of space and cosmos. As a knowledge technology, scientific cartography[5] serves to unite a myriad of sites, places, and landscape features such as mountains and coastlines into a coherent phenomenon: geographical space. It is from this conceptualization of geographical space that I make the argument that there was no global space prior to its cartographic assemblage.

Turning the World Political

The Ottoman conquest of Constantinople in 1453 disrupted the trade patterns in and around the Mediterranean because the Ottomans came to control, or mediate, much of the lucrative trade with Asia. This provided an incentive for the West European rulers to seek alternative trade routes, and in particular Spanish and Portuguese rulers competed to establish and control westward trade routes along the west coast of Africa and the Atlantic islands. During the 1450s, Portugal claimed a monopoly on the Guinea trade on the grounds of being the first Europeans to discover these places. This right was granted by papal bulls.[6] A subsequent war of succession between Spain and Portugal led to the Treaty of Alcáçovas in 1479, which, interestingly, divided the contested areas in the Atlantic and East Africa into a Spanish and a Portuguese sphere. Portugal maintained its dominance at sea and Spain refrained from interfering in the Guinea trade. The Treaty of Tordesillas between Portugal and Spain from 1494 developed, on a global scale, the idea of dividing contested areas into spheres of legitimate possession.

Returning from the first voyage to the Americas, Christopher Columbus's fleet was forced to seek shelter in a Portuguese port in the Azores as a consequence of adverse weather conditions. Being suspicious of Columbus's voyage, the Portuguese authorities laid claim to his discoveries under the Treaty of Alcáçovas.[7] In response, Spain sought papal support and received it. Four bulls were issued by the pope, and the third—*Inter Caetera*—drew a boundary line that laid the foundation of the Treaty of Tordesillas ratified the subsequent year.[8] In this treaty it was agreed that

> a boundary or straight line be determined and drawn north and south, from pole to pole, on the said ocean sea, from the Arctic to the Antarctic pole. This boundary or line shall be drawn straight, as aforesaid, at a distance of three hundred and seventy leagues west of the Cape Verde Islands, being calculated by degrees. ... And all lands, both islands and mainlands, found and discovered already, or to be found and discovered hereafter ... shall belong to, and remain in the possession of, and pertain forever to, the said King of Portugal and his successors.[9]

The treaty then describes the principle of the east-west division. It is significant for a number of reasons. First, it renders the whole world a space for Spanish and Portuguese expansive trade and conquest by inserting the world map as its main reference (boundary from pole to pole). Second, it divides this world according to an abstract line of longitude that does not take into account what already exists in those places that might fall under the auspices of the Spanish or Portuguese crowns. As such, it ties law and space together in a particular way that decides both current and future "discoveries." The treaty refers to an abstract model of space where geographical details were not yet known. But with the expectation that all places can be located according to the grid of latitude and longitude, the treaty also pre-empts future controversies over spatial possession as authority over new land will simply be a matter of location within the matrix. In consequence, the treaty introduced a new logic where the political boundary came to refer to a map, or rather a cartoscientific assemblage of space. Politics no longer primarily corresponded with sociopolitical relations, or "the reality on the ground," but instead with a reality derived through cartographic means. To illustrate, it was already decided that Brazil would belong to the crown of Portugal even prior to its "discovery" in 1500 because it was located on the Spanish side of the demarcation line. It was thus the Treaty of Tordesillas, based on a cartographic reality of the world, that came to decide "the reality on the ground," and not the other way around. Therefore, in the years to come, legitimate claims to possession became inseparable from determining the location of longitudes and latitudes and deciding the location of coastlines and islands.

This shift in the legal and conceptual perception of the scope for European power was both informed by, and accelerated, what Walter Mignolo calls a cartographic revolution in Europe.[10] The adoption and translation of Ptolemy's *Geography* in the first decade of the fifteenth century is often noted as a symbolic starting point for a new way of mapping in Europe.[11] He famously laid out principles for geometric projections of geographical space onto a map based on a graticule of longitude and latitude as the ordering principle. Being an abstraction, the graticule allows the terrestrial world to become the totality that frames human activity even at a point where this space is as yet unknown.

With Tordesillas, the globe takes on a new meaning and the science of measurement becomes crucial for the politics of sovereignty. In principle, the abstract framework of the Ptolemaic globe and the legality sanctioned by the *Inter Caetera* papal bull turned boundary issues into a question of measuring geographical positioning and then deciding sovereignty according to the treaty. In 1515, for instance, a group of Portuguese were imprisoned for having violated Spanish rights by landing at the Cape of St. Augustine in Brazil, but controversy arose as it was not actually known where this cape was located in relation to the demarcation line. In response to this particular problem, a council of scientists and experts was assembled to determine whether the Cape of St. Augustine was on the Spanish or the Portuguese side of the demarcation line.[12] Within the schematic, the cartographic settlement of the boundary precedes territorial divisions on the ground.[13]

Turning the Globe Political

As the Treaty of Tordesillas drew the boundary from "pole to pole" on a two-dimensional map, it did not take into account that the Earth is a sphere. What happened if Spain sailed west and continued? The primary motive for exploration was trade, especially in spices, and the most valuable locus was the island group of the Moluccas in contemporary Indonesia. They were reached in 1515 by the Portuguese sailing east, and only later by Magellan's Spanish expedition sailing west in 1521.[14] This disrupted the settlement of the Treaty of Tordesillas because both countries could now claim the right to the island under the settlement of this treaty. To reach an agreement on the demarcation line that would run on "the other side of the Earth," negotiations commenced between representatives of the two nations during the 1520s.

These negotiations introduced the globe as a stage and a practical tool for international politics. Two delegations were launched from the respective sides, and they presented a large collection of maps and globes in order to support their claim to the disputed islands. Prolific cartographers such as Diego Ribeiro, who had been greatly involved in planning Magellan's journey,[15] and the Reinel brothers on the Portuguese side featured among the delegates. One of the key disputes was the size of the Earth, as the width of the Pacific would decide whether the islands would fall on one side or the other. Perhaps unsurprisingly, it was not possible to find a technical solution to the dispute; yet the interesting thing is the attempt. The question was settled with an agreement codified in the Treaty of Saragossa ratified in 1529. Charles V gave up his claim to the islands in return for compensation in gold, and the Spanish court negotiated a clause that allowed the settlement to be renegotiated if new geographical evidence should occur that would support the Spanish claim.[16] The agreement was tied up in a map that had to be recognized by both sides, who also agreed that the map "shall also designate the spot in which the said vassals of the said Emperor and King of Castile shall situate and locate Molucca, which during the time of this contract shall be regarded as situated in such place."[17]

The image of the globe was not an invention of the Renaissance, but the "practical use" to which it was put represented a significant transformation. In preceding periods, the globe had been adopted to signal universality and act as a symbol of power.[18] With the treaties of Tordesillas and Saragossa, the globe—still epitomizing universality—was becoming a political space for European empires in the making. This process, however, required more than an abstract model of the globe. As the globe became the theater of European politics, it became necessary to assemble a new global geography, because a landscape must first be mapped and made familiar for it to be navigated and controlled. That is, making the globe a practical, political space required its assemblage through cartographic means, and it was with the treaties of Tordesillas and Saragossa that politics began referring to a cartographically derived global space.

Assembling the Globe

In *Pandora's Hope*, Latour notes how navigating the landscape at ease presupposes previous mapping of that space.[19] If the maps are taken away and cartographic conventions confused, "our four scientists would be lost in the landscape and obliged once more to begin all the work of exploration, reference marking, triangulation, and squaring performed by their hundreds of predecessors. Yes, scientists master the world, but only if the world comes to them in the form of two-dimensional, superposable, combinable inscriptions."[20] Latour describes the work of contemporary scientists working in the field, but the imagined situation of scientists operating without their maps resembles that of the Iberian dynasties around 1500 who had little knowledge of the geography of the globe.

For Latour, knowledge is akin to familiarity. This implies that the significance of exploration is not to discover new lands but to bring them "back home" in terms of knowledge that will allow a return to the place in question.[21] It is all about the possibility of *coming back*. Bringing back places means that they need to be recorded in a manner that allows them to be combined with existing knowledge. For Latour, this means that places need to be made mobile, kept stable, and made combinable.[22] Hence, places, lakes, hills, and other geographical features have to be rendered mobile in order to constitute a whole. This enables people who have the accumulated knowledge to be able to send expeditions out to places, of which they have no personal experience, and be reasonably confident of the expeditions arriving at these places and returning home.

Establishing geographical knowledge in this manner needs to be coordinated by central institutions where calculations are made and the disparate places are assembled into a coherent expression of knowledge. At least that is the aim. In the wake of the settlement of Tordesillas, both the Spanish and the Portuguese authorities established institutions where they kept and developed "master maps" that assembled all the disparate pieces of information that were primarily recorded by sailors. The *Padreo Real* and the *Padron Real* were, respectively, the master charts of the Casa de Mina in Lisbon and the Casa de Contratación in Seville. The two crowns used these charts "to keep knowledge of new discoveries within the control of the state and to ensure the standardization of knowledge, so that errors and inconsistencies among charts could be eliminated and they could be revised and updated as new discoveries were made."[23] The maps were attempts to create a centralized knowledge framework that would allow pilots, by their own means, to return to any location that had been discovered and to ensure that this framework was regularly updated.

The Spanish *Padron Real* consisted of "a large world map and of a book of charts of considerable size covering specific routes."[24] It was managed by the Casa de Contratación (House of Trade), which was established in 1503 to control Spanish overseas trade and colonization. In effect it worked as a department of government responsible for, among other things, commerce, a school of navigation, and a hydrographic bureau.[25] The latter was established in 1508, with the famed explorer and cartographer Amerigo Vespucci as the first "pilot major" responsible for the *Padron Real*. Partly to remedy the problem of poor duplicate maps being sold in the Spanish ports, Vespucci was instructed to create an official master map to minimize errors.[26] David Turnbull quotes the instructions given to Vespucci at length:

> We command that a Padron General be made and, so that it should be more accurate, we command our officials of the Casa de la Contratación that they assemble all our pilots, the most skilled captains at the time, and that the said Amerigo Vespucci, our pilot major being present, a padron of all the lands and islands of the Indies hither to discovered and belonging to our kingdoms and seignories be drawn up and made. ... when they find new lands or islands or shoals or new harbours ... all shall be registered in the proper place in the padron real, in order that navigators be better advised and cautious.[27]

In that respect the *Padron* worked as a mediator between the pilots and the spatial locations they were exploring. On returning from the Indies, the pilots were obliged—under threat of heavy punishment—to submit their log to the Casa, where at least once a year the *Padron* was updated, and in turn new charts were distributed to navigators sailing to the New World.

In practice, the *Padron Real* was not entirely successful, because of epistemic complexities in its setup and because the *Casa* never achieved an effective monopoly on issuing charts.[28] Nevertheless, while being unable to establish a sustainable framework that could bring the entire globe together in a single map located in Seville, the *Padron* represents an early and costly attempt to record "the bearings of all lands."[29] In the context of Latour's notion of space and knowledge, the institutionalized master maps should be understood as a process of translation, where the concept of the globe via a new cartographic regime is assembled to accommodate legal-political ambitions. During the sixteenth century, cartographic practice gradually developed from a concern with sovereignty and the desire to produce a navigable global space to questions pertaining to governance and, eventually, establishing a universal geographical nature—whose essence was captured through geometry—as the spatial stage for politics.

Cartographic Encounters

The Spanish Crown faced a challenge of governing after the conquest of New Spain and Peru, and this increased the need for spatial knowledge. Governing European possessions meant governing a space within the reach of the monarch. Isabel and Ferdinand, for example, had traveled throughout their realm during their time in power in order to maintain a presence there. The new possessions, in contrast, were beyond the physical reach of the monarch's body.³⁰ Therefore, the court needed to obtain spatial "objective" knowledge, which lessened the dependence on local governors and indigenous knowledge. In other words, it was thus necessary to make the colonies present at the center of the empire.

The Council of the Indies was responsible for overseeing the government of the transatlantic empire and it did so "in superbly bureaucratic style, various instructions and questionnaires poured from the Council's desks to find their way to the remotest New World jurisdictions."³¹ Various surveys were commissioned and instructions issued to local governors to define the new possessions according to a grid system of latitude and longitude and obtain geographical details and local maps.³² From the 1570s, the cosmographer Juan López de Velasco came to coordinate what is known as the *Relaciones Geográficas*.³³ The *Relaciones* contained a large number of questionnaires asking local officials and governors to provide descriptions of the geography, history, mythology, and topographical mapping. Included was a detailed instruction of how and when to monitor a lunar eclipse.³⁴

If this ambitious project had been successful, colonial officials would have supplied "López de Velasco with accurate topographical and coastal maps, as well as precise lunar observations [that would have provided] ample information to make both geographic and chorographic maps of this crown jewel of Spain's colonial empire, thus making this part of the New World visible to its absent king."³⁵ This would have provided the state with a much-needed tool of governance. In the instruction to the governors of the *Relaciones Geográficas*, King Philip II wrote: "so that the Council can attend to their good government, it has seemed a proper thing to decree that a general description be made of the whole condition of our Indies, islands, and their provinces, the most accurate and certain possible."³⁶

Yet the project did not succeed. The *Relaciones* were based on a strictly Euclidian framework organized around the grid of longitude and latitude and aimed to produce disparate spatial data that were compatible (that is stable, mobile, and combinable, as discussed above). However, the questionnaire respondents did not render the world mobile in such a sense. The almost two hundred replies were all very different, incompatible both with each other and with the rational framework prepared "back home" by Velasco. He had, for example, written the instructions on the lunar eclipse observations so that a layperson would be able to return "scientific spatial data" required by the "experts" back home. Yet very few observations were returned, and although some were fairly accurate, the project did not succeed in establishing a precise network of positions.³⁷

Equally disappointing, from Velasco's point of view, were the topographical maps. The majority of these had been painted by Native Americans who were drawing heavily on their own map-making traditions with their associated iconography.[38] The result appeared as an intricate hybrid of new cartographic conventions and the indigenous traditions that were largely incommensurable with the Ptolemaic episteme of map-making. On the other hand, these hybrid responses proved that the immediate encounter between the two cultures was not antagonistic. Most of the maps contained a mix of the Ptolemaic style of the Spaniards and the cartographic mode of the natives, building on a social projection where societal hierarchies and relations provide the map's ordering principle.[39] These maps were of little help for the governing ambitions of the Spanish court, yet the process behind them clearly illustrates the challenges of assembling a unified global space and the need to mobilize all sites according to a singular mode of calculation.

Conclusion

Even though there was a widespread concept of a globe prior to the Renaissance, its meaning changed with the advent of the treaties of Tordesillas and Saragossa. But in order to be navigable and governable, global space had to be assembled through laborious surveying and calculative practices. When the Spanish and Portuguese strove so industriously to map the globe during the sixteenth century, their aim was to assemble a cartographic global space that would allow them to navigate and compete on a global scale. This illustrates the flaws of the common notion of global space as simply waiting to be flooded by European mariners, merchants, and missionaries. In both popular and academic discourse, it is curious how the globe is often considered a more natural space than particular political spaces, such as territory, that have acquired a connotation of stasis and artificiality. Space can be understood as natural, obviously, only if it is detached from the social.

For social life, the globe is not a more natural space for politics than territory. Global space should not be considered as something eternally present bringing unity to humanity; spatial relations have to be constructed, not simply in terms of conceptualization or connections between people, but in processes where the material environment is fabricated as a thing in itself. As pointed out by Latour, thinking space and time independently as a frame of reference *inside* which events occur "makes it impossible to understand how different spaces and different times may be produced *inside the networks* built to mobilize, cumulate and recombine the world."[40] It was inside the Casa de Mina in Lisbon and the Casa de Contratación in Seville that global space was being assembled from the many sources and recordings that were made available there. It was these practices that enabled networks of trade and conquest to expand, illustrating again, in Latour's words, that "space is something generated *inside* the observatory."[41]

Jeppe Strandsbjerg is Editor-in-Chief with DJØF Publishing and a former Associate Professor of International Relations at the Copenhagen Business School, Denmark. He has primarily written on the concept of space in International Relations, the relationship between space and state formation, and in particular on the significance of cartography.

NOTES

1. For further discussions of the globe, see in particular the chapters by Stefan Willer, Alfred Hiatt, Kari van Dijk, Helge Jordheim, Siv Frøydis Berg, and Espen Ytreberg in this volume.
2. Examples are plenty. For an influential example in the globalization literature, see Jan A. Scholte, *Globalization: A Critical Introduction* (Basingstoke, 2005); for a historical account of Europe that represents a similar approach to global space, see Eric R. Wolf, *Europe and the People without History* (Berkeley, 1990).
3. There might be a danger, however, that scholarship emphasizing the significance of Tordesillas reproduces another mythological transition, just like the discipline of International Relations has reified the Treaties of Westphalia beyond historical recognition. I owe this point to Nisha Shah.
4. Jerry Brotton, *Trading Territories: Mapping the Early Modern World* (London, 1997); Denis E. Cosgrove, *Apollo's Eye: A Cartographic Genealogy of the Earth in the Western Imagination* (Baltimore, MD, 2003); Bruno Latour, *Science in Action: How to Follow Scientists and Engineers through Society* (Milton Keynes, 1987); Bruno Latour, *Pandora's Hope: Essays on the Reality of Science Studies* (Cambridge, MA, 1999).
5. I consciously avoid the term "modern cartography" to describe the cartographic trends in Europe from the Renaissance onward, as "scientific" or "geometric" provide a more apt description of this mode of cartography.
6. J. H. Parry, *The Age of Reconnaissance: Discovery, Exploration, and Settlement, 1450–1650* (London, 2000), 134.
7. Ibid., 151.
8. Ibid., 150–52.
9. "Treaty between Spain and Portugal Concluded at Tordesillas," Avalon Project, retrieved 10 June 2013 from http://avalon.law.yale.edu/15th_century/mod001.asp.
10. Walter D. Mignolo, *The Darker Side of the Renaissance: Literacy, Territoriality, and Colonization* (Ann Arbor, 1995), 219–58.
11. Raleigh A. Skelton, *Decorative Printed Maps of the 15th to 18th Centuries: A Revised Edition of Old Decorative Maps and Charts* (London, 1965), 35.
12. Ursula S. Lamb, "The Spanish Cosmographic Juntas of the Sixteenth Century," *Terrae Incognitae* 6 (1974): 53.
13. For further discussions of territory, see in particular the chapters by Andreas Philippopoulos-Mihalopoulos and Stefan Willer in this volume.
14. Marcel Destombes, "The Chart of Magellan," *Imago Mundi* 12, no. 1 (1955): 66.
15. Brotton, *Trading Territories*, 133.

16. Ibid., 136.
17. Ibid., 137, quoting Frances G. Davenport, *European Treaties Bearing on the History of the United States and Its Dependencies* (Washington, DC, 1967).
18. Cosgrove, *Apollo's Eye*, 11.
19. Latour, *Pandora's Hope*, 28–29.
20. Ibid., 29.
21. Latour, *Science in Action*, 217.
22. Ibid., 223.
23. David Turnbull, "Cartography and Science in Early Modern Europe: Mapping the Construction of Knowledge Spaces," *Imago Mundi* 48, no. 1 (1996): 7.
24. Lamb, "Spanish Cosmographic Juntas," 57.
25. Clarence H. Haring, *Trade and Navigation between Spain and the Indies in the Time of the Hapsburgs* (Gloucester, MA, 1964), 32.
26. Ibid., 306.
27. Turnbull, "Cartography and Science," 11.
28. Haring, *Trade and Navigation*, 307.
29. Latour, *Science in Action*, 224.
30. Barbara E. Mundy, *The Mapping of New Spain: Indigenous Cartography and the Maps of the Relaciones Geograficas* (Chicago, 1996), 8.
31. Clinton R. Edwards, "Mapping by Questionnaire: An Early Spanish Attempt to Determine New World Geographical Positions," *Imago Mundi* 23, no. 1 (1969): 17.
32. Mundy, *Mapping of New Spain*, 12.
33. Howard F. Cline, "The *Relaciones Geográphicas* of the Spanish Indies, 1577–1586," *Hispanic American Historical Review*, August (1964): 346.
34. Mundy, *Mapping of New Spain*, 18.
35. Ibid., 22.
36. Cline, "*Relaciones Geográphicas* of the Spanish Indies," 363.
37. Edwards, "Mapping by Questionnaire," 22–27.
38. Mundy, *Mapping of New Spain*, 215.
39. Ibid., xiv–xvi.
40. Latour, *Science in Action*, 228; emphasis in the original.
41. Ibid., 229; emphasis in the original.

BIBLIOGRAPHY

Brotton, Jerry. *Trading Territories: Mapping the Early Modern World*. London: Reaktion, 1997.

Cline, Howard F. "The *Relaciones Geográphicas* of the Spanish Indies, 1577–1586." *Hispanic American Historical Review*, August (1964): 341–74.

Cosgrove, Denis E. *Apollo's Eye: A Cartographic Genealogy of the Earth in the Western Imagination*. Baltimore, MD: Johns Hopkins University Press, 2003.

Davenport, Frances G. *European Treaties Bearing on the History of the United States and Its Dependencies*. Washington, DC: Carnegie Institution of Washington, 1967.

Destombes, Marcel. "The Chart of Magellan." *Imago Mundi* 12, no. 1 (1955): 65–88.
Edwards, Clinton R. "Mapping by Questionnaire: An Early Spanish Attempt to Determine New World Geographical Positions." *Imago Mundi* 23, no. 1 (1969): 17–28.
Haring, Clarence H. *Trade and Navigation between Spain and the Indies in the Time of the Hapsburgs*. Gloucester, MA: Peter Smith, 1964.
Lamb, Ursula S. "The Spanish Cosmographic Juntas of the Sixteenth Century." *Terrae Incognitae* 6 (1974): 51–64.
Latour, Bruno. *Pandora's Hope: Essays on the Reality of Science Studies*. Cambridge, MA: Harvard University Press, 1999.
———. *Science in Action: How to Follow Scientists and Engineers through Society*. Milton Keynes: Open University Press, 1987.
Mignolo, Walter D. *The Darker Side of the Renaissance: Literacy, Territoriality, and Colonization*. Ann Arbor: University of Michigan Press, 1995.
Mundy, Barbara E. *The Mapping of New Spain: Indigenous Cartography and the Maps of the Relaciones Geograficas*. Chicago: University of Chicago Press, 1996.
Parry, J. H. *The Age of Reconnaissance: Discovery, Exploration, and Settlement, 1450–1650*. London: Weidenfeld & Nicolson, 2000.
Scholte, Jan A. *Globalization: A Critical Introduction*. Basingstoke: Palgrave Macmillan, 2005.
Skelton, Raleigh A. *Decorative Printed Maps of the 15th to 18th Centuries: A Revised Edition of Old Decorative Maps and Charts*. London: Spring Books, 1965.
Stevenson, Edward L. "The Geographical Activities of the Casa de la Contratacion." *Annals of the Association of American Geographers* 17, no. 2 (1927): 39–59.
Strandsbjerg, Jeppe. "Cartopolitics, Geopolitics and Boundaries in the Arctic." *Geopolitics* 17, no. 4 (2012): 818–42.
———. *Territory, Globalisation and International Relations: The Cartographic Reality of Space*. Basingstoke: Palgrave, 2010.
Thrower, Norman J. W. *Maps and Civilization: Cartography in Culture and Society*. Chicago: University of Chicago Press, 1999.
Turnbull, David. "Cartography and Science in Early Modern Europe: Mapping the Construction of Knowledge Spaces." *Imago Mundi* 48, no. 1 (1996): 5–24.
Wolf, Eric R. *Europe and the People without History*. Berkeley: University of California Press, 1990.

▶• 21 •◀

The Individual and the "Intellectual Globe"

Francis Bacon, John Locke, and Vannevar Bush

Richard Yeo

In the *Atlantic Monthly* of July 1945, Vannevar Bush, the American engineer and wartime science advisor to the president, proposed that information derived from various sources could be conveniently stored on microfilm. He imagined a machine that stored and retrieved reels of specially selected information:

> Consider a future device for individual use, which is a sort of mechanized private file and library. It needs a name, and, to coin one at random, "memex" will do. A memex is a device in which an individual stores all his books, records, and communications, and which is mechanized so that it may be consulted with exceeding speed and flexibility. It is an enlarged intimate supplement to his memory.[1]

The storage capacity of the memex would be considerable: "Only a small part of the interior of the memex is devoted to storage, the rest to mechanism. Yet if the user inserted 5000 pages of material a day it would take him hundreds of years to fill the repository."[2] On this basis, Bush declared that "The *Encyclopaedia Britannica* could be reduced to the volume of a matchbox. A library of a million volumes could be compressed into one end of a desk."[3] However, this is not what he intended to do because he did not envisage the memex as a new way of storing older selections and arrangements of information and knowledge. Instead, he regarded it a personal, even a private device in the battle against information overload—a problem not adequately addressed, in his opinion, by library catalogues, or encyclopedias and their classification and organization of subjects.[4] Bush was preoccupied with the needs of individuals (such as himself) who wanted to keep track of their own information and thoughts gathered for specific purposes. He predicted the emergence of new sets of information drawn from a great variety of sources and tailored to the interests and projects of the individual owner of a memex:

> Wholly new forms of encyclopedias will appear, ready-made with a mesh of associative trails running through them, ready to be dropped into the memex and there amplified. The lawyer has at his touch the associated opinions and decisions of his whole experience. ... The physician, puzzled by a patient's reactions, strikes the trail established in studying an earlier similar case, and runs rapidly through analogous case histories, with side references to the classics for the pertinent anatomy and histology.[5]

Bush's allusion to "new forms of encyclopedias" may seem to invoke the traditional interest, pursued from ancient Greece to the European Enlightenment, in mapping the contours of the "intellectual globe," conceived as the complete body of human knowledge.[6] However, Bush was not deferring to the notion of a circle of knowledge (*encyclios paideia*), other ideas about systematic relationships among subjects, or preferred pathways through knowledge.[7] He was not concerned with disciplinary relationships but with the mental associations in the individual's mind, as registered by past search "trails" (as he called them) preserved in the memex. His key notion was "associative indexing," which, he explained, was "a provision whereby any item may be caused at will to select immediately and automatically another. This is the essential feature of the memex. The process of tying two items together is the important thing." Bush also spoke, as we do now, of "linking" items.[8] The memex allowed these search trails to displace all concern with classification and conceptual genealogy. Although critics at the time indicated that users of the device depended, at least initially, on general subject categories and sub-divisions provided by library catalogues and encyclopedias, the appeal today of both Wikipedia and Google confirms the prescience of Bush's view. Indeed, Google (and other online corporations, such as Amazon) have taken the tracking and predicting of personal choice and interest further than Bush imagined.

Does the traditional concept of an "intellectual globe" continue to serve any purpose? Certainly, it seems, for the tasks of finding and retrieving information, the availability of fingertip searches of words or short sequences of letters has severely lowered the utility of subject catalogues and the indexes of printed reference works. In this sense, as Bush anticipated in 1945, the individual can now be the center of his or her own intellectual world. However, this is precisely the issue confronted by earlier reflections on the world of knowledge and learning: namely, how did the individual relate to the "intellectual globe," conceived as the collective knowledge of mankind? What parts of this world were fundamental, in what order should they be approached, and how many should be attempted? In this chapter I consider the views of

Francis Bacon and John Locke, two early modern English figures attached, in retrospect, to the Enlightenment encyclopedic project.

Francis Bacon

In the "Preliminary Discourse" (1751) to the *Encyclopédie* (1751–80), Jean le Rond d'Alembert, with the agreement of Denis Diderot, expressed debts to Bacon for his classification of knowledge, and to Locke for his analysis of human knowledge in terms of constituent ideas and their combinations. Indeed, d'Alembert and Diderot adopted Bacon's classification in terms of governing mental faculties: thus memory, imagination, and reason controlled, respectively, the fields of history, poetry, and philosophy.[9] Bacon's approach involved the idea of *homo faber*, "man the maker"—in this case, the mind as the maker of knowledge (apart from revealed knowledge).[10] Enlarging on this, the French *philosophes* argued that because humans *made* knowledge (as opposed to the objects and structures of the natural world), they could arrange it in ways that suited their purposes. D'Alembert believed that since the Scientific Revolution of the seventeenth century, knowledge had progressed by intense specialization within limited domains and that "the infinitely varied branches of human knowledge" formed "a truly unified system."[11] But when thinking about relationships between various disciplines, d'Alembert adopted a seemingly cavalier attitude, saying that, as with "general maps of the globe," these connections could be represented in various, even arbitrary, ways. He declared that "one can create as many different systems of human knowledge as there are world maps having different projections."[12] Although Bacon also contended that there were several plausible ways of classifying the "sciences" (in the sense of branches of scholarly inquiry), he affirmed the importance of this task and announced that his own attempt was crucial both for the advancement of learning and for the intellectual and moral benefit of those individuals who pursued, or used, knowledge. Additionally, when he (and also Locke) contemplated the branches of knowledge, they recognized that each individual could feasibly know only a small portion of it. In their view, this entailed intellectual and moral decisions about, for example, whether general or specific knowledge should be sought.

In about 1592, Bacon told Lord Burghley that "I have taken all knowledge to be my province."[13] In the *Novum organum* (1620), he said that although the things he addressed are "quite new," they "are framed on an extremely ancient archetype, i.e., the very world itself, and the nature of things and of the mind."[14] Bacon accepted the challenge of mapping the world of knowledge produced by the mind so as to improve its fit with "the very world itself." He concluded his *Advancement of Learning* (1605) on this point: "Thus have I made as it were a small Globe of the Intellectuall world, as truly and faithfully as I coulde discover, with a note and description of those parts which seeme to mee, not constantly occupate, or not well converted by the labour of Man."[15] In 1612, in *Descriptio globi intellectualis*, he restated the case for his classification of knowledge by reference to the three mental faculties by which it was acquired, contending that "there cannot be others or any more than these."[16] Far more so than d'Alembert, Bacon regarded this delineation of the intellectual world as a guide for the advancement of the sciences. He stressed that individuals seeking particular knowledge needed to be aware of what had already been done, what needed to be done, and how the various disciplines related to each other. It is also important to appreciate that Bacon made an a priori assumption that there was a unity among the several branches of knowledge, stressing that the divisions he drew must always be seen rather as "*lines* & *veines*, then [than] for *sections* and *separations*: and that the continuance and entireness of knowledge be preserved."[17] This conviction did not rest, as it did for d'Alembert, on confidence about the power of the geometric, or mathematical, method when applied to the empirical and physical world. Rather, Bacon insisted that general and synthetic doctrines must be founded on a solid gathering of information in what he called "natural histories," and that this entailed a proper order of inquiry.[18] In 1674 Robert Boyle agreed that Bacon offered a reliable compass: he spoke of "that great Restorer of Physicks, the illustrious *Verulam*, who has trac'd out a most useful way to make Discoveries in the Intellectual Globe, as he calls it."[19]

Bacon's idea of an intellectual globe was elaborated in the title-pages of two of his works: the posthumously published *Sylva sylvarum* (1627) and the English translation by Gilbert Watts in 1640 of the *De dignitate et augmentis scientiarum* (1623). The engraved illustrations pay homage to Simon van de Passe's famous title-page for the *Instauratio magna* (1620) with its image of a ship sailing through the Pillars of Hercules (at the entrance to the straits of Gibraltar) in search of the *terra incognita*, and also new knowledge.[20] However, the two later images introduced the notion of an intellectual globe that complements, at least potentially, the physical globe explored by travel and understood by science. In *Sylva sylvarum*, the *mundus intellectualis* is depicted as a globe between the two pillars (Figure 21.1).[21] In Watts' translation of *De augmentis*, this globe is placed in the top right corner, facing, and in communication with, the *mundus visibilis* (Figure 21.2). Watts assured readers that Bacon believed that "the Intellectual Globe, and the Globe of the World, intermix their beams and irradiations in a direct line of projection, to the Generation of Sciences." He said that this would come about by "bringing in, a new Primum Mobile, into the Intellectual Globe of Sciences."[22] This new prime mover was the reform in method and attitude demanded by Bacon's

Figures 21.1 and 21.2. Illustrations from Francis Bacon's *Sylva sylvarum or a Naturall Historie, in Ten Centuries* ([1627] 1651 edition) and *Of the Advancement and Proficience of Learning* ([1605] 1640 edition). Published with permission by Rare Books & Special Collections, University of Sydney Library.

"Great Instauration"—one that involved many people and that was to be a work more "of time than of talent."[23]

In discussing the ways in which Aristotle and other ancient teachers set out guidelines for thinking, especially in logic, Bacon acknowledged the appeal of a fixed, and incontestable, starting point. He developed this into a more general observation, namely that all men "have a desire, to have an *Atlas* or Axel tree within; to keep them from fluctuation; which is like to a perpetuall peril or falling."[24] I suggest that we can consider his intellectual globe as an attempt to provide such an anchor point for individuals, especially for those engaged in empirical inquiry that, in his estimate, lacked the counterpart of the rules and precepts established for logic and rhetoric.

In Bacon's time and into the seventeenth century, individual scholars such as Joseph Scaliger (1540–1609), Isaac Casaubon (1559–1614), and John Selden (1584–1654) were admired for their universal learning.[25] However, for Bacon, such polymathy was not a useful model for the reform of knowledge. First, it was unfeasible for the great majority of individuals who, although not likely to attain profound learning, nevertheless could contribute to the collective task of advancing knowledge, especially natural knowledge, or science; and second, it did not encourage new inquiry. This called for a radical change in intellectual training, so that the traditional "relationship of master and pupil" was replaced with that of "discoverer and improver of discoveries." Bacon alleged that the present stagnant condition of the sciences had been caused by "nothing more than the audacity of the few, and the idle slackness of the rest."[26] As he imagined it, the task was to fill out the intellectual globe so that it matched and explained the terrestrial, so that sciences accounted for the world of nature, and perhaps also for the social world. This endeavor was necessarily a collaborative one, extending over generations. It needed direction, and a survey of the kinds of knowledge was one such aid. Bacon complained that this had not been adequately attempted. For example, elaborate trees and Ramist diagrams were merely ways of arranging the poor stock of extant bookish knowledge, which itself was shallow and repetitive; and most traditional schemata outlined only a pedagogic order of study rather than a plan for research. His map of the intellectual globe promised to direct the efforts of those who had special knowledge of a topic, or mastery of a skill or art. Bacon adopted the role of the scholarly individual able to take a general view, albeit without claiming polymathic status: "Expert Men can Execute, and perhaps Judge of particulars, one by one; But the generall Counsels, and the Plots, and Marshalling of Affaires, come best from those that are *Learned*."[27]

Given Bacon's damning assessment of past intellectual progress, the lessons he drew from the historical record were mainly negative, such as what to avoid. In contrast, his positive advice on how to proceed was normative and heavily prescriptive. Bacon averred that the sciences developed in a definite sequence. Thus, his sub-divisions of subjects within the three main domains of knowledge—philosophy, history, and poetry—set out a fundamental structure designed to avoid category errors. Bacon stressed that the path of discovery must respect both the integrity and interdependence of the various sciences: natural history supported natural philosophy and so on up to the most abstract science, metaphysics, which "is charged with least multiplicitie." This "connexion, or concatenation" of knowledge gave some assurance that "the Notions and conceptions of Sciences" could be reduced to a manageable number, and so the individual, although confined to one short life, and able to master only a limited portion of knowledge, could appreciate the harmony of its parts. However, there was no secret that allowed one individual to embrace all the sciences; rather, the collective work of many individuals produced an intellectual pyramid that we can each admire.[28] Bacon allowed the individual to be either a spectator of or a small contributor to a long-term project that was not "beyond the capacity of mere mortals" because "its completion is not confided entirely to a single age but to a succession of them."[29]

John Locke

Like many other early modern thinkers, Locke was interested in what he called "the Division of the Sciences."[30] Indeed, during the 1670s he drew up several schemata that displayed the various branches of knowledge according to either the major disciplines and subjects or to the *ways* of knowing. In the latter, which resemble Bacon's reference to mental faculties, Locke gave the main divisions as *cognoscendorum, reminiscendorum,* and *agendorum*—thereby indicating that knowledge can be acquired by thinking, by remembering (largely through historical records), and by making practical or technical interventions.[31] But Locke granted a license to choose a division of subjects that suited an individual's purpose, a permission he emphasized in a journal entry of 1677, saying that such classification "perhaps will be best done by every one himself for his owne use as best agreeable to his owne notions; though the nearer it comes to the nature & order of things it is still the better."[32] The implication is that such categories can be functional, assisting organization and retrieval of information, such as that stored in notebooks. Indeed, in an anonymous French publication of 1686 about his way of making commonplace books, Locke suggested that separate notebooks be kept for three main branches of knowledge: physical knowledge, moral knowledge, and a third type concerning the use of signs, such as words.[33] When he settled on this tripartite schema of the "Sciences" in the last chapter of his *Essay* (1690), he rendered these branches as "*natural Philosophy,*" "*Ethicks,*" and "*the Doctrine of Signs,*" describing them as "the three great Provinces of the intellectual World, wholly separate and distinct one from another."[34] Given this view, it is not surprising that Locke, in contrast to Bacon, was unwilling to posit any discernible unity of the branches of knowledge, or at least not one that could direct particular inquiries, and still less one that might encourage older polymathic aspirations to universal learning.

In Locke's assessment, the human predicament was that of being caught between the folly of universal knowledge and the danger of limited exposure to a wide range of ideas and opinions. In 1677, while living and traveling in France, he made a long entry in his journal in which he considered how a person should cultivate, and balance, both body and mind in the pursuit of truth. Here Locke pondered the relation of the individual mind to the "provinces of the mundus intelligibilis as I may call it."[35] He began by questioning the ambition of universal learning, declaring that "the extent of knowledge or things knowable is so vast, our duration here so short, and the entrance by which the knowledge of things gets into our understanding so narrow, that the time of our whole life would be found too short" to attain such a goal.[36] He noted that the "most knowing men," engaged in a life of study, have all felt doubt, difficulty, and a sense of inadequacy.[37] When he returned to this theme in later published writings, Locke made some allowance for the difference between polite learning and the quest for *new* scientific knowledge, but nevertheless maintained that the problem was a general one.[38] Although he did not object to indulging "a taste of every sort of knowledge," Locke underlined clear limits and risks: "This is an excellency, indeed, and a great one too, to have a real and true knowledge in all, or most of the objects of contemplation. But it is what the mind of one and the same man can hardly attain unto."[39]

There was also an opposite, and equally dangerous, tendency: that of intellectual narrowness. In the *Conduct of the Understanding* (1697), Locke warned that even "men of study and thought" can go astray when they confine their interests and ideas to limited topics and sources of information:

> They converse but with one sort of men, they read but one sort of books, they will not come in the hearing but of one sort of notions: the truth is, they canton out to themselves a little Goshen, in the intellectual world, where light shines, and, as they conclude, day blesses them; but the rest of that vast expansum they give up to night and darkness, and so avoid coming near it. They ... will not venture out into the great ocean of knowledge.[40]

Locke tried to arbitrate between polymathic ambition and these tiny intellectual cantons. In early modern culture, the prestige of general learning was still strong—as seen in Bacon's adoption of this ideal when mapping the fields of knowledge. However, when the founding members of the Royal Society of London (from 1660) contemplated the extensive collection of empirical information that Bacon demanded, they were anxious about its implications for the individual inquirer. As Thomas Sprat put it in his quasi-official *History* (1667), the problem was that the "infinite *Observations*" required were impossible for "any single mind" to comprehend, and so he reported the preference for "*Companies* before *single endeavours* in *Philosophical* matters."[41] Locke also endorsed collaboration but realized that intellectual advances derived from passionate curiosity were often necessarily focused on one question, or within one subject:

> It is not amiss that every one should relish the science that he has made his peculiar study. ... But the contempt of all other knowledge, as if it were nothing in comparison of law or physic, of astronomy or chemistry, ... coops it [i.e., the understanding] up within narrow bounds, and hinders it from looking abroad into other provinces of the intellectual world.[42]

Locke's prescriptions thus ruled out any easy path to knowledge. Not only was universal knowledge a futile dream, but the collective knowledge of humanity did not transfer in any simple fashion to particular individuals:

> For, I think, we may as rationally hope to see with other Mens Eyes, as to know by other Mens Understandings. ... The floating of other Mens Opinions in our brains makes us not one jot the more knowing, though they happen to be true. ... In the Sciences, every one has so much, as he really knows and comprehends: What he believes only, and takes upon trust, are but shreds; which however well in the whole piece, make no considerable addition to his stock, who gathers them.[43]

On this view, each person must seek out his or her own knowledge of the world; books should be read, observations and experiments undertaken, and conversations enjoyed, but in the end doctrines and theories should receive assent only after proper comprehension.

Lessons from the Early Moderns

In sum, both Bacon and Locke identified the task of bringing the intellectual and visible worlds into alignment as a collective one to which individuals contribute in various measures. Bacon believed that this was most effectively done with reference to an appropriate framework, such as that supplied by his intellectual globe. He claimed that all individuals share the results consolidated by the pyramid of the sciences built by others over a long period of time. Locke's conclusion was less sanguine: he accepted the importance of collective effort, warning of the dangers of intellectual Goshens; but he placed a heavy onus on each individual who, in spite of limited knowledge, must assent, with moral responsibility, to the portions of knowledge and science he or she used. For Locke, more so than Bacon, the relationship of the individual to the world of knowledge posed a major dilemma.

Vannevar Bush has been seen as a pioneer of hypertext and the convenient processing of digital information; but he must also be identified as one who erased earlier concerns about the relation of individual understanding to the "intellectual globe." Some thirty years after Bush's paper, Mortimer Adler's construal of the role of the *Encyclopaedia Britannica* indicated that these concerns were not entirely outdated. Adler averred that "the whole world of knowledge is a single universe of discourse," and he sought to depict a revised circle of knowledge—"a figure in which one can go from any point, in either direction, around the circumference."[44] But Bush had already lost interest, and he took d'Alembert's acknowledgment of the arbitrary and functional nature of maps of knowledge to an extreme, dismissing these as irrelevant and making the individual alone the point of reference for interaction with the accumulated archive of information. He was content to offer his memex as a personalized Goshen formed by the tracks of the individual's own searches. In doing so he was, ironically, indebted to Bacon and Locke. These two major figures had removed polymathy or universal learning as a feasible ideal, and they acknowledged specialist knowledge as the emerging source of intellectual authority. However, they also believed that each person had a responsibility to be aware of the scope and limits of various disciplines, and the consilience or otherwise of claims made by rival methods and theories. If we wish to consider how individuals could, or should, appreciate the boundaries of disciplines and the contours of the world of knowledge, then these early modern deliberations are worth retention and consideration.

Richard Yeo is a historian of science, a Fellow of the Australian Academy of the Humanities, and Emeritus Professor at Griffith University, Brisbane. His books include *Defining Science: William Whewell, Natural Knowledge and Public Debate in Early Victorian Britain* (Cambridge University Press, 1993); *Encyclopaedic Visions: Scientific Dictionaries and Enlightenment Culture* (Cambridge University Press, 2001); and *Notebooks, English Virtuosi, and Early Modern Science* (University of Chicago Press, 2014).

NOTES

1. Vannevar Bush, "As We May Think," *Atlantic Monthly*, July (1945): 106–7. Bush's choice of name has been interpreted as a contraction of either "*mem*ory *ex*tended" or "*mem*ory ind*ex*." His idea is now, in retrospect, often regarded as a forerunner of hypertext. On this, and more generally, see Richard Yeo, "Before Memex: Robert Hooke, John Locke, and Vannevar Bush on External Memory," *Science in Context* 20 (2007): 21–47.
2. Bush, "As We May Think," 107; on the method of scanning, see 105–6.
3. Ibid., 103.
4. Ibid., 102. On this theme, see Richard Yeo, *Encyclopaedic Visions: Scientific Dictionaries and Enlightenment Culture* (Cambridge, 2001).
5. Bush, "As We May Think," 108.
6. For further discussions of the dictionary and the encyclopedia, see in particular the chapters by Nora Eggen and Sanja Perovic in this volume.
7. See L. M. de Rijk, "γκύκλιος παιδεία: A Study of Its Original Meaning," *Vivarium* 3 (1965): 24–93.
8. Bush, "As We May Think," 107.
9. Jean le Rond d'Alembert, *Preliminary Discourse to the Encyclopedia of Diderot*, trans. Richard N. Schwab with Walter E. Rex (Chicago, 1995), 143–57.
10. Antonio Perez-Ramos, *Francis Bacon's Idea of Science and the Maker's Knowledge Tradition* (Oxford, 1988).
11. D'Alembert, *Preliminary Discourse*, 5; see also 47.
12. Ibid., 48–49.

13. Francis Bacon, "Letter to Lord Burghley," in *Francis Bacon: The Major Works*, ed. Brian Vickers (Oxford, 2008), 20.
14. Francis Bacon, "Dedication to James I," in *The Oxford Francis Bacon*, vol. 11, *The Instauratio magna, Part II: Novum organum and Associated Texts*, ed. Graham Rees (Oxford, 2004), 7.
15. *The Oxford Francis Bacon*, vol. 4, *The Advancement of Learning*, ed. Michael Kiernan (Oxford, 2000), 192. Bacon also referred to a "faithfull perambulation of learning, with an inquiry what parts therof lye fresh and wast[e], and not improved & converted by the Industrie of man" (61).
16. Francis Bacon, *Descriptio globi intellectualis*, in *The Oxford Francis Bacon*, vol. 6, *Philosophical Studies c. 1611–c. 1619*, ed. Graham Rees (Oxford, 1996), 98–99; also Francis Bacon, "A Description of the Intellectual Globe," in *The Works of Francis Bacon*, vol. 5, ed. James Spedding et al. (Stuttgart, 1963), 504.
17. Bacon, *Advancement of Learning*, 93.
18. Francis Bacon, *Parasceve, ad historiam naturalem, et experimentalem* [A Preparative to a Natural and Experimental History], in *The Oxford Francis Bacon*, vol. 11, 451–53.
19. Robert Boyle, *The Excellency of Theology, Compared with Natural Philosophy* (1674), in *The Works of Robert Boyle*, vol. 8, ed. Michael Hunter and Edward B. Davis (London, 1999–2000), 75.
20. Francis Bacon, *Sylva sylvarum or a Naturall Historie, in Ten Centuries: Published after the Author's Death by William Rawley* (London, 1627).
21. For comments on both images, see Margery Corbett and Ronald Lightbown, *The Comely Frontispiece: The Emblematic Title-Page in England 1550–1660* (London, 1979), 185–89.
22. Gilbert Watts, "Favourable Reader," in Francis Bacon, *Advancement and Proficience of Learning*, trans. Gilbert Watts (Oxford, 1640), sig. ¶¶2r and the first page (facing sig. ¶3v).
23. Bacon, "Dedication to James I," 6–7.
24. Bacon, *Advancement of Learning*, 114. This draws on the fable of Atlas in Homer's *Odyssey* and Virgil's *Aeneid*.
25. Yeo, *Encyclopaedic Visions*, 9–12.
26. Bacon, "*Great Instauration* preliminaries", in *The Oxford Francis Bacon*, vol. 11, 13.
27. Francis Bacon, "Of Studies," in *The Oxford Francis Bacon*, vol. 15, *The Essayes or Counsels, Civill and Morall*, ed. Michael Kiernan (Oxford, 1985), 152. See also his *Advancement of Learning*, 11, for the negative appraisal of "Emperique Statesmen, not well mingled with men grounded in Learning."
28. Bacon, *Advancement of Learning*, 85; see also Francis Bacon, Translation of *De augmentis scientiarum*, in Bacon, *Works*, vol. 4, 361 on "uniting the axioms of sciences into more general ones."
29. Bacon, "*Great Instauration* preliminaries", 25.
30. John Locke, *An Essay Concerning Human Understanding*, ed. Peter H. Nidditch (Oxford, 1975), IV.xxi.

31. See, for example, Bodleian Library, Oxford, MS Locke c. 28, fols. 50–51 (of 1677); and Richard Yeo, *Notebooks, English Virtuosi, and Early Modern Science* (Chicago, 2014), chap. 7.
32. Bodleian Library, Oxford, MS Locke, f. 2, pp. 128–29 (5 April 1677).
33. In the French version these are *la Morale, & la Physique*; the third is *la science des signes*. [John Locke], "Methode nouvelle de dresser des recueuils: Communiquée par l'auteur," *Bibliothèque Universelle et Historique* 2 (1686): 326.
34. Locke, *Essay Concerning Human Understanding*, IV.xxi.2–5.
35. Bodleian Library, Oxford, MS Locke, f. 2, p. 86 (26 March 1677).
36. Ibid., 85. See also p. 42 (8 February 1677) under the heading "Understanding": "Our minds are not made as large as truth nor suited to the whole extent of things."
37. Ibid., 86. On this theme, see Richard Yeo, "Hippocrates' Complaint and the Scientific Ethos in early Modern England," *Annals of Science* 75 (2018): 73-96.
38. Richard Yeo, "John Locke and Polite Philosophy," in *The Philosopher in Early Modern Europe: The Nature of a Contested Identity*, ed. Conal Condren, Stephen Gaukroger, and Ian Hunter (Cambridge, 2006), 254–75.
39. John Locke, *Of the Conduct of the Understanding* (1697), in *The Works of John Locke*. A new edition, corrected, vol. 3 (London, 1823), 238–39 (section 19).
40. Ibid., 209 (section 3). Before the Exodus, the Jews lived in the "Land of Goshen" in Egypt (Genesis 45:9–10 and 47:27).
41. Thomas Sprat, *The History of the Royal Society of London, for the Improving of Natural Knowledge* (London, 1667), 102.
42. Locke, *Of the Conduct of the Understanding*, vol. 3, 244 (section 22).
43. Locke, *Essay Concerning Human Understanding*, I.iv.23.
44. Mortimer J. Adler, "The Circle of Knowledge," in *Encyclopaedia Britannica*, 15th ed., vol. 1, *Propaedia* (Chicago, 1974), 5–8.

BIBLIOGRAPHY

Adler, Mortimer J. "The Circle of Knowledge." In *Encyclopaedia Britannica*, 15th ed., vol. 1, *Propaedia*, 5–8. Chicago: Encyclopaedia Britannica, 1974.

Bacon, Francis. *Translation of De augmentis scientiarum*. In *The Works of Francis Bacon*, vol. 4, edited by James Spedding, Robert L. Ellis, and Douglas D. Heath, 273–498. Stuttgart: F. Frommann Verlag G. Holzboog, 1963. Reprint of 1857–74 edition; vol. 5, 3–123.

———. "Dedication to James I." In *The Oxford Francis Bacon*, vol. 11, *The Instauratio magna, Part II: Novum organum and Associated Texts*, edited by Graham Rees, 6-9. Oxford: Clarendon Press, 2004.

———. *Descriptio globi intellectualis*. In *The Oxford Francis Bacon*, vol. 6, *Philosophical Studies c. 1611–c. 1619*, edited by Graham Rees, 95–169. Oxford: Clarendon Press, 1996.

———. "A Description of the Intellectual Globe." In *The Works of Francis Bacon*, vol. 5, edited by James Spedding, Robert L. Ellis, and Douglas D. Heath, 503–44. Stuttgart: F. Frommann Verlag G. Holzboog, 1963. Reprint of 1857–74 edition.

———. "Letter to Lord Burghley." In *Francis Bacon: The Major Works*, edited by Brian Vickers, 20. Oxford: Oxford University Press, 2008.
———. "Of Studies." In *The Oxford Francis Bacon*, vol. 15, *The Essayes or Counsels, Civill and Morall*, edited by Michael Kiernan, 152–54. Oxford: Clarendon Press, 1985.
———. *The Oxford Francis Bacon*. Vol. 4, *The Advancement of Learning*. Edited by Michael Kiernan. Oxford: Clarendon Press, 2000.
———. *The Oxford Francis Bacon*. Vol. 11, *The Instauratio magna, Part II: Novum organum and Associated Texts*. Edited by Graham Rees. Oxford: Clarendon Press, 2004.
———. *Parasceve, ad historiam naturalem, et experimentalem* [A Preparative to a Natural and Experimental History]. In *The Oxford Francis Bacon*, vol. 11, *The Instauratio magna, Part II: Novum organum and Associated Texts*, edited by Graham Rees, 448–85. Oxford: Clarendon Press, 2004.
———. "Great Instauration preliminaries." In *The Oxford Francis Bacon*, vol. 11, *The Instauratio magna, Part II: Novum organum and Associated Texts*, edited by Graham Rees, 2–25. Oxford: Clarendon Press, 2004.
———. *Sylva sylvarum or a Naturall Historie, in Ten Centuries: Published after the Author's Death by William Rawley*. London: J. H. for William Lee, 1627.
Boyle, Robert. *The Excellency of Theology, Compared with Natural Philosophy* (1674). In *The Works of Robert Boyle*, vol. 8, edited by Michael Hunter and Edward B. Davis, 3–98. London: Pickering & Chatto, 1999–2000.
Bush, Vannevar. "As We May Think." *Atlantic Monthly*, July (1945): 101–8.
Corbett, Margery, and Ronald Lightbown. *The Comely Frontispiece: The Emblematic Title-Page in England 1550–1660*. London: Routledge & Kegan Paul, 1979.
D'Alembert, Jean le Rond. *Preliminary Discourse to the Encyclopedia of Diderot*. Translated by Richard N. Schwab with Walter E. Rex. Chicago: University of Chicago Press, 1995.
De Rijk, L. M. "γκύκλιος παιδεία: A Study of Its Original Meaning." *Vivarium* 3 (1965): 24–93.
Locke, John. *An Essay Concerning Human Understanding*. Edited by Peter H. Nidditch. Oxford: Clarendon Press, 1975.
———. *Of the Conduct of the Understanding* (1697). In *The Works of John Locke*. A new edition, corrected., vol. 3, 205–89. London: T. Tegg et al., 1823.
[Locke, John]. "Methode nouvelle de dresser des recueuils: Communiquée par l'auteur." *Bibliothèque Universelle et Historique* 2 (1686): 315–40.
Perez-Ramos, Antonio. *Francis Bacon's Idea of Science and the Maker's Knowledge Tradition*. Oxford: Clarendon Press, 1988.
Sprat, Thomas. *The History of the Royal Society of London, for the Improving of Natural Knowledge*. London: Royal Society, 1667.
Watts, Gilbert. "Favourable Reader." In Francis Bacon, *Of the Advancement and Proficience of Learning*, translated by Gilbert Watts, sig.¶¶2ʳ and the first page (facing sig. ¶3ᵛ). Oxford, 1640.
Yeo, Richard. "Before Memex: Robert Hooke, John Locke, and Vannevar Bush on External Memory." *Science in Context* 20 (2007): 21–47.
———. *Encyclopaedic Visions: Scientific Dictionaries and Enlightenment Culture*. Cambridge: Cambridge University Press, 2001.

———. "John Locke and Polite Philosophy." In *The Philosopher in Early Modern Europe: The Nature of a Contested Identity*, edited by Conal Condren, Stephen Gaukroger, and Ian Hunter, 254–75. Cambridge: Cambridge University Press, 2006.

———. *Notebooks, English Virtuosi, and Early Modern Science*. Chicago: University of Chicago Press, 2014.

Part V

MAKING THE WORLD

▶• 22 •◀

The World as Sphere

Conceptualizing with Sloterdijk

Kari van Dijk

The World as a Whole

Even before scientific evidence convinced us to think of our world as a sphere, the world was represented in terms of roundness. A famous example is the Hereford *mappa mundi*.[1] The reason for this is evident: the world has always been imagined and conceptualized in terms of totality,[2] as something central to human existence from which nothing is missing, something that lacks nothing and contains everything—including us as human beings. Because that which contains everything and lacks nothing must be whole,[3] it comes as no surprise that what we conceptualize as "the world" has been and still is associated with roundness, for there has not been a more powerful symbol of wholeness throughout the ages and all kinds of different cultures than the sphere. In European philosophy, wholeness has often been imagined as parts coming together to make up a whole.[4] Interestingly, this basic understanding of wholeness, namely of parts coming together to make up a round whole, does play a certain role whenever those of us conditioned by a European cultural context think of the world. For whatever our particular perception of the world is, we inevitably imagine a sphere-like shape, indicating a finite collection of everything there is, everything known to us, or, more specifically, everything that is meaningful to us. In 2011, the Haus der Kunst in Munich showed a retrospective of works by American artist Matt Mullican (1951) called *Organizing the World*. For Mullican, the world consists of many parts that are all meaningful entities in themselves and that should all be taken into consideration in order to do justice to the whole of our human experience of the world. Although Mullican's project "dovetails with the immoderate as well as unfulfillable claim to collecting everything that exists,"[5] his work shows quite clearly that the notion of the world as a (round) whole, consisting of many parts that essentially belong together, still has a powerful grip on us.

World-Making in the Age of Disenchantment

In *Globen* ("Globes"), the second part of his *Spheres* trilogy, German philosopher Peter Sloterdijk refers to an ancient mosaic showing philosophers pondering a sphere.[6] The world having become larger and less unequivocal in antiquity, Sloterdijk shows how conceptual strategies were invented in order to cope with a world that had begun to lose some of its self-evidence: the era of metaphysical globalization was born.[7] Thinking about the world is not the same as being in it, but in antiquity, thinking never meant that the sensation of being enveloped in a warm, well-tempered cosmos was ever in danger.[8] Being-in-the-world at that point answered to being immersed in a resonating, responsive cosmos, in which all parts of the shared world were animated and bound together by one or more shared focal points, be they gods or magic.[9] The resonance of this premodern equilibrium between self and world was guaranteed by what American philosopher Charles Taylor has called the "porous" or "embedded self."[10] "Embedded" in a resonated cosmos it did not think it could influence, the porous self did not experience any boundaries between itself and its surroundings and was either unable or unwilling to imagine itself "outside of a particular context," that is, outside of the world it shared with its fellow inhabitants.[11] However, in the wake of what Taylor calls "the great disembedding," dramatic changes started to affect the porosity of the relationship between self and world.[12] Concentrating on a "movement which gathers steam in the late mediaeval period," Taylor shows how certain forces within Latin Christendom began to feel dissatisfied with the fact that the drive toward perfection inherent to Christianity did not extend itself to the whole of society but was restricted to only a small group fully dedicated to such a drive.[13] In Taylor's view, this fundamental dissatisfaction generated an impulse to reform society as a whole, aiming at reshaping society in such a way that would make *all* "parts" embark on the voyage toward inner perfection. The relationship between self and world changed fundamentally because of this, in the sense that the cosmos in which the "porous" self formerly had felt itself immersed slowly but surely became an *object* for what Taylor calls the "work of reform," that is, an in its essence revolutionary project through which late medieval theologians and thinkers sought to change society as a whole.[14] Of course, this objectification necessarily led to a growing distance between self and world. Thus, a gradual disembedding of the self from the world took place, a world that was no longer felt to be perfect the way it was but that had to be improved according to a God-given road map. As a consequence, the importance of the individual mind as a crucial agent for envisioning a different, better world rose, and the "buffered self" began to emerge. This was a self that was able to imagine itself outside of the world, that focused entirely on its individual salvation, and that thereby began to draw distinct boundaries between self, world, and other(s). To Taylor, this change in the relationship between self and world marks the beginning of a process German philosopher Max Weber has called the disenchantment with the world, the *Entzauberung der Welt*.[15] By disenchantment, Weber refers to a process of intellectualization and rationalization caused by scientific discoveries at the dawn of modernity that led to the emergence of a subject that wanted to take possession of the world, aiming at controlling it by making it calculable.[16] Taylor and Weber take different views as far as the cause of disenchantment is concerned, but both understand *Entzauberung* as a process through which the gap between self and world has begun to widen. Sloterdijk, also writing in the tradition of Weber, arrives at similar conclusions with regard to the changed relationship of self and world in modernity.

Humans are sphere-builders (i.e., world-makers) in Sloterdijk's philosophy, because they need immunizing strategies in order to cope with a world that very often does not meet their needs.[17] In medieval times, Christianity functioned as a giant immunizing macrosphere in which all "parts" were infused with shared values and perspectives, and thus people felt protected by their faith in an omnipresent God who structured their world.[18] But in the wake of what Sloterdijk calls terrestrial globalization, meaning the era in which scientific evidence shook long-cherished religious beliefs and made conquistadores, scientists, cartographers, and missionaries go out into the world to see for themselves, the relationship between self and world changed.[19] Combined with developments from within Christian theology that—already before terrestrial globalization had been set in motion—inspired doubts about the finite nature of the cosmos, the disenchanted self had to face a world in which it felt less and less at home.[20] Dutch writer Joke J. Hermsen, in referring to Sloterdijk in one of her novels, speaks of the bursting of the divine bell with regard to this process: suddenly, cold air was entering the well-tempered macrosphere, causing disturbance in an order that for a long time had seemed never-changing and incontestable.[21] As Hermsen states, the self was from then on not so much *in* the world as it was *on* it, that is, moving around the world, measuring it, looking at it with cold, scientific eyes.[22] At the same time, the West set about conquering the whole of the then known world, "cloning" itself by forcing its own (Christian) worldview and mode of being-in-the-world onto the rest of the globe.[23] This process has ultimately led to what Sloterdijk describes as the third phase of a globalization process of which we now for the first time see the full consequences: the era of telecommunicative or electronic globalization, in which "all" parts of the world, be they regions, countries, or citizens, obey the rules of a late capitalistic clock that ticks in exactly the same manner wherever a transaction is being processed.[24] Thus, a *Weltinnenraum* ("world interior") has been created, a mega-sphere governed by a logic of sameness and unity.[25] Being heir to poststructuralist thinkers like Deleuze and Derrida, Sloterdijk leaves no doubt that we urgently need to revise the way we build our world(s). But in order to come up with different strategies to conceptualize the world, it is important to look into the reasons why modern people have felt a need to create a world that would be whole and one.

Craving for Unity

In *Blasen* ("Bubbles"), the microspherological core of his philosophy of spheres, Sloterdijk inquires into what it is that makes us essentially human. Surprisingly, he starts *in utero*: from the moment the fetus starts developing in the uterus, it lives enclosed in a well-tempered interior that protects its vulnerable inhabitant from anything that could harm it. Continually experiencing that everything it could possibly need is being provided for, it also senses the presence of a nameless companion that is always there: the placenta, feeding the fetus and providing it with an awareness of structure that tells it from the beginning *that it is not alone*.[26] This experience—only sensed, not known—is extremely important in the context of Sloterdijk's philosophy. For there, in the uterus, the foundation of what Sloterdijk sees as our utmost human capacity is laid. If we are humans, we are so because of the fact that we "know" from the moment we have been infused with life that being is about sharing and not being alone. The moment of birth, however, makes us suddenly lose the benign, well-tempered environment once so pleasing. Being separated from the placenta and confronted with a world so very different in atmosphere from where we originally came from, human life from then on is all about the attempt to compensate for the loss of an environment that we will never regain but that we can at least hope to rebuild *conditionally*.[27] This compensatory pattern calls to mind one of the most famous texts of Western metaphysics, namely Plato's *Symposion*. As it turns out, Sloterdijk refers quite often to this text in *Blasen*.[28] In the *Symposion*, Plato lets Aristophanes tell the tale of how humans once were godlike, powerful spherical beings that started to pose a serious threat to the gods. Because of this, their hubris was punished by Zeus, who weakened them by cutting each human being in half.[29] Since that day, humans have been trying to recover their former, lost wholeness by searching for their corresponding and complementing "other half" with whom it might become possible to reconstitute the lost wholeness.[30] Desire to Plato, then, is an attempt to regain wholeness: by desiring, humans try to overcome the severe fragmentation they have been subjected to.[31] Sloterdijk invokes this pattern in *Blasen* in the sense that Plato's first phase of the triadic structure of original wholeness, fragmentation, and regained wholeness is now located in the maternal uterus, where the fetus and its mute companion, the placenta, echo Plato's original, perfect human beings, unconscious of desire, lacking nothing. Zeus's primal cut, that is, the phase of fragmentation in the *Symposion*, is transformed into the moment of birth by Sloterdijk, in the sense that the fetus suddenly finds itself separated from its life-giving companion and is confronted with an external coldness it was never really prepared for. Subconsciously remembering the silent, intimate togetherness it once had in the uterus, the new-born human being will then, from the moment of its birth, try to recreate the fullness it once experienced by building spheres, fragile "round worlds" that only come into being when (at least) two human sphere-builders, driven by the same desire to regain a lost wholeness, meet and start building microspheres together. However, despite the similarities that exist between Plato's account of love and Sloterdijk's retelling of the age-old triad of original wholeness, fragmentation, and regained wholeness, Plato and Sloterdijk differ quite substantially from each other in the way they deal with the phenomenon of difference.[32]

In the *Symposion*, that which is cut in two halves is a perfect, godlike wholeness. Being suddenly marked by fragmentation, and thus by difference, Zeus's primal cut turns the original sphere-like creatures into humans, making them experience lack and consequently desire. This original wholeness, forever lost after fragmentation, is described and referred to in terms of an unbroken unity, which means that to Plato, love is a primal force through which humans try to overcome their human, imperfect, desiring state in favor of a condition without lack and desire.[33] World-making, be this on a micro- or macrospherological level, functions the same way in Sloterdijk's philosophy in the sense that it is a compensatory process through which the experience of a lost wholeness (say, the loss of the well-tempered interior the fetus shared with the placenta in the uterus, or the bursting of God's sheltering bubble at the dawn of modernity) has to be counterbalanced.[34] Thus, the macrospherological interior as shaped through terrestrial globalization leading up to the *Weltinnenraum* of our present age, namely an undivided whole leaving no room for differences, seems to find its most primal cause in what Plato describes as our human urge to compensate for an original loss. By attempting to turn the whole of the world into one, modern people have tried to compensate for the loss of at least two well-tempered interiors and have thereby stayed "true" to what Plato in his *Symposion* identifies as the most primal urge in life: the need to turn that which is fragmented, that is, different, into one.

Wholeness ≠ Unity

If the concept of the world as discussed above—that is, one that comprises everything there is and everything that exists—necessarily stems from emerging fractions and ruptures that separate one thing or human being from the other, then the world cannot be one but must necessarily be marked by difference. In recent years, the equation of wholeness with unity has made way for a different understanding of wholeness. Thus, thinkers like Sloterdijk, Wilhelm Schmid, and Luce Irigary have been searching for and working toward a wholeness that would no longer be one.[35] As far as Sloterdijk is concerned, his reworking of the concept of wholeness becomes apparent when looking into the concept of the sphere at a microspherological level. When describing the well-tempered environment in which the fetus slowly develops while being in the uterus, Sloterdijk stresses that the fetus experiences the presence of its silent companion, that is, the life-giving placenta, as a "with," a *Mit*. This sensed presence of something other with which the fetus shares its first interior makes the fetus experience itself as an "as well," an *Auch*. It is this primal *Hier-Dort-Struktur* ("here-there structure") that conditions the fetus to be a future sphere-builder, that is, a creator and inhabitant of shared round worlds.[36] Infusing us with subconscious, prelogical "knowledge" of how to succeed in building immunizing spheres together with fellow human beings, the prenatal *Hier-Dort-Struktur* suggests to us from the beginning that relating to something or someone other can neither be understood entirely in terms of unity nor entirely in terms of difference but must be based on a kind of bonding that eludes unequivocal concepts like unity or difference. With each and every sphere created, the lost relationship to the first "companion" we ever had is re-enacted, but the difference is that now these postnatal round worlds are the result of a joint activity by (at least) two subjects that are all imperfect, desiring human beings marked by difference and striving to regain at least something of the primal fullness now forever lost to him or her. Interestingly, the creation of these immunizing round worlds through which people can feel sheltered and protected does entail the possibility of participating in a shared experience of wholeness.[37] Still, people should never forget that spheres, like bubbles, are very fragile entities that can burst at any time—an aspect Sloterdijk stresses quite often.[38] Compared to the triadic structure in Plato's *Symposion* (original wholeness/unbroken unity, fragmentation, and regained wholeness), it is evident that in Sloterdijk's philosophy, fragmentation and difference are the foundation of sphere-building, and there seems to be no intention whatsoever in Sloterdijk's philosophy for this condition to be overcome. Sphere-building and world-making, then, are grounded in fragmentation and/or difference and can only be conceived of on the basis of that which is no longer one. It is this feature which makes the concept of the sphere a productive tool with regard to the challenge implied by a different conceptualization of the world.

On the Difficulty of Accepting Difference in a World That Is Not One

When German philosopher Markus Gabriel claims that the world does not exist, he refers to the fact that the concept of the world, understood as a whole that comprises everything there is, will never be accessible to humans—if only because being in the world and thinking about the world are two different things that both necessarily belong to the concept of the world if it is to comprise all there is, but that presupposes two very different relationships from self to world that cannot be enacted at the same time.[39] Also, humans are different from each other and have different perspectives, which means that how one person imagines or conceptualizes the world will in most cases be very different from how another person envisions the world. Since postmodernity, all has become a question of perspective, which at best means that it might be legitimate to speak of a multiplicity of worlds.[40] This line of thought is very central to Sloterdijk's thinking as well. Sloterdijk's philosophy of spheres can be described as a big wake-up call to our globalized world(s) in which everything seems so connected but in which so little real nearness and intimacy remain. In referring to Plato's *Symposion*, Sloterdijk wants to rekindle the *Ergänzungszauber* ("supplementary magic") by reminding us of our innate ability to create "bubbles," fragile well-tempered interiors through which we might become able to cope with the irreversible consequences of our disenchanted modern world.[41] In *Schäume* ("Foams"), the third part of his trilogy, Sloterdijk invokes the image of foam to make the structure of today's multifocal world apprehensible: if bubbles are the stuff our world(s) are made of on a microspherological level, then foam shows us that the world as we know it today consists of a multiplicity of worlds that are all very different from one another.[42]

One of the domains in which difference makes itself felt most acutely at present is the field of religion. In *A Secular Age*, Taylor highlights three key features of secularity, the third of which is about the "conditions of belief" in today's globalized world.[43] Secularization having led to a "move from a society where belief in God is unchallenged and indeed, unproblematic, to one in which it is understood to be one option among others, and frequently not the easiest to embrace," Taylor shows how secularization has set a global process in motion that cannot be turned back and that has left visible traces in the subjective realities of believers and non-believers alike.[44] Whether you believe or not, Taylor contends, our secularized world continually confronts us with fellow human beings who take different views on things, which means that one's own view is always in danger of being challenged. For that reason, "naïveté" seems to have become "unavailable to anyone, believer or unbeliever alike."[45] But even if the secular has become such a defining feature of our globalized world, there can be no doubt at present that religion has once more become a topic no one seriously dealing with the challenges of today's world can afford to avoid. Thus, a "return of religion" has been widely proclaimed, causing even convinced atheists like Alain de Botton to ask what aspects of religious life may have been lost to our present world and how they could be "fruitfully ... applied to the problems of secular society."[46] The approach de Botton chooses is certainly a rare phenomenon in a world in which "the presumption of unbelief has become dominant" and has "achieved hegemony" in trendsetting circles frequented by academics and intellectuals.[47] In 2009, Dutch best-selling author Kluun wrote a book called *God is gek: De dictatuur van het atheïsme* in which he criticizes the way in which famous Dutch talk show hosts, well-known debaters, and intellectuals time and again proclaim the allegedly undisputable fact that God does not exist.[48] In this context, it comes as no surprise that Kluun also refers to Richard Dawkins, in whom Kluun as well as other intellectuals see a militant atheist at work who argues more convincingly for his allegedly non-questionable case, so it seems, than any advocate of whatever religious view ever did before him.[49] However, if the world is a whole, and this world more than ever reveals itself to be made up of many different "parts," that is, different views, opinions, and convictions, then it is necessary to reconsider the way we have been conceptualizing the world. Returning to Sloterdijk's concept of the sphere, I would like to suggest that this concept can be used as an impulse toward a new conceptualization of the world. Sloterdijk's small, cohabited, "round worlds" only come into being when two imperfect human beings, each marked by fragmentation and difference, start building a fragile, sheltering interior they can feel at home in but that will never be everlasting or even perfect. Sphere-building or world-making, then, is about accepting difference and leaving room for that which is different. All around the globe, different cultures and religions have given and still give evidence of the fact that humans need a concept like the world to express wholeness, indicating and outlining a conceptual space that comprises and includes everything there is or that is meaningful to us. The world, then, if only as a concept, *does* exist—but it is a whole not shared by all and marked by difference.

Kari van Dijk, PhD, works at the Munich office of Mynewsdesk. Among her most important recent publications are "Auf Schienen zur Kunst. Zum

Motiv der Zugfahrt in *Wo Europa anfängt, Das nackte Auge* und *Schwager in Bordeaux*," in *Eine Welt der Zeichen. Yoko Tawadas Frankreich als Dritter Raum*, edited by Bernard Banoun and Christine Ivanovic (Iudicium Verlag GmbH, 2015), and *Unvollkommene Androgynie. Menschliche Stimmen bei Ingeborg Bachmann, Elizabeth Murray und Yoko Tawada* (Facilitair Bedrijf RU Nijmegen, 2012).

NOTES

1. Peter Barber and Tom Harper, *Magnificent Maps: Power, Propaganda and Art* (London, 2010), 14.
2. Arnim Regenbogen and Uwe Meyer, eds, *Wörterbuch der philosophischen Begriffe* (Darmstadt, 1998), 723.
3. Plato, *Symposium*, 201a. Translated by Robin Waterfield, Oxford: Oxford University Press, 2009
4. Starting with Plato, as Harte shows. Verity Harte, *Plato on Parts and Wholes* (Oxford, 2005), 5.
5. "Matt Mullican 'Organizing the World' at Haus der Kunst, Munich," *Mousse Magazine*, retrieved 2 February 2018 from http://moussemagazine.it/matt-mullican-organizing-the-world-at-haus-der-kunst-munich/.
6. Peter Sloterdijk, *Sphären*, vol. 2, *Globen: Makrosphärologie* (Frankfurt am Main, 1999), 13–14. For further discussions of the globe, see in particular the chapters by Stefan Willer, Alfred Hiatt, Jeppe Strandsbjerg, Helge Jordheim, Siv Frøydis Berg, and Espen Ytreberg in this volume.
7. Peter Sloterdijk, *Sphären*, vol. 3, *Schäume: Plurale Sphärologie* (Frankfurt am Main, 2004), 20; Kari van Dijk, "Sphären-Bilden im Globalisierungsschaum: Betrachtungen zu Yoko Tawads Erzählung *Das nackte Auge* und Peter Sloterdijks Sphären-Trilogie," in *Nur Narr? Nur Dichter? Über die Beziehungen von Literatur und Philosophie*, ed. Roland Duhamel and Guillaume van Gemert (Würzburg, 2008), 343–73.
8. Markus Gabriel, *Warum es die Welt nicht gibt* (Berlin, 2013), 22.
9. Drawing quite heavily on Heidegger in the first part of the trilogy, *Blasen*, Sloterdijk endeavors nothing less than to come to a new understanding of what it means to be-in-the-world (*In-der-welt-Sein*). In defining human beings as builders of *Rundwelten* ("round worlds"), however, being-in-the-world to Sloterdijk apparently no longer answers to a condition that humans simply find themselves conditioned by: that is, *worlds have to be built*. Peter Sloterdijk, *Sphären*, vol. 1, *Blasen: Mikrosphärologie* (Frankfurt am Main, 1998), 28, 336–45.
10. Charles Taylor, *A Secular Age* (Cambridge, MA, 2007), 35, 147.
11. Ibid., 35–41, 149.
12. Ibid., 146.
13. Ibid., 61. For further discussions of religion, see in particular the chapters by Nora Eggen, Oddbjørn Leirvik, Chenxi Tang, Kyrre Kverndokk, Erling Sandmo, and Alfred Hiatt in this volume.

14. Taylor, *Secular Age*, 61.
15. Max Weber, "Wissenschaft als Beruf," in *Max Weber: Wissenschaft als Beruf 1917/1919, Politik als Beruf 1919*, ed. Wolfgang J. Mommsen et al. (Tübingen, 1994), 22. Taylor, *Secular Age*, 25, refers to this concept explicitly. It should be noted, though, that Taylor's theory about the origins of disenchantment differs substantially from Weber's perspective in the sense that Weber holds the emergence of a scientific approach to the world solely responsible for the changed relationship between self and world.
16. Weber, "Wissenschaft als Beruf," 9.
17. Van Dijk, "Sphären-Bilden im Globalisierungsschaum," 372.
18. Weber, "Wissenschaft als Beruf," 9.
19. Sloterdijk, *Globen*, 801–1007; Peter Sloterdijk, *Im Weltinnenraum des Kapitals: Für eine philosophische Theorie der Globalisierung* (Frankfurt am Main, 2005), 11–46.
20. Sloterdijk, *Globen*, 465–592.
21. Joke J. Hermsen, *De profielschets: Een roman* (Amsterdam, 2004), 262.
22. Ibid., 261.
23. Sloterdijk, *Globen*, 928.
24. Sloterdijk, *Schäume*, 20.
25. Sloterdijk, *Im Weltinnenraum des Kapitals*, 25–27.
26. Sloterdijk, *Blasen*, 360. Here, Sloterdijk draws on insights from psychoanalytical theories about the prenatal relationship between mother and child (216). See also the following passage from a conversation with Hans-Jürgen Heinrichs: "Ich denke jetzt vor allem an das, was während der beiden letzten Generationen an psychoanalytischer und palöopsychologischer Forschung zutage gebracht worden ist, an diesen imposanten Komplex aus Erkenntnissen über die psychodynamischen Gewebe der frühen Mutter-Kind-Beziehung—ich erwähne hier nur die Strömungen der prä- und perinatalen Psychologie zwischen Gustav Hans Graber und Ludwig Janus, die sich in letzter Zeit zu einer konsolidierten Disziplin entwickelt hat." ("I am now thinking primarily of what has been brought to light of psychoanalytical and paleopsychological research during the last two generations, more precisely, the imposing complex of insights into the psychodynamic fabric of the early mother-child relationship—I will here mention only the curents in pre- and perinatal psychology associated with Gustav Hans Graber and Ludwig Janus, which have recently developed into a unified discipline.") Peter Sloterdijk and Hans-Jürgen Heinrichs, *Die Sonne und der Tod: Dialogische Untersuchungen* (Frankfurt am Main, 2001), 153. Translated here by Helge Jordheim and Erling Sandmo.
27. Van Dijk, "Sphären-Bilden im Globalisierungsschaum," 351–52.
28. For a detailed rendering of the frequent intertextual references Sloterdijk makes to the *Symposion* throughout his work, see Kari van Dijk, "Unvollkommene Androgynie: Menschliche Stimmen bei Ingeborg Bachmann, Elizabeth Murray und Yoko Tawada" (PhD dissertation, Radboud University, Nijmegen, 2012), 107–15.
29. Plato, *Symposium*, 190c-d.
30. Ibid., 191b-192e.
31. In the *Symposion*, three different original human races are mentioned that all share this same pattern of desire but that differ qualitatively in the sense that one race was

entirely male, one entirely female, and one androgynous, that is, male and female at the same time (Plato, *Symposium*, 189d-190b). In the case of homosexual love, desire is an attempt of two wholly identical male or female "halves" that both strive to regain their lost wholeness. In the case of heterosexual love, both "halves" differ qualitatively from each other as one "half" is male whereas the other is female. Despite the differences that exist between one type of desire and the other, all three modes of love are governed by the same urge to overcome fragmentation and/or difference.

32. Sloterdijk and Heinrichs, *Die Sonne und der Tod*, 147.
33. Plato, *Symposium*, 191b-192e.
34. Van Dijk, "Sphären-Bilden im Globalisierungsschaum," 352, 370.
35. Wilhelm Schmid, *Mit sich selbst befreundet sein: Von der Lebenskunst im Umgang mit sich selbst* (Frankfurt am Main, 2004), 109; Luce Irigary, *The Way of Love* (London, 2002), 106. For Irigary, see for example van Dijk, "Unvollkommene Androgynie," 194-18.
36. Sloterdijk, *Blasen*, 359-60.
37. Dijk, "Unvollkommene Androgynie," 113-14.
38. On the first page of *Blasen*, Sloterdijk refers to a mezzotint by G. H. Every, showing a young child watching soap bubbles in the sky. Sloterdijk, *Blasen*, 16.
39. Gabriel, *Warum es die Welt nicht gibt*, 18-22.
40. Ibid., 17.
41. Sloterdijk, *Blasen*, 213.
42. Sloterdijk, *Schäume*, 23.
43. Taylor, *Secular Age*, 3.
44. Ibid.
45. Ibid., 21.
46. Alain de Botton, *Religion for Atheists: A Non-believer's Guide to the Uses of Religion* (London, 2012), 19.
47. Taylor, *Secular Age*, 13.
48. Kluun [Raymond van de Klundert], *God is gek: De dictatuur van het atheïsme* (Amsterdam, 2010), 9.
49. Ibid., 28. Cf. Peter Strasser, "Nobody is Perfect," in *Wozu Gott? Religion zwischen Fundamentalismus und Fortschritt*, ed. Peter Kemper et al. (Frankfurt am Main, 2009), 157-68, at 166; de Botton, *Religion for Atheists*, 18.

BIBLIOGRAPHY

Barber, Peter, and Tom Harper. *Magnificent Maps: Power, Propaganda and Art*: London: British Library, 2010.
De Botton, Alain. *Religion for Atheists: A Non-believer's Guide to the Uses of Religion*. London: Penguin Books, 2012.
Gabriel, Markus. *Warum es die Welt nicht gibt*. Berlin: Ullstein, 2013.
Harte, Verity. *Plato on Parts and Wholes*. Oxford: Oxford University Press, 2005.
Hermsen, Joke J. *De profielschets: Een roman*. Amsterdam: De Arbeiderspers, 2004.

Irigary, Luce. *The Way of Love*. London: Continuum, 2002.
Kluun [Raymond van de Klundert]. *God is gek: De dictatuur van het atheïsme*. Amsterdam: Uitgeverij Podium, 2010.
Plato. *Symposium*. Translated by Robin Waterfield, Oxford: Oxford University Press, 2009.
Regenbogen, Arnim, and Uwe Meyer, eds. *Wörterbuch der philosophischen Begriffe*. Darmstadt: Wissenschaftliche Buchgesellschaft, 1998.
Schmid, Wilhelm. *Mit sich selbst befreundet sein: Von der Lebenskunst im Umgang mit sich selbst*. Frankfurt am Main: Suhrkamp, 2004.
Sloterdijk, Peter. *Im Weltinnenraum des Kapitals: Für eine philosophische Theorie der Globalisierung*. Frankfurt am Main: Suhrkamp, 2005.
———. *Sphären*. Vol. 1, *Blasen: Mikrosphärologie*. Frankfurt am Main: Suhrkamp, 1998.
———. *Sphären*. Vol. 2, *Globen: Makrosphärologie*. Frankfurt am Main: Suhrkamp, 1999.
———. *Sphären*. Vol. 3, *Schäume: Plurale Sphärologie*. Frankfurt am Main: Suhrkamp, 2004.
Sloterdijk, Peter, and Hans-Jürgen Heinrichs. *Die Sonne und der Tod: Dialogische Untersuchungen*. Frankfurt am Main: Suhrkamp, 2001.
Strasser, Peter. "Nobody is Perfect." In *Wozu Gott? Religion zwischen Fundamentalismus und Fortschritt*, edited by Peter Kemper, Alf Mentzer, and Ulrich Sonnenschein, 157–68. Frankfurt am Main: Suhrkamp, 2009.
Taylor, Charles. *A Secular Age*. Cambridge, MA: Belknap Press of Harvard University Press, 2007.
Van Dijk, Kari. "Sphären-Bilden im Globalisierungsschaum: Betrachtungen zu Yoko Tawads Erzählung *Das nackte Auge* und Peter Sloterdijks Sphären-Trilogie." In *Nur Narr? Nur Dichter? Über die Beziehungen von Literatur und Philosophie*, edited by Roland Duhamel and Guillaume van Gemert, 343–73. Würzburg: Königshausen & Neumann, 2008.
———. "Unvollkommene Androgynie: Menschliche Stimmen bei Ingeborg Bachmann, Elizabeth Murray und Yoko Tawada." PhD dissertation, Radboud University, Nijmegen, 2012.
Weber, Max. "Wissenschaft als Beruf." In *Max Weber: Wissenschaft als Beruf 1917/1919, Politik als Beruf 1919*, edited by Wolfgang J. Mommsen, Wolfgang Schluchter, and Birgitt Morgenbrod, 1–23. Tübingen: J. C. B Mohr (Paul Siebeck), 1994.

▶• 23 •◀

The Fontenellian Moment

Revisiting Seventeenth- and Eighteenth-Century Worlds

Helge Jordheim

Introduction: Luhmann's *Erdball*

In debates on globalization and globalization theory, "world society" is one of the key concepts routinely evoked to map the political, social, cultural, and economic implications of global communication. One of the earliest definitions can be found in an essay by the German systems theorist Niklas Luhmann, published in 1971, with the German title *Die Weltgesellschaft*. The main claim of Luhmann's essay is that during the last centuries a "world society" has emerged, which is completely different from previous so-called old European societies, mainly because world society has no regional or geographic borders, but comprises the entire world.[1] This world society is a "social system," constituted by functionally differentiated systems of communication, concerned either with money, power, truth, or love.[2] Toward the end of Luhmann's essay, however, another concept of the world emerges, apparently not by intention or device, but as an afterthought, almost like a semantic leftover from the main conceptual work:

> So far we have proceeded in a naïve way with regard to the concept of the world, as if we were talking about the globe and its firmament [*den Erdball und sein Firmament*]. To think in this way corresponds to the ordinary experience of the world, accompanying all life and activity. However, this experience of the world has its own history und can always be analyzed again. And the concepts of the world that thus become visible vary in a non-contingent way.[3]

In this passage, the concept of "world" is split in two. On the one hand, there is the reflexive, highly sophisticated, and complex *Weltgesellschaft*, a theoretical high point of systems theory, coined in order to name a radically new and different historical situation. On the other hand, there is the "naïve" conceptualization *Erdball*—which in English must be rendered by the less distinct "globe," but which literally translates into "earth ball"—corresponding, as Luhmann puts it, "to the ordinary experience of the world, accompanying all life and activity."[4]

In Luhmann's essay, the two concepts of "world" are also separated by a kind of time lag. In the discourse on globalization and world society, still in its early beginnings in 1971, Luhmann observes a lag between the proliferating, ever-expanding discourse on globalization, in which new concepts and discursive strategies are developed to describe the accelerating changes of globalization, and the way "we" keep referring to the world itself in categories that are themselves old, outdated, and taken from ordinary, everyday, unscientific discourse. Thus, two rhythms of conceptual change are contrasted: on the one hand, the quick, accelerating rhythms of conceptual innovation and turnover in the highly specialized globalization discourse, unfolding in the social, legal, and human sciences from the 1970s and onward; on the other hand, the slow, long-term changes and the relative historical stability and continuity of what Luhmann calls the "ordinary experience of the world," which can be presumed to indicate the world of social practice, popular culture, education, public debate, and so forth.

Almost forty years after Luhmann published his essay, innumerous books and research projects have set out to discuss and clarify what he meant by *Weltgesellschaft*, with mixed results.[5] In this chapter, however, the naïve and ordinary, old, stable, continuous, seemingly obsolete, or at least belated concept of the *Erdball* will be the target of conceptual and genealogical investigations.[6] By drawing on insights from conceptual history and book history, the chapter will identify a moment in the history of the concept of the world when this specific version of the concept, in which very different forms of knowledge as well as different semantic traditions converge, takes center stage. This moment is linked to a particular writer and, even more significantly, to a particular book, which became a cultural event that even to this day—over three hundred years later—has influenced how the world is conceptualized.

The Fontenellian Moment

The book in question was first published in Paris in 1686, with the striking, if not entirely original title *Entretiens sur la pluralité des mondes* (Conversations on the plurality of worlds). The author, Bernard de Fontenelle, was a well-known writer at the time, who had written in most of the popular literary genres, such as poems, tragedies, comedies, and dialogues, more or less successfully.

Later he was to become the permanent secretary of the Academie des Sciences in Paris. The *Entretiens*, his most famous work, became an instant success, both in France and abroad. Only two years after the French first edition was published, three English editions were circulating, translated and published by central figures in English print culture. In Fontenelle's lifetime—he lived for a hundred years, from 1657 to 1757—the *Entretiens* was published in no fewer than thirty-three French editions, with several additions and revisions, and was translated into several languages. Among the translators were some of the most famous writers of seventeenth- and eighteenth-century Europe, such as the English dramatist and novelist Aphra Behn, and the leading figure of German classicism, Johann Christoph Gottsched.

The immediate success of the book was due both to its scientific content and to the way it was written. As stated in the title, Fontenelle's work employs the form of the conversation, taking place between a philosopher, clearly the voice of the author himself, and a certain Marquise de G., who in later research has been identified as modeled on the Marquise de la Mésangère, as they stroll around a Rococo garden surrounding a palace, talking and flirting. In this scene, so familiar from contemporary French and European literature, what stands out is the subject of their elegant, learned, and flirtatious conversation: the universe. Stars and planets are not—at least not only—an excuse for romantic reveries, but also objects of cosmological and astronomical discourse, unfolding in the course of five, in later editions six, evenings.

In the *Entretiens*, Fontenelle mounts a strong defense of a Copernican and heliocentric cosmology, based on a Cartesian, completely mechanistic physics, which he systematically strips of all traces of Aristotelian or Christian teleology. According to his theory, the universe is made of an infinite multitude of *tourbillions*—"whirlwinds" or "whirlings," as Aphra Behn names them in her translation—each with a star in its center. Our solar system, Fontenelle argues, is one such *tourbillion*. Furthermore, every planet has its own *tourbillion*, and this is why the moon can be seen to circumnavigate the Earth.

But what really catches the imagination of the European reading audience, from England to Russia, from Sweden to Italy, is the fundamental claim that each planet is also a *world*; hence, in the universe there is not one, but a plurality of worlds. Already half a century earlier, in 1638, the Anglican clergyman and later Bishop of Chester, John Wilkins, had published his *A Discovery of a World in the Moone*, republished only a few years later with the explanatory subtitle "Discourse tending to prove that 'tis probable that there may be another World in the Moone." But Fontenelle's particular mix of scientific discourse and elegant dialogue had a much wider and more lasting effect on readers and changed the concept of the world in a much more pervasive way.

In the conceptual history of "world," there is a period of a little more than a hundred years that we can usefully refer to as "the Fontenellian moment," a

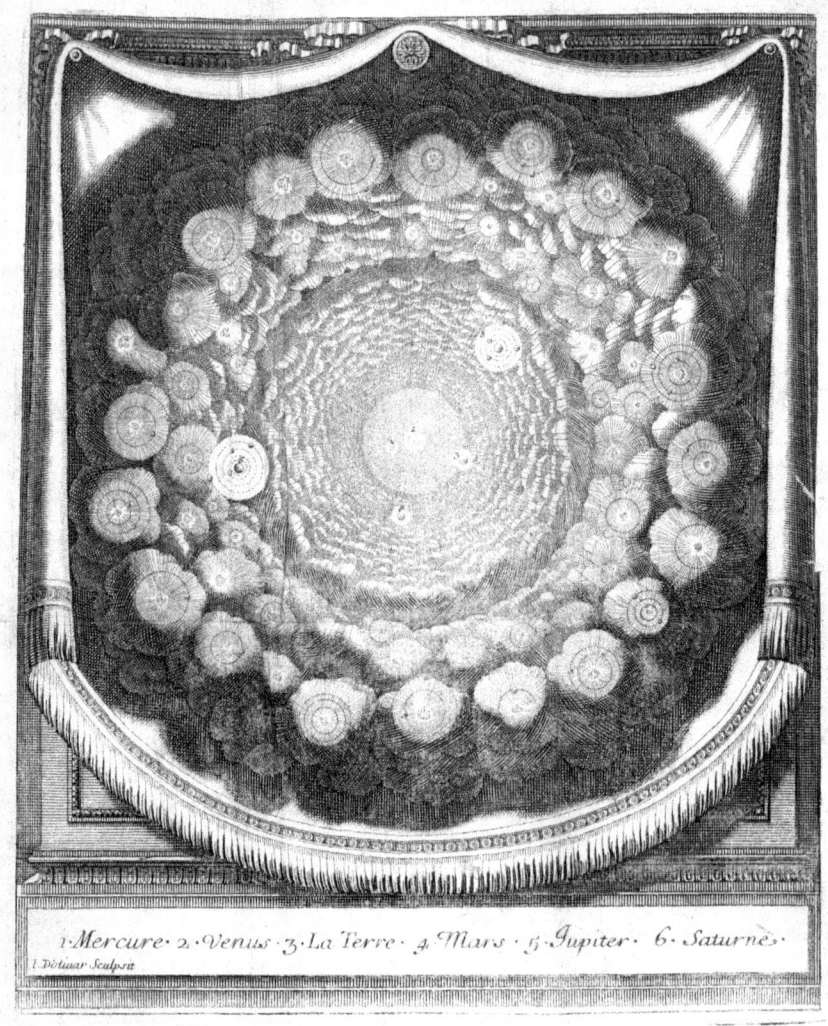

Figure 23.1. Juan Olivar's illustration to the first edition of Fontenelle's *Entretiens*. Courtesy of the University of Oslo Library.

term inspired above all by J. G. A. Pocock's "Machiavellian moment," which sought to track the enduring influence of the Florentine political theorist.[7] To speak similarly of a "Fontenellian moment" means to zoom in on a period when the concept of the world is vehemently debated in most European countries, across various fields of knowledge and different social and intellectual milieus. At the center of these exchanges, which Michael Sauter refers to as "the Plurality of Worlds debate,"[8] stands Fontenelle's *Entretiens*. In this

French work and its numerous translations, the semantics of world and planet are combined in a way that has major consequences for Enlightenment and post-Enlightenment anthropology.

There are different ways of mapping the effects and trajectories of Fontenelle's reconceptualization of the concept of the world, by means of a rhetoric of "plurality" that deeply affects both the meanings and uses of the concept. This chapter will explore, albeit briefly and tentatively, how the circulation and translation of Fontenelle's *Entretiens* becomes the scene of radical transformations of the semantics and pragmatics of the concept "world." More precisely, I will target specific seventeenth- and eighteenth-century translations, mainly into English and German but also Danish, and investigate how their ways of translating key terms and passages can be understood as responses and contributions to this reconceptualization of the world. By investigating how different translators react to the building of the plural worlds, as well as to the use of the word "system" to describe the nature of this plurality, we can hope to learn more about the kind of conceptual intervention that Fontenelle's work came to represent, and not least about the "world" concept that emerged from this debate. After 1800, this concept came to represent a "road not taken" because of both anthropocentric reduction (discussed in the introduction to this volume) and academic specialization. In recent discussions on globalization and the climate crisis, however, as we shall see toward the end of this chapter, a new concept of the world is emerging, heralded by Luhmann in 1971, which invokes some of the meanings and usages pioneered in Fontenelle's *Entretiens*.

World in Plural

In the *Entretiens*, Fontenelle discusses, explains, and defends the Copernican and Cartesian revolutions, which transformed the universe from a divine, geocentric, and meaningful order to a mechanistic, heliocentric, and atomistic system. Little of this was new to his readers, but he laid it out in an accessible and elegant literary style and with a talent for writing dialogues that was unprecedented in this field of knowledge.

Fontenelle's main contribution, however, lay on the conceptual level, primarily in the building of the plural, in the shift from "world" to "worlds." Beginning with the question of whether blondes or brunettes are the more beautiful and alluring, the conversation between the philosopher and the marquise by analogy moves on to the benefits of day and night, until the philosopher suddenly exclaims, in Behn's English translation from 1688, that he "cannot forgive his [i.e., the Sun] taking from him the sight of all those Worlds that are there."[9] Surprised, almost shocked by the use of the plural, the marquise exclaims, "Worlds ... what Worlds?"[10] Or in the French original, *Qu'appelez-vous tous ces Mondes?* ("What do you call all those worlds?").[11] Already here the translation deviates from the original in interesting ways, which we will return to later. At this point the philosopher realizes that the cat is out of the bag and discloses his theory about the plurality of worlds, apologizing in advance for his "weakness" (in Behn's translation, or in the French original, *ma folie*, directly translated "my madness"): "Alas, said I, I am sorry that I must confess that I have imagined to myself, that every Star might perchance be another world."[12] Then, addressing the reader, not the marquise, the philosopher sums up the gist of his theory in a passage that reads almost like an entry in a dictionary, to make sure that there will not be any misunderstandings about his use of the terms in question:

> Car à une personne comme elle, qui ne sçavoit rien en matiere de Phisique, il faloit prendre les choses de bien loin, pour luy prouver que la Terre pouvoit être une Planète, et les Planètes autant de Terres, & toutes les Etoiles des Mondes.[13]

And in Behn's translation:

> I knew not where to begin my discourse for to prove to her (who understood nothing of Natural Philosophy) that the Earth was a Planet, all the other Planets so many Earths, and all the Stars Worlds, it was necessary for explaining myself, to bring my Arguments a great way off.[14]

Obviously, both Fontenelle and his translator use the passage to clarify how the pluralization of "world" fits in with the rest of the cosmological terminology. Until now, *Terre* or "Earth" has been the proper noun for the only planet that could qualify as a world, but from now on *terre* ("earth") will be used as a common noun to designate the possible existence of numerous different planets. Later in the first conversation Fontenelle gives the marquise a more detailed description of the roles of the stars: they are worlds only to the extent that they give light and warmth to those other "earths." If Fontenelle expected shock and incredulity from his readers in response to the pluralization of "world," he made sure to anticipate these feelings by means of the initial reactions of the marquise, which, however, soon turns into curiosity and fascination.

The shockwaves produced by the forming of the plural "worlds" reverberate in the different translations, depending both on the political and the linguistic contexts. In 1687 and 1688, no fewer than three English translations were published: the Dublin edition by by a nobleman and knight with the initials W. D. from 1687, entitled *A Discourse of the Plurality of Worlds*; the London edition from 1688 by John Glanvill, simply *A Plurality of Worlds*; and the other London edition from 1688, Aphra Behn's aforementioned *A Discovery of New Worlds*. Even in these three contemporary English-language versions, however, the meaning of the term "world" differs. In his preface, the translator with the initials W. D. places Fontenelle's work in the colonial rivalries between England and France and claims that the English, who beat the French to the other "New World," America, will beat them to these new worlds as well.[15] His semantics of "world" must have seemed both familiar and reassuring to his readers. Behn adopts a similar conceptual structure for her title, though less focused on colonialism than on discovery, as she reuses John Wilkins' title for his aforementioned *A Discovery of a World in the Moone* from 1638.

For obvious historical and political reasons, the same imperialist and colonialist semantics of "worlds," employed to fit the experiences and ambitions of the British readers, did not seem to offer itself to the German and Danish translators. As opposed to their English colleagues, they did everything they could to avoid the plural of "world," in what can be interpreted as an attempt to avoid offending the readers' religious and moral sensibilities. For the German translation, published in 1726 in Leipzig, the translator Johann Christoph Gottsched, the most famous German proponent of French classicism, chose the title *Herrn Bernhards von Fontenelle Gespräche von Mehr als einer Welt, zwischen einem Frauenzimmer und einem Gelehrten* (Bernard de Fontenelle's conversations on more than one world, between a madam and a scholar).[16] Instead of going with the plural *Welten*, Gottsched decides to reformulate the title using the stylistically much less elegant, but also much vaguer and less provocative *mehr*, in English "more": "more than one world." In the German title, the plurality of worlds remains a speculative possibility more than a scientific hypothesis, a suggestion or suspicion more than a claim or an assertion. Even more importantly, the relativizing effect involved in pluralizing something that was believed to be unique—God's singular creation—is seriously dampened when the one world, the world in singular, is kept as the standard and figure of comparison. Other worlds, Gottsched implies, can only be labeled "worlds" if they are similar to the one we know and measure up to it. Hence, the one singular world, God's earth, remains the center not of the universe, but of the process of conceptualization.

The Danish translation by Friderich Christian Eilschow, published in Copenhagen in 1748, follows Gottsched and adopts the title *Bernhard Fontenelles Samtaler Om Meer end een Verden* (Bernard Fontenelle's conversations about more than one world).[17] Again, "more" (Danish *meer*) is used to replace the plural "worlds." Indeed, the entire Danish translation is so close to Gottsched's German translation that the claim stated in the subtitle that the work is a translation of the latest French edition comes across as rather unlikely. Even more revealing, however, is the Danish translation printed in 1764, which reuses Eilschow's translation but repackages it completely, replacing the Christian iconography adorning the first edition with French Rococo gardens and castle, and also changes the title to *Samtaler om Flere end*

Figures 23.2 and 23.3. The two Danish editions of Fontenelle's *Entretiens*, from 1748 (left) and 1764 (right). Courtesy of the University of Oslo Library.

een Verden, which also translates to English as "Conversations about more than one world," though with a slight but significant twist. If the combination of *meer* and the numeral *een* had not made it sufficiently clear to Danish readers that the title refers to a "plurality" of separate independent worlds, not just augmentations of or parallels to our own, the explicitly quantitative *flere* ("more, several") can be seen to remove any doubt, in spite of the reluctance of the translators to use the plural.

The response to Fontenelle's *Entretiens* and more specifically to the building of the plural "worlds" in the German and Danish translations represents a quite ingenious attempt to avoid the use of the plural altogether. This translational shift may partly be explained by the different etymologies of the Romanic *monde* and Germanic *Welt*. In the entry "Welt" in the dictionary of untranslatable philosophical terms, Pascal David points out that the French *monde* comes from Latin *mundus*, which is originally a cosmological term, defining the totality of which the subject is only a part. In Roman times, *mundus* was used to describe naturalistic and empiricist worldviews, for instance in Pliny the Elder and Lucretius, while Christians used the more temporal word *saeculum* (a word that originally referred to the lifespan of a generation). The

Germanic *Welt* or *verden*, on the other hand, has quite another etymology, composed of the Latin word for "man," *vir*, and the Germanic *alt*, meaning "age." Hence, the original meaning of *Welt* was "age of man"—a temporal and phenomenological concept, not a spatial and cosmological one.[18] This anthropocentric concept of the world—in which man, in terms of human life and experience, was always included, even presupposed as an integral part of the conceptual meaning—comes across as much harder to pluralize, to put into a context of a plurality of worlds than the French cosmological *monde*.

Half a century later, the plural *Welten* does finally appear in the German title of Fontenelle's work. By then, however, the work itself had changed. *Dialogen über die Mehrheit der Welten* (Dialogues on the plurality of worlds), published in Berlin in 1780, is a completely different translation from the one published in 1726. It is filled with scholarly diagrams and scientifically updated measurements of the distances between the planets, as well as scholarly annotations, published by one of the most admired astronomers in the Europe of his day, Johann Elert Bode of the Academy of Sciences in Berlin.[19]

Along with the differences in publishing context and paratextual elements, the inclusion of the plural *Welten* in the title serves as an indication that by

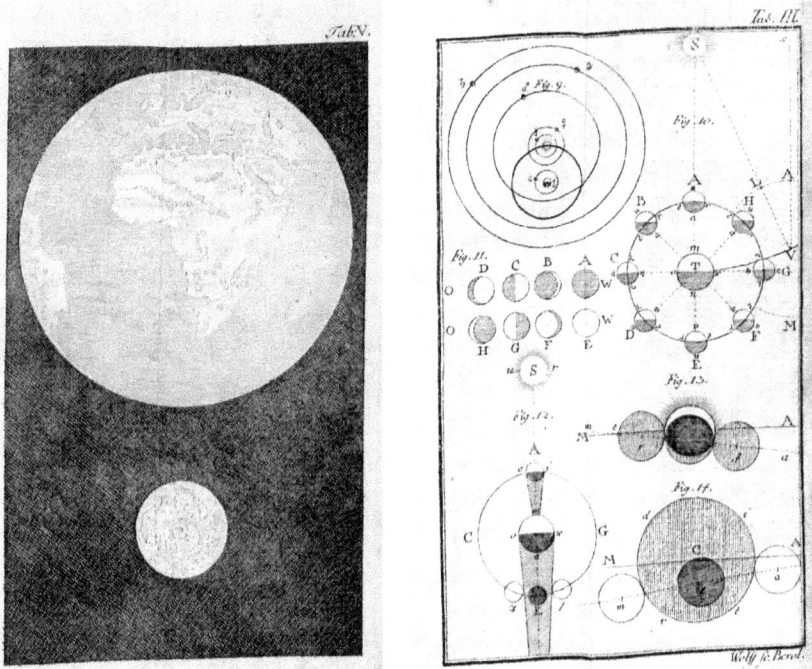

Figures 23.4 and 23.5. Illustrations to the 1780 Berlin edition of Fontenelle's *Entretiens*. Courtesy of the National Library of Norway.

the end of the century Fontenelle's *Entretiens* had been incorporated into the new order of knowledge about to emerge, in which the sciences of man and the sciences of nature were separated into different disciplines, with "celestial anthropology," to use Sauter's term,[20] giving way to the scientific discipline of astronomy.

Plurality of Worlds: System or Edifice

As soon as the concept "world" shifts from singular to plural, the question arises how these worlds are organized, how they relate to one another, and which rules or principles apply. Again, the translators chose to see this differently, with consequences going far beyond linguistic or stylistic choices.

For the second edition of her translation of Fontenelle's *Entretiens*, published posthumously in 1700 in the second volume of her collected works, Behn or her editor decided on an entirely new title: *A Theory or System of Several New Inhabited Worlds Lately Discover'd and Pleasantly Describ'd, in Five Nights Conversation with Madam the Marchioness of *******.[21] The pragmatic paratextual role of the new title is partly to insist on the fact that the worlds are "inhabited," thus introducing Fontenelle's definition of "world," but more importantly it qualifies the entire work in a new way by adding "A Theory or System." That the word "system" is introduced in the title is in itself not very surprising, since it is definitely one of the key concepts of the *Entretiens* alongside "world," "earth," and "universe." At the same time, the choice of title points the analysis of the conceptual innovations of the *Entretiens* and their responses from translators and readers, both implicit and explicit, in another direction.

At the end of the preface, Fontenelle states that there is one group of readers he wants to address in particular, that is, the religious ones, and he writes, in Glanvill's quite literal translation:

> They are those scrupulous Persons, who imagine, that the placing of Inhabitants any where, but upon Earth, will prove dangerous to Religion: I know how excessively tender some are in Religious Matters, and therefore I am very unwilling to give any offence in what I publish to People, whose opinion is contrary to that I maintain: But Religion can receive no prejudice by my System, which fills an infinity of Worlds with Inhabitants, if a little error of the Imagination be but rectify'd.[22]

This little "error" concerns the belief that the inhabitants of the moon must by necessity be "Men made as we are"—when they indeed might be something else completely, another kind of species. The key word in this passage, however, is "system," "my system," as Glanvill translates it, or in the French original, *ce Sistême, où je remplis d'Habitans une infinité de Mondes* ("this system, where I fill an infinity of worlds with inhabitants").[23] In the French original, the originator of the system appears in the pronoun *je*, posing as the subject in the relative clause; in the English translation, he appears in the main clause in the possessive pronoun "my." In both cases, however, the philosopher himself, a thinly disguised version of the author Fontenelle, assumes responsibility for the existence and contents of the system: it is *his* system, *he* is the one who fills it with inhabitants, not God or any other authority.

On the one hand, "system" refers to the system of Copernicus or any other cosmological theory at hand at the moment. But in the seventeenth and eighteenth centuries, "system" also refers to a way to organize knowledge more generally, a completely rational organization of all that is known about a particular subject, different from the bodies of knowledge inherited from scholasticism and Aristotelianism, which were governed by a kind of inherent transcendent meaning or teleology. As an unknown author writes in the *Encyclopédie*—which was in itself, of course, one of the most influential systems of knowledge in the period—a system "is nothing more than the arrangement of the different elements of an art or a science in an order that makes them mutually dependent."[24] This "mutual dependency" excludes all supernatural, mythological, and religious explanations, simply because they do not fit into the system and its structure and logic. In this sense, Cliff Siskin argues that the "system" of the seventeenth and eighteenth centuries should be understood as a genre, indispensable to the ambitions of the Enlightenment.[25]

Turning to Gottsched's 1726 German translation, a significant change of conceptual meaning has taken place. The word "system" has been replaced by the word *Weltgebäude* ("world edifice"), reintroducing both subtly and effectively a well-known Christian metaphor: God as architect. Whereas Fontenelle and his English translators use "system" in an individualistic, perspectivist meaning, referring to the author as sole originator and constructor and to the world as a set of mutual dependencies, Gottsched replaces "system" with "edifice" and reintroduces a transcendent, theological superstructure, in which God reappears as the prime mover and architect. In this way he returns the concept of the world to the semantic opposition between God and world, from which Fontenelle has taken pains to dislodge it.

The World from Outside

By means of the plural "worlds" and the genre label "system," the world is conceptualized in a way that fuses cosmological and anthropological claims and sparks the Enlightenment imagination. That the universe contains several worlds that are inhabited by creatures not unlike humans means that the character of our own world and of its inhabitants changes radically. Both are secularized, decentered, and relativized. The world is stripped of its religious meanings and contexts; it is made relative to something else, other planets and their inhabitants, and it is removed from the center of the universe, not just in a purely spatial sense, but also phenomenologically and anthropologically. Finally, the world is made into something limited, it is given a real and tangible outside. According to this "celestial anthropology," the inhabitants of the Earth, the humans, are just one of many peoples, or rather species, who inhabit the universe.

From this fusion of cosmology and anthropology follows a secularized, decentered, and relativized epistemology. To acknowledge the totality of the Earth, we need to observe it from the outside, to find a point of view in space from where we can study this particular world. In Fontenelle's *Entretiens* the epistemological advantages of the inhabitants of different planets become the topic of one of the disagreements between the philosopher and the marquise, here in Behn's translation:

> 'Tis even so, said I, we would judge of all, but are still ill placed to take our view; in judging of ourselves we are too near, in judging of others too far off. The middle place between the *Moon* and the *Earth* is the best to take a right prospect of both; and better it would be to be simply a Spectator of the *World* than an Inhabitant.[26]

Indeed, this idea of being a spectator of the world rather than an inhabitant, of observing humanity from outside, rather than being part of it, is closely and inextricably linked to the idea that there is a plurality of worlds, other planets from where the Earth can be observed by the inhabitants of these planets. In this way, the Fontenellian moment can also be seen as a condition of possibility for Herder's and Humboldt's attempts at viewing our world from outside, from an unspecified point in the universe, zooming in on the Earth from among distant stars and nebulas, as we discussed in the introduction. In the *Entretiens*, however, this turn to epistemology remains overshadowed by the anthropological effect of the theory of the plurality of worlds, by which man is turned into a liminal being, much to the offense of the marquise:

> I shall never be satisfy'd, said the *Marquiese*, with the Injury we do the Earth, in being to favorably engag'd for the Inhabitants of the moon, unless you can assure me that they are as ignorant about their Advantages as we are of ours, that they take our Earth for a Star, without knowing that the Globe that they inhabit is one also.[27]

At stake is again the privileged position of man, dependent on the possibility of knowing the truth about the universe.

Conclusion: Planet-Talk in the Enlightenment

The Fontenellian moment and the Plurality of Worlds debate are examples of what the postcolonial critic Gayatri Spivak labeled "planet-talk" and "planet-thought" in her trailblazing essay *Death of a Discipline* from 2003. In the conversation between the philosopher and the marquise in the garden outside Paris, we witness how, to use Spivak's words, the planet "overwrites the globe," how the reference to "differentiated political space"—at the end of the seventeenth century, this would mean colonies and emerging nation-states—is replaced by a reference to "undivided 'natural' space."[28] In spite of vast theoretical differences, Spivak's dichotomy of globe and planet seems to echo Luhmann's *Weltgesellschaft* and *Erdball*. Whereas Luhmann in 1975 wanted to theorize world society, Spivak, thirty years later, by which time globalization had become the most theorized phenomenon of the human and social sciences, ventures to shift our attention to the planet, mostly for normative and political reasons. She continues:

> If we imagine ourselves as planetary subjects rather than global agents, planetary creatures rather than global entities, alterity remains underived from us; it is not our dialectical negation, it contains us as much as it flings us away. And thus to think of it is already to transgress, for, in spite of our forays into what we metaphorize, differently, as outer and inner space, what is above and beyond our reach is not continuous as it is not, indeed, specifically discontinuous. We must consistently educate ourselves into this peculiar mindset.[29]

Only five years later, this education into a planetary mindset took a new, slightly different turn in Ursula Heise's book *Sense of Place, Sense of Planet*, which expands the concepts of alterity to encompass not only other humans, but animals, plants, and indeed, by drawing heavily on science fiction, other planets and their inhabitants. Thus, the idea of "planet-thought"—or as Heise puts in, in reference to Benedict Anderson, "imagining the planet"—becomes a vehicle for environmentalism, ecocriticism, and posthumanism.[30]

But in spite of Spivak's claim that "historical reckoning remains crucial to our task,"[31] neither she nor Heise ventures much beyond their own contemporary contexts in order to find out if the conceptualizations of the world they are developing have a prehistory or even a genealogy—and in fact, they do. In spite of Luhmann's contention, there is nothing "naïve" or "ordinary" about the idea of the *Erdball*. It is a complex, multifaceted idea that was developed in the *res publica literaria* of the seventeenth and eighteenth centuries, until it succumbed, as mentioned above, to the "anthropological reduction" that began with Kant and continued through the entire nineteenth and twentieth centuries, as well as to the demands of academic specialization. At the time of its emergence, the cosmological and anthropological assemblage of the *Erdball* was a product of multiple linguistic and conceptual genealogies, specific to both academic and national cultures. One point of convergence of these genealogies was Fontenelle's *Entretiens sur la pluralité des mondes*. In certain ways, this was a trivial and, indeed, "ordinary" text, but it sparked a transformation of the concept of the world across several European languages.

Helge Jordheim is Professor of Cultural History in the Department for Culture Studies and Oriental Languages, University of Oslo. He has published widely on eighteenth-century intellectual culture in Europe as well as on the history of concepts and the theory of history. His most recent book is a transnational history of the concepts of civility and civilization, written with an international team of scholars (*Civilizing Emotions*, Oxford University Press, 2015). At present he is writing a book on the cultural history of time in the seventeenth and eighteenth centuries.

NOTES

1. Niklas Luhmann, "Die Weltgesellschaft," in *Soziologische Aufklärung*, vol. 2, *Aufsätze zur Theorie der Gesellschaft*, 5th ed. (Wiesbaden, 2005), 63–88.
2. Ibid., 74.
3. Ibid., 80, my translation.
4. For further discussions of the globe, see in particular the chapters by Stefan Willer, Alfred Hiatt, Jeppe Strandsbjerg, Kari van Dijk, Siv Frøydis Berg, and Espen Ytreberg in this volume.
5. See, e.g., Bettina Heintz, Richard Münch, and Hartmann Tyrell, eds, *Weltgesellschaft: Theoretische Zugänge und empirische Problemlagen*, special issue, *Zeitschrift für Soziologie* (Stuttgart, 2005).
6. The most ambitious attempt to write the history and philosophy of this concept of the world is found in the second volume of the "spherology" of the German philosopher Peter Sloterdijk, in which, however, Fontenelle and his work are not discussed at any length. See Peter Sloterdijk, *Sphären*, vol. 2, *Globen: Makrosphärologie* (Frankfurt am Main, 1999).
7. J. G. A. Pocock, *The Machiavellian Moment* (Princeton, NJ, 1975).
8. Michael J. Sauter, *The Liminality of Man: Astronomy and the Birth of Anthropology in the Eighteenth Century* (Mexico City, 2010), 41.
9. Fontenelle, *A Discovery of New Worlds. From the French. Made English by Mrs. A. Behn.* ... (London, 1688), 5.
10. Ibid., 5–6.
11. Bernard de Fontenelle, *Entretiens sur la pluralité des mondes* (Paris, 1686), 14.
12. Fontenelle, *A Discovery*, 6.

13. Fontenelle, *Entretiens*, 16–17.
14. Fontenelle, *A Discovery*, 8.
15. Fontenelle, *A Discourse of the Plurality of Worlds*. Written in the French by the most Ingenious Author of the Dialogues of the Dead and Translated into English by Sir W. D. Knight (Dublin, 1687).
16. Fontenelle, *Herrn Bernhards von Fontenelle Gespräche von Mehr als einer Welt, zwischen einem Frauenzimmer und einem Gelehrten*. Nach der neuesten Französischen Auflage übersetzt von Joh. Chr. Gottscheden (Leipzig 1726).
17. Fontenelle, *Bernhard Fontenelles Samtaler Om Meer end een Verden. Imellom et Fruentimmer og en lærd Mand*. Af det nyeste Franske Oplag oversatte paa *Dansk* …af Friderich Christian Eilschow (Copenhagen, 1748).
18. Pascal David, "Welt," in *Vocabulaire européen des philosophies: Dictionnaire des intraduisibles*, ed. Barbara Cassin (Paris, 2004), 1389–96.
19. Fontenelle, *Dialogen über die Mehrheit der Welten*. Mit Anmerkungen und Kupfertafeln von Johann Elert Bode, Astronom der königl. Akademie der Wissenschaften zu Berlin (Berlin 1780).
20. Sauter, *Liminality of Man*, 5.
21. Fontenelle, *A Theory or System of several new-inhabited Worlds lately discover'd and pleasantly describ'd, in five Nights conversation with Madam the Marchioness of* ****** (London, 1700).
22. Fontenelle, *A Plurality of Worlds*…. Translated by John Glanvill (London, 1688), preface, n.p.
23. Fontenelle, *Entretiens*, preface, n.p.
24. "Systeme (Metaphysique)," ARTFL Encyclopédie Project, retrieved 6 February 2018 from http://artflsrv02.uchicago.edu/cgi-bin/philologic/getobject.pl?c.14:2608.encyclopedie0513.
25. Cliff Siskin, "Mediated Enlightenment: The System of the World," in *This Is Enlightenment*, ed. Cliff Siskin and William Warner (Chicago, 2010), 164–72.
26. Fontenelle, *A Discovery*, 45.
27. Ibid.
28. Gayatri Chakravorty Spivak, *Death of a Discipline* (New York, 2003), 72.
29. Ibid.
30. Ursula K. Heise, *Sense of Place, Sense of Planet* (Oxford, 2008), 5.
31. Spivak, *Death of a Discipline*, 72.

BIBLIOGRAPHY

Bode, Johann Elert. *Dialogen über die Mehrheit der Welten. Mit Anmerkungen und Kupfertafeln von Johann Elert Bode, Astronom der königl. Akademie der Wissenschaften zu Berlin*. Berlin: Christian Friedrich Himburg, 1780.

David, Pascal. "Welt." In *Vocabulaire européen des philosophies: Dictionnaire des intraduisibles*, edited by Barbara Cassin, 1389–96. Paris: Seuil/Robert, 2004.

Fontenelle, Bernard de. *Entretiens sur la pluralité des mondes*. Paris: C. Blageart, 1686.

———. *A Discourse of the Plurality of Worlds*. Written in the French by the most Ingenious Author of the Dialogues of the Dead and Translated into English by Sir W.D. Knight. Dublin, Printed by Andrew Cooke and Sam. Hather and William Normann Bookbinder to his Grace the Duke of Ormond, 1687.

———. *A Discovery of New Worlds*. From the French. Made English by Mrs. A. Behn. To which is prefixed a PREFACE by way of ESSAY on Translated PROSE; wherein the Arguments of Father Tacquet, and others, against the System of *Copernicus* (as to the Motion of the Earth) are likewise considered, and answered: Wholly new. London, Printed for William Canning in his Shop at the Temple-Cloysters, 1688.

———. *A Plurality of Worlds*. Written in French by the author of the *Dialogues of the Dead*. Translated into English by Mr. Glanvill. London, Printed for R. Bentley and S. Magnes, in Russel-Street, in Covent-Garden, 1688.

———. *A Theory or System of several new-inhabited Worlds lately discover'd and pleasantly describ'd, in five Nights conversation with Madam the Marchioness of *******. Written in French by the famous Mons. Fontanelle. I: *Histories, Novels and Translations*. Written by the most Ingenious Mrs. Behn. The Second Volume. The greatest part never before printed. London: Printed by W.O. for S.B. and sold by M. Brown at Gross-keys on Ludgate-hill, 1700.

———. *Herrn Berhnards von Fontenelle Gespräche von Mehr als einer Welt, zwischen einem Frauenzimmer und einem Gelehrten*. Nach der neuesten Französischen Auflage übersetzt von Joh. Chr. Gottscheden, Leipzig Verlegts Bernhard Christoph Breitkopf, 1726.

———. *Dialogen über die Mehrheit der Welten*. Mit Anmerkungen und Kupfertafeln von Johann Elert Bode, Astronom der königl. Akademie der Wissenschaften zu Berlin. Berlin 1780. Bey Christian Friedrich Himburg.

———. *Bernhard Fontenelles Samtaler Om Meer end een Verden. Imellom et Fruentimmer og en lærd Mand*. Af det nyeste Franske Oplag oversatte paa Dansk, med Figurer oplyste, med Professor Gottschedenes og egne nye Anmerkninger forsynede af Friderich Christian Eilschow, Phil. Mag. Kiøbenhavn, 1748. Trykt hos Christoph Georg Glasing, og findes hos hannem tilkiøbs.

———. *Bernhard Fontenelles Samtaler Om Flere end En Verden. Imellom et Fruentimmer og en lærd Mand*. Af det nyeste Franske Oplag oversatte paa Dansk, med Figurer oplyste, med Professor Gottschedenes og egne nye Anmerkninger forsynede af Friderich Christian Eilschow, Phil. Mag. Kiøbenhavn, 1748. Trykt hos Nicolaus Møller.

Gottsched, Johann Christoph. *Herrn Bernhards von Fontenelle Gespräche von Mehr als einer Welt, zwischen einem Frauenzimmer und einem Gelehrten. Nach der neuesten Französischen Auflage übersetzt von Joh. Chr. Gottscheden*. Leipzig: Bernhard Christoph Breitkopf, 1726.

Heintz, Bettina, Richard Münch, and Hartmann Tyrell, eds. *Weltgesellschaft: Theoretische Zugänge und empirische Problemlagen*, special issue, *Zeitschrift für Soziologie*. Stuttgart: Lucius & Lucius, 2005.

Heise, Ursula K. *Sense of Place, Sense of Planet*. Oxford: Oxford University Press, 2008.

Luhmann, Niklas. "Die Weltgesellschaft." In *Soziologische Aufklärung*, vol. 2, *Aufsätze zur Theorie der Gesellschaft*, 5th ed., 63–88. Wiesbaden: VS Verlag für Sozialwissenschaften, 2005.

Pocock, J. G. A. *The Machiavellian Moment*. Princeton, NJ: Princeton University Press, 1975.

Sauter, Michael J. *The Liminality of Man: Astronomy and the Birth of Anthropology in the Eighteenth Century*. Documentos de Trabajo del CIDE 66. Mexico City: CIDE, 2010.

Siskin, Cliff. "Mediated Enlightenment: The System of the World." In *This Is Enlightenment*, edited by Cliff Siskin and William Warner, 164–72. Chicago: University of Chicago Press, 2010.

Sloterdijk, Peter. *Sphären*. Vol. 2, *Globen: Makrosphärologie*. Frankfurt am Main: Suhrkamp, 1999.

Spivak, Gayatri Chakravorty. *Death of a Discipline*. New York: Columbia University Press, 2003.

▶• 24 •◀

Fixating the Poles

Science, Fiction, and Photography at the Ends of the World

Siv Frøydis Berg

What is to be found at the end of the world? What does it look like? Stories and fantasies about the land of eternal ice, and what could be found there, have existed since ancient times. Western understandings of the Arctic have been shaped by the interplay of expectations and experiences: our expectations of the Arctic constitute a history of repetition, of the constant return to fixed topoi and intertextuality.[1] In the nineteenth century, however, the ends were actually seen. New images were produced, reproduced, and spread.

Due to the polar expeditions, the Arctic gained new attention, producing a wealth of texts, images, and maps of the northern and southern extremes of the planet. The expectations of what existed there changed. Ideas of open, almost endless areas to discover and investigate were gradually transformed into knowledge of points, spots, goals for explorers and nations to conquer, culminating in the final placing and claiming of the poles themselves. The polar explorers brought into existence something that had not been there before: a new Arctic geography. The visual evidence of what they found made a huge impact. In this picture, photography was the perfect witness.

Until the end of the eighteenth century, the visual reports from the Arctic were based on drawings, made on the spot and developed for printing. As photographic technology developed, photography took over, and the final deciding factor was the fixation of silver salts. Optics, cameras, and chemical reactions on photosensitive surfaces were already familiar, but with chemical fixation, the photographers could control the developing process. It made it possible to preserve or freeze the picture that emerged before everything went black, or white. It was like nature pictured nature; William H. F. Talbot, one of the inventors, called photography "nature's paintbrush." But what sorts of drawings could "nature's paintbrush" make? Interpretation, contents, or opinions in the photographs are also a question of fixation, as are the photographer's choice of motifs, caption, and context.

At the end of the nineteenth century the photograph assumed the scale of a mass medium. Gradually, the photographs went from being singular objects, usually mounted on cardboard, to become omnipresent copies. Reproduced photographs were displayed on postcards, posters, labels and packaging, in advertisements and newspapers, in books and picture booklets, and as glass slides for slideshows. They were spread to a constantly widening audience. New technologies, such as halftone printing, and new press and distribution systems made it possible to print and distribute the pictures faster.

The fixating of the poles, the transformation of the poles into places, is also a story about staging, by means of cartography and photography. The interplay of expectations and experiences was driven by a complex apparatus of a new public sphere, where literature, art, science, media history, and photography all played important parts.

A New Polar Scene

The end of the Napoleonic Wars in 1815 left the British Empire with an enormous surplus of ships, men, officers, and equipment in need of an occupation. Now they were to be used to explore the most remote areas of the globe—deep Africa, the high North.[2] The Arctic was a space of nature that became available both for empire and nation building, but also for scientific exploration, mapping, and discovery. In 1818, four British Navy ships set sail toward the North, and three intensive decades of grand polar expeditions began.

As the British polar expeditions prepared for and sailed northward, the visual, aesthetical, and literary investigations of the Arctic *ou-topos* were intensified. In 1820, Robert Barker successfully exhibited giant painted panoramas of the Far North at Leicester Square, introducing a broad audience to images of what the polar explorers should expect.[3] Pictures of the "real North" were soon available at low prices, thanks to the well-documented alliances between key figures in the navy and leading publishing houses. In 1821, the public could buy Sir William Edward Parry's *Journal of a Voyage for the Discovery of a North-West Passage from the Atlantic to the Pacific*. No expenses were spared when it came to the quality of the illustrations, drawn and engraved from sketches made on the spot—like the beautiful *Winter Harbour* (Figure 24.1). Caspar David Friedrich depicted another Arctic landscape. The iconic oil painting *Das Eismeer*, presented in Prague in 1824, shows the wreck of one of Parry's ships, the HMS Griper, crushed between icy shards after the impact, its stern barely visible.

Figure 24.1. The famous *Winter Harbour* was drawn and engraved from a sketch made on the spot by Lieut. Beechey, 1821. The image was published in Parry's expedition report, popular among a general audience and polar travelers, like Nansen and Amundsen. Published in William E. Parry, *Journal of a Voyage for the Discovery of a North-West Passage from the Atlantic to the Pacific; Performed in the Years 1819–20, in His Majesty's Ships* Hecla *and* Griper *under the Orders of William Edward Parry* (London, 1821), 122. Reprinted with permission. Courtesy of the National Library of Norway.

Several critics have investigated and tried to encircle the romantic fascination with the Arctic north. Ryall et al. coined the term "Arcticism," as a nod to Edward Said's famous "Orientalism."[4] Jen Hill has pointed out that the Arctic was like a blank sheet, a place made for representations of different kinds.[5] In her description of early nineteenth-century visual interpretations of the Arctic, she emphasizes the endless stretches of whiteness. Russell Potter, focusing on the eighteenth-century panoramas and visual culture of the Arctic, makes a point of the *silence*.[6] During the eighteenth century, the conceptualization of the Arctic turned toward what Chauncey Loomis has labeled "the Arctic sublime."[7] The Arctic was beyond physical reach for most people—and thus paradoxically at the same time available to everyone. The Arctic became a space particularly suited for metaphysical, artistic, and scientific speculation.

At the same time, natural landscape in general and the Arctic scenery in particular appealed strongly to the romantic preoccupation with the notion of the underlying. The years around 1820 saw the rise of a distinctive British romantic tradition that combined literature, science, and exploration.[8]

The British expeditions between Greenland and North America searched for the Northwest Passage, but their main objective was to locate the magnetic North Pole. The coils not only affected the Northern Lights, but disturbed ships' compasses. International shipping needed cartographic improvements for exact navigation, but to be able to hold a steady course was essential, and so the knowledge of the magnetic poles was of great importance.

Magnetism was a central issue for science and polar expeditions, but can also be found as an ambiguous, but not yet fully investigated metaphor in the literature on the Arctic. Metaphors could link science, expeditions, natural forces, and mindscapes of literary experimentation, and connect them explicitly to the Arctic. Samuel Taylor Coleridge did this, in his poem *The Ancient Mariner* (1797–98), as did Anne Eleanor Porden in *The Arctic Explorers* (1818). The literary Romantics were "obsessed with ideas of polarity," writes Peter Kitson. He points out that in the discussion of these metaphors, neither the science of terrestrial magnetism nor the material contexts of polar exploration are yet fully taken into account.[9]

No-one explored the Arctic sublime more efficiently than Mary Shelley, whose *Frankenstein* presented the quintessential romantic interpretation of Arctic geography. More than anyone, she aligned the metaphor of magnetism to the polarity of life and death, and saw lifelessness and danger in the Arctic landscape.

Imaging the Land of Eternal Ice

In *Frankenstein, or the Modern Prometheus* (1818) the two main narratives—those of Frankenstein and the Monster—are framed by a third story, in which the polar captain Walton recalls his voyage to the North. This third account was written between 1816 and 1818, while the newspapers were filled with news of the British Navy's polar preparations. Walton's letters to his sister first tell the tale of Dr Frankenstein, then the tale of the Monster, before he finally leads the reader back to the Arctic. By starting and ending her novel there, Shelley parallels the projects of Walton and Frankenstein, connecting them to lifeless nature and the fateful search for scientific knowledge.

In the novel, Walton stubbornly heads north. He overhears the increasing desperation of the crew, and ignores the ice slowly freezing them in as he cultivates his image of the polar regions as pure beauty and delight. In his letters he continues his utopian expectations: "sailing over a calm sea, we may be wafted to a land surpassing in wonders and in beauty every region hitherto discovered on the habitable globe."[10] As the non-fictional explorers, Walton would test old theories of the open sea, perhaps also to find the Northwest Passage and the magnetic North Pole. Still, his interest in magnetism goes beyond discovery for the sake of navigation. Searching the Arctic landscape, he wants nothing less than to solve the old riddle of magnetism, going back to Thales and the subject of a whole range of conflicting scientific theories: "What may not be expected in a country of eternal light? I may there discover the wondrous power which attracts the needle; and may regulate a thousand celestial observations, that require only this voyage to render their seeming eccentricities consistent for ever."[11]

As Peter Kitson notes, it is not clear which theory of earth magnetism Walton supports: it could be a central magnetic core in the Earth, as proposed by Halley (1682) and later by Erasmus Darwin, or a solar origin of the magnetic force, as suggested by Adam Walker.[12] Philosophical statements like those of William Gilbert may be more relevant in this setting: in his highly influential work on electric and magnetic phenomena, *De magnete* (1600), he placed magnetic power in the inner sphere of the globe and suggested that magnetism was nothing less than the soul of the Earth.[13] Gilbert described the properties of the lodestone or magnetic iron, compared the polarity of the magnet to the polarity of the Earth, and found that a perfectly spherical lodestone aligned with the Earth's poles would spin on its axis, like the Earth. Magnetism, then, appeared as the unmoved core prime mover, thus challenging both the notion of God and the traditional cosmologist view that the Earth was the center of the universe.

To Shelley's readers, the metaphorical sets of meaning would have been obvious. The powers attracting the magnetic needle could easily be associated with the "spark of life" that Frankenstein discovered, isolated, and infused in a lifeless creature that "dark and dreary night of November."[14] The projects of Walton and Frankenstein offer two closely connected versions of the quintessence of romantic endeavor: what is the origin of life?[15] Both projects connect it to nature, and both tie the novel to contemporary politics, religion, and science. Was it possible, as the radical materialists claimed, that life was a material substance, and thus a possible object for scientific examination? Or were the vitalists correct when they argued that both life and soul were affairs of God and beyond human reach?[16]

As interesting as the spark itself is the space in which Shelley lets her explorers search for it. Where Walton sought the origin of magnetism in the land of eternal ice, Frankenstein induced life in dead body-parts. Frankenstein selected parts for his "human being in perfection" that were as beautiful as the Arctic nature: "his hair of a lustrous black, and flowing; his teeth of a pearly whiteness."[17] Snatched from graveyards and picked from charnel houses, each piece was cut from different, anonymous dead bodies, leaving no possible traces of their former owners. At the very moment of animation, however, the beauty disappears: death was beautiful, life was filled with horror. Two variations on the same theme meet in the moment of animation: the scientific instrumental approach toward nature, and the gothic fascination with death and its aestheticization.

It is the sight of the Monster that finally convinces Walton to turn the ship and abandon his quest. The Monster, however, finally comes home, leaving a powerful gothic expression of nature and of the Arctic sublime. Created by lifeless nature, he returns to the lifeless masses of frozen ice—finally disappearing and thus ending the novel "in darkness and distance."[18] The pursuit of life is connected to death, and death to the lifeless matter of Arctic nature.

In the preface to the 1831 version, Shelley writes that her ambition was to write a novel "which would speak to the mysterious fears of nature, and awaken thrilling horror."[19] Gothic novels like *Frankenstein* explored the potential of emotions through the experience of horror. These feelings were provoked in particular by what Edmund Burke, among others, labeled "the sublime."[20] At the same time, as Roy Porter points out, the sublime was "terror in safety"—the reader could experience it from his armchair.[21]

The experience of the Arctic sublime took another twist for the British audience when the fate of the lost Franklin expedition (1845) came to light, almost thirty years after *Frankenstein*. In terror and disbelief, the armchair traveler learned that men of science and civilization were driven into disaster, death, and "the last resource," cannibalism. The Franklin disaster was a major event in the history of the public interest in polar exhibitions.[22] It activated the early myths about the Arctic. Despite several successful earlier polar expeditions, which made the British the leading polar nation of the world, public reactions were also deeply informed by aesthetical interpretations and novels like Shelley's *Frankenstein*, creating myths of science, imagination, and Arctic geography.

Another novel is worthy of a brief mention: in 1886, Jules Verne zoomed in on the Arctic region by presenting a literary encircling of the very "heart of whiteness," the North Pole. In *The Adventures of Captain Hatteras*, Hatteras actually reaches the pole. Nodding to Shelley and theories of earth magnetism, Verne investigated the pole as if it held the answers to the riddle of the Earth itself. Hatteras follows the theories of the open sea, but he imagines the pole itself as a volcanic island and a passage to a subterranean world. The protagonist collapses at the very moment of conquest: as in *Frankenstein*, the sight of the innermost secrets of Earth and life is irrevocably tied to hubris, danger, and madness.

Written as a polar expedition report, *Hatteras* draws on knowledge from the Ross, Scoresby, and Franklin expeditions. It is packed with references to contemporary science and geography. Hatteras's fictional expedition also has remarkable similarities to Fridtjof Nansen's *Fram* expedition to the North Pole thirty years later. Hatteras's vessel is called *Forward*, corresponding to the meaning of the Norwegian word "Fram." Like *Fram*, *Forward* was designed "for enormous pressures" in order to resist the pack ice. She freezes in the polar ice, and drifts with the ocean current toward the geographical North Pole. In both expeditions the captain leaves his ship to reach the pole by foot or by sleigh. Verne's novel was part of *Fram*'s library, and in an interview with *Le Monde*, Nansen confirmed that he had read it "over and over again." The admiration was mutual. As Verne said on another occasion, Nansen had conducted the journey he had only imagined.[23]

Exploring the Nature Farthest North: Nansen the Photographer

Among the myths and stories of the Arctic North, the reports from the polar explorers themselves held a particular position. Unlike the literary and artistic explorers, they had actually been there. At the same time, these reports were necessary stagings for the polar explorers, both to secure publicity and thus funding for their projects, and to have the armchair reader witness and recognize their achievements. Heroics presuppose narrative.

During the eighteenth century, pictures in reports were drawings, often by known artists after sketches made on the spot. At the end of the century, however, the visualizations of the Arctic took a new turn. Advancement in photographic technology and halftone printing made it possible to print photographs and text together. More efficient distribution systems made photography potentially omnipresent. Photography was the perfect witness where human witnesses were absent. An advanced photographer like Fridtjof Nansen could stage his achievement more convincingly than anyone before him.

Nansen never reached the North Pole, but for a long time no-one had come closer than he had as he traveled by sleigh with his companion Hjalmar Johansen during the first *Fram* expedition (1893–96). In words and pictures, Nansen maintained the image of the sublime Arctic, and played along with the public's expectations of the ambiguous Arctic nature. In his costly but bestselling travel narrative, *Farthest North*, intended for a wide audience, the image of the modern scientist was fused with the image of the skiing, national polar hero—useful both for Norwegian nation building and in the international competition among polar nations.

In *Farthest North*, Nansen described his inner longing for the North in a manner that is strikingly similar to that of the earlier fictive polar expeditions.

Nansen combined the tradition of the sublime with Norse mythology, and compared the polar regions with the misty, mythic lands of Niflheim, the Norse kingdom of death. He wrote himself into a common history of great feats and heroics, emerging as the modern hero of the late nineteenth century, the scientist:

> Why did we continually turn to attack? There, in the darkness and cold, stood Helheim, where the death-goddess held her sway; there lay Nåstrand, the shore of corpses. Thither, where no living being could draw breath, thither troop after troop made its way. To what end? Was it to bring home the dead, as did Hermod when he rode after Baldur? No! It was simply to satisfy man's thirst for knowledge. Nowhere, in truth, has knowledge been purchased at greater cost of privation and suffering. But the spirit of mankind will never rest till every spot of these regions has been trodden by the foot of man, till every enigma has been solved.[24]

By planning to drift with the ocean currents and ice, Nansen broke with all previous polar expeditions, which in his view had fought against the forces of nature. With *Fram*, Nansen wrote, he will "... work with and not *against* them."[25]

According to Robert G. David, Nansen's journey with *Fram* represented the triumph of the white explorer.[26] Nansen was praised as a pioneer of marine biology, glaciology, and oceanography, but more important in the present context is his groundbreaking descriptions of the geography and nature "farthest north." In many ways, this expedition established the standard for the exploration of Arctic nature, and for documenting and representing the nature at the end of the world. This is not least a result of Nansen's expert use of photography.

As early as 1890, Nansen had stated that "a necessary addition to the outfit of a modern exploring expedition is, of course, a photographic apparatus."[27] *Fram* was designed to resist the pack ice, but also for photographic work. It was equipped with a darkroom, a large camera with glass plates, and several small instant cameras, which Nansen used on hazardous sleigh rides. Experiences from urban photo studios—frequently used by explorers for staging themselves as polar heroes or scientists before they actually set out on their journeys—were of the essence in the polar regions, this time with the real Arctic Ocean as backdrop.[28]

Farthest North contained an unusual number of photographs of scientific activities: brazing of depths down to 3,500 meters, measurements of temperature in the ocean and on land, observations of meteorological and astronomical phenomena, and the sampling of various organisms and minerals above and below the surface of the sea. They are not scientific photographs in the sense that they document scientific discovery; they document photographic

Figure 24.2. Unknown photographer/Fridtjof Nansen, Polhavet, 12 July 1894. Published in Nansen's bestseller, *"Farthest North": Being the Record of a Voyage of Exploration of the Ship* Fram *1893–96 and of a Fifteen Month's Sleigh Journey,* vol. 1 (Westminster, 1897): "Reading the Temperature with a Lens. 12 July, 1894 (from a photograph)." Courtesy of the National Library of Norway.

staging of science, the polar researcher posing as scientist and modern hero. The backdrop is the Arctic, open and accessible to scientific intervention and curiosity. Instruments and installations are present as photographic props and point to a diversity of scientific approaches that all penetrate deeper into nature than any photograph can capture (Figure 24.2).

Another visual image of the polar regions could be found in the scientific report from the expedition, the prestigious *Norwegian North Polar Expedition: 1893–1896 Scientific Results,* published in six volumes from 1900 to 1908. The report contains only two photographs, an overview picture of a fossil excavation site and a photograph of two rare rose seagulls that Nansen had shot. All the other illustrations are drawings. Nansen the scientist followed the demands of the tradition and did not use photography as scientific evidence.

Fixating the Southern Pole: Amundsen's Tent

On 18 January 1912, Robert Falcon Scott wrote in his diary:

> All the day-dreams must go, all the dreams predicated on the vacancy of this imaginary place. The void has let them down. The mad geometricians were right. Jules Verne was right, Poe was right. There is something at the South Pole. It is a Norwegian Flag.[29]

The geographical conceptualization of the world culminated with the final conquest and visual construction of the poles. A new understanding of the pole as something concrete, a definite place in the world, emerged at the beginning of the twentieth century, by means of an increasingly advanced apparatus of photography, media, public expectations, scientific demands, and visual culture. The telegraph made the distance between the polar regions and civilization shorter; messages went faster. The media participated in shaping expeditions—they created races for a whole world to follow and set up specific destinations. The race was on in several arenas simultaneously—in the ice fields, in the public—and the participants were the explorers, the new media, the newspapers, and the armchair travelers.

The polar expeditions were transformed from research journeys to media events. The polar explorers knew the game. Intimately connected to the media and to public expectations, they staged themselves *and* the end of the world. The Cook-Peary controversy made it clear that scientific evidence meant everything, and they knew the importance of keeping control of the story and winning what Roland Huntford has called the "race to the cable head."[30] Winning a race was a question of producing acceptable evidence so that the conquest could be confirmed by a broad public and established as a matter of fact: this is what it looks like at the end of the world! But then, how to do it? How to visualize the invisible, the white void?

In model worlds, like globes and maps, the cartographic poles are particularly visible and appear as spots, self-evident and hypnotic ends. In the whiteness of the Arctic, however, these spots are not only invisible, but hard to locate. The geographical pole was considered to be an area more than a point, and in continuous motion. In addition, it was well known that Earth was not completely circular, and perhaps the axes were not stable. The rotation area revolved around a middle position, but shifted slightly each day. This did not make it easy to determine the cartographic position of the poles, which became targets for the polar explorers.[31]

When the news of the conquered North Pole reached Roald Amundsen, he changed his plan of going there himself on *Fram*. No-one would pay for a record that had already been set, so he aimed for the South, challenging Scott and his men to a race. Neither Amundsen nor his men expected to locate the exact pole, or believed that "the few miles which possibly separated us from it could be of the slightest importance."[32] The localization of the South Pole was based on meticulously recorded tables with observations of solar elevation. In addition, Amundsen made a most interesting visual representation

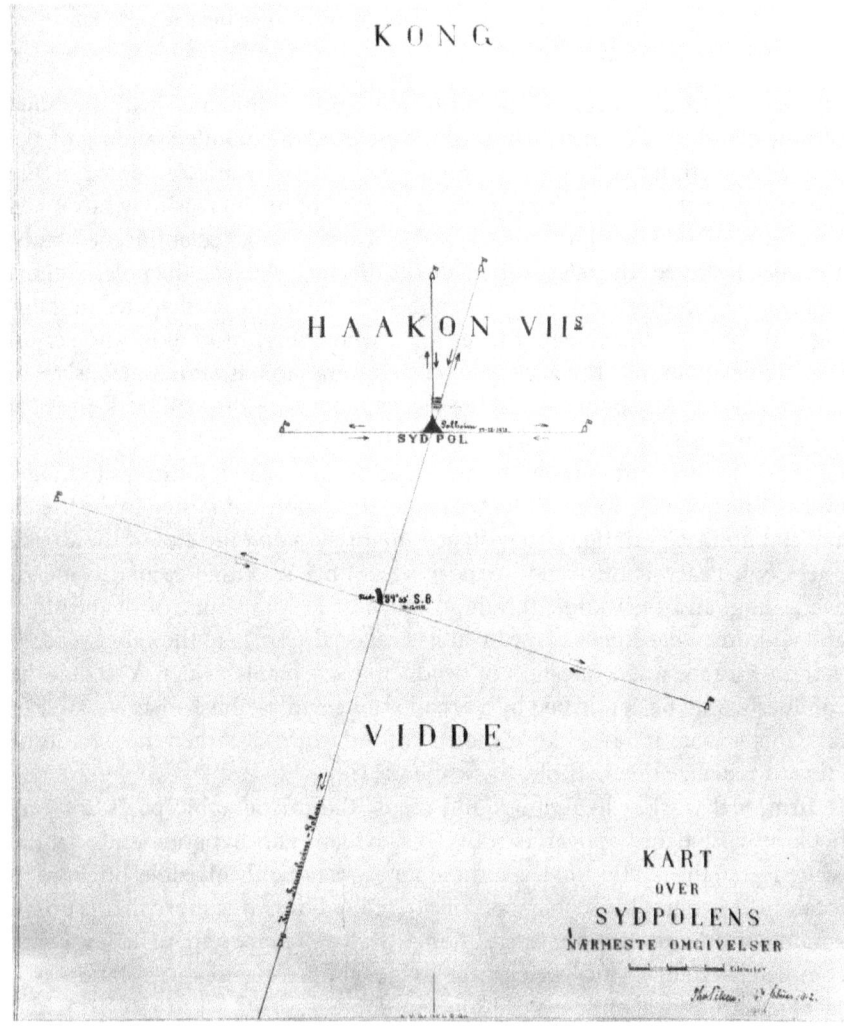

Figure 24.3. Ski tracks, flags, and tent. Thorvald Nilsen's drawing of the first *Chart over the Immediate Surroundings of the South Pole*, 6 February 1912. Photo: Jan Haug. The Royal Court. Published in Roald Amundsen, *The South Pole: An Account of the Norwegian Antarctic Expedition in the "Fram" 1910–1912*, vol. 2 (London, 2010). Reprinted with permission.

of the cartographic South Pole, on the white sheet of the Arctic landscape (Figure 24.3). Camp *Polheim* was encircled, twice. Amundsen wrote: "The encircling was accomplished in this way: Three men went out in three different directions, two at right angles to the course we had been steering, and one in continuation of that course."[33] They planted a flag at the end of each ski track before returning. The ski tracks in the snow, the flags, and the tent were abstracted to pencil lines on a blank sheet of paper, the first "Chart of the Immediate Surroundings of the South Pole."[34] There was nothing there before they came, and there is nothing represented on this map that was not brought there by those who invented it.

A fixed set of polar props was already established in polar history when Amundsen reached the pole: the flag and the tent.[35] A flag on a *pole* could fixate points, but this was not sufficient to create a spot, a place. A recognizable sign of habitation was needed, and the triangular tent was perfect for the purpose. The props that illustrate the place coincide with what the audience would recognize as essential attributes of the polar hero: a fur hood, skis, tents, and flags, against a backdrop of a barren, icy landscape.

The first printed photograph in a Norwegian newspaper showed the scientific placing of the South Pole: the scientist, his measuring instruments, and the Norwegian flag. The most famous image shows four men standing by a tent (the photograph mentioned here is reproduced in Espen Ytreberg's chapter in the present volume as Figure 25.2). It is an icon of a proud and independent Norway, a polar nation, retouched and reprinted, again and again.[36] In Amundsen's staging of the South Pole, the abstract systems of cartography and photography mutually confirm each other. Together, map and photographs visualized a place that was new to the world.[37]

Amundsen left behind the Norwegian flag and a small extra tent, containing a letter for Scott in which he asked him to mail another letter, to the king. What was for Scott "a terrible disappointment" was for Amundsen a confirmation that the South Pole was conquered. Scott confirmed Amundsen's discovery with his own famous photography of his company in front of Amundsen's tent (Figure 24.4). The film, discovered eight months later, a few meters away from the frozen bodies of Scott and two of his companions, was sensational media material.[38] Contrary to the scientific calculations and photographic evidence, the response of the media was utterly unpredictable. In the readings of the public, the photograph of Scott and his men at Amundsen's South Pole immediately coincided with the old image of the Arctic sublime: death and madness at the end of the world.

The conceptualization of the Arctic culminated in the photographic and media-driven fixation of the geographic poles, manifested visually by the cartography, but also what Lund has labeled the "photographic pole." As the polar explorers staged themselves and their conquests for acceptance by

Figure 24.4. Fixating, re-photographing, and thus confirming the place of the South Pole: Scott and his company at Amundsen's tent. Herbert G. Ponting wrote on the reverse: "This print was made from a negative in the roll film which lay for 8 months beside Scott's body before it was found by the Search Party. Later developed." He later described Scott's negatives as "probably the most tragically interesting photographs in the world."[39] Lieut. Bowers, *Discovery of Amundsen's tent at the South Pole by Captain Scott's party*, 18 January 1912. Courtesy of the National Library of Norway.

a broad audience, they brought something into the world that had not been there before. The poles were staged constructions, legitimized by scientific and publicly acceptable evidence. The photographs of the Arctic nature and the photographic poles are part of a larger historical picture, where new stories and expectations interact with the old, transcending the purely visual. The polar scene—the end of the world—was brought into being by voyages of discovery, aesthetical and scientific investigations, and by myths, public expectations, and armchair experiences.

Siv Frøydis Berg is a Research Librarian at the Norwegian National Library and has a PhD in Intellectual History. She has published on polar photography, twentieth-century health conceptions, future thinking from Shelley to Dolly the sheep, and now focuses on early modern epistolary genres. Among her publications are *Norske polarheltbilder 1888–1928* [*Images of Norwegian Polar Heroes 1888–1928*] (Forlaget Press/Nasjonalbiblioteket, 2011, co-edited with Harald Ø. Lund) and *All verdens kunnskap: leksikon gjennom to tusen år* [*All the World's Knowledge: Two Thousand Years of Encyclopedias*] (Forlaget Press/Nasjonalbiblioteket, 2012, co-edited with Helge Jordheim and Øivind Berg.

NOTES

This chapter is based on a physical and online exhibition about polar hero photographs and images at the National Library of Norway, also resulting in Harald Østgaard Lund and Siv Frøydis Berg, eds, *Norske polarheltbilder 1888–1928* (Oslo, 2011). My warmest thanks go to my co-editor.

1. Anka Ryall, Johan Schimanski, and Henning Howlid Wærp, *Arctic Discourses* (Newcastle upon Tyne, 2010), x.
2. For further discussions of the globe, see in particular the chapters by Stefan Willer, Alfred Hiatt, Jeppe Strandsbjerg, Kari van Dijk, Helge Jordheim, and Espen Ytreberg in this volume.
3. Russell A. Potter, *Arctic Spectacles: The Frozen North in Visual Culture, 1818–1875* (Seattle, 2007), 5ff.
4. Ryall et al., *Arctic Discourses*, x.
5. Jen Hill, *White Horizon: The Arctic in the Nineteenth-Century British Imagination* (New York, 2008), 3.
6. Potter, *Arctic Spectacles*.
7. Chauncey A. Loomis, "The Arctic Sublime," in *Nature and the British Imagination*, ed. U. C. Knoepflmacher and G. B. Tennyson (Berkeley, 1997), 95–112.
8. Tim Fulford, Debbie Lee, and Peter J. Kitson, *Literature, Science and Exploration in the Romantic Era: Bodies of Knowledge* (Cambridge, 2006). For further readings on magnetism, see Vidar Enebakk, "Hansteen's Magnetometer and the Origin of the Magnetic Crusade," *British Journal for the History of Science* 47, no. 4 (2014): 1–22. Eric G. Wilson documents the imaginative possibilities for the empty poles, and the metaphoric available to Romantics through new understandings of science in *The Spiritual History of Ice: Romanticism, Science, and the Imagination* (New York, 2003). For the broader cultural ramifications of Arctic exploration, see Robert G. David, *The Arctic in the British Imagination, 1814–1914* (Manchester, 2000); Francis Spufford, *I May Be Some Time: Ice and the English Imagination* (London, 1996).
9. Peter J. Kitson, "Theories of Terrestrial Magnetism and the Search for the Poles," in Fulford et al., *Literature, Science and Exploration*, 168.
10. Mary Shelley, *Frankenstein, or the Modern Prometheus: The 1818 Text* (Oxford, 1994), 5.
11. Ibid., 6.
12. Kitson, "Theories of Terrestrial Magnetism."
13. Val Dusek, *The Holistic Inspirations of Physics: The Underground History of Electromagnetic Theory* (New Brunswick, NJ, 1999), 141ff.

14. Shelley, *Frankenstein: The 1818 Text*, 38.
15. Marilyn Butler, "*Frankenstein* and Radical Science," in *Frankenstein: Mary Shelley*, ed. J. Paul Hunter (New York, 1996), 302–13.
16. The "spark of life" and "raw material" are discussed at length in Siv Frøydis Berg, "Ny teknologi, gamle forestillinger: Kloning og kunstige mennesker i Shelleys *Frankenstein*, Goethes *Faust II* og Huxleys *Brave New World*" (PhD dissertation, University of Oslo, 2010).
17. Shelley, *Frankenstein: The 1818 Text*, 39.
18. Shelley, *Frankenstein: The 1818 Text*, 191. For further discussions of monsters and monstrosity, see in particular the chapters by Erling Sandmo and Karl G. Johansson in this volume.
19. Mary Shelley, *Frankenstein, or the Modern Prometheus* (London, 1831), viii–ix.
20. Edmund Burke, *A Philosophical Enquiry into the Origins of Our Ideas of the Sublime and the Beautiful*, ed. Adam Philip (Oxford, 1998).
21. Roy Porter, *Enlightenment: Britain and the Creation of the Modern World* (London, 2001), 226.
22. Potter, *Arctic Spectacles*, 5.
23. Per Johan Moe, "Hatteras—Nansen," *Norsk Jules Verne* (blog), 2 August 2010, http://julesgverne.wordpress.com/about/hatteras-nansen.
24. Fridtjof Nansen, *"Farthest North": Being the Record of a Voyage of Exploration of the Ship* Fram *1893-96 and of a Fifteen Month's Sleigh Journey*, vol. 1 (Westminster, 1897), 2–3. See also Silje Solheim Karlsen, "Litterære helteportretter," in Lund and Berg, *Norske polarheltbilder*, 46–47.
25. Nansen, *Farthest North*, 17.
26. David, *The Arctic in the British Imagination*, 117.
27. Fridtjof Nansen, *The First Crossing of Greenland*, vol. 1 (London, 1890), 69.
28. Lund and Berg, *Norske polarheltbilder*.
29. Scott, quoted after Spufford, *I May Be Some Time*, 331.
30. Roland Huntford, *Scott and Amundsen: The Last Place on Earth* (London, 2009), 529.
31. At the beginning of the nineteenth century, both polar researchers and the public were well aware of the many types of poles: the magnetic poles, cold poles, the Pole of Inaccessibility, and the geographic poles.
32. Roald Amundsen, *The South Pole: An Account of the Norwegian Antarctic Expedition in the "Fram" 1910-1912*, vol. 2 (London, 1912), 121.
33. Ibid., 125–26.
34. Ibid., 451.
35. Lund and Berg, *Norske polarheltbilder*, 262–269.
36. Lund and Berg, *Norske polarheltbilder*, 270–281. For further discussions of Amundsen's South Pole expedition, see in particular the chapter by Espen Ytreberg in this volume.
37. Photography, Nansen, 86° 13' 36" n.br, Polhavet, 8 April 1895, reproduced as "Our Farthest North Camp" (drawing by Lars Jorde), in Nansen, *Farthest North*, 58; Earnest H. Shackleton, "The Farthest South Camp after Sixty Hours Blizzard," in Earnest H. Shackleton, *The Heart of the Antarctic: Being the Story of the British Antarctic*

Expedition 1907–1909, vol. 1 (London, 1909), 346; Frederick A. Cook, *Camping Outfit*, September 1898, reproduced as "The Belgica in September: The New Tent and the Pack Travelling Outfit," in *Through the First Antarctic Night 1898–1899: A Narrative of the Voyage of the "Belgica" among Newly Discovered Lands and Over an Unknown Sea about the South Pole* (London, 1900), 328.

38. Beau Riffenburgh, *The Myth of the Explorer: The Press, Sensationalism, and Geographical Discovery* (Oxford, 1994), 164–65.
39. Herbert G. Ponting, *The Great White South: Travelling with Robert F. Scott's Doomed South Pole Expedition* (New York, 2001), 278.

BIBLIOGRAPHY

Amundsen, Roald. *The South Pole: An Account of the Norwegian Antarctic Expedition in the "Fram" 1910–1912.* Vol. 2. London: John Murray, 1912.

Berg, Siv Frøydis. "Ny teknologi, gamle forestillinger: Kloning og kunstige mennesker i Shelleys *Frankenstein*, Goethes *Faust II* og Huxleys *Brave New World*." PhD dissertation, University of Oslo, 2010.

Burke, Edmund. *A Philosophical Enquiry into the Origins of Our Ideas of the Sublime and the Beautiful.* Edited by Adam Philip. Oxford: Oxford University Press, 1998.

Butler, Marilyn. "*Frankenstein* and Radical Science." In *Frankenstein: Mary Shelley*, edited by J. Paul Hunter, 302–13. New York: W. W. Norton, 1996.

Cook, Frederick A. *Through the First Antarctic Night 1898–1899: A Narrative of the Voyage of the "Belgica" among Newly Discovered Lands and Over an Unknown Sea about the South Pole.* London: William Heinemann, 1900.

David, Robert G. *The Arctic in the British Imagination, 1814–1914.* Manchester: Manchester University Press, 2000.

Dusek, Val. *The Holistic Inspirations of Physics: The Underground History of Electromagnetic Theory.* New Brunswick, NJ: Rutgers University Press, 1999.

Enebakk, Vidar. "Hansteen's Magnetometer and the Origin of the Magnetic Crusade." *British Journal for the History of Science* 47, no. 4 (2014): 1–22.

Fulford, Tim, Debbie Lee, and Peter J. Kitson. *Literature, Science and Exploration in the Romantic Era: Bodies of Knowledge.* Cambridge: Cambridge University Press, 2006.

Hill, Jen. *White Horizon: The Arctic in the Nineteenth-Century British Imagination.* New York: State University of New York Press, 2008.

Huntford, Roland. *Scott and Amundsen: The Last Place on Earth.* London: Abacus, 2009.

Karlsen, Silje Solheim. "Litterære helteportretter." In *Norske polarheltbilder 1888–1928*, edited by Harald Østgaard Lund and Siv Frøydis Berg, 46–47. Oslo: Forlaget Press/Nasjonalbiblioteket, 2011.

Kitson, Peter J. "Theories of Terrestrial Magnetism and the Search for the Poles." In *Literature, Science and Exploration in the Romantic Era: Bodies of Knowledge*, edited by Tim Fulford, Debbie Lee, and Peter J. Kitson, 149–75. Cambridge: Cambridge University Press, 2006.

Loomis, Chauncey A. "The Arctic Sublime." In *Nature and the British Imagination*, edited by U. C. Knoepflmacher and G. B. Tennyson, 95–112. Berkeley: University of California Press, 1997.

Lund, Harald Østgaard, and Siv Frøydis Berg, eds. *Norske polarheltbilder 1888–1928*. Oslo: Forlaget Press/Nasjonalbiblioteket, 2011.

Moe, Per Johan, "Hatteras—Nansen." *Norsk Jules Verne* (blog), 2 August 2010. http://julesgverne.wordpress.com/about/hatteras-nansen.

Nansen, Fridtjof. *"Farthest North": Being the Record of a Voyage of Exploration of the Ship* Fram *1893–96 and of a Fifteen Month's Sleigh Journey*. Vol. 1. Westminster: Constable, 1897.

———. *The First Crossing of Greenland*. Vol. 1. London: Longmans, Green, 1890.

———. *Norwegian North Polar Expedition: 1893–1896 Scientific Results*. 6 vols. London: Longmans, Green, 1900–1908.

Parry, William E. *Journal of a Voyage for the Discovery of a North-West Passage from the Atlantic to the Pacific; Performed in the Years 1819–20, in His Majesty's Ships* Hecla *and* Griper *under the Orders of William Edward Parry*. London: Murray, 1821.

Ponting, Herbert G. *The Great White South: Travelling with Robert F. Scott's Doomed South Pole Expedition*. New York: Cooper Square Press, 2001 [1921].

Porter, Roy. *Enlightenment: Britain and the Creation of the Modern World*. London: Penguin, 2001.

Potter, Russell A. *Arctic Spectacles: The Frozen North in Visual Culture, 1818–1875*. Seattle: University of Washington Press, 2007.

Riffenburgh, Beau. *The Myth of the Explorer: The Press, Sensationalism, and Geographical Discovery*. Oxford: Oxford University Press, 1994.

Ryall, Anka, Johan Schimanski, and Henning Howlid Wærp. *Arctic Discourses*. Newcastle upon Tyne: Cambridge Scholars Publishing, 2010.

Shackleton, Earnest H. *The Heart of the Antarctic: Being the Story of the British Antarctic Expedition 1907–1909*. Vol. 1. London: William Heinemann, 1909.

Shelley, Mary. *Frankenstein, or the Modern Prometheus*. London: H. Colburn and R. Bentley, 1831.

———. *Frankenstein, or the Modern Prometheus: The 1818 Text*. Oxford: Oxford University Press, 1994.

Spufford, Francis. *I May Be Some Time: Ice and the English Imagination*. London: Faber and Faber, 1996.

Verne, Jules. *The Adventures of Captain Hatteras*. Oxford: Oxford University Press, 2005.

William, Gilbert. *De magnete*. New York: Dover, 1991 [1600].

Wilson, Eric G. *The Spiritual History of Ice: Romanticism, Science, and the Imagination*. New York: Palgrave Macmillan, 2003.

25

The Norwegian Who Became a Globe

Mediation and Temporality in Roald Amundsen's 1911 South Pole Conquest

Espen Ytreberg

Outlining the Explorer

The film sequence is a simple one: for little more than a minute in Kristiania (modern-day Oslo) in 1913, a still camera registers a blackboard that fills the screen.[1] After a few seconds a man enters stage left, in his hand a crayon. Swiftly and assuredly he draws a globe on the blackboard, with feet and arms added to make a person.[2] The man doing the drawing then reveals himself as an effective portraitist, sketching the characteristically large nose and deeply furrowed features of the polar explorer Roald Amundsen, whose expedition team was the first to reach the South Pole, on 14–16 December 1911. The man then carefully draws the Norwegian flag held high in Amundsen's right hand. To round off, the extreme North and South are named on the globe-torso, and some contours of continents are suggested. Before exiting stage right, the portraitist signs off at the bottom of the blackboard with a colloquial naming of the famous explorer as "Han Roald," with the Norwegian pronoun *han* ("he") used here as both a term of familiarity and an informal honorific: both "Roald, one of the guys" and "*the* Roald."

There is something bold and assertive in the way Amundsen's physique is extended in this cartoon to the size of the world, encompassing it and melting together with it. Clearly something is being said here about national pride and the achievements of an eminent Norwegian in the world. But toning-down effects seem to be applied as well. There is the colloquial use of Amundsen's first name. Also, something playful seems to be going on in the cartoonist's toying around with the distended torso of Amundsen's figure, blowing him up to mildly comic effect. It is as if Amundsen has accidentally swallowed a globe. Maybe it will need to come out again, somehow.

Figure 25.1. Sverre Halvorsen drawing Roald Amundsen. Still image captured from the film *Roald Amundsens sydpolsferd*. Courtesy of the National Library of Norway.

The man drawing is Sverre Halvorsen, a professional cartoonist well-known by the readers of Norwegian newspapers and magazines in the early twentieth century. The film sequence was done for the variety theatre Circus Tivoli in Kristiania. The year before, in 1912, Roald Amundsen had returned from Antarctica, having traveled with his *Fram* team to become the first to reach the absolute 90° S. This made him the winner of what newspapers came to call the "Race to the Pole," beating Robert Falcon Scott's Terra Nova Expedition. Amundsen, already famous in Norway and somewhat known abroad, now became famous abroad as well and a national figurehead in Norway. The tale of his conquest became common property, as did his characteristic, furrowed, and eagle-nosed countenance. Sverre Halvorsen was only one of many—photographers, draftsmen, painters, filmmakers, and makers of stamps—who lined up at this time to render Amundsen's likeness for media audiences. The short film sequence of Halvorsen drawing was part of a popular sub-genre in early film entertainment: cartoonists doing a drawing of contemporary subject matter, usually photographed using a time-lapse technique for a moderate fast-forward effect.[3]

This film sequence was a small cog in a wheel of cultural industries that at the time spun ever larger and faster, with the rapid spread of a number of new media forms from the second half of the nineteenth century (photography, film, magazines, popular newspapers, and also radio from the 1920s on). Sverre Halvorsen's cartoon, the filming of it, and the display of that film in Norwegian cinemas all speak to the heavily mediated character of the South Pole conquest event. This could be said also of other polar conquests of the late nineteenth and early twentieth centuries. The importance of mediation to them has been well documented internationally, particularly for newspapers.[4] The South Pole conquest, its investments, uncertainties, braveries, and competitive motifs, was a major international news story in the period 1910–12. Photography played a key role, particularly in documenting the moment of conquest. A flag formed the centerpiece of all six extant photographs from the South Pole point. Mediated flags provided a means of communication between the expedition and a Norwegian nation that had become politically independent only six years earlier, and that looked to Amundsen and his men for affirmations of Norway's place in the world. When Sverre Halvorsen draws Amundsen holding a Norwegian flag high, he refers back to those flags held high at the South Pole.

Among the constraints imposed by the media situation of the early twentieth century was a dearth of information available about international events such as the South Pole conquest, since they happened largely out of the reach of media of mechanical registration (film, photography) and outside the range of media of immediate distribution (telegraph, and partially newspapers). Media events of the early twentieth century lacked the technological affordances that electronic and digital media would later bring, particularly the immediate, "real-time" distribution and reception of unfolding events.[5] This does not mean that events preceding electronic and digital media were necessarily less mediated; recently this point has been argued forcefully by Frank Bösch.[6] Rather, the South Pole conquest was differently mediated, and this chapter points to some of the ways in which mediation worked within that event. The emphasis is on temporal relationships between a main event (the act of conquest proper) and a series of re-stagings of that main event after the fact, spanning several years. Also, the chapter argues that in this space of time, first an articulation and then a change of that articulation took place concerning Norway's place in the "civilized world."

"A Place in the Forefront among Cultured Nations"

Norwegian official political discourse on the expedition and newspaper coverage of it were both dominated by sentiments of national pride. In 1912, after the success of the South Pole conquest, Norway's parliament awarded Roald Amundsen an annual allowance termed a "national reward." In the same year, its president addressed a parliament session, expressing a collective "pride that these men are our fellow Norwegians and have once more brought glory to the name of Norway."[7]

At the time, Norwegian nationalist sentiment and discourse was at something of a high point. Only a few years before the conquest, in 1905, Norway had become an independent country, breaking out of a union with Sweden. This was a time of nationalist affirmation but also a time of searching for ways to conceive of the new nation's place in the world. Norway was a relative latecomer to a process more general to the wave of nation-state formations and nationalisms that had marked the nineteenth century. In different ways, these processes all involved articulations of the relationship between nation and world. Major nations typically conceived of themselves as political and cultural world leaders, via the practices and discourses of colonialization and empire on a global scale. For instance, the celebrations of Queen Victoria's Golden Jubilee and Diamond Jubilee in 1887 and 1897, respectively, have been interpreted as acts of promoting Britain's commanding world presence, cases of "empire on parade."[8]

For a minor, young, and marginal nation such as Norway in the early twentieth century, the task of working out how one's nation related to the world had to be dealt with differently. In a valuable discussion,[9] historian Narve Fulsås has pointed out that the advocates of polar exploration sought to reconcile discourses of the national and the universal. One was about promoting the nationalist competitive instinct, where nations fought against one another in the "race for the Pole," and where "each country now sides with its man," as Leon Amundsen, Roald's brother and agent, said at the time.[10] Lacking the power and glory of empire, Norwegians built an account in which it was precisely their skills from the margins that allowed them to win the race over the empire par excellence. As one parliamentarian noted, "Just in this area we know we can claim for our small nation of people a place in the forefront among cultured nations."[11]

As for the universal, polar explorations of both Norwegian and other nationalities also routinely included scientists and scientific programs. They appealed to scientific values of seeking truth and advancing human knowledge, and the expeditions' legitimacy, particularly in the eyes of their funders, rested heavily on such universalist appeals. At stake here, for the contemporary advocates of conquest per expedition, was the spread throughout the "civilized world" of knowledge about the world's farthest reaches. It was thus quoted with approval in several of the Norwegian newspapers when *Wiener Fremdenblatt* wrote: "The entire civilized world partakes in Norway's triumph. All nations agree in their admiration for the men who in the service of an idea have been prepared to make any sacrifice in order to expand human knowledge."[12]

A vital force was lent to this notion of expanding knowledge among nations by the fact that it was done via a conquest of the natural world's farthest reaches. The conquests of the geographic poles had limited scientific and trade significance but were rich in symbolic potential. The poles were the ultimate white spot on the map—"ultimate" both in the sense that no one had been there, and in that these were areas of snowy and icy extremity. They involved immense and forbidding expanses, they posed the greatest and most unknown danger. Following the deaths of numerous explorers, the polar regions had attained an air of dangerous finality. Because the poles were places at the ends of the world, and because getting there could be seen as a triumph of humanity over nature's greatest challenges, they presented a privileged point from which to address the nation and the world.

Making a Place out of Nowhere

Nothingness is a difficult phenomenon to handle, as Arne Melberg has pointed out in a discussion of travel literature.[13] The geographical South Pole, at 90° S, looked almost as white and undifferentiated to its explorers as it did on the maps. It lies on the Central Antarctic Plateau, which is a vast, flat, highland plain. This plain presents to the eye not much more than a whitish expanse, a sky and a horizon line. When the weather is bad, and it routinely is, the horizon disappears and white-out conditions ensue. Marking a place out in such conditions of course involves considerable trekking skill, but also much more. Elaborate measuring technologies are needed to find the precise location of the geographic South Pole, and elaborate media technologies are needed if one wants to communicate the conquest to absent audiences, meaningfully and authoritatively. Roald Amundsen sorely needed to prove beyond doubt that he had actually been at the precise 90° S. He was acutely aware of the drawn-out and inconclusive battle that Robert Peary and Frederick Cook had become embroiled in, over who had made it first—if any of them—to the geographic North Pole. Consequently, the *Fram* South Pole Expedition was always planned with a view to documenting and distributing evidence about the conquest once it had been made. The expedition had brought cameras for both photography and film, but the film camera could not be carried all the way to the pole. The evidence thus came to rest heavily on photographs taken around the geographic South Pole.

Only six photographs have survived from the period 14–16 December, since the team members were relative amateurs in handling the portable Kodak they had brought.[14] For the expedition team, this period was dominated by two sets of activities. In a series of measurements, they sought to ascertain precisely the position of the geographic South Pole, a task made

Figure 25.2. Roald Amundsen, his crew, and the tent at the approximate South Pole on 16 December 1911. Photograph, available via Wikimedia Commons: https://en.wikipedia.org/wiki/Amundsen%27s_South_Pole_expedition.

difficult by limitations in the available technology, so that at least three different spots were identified inside the three-day period.[15] They came closest (probably within a few hundred meters) on the third and last attempt. By this time they were in a hurry to return, so the photographs documenting the spot and celebrating the conquest are actually from positions somewhat further away. If measurement technology kept frustrating them, the photographs counteracted that frustration, introducing a strong common symbolism and sense of eventfulness. All the photographs feature expedition members posing in postures of acknowledgment or possession, showing off their equipment, dogs, and sleds. And crucially, they all feature the Norwegian flag waving from a pole, centrally placed in the photograph's composition.

In these photographs, the flag is a highly dense symbol. (It already was, of course, but here even more so.) The planting of a flag conventionally signals the annexation of territory, the establishment of what Amundsen called "the little Norway on the South Pole."[16] In this case it also does the crucial job of defining a visible and legible place in the nowhere landscape of the Central Antarctic Plateau. In addition, conspicuously planted as it is, the flag also indicates the spot of the geographic South Pole. And, of course, the flag symbolizes Norway, the entity on whose behalf the conquest is made. One might say the flag represents the parties in a communication process: the expedition members, headed by Amundsen, who originated the message of conquest; the highly deictic message itself (*this* is where the spot is, *we* made it *here*); and the absent audiences of Norway and the "civilized world." Amundsen was keenly aware of the importance of this symbolism, and of the event-character it imparted: "After this first act [the expedition members shaking hands upon arrival at the South Pole spot] we set upon the most momentous and solemn event of the whole journey—the planting of our flag. ... 'We plant you, O dearest flag, on the South Pole, and we name this plain on which it lies the King Haakon VII Plain.'"[17] Although the moment of conquest was of course a climax in itself, it was also a starting-up moment, for the process of communicating the climax and making it the event it would eventually become.

Narrating the Event

In his book-length account of the conquest, Roald Amundsen was quite clear and explicit on the fundamental importance of communicating the event. He wrote this about the mood of the expedition team after setting off from the South Pole continent toward Tasmania, to wire news of a successful conquest:

> In the stage we now found ourselves, with our primary goal achieved, one might perhaps expect a certain relaxation of the mood. But this did not happen. The fact of the matter was that our achievement would only have lasting value when it was brought to the knowledge of humanity, and this transmission needed to happen within the least possible amount of time.[18]

Narration is a powerful means of making what happens eventful, as Reinhart Koselleck has argued.[19] In the case of the South Pole conquest, media were key to telling the event both as it was unfolding and after the fact.

The narration of the event as it unfolded was done primarily in the newspapers, although they were up against a dearth of information. At the time, the wire was the only medium capable of an immediate distribution of information over global distances. However, there were no wire stations on the Antarctic continent, so journalists had to wait for the rare occasions when expedition ships returned intermittently to civilization for supplies. Months would pass between each news wire. In other words, there was no way of imparting the quality of temporal immediacy that impresses itself on us today when major mediated events happen. However, the interval between the event of conquest and the reporting of it was one where eventfulness could be actively built up, via narratives of suspense and uncertainty. Coverage of the event in Norwegian newspapers intensified markedly when it became clear in March 1911 that Amundsen's and Scott's expeditions were engaged in what could be seen as a head-on race. Wrote *Aftenposten*: "The main question, one that has occupied all Norwegians and all who have keenly followed Roald

Amundsen's *Fram* Expedition, has been this: Which route will he choose? ... Today a telegram from Scott's expedition, having just arrived in New Zealand, has cleared the issue: Roald Amundsen has chosen the English route. ... Amundsen has made the sensible choice for he who wishes to compete with success in the exciting race for the Pole."[20] Reports such as these could be seen to build audience identification with the explorers that relied on a sense of the simultaneous. Audiences were invited to feel that their peaceful daily lives in Kristiania and London were being lived just as their explorer-heroes were braving extreme hardships at the other end of the globe, on their behalf.

Benedict Anderson has famously argued the importance of "imaginary communities" for nationalism. He has pointed to the foundational importance of news media with their daily, nationwide mass distribution and consumption for establishing a sense that we have something in common with people we have not met and will never meet. Interestingly, Anderson speaks of nationalism as involving a specifically modern sense of simultaneity. We live our lives according to a linear, homogeneous sense of clock-time; but media also enable experiences of community that are "transverse, cross-time," as he puts it.[21] The South Pole conquest involved an effort to stretch the bond of national community to the other side of the globe, and a corresponding extension of the sense of simultaneity. It was, in a sense, the national community writ large, stretched to encompass the globe, somewhat like Roald Amundsen's cartoon torso.

The Lecture Tours: Events after the Event

As for narrating the event after the fact, this took very elaborate forms in the case of the South Pole conquest. When the news of conquest broke on 8 March 1912, it dwarfed all other stories in the Norwegian press and received significant international coverage. The conquest proper was followed by a series of what one may call secondary events, in the form of public lectures by Roald Amundsen. The lectures were important as generators of revenue for Amundsen, but also for the basic legitimacy claims of the conquest. With the help of an active use of photography and film, the lectures re-staged, affirmed, and celebrated the process and moment of conquest. Roald Amundsen's first public lecture after the South Pole conquest, for the Norwegian Geographical Society on 9 September 1912, was a major Norwegian public event in itself.[22] It was attended by the Norwegian king and queen, at the head of various representatives of the national elite, and was widely reported in the newspapers. It kicked off the first of a series of lecture tours that would take Amundsen through the southern part of Norway, then to the Continent, England, and the United States, until the beginning of 1914.

The lecture of 9 September 1912 was extensively covered by Norway's main newspapers, and the reports were marked by nationalist pride.[23] The context established was national, in the sense of an occasion made for, and shared by, Norwegians. *Aftenposten* described a "wave of excitement washing through our land," and "an honor shared by most all in the nation."[24] It is interesting to note a lack of attention to an international context, both in Amundsen's talk itself[25] and in the newspapers' coverage of this event. There was no mention of the "cultured nations" or the "civilized world"; no mention of Norway leading the world, nor of the "race for the Pole" with England. This is not to say that such notions ceased to be expressed in Norwegian public life at the time, but at least in the context of commentary on the South Pole conquest they did not seem to have been important. This tendency was confirmed in the series of newspaper reports made by *Aftenposten* and *Dagbladet* as Amundsen started on the Norwegian leg of his lecture tour: the context was resolutely national while the world receded from sight, so to speak.

What came instead was an embedding of the conquest event in local contexts. When Amundsen went on tour to the towns of southern Norway, the media event of his visit became an event not just for and about Amundsen, but also for that town and local area itself. In this process, the role of interpersonal public communication in the event was central. While the lecture itself was heavily mediated, the delivery of the lecture by Amundsen was an occasion of both interpersonal and public communication. It would usually be both preceded and followed by salutary speeches, and mayors, magistrates, and schoolmasters also made speeches in public places to gathered crowds. Marching bands, children clutching flags, and sports association members would greet Amundsen as he stepped off the train or boat. Processions were made through the town, the streets lined with flags and torches, crowds cheering them along and joining in at the tail end.[26] When Amundsen came, this seems to have been an occasion for everyone to go out and celebrate him. There was certainly also a celebration of the nation; the waving of national flags was ubiquitous and near-compulsory. At the same time, the emphasis seems to have been on the collective diversion of enjoying pomp, circumstance, and celebrity, as much as on matters national and international. Said *Dagbladet*: "Amundsen brings festivity wherever he goes."[27]

As celebrations with a frame of reference that was partly national and partly local, Amundsen's public lecture events in Norway were markedly different from the world-encompassing discourse that had surrounded the conquest event itself. The attempt to reconcile nation and world seems to have receded as a pressing concern. And largely, the local took precedence over the national, as the notaries of Larvik, Drammen, Fredrikstad, Stavanger, and Trondheim surrounded Amundsen and the crowds surged in to make their mark on the proceedings. In this process, the category of the national itself seems to have shifted somewhat. The explicitly nationalistic, outwardly assertive discourse connected with the "Race to the Pole" was replaced by a celebratory, upbeat, and participative approach where national symbolism was more of a backdrop. Discussing the case of historical "disaster events" such as the 1755 Lisbon earthquake and the 1900 Galveston hurricane, Anders Ekström has argued that mediation of these events over time involved a "tendency to draw the sublime into the domain of the ordinary."[28] Something roughly similar may have been going on in the case of the South Pole conquest: a movement from the sublime, or at least the unique, moment of conquest on a worldwide scale to a series of local re-enactments.

The end result was a form of "soft" nationalism prevalent in Norway also today, although hardly unique to this country: cheering rather than aggressive, patriotic rather than jingoistic, fronted by children waving flags rather than by soldiers in rank. Because the nationalism aspect of Amundsen's lecture tour events was implicit more than elaborated on, it seemed apolitical, in the sense of being removed from the factions and dilemmas of current politics. As Narve Fulsås has pointed out, this lent it a quality of national unification, which in the end may have been at least as politically potent.[29] We may see this implied, celebratory nationalism as a course taken because Norway's repertoire of gestures of national conquest on a world stage was always going to be severely limited.

The process of domesticating this event over time, both literally and figuratively, can be read into that short film sequence where Sverre Halvorsen draws Amundsen's portrait. Halvorsen conjures up something of a rare sight: Amundsen smiling. In the other film sequences from Amundsen's South Pole expedition, and in the extant photographic material, one mostly sees a stern figure. Amundsen's biographers agree in portraying him as somewhat aloof in public settings, and as gradually more and more unhappy and conflicted in his relationships with public life.[30] The act of putting a smile on his face, then, may be about emphasizing the friendly, accessible, and everyday character of what he represented in a wider sense. In combination with the rotund, somewhat comical world-torso, that smile worked to lessen the sense of distance between Amundsen and the popular audiences of his cinema films. It seems to carry the message that his conquest was ultimately a gesture of closeness with regular Norwegians more than an act of worldwide reach.

Espen Ytreberg is Professor of Media Studies in the Department of Media and Communication, University of Oslo. In recent years he has published several articles on the South Pole case and on historical media events, including "The 1911 South Pole Conquest as Media Event and Media Ensemble," *Media History* 20 no. 2 (2014); "Toward a Historical Understanding of the

Media Event," *Media Culture & Society* 39, no. 3 (2016); and "Networked Simultaneities in the Time of the Great Exhibitions: Media and the 1914 Oslo Centenary Jubilee Exhibition," *International Journal of Communication* 10 (2016).

NOTES

1. The sequence is available on the DVD *Roald Amundsens sydpolsferd (1910-1912)* (Oslo, 2010). On the South Pole films and lectures, see Jan Anders Diesen, "The South Pole Film," in *Roald Amundsen's South Pole Expedition 1910-1912: On the Expedition Film and the Iconic Photograph*, bilingual booklet (Norwegian and English) published with the DVD *Roald Amundsens sydpolsferd (1910-1912)* (Oslo, 2010), 101-54. On the photographs, see Harald Østgaard Lund, "The South Pole Photograph," in *Roald Amundsen's South Pole Expedition*, 167-78; Harald Østgaard Lund and Siv Frøydis Berg, eds, *Norske polarheltbilder 1888-1928* (Oslo, 2011).
2. For further discussions of the globe, see in particular the chapters by Stefan Willer, Alfred Hiatt, Jeppe Strandsbjerg, Kari van Dijk, Helge Jordheim, and Siv Frøydis Berg in this volume.
3. Gunnar Strøm, "Caricatures, Cartoons and Advertisements: The Pioneers of Nordic Animated Film," in *Nordic Explorations: Film before 1930*, ed. John Fullerton and Jan Olsson (Stockholm, 1999), 114-36.
4. See, for example, Beau Riffenburgh, *The Myth of the Explorer: The Press, Sensationalism, and Geographical Discovery* (Oxford, 1994); Michael F. Robinson, *The Coldest Crucible: Arctic Exploration and American Culture* (Chicago, 2006); Frank Bösch and Patrick Schmidt, eds, *Medialisierte Ereignisse: Performanz, Inszenierung und Medien seit dem 18. Jahrhundert* (Frankfurt am Main, 2010).
5. For a definition of the media event that emphasizes the liveness and real-time affordances of broadcasting, see Daniel Dayan and Elihu Katz, *Media Events: The Live Broadcasting of History* (Cambridge, MA, 1992).
6. For example, Frank Bösch, "Europäische Medienereignisse," *Europäische Geschichte Online*, retrieved 3 December 2010 from http://www.ieg-ego.eu/boeschf-2010-de. See also Friedrich Lenger and Ansgar Nünning, eds, *Medienereignisse der Moderne* (Darmstadt, 2008).
7. Quoted in Narve Fulsås, "En æressag for vor nation," in *Norsk polarhistorie*, vol. 1, *Ekspedisjonene*, ed. Einar-Arne Drivenes and Harald Dag Jølle (Oslo, 2004), 217.
8. See discussion and references in Meike Hölscher and Jan Rupp, "Empire on Parade: Queen Victorias Thronjubiläen," in Bösch and Schmidt, *Medialisierte Ereignisse*, 160-79.
9. Fulsås, "En æressag."
10. Quoted in Tor Bomann-Larsen, *Roald Amundsen: En biografi* (Oslo, 1998), 146.
11. From a parliamentary debate quoted in *Aftenposten*, 13 March 1912, as quoted in Merete Habberstad, "Myten om polfareren: En studie av pressedekningen av fire polarekspedisjoner gjennom hundre år" (Master's thesis, University of Oslo, 1995), 69.

12. Quoted from *Aftenposten, Dagbladet*, and *Verdens Gang*, 9 March 1912, in Habberstad, "Myten om polfareren," 74.
13. Arne Melberg, *Å reise og skrive: Et essay om moderne reiselitteratur* (Oslo, 2005), 224.
14. See the detailed discussion in Lund, "The South Pole Photograph." The photographs are available via the search facilities of the National Library of Norway at http://www.nb.no/nbsok/search (using the search term "Sydpolen").
15. Roald Amundsen, *Roald Amundsens dagbøker: Sydpolsekspedisjonen 1910-1912* (Oslo, 2010), 312-13. Roland Huntford, *Scott and Amundsen* (London, 1980), presents the most detailed discussion.
16. Roald Amundsen, "The South Pole Lecture," in *Roald Amundsen's South Pole Expedition*, 164.
17. Roald Amundsen, *Sydpolen: Den norske sydpolsferd med Fram 1910-1912* (Oslo, 2003), 491.
18. Ibid., 534.
19. Reinhart Koselleck, "Representation, Event, and Structure," in *Futures Past: On the Semantics of Historical Time* (New York, 1985), 105-14.
20. *Aftenposten*, 28 March 1911. All newspaper quotations in this chapter are translated by the author. For a more extended discussion of the newspaper coverage, see Espen Ytreberg, "The 1911 South Pole Conquest as Historical Media Event and Media Ensemble," *Media History* 20, no. 2 (2014): 1-15.
21. Benedict Anderson, *Imagined Communities: Reflections on the Origin and Spread of Nationalism* (London, 1983).
22. See the account in Diesen, "The South Pole Film," 121-29.
23. Arguments in this section rest on an analysis of coverage in the leading daily newspapers *Dagbladet* and *Aftenposten* between 1 September and 5 October 1912.
24. *Aftenposten*, 10 September 1912.
25. Amundsen, "The South Pole Lecture."
26. As for instance in Amundsen's visit to the town of Larvik, reported in *Aftenposten*, 18 September 1912.
27. *Dagbladet*, 15 September 1912.
28. Anders Ekström, "Exhibiting Disasters: Mediation, Historicity and Spectatorship," *Media, Culture & Society* 34, no. 4 (2012): 473.
29. Fulsås, "En æressag," 221-23.
30. Bomann-Larsen, *Roald Amundsen*; Alexander Wisting, *Roald Amundsen: Det største eventyret. En biografi* (Oslo, 2011).

BIBLIOGRAPHY

Amundsen, Roald. *Roald Amundsens dagbøker: Sydpolsekspedisjonen 1910-1912*. Oslo: Frammuseet/Nasjonalbiblioteket, 2010.

———. "The South Pole Lecture." In *Roald Amundsen's South Pole Expedition 1910-1912: On the Expedition Film and the Iconic Photograph*, bilingual booklet (Norwegian and

English) published with the DVD *Roald Amundsens sydpolsferd (1910-1912)*, 155-66. Oslo: Norwegian Film Institute/National Library of Norway, 2010.

———. *Sydpolen: Den norske sydpolsferd med Fram 1910-1912*. Oslo: Kagge Forlag, 2003.

Anderson, Benedict. *Imagined Communities: Reflections on the Origin and Spread of Nationalism*. London: Verso, 1983.

Bomann-Larsen, Tor. *Roald Amundsen: En biografi*. Oslo: Cappelen, 1998.

Bösch, Frank. "Europäische Medienereignisse." *Europäische Geschichte Online*. Retrieved 3 December 2010 from http://www.ieg-ego.eu/boeschf-2010-de.

Bösch, Frank, and Patrick Schmidt, eds. *Medialisierte Ereignisse: Performanz, Inszenierung und Medien seit dem 18. Jahrhundert*. Frankfurt am Main: Campus Verlag, 2010.

Dayan, Daniel, and Elihu Katz. *Media Events: The Live Broadcasting of History*. Cambridge, MA: Harvard University Press, 1992.

Diesen, Jan Anders. "The South Pole Film." In *Roald Amundsen's South Pole Expedition 1910-1912: On the Expedition Film and the Iconic Photograph*, bilingual booklet (Norwegian and English) published with the DVD *Roald Amundsens sydpolsferd (1910-1912)*, 101-54. Oslo: Norwegian Film Institute/National Library of Norway, 2010.

Ekström, Anders. "Exhibiting Disasters: Mediation, Historicity and Spectatorship." *Media, Culture & Society* 34, no. 4 (2012): 472-87.

Fulsås, Narve. "En æressag for vor nation." In *Norsk polarhistorie*, vol. 1, *Ekspedisjonene*, edited by Einar-Arne Drivenes and Harald Dag Jølle, 173-226. Oslo: Gyldendal, 2004.

Habberstad, Merete. "Myten om polfareren: En studie av pressedekningen av fire polarekspedisjoner gjennom hundre år." Master's thesis, University of Oslo, 1995.

Hölscher, Meike, and Jan Rupp. "Empire on Parade: Queen Victorias Thronjubiläen." In *Medialisierte Ereignisse: Performanz, Inszenierung und Medien seit dem 18. Jahrhundert*, edited by Frank Bösch and Patrick Schmidt, 160-79. Frankfurt am Main: Campus Verlag, 2010.

Huntford, Roland. *Scott and Amundsen*. London: Hodder and Stoughton, 1980.

Koselleck, Reinhart. "Representation, Event, and Structure." In *Futures Past: On the Semantics of Historical Time*, 105-14. New York: Columbia University Press, 1985.

Lenger, Friedrich, and Ansgar Nünning, eds. *Medienereignisse der Moderne*. Darmstadt: Wissenschaftliche Buchgesellschaft, 2008.

Lund, Harald Østgaard. "The South Pole Photograph." In *Roald Amundsen's South Pole Expedition 1910-1912: On the Expedition Film and the Iconic Photograph*, bilingual booklet (Norwegian and English) published with the DVD *Roald Amundsens sydpolsferd (1910-1912)*, 167-78. Oslo: Norwegian Film Institute/National Library of Norway, 2010.

Lund, Harald Østgaard, and Siv Frøydis Berg, eds. *Norske polarheltbilder 1888-1928*. Oslo: Forlaget Press/Nasjonalbiblioteket, 2011.

Melberg, Arne. *Å reise og skrive: Et essay om moderne reiselitteratur*. Oslo: Spartacus, 2005.

Riffenburgh, Beau. *The Myth of the Explorer: The Press, Sensationalism, and Geographical Discovery*. Oxford: Oxford University Press, 1994.

Roald Amundsen's South Pole Expedition 1910–1912: On the Expedition Film and the Iconic Photograph. Bilingual booklet (Norwegian and English) published with the DVD *Roald Amundsens sydpolsferd (1910–1912)*. Oslo: Norwegian Film Institute/National Library of Norway, 2010.

Roald Amundsens sydpolsferd (1910–1912). DVD. Oslo: Norsk filminstitutt, 2010.

Robinson, Michael F. *The Coldest Crucible: Arctic Exploration and American Culture*. Chicago: University of Chicago Press, 2006.

Strøm, Gunnar. "Caricatures, Cartoons and Advertisements: The Pioneers of Nordic Animated Film." In *Nordic Explorations: Film before 1930*, edited by John Fullerton and Jan Olsson, 114–36. Stockholm: Aura/John Libbey, 1999.

Wisting, Alexander. *Roald Amundsen: Det største eventyret. En biografi*. Oslo: Kagge Forlag, 2011.

Ytreberg, Espen. "The 1911 South Pole Conquest as Historical Media Event and Media Ensemble." *Media History* 20, no. 2 (2014): 1–15.

Index

'Abqariyyat al-Masīh (al-'Aqqad), 59
'Abqariyyat Muhammad (al-'Aqqad), 58–60
academia: beliefs in, 2; conflict studies, 159; cosmology in, 41, 349; education, 66, 340–43, 348–50; ethics in, 112; globalization in, 339–43, 348–50; GLP for, 161; hegemony of, 90n14; history in, 4, 218; *The History of Creation* (Haeckel), 95; the intellectual globe in, 20; metaphors in, 47–48; methodology of, 32–33, 37n9; politics of, 16–17, 27–28, 74; semantics in, 17–18, 42–43; Treaty of Tordesillas (1494) in, 308n3
The Academy (Wedmore), 244
Adam of Bremen, 290–95
Adler, Mortimer, 319
Gustavus Adolphus (King), 278–79
Advancement of Learning (Bacon, F.), 313–14
The Adventures of Captain Hatteras (Verne), 361–62
Ahlström, Stellan, 245–46
ʾālam, 41–44, 45–46
Albertus Magnus, 263
d'Alembert, Jean le Rond, 186–87, 313–14, 319–320
Algeria, 81–83
Althusser, Louis, 131
Amundsen, Leon, 376
Amundsen, Roald, 365–68, 373–82

The Ancient Mariner (Coleridge), 359
Ancient Society (Morgan), 160
Anders, William, 13
Anderson, Benedict, 200, 380
anthropology, 3, 11–14, 30, 36
L'an V de la révolution algérienne (Fanon), 82–83
Appiah, Kwame Anthony, 221–22
al-'Aqqad, 'Abbas Mahmud, 58–61
Aquinas, Thomas, 112–13, 115, 120
Arabic, 29–30, 33, 40–46, 57–58, 61. See also Islam
Arab Spring, 62–63
the Arctic. See the Poles
The Arctic Explorers (Porden), 359
Arendt, Hannah, 66–72, 75–76, 205–8
Ari Þorgilsson, 290
Aristotle, 44, 263
art, 245–46, 276–77, 327–28, 357–58, 374–75
al-'Askarī, Abū Hilāl, 41–42
Auerbach, Erich, 209n14
Augustine (Saint), 9
authority: biblical analogies as, 229–30; in exile, 199–200; in Germany, 200–201, 205–6; ICOMOS as, 217–19; in Islam, 58; knowledge and, 48; religion and, 61–62, 120, 233, 278; for world literature, 247–48
avant la lettre, 155–56

Bacon, Francis, 312–20, 321n15
Bacon, Roger, 263
Balandier, Georges, 81, 90n4
al-Balkhī, Muqātil b. Sulaymān, 41–42
Bandarín, Francesco, 214–15
Bandung Conference, 81–82, 86
Bartelson, J., 144
Bataille, Georges, 191
Bayle, Pierre, 18, 184–92
Becker, Gary, 125
Behaim, Martin, 264–65
Behn, Aphra, 341, 343–45, 350
Beitz, Charles, 137
Belgrade Conference, 91n23
Benveniste, Émile, 32–33
the Bible, 55–56
biblical analogies, 228–30, 233–35
Biering, Christian Henrik, 226–31, 234–36
biographies, 204–5
biology, 96–97, 99
Bjarni Herjólfsson, 291–92
Bjørnson, Bjørnstjerne, 246
Bloch, Ernst, 206–7
Blumenberg, Hans, 6
Bode, Johann Elert, 13, 347
Boethius, 261, 265–66
Bösch, Frank, 375
Botton, Alain de, 334
Bourdieu, Pierre, 126–27
Boyle, Robert, 314
Bracon, Francis, 20
Brand (Ibsen), 242–45, 248
Braun, Hermann, 4–5, 13
Brotton, Jerry, 300
Brown, Michael Barratt, 87
Buchanan, Keith, 86–87
Buchman, David, 47, 50n32
Buck, C. D., 30
Burghley (Lord), 313
Bush, George H. W., 15
Bush, Vannevar, 311–13, 319–20

Calderini, Simonetta, 42
Capital (Marx), 124, 128–31
capitalism, 90n14, 95, 123–32
von Carlowitz, Hans Carl, 95
Carlyle, Thomas, 58–59, 242–43

Carson, Rachel, 95
Carta marina (Olaus Magnus), 274–83, 284n2
Carter, Jimmy, 140
cartography, 299–307, 308n5
cartoons, 374–75
Casanova, Pascale, 240–41, 245–46, 248
Casaubon, Isaac, 315–16
case studies, 18, 72–75, 78n10
center-periphery relations, 240–41
Chakrabarty, Dipesh, 241
Chambers, Ephraim, 186–87
Charles V (King), 303
Chart over the Immediate Surroundings (Nilsen), 366
Christ, Jesus, 58–62
Christianity, 58–62. *See also* religion
Churchill, Winston, 15
Cicero, Marcus Tullius, 112, 115, 258–59, 264
civilization, 201
Clam, Jean, 171–72
closed nostalgia, 203
Cold War, 79–80, 84, 88–89, 103, 140
Coleridge, Samuel Taylor, 359
colonialism, 80–81, 84–87, 114–15, 159, 299–307
Columbus, Christopher, 155, 203, 301
Commentarius (Macrobius), 260–62
Commoner, Barry, 96–97
communication, 31–32, 34–35, 184
Conduct of Understanding (Locke), 318
conflict studies, 159
conscience, for humanity, 54–63
Constanza, Robert, 124–25
Cook, Frederick, 377
Cosgrove, Denis, 300
cosmology, 13–14, 41, 341–43, 349, 350
cosmopolitanism, 220–22
counter-history, 190–92
Cox, Robert, 141
critical thinking, 70, 71–72
criticism, 209n14, 215–16, 240–48
Critique de la raison dialectique (Sartre), 83–84
culture: in anthropology, 30, 36; beliefs in, 38n18; biblical analogies for, 228–29;

cultural relativism, 144; formative moments in, 33–34; geography and, 9–10, 220; of Germany, 206–7; globalization and, 62–63, 69, 99–101, 161, 182–83, 191–92, 215, 217, 221–22; history and, 213–14; intercultural education, 66–67, 69–70; of knowledge, 4; learning about, 74–75; metaphors in, 94–95; Norse culture, 286–95; *The Origin of the Family, Private Property, and the State* (Engels), 160; the Poles in, 359–62; politics and, 2, 75–76, 218–19; psychology of, 210n16; Underwater Cultural Heritage, 220; UNESCO, 125–26, 212–22; of US, 206–7; world heritage as, 212–16; of world literature, 243–45. *See also* society

damīr, 57–58
Les damnés de la terre (Fanon), 82–87, 91n20
Damrosch, David, 243, 247
Darwin, Erasmus, 360
David, Pascal, 346–47
David, Robert G., 363
Dawkins, Richard, 334
De augmentis (Bacon, F.), 314–15
Debes, Lucas, 232
De Caelo (Aristotle), 263
De consolatione philosophiae (Boethius), 261, 265–66
de' Conti, Niccolò, 268
De essentiis (Hermann of Carinthia), 266
De Indis (Grotius), 115–17, 119
De iure belli ac pacis (Grotius), 119–20
De la démocratie en Amérique (Tocqueville), 159–60
Deleuze, Gilles, 173–78, 330
Deloria, Vine, Jr., 155
De magnete (Gilbert), 360
democracy, 147–48, 154–61
Denmark: Biering for, 226–31, 234–36; Pontoppidan for, 226–27, 231–36
De Officiis (Cicero), 115
Derrida, Jacques, 330
Descriptio globi intellectualis (Bacon, F.), 314

diachronic analysis, 72
dictionaries, 30, 183–92, 244
Dictionary of Selected Synonyms (Buck), 30
Dictionary of Theater (Pickering), 244
"Dictionnaire critique" (Bataille), 191
Dictionnaire des athées anciens et modernes (Maréchal), 190–91
Dictionnaire des idées reçues (Flaubert), 191
Dictionnaire historique et critique (Bayle), 184–87
Dictionnaire philosophique (Voltaire), 185–86
Diderot, Denis, 186–87, 313
Diogenes, 208–9
A Discovery of a World in the Moone (Wilkins), 341, 344–45
disenchantment, 328–30, 336n15
Documentary Heritage, 220
A Doll's House (Ibsen), 240–41, 248
Douzinas, Costas, 145, 147
Dragmaticon Philosophia (William of Conches), 261–63
"Dream of Scipio" (Cicero), 258–59
Dworkin, Ronald, 136

Earth, 257–58, 261–64, 327–34
Earth Day, 101
earthquakes, 227–31, 231–35, 382
Earth theory, 233–34
Eckermann, Johann Peter, 242
ecology, 94–103
economics: *Capital* (Marx), 124, 128–31; case studies of, 18; history of, 97–98; *Macroeconomics and Health* (Sach), 131; OECD, 125–26; philosophy of, 123–24; of poverty, 102–3; as science, 130; *Small Is Beautiful* (Schumacher), 124–25; social history and, 38n17; *Theories of Surplus Value* (Marx), 128–29; World Bank, 126, 143. *See also* capitalism
education, 66, 340–43, 348–50. *See also* academia
Educational, Scientific and Cultural Organization (UNESCO), 125–26, 212–22
Egypt, 57–58, 62–63
Eilschow, Friderich Christian, 345–46

Eiríks saga rauða (Eiríksson), 290–91, 293
Ekström, Anders, 382
empathy, 105n34
Encyclopedia Britannica, 311–12, 319–20
Encyclopédie (d'Alembert/Diderot), 186–87
Engels, Friedrich, 160
englobing, 191
the Enlightenment, 349–52
Entretiens sur la pluralité des mondes (Fontenelle). *See* Fontenelle
Entzauberung der Welt (Weber), 329
environmentalism, 15–16
Epictetus, 208
epistemology, 45–47, 95, 159–61, 279–81, 350
ethics, 139, 149n10; in academia, 112; cultural relativism, 144; geography and, 101–3; justice, 172–73, 176–78; politics of, 137, 141, 154–55; psychology of, 129, 138; religion and, 61–62; in science, 376–77
ethnicity, 75–76
The Ethnological Notebooks (Marx), 160
Etymologiae (Isidore), 288
etymology, 27–36, 42–43
Europe: Cold War for, 84, 88–89; colonialism for, 159, 299–307; for geography, 274; Germany and, 246; globalization of, 220–21; politics of, 81–82; US compared to, 75
exile, 19, 199–208, 209n14
exploration, 20–21, 362–68, 373–82

faith, 58
Fanon, Frantz, 82–88
Feuerbach, Ludwig, 56–57
Flaubert, Gustave, 191
Fontenelle, Bernard de, 13–14, 351–52; concepts and, 343–48; education and, 340–43, 348–50
Fool's Cap Map, 10–11
formative moments, 33–34
France, 79–89, 205–6, 212–13, 221–22, 245–46
Frankenstein (Shelley), 359–61
frontiers. *See* geography; world heritage

Fulsås, Narve, 376, 382
Fusoris, Jean, 268

Gabriel, Markus, 333
Galbraith, Kenneth, 103
Gandhi, Mahatma, 55, 60–61, 102
generations, 213–14
geography, 365–68; Adam of Bremen for, 290–95; Bayle for, 184–87; cartography, 299–307; culture and, 9–10, 220; ethics and, 101–3; Europe for, 274; *Geographia* (Ptolemy), 268, 302; history of, 182–84, 190–92; knowledge of, 20, 187–90, 304; law and, 117–18; in middle ages, 292; omens from, 231–35; philosophy and, 21n3; politics of, 86–87; psychology of, 203; Ptolemy for, 274–75; science of, 356–57; technology for, 357–64; topology and, 171–72; world heritage and, 216–20. *See also* globes; maps
geology, 236
geopolitics, 40–41
Germanus, Nicolaus, 268
Germany, 89n1, 200–201, 205–7, 246
Gesner, Conrad, 282
al-Ghazālī, Abū Ḥāmid, 40–48
Ghosts (Ibsen), 248
Gianotti, Timothy J., 47–48
Gilbert, William, 360
Glanvill, John, 344–46, 348–49
globalization: in academia, 339–43, 348–50; Arab Spring in, 62–63; beliefs and, 10–13, 15–17, 55–56, 182, 220, 349–50; Cold War and, 103, 140; culture and, 62–63, 69, 99–101, 161, 182–83, 191–92, 215, 217, 221–22; of ecology, 94–103; the Enlightenment and, 351–52; environmentalism in, 15–16; of Europe, 220–21; hegemony from, 137–38; history of, 1–3, 186; human rights and, 144–47, 150n17; international law and, 111–12; for Islam, 40–41; for labor, 19–20; migration and, 117; of nationalism, 380–82; for nature, 98–99; philosophy and, 101–2, 148, 343–48; of politics, 142–43, 156–59, 299–307; of religion, 329–30; science of, 13–15;

spatial justice and, 172–76; trade and, 118
globes, 255–56, 264–69, 299–300, 303
GLP. *See* Great Binding Law of Peace
GNP. *See* gross national product
God is gek (Kluun), 334
Goethe, Johann Wolfgang von, 242–43
Gosse, Edmund, 241–43, 245, 247
Gossouin of Metz, 264
Gothorum Sveonumque historia (Johannes Magnus), 275–76
Gottsched, Johann Christoph, 341, 345, 349
Grand dictionnaire historique (Moreri), 185
Great Binding Law of Peace (GLP), 155–59, 161, 162n7
Great Ireland, 291
Greenland, 289–95
gross national product (GNP), 103
Grotius, Hugo, 111–21
Grundbegriff, 29, 35, 37n7
Guattari, Félix, 173–78

Hadrian's Wall, 216–17
Haeckel, Ernst, 95
Hallward, Peter, 177–78
Halvorsen, Sverre, 374–75, 382
Hamsun, Knut, 248
Haudenosaunee Confederacy. *See* Great Binding Law of Peace
health, 131
Hedda Gabler (Ibsen), 245
Hegel, Frederik V., 247
Hegel, George Wilhelm Friedrich, 56
hegemony, 68–69, 90n14, 137–38
Heidegger, Martin, 67, 178, 269
Heilbroner, Robert, 102–3
Heimskringla (Snorri Sturluson), 287–89
Heine, Heinrich, 207
Heise, Ursula, 351
Hesiod (poet), 116
Herder, Johann Gottfried, 11, 350
Hereford map, 7–9, 274, 327
heritage, 212–22
Hermann of Carinthia, 266
hermeneutics, 47–48
Hermsen, Joke J., 329–30

Herodotus, 284n12
Hier-Dort-Struktur, 332–33
Hill, Jenn, 358
history: in academia, 4, 218; beliefs and, 17–21, 27–36, 71, 75–76, 341–42; of capitalism, 95, 123–24; of cartography, 300; of communication, 31–32; of criticism, 242–45; culture and, 213–14; of democracy, 154–56; of economics, 97–98; *Eiríks saga rauða* (Eiríksson), 290–91, 293; of exploration, 20–21; of geography, 182–84, 190–92; geology and, 236; of globalization, 1–3, 186; of globes, 264–69; of GLP, 155–59; *Gothorum Sveonumque historia* (Johannes Magnus), 275–76; *Grand dictionnaire historique* (Moreri), 185; *Historia animalium* (Gesner), 282; *Historia de gentibus septentrionalibus* (Olaus Magnus), 275, 279–83; *Historia Norwegie*, 294–95; historical clarification, 6; *History* (Sprat), 318; of history, 187–90; *The History of Four-Footed Beasts and Serpents* (Topsell), 282; of humanity, 119–21; of human rights, 138–43; imperialism in, 216–20; of international law, 112–14; *Íslendingabók*, 289–90, 292; of knowledge, 2–3, 7–10; of language, 35, 88–89; of law, 160; *Livre des merveilles du monde* (Mandeville), 264; *Le Livre du ciel et du monde* (Oresme), 264; of maps, 7–11, 19–20, 186–87; of modern condition, 268–69; of Ottoman Empire, 300–301; of philosophy, 3–4, 11, 55–57, 317–20; of photography, 362–64; *Poetic Thoughts on the Destruction of Lisbon* (Biering), 227–31; of the Poles, 356–59, 362–68, 370n31; politics of, 221–22; psychology of, 204; religion and, 235–36, 258, 278–79, 290; of satire, 242–43; of science, 231–36, 263–64, 313–20, 349, 359; of semantics, 5–7; of society, 35–36, 38n17, 88–89; of spatial justice, 168–72; of temporality, 279–80; of the Third World, 79–80; translation in, 343–52; *Treatise on the Novelty of the*

history (cont.)
  World (Pontoppidan), 231–36; Vínland sagas in, 286–95; of war, 281–82; "We Refugees" (Arendt), 205–6; of world literature, 242–43
The History of Creation (Haeckel), 95
Horowitz, Irving Louis, 88
human capital, 125–26
The Human Condition (Arendt), 67–69
humanity, 89n1; conscience for, 54–63; criticism of, 215–16; formative moments in, 33–34; history of, 119–21; nature for, 96–97; philosophy and, 16–17, 330–31, 335n9; semantics for, 14–15
human rights, 125–26, 142–43, 147–48, 150n12, 150n17; philosophy of, 136–38, 149n10; Universal Declaration of Human Rights (1948), 54–55, 62, 139–41, 144–46, 149n10, 156
Humboldt, Alexander von, 12–13, 16, 350
Hunt, Lynn, 136–37
Huntford, Roland, 365
Huntington, Samuel, 159–60
Husayn, Kamil, 58–62
Hussein, Saddam, 15

Ibsen, Henrik, 18, 240–48
Iceland, 289–90
ICOMOS. *See* International Council on Monuments and Sites
identity politics, 62–63, 69–70, 84–86, 100–101
L'image du monde (Gossouin of Metz), 264
imperialism, 216–20
Indonesia, 81–82
Instauratio magna (van de Passe), 314
intellectual globe, 20, 311–20
intercultural education, 66–67, 69–70
International Council on Monuments and Sites (ICOMOS), 217–19
international law, 111–21
Irigary, Luce, 332
al-Iṣfahānī, Al-Rāghib, 42–43
Isidore of Seville, 287–88
Islam, 40–48, 58–61
Íslendingabók, 289–90, 292
Italy, 126–27

Jacobson, Jens Peter, 240–41
Jankélévitch, Vladimir, 203, 207
Jefferson, Thomas, 138–39, 160
Jeffery, Arthur, 42
Jennings, Frances, 161–62
Jesch, Judith, 292–93
Johannes Magnus, 275–76
Johansen, Hjalmar, 362
Joyce, James, 248
jurisdiction, 119–20
justice, 172–73, 176–78. *See also* law

Kafka, Franz, 207
Kant, Immanuel, 56, 351–52
keywords, 33–34, 37n5, 72–73
Khalid, Khalid Muhammad, 58–61
Kircher, Athanasius, 232
Kitson, Peter, 359–60
Kluun (philosopher), 334
Knight, W. D., 344–45
knowledge: authority and, 48; communication of, 34–35; *Conduct of Understanding* (Locke), 318; culture of, 4; *Encyclopedia Britannica*, 311–12, 319–20; *Encyclopédie* (d'Alembert/Diderot), 186–87; of geography, 20, 187–90, 304; of heritage, 214; history of, 2–3, 7–10; learning and, 321n15; maps and, 183–84, 313–14; methodology for, 29; philosophy and, 184–85; science of, 154; semantics and, 183–84
Koestler, Arthur, 96
Kojève, Alexandre, 184
Kollektivsingular, 2
Koselleck, Reinhart, 2, 5, 14–15, 71, 379; damīr for, 57; *Grundbegriff* for, 29, 35, 37n7; temporality for, 227
Küng, Hans, 59

labor, 19–20
language, 90n4; of 'ālam, 42–43; beliefs and, 84–89; Cold War for, 84, 88–89; dictionaries, 183–92; *Dictionary of Selected Synonyms* (Buck), 30; for education, 66; etymology, 27–36, 42–43; history of, 35, 88–89; of inclusion, 99–100; methodology and, 71–72;

psychology of, 32–33; for refugees, 209n12; science of, 28; symbols in, 28–29; synonyms, 29–30; technical terms in, 28, 37n2; in Universal Declaration of Human Rights (1948), 54–55. *See also* semantics
Larrington, Carolyne, 293–94
Latour, Bruno, 303–5
law, 111–21, 142, 155–61, 162n7
Lazare, Bernard, 207
learning: beliefs in, 66–67, 70–72; case studies for, 72–75, 78n10; about culture, 74–75; intercultural education, 69–70; knowledge and, 321n15; phenomenology in, 67–69; plurality in, 75–76
Lefebvre, Henri, 21n3
Leifr Eiríksson, 290–92
Leopardi, Giacomo, 202, 204
Lie, Jonas, 246
Leibniz, Gottfried Wilhelm, 175–76
the Limes, 217–20
Lincoln, Abraham, 207
Linnaeus, Carl, 231
Lisbon (Portugal), 226–35, 382
Livre des merveilles du monde (Mandeville), 264
Le Livre du ciel et du monde (Oresme), 264
Locke, John, 201, 312–13, 317–19
López de Velasco, Juan, 306–7
Love's Comedy (Ibsen), 242–45
Luhmann, Niklas, 18, 168–72, 182–83; philosophy of, 343; world society by, 339–40, 351–52
Lyotard, Jean-François, 170

Macrobious, 258–62
Macroeconomics and Health (Sach), 131
Magellan, Ferdinand, 303
Making Democracy Work (Putnam), 126–27
al-Makkī, Abū Ṭālib, 44
Mandeville, John, 264
maps: Amundsen, R., for, 373–82; beliefs from, 148; *Carta marina* (Olaus Magnus), 274–83; epistemology of, 279–81; Fool's Cap Map, 10–11;

Hereford map, 7–9, 274, 327; history of, 7–11, 19–20, 186–87; *L'image du monde* (Gossouin of Metz), 264; knowledge and, 183–84, 313–14; by Macrobius, 258–61; Norse maps, 287–88; *Padron Real*, 304–5; *Pandora's Hope* (Latour) about, 304–5; Psalter map, 266–67; religion in, 266–67; symbols in, 282–83. *See also* globes
Marco Polo, 268
Marcus Aurelius, 209n14
Maréchal, Sylvain, 190–91
Mare Liberum (Grotius), 115
Marx, Karl, 124, 128–32, 160
mass society, 209n14
materialism, 168
Melberg, Arne, 377
memex, 311–12, 320n1
Metamorphoses (Ovid), 116
metaphors, 4–7, 47–48, 94–95
methodology: of academia, 32–33, 37n9; for anthropology, 3; for beliefs, 17; for critical thinking, 71–72; of diachronic analysis, 72; for knowledge, 29; language and, 71–72; of synchronic analysis, 71–72
middle ages, 255–56; Earth in, 261–64; feet in, 257–61; geography in, 292; globes in, 264–69; water in, 261–64
Mignolo, Walter, 302
migration, 117
Miller, J. D. B., 88
Mincer, Jacob, 125
minorities, 72–76, 209n12
Mishkāt al-anwār (al-Ghazālī), 40, 45–47
modern condition, 86, 111–12, 138; cartography in, 308n5; generations in, 213–14; history of, 268–69; human rights and, 150n12; intellectual globe in, 319–20; spatial justice and, 176–78
Moosa, Ebrahim, 47
moral philosophy, 55–57
Moreri, Louis, 185
Moretti, Franco, 241, 248
Morgan, Henry Lewis, 160
Moro, Anton Lazzaro, 234
Moyn, Samuel, 137, 140–42, 150n19

Muhammad, 58–61
Mullican, Matt, 327–28
multiculturalism, 72–73
multi-perspectivity, 69–71
multiverse, 44–48
Muslims. *See* Islam
Mutua, Makau W., 144–45
mutual respect, 69–70

NAFTA. *See* North Atlantic Free Trade Agreement
Nakamura, Kojiro, 46
Nancy, Jean-Luc, 171–73
Nansen, Fridtjof, 362–64
nationalism, 62–63, 200, 380–82
natural capital, 124–25
natural law, 113–14
nature, 96–99
networks, 76, 78n10
Neuzeit. *See* temporality
New Left Review (journal), 86–87, 91nn22–23
Niels Lyhne (Jacobsen), 240–41
Nietzsche, Friedrich, 12
Nilsen, Thorvald, 366
non-violence, 55, 60–61
normality, 72–73
Norse culture, 286–95
North Atlantic Free Trade Agreement (NAFTA), 150n31
North Pole, 362–64, 377
Norway, 240–48, 286–95, 362–68, 373–82
nostalgia, 19, 201–5, 208
Notker, 265–66
Novum organum (Bacon, F.), 313–14

Obama, Barack, 161
observation, 168–72
OECD. *See* Organization for Economic Cooperation and Development
Olaus Magnus, 274–83, 284n2
omens, 226–36
On Heroes and Hero-Worship (Carlyle), 58–59
Oresme, Nicolas, 264
Organization for Economic Cooperation and Development (OECD), 125–26

Organizing the World (Mullican), 327–28
The Origin of the Family, Private Property, and the State (Engels), 160
Ottoman Empire, 300–301
Ovid, 116

Padron Real, 304–5
pariahs, 206
Paris, 245–46
Parry, William Edward, 357–58
Paulsen, John, 246
Peary, Robert, 377
Peau noire, masques blancs (Fanon), 82
Peer Gynt (Ibsen), 242–45, 248
phenomenology, 67–69, 231–36
philosophy: anthropology in, 11–12; beliefs and, 243; of capitalism, 128–32; of colonialism, 114–15; *Conduct of Understanding* (Locke), 318; *Critique de la raison dialectique* (Sartre), 83–84; *De consolatione philosophiae* (Boethius), 261, 265–66; of democracy, 156–59; *Dictionnaire philosophique* (Voltaire), 185–86; *Dragmaticon Philosophia* (William of Conches), 261–63; of economics, 123–24; in Egypt, 57–58; of the Enlightenment, 349–50; from France, 212–13; geography and, 21n3; globalization and, 101–2, 148, 343–48; history of, 3–4, 11, 55–57, 317–20; *The Human Condition* (Arendt), 67–69; humanity and, 16–17, 330–31, 335n9; of human rights, 136–38, 149n10; the intellectual globe in, 20; of jurisdiction, 119–20; Kluun for, 334; knowledge and, 184–85; *Kollektivsingular in*, 2; of Luhmann, 343; Macrobius for, 258–59; *Making Democracy Work* (Putnam), 126–27; of modern condition, 138; moral philosophy, 55–57; of natural law, 113–14; networks for, 76, 78n10; non-violence, 55, 60–61; of observation, 168–72; *Philosophia* (William of Conches), 261; physics and, 44–45; in politics, 159–61; of religion, 55–56, 328–29; science and, 6–7, 99–100; of

secularization, 9, 333–34; skepticism, 137–38, 144; *Sociologie d'une révolution* (Fanon), 82–83; technology and, 12–13; *Les Temps Modernes* (Sartre), 86; theology and, 45; utopia, 142; *What is The Third Estate?* (Sieyès), 80
photography, 362–64, 367–68, 377–79
physics, 44–46
Pickering, David, 244
plane of immanence, 174–75
Plato, 261, 330–33, 336n31
plurality, 75–76, 342–50
Pocock, J. G. A., 341–42
Poetic Thoughts on the Destruction of Lisbon (Biering), 227–31
the Poles, 360–61; history of, 356–59, 362–68, 370n31; North Pole, 362–64, 377; South Pole, 366, 373–82
politics: of academia, 16–17, 27–28, 74; of beliefs, 36; of Cold War, 79–80; of colonialism, 80–81; culture and, 2, 75–76, 218–19; of democracy, 147–48; of ethics, 137, 141, 154–55; of Europe, 81–82; of geography, 86–87; geopolitics, 40–41; globalization of, 142–43, 156–59, 299–307; of history, 221–22; identity politics, 62–63, 84–86, 100–101; law and, 142; *Making Democracy Work* (Putnam), 126–27; nationalism, 62–63, 200; *New Left Review* (journal), 86–87, 91n22; *The Origin of the Family, Private Property, and the State* (Engels), 160; philosophy in, 159–61; political clarity, 6; of religion, 207; of semantics, 215–16; of the Third World, 85–87; of war, 97–98
Pontoppidan, Erik, 226–27, 231–36
Popkin, Richard H., 185
Porter, Roy, 361
Portes, Alejandro, 127
Portugal, 226–35, 300–307, 382
Potter, Russell, 358
poverty, 102–3, 149n10
The Pretenders (Ibsen), 248
private law, 114–15
property, 114–21, 160
Proudhon, Pierre, Joseph, 130
Proust, Marcel, 201

Psalter map, 266–67
psychology: in Arabic, 57–58; of beliefs, 28–29; of capitalism, 131–32; conscience, 54–63; of culture, 210n16; of disenchantment, 328–30; empathy, 105n34; of ethics, 129, 138; of exile, 200, 202, 205–7, 209n14; of geography, 203; of history, 204; of language, 32–33; of loneliness, 206; of modern condition, 111–12; of nostalgia, 201, 204–5; of pre-assumptions, 71; psychoanalysis, 336n26; of sustainability, 214; of synonyms, 29–30; of the Third World, 87–88
Ptolemy, Claudius, 268, 274–75, 302
public law, 114
Purchart, Abbot, 266
Putnam, Robert, 126–27

Qur'ān, 41–42, 61–62

Rappaport, Rhoda, 232
al-Rāzī, Fakhr al-Dīn, 44
reality, 67–68
The Red Room (Strindberg), 240–41
refugees, 205–6, 209n12
Relaciones Geográficas (López de Valesco), 306–7
religion: 'ālam in, 41–42; authority and, 61–62, 120, 233, 278; beliefs in, 46–47; the Bible, 55–56; ethics and, 61–62; faith in, 58; globalization of, 329–30; history and, 235–36, 258, 278–79, 290; Islam, 40–48; law from, 112; in maps, 266–67; philosophy of, 55–56, 328–29; politics of, 207; Qur'ān, 41–42; science and, 8–9, 231, 274–75; Sunni orthodoxy, 45–46; symbols in, 277–80; synonyms in, 33
Remigius of Auxerre, 287–88
respublica christiana, 111
Ribeiro, Diego, 303
Richter, Herman, 284n2
Rifkin, Jeremy, 105n34
Roman Empire, 212–22
Ross, David, 91n23
Rousseau, Jacques, 56
Ruhkopf, Julie, 245

Saalburg fort, 218
Sachs, Jeffrey, 131
SADC. *See* Southern African Development Community
Safi, Omid, 44–45
Said, Edward, 200, 206–7, 209n14, 358
Saint-Exupéry, Antoine de, 170
St. Leger, William, 244
Saleh, Walid A., 43
Sartre, Jean-Paul, 83–88, 91nn19–20
satire, 242–43
Sauter, Michael, 342–43, 348
Sauvy, Alfred, 79–81, 83–86, 89nn1–2, 101–2
Scaliger, Joseph, 315–16
Scandinavia. *See* Denmark; Norway; Sweden
Schmid, Wilhelm, 332
Schultz, Theodore, 125
Schumacher, E. F., 124–25
Schütz, Alfred, 199–200, 208
science, 370n31; for beliefs, 100–101; biblical analogies for, 233–35; *Conduct of Understanding* (Locke), 318; cosmology as, 341–43; *De essentiis* (Hermann of Carinthia), 266; *A Discovery of a World in the Moone* (Wilkins), 341; of earthquakes, 231–35; Earth theory, 233–34; economics as, 130; ethics in, 376–77; of geography, 356–57; of globalization, 13–15; globes and, 255–56; history of, 231–36, 263–64, 313–20, 349, 359; of knowledge, 154; of language, 28; *Livre des merveilles du monde* (Mandeville), 264; *Le Livre du ciel et du monde* (Oresme), 264; *Norwegian North Polar Expedition* (Nansen), 364; philosophy and, 6–7, 99–100; Ptolemy for, 268; religion and, 8–9, 231, 274–75; semantics in, 257–58; UNESCO, 125–26, 212–22
Science and Survival (Commoner), 96–97
Scott, Robert Falcon, 365–68, 374, 379–80
secularization, 9, 333–34
Selden, John, 315–16
self-equality, 208–9

semantics: in academia, 17–18, 42–43; of ʾālam, 42–43; beliefs and, 36; etymology, 27–36; history of, 5–7; for humanity, 14–15; knowledge and, 183–84; of minorities, 72–73; politics of, 215–16; in science, 257–58; synonyms and, 37n6; of the Third World, 88–89; in translation, 29
Shakespeare, William, 246
Shelley, Mary, 359–61
Shklar, Judith, 200–201
Sieyès, Emmanuel-Joseph, 80, 89n2
Silent Spring (Carson), 95
skepticism, 137–38, 144
Sloterdijk, Peter, 328–33, 335n9, 336n26, 352n6
Small Is Beautiful (Schumacher), 124–25
Smith, Adam, 125
Snorri Sturluson, 287–89
society, 339–40, 351–52; history of, 35–36, 38n17, 88–89; social capital, 126–28; social relationships, 205
Sociologie d'une révolution (Fanon), 82–83
Southern African Development Community (SADC), 150n31
South Pole, 373–82
Spain, 300–307
spatial justice, 168–78
sphere, 327–34
Spinoza, Baruch, 178
Spivak, Gayatri, 351
Sprat, Thomas, 318
Steger, Manfred, 1–2
Strindberg, August, 240–41, 246
Sukarno (President), 81–82
Summa Theologica (Aquinas), 115
Sunni orthodoxy, 45–46
sustainability, 214–15
Sweden, 274–83
Sylva sylvarum (Bacon, F.), 314–15
symbols, 28–29, 277–80, 282–83, 284n12
Symposion (Plato), 330–33, 336n31
synchronic analysis, 71–72
synonyms, 29–30, 33, 37n6
systems theory, 248

Talbot, William H. F., 356–57
Tasmania, 379
Taylor, Charles, 328–29, 333–34, 336n15
technical terms, 28, 37n2
technology, 12–13, 303, 311–12, 320n1, 357–64
temporality, 14, 226–27, 235–36, 240–42, 279–80
Les Temps Modernes (Sartre), 86
Thant, Sithu U, 97
theology, 45
Theories of Surplus Value (Marx), 128–29
the Third World, 79–89, 89n2
Thomsen, Rosendahl, 240, 247–48
Thornhill, Christopher, 143
Timaeus (Plato), 261
Tocqueville, Alexis de, 159–60
topography, 232
topology, 171–72
Topsell, Edward, 282
trade, 118, 150n31
translation, 29, 50n32, 343–52
Treatise on the Novelty of the World (Pontoppidan), 231–36
Treaty of Tordesillas (1494), 299–300, 302–4, 307, 308n3
Turnbull, David, 305

UN. *See* United Nations
Underwater Cultural Heritage, 220
UNESCO. *See* Educational, Scientific and Cultural Organization
Union of Soviet Socialist Republics (USSR), 79–80, 84, 88–89, 103, 140
United Nations (UN): UNESCO, 125–26, 212–22; Universal Declaration of Human Rights (1948), 54–55, 62, 139–41, 144–46, 149n10, 156
United States (US), 75, 88–89, 206–7
unity, 330–33

urbanization, 100–101
utopia, 142

van de Passe, Simon, 314
Varnhagen, Rahel, 207
"Venice Charter," 218–20
Verne, Jules, 361–62
Vespucci, Amerigo, 305
Vínland sagas, 286–95
Vogelaar, Harold, 62
Voltaire, 185–86

Wages of Labor (Marx), 130–31
Walker, Adam, 360
Wallingford, John of, 255–57
war, 96–98, 118–21, 281–82. *See also* Cold War
water, 257–64
Weatherford, Jack, 161–62
Weber, Max, 329, 336n15
Wedmore, Fredrick, 244
Weltgesellschaft, 18, 168, 170–72, 176, 339–40
"We Refugees" (Arendt), 205–6
What is The Third Estate? (Sieyès), 80
Who are We? (Huntington), 159–60
wholeness, 330–33
Wilhelm II (emperor), 218
Wilkins, John, 341, 344–45
William of Conches, 261
Winter Harbour (Friedrich), 357–58
Works and Days (Hesiod), 116
World Bank, 126, 143
world heritage, 212–22
worldliness, 66–69, 73, 75–76
world literature, 240–48, 359–62
world society, 339–40, 351–52
Worsley, Peter, 86–88, 90n14

Yugoslavia, 86–87

www.ingramcontent.com/pod-product-compliance
Lightning Source LLC
Chambersburg PA
CBHW071329080526
44587CB00017B/2779